Burma in Revolt

Burma in Revolt

Opium and Insurgency Since 1948

Bertil Lintner

Westview Press

BOULDER • SAN FRANCISCO • OXFORD

White Lotus

BANGKOK

Maps by the Creative Partnership, Bangkok

Copyright © 1994 by Westview Press, Inc.

Published in 1994 in the United States of America by Westview Press, Inc., 5500 Central Avenue, Boulder, Colorado 80301-2877, and in the United Kingdom by Westview Press, 36 Lonsdale Road, Summertown, Oxford OX2 7EW

Published in 1994 in Thailand by White Lotus Co., Ltd., G.P.O. Box 1141, Bangkok 10501, Thailand

Library of Congress Cataloging-in-Publication Data
Lintner, Bertil.
  Burma in revolt : opium and insurgency since 1948 / by Bertil
Lintner.
    p. cm.
  Includes bibliographical references and index.
  ISBN 0-8133-2344-4
  1. Burma—Politics and government—1948– 2. Burma—History—
Autonomy and independence movements. 3. Burma—Ethnic relations.
4. Minorities—Burma. 5. Opium trade—Burma. I. Title.
DS530.4.L55   1994
959.105—dc20   94-25846
                                                                                              CIP

ISBN 974-8496-19-8 (Thailand)

Printed and bound in the United States of America

10   9   8   7   6   5   4   3   2

Contents

Author's Note

The annual production of opium in the Burmese sector of the Golden Triangle totalled some thirty tons when Burma became independent from Britain in 1948. The country was then a promising young democracy with a bustling free-market economy. The living standard was one of the highest in Asia and the level of education far surpassed that of its then backward neighbours such as Thailand.

Forty years later, Burma was listed as one of the poorest nations in the world; in October 1987 the government in Rangoon even had to apply for Least Developed Country status with the United Nations. Higher education lags far behind even Bangladesh to the west, and all universities and colleges have in any case been closed most of the time since June 1988 (as well as being closed, off and on, in the 1960s and 1970s). Even more startlingly, according to American estimates, the 1992–1993 harvesting season yielded at least 2,575 tons of raw opium, an 8,000% increase since 1948.

Insurgencies in Thailand and Malaysia, which at one time threatened to overthrow the regimes in those countries, have been resolved by a combination of military pressure, political concessions and economic incentives. In Burma, the conflict between the central government in Rangoon and the country's many ethnic minorities entered its 47th year in 1994 with no end in sight. The government has over the past four years struck a number of cease-fire agreements with some of the major groups which has reduced the scale of the fighting, but the ethnic rebels have not been offered any political concessions. According to the terms of these cease-fires, the insurgents have also been allowed to retain their arms and control over their respective areas; the ethnic problem has been frozen rather than solved. Burma today has at least 50,000 armed rebels and ex-rebels who are not under any central governmental control.

While other countries in the region are developing into freer, more open societies, once-democratic Burma has been ruled by a military dictatorship since 1962.

The complex nexus between the drug problem, military rule and Burma's civil war has hardly been considered when international narcotics agencies have discussed the drug problem in the Golden Triangle. The emphasis has been on showcase "crop substitution programmes" (UN agencies) or support for the military government's supposed "campaigns against drugs" (the US Drug Enforcement Administration).

Two US researchers, Alfred W. McCoy and Alan A. Block, have aptly pointed out that the failure of Western drug policy is due mainly to a fundamentally wrong approach: "treating global narcotics trafficking as if it were a localised vice such as pornography or prostitution". Consequently, millions of dollars have been wasted on largely meaningless projects, while the opium production is increasing steadily, year by year—and almost no attempts have been made to address the underlying historical, social and economic factors behind the drug explosion in areas such as the Golden Triangle.

The aim of this book is to explain how Burma's booming drug production, insurgency and counter-insurgency interrelate—and why the country has been unable to shake off thirty years of military rule and build a modern, democratic society. Burma's ethnic strife is not a peripheral problem confined to the country's border areas: it is a central issue. Without a lasting solution to the ethnic question and the civil war, Burma will remain a source of political despair—and drugs from its sector of the Golden Triangle will continue to flood the markets of the world.

Introduction and Acknowledgements

I made my first clandestine journey into rebel-held areas of Burma in January 1981. Carrying a knapsack on my back, I caught a bus from Bangkok's Southern Bus Terminal and travelled out 120 kilometres west to Kanchanaburi on the River Kwai, where Allied prisoners built the fabled bridge during World War II. That was as far as public transport went at that time.

After spending a night in a rat-infested hotel near the market in Kanchanaburi, I boarded a Land-Rover, named rather grandly "the Land Tour Company", and began a gruelling, ten-hour journey along a narrow, winding dirt road through dense forest towards Sangkhlaburi, 225 kilometres further up the river. Sangkhlaburi in those days was a pleasant, picturesque town, located amidst the jungles surrounding the upper reaches of the River Kwai. It consisted of half a dozen rows of wooden shophouses and a truck stop, where vehicles of World War II vintage gathered in the morning. But the main landmark was an impressive wooden structure spanning the river, which resembled a mini replica of the Golden Gate Bridge.

My goal was a trim Baptist Mission compound on the opposite bank of the Kwai. I arrived there exhausted in the late afternoon, and looked up my only contact, given by some friends in Bangkok: Benny Htoo, a former police officer from Burma who in 1949 had joined the rebellion of the ethnic Karen minority to which he belonged. He had fought for several years with the forces of the Karen National Union (KNU) in the hills of Burma, and later retired with his wife, children, grandchildren and a number of other relatives to a house adjoining the missionary hospital in Sangkhlaburi.

At first I had some difficulty locating where he lived, but while walking along a dusty path, I caught sight of an elderly gentleman trimming his hedge. He appeared educated and I politely asked him in English for directions. He lowered his secateurs and replied in flawless Queen's English: "Ah, young man, are you looking for Benny's? That's right over there." He pointed towards a brown-stained house down the village road.

The man at the hedge, I later learned, was Saw Henson Kya Doe, a Sandhurst-trained former brigadier-general of the Burma Army. He had gone underground in the late 1960s to fight against the military government in Rangoon and later settled in Sangkhlaburi.

I met Benny, a jovial and extremely hospitable man in his sixties, and stayed in his house overnight. Early the next morning, I started walking along a dusty path through the jungle towards my final destination: Three Pagodas Pass on the Thai-Burma border. It took me all morning to cover the last twenty-five kilometres up to the pass. Following a rutted dirt-track through the jungle, I laboured under the blazing sun, passing only a few, tiny villages of bamboo huts along the way. When I finally spotted the three small white pagodas—which have given the pass its name—in a glade in the forest, I was met by two young, tough-looking guerrillas riding bareback together on a pony.

Noticing their automatic weapons, I thought it prudent to stop. They spoke a language I had never heard before, but from the tone of their voices I gathered they wanted to know who I was and where I was heading. Feebly, I replied: "Yoo Shoo, Saw Yoo Shoo," the contact name Benny had given me. I was promptly escorted by two other armed guards to Yoo Sho's bamboo house.

My new host turned out to be a former Union Military Police officer. He had disappeared into the jungle to join the KNU when the Karen uprising broke out in 1949, never to return to "civilisation" again. Together with his wife Elsie (who died of cancer a few years later) he made my stay at Three Pagodas Pass both pleasant and educational. From him I received my first introduction to Burma's decades-long civil war, its tragedies as well as its complexities.

Later, from my base in the northern Thai city of Chiang Mai, I made many more illegal trips across the border into rebel-held areas of eastern Burma. In April 1981, I spent almost a month with Shan guerrillas in the hills across the border from Mae Hong Son in northwestern Thailand. This was when I met Hseng Noung, the woman guerrilla soldier who later, in 1983, became my wife. Together, we visited practically every other ethnic rebel army in Burma that was based within reach of the Thai border: the Karennis, the Pa-Os, the Mons, the Was and the Lahus.

We also travelled to the Bangladesh-Burma border in early 1984 to look into the Muslim question in Arakan. At that time, very few journalists were paying much attention to the seemingly bizarre, Burmese sideshow. People perceived events in Cambodia, Vietnam and even Laos and Thailand as far more important.

Hardly anyone else, apart from the magazine I had begun writing for in 1982, the *Far Eastern Economic Review*, was interested when in March 1985 my wife and I left Bangkok for India to embark on our most challenging trek thus far: to cross the ethnic guerrilla areas of northern Burma, from the wild Naga Hills to Kachin State in the northernmost corner of Burma, and on to the communist-controlled territory adjacent to the Chinese frontier in the northeast. Somehow, we succeeded. During our eighteen-month journey on foot, and by elephant, mule, bicycle and river boat, we covered 2,275 kilometres through some of the most remote and least accessible parts of the country.

We became the first journalists to reach areas controlled by the Kachin Independence Army in the far north and the then-powerful Communist Party of Burma in northeastern Shan State. We emerged through Sipsongpanna in southern China in April 1987, and returned to Bangkok to do our stories and to write *Land of Jade*, a book about our experiences in the insurgent-held north of Burma.

Not long afterwards, central Burma erupted. Hundreds of thousands of people in towns and even villages across the country took to the streets to vent years of pent-up frustration with a xenophobic military regime which had turned what was once Southeast Asia's richest country into an economic and political wreck. The uprising was drenched in blood. Thousands of men, women and children were gunned down in Rangoon and elsewhere as the army sprayed automatic rifle-fire into crowds of unarmed demonstrators. The present regime, the State Law and Order Restoration Council, assumed power.

I chronicled these dramatic events in *Outrage: Burma's Struggle for Democracy*, which is based mainly on interviews with people who participated in the Burmese pro-democracy movement of 1988–89. Forgotten Burma was suddenly back on the map again. Even the minority issue received the attention it deserved when, in the wake of the massacre in Rangoon, pro-democracy activists from the urban areas arrived in rebel-held territory along the Thai border.

It was then that I decided to write this book about Burma's civil war, to put the fighting into a historical perspective and to do my best to rectify many of the myths and misconceptions which surround the decades-long conflict. I wanted to explain why once prosperous Burma had fallen into social, political and economic ruin, and why it had become the world's biggest producer of heroin.

Again, as with *Outrage*, I decided to base this book on interviews with people who had participated in the movement rather than rely on largely inaccurate newspaper reports. I had already collected thousands of pages of notes during my many trips to the Thai border and our long trek through the north. I supplemented these with more interviews in 1991, 1992 and 1993 in Thailand, China, the US, Bangladesh and India. Rebels and former rebels were more than willing to cooperate with me, and they often went out of their way to collect the information I requested, or to introduce me to other veterans of the civil war.

It was a far more difficult task to get Rangoon's side of the story. Burma's military government remains one of the most reclusive regimes in the world, and although I did manage to visit Rangoon twice in 1989 (I had previously visited the country legally in 1977, 1979 and 1981), my repeated visa applications since then have been routinely rejected, or simply not answered. Fortunately, I was able to meet in Bangkok a number of retired Burma Army officers who had taken part in counter-insurgency operations in the northeast of the country and against the Karens on the Thai border. Otherwise, I have had to rely on official Burmese publications and newspapers for the Burma Army's version of events.

Since Burma's civil war may be one of the most confusing issues in Asia today, with its many armed groups, factions and fronts, I have added four appendices which I hope will serve as useful references for journalists, scholars and diplomats alike: a chronology; a reasonably complete list of rebel groups; biographies of major leaders of the insurgency; and a list of independent Burma's founding fathers, the legendary Thirty Comrades, and their fates.

This book would not have been possible without my patient wife, Hseng Noung, who helped me interpret numerous interviews and translate documents from the original Burmese into English. David Steinberg of Georgetown University, Josef Silverstein of Rutgers University, Alfred McCoy of the University of Wisconsin at Madison, Mary Kay Magistad of National Public Radio and the *Washington Post*, Robert Karniol of *Jane's Defence Weekly* and my old friend Chao Tzang Yawnghwe, who read parts of both the early draft and the finished manuscript, offered helpful criticisms. I am also grateful to Pippa Curwen for proofreading the text and tidying up my English, and to the Open Society Institute in New York for financing the production of this book. But, above all, I wish to thank the John D. and Catherine T. MacArthur Foundation for providing a research grant, which enabled me to take time off from my regular work as a journalist to write this book.

Bertil Lintner
Bangkok

Prologue:
Murder in the Secretariat

On the morning of 19 July 1947 a green-painted army jeep came speeding through the streets of Rangoon. Its occupants were dressed in military fatigues and were brandishing tommy-guns and other semi-automatic weapons. No one paid much attention to them; World War II had just ended and military-looking people were no strange sight in the Burmese capital.

The jeep stopped outside the Secretariat, a Victorian-style, redbrick building in central Rangoon. Security was tight, as the Governor's Executive Council, the pre-independence *de facto* Burmese cabinet led by Aung San, was in session. Aung San, the architect of Burma's imminent freedom from British colonial rule, had been warned that his life might be in danger, but somehow the gunmen aroused no suspicion as they drove through the central porchway and entered the Secretariat complex.

The hitmen, guns in hand, jumped out of the jeep and half-ran towards the main building. They hurried upstairs and on reaching the room where the cabinet was meeting, they pointed their guns at the assembled ministers, shouting: "Remain seated! Don't move!" Aung San rose to his feet—and the men opened fire. The shooting continued for about thirty seconds, and the uniformed men left the building, jumped into their jeep outside and accelerated away.

It was 10:37 A.M. Other people in the Secretariat were soon jostling in through the open doorway. The pungent smell of carbide and fumes of heavy smoke filled the room. Tables and chairs were overturned and soiled with blood. Nine bullet-ridden bodies lay on the floor: Aung San; his close friend and erstwhile student leader Thakin Mya; Ba Choe, the former editor of the nationalist *Deedok* journal and now a prominent statesman; Razak, a Muslim school principal and politician; Aung San's elder brother Ba Win; Mahn Ba Khaing, one of the few ethnic Karens to have participated in mainstream Burmese politics; and Sao Sam Htun, the *saohpa*, or prince of the Shan State of Möng Pawn, who had taken part in the efforts to amalgamate the minority-inhabited frontier areas with Burma proper. There was also Ohn Maung, a deputy secretary of the Ministry of Transport, who had entered the conference room to submit a report when the assassins struck, and Ko Htwe, Razak's eighteen-year-old bodyguard.

The nation was plunged into grief. Its most competent leaders, who had been preparing to take over Burma after the British, were dead before the country had even become independent. Aung San, the national hero, the *Bogyoke* or General, was only thirty-two and left behind his wife, Khin Kyi, and three small children: two sons and a two-year-old daughter.

On the same day, the Rangoon police arrested U Saw, a right-wing politician who had been Aung San's main rival for the premiership of independent Burma, and charged him with murder. U Saw was convicted and hanged in May 1948.

U Nu, the deputy leader of Burma's main political party at that time, the Anti-Fascist People's Freedom League—which had been founded by Aung San shortly after World War II—took over as prime minister. He was a devout Buddhist and an outstanding intellectual, but hardly the strong leader Burma needed during its first, difficult years of independence.

The full impact of Aung San's assassination was not truly fathomed until many years later. Despite his youth, he was already a veteran of Burma's struggle for independence. In 1936, he had been the key leader of a student strike at Rangoon University, participated in the formation of the *Dohbama Asiayone*—Burma's most intensely nationalistic organisation prior to World War II—and linked up the movement with workers in the oil fields and peasants in the countryside. He had left secretly for Tokyo in 1940 and returned to Burma to gather recruits for military training in Japan. The group, known as the "Thirty Comrades", set up the Burma Independence Army in Bangkok on 26 December 1941 and entered Burma with the Japanese soon afterwards.

He later turned against the Japanese and contacted the Allies, and when the Japanese were forced out in May 1945, Aung San had become Burma's national hero. The Thirty Comrades came to occupy an almost mythical role in modern Burmese history; they were the fathers of Burma's independence as well as its armed forces.

On 12 February 1947, five months before his assassination, Aung San had signed an agreement with leaders of the Shan, Kachin and Chin ethnic minorities in the market town of Panglong in the Shan states, paving the way for the proposed Union of Burma under a federal constitution. The ethnic minorities in Burma's frontier areas were traditionally deeply distrustful of the Burmans in the central plains, and many were downright worried that they would come under Burman domination when the British withdrew.

Some minorities, notably the Karens, did not even participate in the Panglong Conference, but they had their own legal, political organisation, the Karen National Union, and informal negotiations were in progress in Rangoon.

In the mainstream political arena, the situation was also extremely volatile in the late 1940s. The well-organised Communist Party of Burma (CPB) had played an important role in the anti-Japanese struggle and emerged from the war as one of the country's most powerful political organisations.

Against the Communists stood the Socialists, who in a Burmese context were more right-wing than most other political groups during the post-World War II era. Despite their name, the Socialists were a well-organised, non-communist grouping that competed with the CPB for control over the workers and the peasants and their organisations.

But Aung San's position was unique even in this field. He happened to be the brother-in-law of the CPB leader, Thakin Than Tun, and enjoyed at the same time an excellent relationship with Socialist stalwart Kyaw Nyein, with whom he had served on the same executive committee of the Rangoon University Students' Union in the 1930s.

With Aung San as a neutralising factor gone from the political scene, the confrontation between the Communists and the Socialists escalated, and the minorities lost perhaps the only Burman political leader they had ever trusted. Independence finally came at the auspicious hour of 4:20 A.M. on 4 January 1948; the timing had been carefully selected by Burma's astrologers, whom even the Western-educated political leaders often consulted. The Union Jack was lowered and the last British soldier marched past, accompanied by a military band playing "Auld Lang Syne".

As no single person any longer enjoyed the respect and undisputed loyalty given to Aung San among the rank and file as well as the officer corps of the armed forces, power struggles ensued. By mid-1948, most units had mutinied and turned their guns against the government in Rangoon. The Communists also went into armed rebellion—and were followed by the Karens, the Mons, the Karennis and some other ethnic minorities who resorted to armed struggle, demanding independence or autonomy for their respective areas. The disintegration of Burma had begun.

1

"The Rangoon Government"

On 2 April 1948, the sound of gunfire broke the bucolic peace of Paukkongyi, a tiny village near Pegu in the central Burmese dry zone. A Burma Army patrol had discovered that a group of Communists, who had just escaped a crackdown on their movement in Rangoon, were hiding out in the village. Armed with pistols and shotguns, they fought back when the government troops launched an attack. The gun battle lasted for about an hour, before the poorly armed Communists beat a retreat into the forested hills southwest of Paukkongyi. The first regular battle in Burma's decades-long civil war had taken place.

The Communist Party of Burma (CPB) had operated openly until 28 March of that year. Its headquarters had been located in a two-storey, white-plastered brick building at 138 Bagaya Street in Kemmendine, a relatively plush Rangoon suburb. Previously a pawn shop owned by a Chinese merchant, the house had been acquired by the CPB shortly after the Japanese withdrawal from Rangoon in May 1945. A big room downstairs housed the CPB's printing press and the editorial office of its *Communist Daily* newspaper, the theoretical journal *Pyithu Ana* "People's Power" and other party publications.

The central committee and the politburo had met almost daily in a meeting hall upstairs, where the party's second congress had been held in July 1945. Revolutionary posters adorned the walls and there was always febrile activity as party members came and went. Youthful Red Guards in semi-military fatigues, sporting caps with a red star and arm bands with the hammer and the sickle, guarded the premises. These Red Guards were mostly young Communists who had served with Aung San's militia, the People's Volunteer Organisation, prior to the CPB's expulsion in October 1946 from the national front, the Anti-Fascist People's Freedom League (AFPFL).

The party leaders were all relatively young men in their late twenties or early thirties. Most of them had been student activists in the turbulent 1930s, when the *Dohbama Asiayone* dominated Burmese politics. Some had fought against the Japanese during the war. One of them was Thakin Than Tun, a short, burly schoolteacher from Pyinmana, a dusty town on the Rangoon–Mandalay railway in the central plains. He became the general secretary of the party and later led it underground. Thakin Than Tun was married to Daw Khin Khin Kyi, the sister of Aung San's wife, Daw Khin Kyi. He had a reputation for being honest, forthright and uncompromising.

The party's main theoretician at this time was Hamendranath Ghoshal, a Burma-born, upper-caste Bengali Brahmin. His father had moved to Burma in the wake of the British crackdown on the so-called "terrorist movement" of militant nationalists in his native Calcutta at the turn of the century.[1] One of the original founders of the party, Ghoshal and five other young activists had first met in a small flat in Rangoon's Barr Street on 15 August 1939 to set up the CPB.

Present at that time, and still active in the 1940s, was also Thakin Thein Pe. He had served as councillor for agriculture and rural economy or, in effect, minister in Aung San's pre-independence cabinet from September to October 1946, the highest post ever held by a Communist in the British Empire. Thakin Thein Pe was a good-looking, bespectacled intellectual who charmed most women he met.

This was a quality he shared with Thakin Soe, Burma's most radical Communist. Soe had been expelled from the CPB in early 1946 and set up his own Communist Party (Red Flag). He subsequently went underground in Dedaye north of Thegon in the Irrawaddy delta region, where he had fought against the Japanese during World War II. His small squads of men, mostly old followers from the anti-Japanese struggle, who were armed with weapons left over from the war, were already carrying out small-scale guerrilla attacks in the countryside by the end of 1946.

Thakin Soe, a cheerful, stout-bodied Mon from the Moulmein area in the southeast, was an excellent classical singer and violinist. He had worked for the Burmah Oil Company at Syriam, across the river from Rangoon, for fourteen years before becoming an armed revolutionary in 1946.

One of the most serious of the young Communists in Bagaya Street in the late 1940s was Thakin Ba Thein Tin, the 34-year-old, stoney-faced son of a petty Chinese trader from Tavoy and an ethnic Burmese mother. An avid reader of Marxist classics, and well-versed in European literature as well, he had joined the party shortly after the first meeting in 1939. When the widely respected student leader and trade unionist Thakin Ba Hein had died from malaria at the age of thirty-three in November 1946, Ba Thein Tin was elected to the three-man politburo, which also included Thakin Than Tun and Ghoshal.

"At first, we had no weapons there," says Khin Maung Gyi, then a twenty-year-old student activist and party member. "But as the situation became more tense in late 1947, we stocked the office with tommy-guns and Canadian-made .38 revolvers."[2]

The government became increasingly nervous as Communist-inspired labour unrest proceeded to shake Burma in February 1948. A strike at the Burmah Oil Company had led to clerks and office workers in Rangoon walking out as well. Thakin Than Tun, Thakin Ba Thein Tin, Ba Hein's widow, Khin Gyi, and a few other CPB leaders had just attended the 2nd Congress of the Communist Party of India and a youth conference in Calcutta. The CPI congress in particular had advocated a more militant line than before.

In India, a rural rebellion had broken out in Telengana in Hyderabad State in 1946 and was still continuing when the Calcutta meetings were held. When the CPB delegates returned to Burma in mid-March, a massive peasant rally was organised in Pyinmana. A crowd of more than 70,000 people listened to speeches by Thakin Than Tun and passed resolutions supporting the strikes in Rangoon.

On 12 March militant Socialists, staunch opponents of the CPB, gathered at Bandoola Park near the City Hall in central Rangoon. Speakers at the public meeting made impassioned appeals, urging the people to attack newspapers which they considered pro-communist and therefore, in their view, anti-national. Crowds armed with daggers, cudgels and axes stormed into the editorial offices of the *Pyithu Hittaing* ("People's Forum"), run by *Journalgyaw* Ma Ma Lay, the widow of a well-respected Burmese newspaperman, *Journalgyaw* Chit Maung.

The offices of *Oway* and the *Seepwayey* ("The Economist") were also ransacked by angry mobs. Communist leader Thakin Than Tun had already told his opponents in no uncertain terms what would happen if the Socialists came close to his headquarters: "If they dare to come and attack us, we shall fill the Bagaya Chauk [a small gully near their party headquarters] with the bones of the Socialists."[3] He also openly challenged the prime minister himself, branding him a "fascist" and adding: "Thakin Nu wants to live in peace. So let us send him to the most peaceful place." In a Burmese context, this meant the grave.[4]

The country was in turmoil, and finally, on 25 March, Prime Minister U Nu ordered the arrest of the increasingly troublesome Thakin Than Tun. Perhaps predictably, the Communist leader reacted with defiance. On the day of his supposed arrest, he addressed a 3,000-strong crowd of workers in central Rangoon.

Two days later, U Nu issued an ultimatum to the CPB:

> We have waited till now before taking action under the law, but our patience is about to end. As the threat is that the Communists will resist by force the application of law to the strikers ... [we must] prevent with our lives the possibility of a civil war [and seek] a union of the progressive elements in the

country and form a united front with a united programme . . . . This . . . has
been accepted by the AFPFL as well as by the Socialist Party and we commu-
nicated the proposals to the CPB. A reply is due at 4 P.M. today.[5]

When no response was forthcoming from the Communists, U Nu instructed his powerful home minister, Socialist leader Kyaw Nyein, to raid
the CPB's headquarters in Bagaya Street.

On the morning of the 28th, the atmosphere was ominous. The CPB had
learned about the order in advance through their own people in the Home
Ministry.

"Usually a car would come and pick us up at our homes to take us to
our party headquarters," recalls politburo member Thakin Ba Thein Tin.
"But that morning no one came. We waited until 10 A.M. and then sent a
young party member to find out what was going on. He returned, telling
us that the police had raided our headquarters. Our driver had escaped."

At 11:30 A.M., the politburo issued instructions to all party leaders to
leave Rangoon as soon as possible and move to rural areas, where armed
struggle was to be organised. This decision to go underground was far
more serious than that taken by Thakin Soe and his Red Flag radicals two
years earlier, which had led to only a few skirmishes with the police. The
CPB was one of the most powerful political organisations in Burma at that
time. Now, it was civil war.

According to Thakin Ba Thein Tin, not everyone in the party's top leadership supported the move. Ghoshal, whose main political constituency
was the mostly Indian proletariat in Rangoon, had been the mastermind
behind the strikes in February, and he wanted to continue the urban struggle. On the other hand, Than Tun and Ba Thein Tin, who had just returned
from India and were inspired by the Telengana example, advocated armed
struggle in the rural areas.[6]

While many cadres immediately heeded the order issued on the 28th,
several CPB leaders remained in hiding in Rangoon, moving from safe house
to safe house to evade arrest. But one by one, the members of the central
committee also slipped out of Rangoon. Thakin Than Tun went in disguise
by train, protected by sympathetic railway workers. Thakin Ba Thein Tin
left by car and Ghoshal simply caught the bus to Toungoo. It was mid-
April and *Thingyan*, the yearly water festival, was being celebrated throughout the country. The CPB leaders took advantage of the usual chaos and
confusion surrounding the festivities.

By the end of April, all central committee members had managed to
escape from Rangoon. Although more than 300 party members and organisers had been apprehended by the police during the sweeps in late March
and early April, only one member of the central committee, Red Guard
leader Thein Dan, was arrested.

The top leadership was assembled again in May in Kyaukgyi-pauk near Toungoo, a town on the main railway line from Rangoon to Mandalay. The decision to resort to armed struggle was accepted and Ghoshal pledged to follow the majority line. A central military commission for the "People's Liberation Army of Burma" was formed and various strategies discussed. There were plenty of arms in the countryside, left over from World War II, and the CPB already had a strong support base in the Pyinmana area, to where the leaders moved shortly after the Kyaukgyi-pauk meeting.

Ye Tun was a CPB organiser in Pyinmana in the 1940s. The area had been dominated since pre-war days by powerful landlords, and the party had mobilised thousands of landless peasants to refuse to pay rent to the land-owners: "Party members and farmers also used to enter the fields in large numbers, armed with ploughs. There were many fields where the peasants paid no rent, and therefore it was not legal to grow anything there. But our party workers and the peasants would quickly plough the field and plant seedlings. Once planted, the police did not dare to take the seedlings away. No one was allowed to destroy a planted field. In this way, land was actually confiscated from the landlords and handed over to the tillers."[7]

The "plough struggles", as they became known, sometimes developed into armed conflicts. This was the case in March 1947, when "Operation Flush" was mounted to suppress a short-lived peasant rebellion in the Pyinmana area. The local uprising was most probably instigated by the CPB and it led to Burma's first counter-insurgency campaign. The operation was commanded by one Col. Ne Win of the 4th Burma Rifles (Burifs), who struck with a heavy hand. This did little to enhance already diminishing sympathy for the central administration.[8]

Anti-government sentiments were further fuelled by allegations of out-right robbery by the 4th Burifs during the offensive. According to Thaung Htut, a native of Pyinmana: "Valuables stolen in the villages were sold by army officers to Daw Pu, a Muslim jewellery dealer and money-lender in Pyinmana. She as well as the officers of the 4th Burifs became rich as a result of the campaign."[9] The Pyinmana countryside was bubbling with discontent, and there was now even more fertile ground for Communist propaganda.

Part of the reason why the CPB was so strong in the Pyinmana area could also, somewhat ironically, be attributed to the fact that two of the best-known party organisers there, Mya Than and Mya San, were grand-sons of Daw Chan, one of the biggest landowners in central Burma in the 1930s. "It doesn't matter in what direction you point, your finger will al-ways settle on Daw Chan's land," went a local saying in Pyinmana. The fact that her grandsons led the struggle of the landless peasants may seem contradictory, but in rural Asia such feudal allegiances are often more im-portant than ideology.

The nucleus of the Communist army that was being organised in Pyinmana in May 1948 was drawn from two quarters. The first group, and the only ones with a military background, were ex-Burma Defence Army (BDA) personnel, who had fought the Japanese and returned home—with their weapons—when the war was over. But the main force consisted of what Ye Tun terms "converted dacoits": "The Pyinmana area was notorious for dacoits. They organised the villagers and armed them. Some bands had more than 100 men with guns. When they robbed, they robbed entire villages, not just a house or two. Therefore, it was a kind of robbery of one village by another."

These dacoits were organised by the CPB and supposedly given "proper guidance" by its political commissars. But some bands shifted sides as it suited them, and Ye Tun readily admits that it was not an easy task to "convert" these highway robbers into disciplined Marxist guerrillas: "The former BDA men were easier to control. They had fighting experience and were soldiers, not ex-bandits."

And fighting did indeed break out shortly after the first skirmish at Paukkongyi on 2 April, as CPB units attacked police stations in central Burma in search of more arms. Synchronised raids were carried out in Pegu, Myingyan and Toungoo in the central plains, and near the delta town of Bassein as well as in the Arakan area in the west. By May, regular battles were being fought between Communist insurgents and government forces.

The first side to crack under the pressure of armed conflict was not, hardly surprisingly, the hardened ideologues of the CPB. Rifts within the ranks of the government's army soon became apparent after more than a month of bloody clashes. On 15 June, twenty-one privates of the 1st Burifs at Waw in Pegu District defected to the CPB, bringing their firearms with them. In nearby Abya Buda, thirty-one soldiers shot their officer and went over to the Communists.

The following day, more troops from the 1st Burifs at Myitkyo, Pegu, followed their comrades underground, and so did elements from the 6th Burifs. A large chunk of territory around Waw, Daik-U and Thanatbin in central Burma was suddenly under firm Communist control; the first "liberated area" had been established.

Discontent soon spread to the People's Volunteer Organisation (PVO), an association of war veterans that had been set up on 1 December 1945. Known in Burmese as *Pyithu Yebaw Ahphwe*, it had in effect become a militia force loyal to Aung San before his assassination on 19 July 1947. It later split into two factions: a "Yellow Band" PVO led by Bohmu Aung, one of the Thirty Comrades who was close to the Socialist Party, and the much more left-leaning "White Band" PVO led by another of the Thirty Comrades, Bo La Yaung, and Bo Po Kun, also a veteran of World War II.

The White Band PVO went underground on 28 July 1948, taking with them 4,000 men, or approximately 60% of the PVO's total main force.[10] The White PVOs gathered east of Syriam, across the Rangoon river from the capital itself, and dug bunkers and trenches. It was only after the frigate *Mayu* had pounded their positions from the river that the PVO withdrew from the immediate vicinity of Rangoon.[11]

The rift within the military escalated further in July as the cabinet resigned and a power struggle broke out within the top leadership of the regular army. According to an agreement signed in Kandy, Ceylon (now Sri Lanka), between the British and the Burmese nationalists in September 1945, independent Burma's army would consist of a total of 12,000 men.

It would be made up of four Burman infantry battalions, as well as other units from the former colonial army so that old sepoys would be attracted to re-enlist: two each from the Chins, the Kachins and the Karens; one field artillery regiment, an armoured car regiment and various reserve and ancillary units and services such as the engineers.[12] But the Communists had infiltrated the 1st and 3rd Burma Rifles and the loyalty of the ethnic battalions was always in question, especially in view of the turbulent political scene that had emerged in 1948.

Home Minister Kyaw Nyein called on U Nu, the prime minister, with an urgent request. The army needed strong leadership to face the crisis, and Kyaw Nyein demanded that either Ne Win or Bo Zeya be appointed defence minister. At thirty-seven, Ne Win was the senior of the two (Bo Zeya was only twenty-eight), but both belonged to the Thirty Comrades. Kyaw Nyein advocated the former: "The only battalion you can rely on is Bo Ne Win's 4th Burma Rifles."[13]

Ne Win got the post, while Bo Zeya together with Bo Ye Htut, another of the Thirty Comrades, showed their dissatisfaction by staging a mutiny. The first unit to rise up was the 1st Burifs in Thayetmyo on 8 August. The following day, they took over the nearby town of Prome and began marching down towards Rangoon. The tiny Burmese air force had only two or three fighter aircraft, but it remained loyal to U Nu's government. They caught the mutineers in the open at Kyungale, north of Tharrawaddy, and strafed them with machine guns and cannon.

U Nu himself recalls in his autobiography *Saturday's Son*: "It was afterwards reported they had time to take cover after hearing the sound of aircraft engines, but they believed Rangoon had already fallen and the planes had come to greet them, so they simply stood in the open field and were killed . . . Almost the entire vanguard of the First [Burma] Rifles became casualties."[14]

On the 10th, 350 officers and privates from the 3rd Burifs, led by Bo Ye Htut, and the Number 3 General Transport Company at Mingaladon airport north of the capital joined the mutineers, and a convoy of thirty-two trucks rumbled towards Rangoon. Optimism ran high among the gun-wielding young soldiers: "We were certain we were going to capture the capital. We thought there was nothing that could stop us. The troops sang patriotic songs from World War II as the convoy advanced on Rangoon."[15]

But the authorities again responded forcefully by extensive use of aircraft, the only superior force they had left. Sustained airstrikes managed to halt the mutineers at Wanetchaung, just north of the capital. They retreated to Prome—and linked up with the Communists. The Revolutionary Burma Army (RBA) was formed from the former 1st and 3rd Burifs, plus the transport company.

Bo Zeya became the overall commander and allied his troops with the Communists; the combined force was now equipped with machine-guns, mortars, cannons, trucks and even armoured vehicles. They felt confident enough to attack major towns, not just isolated police stations. Like Thakin Soe, the youthful, bespectacled Bo Zeya was an outstanding violinist who composed his own love songs as well.

Meanwhile, the Karen ethnic minority was growing increasingly restive. Many Karens were Christians, converted by mainly American missionaries in the nineteenth century, and there had never been any love lost between them and the Burmans. The Karens had been loyal subjects of the Empire and many of them had fought with the Allies at a time when the Burman nationalists were still siding with the Japanese.

The Karens carried out guerrilla warfare in their rugged hills along the Thai border, ambushing Japanese units and providing the Allies with useful intelligence. Towards the end of the war, large numbers of Karens were recruited into the Burma section of Force 136, Allied-led Special Forces units that carried out attacks behind Japanese lines in Southeast Asia. Burman nationalists, encouraged by the Japanese, attacked Karen villages, and scores of innocent people were butchered.

Shortly after the Japanese invasion in 1942, Bo Tun Hla, an officer in the pro-Japanese Burma Independence Army (BIA; the BDA's predecessor), shot seventeen Karen elders at Papun in the Karen Hills. This was where guerrilla forces led by a British officer who had stayed behind, Hugh Seagrim, were active. In Myaungmya in the Irrawaddy delta region, 150 Karens were slaughtered by the BIA, including a former cabinet minister, Saw Pe Tha, his English wife and their children.

These reprisals against the Karen civilian population were so brutal that Seagrim surrendered to the Japanese rather than see them continue. He was executed—beheaded—by the Japanese shortly afterwards. His self-sacrifice on the Karens' behalf made a strong impression. Many Karens even today talk fondly of their "Grandfather Longlegs". [16]

Centuries of mutual mistrust between the Burmans and the Karens became even more apparent when Burma's independence process began. Led by Saw Ba U Gyi, a bearded, charismatic lawyer, the Karen National Union (KNU) was set up in February 1947 when several hundred representatives from the Karen-inhabited areas of the Irrawaddy delta region and the eastern hills close to Thailand met in the capital, Rangoon.

Even before World War II, many Karens, favoured by the British because of their courage and loyalty, had served with the colonial army and police force. Their discipline and fighting experience made them confident they would be able to stand up against the majority Burmans. Not surprisingly given their pro-British stance, the Karens wanted a separate state which would remain within the Commonwealth.[17]

Thousands of Karens still held weapons from the war, and when the governor, Sir Hubert Rance, addressed the subject in a letter dated 29 June 1947, Saw Marshall Shwin, a Force 136 veteran, responded by referring to wartime massacres by the Burman nationalists of the BIA: "With the painful memories of Myaungmya and Papun atrocities and other Burmese persecutions first in mind [the Karens] are not going to give up any arms for any pretext whatsoever."[18]

In July 1947 the KNU formed its own militia, the Karen National Defence Organisation (KNDO), which was commanded by Mahn Ba Zan, a school teacher from Maubin in the delta, and Saw Sankey, a former captain in Force 136. The KNDO and the KNU were headquartered on Ahlone Road in Sanchaung, a Rangoon suburb. KNDO militiamen in uniform, a bugle and cock on their cap badge, carried out daily drills in full view of the public on the lawn outside the office.

The KNU had boycotted the general election in April 1947 although they continued negotiations with the central government after Burma's independence in January 1948. Suspicions ran deep and the formation of the KNDO was a clear indication that the Karens were preparing for armed struggle to obtain a separate state. They were soon joined by the Mons, an ethnic minority living mainly in the coastal areas around the southeastern port city of Moulmein. Unlike the Karens, the Mons have a long and distinguished literary and cultural history. Distant relatives of the Khmers of Cambodia, they had built their own empires before the Burmans took over the Irrawaddy plain.

In March 1948 Mon nationalists set up the Mon National Defence Organisation (MNDO), modelled after the KNDO, with which they cooperated closely. As the situation was dederiorating, Mon and Karen nationalists met secretly and in August they began collecting arms in the Moulmein area. "We got the arms from various village defence forces in the countryside," recalls Nai Shwe Kyin, one of the Mon leaders at the time. "The commissioner in Moulmein summoned us and ordered the surrender of our arms."[19]

When that did not happen, Nai Shwe Kyin and sixteen other Mon leaders were arrested in a crackdown of Moulmein on 26 August. But their sojourn in jail turned out to be a brief one: KNDO militiamen in collaboration with the Karen-dominated paramilitary Union Military Police simply took over the whole town of Moulmein on the 31st and released the prisoners. Thaton had been captured on the previous day, and an ethnic rebellion in the border areas seemed inevitable—to add to the CPB uprising, the army mutinies and the PVO insurrection which were already in full swing across the central plains.

Moulmein was captured without a single shot being fired, but it was handed back peacefully to the government a few days later when U Nu promised to set up a commission to look into the possibility of granting the Karens local autonomy within the Union of Burma.

However, such attempts to placate the rebellious Karens were effectively thwarted when Burman members of the Auxiliary Union Military Police went on a murderous rampage in the Palaw area south of Moulmein. Many Karens are Christians, mainly Baptists, and it was Christmas Eve. Simultaneously, armed policemen burst into churches in eight villages where Karen Christians were attending the Christmas service. More than eighty men, women and children were butchered. Some say as many as 200 died in the carnage.

Then, in early January 1949, other police units, led by a Socialist hardliner, Bo Sein Hman, bombarded a Karen village in Taikkyi township, sixty kilometres south of Rangoon. The Rangoon daily *The Nation* reported on the 16th that twenty houses had been destroyed and over 150 Karens killed, among them 30 who had been lined up outside the village and executed in cold blood.

Ne Win's 4th Burma Rifles, which remained steadfast in its support for the government in Rangoon, joined the carnage and burnt the American Baptist Mission School in Maubin in the Irrawaddy delta. According to British historian Hugh Tinker: "All over the Delta the night sky turned red as villages burned. The Government looked on, seemingly helpless."[20]

The reason for these senseless killings is hard to ascertain. Tinker suggests that the Burman attacks were instigated by the PVO claiming to represent the government and were not necessarily condoned by higher military authorities. As the PVO was composed of ex-BIA troops, it could thus have been an extension of the Karen-Burman conflict during the Japanese occupation.

Communal tension escalated even further when an incident involving the KNDO took place in a Burman village, seventy-five kilometres south of Rangoon. U Nu writes in his autobiography:

> The Karens raided the village, took all valuables and executed six men in public. After the KNDO raiders had left, the villagers saw a steamer, with an empty cargo boat in tow, passing by, and frantically signalled it to stop. The

steamer had discharged its cargo in Bassein and was returning to Rangoon. There was a police escort on board. Learning of their terrible misfortune, the police brought the villagers to Rangoon. The following morning, a full account of the atrocities appeared in exaggerated form in the newspapers.[21]

A particularly ugly incident took place in early 1949. A hundred Karen men, women and children near the KNDO headquarters in Ahlone were seized by ordinary Burman townspeople and were imprisoned inside the Christian Church near Mission Road in the Rangoon suburb. U Nu received a curt telephone message from the police: "The mob intends to pour petrol on the building and set it ablaze."[22]

The crisis was defused only by the arrival on the scene of U Nu himself. Meanwhile, however, it was hardly a secret that the Socialists, who were included in the government, were secretly negotiating with the army mutineers, the PVO and even the CPB to obtain their cooperation against the KNDO, thus underlining that ethnic divisions were more important than political conflicts between different Burman groups. Whatever the case, the Karens felt threatened. They moved their headquarters from Sanchaung to a large, colonial-style brick building in Insein, a township with a large Karen population just twelve kilometres north of Rangoon.

Hundreds of KNDO militiamen, led by Saw Ba U Gyi and Mahn Ba Zan, gathered in Insein and began disarming government officials stationed there and in the nearby townships of Gyogon and Thamaing. Late at night on 30 January 1949, the government issued a decree outlawing the KNDO. Troops were dispatched the following morning to Insein to enforce the order. Two armoured cars appeared at Ywathit road junction leading to Gyogon, and fired their guns into Insein. The KNDO clashed with the advancing troops—and the long and bitter civil war between the Rangoon government and the Karens had begun.

Three days later, the entire township of Insein, including the local armoury, had been taken over by the KNDO, and for a day the Karens also held the nearby Mingaladon airport. Insein also happens to be the location of Rangoon's best-known prison, the notorious Insein Jail, and on 2 February, more than 500 prisoners were released by the Karen rebels.

Among them was a convicted murderer, an ethnic Karen named Saw Seaplane. He immediately joined the fighting and later became a prominent rebel leader. Those released also included Capt. David Vivian, a British officer who had been convicted of supplying Aung San's assassins with weapons. Even he joined the KNDO. A new headquarters was established on Rifle Range Road at the foot of Seminary Hill, a hillock on which the Christian missionaries had built a renowned bible school in the 19th century.

Karen troops took up positions all around Insein. Trenches were dug, bunkers constructed and roadblocks erected along the roads leading south to

Rangoon. Kaser Doh, then a 23-year-old KNDO soldier, was there: "We had only one armoured car, eight Oerlikon guns, which we had captured from Mingaladon airport, four 0.5 machine-guns, one two-pounder and some grenade launchers. Most of us were armed with .303 Enfield rifles, Sten guns and pistols. And the enemy bombarded us from every side with twenty-five and eighteen pounders, armoured cars and Sherman tanks. Aeroplanes carried out daily bombing missions from their base at Mingaladon and a government gunboat pounded Insein from its position in the Hlaing river."[23]

Although the bombardment was massive, spirits remained high among the 10,000 inhabitants of Insein and the 2,000 KNDO troops defending the tiny enclave just north of Rangoon. Housewives prepared packets of cooked rice and fish paste, or *ngapi*, for the troops, and girls drove jeeps to deliver the rations to the boys in the trenches along the outer defence lines. Food was never a problem; Insein was the site of several rice mills, and the godowns were quickly taken over by the KNDO. *Ngapi* was brought in clandestinely from Karen villages in the Irrawaddy delta region, southwest of Rangoon and close to the Bay of Bengal.

The church bells in Insein rang every morning as the local Christian population gathered to pray for the troops. Vast stocks of ammunition and a few heavy guns had been captured from the Mingaladon armoury when the airport was raided. The Karen fighters held their positions behind train engines and railway carriages at the locomotive workshop in the suburb, only 200 metres away from the nearest government artillery position.

Saw Ba Thin, a 21-year old KNDO soldier from Henzada who had joined the fighting, was in charge of two sections of troops defending the road leading from Gyogon to the Bible School in Insein. He recalls: "When we returned to headquarters to get more ammunition, we had to cross a huge football field. The Burmese knew this and always fired their Bren guns towards us. We often had to crawl in the ditches along the roads to avoid the machine-gun fire." Saw Ba Thin was armed with a British rifle of World War II vintage and carried a Smith & Wesson revolver in a holster at his hip. "They called me 'the cowboy'," he says, laughing at the memory.[24]

Despite such youthful bravado, casualties were extremely heavy. The wounded were taken to a makeshift field hospital which had been set up in the premises of the General Technical Institute in Insein. Medicines were scarce, but many Karens in government service came to join the KNDO when they heard about the fighting. Dr. Marcus Paw, the Karen chief medical examiner of Burma, showed up in Insein to treat the wounded, as did numerous Karen nurses from hospitals and clinics all over Rangoon.

When Lydia, an eight-year-old Karen schoolgirl from Insein, got tired of staying in the trenches all day, she used to go out with her friends to a mango plantation in the township's Ywama quarter: "Mangoes were in season and we climbed the trees to pick the fruit. But we had to run when the gunboats in the Hlaing river fired their Bofors cannons into Insein. One of my friends, another schoolgirl, was hit by shrapnel but survived. It was always eerie to go to the mango plantation because it was there the Karens buried their dead."[25]

The fighting continued for weeks, and soon spread to other parts of the country. The Karens in Insein had hoped that Karen battalions in the Burma Army would mutiny and provide them with badly needed reinforcements. This was indeed the case. Already on 25 January, a few days before the siege of Insein, the battle-hardened 1st Karen Rifles, led by Lieut.-Col. Min Maung, had defected and declared that they would join the KNDO; they had been stationed at Toungoo on the Rangoon–Mandalay railway line.

On 5 February, the 2nd Karen Rifles, who were fighting the CPB in the Prome area, also switched sides. They boarded twenty buses and set off for Insein, capturing the towns of Nattalin and Zigon on the way. But they never reached their destination: government forces ambushed them at Wetkaw bridge near Tharrawaddy and they had to retreat.

A few troops from the 1st Karen Rifles in Toungoo did manage to reach Insein, but the main force was stopped at Payagyi east of Rangoon. The 3rd Karen Rifles, stationed in Mandalay and Maymyo in the north, were disarmed and interned. And although they had remained loyal to the government, the three top Karen officers in the Burma Army had already been retired on 1 February, the day after the battle for Insein began.

The commander in chief, Lieut.-Gen. Smith-Dun, was replaced by Lieut.-Gen. Ne Win of the loyal 4th Burma Rifles. The chief of the air force, Wing Commander Samuel Shi Sho, was also dismissed, as was Brig.-Gen. Henson Kya Doe, a Karen who had joined the BIA during the Japanese occupation and after independence had become chief of operations.

Despite these initial victories over the insurgents, the threat to Rangoon became all the more apparent when one of the most loyal units of the Burma Army defected: the 1st Kachin Rifles. They had fought more intensely against the CPB than any other unit of the army, and their 27-year-old commander, Naw Seng, a decorated World War II hero, had earned the nickname "the terror of the Pyinmana Communists". But the mood turned when he was ordered to attack the Karen-held town of Toungoo.

Despite his youth, Naw Seng was already the most battle-hardened and also perhaps the ablest commander in the Burma Army. But the Kachins are Christians like many Karens, and Naw Seng had no desire to fight them on behalf of the Burmans, whom he in any case never fully trusted. On 21 February, he took his entire battalion and went over to the Karens. He joined forces with the mutineers from the 1st Karen Rifles in Toungoo, led by Lieut.-Col. Min Maung, and marched north, occupying one town after another.[26]

Tamla Baw, a young lieutenant in the 1st Karen Rifles, had fought against the CPB in Pyinmana, Toungoo and Pegu before his unit mutinied. He joined the "Upper Burma Campaign" as the combined effort was called. It seemed almost impossible to reinforce the Karens in Insein, so the only sensible thing to do from their point of view was to carry out diversionary attacks elsewhere in the country. The garrison town of Meiktila in the north fell to the combined Karen-Kachin force on 20 February. Tamla Baw remembers: "We travelled on foot, and by truck, bus and train. There was no real aim or coordination—but a lot of imagination. When we captured Meiktila, we also took over the air base there, including two Dakotas along with some English and American pilots who were flying for the Burmese Air Force. A platoon of Karens boarded one of the planes and a Kachin platoon the other. We flew to Ani Sakhan, a major army base at Maymyo in the hills northeast of Mandalay. Expecting some important visitors from Rangoon to arrive in the planes, all the officers were out to greet them."[27]

But instead, gun-wielding Kachin and Karen insurgents emerged from the planes. They arrested the officers and took over the town, a picturesque hill station built by the British in the late nineteenth century, complete with Victorian brick buildings, golf courses and a botanical garden. Many Karen insurgents were in jail in Maymyo; they were released and rejoined the uprising.

While some insurgents stayed in Maymyo, the main force returned to the plains below where, on 13 March, they captured Mandalay, the second largest city in the country. It had been defended by 3,000 supposedly loyal PVOs, whose attitude was in fact purely opportunistic. After the fall of Mandalay, it was hard to judge exactly which side they were on, and the situation was further complicated by the presence of cadres from the CPB as well as the Red Flags. Before Mandalay fell, more than 200 PVOs had been released from the city jail and armed by the authorities. The remaining prisoners—mostly CPB members and followers of Thakin Soe—were also set free when the Karen-Kachin force marched in.

Nai Shwe Kyin, who was in upper Burma at the time, recalls: "Mandalay was reoccupied by government forces in early April, but through trickery, not an actual military operation. The PVOs were staying in the old fort in the centre of the city, and they were contacted by the government through intermediaries, mostly Buddhist monks. Rangoon played on nationalistic feelings: "You have to liberate the city from the savage Christian Kachins and Karens." They also knew that the CPB and the Red Flags were not on good terms. So one day, the PVOs and monks came in jeeps, pretending they were CPB members and shouting abuse at the Red Flags. The next day, they would pretend they were Red Flags and shouted abuse at the CPB. The outcome was complete chaos. No one knew who was in charge of Mandalay and mobs took advantage of the confusion and looted all the shops in town. Eventually, infighting broke out and the government recaptured Mandalay."

Naw Seng, Min Maung and the others decided to make a push for Insein and Rangoon to relieve the beleaguered KNDO forces there. Thousands of rebel troops marched south and reached Pegu, only eighty kilometres north of the capital. The situation was serious, and U Nu summoned the ablest commander he had left in the army, Brig.-Gen. Kyaw Zaw, the only one of the Thirty Comrades, apart from Ne Win, who was still in active service.

Kyaw Zaw promised that every gun and every soldier he could find would be sent to the Pegu front with orders to fight to the death. U Nu and Kyaw Zaw together boarded a military aircraft and landed at an airstrip 25 kilometres from Pegu to inspect the defence lines. The advance was blocked; on 1 May Naw Seng and his troops withdrew towards Toungoo.

But the defection of Naw Seng's 1st Kachin Rifles and the Karen battalions had considerably weakened the government's counter-insurgency capabilities. Significantly, within four days of Naw Seng's mutiny, the CPB simply walked into Pyinmana and took over the town.

On the same day, 20 February, the town of Yamethin was also captured by Communist forces. Three days later, the CPB took over Myingyan town, and PVOs and RBA forces captured the oil field area of Yenangyaung and Chauk, west of Mandalay, depriving the government of one of its most important sources of revenue.

Magwe and Minbu, two dusty towns in the central dry zone, were occupied by the insurgents on the 25th, and in March the CPB marched into Pakokku, a market town on the banks of the Irrawaddy river between Mandalay and the oil fields of Yenangyaung and Chauk.

In Insein, meanwhile, Kaser Doh was on duty on the main road south of the town: "For three consecutive days in early April, we had heard nothing but the rumblings of gunboat shelling, tank fire, field batteries and mortars. But then, at eight in the morning on the 5th, a jeep with a white flag appeared on the road. It was followed by two saloon cars. They stopped at our roadblock and an army officer stepped out. He was accompanied by diplomats from the Indian and Pakistani embassies in Rangoon and Ah Mya, a Karen Anglican bishop from Rangoon. They said they had been sent to deliver a letter from the government to Saw Ba U Gyi. I radioed our war office in Insein and was told to let them through."

The delegation proceeded to the KNDO headquarters, where a two-hour meeting with Saw Ba U Gyi and his associates ensued. U Nu had appealed for peace and invited the Karen leadership to Rangoon for negotiations. Both sides agreed to a cease-fire for three days.

The following day, Saw Ba U Gyi went to Rangoon, driven in a jeep and accompanied by armed bodyguards and a wireless radio operator. He wore his characteristic green beret, and onlookers immediately recognised the bearded leader of the Karen rebels as they drove up to the old Governor's

House on Mission Road in the capital. He was met there by the prime minister U Nu and Lieut.-Gen. Ne Win, the new army chief.

Although U Nu had a reputation for being fairly sympathetic to Karen demands, his attitude this time was unusually uncompromising, suggesting that he was under severe pressure from his army commanders to deal harshly with the KNDO. After all, Naw Seng's combined Kachin-Karen force was at that moment heading south from Mandalay towards Rangoon. "No concessions were offered; on the contrary, U Nu demanded unconditional surrender. Saw Ba U Gyi left in disgust on the third day," according to Kaser Doh.

Government records from these informal peace talks say that Saw Ba U Gyi and Lieut.-Gen. Ne Win on 6 April signed a preliminary treaty suggesting an amnesty for all Karens who had joined the rebellion and allowing Karen civilians to keep some weapons for their own protection. This proposal was transmitted to Insein by Saw Ba U Gyi's radio operator. The reply from headquarters contained a set of demands, including one for a nationwide ceasefire and the right of the various rebel groups to retain their arms and territories for the duration of the proposed peace talks. This was rejected by U Nu and Lieut.-Gen. Ne Win.[28]

Whatever the case, disappointment among the Karens turned into fury when they discovered that the battered Burma Army had used the three-day ceasefire to bring down reinforcements by plane from garrisons in upper Burma, including Meiktila, which had been recaptured on 22 March.

During the fighting in Insein, the airport had not been safe for the government to use; it had even been occupied by the KNDO for a day. And although the Karens had suffered badly during the fighting, casualties on the government's side were believed to be much higher. "Morale was low among the Burma Army. The defence perimeter around Insein was a graveyard, littered with corpses, and this was only twelve kilometres from Rangoon," claims Kaser Doh. Three companies of elite Gurkha troops attacked Insein as soon as the ceasefire was over on the 9th.

On 21 May, the Karen leadership held a crisis meeting. They were running short of ammunition, and the ceasefire had strengthened the position of the Burma Army. More than 500 Karens, soldiers as well as civilians, had died in the fighting, and reinforcements from the Karen and Kachin battalions who had rebelled against the government did not seem able to advance anywhere near the capital. The KNDO decided to withdraw from Insein.

Under the cover of darkness in the early hours of 22 May, one Karen platoon after another slipped out of Insein. All night, the sound of roaring truck and jeep engines could be heard as the Karens evacuated Insein. Some units crossed the Hlaing river by boat; the plan was to regroup in the Irrawaddy delta region, where the main Karen population lived.

The delta, with its maze of rivers, islands, rich rice-lands, fruit orchards, jungles and mangrove swamps, was ideal country for guerrilla warfare, and this was the Karens' next strategy, following the failure of conventional battles. Other units headed north to the Pegu Yoma mountains, and to the Karen-inhabited eastern hills near the Thai border.

Despite the rather noisy evacuation, the government forces that besieged Insein did not interfere. "They probably thought that Karen reinforcements were arriving," an Insein veteran remembers.[29] Indeed, when Karen community leaders in Insein informed the troops that the rebels had left the town, they were met with disbelief. It was not until noon on the 22nd that government forces entered Insein, only to find it empty of KNDO troops. The town was once again in government hands after a 112-day, bloody siege that had cost nearly 1,000 lives.

But the war was far from over. More than half of the country was still occupied by insurgents, and almost every treasury had been looted. Even Rangoon was insecure, albeit for different reasons. According to U Nu: "In the capital itself, the administration wobbled. There were daylight robberies in the heart of town."[30]

U Nu realised that his government would not survive unless outside support could be mustered. In June, he flew to New Delhi for urgent talks with his Indian counterpart, Jawaharlal Nehru. U Nu later wrote somewhat obliquely: "Pandit Nehru treated me with great considerateness and I returned pleased."[31] Indian arms shipments began arriving in Rangoon a few weeks later, and the government felt more confident. The capital, at least, was safe.

In the countryside, however, the situation was still serious. On 25 August, the CPB announced that their "liberated area embraces 71,000 square miles [183,890 square kilometres] with a population of over six million people".[32] The Karens had taken over large tracts in the Irrawaddy delta region, and the Mons were active in the Moulmein area.

Smaller rebellions had also broken out in the Karenni states, home of the Red Karens, a Karen sub-tribe, and among the Karen-related Buddhist Pa-Os in southern Shan State. The Karennis were steadfastly maintaining that their area was already "independent" and they had no wish to join the Union. Led by the *sawphya* (prince) of Kyebogyi state, Saw Shwe, the Karennis were resisting the Burma Army's attempts to incorporate their area into Burma, and the KNDO gave them full support. The Pa-Os had been swept into the rebellion when Naw Seng's combined Karen-Kachin force entered their hilly country in the southern Shan states in August 1949.

Meanwhile, in the Arakan area in the west, near the border with East Pakistan (now Bangladesh), Muslim *mujahids*, and local Buddhists led by U Sein Da, a former monk, were also waging local guerrilla struggles against the increasingly isolated government in Rangoon.

By the end of the rainy season of 1949, U Nu's administration was actually in control of little more than the capital and was therefore aptly referred to as "the Rangoon Government". Minn Latt, a CPB intellectual who later went to study in Prague, recounted from exile his travels through the "liberated areas" of central Burma in that year:

> I remember making a journey from one major [CPB] base to another, covering about 200 miles [320 kilometres] and not encountering a single enemy. Of course, we did not always travel on fine asphalt roads and rails: for the most part we were on the fields, in the jungles, and going over the mountain ranges. Contact between one base and another may have been difficult and slow, but never impossible.
>
> We walked for a great part of our journey. Sometimes we had to take small Burmese canoes called *bauk-tu*. If we had a good *bauk-tu*, all we had to do was to sit still, but if by chance a man found himself in one that leaked, woe betide that man. He would have to keep bailing the water out non-stop. The only thing he could console himself with was that the rains were not coming down. But sometimes they did!
>
> Then we also rode carts drawn by oxen. There are no tarred roads between villages, hence in many parts motorised traffic is impossible. Even in summer, when motor vehicles make their way to villages near the highway, they have to follow the cart-tracks. Thus, in this people's war, the farther a village is away from the highway, the safer it becomes from motorised surprise attacks. In some places, oxen are unable to pull carts through the mud and swamps. Here buffaloes with immense horns take their place. The villagers are always willing to place their means of transport in the hands of their heroic fighters.
>
> We also travelled by military lorries when we came to roads which were controlled by ourselves; we had captured a lot of vehicles from the enemy, including armoured cars and light tanks. Railway was also a means we took. We travelled for about 25 miles [40 kilometres] by rail, driven by revolutionary workers. It was a pity we did not have a chance to travel by motor launches run by the "People's Transport Service", launches that once belonged to the Irrawaddy Flotilla Company.
>
> But in the jungles and mountains, none of the abovementioned means of transport, except, of course, travelling on foot, was possible. We had taken elephants there: elephants, those gigantic creatures that can be conquered by tiny men. They are very useful in jungles and mountains, though they can carry less on their backs than by hauling. They can easily drag huge trunks of timber, but on their backs, they will be able to carry only about six or seven hundred pounds [270–310 kilograms]. They make their way through the jungles, clearing their route through overhanging bamboos. Slowly but firmly, they pick their way along the dangerous paths, which are no wider than their own feet.
>
> Once the *mahout* [elephant driver] gave me command of the beast and slid down holding the huge ears. This man had terrible bouts of malaria attack-

ing him every now and then. When the attacks came, he would slide off from the elephant and lie down on the wayside covering himself with his *longyi* [sarong]. His fellow *mahouts* would pay no attention to this. "It is nothing unusual." A few minutes later, he would appear somewhere in the front, by means of a short-cut, and nimbly climb up again onto the neck of the animal. As I guided the elephant, I looked at the long line of animals. On their hips were branded the marks of the teak companies they had once belonged to.[33]

Predictably, the government painted a completely different picture of the rebel forces. The official publication *Burma and the Insurrections*, published in September 1949, stated that the rebels

allege themselves to be fighting for the oppressed masses; surely then they must have a proletarian discipline. But no. In Pegu District, Communists loot villages which support the PVO. PVOs loot all. In Tharrawaddy District, Communists flushed with power, murder people for personal grievances. Many Communist sympathisers are alienated because their personal friends molest their womenfolk. One supreme example is the case of a woman who with her husband had actively helped the Communists seize the town, but who later committed suicide because the Communist leader whom she and her husband had fed and sheltered raped her.[34]

The polarisation of Burmese society appeared complete after barely a year of independence. In December 1948, U Nu issued a desperate appeal to the CPB to come to the negotiating table. His old comrades from student days in the 1930s and the early nationalist struggle—Bo Zeya, Bo Ye Htut, Bo Thein Dan and Bo Thet Tun—were personally invited to talks in Rangoon. The rebel leaders promised to send a reply by 15 March 1949.

On 24 March, the rebels met in Prome to set up a united front, comprising the CPB, Thakin Soe's Red Flags, the PVO, the RBA and local Arakanese insurgents led by Sein Da. On the same day, a statement was issued in response to U Nu's plan for talks: the prime minister would be arrested and arraigned befor a "People's Court".[35]

Both sides were accusing each other of atrocities and boasting about "imminent victory". The Communists were so confident that their leader, Thakin Than Tun, proudly declared: "If we continue to fight with industriousness and determination, we will surely defeat the enemy within two years."[36] And on 19 July 1949, the second anniversary of the assassination of Aung San, U Nu, beleaguered in the capital Rangoon but waiting for more Indian assistance, called on the nation to unite behind his slogan "Peace Within One Year!"[37] Neither of these bold claims turned out to be even remotely close to the truth.

2

The Burmese Jigsaw

Calcutta, the old capital of Britain's Indian Empire, with its impressive Victorian buildings, spacious colonnades and palmtree-lined avenues, may seem an unlikely venue for an international, Communist-sponsored conference. But it is a city in which all that is magnificent about urban India is to be found side by side with abject squalor: its imperial grandeur, its theatres, its coffee-houses and its bookshops are set against some of the most depressing slums, the most wretched pavement hovels, the most noxious pollution and the most irreparable decay in the world.

An Indian weekly once said that parts of Calcutta seem "a city without hope, a soot-and-concrete wasteland of power-cuts, pot-holes and poverty; yet it inspires some of the country's greatest creative talents." It is therefore not surprising that radical ideas have always flourished in this fertile soil, and Calcutta has been the centre for revolutionary movements in South Asia since the beginning of the nineteenth century.

In February 1948, Communists and other leftists from all over the world gathered in this remarkable city to discuss the situation in a world that was changing rapidly in the wake of World War II. The Soviet Union had not only emerged as one of the winners of the war, but it had also proclaimed itself as champion for the peoples of Asia, Africa and Latin America who were fighting against colonial domination in various forms. Detente with Britain and the US, which in any case had been little more than a marriage of convenience against the Axis powers, was irrevocably over.

At Wiliza Gora in Poland on 22 September 1947, a prominent Soviet theoretician, Andrei Zhdanov, had given a speech on the occasion of the founding of a new organisation that united revolutionary groups from all over the world, the Cominform. He had advocated a much more confrontational line than the global Communist movement had followed since World War II, arguing that the world had become divided into "two camps".

Zhdanov had declared that one was made up of the US, Britain, France, and other "imperialist" powers, while the other camp belonged to the Soviet Union and the newly established "people's democracies" in Eastern Europe. "Progressive" nations and movements had to support this second camp if they were to have Communist support and sympathy. Many Western observers especially saw the newly established Cominform as a reincarnation of the powerful Communist International, the Comintern, of the 1930s.[1]

This new militant tendency permeated the meeting of the Southeast Asian Youth Conference in Calcutta, which had been called under the auspices of the Soviet-controlled World Federation of Democratic Youth (WFDY) and the International Union of Students (IUS). On 19 February, an impressive gathering of representatives from India, Pakistan, Ceylon, Nepal, Burma, Indonesia, Vietnam, the Philippines and Malaya congregated in a building facing Wellington Square in Calcutta's crowded Bowbazar area, the centre of political activity in the city. The meeting hall had been provided by Raja Subodh Mullick, a prominent Bengali nationalist.[2]

Observers and guests had come from Korea, Mongolia, the Soviet Union, Australia, Yugoslavia, France, Canada and Czechoslovakia. Six representatives of the Communist student movement in China unexpectedly showed up in Calcutta as well: they had not been invited, but their request to be included among the delegates was immediately granted, reflecting growing admiration for Mao Zedong's rapid advances in China at the time.[3]

Not all delegates were Communists, however. There were also other Asian nationalists with no particular sympathy for the Soviet Union. Messages of greetings were read out from a wide range of dignitaries such as India's Prime Minister Jawaharlal Nehru, Ho Chi Minh, the Czech Communist leader Klement Gottwald, Mrs. Eleanor Roosevelt—and even U Nu.[4]

But nevertheless the conference remained in Communist hands. Controlling the meeting were Joseph Grohman, the Czech president of the IUS, and Jean Lautissier, a young French Communist who represented the WFDY. The revolutionary bloc was further strengthened by the presence of Australia's fire-brand Communist leader, Lawrence Sharkey, then a controversial figure in the movement, as he was engaged in a bitter dispute with the British Communist Party over revolutionary strategies. CPB Chairman Thakin Than Tun and Politburo member Thakin Ba Thein Tin were in India at this time as well, not to attend the youth conference but as guests of the Communist Party of India (CPI), which was to hold its second congress in Calcutta shortly afterwards.

The CPB's links with India, and West Bengal in particular, had traditionally been very strong. The party had actually begun as an offshoot of the Communist movement in India. The first contact had been established when Thakin Thein Pe studied law in Calcutta from 1936 to 1938. It was during this time in India that he met radical members of the Bengal Students' Federation and, possibly under their influence, wrote his famous novel *Tet Hpongyi* ("The Modern Monk"), which criticised the traditional monastic hierarchy in Burma.[5]

When Thein Pe returned to Burma in 1938, he was accompanied by a prominent Bengali Communist, B.N. Dass, who helped his new-found Burmese comrades establish Marxist study groups in Rangoon and elsewhere.[6] But the firmest link between the Burmese and the Indian Communists was H.N. Ghoshal, who had become one of the party's foremost theoreticians.

Ghoshal was born in Rangoon, but maintained close ties with the Indian Communists. In the second week of December 1947, two months before the Calcutta conference, the CPB sent Ghoshal to Bombay to observe a crucial meeting of the CPI's central committee. There was widespread opposition against the moderate CPI secretary, P.C. Joshi, as the far more militant B.T. Ranadive was gaining support within the party. A rural rebellion had broken out in Telengana in Hyderabad State in 1946 and was still continuing in early 1948. What appeared to be a genuine mass campaign against the landlords and the state autocracy had been set in motion, especially in the two districts of Nalgonda and Warangal.[7]

While in Bombay, Ghoshal gave an interview to the CPI's daily *People's Age*, which contained a critique of the CPB's "rightist" mistakes, and urged the leadership to correct this "deviation".[8] The article appeared on 4 January—which, hardly by coincidence, was Burma's independence day—and it was clearly influenced by the more militant line that the Indian Communists had begun to advocate at this time.[9]

Nevertheless, on his return to Burma, Ghoshal was severely criticised for this "unauthorised" attempt at influencing party policies. He replied that the article, although signed with his Burmese name, *yebaw* Ba Tin, was not written by him but by a CPI leader who wanted to influence his Burmese comrades to adopt a more militant position. Whatever the case, Ghoshal was excluded from the delegations that the Burmese Communists sent to Calcutta in February to attend the youth conference and the CPI's second congress.[10]

On the final day of the youth conference a rally was held in the Calcutta Maidan—a green park in the city centre—and more than 15,000 people showed up. They listened to the radical youth leaders affirm their faith in the final victory of the "peoples of Southeast Asia."[11] In the crowd were four Burmese Communists. Two were official delegates to the youth conference: *yebaw* Aung Gyi and Bo Aung Min,[12] and two participated as observers: Hla Myaing (who surrendered in the 1950s and later became an editor of the state-run *Working People's Daily*), and Khin Gyi, the widow of Thakin Ba Hein, the father of "true" Communism in Burma.[13] Two other leading Burmese Communists, Thakins Than Tun and Ba Thein Tin, later attended the CPI's second congress.

According to most Western historians, this was a major turning point in the history of post-war Communism in Asia. Some observers even go a step further and advocate the theory that the youth conference was the place at which "directives from Moscow" were issued to "start unrest in Asia".[14]

Zhdanov's speech in Wiliza Gora is said to have been the impetus, and the Calcutta youth conference the vehicle for conveying these ideas to the revolutionary movements in Asia. The advocates of this conspiracy theory point to the fact that later the same year Communist-led, armed insurrections indeed broke out in Burma (March), Malaya (June), and Indonesia (September), in addition to already existing conflicts in Vietnam and the Philippines.

The most extreme version of this school of thought is to be found in *Inside a Soviet Embassy: Experiences of a Russian Diplomat in Burma*, which was ostensibly written by a defector from the Soviet embassy in Rangoon. It is, however, more likely that the book was ghosted by his interrogators following the Soviet diplomat's defection to the US in 1960, hence its mixture of apparently genuine reports from inside the embassy—and Western, Cold War-inspired statements such as this one: "the Communist insurrection in Burma . . . had been ordered by Stalin during the infamous 1947 Calcutta Youth Conference along with the Indonesian, Indochinese, Malayan, and Philippine rebellions."[15]

But although there is absolutely no evidence to support this conclusion, it is plausible to assume that the radicalisation of, for instance, the CPI and the CPB that followed arose from a confrontation during the youth meeting—which was also, it should be noted, attended by representatives from Burma's main party, the Anti-Fascist People's Freedom League (AFPFL), and the Indian National Congress.

The young Communists argued that the leaders of their respective countries had achieved a "sham independence" by collaborating with "the imperialists"—which prompted the delegates from the AFPFL and the Indian National Congress to walk out in protest. Some other delegates, notably the Filipinos, even returned home, denouncing the meeting as "Soviet-dominated."[16] The whole affair was in fact so messy that some of the Indian organisers found it necessary to carry firearms to the meeting hall at Wellington Square.[17]

A few days after this rather ill-fated youth conference, the CPI met for its second congress. This meeting went far more smoothly for the militants. Joshi was dismissed from his post and replaced by Ranadive, who in a report to the party stated that "Telengana today means Communists, and Communists mean Telengana".[18]

Thakin Than Tun, the head of the CPB delegation to the congress, thundered in a speech: "Comrades! 1948 . . . will decide the fate of the liberation movements in Southeast Asia." He went on to accuse the U Nu government in Burma of being a "subservient tool in the hands of imperialism", adding that thousands of Communist guerrilla fighters were ready to "swing into action whenever the occasion demands it . . . we are making all-out efforts to prevent civil war. But if the national bourgeoisie, backed by Anglo-Americans, insists on having it, well they will have it."[19]

This new militancy was encouraged by the Yugoslav delegates, Vladimir Dedijer and Radoven Zokovic, whose message was well received by the supporters of the Telengana struggle.[20] But Thakin Ba Thein Tin, who attended the congress, dismisses it as a "cock-and-bull story" that a "conspiracy" was hatched even at this meeting.

He says that the decision to take up arms in Burma was solely the CPB's and unrelated to almost simultaneous uprisings in Malaya, Indonesia and the Philippines. Ba Thein Tin also asserts that the only foreign representatives at the CPI congress were the six CPB delegates, Australia's Sharkey, the two Yugoslavs and a young Russian woman who was introduced to him as "Comrade Olga".[21] The Yugoslav delegates went back to Belgrade after the congress; they did not, as claimed by some historians, go to Burma.[22]

Than Tun returned home by plane after the congress, while Thakin Ba Thein Tin remained in the city for a few days before boarding an ocean liner bound for Rangoon. On his departure, Ranadive accompanied him to the jetty. In parting, Ba Thein Tin said: "You have helped our party a lot. But now we have learned that we have to rely on ourselves. You have the right to criticise us and make suggestions. But it's up to us to accept your criticism, and we won't blame you if we take the wrong steps."[23] Ranadive bid his Burmese comrade farewell, and the two men parted, never to meet again. The CPB went underground on 28 March, while the CPI in the end decided to continue working within India's democratic framework, despite the seeds of revolution that had been sown in Telengana.

US historian Charles McLane, who spent years researching Soviet policics in Asia, writes that the "Soviet response to the ensuing rebellions in Southeast Asia followed no fixed pattern", and even that there was "a perceptible decline in Soviet interest in the Burmese insurrection . . . after the spring of 1949"[24]—statements which effectively contradict the assumption that Stalin had mapped out some "master plan" for Communist seizure of power in Southeast Asia.

The most authoritative account of the meetings in Calcutta in early 1948 has been compiled by Ruth McVey. She argues that we can only say with safety that Zhdanov's "two-camp" theory was introduced at the Calcutta conference.[25] But, she adds, "it does not seem likely that the two-camp message lit the revolutionary spark in Southeast Asia, though it may well have added the extra tinder which caused it to burst into flame . . . the opportunity and incentive for Communist rebellion were already present in the countries where revolt occurred."[26]

In Burma, this was certainly the case. The country had a long tradition of peasant struggles, which had little to do with Zhdanov's speech in Wiliza Gora, or the haphazard meetings in Calcutta in 1948. In modern times, this tradition was revived as soon as the British marched into Mandalay in 1885, ending the last of the Burmese kingdoms and finalising the conquest that had begun with the first Anglo-Burmese war of 1824–26. The king, Thibaw, was led away in captivity and sent into exile in India—but the remnants of the old royal army, some of the surviving princes, court officials, village headmen and even Buddhist monks took up the sword in many regions of the old Burmese kingdom, which had now become a province of British India.

According to US historian John F. Cady:

> Throughout 1886 and 1887, every district of Upper Burma was in a ferment of revolt. Military posts and convoys were attacked, and virtually every male villager was ready to fight. The population accepted the hardships of war and enveloped all rebel movements in a conspiracy of silence.[27]

A year after the British conquest, Sir Charles Crosthwaite, an extremely harsh administrator, was appointed chief commissioner of Burma. He mounted a merciless campaign to suppress the rebellions. Mass executions of so-called "dacoits"—the Burmese would say freedom fighters—took place, and villages showing any sympathy for the rebels were promptly put to the torch. The total number of people killed in battle or executed on being captured, by hangings or decapitation, numbered in the thousands. Aung San's maternal grand-uncle, Bo Min Yaung, led one of these local resistance armies; he was among those captured and decapitated by the British.[28]

But the most serious challenge to the British was centred in the southern Shan States, where the famous Limbin prince—the son of the last crown prince of Burma and a disgruntled member of the royal family—had been in rebellion since the reign of King Thibaw. After the British conquest, the Limbin prince continued to fight and managed to unite several resistance leaders into the so-called "Limbin Confederacy", which reduced much of northern Burma to anarchy and desolation.

It took the British five years and the deployment of 60,000 regular troops and military police to stamp out the insurrections in the north. They could hardly have imagined this when they had first marched into Mandalay with just 500 men. The spirit of nationalism then went into the doldrums for almost two decades, as all leading resistance fighters had been eliminated. But even after Burma had been "pacified", in the colonial jargon, there were local uprisings in the Chindwin and Monywa districts, and skirmishes with small bands of guerrillas never ceased.

The whole pattern of peasant rebellions, dictatorial tendencies and social instability in Burma reflects an extremely complicated historical dichotomy which has persisted as the national dilemma. On the one hand, Burma has a strong authoritarian tradition which, in the past, was represented by the monarchy, and sometimes even by insurgent leaders in the countryside. A Burmese king was "shielded from the eyes of his subjects, wrapped in ritual, and responsible for the [Buddhist] faith; his authority was viewed as semidivine and unbridled", to quote US Burma scholar Josef Silverstein.[29] By the ancient tradition of divine kingship, the monarch wielded unquestioned power over the life and death of his subjects.

Consequently, the people were never consulted and elections of any kind were unheard of. "Authority from above has been accepted by the majority of people, and the leader who holds the palace or seat of government and controls the symbols of authority has the right to rule," continues Silverstein in his analysis. "As a result of this pattern, the people were little concerned with the affairs of the state. The average peasant did not expect the state to do anything to improve his life."[30] In short, the belief in the god-king meant that it was *lese majeste* to suggest or even to imagine any possible limits to his omnipotence.

The state never served as a vehicle for social and economic change. If the state became too oppressive—when, for example, it took an excessive amount of taxes or forced men to fight in needless wars—there was no reason for the individual to rise up against the tyranny. "The political culture of the Burman early was characterised by the people's stoic acceptance of misfortune and the government's excessive demands and victimisation through theft, war and plunder," Silverstein concludes.[31]

The other side of Burma's heritage is represented by a solid intellectual and creative tradition. The yearly cycle in any Burmese village includes a number of *pwes* — the word *pwe* is usually translated to mean a fair, but it is actually much more than that. Every *pwe* worth mentioning includes a theatrical performance, which is vastly enjoyed by all. There are few people in the world who are so fond of culture and drama as the Burmese. Sir J.G. Scott, a Scotsman who wrote about Burma under the pseudonym Shway Yoe in the last century, aptly said that "probably there is no man, otherwise than a cripple, in the country who has not at some period of his life been himself an actor, either in the drama or in a marionette show; if not in either of these, certainly in a chorus dance".[32]

Burma has always had a high literacy rate, and education has been a source of national pride since pre-colonial days. At the age of seven or eight, every Burmese boy was sent to the local monastery to learn to read, write and to memorise Buddhist chants and Pali formulas used in pagoda worship. For girls, education was less universal, but even so, the census for British Burma in 1872 stated that "female education was a fact in Burma before Oxford was founded".[33]

The long and strong tradition of widespread literacy was further enhanced by the introduction of British-style education during the colonial
era. Needless to say, the colonial authorities were mainly interested in procuring a stratum of English-speaking civil servants and skilled clerks for
foreign companies—but the result also included an abundance of newspapers and bookshops with foreign literature. Along with them came strong
Western intellectual influences. The removal of the monarchy in 1885 had
cleared fertile ground for the new ideas. The highly creative Burmese psy-
che flourished and became increasingly politicised. A powerful, intellectual and anti-authoritarian tendency began taking shape which, in many
ways, was as deeply rooted in Burmese tradition as the monarchic system.

By the turn of the century, new nationalist leaders had begun to emerge
from the youthful ranks of Rangoon College, working hand in hand with
others who had set up the first politicised Buddhist societies as early as
1897. The Young Men's Buddhist Association (YMBA) was founded in 1906
by a group of young college students. Soon thereafter senior government
servants and barristers also became members, and within a decade the
YMBA had established itself as a national organisation.

The original plan for a more firmly organised movement crystallised
into the General Council of Burmese Associations (GCBA) in 1917. It drew
its supporters mainly from the educated urban middle class; for instance,
one of its most prominent leaders in the earlier days was Chit Hlaing, the
son of an England-returned barrister.

Dr. Maung Maung, once a renowned Burmese historian, commented on
the emergence of the nationalist movement in his study *Burma's Constitution*:

> The press lent support to the GCBA movement. The *Sun*, of course, shone
> bright, joined by the *New Light of Burma*, the *Liberty*, the *Modern Burma*, the
> *Bandoola Journal*, and a few others in Burmese; the *Observer*, the *New Burma*,
> the *Free Burma*, and the *Rangoon Mail* in the English language.
>
> In the early years, the press was one for the common cause, and journal-
> ists, like barristers, stood in the vanguard of the movement. Newspapers
> were numerous and poor, and editors had to be a little of everything on their
> papers, but they were inspired and dedicated. Only when politics became a
> profession with political jobs to grab and spoils to distribute did some news-
> papers sink to the level of personal or party organs.[34]

Another group of urbanites who became involved in the nationalist
movement at an early stage were, of course, the students. The first peaceful challenge to the colonial authorities—as opposed to the armed insurrections in the late nineteenth century—came from these young, urban intellectuals in December 1920. A bill had been introduced which would pro-

vide Burma with its first resident university, replacing two colleges that had previously been subordinated to the University of Calcutta.

The students and other nationalists had reservations about some details of the bill, including matriculation requirements and tuition costs—but the British lieutenant-governor, Sir Reginald Craddock, turned a deaf ear to the protests. The bill was passed in its original version as the Rangoon University Act on 1 December. Four days later, 500 out of a total of 600 students in Rangoon launched a strike, which was followed by strikes by secondary school pupils in the capital as well as in Mandalay and other towns.

The students camped at the foot of the gold-covered Shwe Dagon pagoda—Burma's holiest shrine, which still dominates the capital's skyline. Despite threats by the Lieutenant-Governor, the public at large helped the strikers enthusiastically. In a statement issued on 8 December, the strikers proclaimed:

> We, the students of the Rangoon and Judson colleges, have entered into a struggle, the end of which no one can yet foresee. But we are firmly convinced of the righteousness of our cause . . . nothing can save the nation but a proud and indomitable stand on the part of Young Burma, with the wholehearted support of the Burmese people.[35]

Not all their demands were met, but the strike ignited a strong flame of nationalism which could not be extinguished. The first national leader to emerge from these early tumultuous years of the reborn Burmese nationalist movement was *Sayadaw* U Ottama, a Buddhist monk who had spent some time in India and Tokyo. He returned to Burma in 1919 and began travelling extensively, preaching patriotism and organising *Wunthanu Athins* ("Nationalist Societies") across the country.

In the Gandhian way, he transformed a basically political issue—nationalism and independence for Burma—into a religious one which appealed even to those who had not received British education. A fiery speaker and agitator, U Ottama attracted a large following of mainly Buddhist monks, who organised demonstrations and meetings. The Imperial Government responded fiercely, bringing in the military police to break up these gatherings.

U Ottama himself was arrested in 1921 because of his militant speeches: he was tried for sedition and sentenced to eighteen months' imprisonment. The impact of this unfair punishment could be felt all over Burma. It was the first time a nationalist had been charged with sedition and, adding insult to injury, he was a Buddhist monk of the eminence of a *sayadaw*, or great teacher: it was a challenge to the dignity of the entire nation. U Ottama was to spend several more spells in prison before his death on 9 September 1939.

The movement took a much more violent turn in 1930 when a revolt broke out in Yetaik village in Tharrawaddy district, where an ex-monk called U Yar Kyaw, a member of the GCBA, was setting up secret societies in the countryside called *Galon Athins*. They were similar to U Ottama's *Wunthanu Athins* but much more masonic in their organisation and way of operating. The *galon* was a powerful bird in Hindu mythology—the garuda in Sanskrit—and these groups attracted many village youths and others from the impoverished countryside, which the splendours of the colonial economy never reached. The people were poor, and they were desperate.[36]

In the meantime, a Burmese, Joseph Augustus Maung Gyi, had been awarded a knighthood and become the first native acting governor (for Sir Charles Innes, who was on home leave in Britain due to illness). Sir Joseph went to the worst affected area, the district of Tharrawaddy north of Rangoon, and held a *durbar* in the town, as he had done in many other places before. At this public audience on 21 December 1930, peasant representatives pleaded to the acting governor to cancel or at least postpone tax collection in the rural areas for a year. Sir Joseph, however, imperiously rejected the request. The following day, the peasants of Tharrawaddy took up arms against the government.

U Yar Kyaw, their leader, was now known as Saya San. He had proclaimed himself king, assuming the presumptuous title of *thupannaka galuna raja* (Illustrious Galon King), and raised an army of disgruntled peasants. With almost bare hands they decided to face the modern guns of the British colonial army: the arsenal of the rebels consisted of no more than 30 firearms, supplemented by hand-made shotguns manufactured from pipelengths and bicycle tubing. Apart from this, they had only cross-bows and spears. According to US Professor Lucien W. Pye:

> The Saya San rebellion which broke out in 1931 conformed to the traditional Burmese political and religious pattern of revolts which sought to establish a new monarchy. Guided by soothsayers and supported by magicians, tattooers and the sellers of protective medicines, amulets and charms, the army raised by Saya San placed him upon a throne under the White Umbrella, which symbolised royalty in old Burma, and convinced themselves that they were invulnerable to mere modern guns and weapons. The movement thrived on ignorance, superstition and readiness to accept a mystical and magical view of the universe, to live on unreasonable and emotional expectations of political success.[37]

The majority of the fighters in Saya San's quixotic *galon* army had risen to recover their land from the hands of money-lenders who had taken over vast tracts of the Burmese countryside during the repression of 1929–30. They may have been naive, but their grievances were real, and as Burmese historian Dr. Htin Aung pointed out: "The only way for the people of Tharrawaddy to end their misery was to rise in rebellion against the British . . . [and] was death not preferable to this misery of poverty under an alien rule?"[38]

Furthermore, their rebellious stance represented a tradition which, in a paradoxical way, was as indigenously Burmese as the subservient acceptance of victimisation through theft, war and plunder which Silverstein has documented. Saya San was the traditional *minlaung* (pretender) to the old Burmese throne, a figure often produced in times of crisis. Given such a leader, even the stoic Burmese would rebel against tyranny.

Saya San first raised his standard at *Alan-taung*—which literally means "the-hill-where-the-flag-flew"—in the rugged, densely forested Pegu Yoma mountain range north of Rangoon, east of Tharrawaddy. A whole battalion of British troops was thrown in against the *galons*. Saya San's headquarters fell and casualties were extremely heavy. But the insurrection spread to twelve out of forty districts, from its epicentre in Tharrawaddy down to the Irrawaddy delta and north to Upper Burma and even to some parts of the Shan States.

The government's forces resorted to brutal suppression: entire villages were razed to the ground, suspected rebels were decapitated and their severed heads displayed as a warning to others. In one particularly gruesome incident, fifteen severed heads were displayed in front of the deputy commissioner's office in Prome. Photographs of the gory exhibition appeared in *The Sun* newspaper, owned and edited by U Saw, and copies were sent to the British parliament.[39]

When the uprising was finally crushed in 1932, more than 10,000 rebels had been killed, 9,000 captured alive and imprisoned, and 128—including Saya San himself and two of his closest associates, Saya Nyan and a hermit called Bandaka—had been hanged. Saya San went to the gallows with his head held high on 28 November 1931. On the government's side there had been no more than fifty casualties, including civil police and officials. Aung San Suu Kyi notes that the rebellion aroused "the patriotic sympathy of the people, who were also repelled by the ruthlessness with which the British dealt with the rebels".[40]

The death sentences were passed by a special tribunal set up by the government to try the rebels. Trials were held in districts where insurrections had occurred, and many nationalistic lawyers eagerly volunteered to defend the accused, most of whom were ordinary, illiterate villagers. But one young pleader stood out among all these lawyers: Maung Saw, a native of Tharrawaddy and an ardent admirer of Saya San. He quickly ascended to prominence following his part in the trial, and the publication of a pamphlet in the form of an open letter to the British Secretary of State. To uphold the glory of Saya San *galons*, U Saw in 1938 raised his own force, named after Saya San's ragtag band of peasant rebels. The personnel of his new *Galon Tat* wore a green uniform and carried bamboo staves.

The abortive peasant revolt left the colonial victors jubilant in their private clubs all over Burma: they ridiculed the naivety of the superstitious rebels, their hocus-pocus and how easy it had been to defeat them. But to the young intelligentsia in Rangoon and elsewhere, the Saya San rebellion provided an invaluable lesson in the art of guerrilla warfare. The hostilities were far from over; the confident colonial authorities could not have foreseen that just ten years hence the tables would be turned.

Even as the peasant rebels were being slaughtered, serious-minded youths had begun discussing how to organise armed resistance against the British. These young men came from the national schools, which had been established after the 1920 student strike, which used Burmese as the medium of instruction. Many of them already had a sound knowledge of Burmese history and literature as well as Buddhism, more so than those who were being educated at European-style schools.[41]

Thus, although the Saya San rebellion was effectively crushed, it nevertheless played a crucial role in paving the way for the eventual success of Burma's independence movement. Despite the fact that Saya San had wanted a return to the world of the old Buddhist kingdom of pre-British days, the young nationalists had noted that most of his followers were, in fact, young monks and impoverished farmers, and the rebellion had clearly demonstrated their potential.

Leftist ideas had already entered Burma from India and Britain, and in one of those many Burmese ironies, the royalties from a book written by Saya San funded the establishment of a library of the first Marxist literature to reach Burma. Most of this literature was brought in by students returning from England, and a number of book clubs, notably the *Nagani* ("Red Dragon") Book Club, were set up in Rangoon and elsewhere. From then onwards, leftist thinking influenced nearly every political organisation in Burma, including the powerful *Dohbama Asiayone* and the prestigious Rangoon University Students' Union (RUSU).

The militant young nationalists called themselves *thakins* or "masters", a title hitherto reserved for the British. By adding this title to their names, they intended to show that they, the Burmese, were the real masters of the country. The centre of their activity was the leafy campus of Rangoon University—and the most prominent student leaders in the mid 1930s were the young group of five: Thakin Nu, Thakin Aung San, Thakin Kyaw Nyein, Thakin Thein Pe, and M.A. Raschid, a Muslim of Indian origin.

A second student strike occurred in 1936 when the RUSU president, Thakin Nu (later U Nu) and his close associate Thakin Aung San were expelled from the campus. The two were eventually reinstated, but by that time the movement had taken a very definite anti-colonial stand. The anti-

British movement, no longer confined to the activities of groups of militant students in Rangoon, spread across the country in the 1930s. The peasants, hard-hit by the collapse of the international rice market in 1930 and burdened by heavy taxes, were rapidly losing their land to money-lenders and absentee landlords. By the end of the decade, Burma was ripe for a nationwide uprising.

Two years after the second student strike at Rangoon University, the young nationalists spearheaded a mass uprising, and 1938 became known as the "Year of the Revolution", or the "1300 Movement", since according to the Burmese calendar it was the year 1300. A strike broke out among militant workers in the Yenangyaung oil fields southwest of Mandalay. In Rangoon, the students took to the streets and demonstrated against the British authorities.

When the police charged the demonstrators, a young student, Aung Gyaw, suffered a bad head wound from a baton blow, and died in hospital shortly afterwards. He was immediately proclaimed a martyr and all over the country the incensed public joined in the protests. In Mandalay, on 15 February 1939, the police opened fire on a huge demonstration, killing seventeen people, of whom seven were Buddhist monks. "Out of this national and class struggle of the Burmese people and working class emerges the Communist Party of Burma," the Burmese Communists declared much later in their official party history.[42]

According to early British documents, the "father of Burmese communism", was Oo Kyaw, the son of a big landowner in Henzada district.[43] After passing the secondary school final in Burma and the London Matriculation in Ceylon, he went to London in 1927 to study for the bar. Already strongly influenced by Bengali revolutionaries and by the India-based League Against Imperialism, he travelled widely in Europe, where he contacted various Communist groups. Oo Kyaw was believed to have been instrumental in sending Marxist literature back to Burma, and through a lively correspondence with a few selected student leaders back home in Rangoon he managed to pull the movement against the British sharply towards the left.

But no communist organisation was established until Thakin Thein Pe returned from India in 1938. The CPB was officially founded on 15 August 1939 when a group of young Burmese intellectuals met in a small flat in Barr Street, Rangoon. Among them were several student leaders from the *Dohbama*: Thakin Aung San, Thakin Thein Pe, Thakin Ba Hein, and Thakin Hla Pe, later known as Bo Let Ya. The charismatic Aung San was elected general secretary and in the official party history this unpretentious meeting in Rangoon is called the CPB's first congress.[44]

Quite independently from the emergence of the Indian- and British-inspired radical student movement among the Burman intellectuals, communist ideas had also penetrated Rangoon's Chinese community in the late 1920s. "Chinese communism" was first introduced into Burma by Wu Wei Sai (alias Wu Ching Sin) and his wife, who arrived in Rangoon in May 1929 from Shanghai.

He became editor-in-chief of a Chinese-language daily newspaper called *Burma News*, while his wife became a teacher at the Chinese-medium Peng Min School in Rangoon. The couple distributed Communist leaflets in Rangoon's Chinatown and built up a small circle of followers. Their activities were discovered in December 1929 when the special branch of the British police intercepted a letter Wu Wei Sai had written in invisible ink to the South Seas Communist Party in Singapore.[45]

His main message appears to have been that there was no fertile ground for communist ideas among the largely business-oriented Chinese community in Burma. Unlike Singapore and Malaya, Burma had very few labourers of Chinese origin: almost all coolies, dockworkers and other manual labourers in Rangoon were Indian. Wu Wei Sai therefore left Burma in 1930 and was never heard of again.

Only half a dozen members remained in a cell with the pretentious name "the Provisional Committee of the Special Division, Burma, Branch of the South Seas Communist Party". Because they were Chinese, the British police were able to have some of them deported to China. A Chinese cell was also established in Pyinmana but neither this group nor the underground Communist movement in Rangoon's Chinatown had any contacts with the radical Burman movement; instead, their links were with the Chinese-dominated Communist parties in Malaya and Singapore.

As far as is known, the Burman nationalists were unaware of the existence of these Chinese cells. Had the two groups established contact in the late 1930s, it is possible that communism might have succeeded in Burma. For, despite their Indian connections, the young Burmese radicals pinned their hopes for help in their struggle against the British on Mao Zedong and his increasingly victorious Communist army in China, but did not know how to contact them.

Then World War II broke out, a few weeks after the first Communist meeting in Rangoon—and the future of Burma was to change in a way that few had expected. In Asia the fighting had actually begun on 7 July 1937 when Japan attacked Chinese troops at the Marco Polo bridge near Beijing. This was the first move of a carefully calculated plan of conquest; the Japanese intended to establish what they called the "Greater East Asia Co-Prosperity Sphere".

What they really wanted, however, was to expand a strengthened Japanese Empire to include China and other East Asian territories. Nationalist Chinese troops, led by Kuomintang President Chiang Kai-shek, were resisting the Japanese advance in China, and Allied forces established a huge supply operation through an overland route that became popularly known as the Burma Road.

Tons of vital war supplies were unloaded from ships in Rangoon, then sent by convoys of trucks over the sun-baked plains of central Burma. The road continued through the Shan hills to Lashio, and on to Kunming in Yunnan, southern China. The Japanese began taking a keen interest in Burma, as war veteran Izumiya Tatsuro describes:

> Firstly, there was the Burma Road as the immediate objective. But apart from this, it had not been long since Burma had been conquered by the British, and there was a strong anti-British movement among the Burmans—who constituted the majority among the many races of Burma—because they were severely repressed by the British. The prospects seemed good for operations in Burma.[46]

Aung San and his younger generation of nationalists had decided to fight for complete independence from Britain—not merely Dominion status within the Commonwealth as some of the older politicians advocated—and they were convinced that this goal could be achieved only through an armed uprising. Aung San was only in his mid-twenties but already a political veteran. He had served as the general secretary of the *Dohbama* and, apart from being one of the founders of the CPB, he was also the founder of the Freedom Bloc, a broader alliance of which veteran politician Dr. Ba Maw was the president—and they looked to the East rather than the West for help.

In March 1940, after serving seventeen days in prison, Aung San represented the Burmese nationalists at a meeting of the Indian National Congress at Ramgarh in India. There he met for the first time the urbane, sophisticated statesman Jawaharlal Nehru and also the much more hot-blooded Bengali nationalist, Subhas Chandra Bose.

On his return to Burma, Aung San discovered that the colonial authorities there had issued a warrant for his arrest. He decided to slip out of the country. Together with a close friend, Thakin Hla Myaing, he stowed away on a Chinese ship in the port of Rangoon with 200 Rupees in his pocket and a dream in his heart.

Aung San wanted to fight for Burma's independence and he had been instructed by other militant *thakins* to go to Shanghai to contact the Chinese Communists led by Mao Zedong. But he was in a hurry—the district superintendent of Henzada, a man called Xavier, had publicly advertised a reward of five Rupees to turn Aung San in—so he and Hla Myaing took the first Chinese ship they could find. They disguised themselves as Chinese deck passengers Tan Luan Shung and Tan Su Taung.[47]

It was 8 August 1940, and the ship happened to be destined for Amoy—a coastal Chinese city which was occupied by the Japanese. The Japanese

tracked them down and instead of ending up with Mao Zedong's partisans in the mountains of China, Aung San and Hla Myaing were taken to
Tokyo.

The Japanese listened carefully to the two young Burmese. They were
promised what they wanted: arms and military training to fight the British. The Japanese took them to Thailand and, while Hla Myaing remained
behind in Bangkok, Aung San, again in disguise, returned to Rangoon in
February 1941.

The following month, he left with four of his comrades. Among them
was close friend Thakin Hla Pe (Bo Let Ya) and Thakin Tun Shein, who
later became Bo Yan Naing and married Dr. Ba Maw's daughter. With the
cooperation of the Daitoa Shipping Company—one of many fronts for Japanese intelligence—they boarded the Shunten Maru, bound for Tokyo.

Military training began in April with just the six of them: Hla Myaing
had returned from Bangkok to join the military exercises, which were held
not in Japan proper but on the Japanese-held Chinese island of Hainan.

In April, seven more young *thakins* were also smuggled out of Burma by
the Japanese on board a ship called Kairu Maru. That batch included Ko Aung
Thein and Thakin Shwe, who were later to be known under their *noms de
guerre* Bo Ye Htut and Bo Kyaw Zaw. In early June, three more *thakins* followed, and in July another two arrived in Hainan. A Burmese drama student
in Tokyo, Ko Saung, had joined the initial meeting but never participated in
the actual military training in Hainan. Including him, there were now nine-
teen young Burmese nationalists preparing to fight for independence.

Then, in July, an unexpected fourth batch of eleven arrived on board the
Koreyu Maru, which belonged to the same Japanese shipping line. This
last group included several members of a minority faction of the *Dohbama*,
the so-called Thakin Ba Sein-Thakin Tun Oke group. Thakin Tun Oke himself was in the last batch, accompanied by Thakin Shu Maung (later to
become Bo Ne Win), who had dropped out of Judson College in 1931 to
work as a clerk in a suburban Rangoon post office. Their arrival caused
some concern among Aung San and his comrades, who belonged to the
majority *Dohbama* faction, which honoured the old nationalist writer Thakin
Kodaw Hmaing.

Frictions soon arose between the original group and the late-comers.
According to Bo Kyaw Zaw: "Aung San and Ne Win quarrelled quite often
[in Hainan] . . . . Aung San was always very straightforward; Ne Win much
more cunning and calculating. But Aung San's main objection to Ne Win
was his immoral character. He was a gambler and a womaniser, which the
strict moralist Aung San—and the rest of us as well—despised. But for the
sake of unity, we kept together as much as we could."[48]

By now it was clear that the initial unity among the *thakins* belonged to
the past. Previously, even though there had been an abundance of different

political parties—the main *Dohbama*, the CPB, the People's Revolutionary Party (PRP), the *Sinyetha* or "Poor Man's Party", and others—these names had meant little since the activities and even the policies of these parties generally overlapped, and since many people were members of two or three parties at the same time. Now, however, various rival factions began to emerge—and the main division of opinion was between the left-leaning Thakin Kodaw Hmaing faction of the *Dohbama* on the one hand, and the extreme right-wing, Axis-oriented Ba Sein-Tun Oke group on the other. Aung San, Bo Let Ya and the more prominent of the *thakins* belonged to the former faction, while Ne Win—who was later to become Burma's military dictator—was one of the most prominent members of the latter.[49]

It should also be noted that the connection with Japan was not established simply because Aung San had caught the wrong ship in Rangoon. Japan's secret activities in Burma had been undertaken by various agents in Rangoon and elsewhere. As early as the 1930s a Japanese naval officer called Shozo Kokubu had made contact with the Ba Sein-Tun Oke faction. In 1940 another nationalist, Dr. Thein Maung, had visited Tokyo on a trip arranged by a Japanese agent in Rangoon, Dr. Tsukasa Suzuki.[50]

However, Thakin Kodaw Hmaing's followers, including Aung San, were suspicious of the Japanese, and the aborted trip to China should be seen as an attempt to find another source of support for the struggle for independence. When that failed, only the Japanese option was open to the young Burmese nationalists.[51]

The Japanese were clearly aware of this, which may help explain why they decided to include the Tun Oke-Ba Sein faction in their training programme. Thakin Ba Sein, the actual founder of the *Dohbama*, had together with Thakin Tun Oke begun contacting the Japanese as early as in 1938. On their recommendation, Ba Sein had already tried to cross the border to Thailand in October 1940, only to be caught and imprisoned.

Whatever the motives of the Japanese, with the arrival of this last batch, they added up to thirty young nationalists. Hence they became known in Burmese history as the Thirty Comrades. Their Japanese commander was Col. Keiji Suzuki, the officer who had apprehended Aung San and Hla Myaing in Amoy. While the only guiding principle of at least the Thakin Kodaw Hmaing faction of the Thirty Comrades was freedom for Burma, Col. Suzuki and Japanese intelligence clearly had other plans in mind.

In order to cut the Burma Road, the Japanese wanted an indigenous Burmese fighting force to boost their chances of success. This intelligence programme was code-named the Minami Kikan, and the young Burmese in Japan unwittingly formed a vital part of it.

In December, twenty-eight of the thirty comrades were transferred to Bangkok; Ko Saung never joined the army and one of the young Burmese, Thakin Than Tin, had succumbed to malaria in Formosa, after the training had shifted to there from Hainan. The Burma Independence Army (BIA) was formally set up in Bangkok on the 26th. Thakin Hla Pe (*aka* Bo Let Ya) later recalled:

> Enthusiasm ran high and each one of us drew blood from the arm to drink an oath of loyalty. That night we had a meeting of all those who had returned from the training camps in Japan, and Aung San suggested that we should each pick an auspicious name that would give pride and confidence and a sense of mission, a name to carry on our march. It was Aung San's idea and not one that we conceived by collective or prolonged thinking. We liked the idea when it was put to us, and at the meeting we made our selections, tried them out, liked them, and felt a few inches taller wearing the new names.[52]

"Bo" was added to all their new *noms de guerre*: It was a military title that commanded respect and authority. Thus, Aung San became Bo Teza (Powerful Officer), Hla Pe assumed the name Bo Let Ya (Right Hand Man), Thakin Aung Than was Bo Setkya (Officer of the Flying Weapon), Shu Maung became Bo Ne Win (Sun of Glory) and so on. The sole exception was Thakin Tun Oke, who assumed a Japanese name.

Col. Suzuki, the commander of the group, was named Bo Mogyo (Thunder). The Japanese officer had wanted a Burmese name also, and his *nom de guerre* was given to him by Aung San himself. But although Mogyo may mean thunder, there is also a much more subtle explanation to Suzuki's Burmese name. A Burmese saying circulated during British rule: *htiyo-ko mogyo pyit mai*. This prophecy literally meant, "a royal dynasty [the British Raj] will be struck by a bolt of lightning".[53]

In early 1942, the BIA entered Burma together with the Japanese army. Apart from the initial twenty-eight, many more Burmese joined in Thailand and along the border. They numbered about 2,300 in the beginning and soon swelled to 30,000 by the time they reached central Burma. On 7 March 1942, Rangoon was captured by the Japanese, aided by the BIA. The British retreated to the northwest, across the border to safety in India. On 1 August 1943, the Japanese granted "independence" to Burma. Dr. Ba Maw, who had led the *Sinyetha* in the late 1930s became *naingandaw adipadi*, or supreme ruler. He also assumed the title *anashin mingyi kodaw*, meaning "Lord of Power, the Great King's Royal Person". After more than a decade of liberal and left-wing influences, Burma's authoritarian tradition had surfaced again in the form of Axis-sponsored *Führerschaft* with tendencies that clearly hinted at National Socialism. Ne Win became commander of the reorganised Burmese nationalist forces, now renamed the Burma National Army (BNA).

Aung San's daughter, Aung San Suu Kyi, has presented probably the best analysis of the nationalist movements of the 1930s in her study *Burma and India: Some Aspects of Intellectual Life Under Colonialism*.[54] Comparing the different intellectual traditions of these two countries, she argues that already in the 19th century India managed to integrate new, mainly Western ideas relatively harmoniously into its development without losing its identity, whereas the much later and less widespread renaissance in Burma fell short of achieving an East-West, old-new synthesis at the intellectual level. Moreover, there was no time to allow political attitudes to mature before World War II broke out.

Aung San Suu Kyi argues:

> With the advance of the Japanese the Burmese had to face a new set of problems. They had to learn how to cope with a fellow Asian race whose achievements they had admired and who professed to be their allies .... It was against a different background from that which had prevailed under the British that the Burmese had to continue their search for a synthesis of ideas and action which would carry their nation to the required goal as an integrated whole.[55]

The myth of European invincibility had been dispelled—which greatly encouraged the Burman nationalists to look back into history in search of their own military tradition instead of developing the more enlightened tendencies which had begun to emerge in the 1930s, but had never taken firm root in Burmese thinking.

But it was wrong to assume that the Allies had given up. From bases in Assam in northeastern India, preparations began for an alternative to the Burma Road to reach out to the Chinese front once again. The immediate solution was to air-lift supplies from Assam across the mountains of northern Burma—"the Hump" in World War II jargon—and into China. The commanders of the ambitious campaign were two generals who deployed vastly different methods of warfare. One was the enigmatic Briton Maj.-Gen. Orde Wingate who led the "Chindits", named after the *chinthe*, the winged stone lions who are the guardians of Burmese temples. The troops were mostly British, but in their ranks also marched Gurkha Riflemen from Nepal, Nigerians of the Royal West African Frontier Force, Chinese from Hong Kong and native soldiers from the Burma Rifles.

Shelford Bidwell, who fought in the Burma Campaign, writes that among the Chindits "there were symptoms of almost religious fervour inspired by their messianic leader".[56] Wingate always carried his Bible with him, and quoted from the Scriptures freely. "His God," writes Richard Rhodes James, another veteran of the Burma Campaign, "was the God of the Old Testament, a preserver, strengthener and deliverer in battle, who defended the Righteous Cause but insisted His soldiers be worthy of His cause".[57]

Wingate always spoke with his eyes fixed on his listeners and "his harsh, metallic voice, his clear and vibrant style with its evangelical Old Testament flavour and biblical turns of phrase, never failed to grip his audience".[58] His ideal was the infantryman and the mode of transport was the mule. Wingate's tactics were essentially evasive and based on guerrilla-style hit-and-run attacks.

The other general, Joseph W. Stilwell, was an abrasive American who earned the nickname "Vinegar Joe" for his short temper. In the small, peace-time army of the US, Stilwell had served as a Chinese interpreter and after spending many years in the East, he became the American officer with the greatest knowledge of Chinese affairs. He was posted as US defence atta-che in China in 1935, and became chief military adviser to China's auto-cratic ruler, Chiang Kai-shek, during his rise to power. Stilwell's plan was for an army of well-equipped, US-trained, Nationalist Chinese troops to advance from India, "clearing the trace of a route through the tangle of forests and mountains and over the great rivers of the extreme north of Burma as far as the Chinese frontier".[59]

Not surprisingly, the two commanders clashed immediately over both tactics and strategy. Stilwell despised the British, whom he always referred to derogatorily as "those Limeys"; Wingate and the British perceived the US China policy as based on a profound misunderstanding of the corrupt and incompetent regime of nationalist Chinese leader Chiang Kai-shek. Although some US military commanders, including Stilwell himself, had at times expressed reservations about Chiang and his ruthless regime, they never wavered in their support for him. The British unequivocally asserted that the Chiang regime "was ready to suck on the seemingly inexhaust-ible udder of American wealth and determined to do nothing in return in the way of attacking the Japanese".[60] Indeed, when the Chinese forces en-tered Burma, they proved to be ill-disciplined and despised by the local people.

Wingate, on the other hand, counted on the loyalty to the British Crown of the many hill peoples inhabiting Burma's frontier areas—the Kachins, the Chins, the Karens and others—who already formed the backbone of the Burma Rifles. On the eve of World War II, only 1,893 of the soldiers of the colonial army were Burmans, compared with 2,797 Karens, 852 Kachins, 1,258 Chins and 2,578 Indians.[61] Many Karens in particular had been in the ranks of the force that had crushed the Saya San rebellion in the early 1930s, and Kachin troops had been used against pro-independence demonstra-tors in Mandalay in 1938.

Burman writers usually accuse the British of having conducted "divide-and-rule" tactics by deliberately isolating the minorities from mainstream Burmese politics. While that may be true, it is also correct to say that the various hill peoples in Burma's periphery have throughout history tended to perceive the Burmans as arch-enemies and untrustworthy. The British did little more than to take advantage of this already existing, centuries-old animositiy.

When the *Dohbama Asiayone* was established in the 1930s, there was a debate among the young Burman nationalists as to what name should be used for the country: the formal, old royal term *myanma* or the more colloquial *bama*, which the British had corrupted into "Burma" and made the official name of their colony.

The nationalists concluded:

> Since the *Dohbama* was set up, the movement always paid attention to the unity of all the nationalities of the country . . . and the *thakins* noted that *myanma naingngan* [the *myanma* state] . . . meant only the part of the country where the Burmans lived. This was the name given by the Burmese kings to their country. But this is not correct usage. *Bama naingngan* is not the country where only the *myanma* people live. It is the country where different nationalities such as the Kachins, Karens, Kayahs, Chins, Pa-Os, Palaungs, Mons, Myanmars, Rakhines, Shans reside. Therefore, the nationalists did not use the term *myanma naingngan* or *myanmapyi* [*myanma* country], but *bama naingngan* or *bamapyi*. That would be the correct term. There is no other term than *bama naingngan* or *bamapyi*. All the nationalities who live in *bama naingngan* are called *bama*.[62]

Thus, the movement became the *Dohbama* instead of the *Dohmyanma*.

Half a century later, in 1989, Burma's new military rulers decided that the opposite was true and renamed the country "Myanmar": "*Bama* . . . is one of the national groups of the Union only . . . *myanma* means all the national racial groups who are resident of the union such as Kachin, Kayah, Karen, Chin, Mon, Rakhine, Bama and Shan."[63] A similar confusion exists in English where some scholars maintain that "Burman" refers to the majority people who inhabit the central plains whereas the term "Burmese" covers the language of the "Burmans"—as well as all citizens of the country, including the minorities.

All these contradictions reflect an inescapable fact which many Burmans are still reluctant to acknowledge: there is no term in any language that covers both the Burmans and the minority peoples, as no such entity ever existed before the arrival of the British in the nineteenth century. Burma, as we know it with its present boundaries, is a colonial creation rife with internal contradictions and divisions.

No authoritative history of the many peoples of Burma and their origin has ever been written, but most historians accept the theory that the present inhabitants of Burma migrated from the north in different waves, and settled in various parts of the country which is known today as Burma. According to the 1931 census—the last proper census ever to be taken in the country—the Burmans made up 60% of the total population.[64] They are believed to have come down from the Tibetan plateau and settled in the Irrawaddy plain between the ninth and the eleventh centuries. They were an agrarian people who established small, relatively self-sufficient villages.

Their first ethnic clash occurred with the Mons, or Talaings, a people related to the Khmers of present-day Cambodia. The Mons had been living in the coastal areas of southern Burma long before the arrival of the Burmans, and they were the first to come into direct contact with Indian civilisation, adopt Theravada Buddhism, develop a written script, and adapt Indian law to their local needs.[65]

In 1067, the Burmese king Anawrahta defeated the Mons and took back with him to his capital at Pagan in northern Burma more than 30,000 Mon scholars, religious leaders, artists and slaves. Under the influence of the subdued Mons, the hitherto rustic Burmans were uplifted socially and culturally, and Pagan became a grand city with thousands of pagodas; the Burmans adopted Buddhism from the Mons and learned their alphabet, which was modified and used to write Burmese.[66]

The Mons were gradually assimilated into the new Burmese kingdom that was emerging. The last separate Mon kingdom, centred on Pegu, was conquered by the Burmans in 1757. But even so, Mon identity persisted and in modern times led to a strong nationalist movement demanding a separate state and autonomy for their area, mainly around the southeastern port city of Moulmein.

Another people also lived in southern Burma when the Burmans arrived about a millennium ago: the Karens, who are believed to have settled in what today is Burma in the sixth or seventh century.[67] Unlike the literate Mons, the Karens have no written account of their early history, but folksongs record their grandfathers crossing "an ocean of sand", which has been interpreted as a reference to a presumed migration from Mongolia, through the Gobi desert, to southern China and into Burma.[68]

The Karens suffered more at the hands of the aggressive Burman invaders than any other people in the region. They were treated as inferiors and, unlike the Mons, discouraged from intermingling with the Burmans. Those Karens who lived under direct Burman rule were forced to provide corvee labour for their new masters, and heavy taxes were imposed on them.[69] There were frequent raids into unadministered Karen territory by the politically more advanced lowland Burmans. Many references are made in Karen folklore to hardship and suffering experienced during their history.

Until the beginning of the nineteenth century, the Karens had no political organisation of their own and most of them were not integrated into any governmental system.

"The position of the Karens before the advent of the British was that of a subject race in true Oriental fashion," writes Karen historian Sir San C. Po.

They were treated as slaves, hence, they made their homes on the mountain-side or on tracts of land far away from the towns and larger villages occupied by the Burmans. High stockades surrounded those Karen villages, and sure death was the fate of all intruders.[70]

This situation was soon to change. In 1810, in New England, the American Board of Commissioners for Foreign Missions was formed, consisting of Congregationalists, Presbyterians and Baptists. At a historic service at Salem, Massachusetts, on 6 February 1812, the board nominated a number of members to travel abroad "for the sake of Christ and the promotion of His Kingdom in some Asiatic Field".[71]

The following year, Adoniram and Ann Judson arrived in southern Burma. To their great astonishment, Karens came down in the thousands from their hills to welcome the missionaries. In Karen folklore, there were obscure references to a "white brother" with a "Holy Book" and a god called "Y'we":

The Karen was the elder brother,
And obtained all the words of God (Y'we),
God formerly loved the Karen nation above all others,
But because of their transgressions, He cursed them,
And now they have no books.
Yet he will again have mercy on them,
And love them above all others.

God departed with our younger brother,
The white foreigner.
He conducted God away to the West.
God gave them power to cross waters and reach lands,
And to have rulers from among themselves.
Then God went up to heaven,
But he made the White foreigners,
More skilful than any other nation.

When God had departed,
The Karens became slaves of the Burmans.
Became sons of the forest and children of poverty;
Were scattered everywhere.
The Burmans made them labour bitterly,
Till many dropped down dead in the jungle,
Or they twisted their arms behind them,
Beat them with stripes, and pounded them with the elbow,
Days without end.[72]

The origin of this astonishing song is uncertain, but the reference to a "white brother" is believed to indicate that the Karens had met Nestorian Christians in China while migrating south. Whatever the reason, it made the Judsons' work much easier than they could ever have expected. Once converted and strengthened spiritually, the Karens struck back at their traditional enemies in the plains. They willingly fought alongside the British against the Burmans when the country was conquered in stages in 1824–26, 1852 and 1885.

Since then, several governments in Asia have branded tribal, Christian communities as "subversive", adhering to a "colonial religion"—and therefore opposed to independence and inclined towards separatism. This could be no further from the truth. The colonial authorities in India, and Burma, actually viewed the Christian missionaries with deep suspicion as they were seen as interfering with the traditional religious belief patterns of these communities—which were often located in sensitive frontier areas. For the first time in history, many of the local people also went to school. The colonial power wanted these areas to be under its direct military administration rather than being controlled by some dubious and unreliable spiritual organisations.

But the British did not miss the opportunity to take advantage of these recently converted minorities. When Burma was made a province of British India, many Karens were recruited into the army and the colonial police. Maj. Enriquez, a British army officer, commented on the Karen at that time:

> Owing to the missionaries' activities, the Karens are often better educated than the Burmans . . . and they have been taught to cooperate and cultivate their racial individuality . . . . Their outside affections . . . are reserved for the British. They have no delusions of Home Rule. The more anti-British the Burmans become, the more passionately loyal are the Karens.[73]

Significantly, the first institute of higher learning in Burma was the Judson College, named after the first American missionaries to the Karens.

The promotion of "His Kingdom" in Asia had given many poor and backward hill tribes a new life; a common creed instead of scattered beliefs in the power of spirits; a written language and their own literature. With this came self-esteem and ethnic pride. The arrival of the missionaries among the Karen and other tribal minorities of Burma had resulted in social, cultural, economic and educational transformation.

At one time, Christian Karens numbered 22% of the student body at the University of Rangoon, while they were only about 2% of the total population of Burma.[74] They took no part in the political activities of the Burman students, but a Karen National Association (KNA) had already been established in 1881—the first political organisation in British India. The KNA was set up four years before the Indian National Congress, and more than twenty-five years before the Burmans formed the YMBA. The KNA was dominated by Christian Karens although they never actually made up more then 15% of the Karen population in Burma. Christians have continued to dominate their political movement ever since, primarily because their education has been superior to that of Buddhist and animist Karens.

Under the colonial regime, many Karens migrated from their hills in the east to the Irrawaddy delta, which was being opened for rice cultivation by the British. These lowland Karens became the most assimilated; many adopted Buddhism as well as Burmese customs and social habits. Even so, the Christians, mostly Baptists but including a fair number of Roman Catholics, were represented in major delta towns such as Bassein, Henzada and Myaungmya—and whether Christians or not, the Karens developed a new consciousness during the colonial era and were no longer willing to accept a subordinate position.[75]

The first demands for a separate Karen State were raised in 1928 by Sir San C. Po, one of the best-educated Karens at the time: "The Burmans have the whole country to themselves. Where have the Karens a place they can call their own? . . . 'Karen Country', how inspiring it sounds!"[76]

According to the 1931 census, there were 1.37 million Karens in Burma, nearly 8% of the population at that time. But the name Karen actually includes a number of different tribes, of which the Sgaw by the end of colonial rule had become the largest and most widely dispersed. They were found all over the Irrawaddy delta, from the area around Prome down to the Arakan coast in the west and the hills along the Thai border in the east.

The other main tribe, the Pwo, lived almost exclusively along the seacoast from Arakan down to Mergui in Tenasserim Division, where they intermingled with the Mons. A third sub-group, the Bwe, were found in the vicinity of Toungoo and in the territory extending from the foothills east of that city into the Karenni states bordering Thailand.

Besides the Karens, the Shans were the most numerous of Burma's many ethnic groups, forming 7% of the population in the 1930s. They are not related to any other ethnic group in Burma. The word "Shan" is actually a corruption of "Siam" or "Syam" and is the name given to them by the Burmans; the letter "m" becomes "n" as a final consonant in the Burmese language. The Shans call themselves "Dtai" (sometimes spelled "Tai" or, across the border in southwestern China, "Dai"), and they are related to the Thais and the Laotians.

The origin of the Thai peoples is still a question of academic controversy, but according to the most reliable and scientifically documented theories, the cradle of the Thai race is to be found in Yunnan and Sichuan in southern China. Chinese historians mention that a Thai tribe called "Great

Mung" inhabited the western part of Sichuan around 2,000 B.C.[77] The Thais, however, called themselves Ailao, and in 122 B.C. they formed a united kingdom in order to counter Chinese incursions from the north, which had become increasingly prevalent since the days of the powerful Emperor Shih Huang Ti's reign (260–247 B.C.).

Thai historian Luang Vichitra Vadhakarn states that the Thais began migrating towards Southeast Asia in 69 B.C. to escape harassment by the Chinese.[78] The Thais who remained in the Ailao kingdom rose successfully against the Chinese emperor in 9 A.D., only to be deprived of their free status two centuries later.

The last unified Thai state in southern China was the kingdom of Nanchao, which covered large areas of southern Yunnan in the 7th century. This kingdom gradually declined, and succumbed to conquest by Kublai Khan in 1253. The movement south which had begun more than a thousand years earlier was now reinforced by hordes of new emigrants, leading to the setting up of Thai kingdoms, principalities and cities all over Southeast Asia:

> From their homes north of the Yangtzekiang, the Thais, due to never ceasing Chinese pressure, emigrated towards the south, southwest and southeast, and spreading out fanwise they invaded and conquered the countries of Yunnan, the Shan States, Upper Burma, Assam and Manipur and to the east and southeast Kweichow, Kwangsi, Kwangtung and the island of Hainan, and finally took possession of Upper Tongking, Laos and the present kingdom of Thailand.[79]

The western group, later referred to as the Shans, descended along the Salween river into the vast high plateau of northeastern present-day Burma. They settled in the valleys between ridges on both sides of the river and established an abundance of principalities, varying in size and importance. The smallest, Namtok, measured thirty-five square kilometres and was inhabited by a few hundred peasants scattered in two or three tiny villages, while the largest, Kengtung, encompassed 32,000 square kilometres, or roughly the size of Belgium, and had a population of several hundred thousand.[80]

The Shan states were never effectively united, but for a short while after the fall of the Burman Pagan dynasty in 1287, the Shans overran most of upper Burma and established their rule over the other ethnic groups. Silverstein writes: "The Shans were direct political rivals of the Burmans for control over the entire area from that period until 1604, when they ceased resisting and accepted indirect rule by the Burmans."[81]

But despite increasing pressure from the Burmese kingdoms in the plains as well as Burmese military presence in some of the principalities, their hereditary chiefs, or *saohpas* (*sawbwa* in Burmese), managed to retain a large degree of sovereignty. Neither Burma nor China was ever able to achieve effective conquest of the fiercely independent Shan princes and their states.[82] Like their Thai and Laotian cousins, the Shans were Theravada Buddhists with their own script, history and centuries-old literature.

Their political status, however, underwent drastic changes in the nineteenth century when Southeast Asia became an arena of competition between the two main colonial powers at that time: the French and the British. While Burma was in the process of being conquered by the British, the French had extended their sphere of influence over Laos in the east. In between lay the wild and rugged Shan hill country with its abundance of principalities and local rulers. Sir Charles Crosthwaite, British chief commissioner of Burma in 1887–90, described the situation in this manner:

> Looking at the character of the country lying between the Salween and the Mekong, it was certain to be the refuge for all the discontent and outlawry of Burma. Unless it was ruled by a government not only loyal and friendly to us, but thoroughly strong and efficient, this region would become a base for the operations of every brigand leader or pretender where they might muster their followers and hatch their plots . . . . To those responsible for the peace of Burma, such a prospect was not pleasant.[83]

To avoid the emergence of an uncontrollable buffer state between the two colonial powers of the time, the British extended their area of conquest in Burma to include the Shan states, which were "pacified" over the years 1885–90. Another main reason that the British decided to precede the French and keep them at bay on the other side of the Mekong was that the trans-Burma trade routes to China passed through the northeastern border areas of the Shan territory.

Several envoys sent by the East India Company to Burma during the period 1700–1824 had reported on the China trade from upper Burma and the Shan states. John Crawfurd, for instance, stated in 1826 that fourteen million pounds of cotton worth £228,000 were exported to China by these routes, supplemented by exports of jade from the Kachin Hills further to the north, amber, rubies, sapphires, edible birds' nests and so on. The trade was balanced by Chinese exports of copper, ironware, brass, tin, lead, gold leaf, medicines, and Chinese luxuries in food and dress.[84]

The two main trade routes to China were the "Ambassador's Road" from Bhamo (now in southern Kachin State) and the legendary Burma Road from Lashio in the northern Shan states to Yunnanfu (now Kunming) in China. The present boundaries of northeastern Burma are, in other words, a direct outcome of nineteenth century rivalry between the French and the British and the struggle for control of the lucrative China trade.

The Shan people, and the numerous hill tribes who inhabit the mountains surrounding their valleys, are today found on all sides of the borders in this region—in Burma, Thailand, Laos, China, and even in northwestern Vietnam. There are also Shans in Kachin State, primarily in Bhamo, Waingmaw, Hopin in the south, and the valley around Putao (Hkamti Long) in the far north of the territory, which was also ruled by a local *saohpa*. In addition, there were two Shan states in northwestern Burma: Singkaling Hkamti and Hsawnghsup (corrupted in Burmese to "Thaungdut").[85]

The thirty or so Shan states on the northeastern Shan plateau achieved a status different from that of Burma proper, which was a directly administered British colony. They became protectorates and the British recognised the authority of the Shan *saohpas*, who enjoyed a status somewhat similar to that of the rulers of the Indian princely states. Each *saohpa* was responsible for administration and law enforcement in his state; he had his own armed police force, civil servants, magistrates and judges.[86]

In 1922 the British created the Federated Shan States and for the first time the Shan area gained a governing body common to all the principalities. The Federated Shan States' Council was established, comprising all the ruling princes and the British governor in Rangoon. The council dealt with such common concerns as education, health, public works and construction. Peace and order was established in the area for the first time in many centuries. In addition to the hereditary *saohpas*, there were also *ngwegunhmus* ("tax collectors") and *myosas* (literally "town eaters", or tax collectors of another kind), who either inherited their titles, or were appointed by the princes to carry out local administration.

Partly because of their separate administrative status, the Shan states were never affected by the pre-war nationalist movement that swept central Burma at the time. The colonial machinery was also very light in the Shan states: the British presence was confined to a chief commissioner in the administrative centre of Taunggyi and a few political officers in the more important states.

On the other hand, very little was done to exploit the rich natural resources of the area and uplift it economically. The major preoccupation of the British in Burma was to develop the lowlands into a granary and rice-exporter for India. The colonial epoch meant for the Shan states peace and stability—but it was also a period of economic and political standstill.[87]

The situation was even more backward in the hills surrounding the Shan valleys. These highlands were inhabited by a variety of hill peoples, mostly of Tibeto-Burman stock—Kachins, Lahus, Lisus and Akhas—who were comparatively recent arrivals in the area. The movement of Kachins from the mountains of southern China and eastern Tibet was still going on when the British entered the area in the early twentieth century. But there were also tribes which had been there at least as long as the Shans, if not before them, such as the Mon-Khmer speaking Palaungs and Was. The Palaungs, who lived mainly in Tawngpeng state in the north, had developed into relatively prosperous tea-growers, while the Was were still head-hunters when World War II broke out: the wild hills they inhabited east of the Salween river, adjacent to the Chinese frontier, were never fully conquered by the British.

According to British researcher G.E. Harvey: "Throughout history the only administered areas on either side of the Burma–China frontier were the valleys and a few main routes. The hills were No Man's Land, even for the Chinese, and the Wa massif was especially *terra incognita*. Nobody ever went there and even the approaches were dreaded, the Salween and Mekong valleys being malaria-ridden—Chinese officers regarded the whole area as a penal station." It was not until 1937 that the British stationed two officers in the Wa Hills to introduce light administration.[88]

The southern Shan states, especially the hills surrounding Taunggyi and Hsi-Hseng, were inhabited by a Karen sub-group, the Thaungthu or Pa-O tribe. Although related to the Karens, they had adopted Buddhism from the Shans and developed their own literature.

To the south of the actual Shan states was another Karen sub-group that had come under Shan influence, but in a different way: the Karennis (literally "Red Karens"), who had remained animist or been converted by Christian missionaries—but who had adopted Shan political culture and established their own principalities ruled by *saohpas*.

The status of the Karenni principalities was even more complex than that of the Shan states, which were protectorates: the Karenni states were recognised as "independent" by an agreement signed in 1875 by T.D. Forsyth, for the British Crown, and Kin Wun Mingyi, the representative of the King of Burma: "It is hereby agreed between the British and Burmese Governments that the state of Western Karenni shall remain separate and independent and that no sovereignty or governing authority of any description shall be claimed or exercised over that State."[89] In reality, however, the Karenni states—Kyebogyi, Kantarawaddy and Bawlake—enjoyed the same status as the Shan states.

In the northeasternmost corner of the Shan states was another colonial anomaly: a district called Kokang which was inhabited by ethnic Chinese of Yunnanese stock. Kokang's mountains are some of the most strikingly beautiful in Southeast Asia; shrouded with mile-high clouds during the rainy season, they strongly resemble traditional Chinese scroll paintings. But the magnificent landscape has always contrasted starkly with the austere life in its villages. The Kokang Chinese live at an altitude where not even dry paddy farming is practicable and they have traditionally had to depend on various cash crops—tea, corn or opium—to buy rice from the more developed valleys.

The local trade in opium was controlled by other Chinese groups, mostly immigrants from Yunnan. Many of these came from the Muslim, so-called Panthay, minority of southern China, descendants of Kublai Khan's Arab and Tartar soldiers who settled in the Dali area of Western Yunnan and married local women.

In 1855, the Panthays rose in rebellion against the emperor in Beijing. The fighting blocked Yunnan for nearly two decades, and it was eventually crushed with a heavy loss of life. Tens of thousands of Yunnanese Muslims were butchered when Beijing reasserted control over the area, and many survivors migrated across the mountains into the northeastern Shan states. Speaking the same dialect as the Kokang Chinese, they settled in the vicinity, mainly in the Panglong-Hopang area immediately south of Kokang proper.[90] Deprived of land to cultivate, the Panthays of Panglong became traders. Since their arrival there more than a century ago, they have been first-class muleteers and opium smugglers.[91]

Yunnan, not Burma, was the main source of opium in East Asia at this time—but although increasing amounts of raw opium were harvested in southern China in the nineteenth century, India had for centuries been the chief producer of the drug for international trading. Some of India's Mughal emperors had tried to tax opium sales to raise revenue for the state. No single organisation, however, in any part of Asia had the will, the networks, or the political and naval power to create new markets before the advent of the colonial powers.

Britain's move to colonise India and other parts of Asia heralded a new era in international opium trading. In 1600, the British East India Compay had been formed with the mission to expand trade contacts between Britain and Asia, and between British spheres of influence in the Far East. In the centuries to follow, this trade had been pursued with much vigour. The stalwart mariners of the East India Company had fought their way into the highly competitive markets of Asia, followed by the armies of Britain's expanding colonial empire.

China, with its teeming millions of people, held the greatest attraction. It was a potential market for the products of the growing British Empire; but, more importantly, China could supply goods that were becoming popular in Europe itself—especially tea. Britain, however, faced severe problems in its trade relations with China. The British had little to offer that the Chinese wanted. In fact, the Chinese wanted only one item from Britain and British India: silver. By the late eighteenth century, every British ship that sailed from India to the Chinese port of Canton (Guangzhou) carried a cargo composed of 90% silver bullion.[92]

By the early nineteenth century, India faced a shortage of silver, and another commodity had to be found. The answer was opium, which grew abundantly in India and which gradually was becoming popular in China.

Opium replaced silver as the currency of trade with the Chinese. The flow of silver from India to China was effectively halted, and after the mid-nineteenth century the silver trade had completely reversed direction. Silver was now going back from China to India to pay for opium and tea.

India's income from the Chinese opium trade paid for constructing grand, imperial buildings in Calcutta, Madras, Bombay and other cities established by the British in India. An opium tax soon produced more than one-fifth of government revenue in the vast empire of British India.[93]

But Britain was far from being China's only opium supplier. Americans also sold Turkish opium to the Chinese. Clipper ships belonging to well-respected firms such as Perkins & Company and Russell & Company of Boston transported immense quantities of opium from the Middle East to China.[94] Persian opium was later imported by any trader in a position to do so. The American merchant W.C. Hunter used one simple phrase to describe the Chinese opium trade between 1835 and 1844: "We were all equally implicated."[95]

The Chinese government tried, at least officially, to suppress the opium trade. Opium was devastating China's population; millions of people became addicted to the drug. Opium smoking had been prohibited in China in 1729; cultivating and importing opium was specifically banned in 1799.[96] But these edicts were ignored by all Western merchants—and the ruling Ching Dynasty was too weak to enforce its policies. Local officials also were too corrupt to obey edicts from the Imperial Court in Beijing.

The Ching emperors tried time and again to stop the inflow of opium and the outflow of hard currency. China's emperor then sent an unusually vigorous official, Lin Zexu, down to Canton to stamp out the trade. Lin demanded that the merchants sign bonds promising never to bring opium to China again, on pain of death. Some American merchants signed, but the British refused.

When the news of the refusal reached Beijing, the emperor banned all trade with British merchants. Lord Palmerston, the British foreign secretary, decided to retaliate: a powerful fleet, with 4,000 soldiers aboard, was assembled. An official declaration said the fleet would "protect British interests".[97]

British warships bombarded the ports along the South China Sea to force the emperor to open them to British merchandise—which was primarily opium from India. But not everyone agreed with this policy. William Gladstone, a young Liberal politician who later became prime minister of Britain, said: "A war more unjust in origin, a war more calculated to cover this country with permanent disgrace, I do not know and I have not read of."[98]

The outcome was the first Opium War between Britain and China, which lasted from 1839 to 1842. China lost, and the victorious British not only forced open China's ports—they also forced China to cede the island of Hong Kong to Britain.

The new colony gave the British a tremendous advantage over other opium traders. Trade with China became a virtual British monopoly; Hong Kong became the most important transfer point for Indian opium entering the vast Chinese market. By 1854, yearly British sales of opium amounted to nearly 80,000 chests, weighing 133 pounds each; China's opium smokers numbered in the millions.[99]

This traffic, organised from Hong Kong, created some of the largest firms in the colony and laid the foundation for many personal fortunes. The most successful of all Hong Kong opium traders during the mid-nineteenth century were two young men: William Jardine and James Matheson. According to veteran Australian journalist Richard Hughes: "They were both Scottish, both religious in the stiff Calvinist way, both scrupulous in financial and personal matters, both indifferent to moralistic reflections on contraband and drugs."[100]

Jardine-Matheson still is one of the largest commercial firms in Hong Kong. Its present-day executives are conventional members of the Hong Kong business world, and few of them like to be reminded how the company's influence originated.[101]

Frictions between the Chinese and the foreigners continued after the acquisition of Hong Kong, and a second opium war was fought from 1856 to 1858; its final phase saw the Anglo-French forces charging into Beijing, where they looted and burned the emperor's famous summer palace. China had lost again, and more territory was ceded to the British. The Kowloon Peninsula was added to the British colony of Hong Kong. This time, China was forced to legalise the opium trade. According to US historian Leonard P. Adams:

> Following the Second Opium War, the Chinese were still diplomatically and militarily unable to stop the drug flow into their country, and Britain continued to peddle increasing amounts of Indian opium. In the peak year of 1880, China imported more than 6,500 tons, most of which was produced in India. However, China began to grow her own on a massive scale in the 1860s. After 1880 the demand for foreign opium decreased, until by 1905 the amount brought in was roughly half the 1880 figure. By the early 20th century, China's annual opium crop was over 22,000 tons.[102]

The areas of China most suitable for growing the opium poppy were in Sichuan and, most importantly, in Yunnan across the border from Burma. There was no shortage of consumers: by 1900 China had 13.5 million addicts consuming 39,000 tons of opium annually.[103] The poppy soon became a valuable cash crop for the the hill tribes of Yunnan, which often were the same as in northern and northeastern Burma. Thai researcher Chiranan Prasertkul argues that the Yunnan opium trade—and the spillover into Kokang and the northeastern Shan states—grew out of the Panthay rebellion in the mid nineteenth century. The social and economic order in Yunnan was disrupted, and the economic benefits of opium were so highly appreciated in times of social upheaval that the opium trade boomed.[104]

Some of the wealth derived from opium was also used to build an enormous system of rice terraces for cultivating paddy in Kokang, which at this time formed a buffer-zone between the Shan states and Yunnan. Although it remained part of China for several centuries, its location in a remote corner of Yunnan made it impossible for the central government to exercise control over the area. To the west, the deep Salween gorge formed a natural barrier between Kokang and the Shan principalities. Kokang was left alone and, over generations, a strong sense of independence was nurtured as a result. The area was consolidated into a single political entity by the Yang clan, which in 1840 had received a copper seal from the governor of Yunnan, giving them the hereditary rights to rule Kokang as a vassal of the emperor in Beijing.[105]

As the trade between Yunnan and British Burma flourished, some of the local Chinese chieftains in Kokang became relatively wealthy. For economic and strategic reasons, the British were becoming increasingly interested in semi-autonomous Kokang, and the area was formally incorporated into British Burma according to the Anglo-Chinese Burma Treaty of 4 February 1897, although its inhabitants were almost exclusively Chinese of the Yunnanese stock.[106]

Nevertheless, the British were no more successful than the Chinese before them in establishing central, governmental control over this remote area east of the Salween and immediately north of the Wa Hills. It could, at best, be described as indirect rule through the British-advised *saohpa* of Hsenwi, west of the river, to whom the local, hereditary ruler of Kokang paid tribute.[107]

In the late nineteenth century, poppy cultivation spread from Kokang into the Wa Hills, and the Panthay Muslims, who lived in Panglong-Hopang in between, conducted mule convoys which carried the drug from the poppy fields to the buyers in major market towns in northern Burma and even further afield.

A British traveller, who went through the Wa Hills and the Panglong-Hopang area during the colonial era, wrote:

Most of [the Panthays] were indistinguishable from the Yunnanese save that they had a mosque and occasionally a *maulvi*. But their inner elite had managed to retain its identity in 1931 when I met them—one or two were 6 ft. tall with straight eyes and aquiline features showing their Arab descent. In that year they were financed by Singapore Chinese and they had 130 mauser rifles with 1,500 mules, exporting opium by the hundredweight into French, Siamese and British territory, each muleload escorted by two riflemen.[108]

By this time, opium had according to Chiranan become "almost the standard medium of exchange in trade" in southern Yunnan, Kokang and parts of upper Burma.[109] The consumers of the drug were mostly ethnic Chinese: local people in Kokang, Panglong-Hopang and across the border in Yunnan, and overseas labourers and other Chinese in Siam (Thailand), Malaya, Singapore and elsewhere in Southeast Asia.[110]

Poppy cultivation was legal, but nevertheless restricted to the wild and mountainous areas east of the Salween river: the head-hunting Wa Hills and in Kokang. Although smuggling and unauthorised trade did occur, the business was tightly controlled by local and British authorities under the 1910 Opium Act and the 1938 Opium Rules.[111]

Officially, opium was a state monopoly, and licences were allotted by the colonial authorities to selected vendors at a fixed fee. At each shop, a Resident Excise Officer was stationed to supervise the sales and see to the disposal of surplus opium every evening. But even so, an early British government report stated that opium revenues "are growing steadily but do not yet cover expenditure."[112] Significantly, the main pre-war anthropological study of the Shans has only one reference to opium: "No religious Shan takes opium, so it is not openly used as a medicine, but native doctors use it occasionally mixed with herbs."[113]

Although most of the income from the opium trade was generated in markets outside the poppy growing area, the *saohpa* of Hsenwi—under whose jurisdiction the newly acquired territory of Kokang fell—collected more revenue than any other Shan prince during the British era.[114]

Another minority also lived under the *saohpa* of Hsenwi, especially in the hills around Kutkai and Namhpakka. The warlike Kachins had managed to migrate that far south before the British were able to control such movements of peoples within their Burmese territories. The first Kachins are believed to have arrived in northern Burma from Tibet more than a thousand years ago. A warlike mountain people, over the centuries they drove the Chins (see below), Palaungs and Shans out of most of the north. The Hukawng Valley was given its name during this conflict: *ju-kawng* in the Jinghpaw Kachin dialect means "cremation mounds", referring to the innumerable mounds where the bodies of the Shans killed by the Kachins were cremated.[115]

According to Henry Noel Stevenson of the Burma Frontier Service

Once the Kachins had established their right to the northern hills by the eviction of the former inhabitants, they set up their own tribal institutions and settled down to consolidate their gains. These tribal ties, which exist up to the present time, were probably established chiefly for protection against their enemies.[116]

Although the Kachins, like the Karens, were comprised of a number of tribes, the distinctions between them have had little divisive effect. There were the Jinghpaw, the Maru, the Lashi, the Atzi, the Lisu and the Rawang— but these represented linguistic groups rather than actual tribes.

Far more important bonds were formed by an intricate system of clans which cut across tribal barriers. Every Kachin belonged to one of five original families: Marip, Maran, Lahpai, N'Hkum and Lattaw. In one way or another, these clans were related in an all-embracing kinship network, the complexities of which were an anthropologist's nightmare. In practice, however, this system bound together a remarkably tight-knit society.[117]

Just before the turn of the century, a Swedish-American Baptist missionary, Ola Hanson, arrived in the Kachin hills. He was not the first Western missionary to the north, but by far the most energetic. The Kachins, until then animists, were converted to Christianity faster than any other ethnic group in Burma. After Hanson had put their language into the Roman alphabet, the Bible was translated into Kachin and they achieved a relatively high literacy rate. Baptist congregations were soon to be found all over the Kachin-inhabited areas of the northern Shan states as well as in the Kachin hills to the north. Pockets of animism survived only in the remote so-called Triangle area between the Mali Hka and Nmai Hka rivers, the headwaters of the mighty Irrawaddy.[118]

Akin to the Kachin were two other Tibeto-Burman tribes in the northwest: the Nagas and the Chins. The latter are also closely related to the Mizos (or Lushais as they used to be called during the colonial era) of northeastern India. Like the Kachins, the Chins were animists until the arrival of Christian missionaries about a century ago. They put Chin into written form as well, using the Roman alphabet. But the difference was that whereas the Jinghpaw dialect became the *lingua franca* of the Kachin tribes, the Chins remained divided by at least forty-four different, mutually unintelligible dialects.

Politically, the northern Chin tribes were ruled by hereditary chiefs and an aristocracy, while many of the southern Chins had a democratic type of organisation.[119] Each village was governed by a council which was elected to represent the main families or residential sections of the village. Contributing to the diversity and lack of ethnic cohesion in the Chin hills was the fact that each village was usually autonomous.

Unlike the Kachins, who were never conquered by any Burman state, the Chins were forced to pay tribute to the kings in Mandalay. But there was never any love lost between the two peoples. According to Chin historian Vumsom:

[The] Zo [i.e. the Chins] refer to [the] Burman as *Kawl* and to the country they inhabit as *Kawlram*, in a somewhat derogatory sense. *Kawl* means "under" or "below", therefore *Kawl* must have originally referred to the plain dwellers. [The] Zo profess low regard for Burmans and Burman social behaviour, but they envy the cleverness of the Burmans and their ability to take advantage of them in many ways . . . . Zo people feel that they are in constant danger of exploitation by the Burmans, and therefore the term *Kawl* for the Burmans is associated with ill-bred, unstable, tricky and treacherous character.[120]

The British recognised the fighting abilities of the Kachins and the Chins at an early stage. Along with the Karens, these two ethnic groups came to make up the backbone of the colonial army in pre-World War II days.

The Nagas inhabited the remote mountain regions immediately to the north of the Chin hills. Like the Chins, they spoke an abundance of local dialects, and were grouped into clans and virtually independent village clusters. Stevenson states that there were approximately 75,000 Nagas in Burma in 1941, and that the greater portion of this number came under "a gentle form of regular administration" only in 1940.[121]

While the Naga tribes on the Indian side of the border were converted to Christianity at about the same time as the Kachins of Burma, and obtained their own Roman script as well, the Burmese Nagas lived in isolation. There were no roads, no towns, only villages on hilltops surrounded by stockades. The Nagas were head-hunters and feared by the plains people. Few ever dared to venture into their wild mountains, and whatever administration existed was exercised from a safe distance in Singkaling Hkamti by the Chindwin river on the plains below.[122]

Socially and politically, the Nagas were torn apart by tribal warfare. Their head-hunting forays were intrinsic to their culture and their visions of virulent manhood. Every Naga village had at least one *morung*, or community hall, where the old men met and adolescent boys stayed until marriage. As soon as a boy reached puberty, he was no longer permitted to sleep in his parents' house but had to move to the *morung*. The walls of these *morungs* were decorated with human skulls: otherwise, the village would feel weak, ashamed and unprotected—and the crops would not be plentiful.

The bringing of heads, followed by days of feasting, were believed to enhance the fertility of the village, and not only in regard to the crops. A girl would never marry a boy who had not taken at least a couple of heads as he would not be considered a real man. Not surprisingly, the Nagas felt no affinity for Burma; most probably, the vast majority of them had never heard of that country, let alone agreed to belong to it.[123]

To the south of the Chin and Naga Hills was a territory which sharply contrasted with this primitive wilderness: the Arakan region, which had been a separate kingdom until it was conquered by the Burmans in 1784. It is believed—nothing is certain in early Burmese history—that the Arakan coast was originally inhabited by Indians. In the 10th century, it was invaded by a people closely related to the Burmans, probably called Kanran, one of the earliest Tibeto-Burman tribes from eastern Tibet to enter present-day Burma.[124] The newcomers mixed with the original inhabitants and formed the kingdom of Arakan. The Arakanese language is an earlier, archaic form of Burmese and the features of the Arakanese reflect their origin: they look like a mixture of Subcontinental people and Mongols.

The Arakan area was separated from Burma by a densely forested mountain range, which made it possible for the Arakanese to maintain their independence until the late eighteenth century. Contacts with the outside world had until then been mostly to the west, which, in turn, had brought Islam to the region. The first Muslims on the Arakan coast were Moorish, Arab and Persian traders who arrived between the ninth and the fifteenth centuries. Some of them stayed and married local women. Their offspring became the forefathers of yet another hybrid race, which much later was to become known as the Rohingyas. They speak a Bengali dialect interspersed with words borrowed from Persian, Urdu and Arakanese.[125]

There is no evidence of friction between them and their Buddhist neighbours in the earlier days. Indeed, after 1430 the Arakanese kings, though Buddhists, even used Muslim titles in addition to their own names and issued medallions bearing the *kalima*, or Muslim confession of faith.[126] Persian was the court language until the Burmese invasion in 1784. Burmese rule lasted until the first Anglo-Burmese war of 1824–26, when Arakan was taken over by the British along with the Tenasserim region of southeastern Burma. The separate identity of the Arakanese was further enhanced by the early introduction of British education, newspapers and other cultural influences which entered the area from Bengal.

When Burma was a part of British India, the rich ricelands of Arakan also attracted thousands of seasonal labourers, especially from the Chittagong area of adjacent East Bengal (now Bangladesh). Many of them found it convenient to stay since there was already a large Muslim population and, at that time, no ill feeling towards immigrants from India proper—unlike the situation in other parts of Burma. At the same time, Buddhist Arakanese migrated to East Bengal and settled along the coast between Chittagong and Cox's Bazar. The official border, the Naaf river, united rather than separated the two British territories.

Against this backdrop of ethnic confusion and centuries of mistrust, modern Burma emerged: a Burman-dominated, central heartland on both sides of the Irrawaddy river, surrounded by a horse-shoe shaped ring of mountain ranges inhabited by altogether more than a hundred different Tibeto-Burman, Mon-Khmer and Tai nationalities. But even inside this "horse-shoe", there were some important minorities: the Indians and the

Chinese, who dominated trade and commerce in virtually every urban centre across the country. Indian influence dates back to the time of the Mon empires, when Buddhism entered Burma along with an alphabet based on South Indian script.

During the British era, thousands of Indians were brought in to work on the railways, in the postal services and in the civil administration. Many were also soldiers in the colonial army. Others were encouraged to settle in the Irrawaddy delta, which became the new centre for Burmese agriculture and rice cultivation. Many Indians also went into business, and being more familiar with modern finance and commerce than the Burmans, they soon came to control a disproportionately large share of the country's economy. Before World War II, 45% of Rangoon's population was of South Asian origin—Hindu, Muslim or Sikh.

The most detested of all immigrants from India were the money-lenders, the majority of whom belonged to the *chettiar*-caste from Madras. The peasants, hard-hit by the crisis in the international rice market in 1930, and burdened by heavy taxes, were rapidly losing their land, chiefly to British banks but also to the *chettiars*. This had been the cause of the Saya San rebellion in the early 1930s, and the nationalist movement that emerged in its wake campaigned not only against the British but even more fiercely against the *chettiars* and the Indians who worked for the colonial administration. Generally speaking, any person of South Asian origin was looked down upon and referred to as *kala*, a pejorative meaning "foreigner" or "Indian".[127]

Not surprisingly, the Burmese have traditionally felt much closer to the Chinese than the Indians. Although the Chinese have been entering Burma for centuries, they have generally intermarried quite freely. The relatively small size of the Chinese community in Burma—estimated at something over 300,000 immediately before the outbreak of World War II—also accounts for the low level of hostility against the Sino-Burmese compared with the situation in other Southeast Asian countries.[128] The urban Chinese—mostly Cantonese and Hokkien—formed part of the mainstream economy of Burma and had little contact with other, upcountry Chinese minorities such as the Panthay Muslims and the Kokang Chinese in the Shan states.

In addition to these larger migrations there was always a constant flow of smaller groups which had been driven from their original habitats by war or famine or both. To complicate matters even further, the Burmese kings usually brought back large numbers of captives taken in battle: this included Thais, Manipuris and even French and Portuguese gunners who were housed in Shwebo in the north. According to Stevenson:

> The main result of this confusion of external and internal strife, the search for
> empty spaces, and the feuds among the kings and princes of early Burma, is

that the whole country is a mass of small pockets of mutually hostile peoples, speaking languages which vary sometimes from village to village within a single tribe, and having customs which differ in minor details to a bewildering degree.[129]

Pax Britannica provided the stability that was needed to keep this intricate jigsaw puzzle of nationalities, tribes, immigrant communities, and linguistic and religious groups functioning as one administrative entity. But World War II pitted many of the nationalities against one another, and old animosities flared anew. In his official history of the *SOE in the Far East*, Charles Cruickshank states plainly that: "the embryo guerrilla movement among the hill tribes in Burma which SOE developed successfully was based as much on hostility to the Burmese of the plains as on loyalty to the British regime".[130]

Australian Burma scholar Andrew Selth adds: "It appears that the hill people were encouraged in their traditional enmity towards the Burmans and in their belief that, on the defeat of the Japanese and return of the British, they would be rewarded for their services in a particular way."[131]

The disruption of the social order was most evident in the north, where the Allied forces were preparing for a counter-offensive against the Japanese. They were willingly assisted by the hill tribes of the area, while Burmans were on the other side of the fence. In Arakan, the Buddhists sided with the BIA and the Japanese, while the Muslims remained loyal to the British.

The Shans by and large stayed out of the war, and their separate status was recognised by the Japanese, who did not include the Shan States in the area under the jurisdiction of their puppet government in Rangoon. Two of the Shan States, Kengtung and Möng Pan, were handed over to the Thais and administered by Gen. Pin Choonhavan, one of Thailand's most powerful army commanders.[132]

The northern war theatre strikingly resembled Stevenson's description of a confusing mish-mash of rival nationalities. The road which Gen. Stilwell wanted to build through this remote corner of Burma was to cross jungles and mountains inhabited mainly by Kachin hill tribesmen that the Japanese had not fully conquered. But there were also Nagas, Chins, Shans, Chinese and even Indians and Burmans.

This road building effort was one of the most ambitious projects ever undertaken in Southeast Asia, adding new outside influences to the already bewildering scene. First went Stilwell's American-trained Chinese divisions, driving the Japanese before them. On either side, in flanking movements, Chinese and American patrols provided security for the road construction teams. On the heels of the Chinese divisions came the trail blazers, marking out the line with axes for the armour-plated bulldozers that followed. Last came the main labour force, who blasted the road, paved it, and constructed steel bridges across the innumerable streams and rivers along the way.

The labour force was also one of the most mixed in the history of road construction anywhere in the world. Lieut.-Col. Frank Owen, a British officer in one of these teams, described the labourers:

> Chinese, Chins, Kachins, Indians, Nepalese, Nagas, Garos slashed, hauled and piled. Negroes drove machines. Black, brown, yellow and white men toiled shoulder-deep in the streams, belt-deep in red mud. In one camp, 2,000 labourers spoke 200 different dialects.[133]

It was the British Empire, with American support, that struck back against the Japanese. Soon weapon-carriers, guns, tanks and infantry columns flowed down the ten metre wide, double-tracked, metalled, trenched, banked and bridged road which Stilwell had initiated. Town after town was conquered, and even the administrative centre of the Kachin hills, Myitkyina, fell on 3 August 1944 after a 78-day siege by the Allies. Stilwell's so-called "Ledo Road" became a new highway stretching from the small town of Ledo in Assam—hence its name—to Kunming, the provincial capital of Yunnan, a total of more than 1,000 kilometres.

But completing this road—and reconquering the north of Burma—would have been impossible without the support of local hill tribesmen, mostly Kachins, who operated under a unit known as Detachment 101. According to retired US army officer Charles M. Simpson:

> Detachment 101 organised and led an irregular force of Kachin tribesmen that ultimately numbered about 11,000 men. They operated deep in the jungle as individual agents, in small groups, or in battalion strength. They kept the Japanese under surveillance, raided, ambushed and harassed without cease. The high command in the theatre credited almost 90% of its intelligence to Detachment 101, and 85% of the Tenth Air Force's targets were designated by them. Detachment 101 counted 5,428 Japanese known killed, and a fair estimate of the real total is closer to 10,000. Once General Joseph Stilwell asked the leader of a successful Kachin ranger guerrilla unit how they could be so sure of the large and exact number of Japanese killed in a particular engagement. The Kachin opened a bamboo tube and dumped a pile of dry ears on the table. "Divide by two," he told Stilwell.[134]

A further effect of the war in the north was its impact on the local opium trade. On the one hand, international attitudes to opium had changed since the days of the free-wheeling trade with China. In London, Christians and liberals had argued intensely and emotionally that the opium trade from

British India was immoral. Their efforts had succeeded in 1917 when India's opium exports to China had been banned. But by then many Chinese warlords were already encouraging China's hill tribes to cultivate poppies so that an annual opium tax would pay for their troops. The Emperor in Beijing had been overthrown by a revolution in 1912, and virtual civil war raged in many parts of China even before the Japanese invasion.

The collapse of the millenia-old Chinese empire had brought chaos and rivalry between several new, republican contenders for power. The Allied forces supported the most powerful warlord—Chiang Kai-shek—against the Japanese, and he relied heavily on drugs to finance his war effort, and to enrich himself. On the battlefields of Asia, Christian and liberal concerns over the immorality of the opium trade meant nothing. In Burma, the opium business simply slipped from the hands of feudal Shan *saohpas*, and colonial tax collectors and bureaucrats—to be absorbed by the mighty war machine that was trying to halt the Japanese advance in the Far East.

During the war in the Kachin hills, opium was used for the first time ever to pay soldiers in northern Burma. When the British first raised the Kachin troops, called Northern Kachin Levies, their policy was to pay for local services in opium. This was done on a limited scale, but when US forces arrived, this changed dramatically. According to Ian Fellowes-Gordon, a British officer who served with the Kachin Levies during the war:

> US Air Force aircraft flew in large quantities of opium from India . . . and distributed it with typical efficiency, in ample, generous doses. Whereas in the Northern Kachin Levies, the *kani* [opium] was given only to villagers in exchange for labour and food, the Americans were now paying a number of their guerrillas with it. The men were entitled to draw pay in cash or in opium. As a result, it was starting to circulate as currency and, rather than being able to cut down the use of it, we [the British] would have to step up ours.[135]

Lasang Ala, a Kachin war veteran, remembers: "Packets of opium were air-dropped by Dakota planes from India along with arms, ammunition, money and rations. Each packet contained 80 *ticals* [1.28 kilograms] of cooked opium. The quality was excellent. It was so solid that we had difficulty in cutting the cakes with our *dahs* [swords]. The opium was distributed by the American commanders to their subordinates who used it for different purposes. First, it was given to villagers to pay for information about enemy movements. Secondly, whenever there was a shortage of cash, opium was used as 'money' to pay for chickens, eggs, rice, salt and so on in the villages. Thirdly, Kachin soldiers under US command could be paid in opium if they asked for it. But generally speaking, opium abuse was not widespread among our Kachin guerrillas. The American officers never smoked it themselves; they only distributed it to the villagers."[136]

Few official accounts of the war in northern Burma mention the role that opium played in the fight against the Japanese. A notable exception, however, is *Behind the Burma Road: the Story of America's Most Successful Guerrilla Force* by W.R. Peers, a commanding officer of Detachment 101, and veteran *Time* correspondent Dean Brelis, who as a young lieutenant served as a field operative for the same American unit. A reconnaissance team was sent to Fort Hertz (Putao today) in northernmost Burma—a place which the Japanese never managed to conquer and where brave Kachin tribesmen every morning hoisted the Union Jack while they were waiting for the British to return.

The trip, the authors said,

> had also given us a firsthand understanding of money and opium as other tools of guerrilla operations. Early as it was then in the Japanese occupation, we found that paper money which the enemy [the Japanese] had distributed was received with indifference; forthwith we gave highest priority to gathering large sums of British silver coins. It was also necessary to enter the opium business.[137]

The two US officers stated quite frankly that their decision to use opium was based on the fact that it would give their troops a "certain amount of freedom, of buying power." They did not question whether it was just or unjust:

> Simply stated, paper currency and even silver were often useless, as there was nothing to buy with money; opium, however, was the form of payment which everybody used. Not to use it as a means of barter would spell an end to our operations. Opium was available to agents who used it for a number of reasons, varying from obtaining information to buying their own escape. Any indignation felt was removed by the difficulty of the effort ahead. If opium could be useful in achieving victory, the pattern was clear. We would use opium.[138]

Elsewhere in Burma, other hill peoples continued their fight against the Japanese for the Allied forces, notably the Karens along the southern border with Thailand. Unlike the Kachins in the north, who fought exclusively against the Japanese and never encountered the Burmese nationalists, the Karens clashed with the forces of the erstwhile BIA. Many Burmans were also eager to take revenge for the Karens' support of the British, including the role they had played in crushing the Saya San rebellion. This was evident in the massacres of civilians which led to the surrender of the legendary Maj. Hugh Seagrim, the British guerrilla leader among the Karens during the early years of the Japanese occupation.

Tamla Baw served with Seagrim at the time of his surrender and subsequent execution at the hands of the Japanese: "He was deeply religious and had a strong personality. Above all, he loved us Karens. When he gave himself up, people wept in the villages."[139]

Resistance among the Karens was revitalised by the arrival of Col. John Cromarty-Tulloch, who had been one of Wingate's closest aides. At the age of 50, he was parachuted into the Karen hills and landed with his monocle still in place. Like Wingate, Tulloch was a deeply religious man with a firm commitment to Burma's hill peoples. He belonged to Force 136, a new unit that had been set up by the British to organise guerrilla resistance behind Japanese lines in Southeast Asia. The Burmese contingent of Force 136 was made up almost entirely of Karen, and Tulloch became their new hero. A specialist in jungle warfare, Tulloch led his Karen guerrillas to pin down nearly 30,000 Japanese troops in eastern Burma.[140]

As the war was going badly for the Japanese, frictions soon became apparent between them and their auxiliary force, the Burmese nationalists. The realities of Japanese occupation had also turned out to be even more brutal than British colonialism, as the Burmese nationalists had discovered much to their dismay. The dreaded Japanese *Kempeitai* intelligence machine was well-trained in torture of anyone suspected of being a "spy". Bo Ne Win of the Thirty Comrades was trained by the *Kempeitai* to perform some of these "duties", together with some of the other fascist-leaning members of the nationalist movement such as Dr. Ba Maw, the puppet head of state, and Thakins Tun Oke and Ba Sein.[141]

But the rest of the Thirty Comrades were disgusted. Ironically, the loosely organised Burmese Communists were the first to contact the Western Allies at a time when Aung San and the non-communists were still siding with the Japanese. This was similar to the situation in British Malaya, where the Communists also cooperated with the colonial power against the Japanese.

Already in July 1941, writing from Insein Jail, Thakin Than Tun and Thakin Soe issued a document known as "the Insein Manifesto" [142] in which they favoured a temporary alliance with the British in the face of the danger of a Japanese attack against Burma—which actually did take place in December of that year. In July 1942, after the Japanese invasion, two Communists, Thakin Thein Pe and Thakin Tin Shwe, reached Calcutta, where they were introduced to Force 136. Secret contacts were made with the nationalists, who were becoming increasingly disappointed with the Japanese.

On 27 March 1945, the Burmese nationalist forces—now renamed the Patriotic Burmese Forces (PBF)—eventually turned their guns against the Japanese. The PBF was about 11,480 strong and immediately received support from the British.[143] For strategic purposes, the country was divided into eight military regions:

No. 1 Region (Prome, Henzada, Tharrawaddy and Insein). Military commander: Aung San; political adviser: Thakin Ba Hein (CPB leader);

No. 2 Region (Pyapon/Eastern Irrawaddy delta). Military commander: Ne Win (one of the Thirty Comrades); political adviser: Thakin Soe (CPB leader);

No. 3 Region (Western Irrawaddy delta). Military commander: Saw Kya Doe (a Karen);

No. 4 Region (South of Toungoo/Hanthawaddy). Military commander: Kyaw Zaw (one of the Thirty Comrades); political adviser: Thakin Chit (PRP leader);

No. 5 Region: (Tavoy-Mergui). Military commander: Tin Tun; political adviser: Thakin Ba Thein Tin (prominent CPB member);

No. 6 Region (Pyinmana-Meiktila). Military commander: Bo Ye Htut (one of the Thirty Comrades); political adviser: Thakin Kyaw Nyein (ex-student leader);

No. 7 Region (Thayetmyo-Minbu). Military commander: Bohmu Aung (one of the Thirty Comrades); political adviser: Thakin Tin Mya (CPB member);

No. 8 Region (Upper Burma): Commander: Bo Ba Htoo.

The set-up reflected the close relationship which now existed between the Communists and virtually all non-communist nationalists—although it would have been a clear exaggeration to say that it was the CPB that actually led the struggle, which the Communists have since claimed.[144]

To coordinate political activities, a front organisation, the AFPFL, was formed in August 1944, comprising nationalists as well as Communists and even some regional groupings. Aung San, Ne Win and Bo Let Ya represented the army; Thakin Soe, Thakin Than Tun and Thakin Tin Mya came from the CPB; and Thakin Ba Swe, Thakin Kyaw Nyein and Thakin Chit were from the PRP. Allied forces in India pushed east, and on 1 May 1945, Rangoon was liberated. The last Japanese forces withdrew from Burma a few months later.

The reorganised PBF was recognised by Lord Louis Mountbatten as "an Allied force" at a meeting in New Delhi on 30 May. The CPB was now at the height of its strength and popularity because of the crucial role the Communists had unquestionably played in the anti-Japanese struggle. During this period, the CPB developed into a true political party, not just a Marxist study group comprising people who spent most of their time working for other parties, as had been the case in 1939–41. In early 1943, Thakin Soe gave a course to twelve followers in the delta town of Pyapon; this event is seen by many scholars as the real origin of the CPB. [145]

In January 1944, another meeting was held in Nyaungkyaung village of Kyaiklat township; it was attended by seven people, including Thakin Soe and Thakin Tin Mya. Thakin Soe was elected secretary general of the CPB.

This meeting is sometimes referred to as the CPB's first congress, but it was not recognised as such by the main party. [146] At this time, however, many prominent Burmese became party members, either temporarily because of the relative popularity of the CPB, or permanently as dedicated Communists. Ne Win belonged to the former group;[147] Bo Ye Htut, Bo Zeya and a few other heroes of the anti-Japanese struggle belonged to the latter.

The war was over—and Burma's democratic process, interrupted by the Japanese occupation, gained momentum once again. Renewed rallies were held in Rangoon to press demands for complete independence for Burma. Sir Reginald Dorman-Smith, the British governor who had spent the war years in exile in Simla, India, returned on 16 October 1945. Well before that, on 19 August, the AFPFL led by Aung San had held a historic mass meeting in the *Nethurein* Cinema Hall in Rangoon, demanding full independence for Burma, outside of the Commonwealth.

The efficiency of the CPB's organisation increased notably in the immediate post-war period. The party was reorganised into an effective Communist organisation at the second party congress, which was held on 20–21 July 1945 in Rangoon. It was attended by more than 120 delegates from all over the country, representing a total of 6,000 party members, not including members of CPB-affiliated mass organisations who numbered in the tens of thousands.[148]

A 21-member central committee was elected; it named Thakin Than Tun chairman of the politburo, and Thakin Thein Pe new general secretary—in absentia since he was still in India. Thakin Thein Pe returned to Burma later that year and assumed leadership of the party. The CPB at this time advocated a peaceful transition to socialism, a line which was later branded "Browderism" after the reformist doctrines of the then chairman of the Communist Party of the United States, Earl Browder.

An extended plenum of the CPB was held in February–March 1946. Thakin Soe, a hardliner who felt his wartime role in the underground entitled him to greater recognition, launched a sharp attack on the party leadership. He seized upon the issue of "Browderism", and submitted a memorandum, accusing Thakin Than Tun and Thakin Thein Pe of advocating the moderate line.

In retaliation, Thakin Than Tun accused Thakin Soe of immorality and "sexual misconduct". Thakin Soe succeeded in forcing his two rivals to step down temporarily. During the leadership vacuum, Soe tried to fill the central committee with his own people—but this backfired when Thakin Than Tun and Thakin Thein Pe returned to power after a few days.[149]

The break between Thakin Soe and the main party was now final and irrevocable; he set up his own Communist Party (Red Flag) and went underground in the Irrawaddy delta to wage a guerrilla war against the British. Some of the other hardline Communists, including Thakin Tin Mya and six members of the central committee, sided with Thakin Soe in the conflict.

The Burmese government later described Thakin Soe in these terms:

> He reads voraciously and writes profusely. He is extremely ruthless in his methods and combines in himself the qualities of a terrorist, a voluminous pamphleteer and a dauntless campaigner . . . . He has a considerable following . . . in Maubin, Pyapon and Hanthawaddy districts and . . . in Pakokku and Lower Chindwin districts.[150]

The question of "Browderism" became more controversial after a meeting between Lord Mountbatten and the Burmese wartime resistance leaders in Kandy in September 1945. Then it was decided to dismantle the large army Aung San and others had built up, and to form a new Burma Army consisting of a mere 4,700 troops. But about 3,500 ex-resistance fighters did not register for regular enlistment and instead formed the *Pyithu Yebaw Ahphwe*, which became known in English as the People's Volunteer Organisation (PVO). In effect, it was a paramilitary force controlled by Aung San.

Nonetheless, the Kandy Agreement was seen by the hardline Communists as a surrender to the British. At this time, Thakin Than Tun argued that the idea of launching open warfare against the British was "unrealistic" and "politically wrong"; he also claimed that the US-UK-Soviet conferences at Teheran, Yalta and Potsdam had laid solid foundations for the peaceful cooperation of all nations within the framework of the United Nations. Given the strong position of the Soviet Union and "the socialist forces" all over the world, armed struggle against "the imperialists" was not necessary.[151]

The CPB, however, had managed to penetrate Burma's fledgling trade union movement. On 1 June 1945, the All-Burma Trade Union Congress (ABTUC) had been set up in Rangoon with a prominent Communist, Thakin Ba Hein, as its first leader. Altogether fourteen trade unions, with a total membership of 11,150 workers, were then affiliated to the ABTUC. On 9 July it applied for membership of the World Federation of Trade Unions. The All-Burma Peasants' Union (ABPU) was another organisation which the Communists had managed to infiltrate.

Under the guise of the ABPU, the Communists mobilised the peasants in "no rent, no taxes" campaigns. They even confiscated land from big landlords and distributed it to the cultivators, which earned them a certain degree of popularity in the countryside. The CPB's own newspaper, the *Kommyunit Nezin*, was widely read in the capital and elsewhere. But it should also be stressed that the Communists were less successful than the PRP (which in August 1945 had become the Burma Socialist Party, the BSP) in recruiting a mass following. The BSP had chosen to work within the AFPFL and strengthen it, which made that party more popular than the CPB among Burma's many leftists.

As a direct result of the war, the frontier peoples had also become more politicised than before: their previous isolation had been broken and they had been exposed to radically new ideas. But they developed a movement that differed considerably from mainstream Burmese politics. As the Burman nationalists had made the tactical mistake of allying themselves with the Japanese during the war, the traditional gap between them and the various frontier peoples had widened; it was not as easy to convince them to join the Union which the nationalists were proposing.

The Karens were especially reluctant to see the British go and to be "handed over" to their traditional enemies, the Burmans, without adequate safeguards. The Kachins in the far north were the heroes of the anti-Japanese campaign, and their commander, the short, stocky warrior Naw Seng had emerged from the war with

> a dream of an independent country, independent like Nepal, and prospering as that gallant country does, by hiring out its fighting men. And certainly Subedar Naw Seng, Burma Gallantry Medal and Bar, would have been the perfect figurehead for what his company commander light-heartedly called "Naw Seng's Kingdom".[152]

The Shans in the northeast had from the early days of British rule enjoyed considerable autonomy, which they were extremely unwilling to let go. The Karennis were, at least nominally, already independent and saw no reason to take part in any negotiations at all.

The first step was taken by the Karens, who on 3 February 1946, less than a year after the end of the war, met in Rangoon to discuss their future. Representatives of three Karen organisations participated: the largely Christian Karen Central Association and the Buddhist-dominated Karen National Association, which both advocated a separate Karen state, and the Karen Youth Organisation, a "disciple of the AFPFL", as the British governor reported back to London at the time.[153]

Despite their differences, the meeting adopted a resolution demanding the appointment of two Karen executive councillors and four legislative councillors.[154] The demands were modest, but voices were also raised for a separate Karen state, encompassing Tenasserim and Irrawaddy Divisions.[155]

The following month, leaders of the Shans, the Kachins and the Chins assembled in Panglong, a small market town in the central Shan states (not to be confused with the Panglong of the Panthay Muslims in the northeastern Shan States) for the first in a series of conferences leading up to the creation of the Union of Burma.

This first meeting was attended by the thirty-four Shan *saohpas*, Thakin Nu from the AFPFL and U Lun speaking for the governor's Executive Council. Representing the governor was Stevenson, the old Burma hand who had joined the Burma Frontier Service in 1926, raised the Chin Rifles after the outbreak of World War II and become director of the Frontier Areas Administration in 1946.

Among the crowd in Panglong could also be seen U Saw, the right-wing politician who had defended Saya San in the 1930s, representing himself. US-born, Namkham-based Dr. Gordon Seagrave—the legendary "Burma Surgeon" whose team of Kachin and Karen nurses had operated round the clock during the siege of Myitkyina in 1944—also attended the conference, speaking on the medical needs of the frontier areas.[156]

Although the Shans were closely related to the Thais, there was no movement to amalgamate the Shan states with neighbouring Thailand. Most Shans remembered the Thai occupation of Kengtung and Möng Pan during the war with bitterness, and they reasoned that they would be better off as a part of the Union of Burma, with constitutional safeguards, than if they became second-rate subjects of the Kingdom of Thailand.[157]

The wily politician U Saw urged the minorities to unite with Burma proper for defence and economic development while retaining full autonomy within their respective areas. That statement was well received, but the minority leaders reacted strongly when Thakin Nu argued that the British had been instrumental in separating some of the minorities from the Burmans and making them hate each other. The Kachin representative retorted in no uncertain terms:

> This we deny emphatically. What have the Burman people done toward the hill peoples to win their faith and love? Did not a section of the Burmese public, who while saying that we all belong to the same race, blood and home call in the Japanese and cause the hill peoples to suffer? If therefore the Burmese want unity with the hill peoples they must change.[158]

This first Panglong Conference decided on a common plan for rebuilding the war-devastated frontier areas. The frontier delegates also set up the Supreme Council of the United Hill Peoples (SCOUHP) to safeguard their interests against the Burmans, who were generally regarded with suspicion. The chairman of the new umbrella organisation of frontier peoples was Sao Shwe Thaike, the *saohpa* of Yawnghwe.

To the regret of many, the Karens participated only as "observers" in the Panglong Conference: they had other objectives in mind. In August, a four-man Karen "Goodwill Mission" consisting of four English-trained lawyers departed for London. Its leader, the 64-year-old veteran Saw Sydney

Loo-Nee, had been a member of the House of Representatives from 1937 and its speaker for a brief period before the Japanese invasion. The delegation's deputy, Saw Po Chit, had also served as an MP and been Minister of Education in 1939. They were accompanied by Saw Thra Din, the 51-year-old President of the Karen Central Organisation, and Saw Ba U Gyi, a dynamic, 42-year-old barrister who had worked together with Aung San for reconciliation with the Burmese during the Japanese occupation.

This well-selected group stated that they wanted "to thank His Majesty's Government and the British people for their deliverance from the Japanese". But they also made it clear they "would, of course, at the same time take the opportunity of stating the Karens' attitude towards the future of political developments in Burma."[159]

The British response to the mission was one of confusion. On the one hand, there were government officials such as Stevenson who sympathised with Karen demands and understood their fears. Some war veterans, who had fought together with the Karens against the Japanese—and the BIA— also felt that the British should not let their erstwhile, loyal allies down.

The official policy, however, was not to support the Karen demands; it was believed that any British backing for demands for a separate Karen state would jeopardise the delicate independence negotiations with Aung San and the AFPFL: "The Secretary of State [for Burma] did not wish to get entangled with Karen political demands which might prove embarrassing and would prefer that the object of the visit of this mission to the UK should be of a private nature to thank HMG for its assistance."[160] Questions were also raised as to whether the mission was "fully representative" of the Karens.

The delegation remained in London throughout the cold, rainy English autumn without accomplishing anything. Sitting in exile in Sangkhlaburi in western Thailand half a century later, Saw Thra Din proudly displays pictures taken during his visit to London. But the most exciting event the British hosts arranged for their Karen visitors appears to have been a visit to the Sunlight Soap Factory outside London.[161]

Almost the only British official who took the mission—and the situation—seriously was Stevenson. Having served for several years with the frontier peoples, he was perhaps in a better position than most other British administrators to understand their sentiments, and he warned at the time that there was a real threat of an armed uprising among the Karens: "I have come to the regrettable conclusion that the present Karen quiescence means simply that they refuse to quarrel with *us*. But if we go, if go we do, the war for the Karen state will start."[162]

Realising that he was talking to deaf ears, Stevenson resigned from the Frontier Areas Administration a few months later. The political situation in Burma was also becoming progressively more serious. The AFPFL had called a general strike in September to press demands for independence. Attempts by the British to patch up the confusion by appointing a new, broader Governor's Council—which included Saw Ba U Gyi representing the Karens, and a CPB leader, Thakin Thein Pe—did not defuse the explosive situation.

The CPB began attacking Aung San personally, accusing him of "betraying the nationalist cause" by participating in the British-initiated pre-independence government—despite the fact that Thakin Thein Pe was also included in that cabinet.

Aung San responded by expelling the Communists—led by his brother-in-law Thakin Than Tun—from the AFPFL on 3 November. He was replaced as AFPFL secretary general by Kyaw Nyein, a Socialist stalwart who was not renowned either for political acumen or an ability to compromise. Communist militiamen who had served with the PVO formed their own force: the militant People's Democratic Youth League, better known as the Red Guards. Dressed in green fatigues with red arm bands emblazoned with a hammer and a sickle, they staged well-disciplined marches in the streets of Rangoon, causing many Europeans in the capital to look on in fear and anticipation.[163]

But Aung San continued his indefatigable struggle for independence. In January 1947, he travelled to London to meet British Labour prime minister Clement Attlee. "We want complete independence. There is no question of Dominion status for Burma," Aung San said in New Delhi on his way to London. But in an attempt to forge national unity, other Burmese political leaders were also included in Aung San's London delegation. The opposition was represented by U Saw and Thakin Ba Sein, another right-wing opponent of Aung San. When an agreement to grant Burma independence was reached on 27 January, both U Saw and Ba Sein refused to sign. But the decision had been taken. Burma was to become an independent republic outside the Commonwealth.

It was within less than a week of the signing of the Aung San-Attlee agreement that more than 700 Karen representatives from all over southern Burma gathered in the Vinton Memorial Hall in Rangoon to review the situation, which in their view was becoming increasingly desperate. The Anglicised barrister Saw Thra Din chaired the stormy and emotional conference, but handed over the leadership to the increasingly militant Saw Ba U Gyi when the Karen National Union (KNU) was formed on 5 February. The KNU's first resolution stated:

> The Karens have through their Goodwill Mission, made known in unmistakable terms to the British Administrators their aspiration for a separate Karen State formed out of Tenasserim Division, Nyaunglebin Sub-Division in Pegu District, [and] including Salween District in the present Frontier Area. His Maj-

esty's Government completely ignored altogether the Memorial submitted since 15 January 1946. The Congress is, therefore, aggrieved at the silence observed on this matter in the [Aung San-Attlee] Agreement, and now fervently requests that due recognition be given to the Karen legitimate aspirations.[164]

Despite all the frustrations and difficulties, some of the minority leaders—although not the Karens—met for a second Panglong conference in the same month. This time it went more smoothly. Aung San himself had travelled up to the Shan states to negotiate with the hill peoples whose delegates had at last decided to join Burma and ask for independence from Britain. On 12 February Aung San and twenty-three representatives of the Shans, the Kachins and the Chins signed the historic Panglong Agreement. This was a key document in post-war relations between the frontier peoples and the central authorities in Rangoon. The day on which the agreement was signed is still celebrated officially every year in Burma as Union Day, a national holiday.

Although they had agreed to join the Union, their traditional desire for local self-government was reflected in the important Clause Five, which dealt with the powers of the central government in Rangoon:

> It will not operate in respect of the Frontier Areas in any manner which would deprive any portion of these areas of the autonomy which it now enjoys in internal administration. Full autonomy in internal administration for the Frontier Areas is accepted in principle.[165]

Moreover, the Shan princes asked for, and were granted, the right to secede from the Union of Burma after a ten-year period of independence— that is, in 1958—should they be dissatisfied with the new federation. This right was also granted to the Karenni states and ensured under the first Burmese Constitution, which at this time was being drafted in Rangoon.[166] The Panglong Agreement as well as the new Constitution further stipulated that a Kachin State be formed, but without the right to secede.

In order to gain a better understanding of the opinions and sentiments of the frontier peoples, the British government in March set up the official Frontier Areas Committee of Enquiry (FACOE). It was a well-intentioned attempt to find a solution to the ethnic crisis, and a broad spectrum of people was invited to listen to all the fears and aspirations of the many peoples of Burma.

Silverstein writes:

> The Committee, composed of Burmans, minority representatives and Europeans, was provided for in the Aung San-Attlee Agreement. The British gov-

ernment chose D.R. Rees-Williams to act as committee chairman and W.B.J. Ledwidge (who originally came from England as Bottomley's associate during the Panglong Conference) to act as secretary. The Burma Executive Council designated U Tin Tut, Thakin Nu, U Khin Maung Gale, and U Kyaw Nyein, the latter three representing the AFPFL. U Kyaw Nyein was later replaced by Saw Myint Thein of the Karen Youth Organisation, an AFPFL affiliate organisation. Representing the Frontier Areas and the minorities were the Frontier Area Councillor, his two deputies, and Saw Sankey of the Karen National Union.[167]

Despite the seemingly broad-based nature of the enquiry commission, it had severe shortcomings. Rees-Williams had practised as a solicitor in Malaya in 1930–34, and was now a Labour MP with little or no knowledge of Burma's minority problems. Arthur Bottomley, another Labour MP, had observed the Panglong Conference in February, but spent most of his time in Burma making friends with Col. Ne Win and other uncompromising, hardline military officers.[168]

The hearings with the Shans went without any major problems. Their spokesman, the Yawnghwe *saohpa* Sao Shwe Thaike, stated straightforwardly: "We want to associate with Burma on the condition that full autonomy is guaranteed in our internal administration."[169] The Kachins reiterated their demand for a separate state within the Union, and the Chins stated, somewhat more vaguely, that they adhered to "the principles of the Panglong Agreement" and that "it is our intention to associate with Burma on a federal basis."[170] Karen spokesman Saw Marshall Shwin was far more sarcastic in his replies to the committee's questions:

> *Thakin Nu*: Do you think if Burma severs her connection from the British you will suffer?
> *Saw Marshall Shwin*: Certainly.
> *U Kyaw Nyein*: Supposing the world situation is such that Burma can stand on her own legs and can defend herself against any possible foreign aggression, would you object to Burma's secession from the British Empire and would you object to joining Burma?
> *Saw Marshall Shwin*: I do not think this is likely to be for a thousand years to come.[171]

Discussions with other, smaller tribes were even more difficult. The headhunting Was had their own views on a union with Burma and the hearings before the FACOE revealed a wide gap between the British or Burman way and their perception of life and society:

> Do you want any sort of association with other people?

—We do not want to join anybody because in the past we have been very independent.
What do you want the future to be of the Wa states?
—We have not thought about that because we are wild people. We never thought of the administrative future. We only think about ourselves.
Don't you want education, clothing, good food, good houses, hospitals etc.?
—We are very wild people and we do not appreciate all these things.[172]

The overall impression of the Enquiry Committee was that the minority peoples were, by and large, willing to join Burma provided there was a federal system which guaranteed internal autonomy in their respective areas. It was agreed to hold elections to a Constituent Assembly, which would draft a constitution for the independent republic that was about to emerge. Out of a total of 255 members, 182 would be elected from non-communal constituencies, 24 from Karen and 4 from Anglo-Burman constituencies, in addition to 45 representatives chosen from the Frontier Areas.[173]

A challenge was posed not only by the Karens but also by the Communists, who were outside the entire process. The CPB's shift from a legal opposition party to an underground insurgent organisation began in April when it decided on a half-hearted boycott of the elections to the suggested Constituent Assembly.

Although the CPB did not participate as an organisation, it fielded twenty-eight candidates, of whom seven were elected: the juggernaut AFPFL captured the remaining non-communal seats. The CPB's reluctance to participate may have been prompted by the realisation that the party would not stand a chance against the AFPFL in free and fair elections. Instead, the party continued to work within the "mass organisations" in order to build up a power base, especially among Burma's peasants and workers.

The KNU also boycotted the election, but for entirely different reasons. Their separatist demands were growing stronger as the constitutional process seemed to leave no provision for a Karen state. The Karen National Defence Organisation (KNDO), an armed militia, was formed on 17 July. Any hopes for British protection had dimmed after Rees-Williams had made some rather insensitive remarks about "the lack of Karen unity"—which had prompted the KNU to issue a strongly worded rebuttal on 25 June.[174] An armed insurrection now seemed inevitable.

Among the Communists, the old peaceful, "Browderist" line was gradually being abandoned as the CPB increased its contacts with the international Communist movement. In February 1947, Thakin Ba Thein Tin—who had replaced Thakin Ba Hein as a member of the politburo after the latter's death from malaria in 1946—and *yebaw* Aung Gyi represented the

party at the British Empire Communist Conference in London, the first
international meeting attended by the CPB. In the region, Communists were
on the march in the Korean peninsula, China, Malaya, Vietnam and the
Philippines.

The mood among communist parties at the time was becoming increasingly militant. They had played a crucial role in the anti-Japanese struggle
throughout the region, and it seemed for them only logical that as the fight
for "national sovereignty" was over, "socialist revolution" would be next
on the agenda. As a direct result of World War II, weapons were also easily
available in virtually every country in the Far East. The militant mood of
the Calcutta Youth Conference reflected this situation.

It was at this crucial time in Burma's modern history that U Saw and his
group of ultra right-wing politicians sent their hitmen to the Secretariat in
Rangoon on 19 July to gun down Aung San and almost the entire pre-
independence cabinet. The AFPFL's vice president, Thakin Nu, later referred to as U Nu, took over as prime minister. In October, he travelled to
London and a second agreement was signed with Clement Attlee, paving
the way for Burma's independence. On 4 January, the prime minister of
the new nation declaimed in a melodramatic address to the nation:

> From the dim and distant days shrouded in the mists of antiquity, born of the
> same mother the Shan, Kachin, Karen, Chin, Mon and the Burman brethren
> have lived in loving friendship, in unity that could not be shattered and in
> freedom that could not be shackled . . . . The freedom we have won is not the
> freedom for a privileged few. This freedom is for all the indigenous peoples:
> for all the sons and daughters of our sacred soil to enjoy . . . .No community,
> no tongues, no creed, no sect divide us and we are one . . . . The Union of the
> Republic of Burma has become an Independent Sovereign State.[175]

But the astute statesman Aung San was gone from the scene, and his
successor U Nu was unable to do much more than to deliver such grossly
inaccurate platitudes. In an attempt to forge national unity, the Shan leader,
Sao Shwe Thaike, had been given the largely ceremonial post of president
of the Union. But such attempts to placate the minorities were soon thwarted
by the inability to solve the Karen issue.

In the remote and isolated Karenni states, resistance to the amalgama-
tion with Burma had already begun. Bee Tu Re, a local leader had on 11
September 1946 proclaimed the United Karenni Independent States (UKIS)
as a local "government", or rather movement, to preserve the "independent" status of the Karenni states of Bawlake, Kyebogyi and Kantarawaddy
in view of Burma's imminent independence.

In November 1947, Saw Maw Reh, another Karenni leader and a veteran of Force 136, formed the Karenni National Organisation (KNO) to

back up the UKIS politically. By the time of Burma's independence, they were collecting arms and ammunition to prepare for the "defence" of their "independent nation".[176]

In the hills of Arakan in the far west of the country, a legendary Buddhist monk called U Sein Da and nicknamed "the King of Arakan" had formed the Arakan National Liberation Party and begun waging guerrilla warfare to regain Arakan's independence. Muslim *mujahids* were active in the same area, but for different reasons. Centuries of harmony between the two religious communities of Arakan had been disrupted by the Japanese invasion.

The Buddhists, encouraged by the occupation army, had carried out acts of violence against the Muslims to punish them for their loyalty to the British. About 80,000 Muslims had fled to East Bengal during the war, where they were interned in refugee camps in Rangpur, Dinajpur and Noakhali. But after independence, they were not allowed to return.[177]

In parts of the Irrawaddy delta, the fiery Thakin Soe's Red Flags were active, ambushing police outposts and and looting local treasuries.

The country was ripe for revolt, and U Nu, although a talented intellectual, was hardly the strong statesman Burma needed during its first difficult years of independence. The attacks on the CPB in late 1947 and early 1948, and certainly the order to arrest Thakin Than Tun on 25 March, could be seen as unnecessary provocations which the more tactful and diplomatic Aung San most probably would have avoided.

The CPB has always claimed that they had to resort to armed struggle in self defence because "the ruling class attacked us".[178] Successive Burmese governments, for their part, have asserted that there was a Communist conspiracy hatched in Calcutta in February 1948. They go on to claim that the "proof" of this is a "thesis" which Ghoshal supposedly brought back from Bombay immediately before the Calcutta meetings.

"The gist of the twenty-seven pages of closely typed document," an official government publication says, "is that the 'independence' is a sham and that under cover of this sham British Imperialism would work a stranglehold on the defence and economic life of the country." Consequently, an armed rebellion had to be launched.[179] This thesis was supposedly "ratified" at a CPB meeting in Pyinmana in March, shortly after the return from Calcutta of Than Tun and the CPB delegation.

Western historians have, almost without exception, accepted that this "thesis" provided the ideological basis for the CPB insurrection that followed within two weeks of the Pyinmana rally. The gross misunderstandings of modern Burmese history began at this juncture. The meeting in Pyinmana was in fact a peasant rally where no "Communist strategy" for "a guerrilla war" was even discussed.

The assembled farmers merely adopted a few resolutions supporting some strikes which the CPB had instigated in Rangoon at the time.[180] The "thesis" has never at any time been circulated by the CPB, which casts serious doubts on its authenticity.[181]

The CPB themselves state that the document is a forgery: "The so-called Ghoshal thesis is a fake concocted by the imperialists. We never adopted a line to wage civil war until the AFPFL government had started their nationwide suppression."[182]

Whatever the case, the explosive situation in Burma shortly after independence hardly needed any outside impetus to develop into an armed conflict. Thesis or no thesis, the CPB had already given up its previous "Browderist" line and the personal, potentially stabilising link the AFPFL had to the CPB through the brother-in-law relationship between Thakin Than Tun and Aung San was gone. There was also no escape from the fact that the minorities had little faith in U Nu's new government.

It is far too facile to explain Burma's tragedy, which has unfolded since 1948, in the context of some evil "conspiracy"—a theme that has been repeated in different variations many times since by several Burmese regimes. The roots of the tragedy do not begin with a call to arms given in a thesis which was purportedly written in Bombay, distributed by the authorities, but never read by the rebels themselves.

The answer is to be found in Burma's own turbulent history; the short-sightedness on the part of the US officers who led the campaign against the Japanese during World War II; the incompetence of the last British administrators; and the ineptitude of the successive governments of independent Burma. It is also to be found in the role which the country came to play as a "secret battlefield" during the Cold War, which began only a few years after the British withdrawal.

ETHNIC MAP OF BURMA

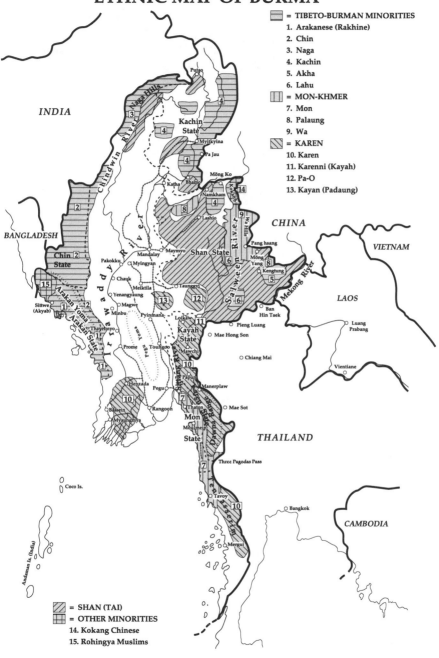

= TIBETO-BURMAN MINORITIES
1. Arakanese (Rakhine)
2. Chin
3. Naga
4. Kachin
5. Akha
6. Lahu

= MON-KHMER
7. Mon
8. Palaung
9. Wa

= KAREN
10. Karen
11. Karenni (Kayah)
12. Pa-O
13. Kayan (Padaung)

= SHAN (TAI)
= OTHER MINORITIES
14. Kokang Chinese
15. Rohingya Muslims

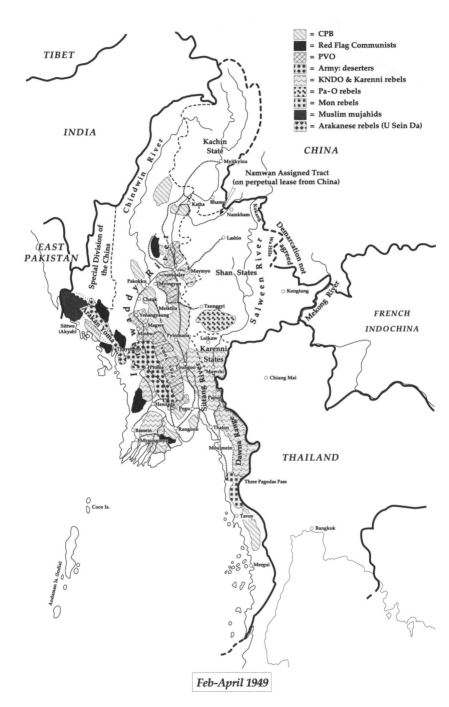

TIBET

INDIA

Kachin State

Myitkyina

CHINA

Namwan Assigned Tract
(on perpetual lease from China)

Chindwin River

Katha Bhamo

Namkham

Kokang

EAST
PAKISTAN

Special Division of
the Chins

Lashio

Demarcation not
agreed

Wa Hills

Salween River

Mandalay Maymyo

Shan States

Pakokku

Myingyan

Chauk

Meiktila

Kengtung

Mekong River

FRENCH
INDOCHINA

Arakan Yoma

Sittwe
(Akyab)

Yenangyaung

Magwe

Minbu

Pyinmana

Taunggyi

Loikaw

Irrawaddy River

Thayetmyo

Prome

Toungoo

Karenni
States

Mawchi

Chiang Mai

Henzada

Pegu

Papun

Sittang River

Bassein

Myaungmya

Rangoon

Thaton

Moulmein

Salween River

Dawna Range

THAILAND

Coco Is.

Three Pagodas Pass

Tavoy

Bangkok

Andaman Is. (India)

Mergui

= CPB
= Red Flag Communists
= PVO
= Army: deserters
= KNDO & Karenni rebels
= Pa-O rebels
= Mon rebels
= Muslim mujahids
= Arakanese rebels (U Sein Da)

Feb-April 1949

3

"Peace Within One Year"

After a year and a half of bitter fighting, the tide began to turn. In the beginning, the insurgents had actually been more numerous than the government's forces. The KNDO fielded at least 10,000 troops in mid-1949, the Communists 10,000–15,000, the PVO approximately 4,000 men and other, smaller insurgent groups another few thousand regulars and irregulars.

But despite the fact that a substantial number of the Karen and Communist forces were deserters from the army and the Union Military Police, the rebels were lacking in discipline and coordination. Their motives for taking up arms against Rangoon were also vastly different: the ethnics fought for self-determination, the CPB for a political ideal, and the PVOs seemed to be eager to fight whoever happened to come in their way.

After the defection to the CPB of the entire 1st Burifs under Bo Sein Tin, 300 officers and men of 3rd Burifs led by Bo Ye Htut and elements of the 6th Burifs under Bo Aung Myint, and the defection to the KNDO of the 1st, 2nd and 3rd Karen Rifles plus the 1st Kachin Rifles, only the 1st Chin Rifles, and some Burman troops, mainly from the 4th and the 5th Burifs, remained loyal to the government.

It was estimated that the army had lost 42% of its personnel and 45% of all its equipment.[1] Dr. Maung Maung, Burma's official historian, paints an even darker picture of the situation during the first year of the civil war: "There were maybe 2,000 soldiers at Gen. Ne Win's disposal [when he took over as commander in chief in early 1949], all scattered in decimated, weak battalions and companies."[2]

Whatever the exact number of troops that remained loyal to the High Command, it was a miracle that the "Rangoon Government" managed to survive. But massive outside assistance, primarily from India, enabled the Burmese government to rebuild its shattered armed forces. According to U Nu:

True to his words, Pandit Nehru sent several shipments of arms, without which Burma might never have recovered. Now the unserviceable guns of the combat troops were replaced, and new units raised and equipped. By November 1949, the army, the civilian police, and the UMP (Union Military Police) felt strong enough to retake towns and villages under rebel occupation.[3]

Whereas the Karens had made up the single largest ethnic component of the armed forces at independence, the Kachins now provided the main recruiting ground for the new units which were being formed. Even though Naw Seng and his 1st Kachin Rifles had joined the Karen rebels, most Kachins had remained loyal to the government: they had, after all, been given their own state under the 1947 Constitution and their political leader, Sinwa Nawng, the *duwa*, or traditional ruler, of Sima had become minister in U Nu's cabinet. These warlike tribesmen from the northern hills also made ideal soldiers, and no less than six battalions of the Kachin Rifles were established in 1949–51, followed by a battalion of Kayah Rifles which enlisted Karennis, Shans and other minorities in the Kayah (Karenni) and Shan states.

Many of the new soldiers also came from the ethnic Chin minority. Like the Kachins, the Chins were a hardy, warlike hill people who had also fought bravely against the Japanese during World War II. In the first year of independence, the Chins had remained astonishingly loyal to the central government in Rangoon. The defence of the capital, during the siege of Insein in early 1949, had actually been in the hands of the 1st Chin Rifles led by Lieut.-Col. Hrang Thio, who was supported by some less battle-hardened units from the Burman-dominated 5th Burifs, commanded by Maj. Saw Myint.[4]

Within a few years after the mutinies of 1948 and 1949, the strength of Burma's armed forces had thus increased to more than 30,000 well-equipped men.[5] As early as September 1948, irregular forces had been drafted into the Burma Territorial Force, called *sitwundan* in Burmese, which soon totalled fifty-two companies.[6]

The powerful Burma Army that emerged from the first few years of civil war was to become a curious combination of two totally disparate traditions, as Dr. Maung Maung, Burma's official historian, points out:

> Some of the senior officers were British trained . . . men who [had] gained combat experience in fighting their way back into Burma [in 1945]. Some were BIA [Burma Independence Army] men who learned the science of war by rule of thumb the hard way from the Japanese at military schools in Burma or Japan. When the Burma Army was built into an effective force after independence the methods of training and warfare adopted were an Anglo-Japanese

mixture. Fortunately, the mixture proved more potent than the original components and it is standing the severest test of jungle warfare.[7]

The local *sitwundan* militias also played a large and important part in fighting the insurgents. Even at the University in Rangoon, students received basic military training and were organised into special University Training Corps (UTC). Gradually, gentle, peaceful Buddhist Burma was becoming a militarised society.

Although many of the new rank and file came from the frontier areas, the high command had been firmly controlled by Burman officers since Lieut.-Gen. Ne Win had taken over from Smith-Dun as commander in chief on 1 February 1949. The army at that time had only two regional commands: the southern led by Brig.-Gen. Aung Thinn, a Burman, and the northern command under Brig.-Gen. Lazum Tang, a Kachin. But in another reshuffle in November, Lazum Tang was replaced by Brig.-Gen. Kyaw Zaw, one of the Thirty Comrades.[8] All were very young and ambitious as life lay ahead of them; Kyaw Zaw was only thirty when he became a regional commander and so were most battalion commanders. Ne Win had not yet turned forty when he was appointed commander in chief of the army.

It was not only India that came to Burma's rescue during this difficult time. Under the Let Ya-Freeman Agreement, signed in Rangoon on 29 August 1947, London was also obliged to provide military equipment as well as facilities for the training of Burmese army, navy and air force personnel in the United Kingdom. Although Burma had almost been written off as lost in 1949, some limited assistance did come through and a selected few Burmese army officers were also taken to Malaya to observe operations against Communist guerrillas in the jungles and hills of the Malayan Peninsula.[9]

During the height of the civil war in 1950, not only India but also Britain provided Burma with thousands of small weapons and arranged with other Commonwealth countries, including Australia, Ceylon and Pakistan, to furnish a loan of £6 million to tide over the state's treasury until the insurgent forces could be suppressed.[10]

Soon after the civil war had broken out, U Nu had also approached the United States for military assistance. After some hesitation, Washington sent ten ex-Coast Guard cutters for use as river patrol craft and other equipment, totalling a modest US$3.5 million in value, which were delivered in November 1950.[11] In addition, Washington had in September agreed to grant US$8–10 million in development assistance over a ten-month period ending 30 June 1951.

The Cold War had just begun, and Washington had not yet formulated any clear strategy to fight communism in Asia. But the British Commonwealth had exactly that purpose in mind when it launched its so-called Colombo Plan, an aid scheme created at a Foreign Ministers' Conference in the Ceylonese capital in January 1950: it was a mini-version of the ambitious, US-directed Marshall Plan which had been designed to contain the influence of the Soviet Union in Europe.

In Asia, the main enemy was China, where Mao Zedong's Communists had emerged victorious in the civil war against the Kuomintang (KMT) in October 1949. If China achieved domination over weaker, neighbouring states such as Burma, Beijing's chances of extending its power to Indonesia and, even more worrisome for Western security planners, perhaps as far as Australia, would be enhanced.

Australia's fears were echoed in a speech by its external affairs minister, Percy Spender, in March 1950:

> Should the forces of Communism prevail and Vietnam come under the heel of Communist China, Malaya is in danger of being outflanked and it, together with Thailand, Burma and Indonesia, will become the next direct objects of further Communist activities . . . . Burma, in particular, is obviously in a condition where active Communist intervention from outside could bring all organised government to a halt.[12]

Burma had chosen not to join the Commonwealth after independence, but it did participate in the Colombo Plan's civilian aid scheme.[13] As for further military assistance from the West, US undersecretary of state James E. Ferb stated quite cautiously in a memorandum for President Harry S. Truman:

> The Departments of State and Defence are agreed that military aid furnished to the Government of Burma shall not be such as to encourage the British to reduce their military assistance or to induce Burmese unwillingness to accept further United Kingdom assistance.[14]

The civil war had been an extremely costly affair. U Tin, minister for finance and revenue, stated in his budget speech in September 1949 that 33 million Kyats had been looted from treasuries all over the country since the fighting broke out in April the year before. The damage to Union property was estimated at 197.8 million Kyats, and the loss of land revenue not collected by the government amounted to 30 million Kyats.[15] Villages across Burma lay in ashes, scores of families had been separated and tens of thousands of refugees had flocked to Rangoon, where they lived in haphazardly built, rickety shantytowns called *kwetthis*.

Both civilian and military aid were important for the reconstruction of Burma. In order to solve the crisis domestically, the Burmese government also realised that not only military pressure should be applied against the insurgents. In a move that startled many of his Western supporters, U Nu had on 25 May 1948 announced a programme for "Leftist Unity" to counter the Communist insurrection by political means. It stated, among other things, that Rangoon wanted to "secure political and economic relations with Soviet Russia and the democratic countries of Eastern Europe in the same way as we are now having these relations with the United States." U Nu's controversial move also included "the refusal of any foreign aid of any kind which will compromise the political, economic and strategic independence of Burma".[16]

U Nu had on 13 June reiterated his plans to unite all "leftist forces", but the only outcome had been an uproar in Britain, where many people thought that Burma was about to become Communist. The foreign secretary, Ernest Bevin, had gone as far as calling in the Burmese ambassador to London to demand an explanation. In Rangoon, an emergency press conference had to be held on 17 June to dispel such fears.

Wise from the bitter lesson of the controversial move—which the Communists had in any case rejected—U Nu went on to launch a social welfare programme to counter leftist propaganda. The devastated economy had to be revived, and the shattered lives of the people rebuilt. The answer was an ambitious plan called *pyidawtha*—"Happy Land"—which in many ways resembled US President Franklin D. Roosevelt's New Deal in the 1930s.

According to the plan, Burma had to industrialise. Emphasis was placed on social welfare programmes such as housing, education and health, and the entire bureaucracy was to be shaken out of its traditional arrogance and complacency by sweeping democratisation of the 10,000 village tracts, 200 townships and 40 districts which made up the local administration of the Union.[17]

The "Rangoon Government" slowly began to reassert its authority as the weakened rebel forces continued to lose ground across the country. After withdrawing from Insein, and after the failure of the Upper Burma Campaign, the KNDO forces managed to regroup in the Irrawaddy delta region southwest of Rangoon, in the Pegu Yoma mountains north of the capital and in the sparsely populated Karen hills in the east, adjacent to the Thai border.

Following the retreat from Insein, Toungoo—the former headquarters of the 1st Karen Rifles—had become the main centre for the Karen rebels. Situated on the main railway line from Rangoon to Mandalay, it was a major town, and the rebel presence there virtually cut the country in half. The Karens controlled a sixty-kilometre stretch of the railway as well, where they sold their own tickets and issued tax certificates for the trains to pass through.

The headquarters area included the site for the KNU's own broadcasting station, which beamed daily fighting bulletins, Karen propaganda and

Christian hymns in Burmese, English and Karen from a 500-watt Helicrafter transmitter. It had been set up by a Canadian signals officer who had served with the British forces in Meiktila. He had joined the Karen rebellion when the KNDO captured the garrison town in February 1949—only to die of typhoid in Toungoo less than a year later.

In mid-March 1950, the government felt strong enough to move against the Karens in Toungoo. Newly equipped government forces marched north from Rangoon, and the town fell on 19 March 1950 after two days of heavy fighting. The Karen rebels retreated into the jungle-clad, malaria-infested hills east of Toungoo along with their entire headquarters, including their main office, the broadcasting station and military high command. A new headquarters was established at Mawchi in the southern Karenni states, eighty kilometres east of Toungoo and just fifty kilometres from the Thai border. For the first time since the Karen rebellion broke out, the Karen headquarters was not in central Burma.

Mawchi was renowned for its tungsten mines and, before World War II, these had been the world's most important source of this valuable mineral. Some of it was smuggled across the border to Thailand, and there exchanged for arms and ammunition. But there was a shortage of rice in the area, and the Karen rebels soon found themselves unable to feed their troops.

The headquarters was moved once again, this time to Papun, a small town in the eastern hills eighty kilometres south of Mawchi. Located on the banks of the Yozilin river, which flows through a narrow strip of cultivated flatland surrounded by rugged, forested mountains, it consisted of 500 houses inhabited by approximately 2,000 people.

A church, a district office and a colonial-style police station, built during the British period, surrounded a lively market place where life went on as usual despite the presence of the rebels. Their radio station, which the rebels had brought with them from Toungoo, continued its broadcasts from this new base in the eastern hills. Following the death of the Canadian officer, an Anglo-Burmese deserter from the Burma Army signals, Samuel Davidson, was placed in charge.[18]

The KNDO remained the main militia force of the KNU, but following the defections of the Karen units from the Burma Army, a more regular set-up, the Kawthoolei Armed Forces (KAF), had been established on 14 June 1949 under the command of Gen. Min Maung, the former commander of the 1st Karen Rifles. Papun now became the "capital" of the Karens' own state, which they called "Kawthoolei", or "Flowerland" in English. But no official proclamation of independence was made, nor was the informal rebel state recognised by any foreign country.

However, a few British adventurers did rally to the support of the KNU. Already in March 1948, two months after independence, the Karens had sent a secret envoy to London to plead their case to Conservative MPs and others who would be in favour of the pro-British Karens. The envoy, Oliver Ba Than, had managed to enlist the support of a few veterans of the Burma campaign who had a special affection for the loyal Karens. On 30 June, a meeting was held at the Westminster Gardens residence of Lieut.-Col. Frank Owen, a veteran of the Burma Campaign who had become editor of the *Daily Mail.*

About forty people showed up at Owen's meeting, mostly senior British ex-servicemen, including another ex-Force 136 officer, Alexander Campbell, who had become a correspondent for the *Daily Mail* after the war; Sir Reginald Dorman-Smith, a former Conservative MP and cabinet minister who had served as governor of Burma in 1941–46; Labour MP Raymond Blackburn; the Rev. J.W. Baldwin, an Anglo-Burmese Seventh-day Adventist minister and Karen sympathiser; Henry Noel Stevenson, who had joined the Burma Frontier Service in 1926, raised the Chin Rifles after the outbreak of World War II and become director of the Frontier Areas Administration in 1946; and Anthony Stonor, a junior officer of the 2nd Battalion of the Welch Regiment who had been stationed in Shwegyin, Kalaw, Pyinmana and Rangoon before independence.

The most colourful of the participants at this meeting in London in June 1948 was the monocled, famous war veteran, Col. John Cromarty-Tulloch, Orde Wingate's close associate who had organised Karen guerrillas for the Allies' Force 136 in the eastern hills during World War II.[19] Together, they formed the "Friends of the Burma Hill Peoples" and Oliver Ba Than had returned to Burma with promises of arms. *Daily Mail* correspondent Campbell had followed shortly afterwards, using his journalistic credentials as a cover, and checked into the Strand Hotel in central Rangoon.

Campbell told the Karens that their hero, Cromarty-Tulloch, had chartered a steamship called SS Henderson, and that the old colonel was going to set course for Burma with arms and ammunition for the Karens[20]. Meanwhile, Stonor, who was twenty-one at the time, had got a job as a planter with a rubber company in Malaya. Two days before he was about to sail for the Far East, news came through that the Karens had occupied Moulmein. This was in August, two months after the meeting in Westminster Gardens:

"I telephoned Tulloch, who told me that he was off to Calcutta and said that when my ship docked at Bombay there would be a message from him and I was to be ready to leave the ship and join him and others who were going to the Karens' aid. My ship, MV Selandia, duly docked at Bombay but there was no message nor any sign of Tulloch, so I carried on, disembarking at Penang, where I landed and joined my estate in Perak. After a week or two, I contacted a Javanese fishing-boat captain who agreed to take me to Moulmein for a sum of money. So I paid the deposit and wrote to Tulloch (who was in England) telling him that I was about to sail for

Moulmein. He wrote back, telling me not to since the Karens had handed back Moulmein to the Burmans. This I had not been aware of as I had been on the high seas at the time it happened."[21]

Only a few in the top Karen leadership appear to have been aware of Tulloch's high-flown plans. One of them was Mika Rolley, a KNU organiser in the Irrawaddy delta region: "That was why we captured Moulmein in October 1948. We had arranged a landing site near Amherst on the sea. But because the government persuaded our leaders to hand back the towns, Tulloch had to turn back. A letter to Campbell in Rangoon was intercepted by the authorities and he was deported back to Britain."[22]

It is, however, uncertain whether Tulloch ever left Britain with his supposed shipload of arms and ammunition. The degree of support he had for his plan was also questionable. The British government was giving lavish military assistance to Rangoon at the time, and Tulloch most probably represented little more than a smaller group of disgruntled war veterans who were emotionally close to the hill peoples and disgreed with official policies.

Whatever the case, a second attempt by Tulloch and his men to send arms and ammunition to the Karens came in July 1950, but, again, few knew about the mission. That month, the KNU summoned a national congress in Papun to draw up plans for the future and to create a more effective organisation in view of the initial setbacks in Insein and elsewhere. About fifty rebel leaders from all over the eastern war zone gathered at Papun. The forces in the delta were represented by Saw Sankey, a former manager of Rangoon Electric Transport who had served with Force 136 during the Japanese occupation and later joined the KNDO, and Mika Rolley. The duo had set off in disguise with their families across the central plain, reaching Papun after a month's journey.

The congress was held in an open bamboo-and-thatch meeting hall that had been specially erected for the occasion on the bank of the Yozilin. The most important outcome of the congress was the formation of a common administration for the KNU's "liberated areas". It was named the Kawthoolei Governing Body, which resulted in the rather unfortunate abbreviation KGB. "We didn't know about the other KGB in those days," said Sgaw Ler Taw, a Karen rebel veteran who attended the meeting in Papun. "But we thought 'governing body' sounded impressive."[23]

On the last day of the congress, the charismatic bearded hero of the Karen uprising, KNU chairman Saw Ba U Gyi, stood up and rather cryptically informed the audience: "I'm now going to pull a political stunt."[24] Gathering his papers and notes, he then left the meeting hall.

Exactly what he meant was not clear to the assembled Karen rebel leaders. But shortly after the meeting was over, he set off for the Thai border town of Mae Sot together with Saw Sankey, a bodyguard of five men—and a mysterious former district duperindendent of police from Maymyo, known only as "Mr. Baker", who had showed up at Papun during the final stages of the congress. Mr. Baker, an Anglo-Indian, had been sent secretly by Tulloch, who was planning to bring the Karen leaders down to Bangkok.

Whether Tulloch, then said to be somewhere in the Far East, was really in a position to arrange a second shipment of arms was unclear. But that was, at least, what Saw Ba U Gyi hoped for. This time, the KNDO was in open rebellion against the Government and they would not repeat the mistake they had made at Moulmein two years before.[25]

On 11 August, the party reached the small village of Taw Kaw Koe near the Thai border, northwest of Mae Sot. Given the secret nature of their mission, they decided to spend the night under the trees of a betelnut plantation on the outskirts of the village, near the Ler Pu Klo river. But the party had been spotted by a Burma Army informer in Taw Kaw Koe, who promptly reported to the nearest garrison the arrival of 'some Karen leaders'.

Troops led by Maj. Sein Lwin of the 3rd Burifs surrounded their bivouac at three in the morning of the 12th. An army officer shouted in the dark to the rebels to surrender. When no response was forthcoming, the troops opened fire. Saw Ba U Gyi, Saw Sankey, Mr. Baker and their bodyguards all died in a hail of bullets.[26]

Saw Ba U Gyi's corpse was taken to Moulmein, where hundreds of local people stormed the civil hospital's mortuary to get a glimpse of the slain, bloody and bullet-ridden Karen leader.[27] After this public display, the body was dropped in the sea to deprive the Karens of any martyr's grave that would become a place of pilgrimage and thus a possible rallying point for the anti-Rangoon resistance.

Baker was also recognised by Burma's military intelligence. But the Burmese authorities never managed to identify Saw Sankey: for years, they believed he was still alive. For some inexplicable reason, they decided that it was the corpse of Capt. David Vivian, the British officer who had been freed by the Karens in Insein in February 1949.[28]

Tulloch by now decided to give up; it is uncertain whether he was as well-connected as he had told Oliver Ba Than and other Karens, or even if he was capable of delivering the goods he had promised. The Karens appear to have believed him; few others did. Ironically, Tulloch was arrested in Britain shortly afterwards for embezzling money that had been entrusted to him for the education of Chaine Dun, the son of Lieut.-Gen. Smith-Dun, the Karen former commander in chief of the Burma Army. Tulloch was tried and found guilty of "fraudulently converting £1,240 entrusted to him for the education of a Burmese boy in this country".[29]

It was suspected that Tulloch had used the money to finance some of his failed attempts to buy weapons for the Karens. If that indeed was the case, and if that sum of money was all that Tulloch had at his disposal, the much-publicised "conspiracy" was little more than a fraud. But it provided the Burmese government with the ammunition it needed to discredit the Karens as "foreign lackeys".[30] Tulloch was the first swindler to contact the Karens and promise aid and assistance which never materialised. This was to happen many times again during the decades of rebellion that followed.

Tulloch, the war hero turned adventurer, died in prison two years later.[31] Only one of his men ever made it to the Karens: the Rev. J.W. Baldwin, who had returned to Burma via Chiang Mai in 1949. He remained with the the KNU in the jungle until 1951, when he died from blackwater fever near Kamamaung, a small village in the eastern hills. Written on his tombstone is the epitaph: "Here lies one who loved the Karens."[32]

Meanwhile, Naw Seng and his band of Karens and Kachins had continued their race through the Shan states. After capturing Taunggyi, they marched north and occupied Lashio on 27 August 1949. The Möng Mit *saohpa* and head of the Shan state government, Sao Khun Hkio, was in the Lashio area at the time, which caused considerable anxiety in Rangoon. The War Office ordered the then northern commander, Brig.-Gen. Lazum Tang, to launch a counter-offensive. Moving northeast from the hill station of Maymyo, Lazum Tang—also a Kachin but loyal to the government—led his forces along the railway line to Lashio, towards the Chinese frontier in the northeast.

"Naw Seng decided to evacuate Lashio. Besides, Naw Seng wanted to continue to his native Kachin hills and start a rebellion there," Zau Mai, one of Naw Seng's old comrades says.

> I joined his forces when they reached my home village near Kutkai, north of Lashio. I was only 17 then, but we village youths looked upon Naw Seng as a hero. On 31 August, we overran Namkham on the Chinese border in the northern Shan states. From there, the road led north to Bhamo and Kachin State. Naw Seng summoned us and we were told that he wanted to occupy the Kachin hills and proclaim a republic which he wanted to call "Pawngyawng". The Karen struggle for independence inspired him to fight for a separate Kachin country as well.[33]

The combined force faced little resistance when it advanced on Namkham. There was one company of government troops at Möng Yu, the junction of the Burma Road to China and the route west to Namkham, another company at Muse and a third at Namkham itself. A typical road-block in those days consisted of a few sandbags, a 50-calibre-machinegun emplacement, and a squad of soldiers every ten or twenty kilometres along the main roads. Naw Seng and his men drove into Namkham in a convoy of trucks.

The local garrison was quickly dealt with; hardly a shot was fired as the government troops abandoned their post.[34] They all escaped unscathed, as did Sao Khun Hkio, who had not even been in Lashio town when Naw Seng had arrived there. He was safe in Möng Mit. U Nu promptly cabled him a message: "Hkio, your worries are over. Come to me in Lashio." U Nu had decided to visit the battle front and there was a happy reunion with Sao Khun Hkio, who travelled up to Lashio to meet him. According to U Nu:

> Namkham was still in rebel hands, and [I] felt compelled to return to Rangoon to find clothing for the troops that was not available in Lashio. The cotton uniform was insufficient protection against the cold, and if soldiers built fires they were easy targets for rebel snipers. Neither the War Office nor Police Supplies could meet the demand for woollens. But the British Army, however, had left woollen blankets for the hospital and these were now requisitioned. Likewise about five hundred hospital uniforms for patients were packed into bundles and conveyed by [me] to Lashio. Road transport to Namkham was slow and uncertain, so Sao Khun Hkio and [I] flew over Namkham and lowered the bundles in a free drop.[35]

Whether the besieged garrison in Namkham received their woollen uniforms is uncertain, but reinforcements were on their way up the old Burma Road from Lashio to Hsenwi—and down from Myitkyina and Bhamo in the north. As they were closing in on Namkham, and the route to Kachin State was no longer clear, Naw Seng decided to move east. But before evacuating Namkham, he took with him some unusual booty. The American doctor, Gordon Seagrave, was running a missionary hospital in Namkham and was training medical staff, mainly from Christian Karen and Kachin communities. Seagrave had become famous during World War II when he and his team of nurses operated around the clock throughout the 78-day siege of Myitkyina during the final stages of the Allies' Burma campaign.

Seagrave, whose family had been missionaries in Burma for generations, had grown up speaking, reading and writing Karen as well as Burmese and remained deeply sympathetic to the Karens ever after. Naw Seng was an acquaintance from World War II. According to Dr. Seagrave's son, Sterling Seagrave: "When Naw Seng and his mixed Kachin-Karen convoy arrived in Namkham, they came as friends, stayed as friends and left as friends. There was a great deal of excitement among the doctors and nurses. There were a few wounded, who were treated—but my father always treated everybody, regardless of politics."[36]

Dr. Seagrave's medical staff were among the best in Burma, and Naw Seng took seven of them with him when he withdrew from Namkham in late September, including Dr. Ba Saw, a Karen who was expected to run the hospital if anything happened to Dr. Seagrave.[37] The Burma Army roared into Namkham forty-eight hours after Naw Seng had left.

According to Sterling Seagrave: "Although there were no insurgents there when they arrived, they stormed the hospital as if it were a military target, roughed up doctors and nurses, and arrested my father. He was charged with treason on a number of counts, including giving aid and comfort (and medical supplies) to the 'insurgents', providing them with a team of doctors and nurses, and—most comic—of 'having them over for tea'. His reply to that charge, before the Burma Supreme Court, was 'I am an American and Americans don't drink tea, they drink coffee'. The treason charges, framed by Ne Win and approved by U Nu, were eventually thrown out by the Supreme Court, and my father exonerated, but only after he had spent more than a year in Rangoon Jail and suffered his first heart attack."[38]

After leaving Namkham, Naw Seng and his men drove southeast to Kutkai, but the road was insecure and they soon had to abandon their vehicles and march into the hills. The villages in the mountains east of Kutkai are almost exclusively Kachin, so Naw Seng was safe for the time being. In November, he formally set up his own rebel army, the Pawngyawng National Defence Force.

A flag was hoisted, the lower part of which was green, symbolising the lush and fertile Kachin country, and the upper part red, which was meant to honour the people who had fallen in the war against the Rangoon government. In the middle were two crossed Kachin *dahs*, or traditional swords, with the letters PNDF superimposed on a white scroll. Pawngyawng was the name Naw Seng wanted to give the independent republic of which he dreamt; it was the mythical progenitor of the oldest Kachin tribes.

"We were about 2,000 to 3,000 men at that time," Zau Mai remembers. "Most of us were Kachins, but there were also quite a few Karens who had followed Naw Seng up into the Shan states, plus a few Shans. We really thought that our independence was at hand."

Somewhat surprisingly, the government's forces left the Burma Road and went after the rebels, into the remote and rugged border mountains around Möng Ko, Möng Hom, Möng Ya and Phong Hseng (or Hpaunghsaing, as the Burmese prefer to call it). Fierce battles raged for several months, and Naw Seng, unable to resupply his troops in these isolated border areas, was running out of ammunition.

Cornered at the border village of Möng Ko, he sent an emissary across the stream in the valley to Man Hai on the Chinese side. Informal talks were held with the local authorities in Man Hai and they agreed to accept Naw Seng's battered PNDF as refugees. On 5 May, Naw Seng's main force of 400 men crossed the frontier into Yunnan. The remaining troops slipped quietly back to their home villages in Kachin State and a handful made it to the Karen hills in the south. The rebellion led by the legendary, swashbuckling Naw Seng was over.[39]

The CPB's "people's war" was not progressing very well either. A "united front", the People's Democratic Front (PDF), comprising the CPB, Thakin

Soe's Red Flag Communists and the PVO had been set up on 24 March 1949 in Prome.[40] The combined "front" had managed to capture the delta town of Henzada, and Tharrawaddy, further to the north, but on 27 August both towns were recaptured by government forces—and soon rifts became evident within the PDF.

When its different members met in Prome in March the following year, open hostilities erupted and the PVO drove the CPB out of Thayetmyo, where the Communists had maintained their own "Military Academy" right in the centre of town. Pakokku, south of Mandalay—in rebel hands for more than a year—returned to full government control on 29 April 1950. Nearly all the towns that had been seized in 1948 and 1949 were back in government hands by the end of the year.

On 1 September, the Communists' People's Liberation Army of Burma and the Revolutionary Burma Army of the 1948 army mutineers formally merged to become the *pyithu tatmadaw* (People's Army) of the CPB. But it was too late to reverse history: the insurrections had failed and the rebels knew that they could not defeat the government's troops in open battle. According to Thakin Ba Thein Tin, a last desperate attempt at attacking an urban centre was made in late 1950:

> We decided to launch a frontal assault on Lewe, between Pyinmana and Yedashe. We mobilised 3,000 men but, although the government force was only 1,000 strong, we failed to capture the town. It was too well-defended with three lines of trenches full of sharpened bamboo stakes. Then we tried to hold a mass rally at Natawgyi, near Myingyan. But the enemy [government forces] arrived at the scene and we lost many of our best cadres. After these two incidents, we decided that it was futile to attack towns and cities, or even to organise mass movements inside urban centres. We decided to study Mao Zedong's theory of the protracted war: to establish base areas in the rural areas first and surround the towns later.[41]

Smaller rebellions among the Mons, Pa-Os, Karennis and in Arakan did not have much impact on the main political scene in Burma. The first three depended on Karen support, and the third was too splintered and factionalised to be of any major significance. The Muslims in Arakan enjoyed some sympathy across the border in East Bengal, but their forces had dwindled from several thousand in 1948 to just a handful by 1950. Their leader, Jaffar Hussain—who was also known as Jaffar Kawwal as he had been a famous practitioner of Qawwali, the devotional music of the Sufis, an ascetic Muslim sect—was assassinated in October 1950.

The new commander of the *mujahids*, Cassim, lacked both the charisma and the popularity of his predecessor. Buddhist insurgents, led by the monk Sein Da, established a foothold in the Arakan Yoma. His men even managed to hold on to a few towns for some years, but their rebellion was localised and never posed any serious threat to Rangoon.

"Peace Within One Year" did not seem that far-fetched after all—when, unexpectedly, an unusual column of armed men marched into the hills of the eastern Shan state of Kengtung in January 1950. Two hundred soldiers from the Nationalist Chinese, or Kuomintang forces, with mules carrying their weapons and equipment, crossed the frontier and set up a temporary camp in the hills surrounding Möng Yang, a small market town about eighty kilometres north of Kengtung city, near the Yunnan frontier. Following the victory of Mao Zedong's Communists, and the proclamation of their People's Republic of China in Beijing on 1 October, 1949, Chiang Kai-shek's main KMT force had retreated to Taiwan, where his "Republic of China" lived on after the loss of the mainland.

Fighting continued for several months in some remote parts of China, including Yunnan, a province rife with warlordism, banditry and opium trafficking. It was not until December 1949 that the Communist People's Liberation Army (PLA) entered the provincial capital of Kunming. The KMT governor of Yunnan, an old political trickster called Lu Han who specialised in smuggling opium and arms, secretly rallied to the side of the Communists.[42]

The two military units defending the province were the 8th and the 26th Armies, commanded by Gen. Li Mi (a.k.a. Peng Chen) and Gen. Yu Chen-wan respectively. Both escaped hurriedly in an aeroplane to Hong Kong when the Communists marched in.[43] The remnants of their forces retreated south, towards the borders with Burma and French Indochina.

Marching over steep mountains and through malaria-infested jungles, they struggled to survive. The Nationalist troops were running short of rations and ammunition. Many were barefoot; some wore sandals made from cloth or rice stalks. There was no way they would make it to the coast and across the sea to Taiwan. Although a small unit had retreated across the border into Burma in January, the other 1,500 to 2,000 survivors marched on aimlessly. Well-armed and well-fed PLA columns were pursuing them, but, given the difficult terrain, even their advance was slow.

The vast majority of the KMT troops would most probably have surrendered, or simply exchanged their tattered uniforms for peasants' clothing and returned home to their villages, had it not been for a remarkable intellectual in their midst: the short, bespectacled Professor Ting Tsuo-shou. A native of Hunan province and educated in France, he was a renowned calligrapher, and he had read all the Chinese classics. Driven by almost quasi-religious fervour, he believed firmly that victory for the Communists would mean an end to the reign of the cultured classes in China.

Ting had actually fled to Taiwan together with Chiang Kai-shek aboard a gunboat in May 1949, just before the fall of Shanghai. The professor had spent a few months on the island, discussing military strategy with Chiang Kai-shek. Despite his frail appearance, Ting was a fiery orator, and he gave ardent anti-Communist lectures at various gatherings in Taiwan throughout the summer of 1949.

Professor Ting then had decided to return to areas in the mainland, where Nationalist forces were still holding out. In late 1949, he found himself in southern Yunnan together with 1,000 men of the 8th Army, commanded in Gen. Li Mi's absence by Col. Li Ko-kwei. Together, the two men mapped out a new strategy. If the KMT were to survive on the Chinese mainland, they would have to do what the Communist revolutionaries had done before them: to establish a base area in the southern parts of Yunnan which the PLA had not yet reached. This was the only chance to one day reconquer China, as Mao and his partisans had done from their base in Yan'an.[44]

They decided that the best choice would be Jinghong (Che Li in Chinese) in Sipsongpanna, near the border with Laos, where KMT militias were still holding out against the PLA. A base area had to be close to supply bases and secure lines of communication, and the Francophone Chinese professor evidently hoped that the colonial authorities in French Indochina—which were battling their own Communist insurgents—would be willing to support his grand plan to fight the new rulers in Beijing. Should the attempt to set up a base area inside Yunnan fail, the KMT could always retreat across the frontier to Laos to regroup, or to ask for asylum.

But before Ting and the KMT forces could reach the vicinity of the Jinghong, the Communists had marched in and occupied the town and all areas east of it up to the Laotian border. Ting and the commanders of what remained of the 26th and 8th Armies held an emergency meeting to find an alternative location for a new base.

There were by now almost no areas left in Yunnan which could be considered safe. They decided to follow the course of the Mekong river, not to Laos but across the frontier into Burma, the only option left to them. Fortunately, some troops from the 93rd Division of the 26th Army were among them—and their commander, Chen Wei-chen, had some knowledge of the conditions of Kengtung in the eastern Shan states, where ten years before he had fought the Japanese with American support.

To avoid being captured and disarmed by the Burmese—which they learned had happened to the first KMT stragglers who had entered the Möng Yang area in January—Ting and more than 1,000 KMT soldiers marched through dense forests and jungles along the Mekong, where it forms the border between Burma and Laos. Eventually, they reached a fertile green valley called Möng Pong.[45] There was rice, fruit and pork in abundance, and the local Shans were friendly, peaceful and hospitable.

A camp was built, hidden in the forest near the village. The hills and jungles of Laos could be seen across the river, and the Thai border was only a few kilometres to the south. It seemed an ideal place for a secret base where they could regroup, and prepare for the reconquest of the Chinese mainland.[46]

They decided not to cross the river, but to remain on the Burmese side of this tri-border junction, where governmental control of remote areas was much more lax than in Laos and Thailand. They had just learned that as many as 5,000 troops from other retreating KMT units had entered Laos at about the same time, only to be disarmed and interned by the French.[47]

The first priority was to re-establish contact with the outside world. Professor Ting and Chen Wei-chen of the 93rd Division removed their uniforms, put on civilian clothes—and boarded a bus to Tachilek, a ramshackle border town on the Thai frontier opposite Mae Sai. The two towns were separated by a small river, over which a bridge of logs had been built during the war. Both Tachilek and Mae Sai were market towns, so Ting and Chen were certain they would meet some trustworthy Chinese there.

While strolling down a dusty street in Tachilek, they spotted portraits of Sun Yat-sen and Chiang Kai-shek inside one of the houses. By good fortune, the house belonged to one Madame Yan, a lady of Yunnanese extraction, whose family had been living in Tachilek for a century. Her husband was the chairman of the Yunnanese Association in Tachilek, and he had been a main local contact for the KMT's intelligence service during World War II.

The Yans introduced Ting and Chen to Ma Shou-i, a prosperous Sino-Burmese trader in town who commanded his own private army of 800 men. He was an accomplished smuggler: in the past, he had sent mule convoys from the Thai-Burma border up to Lancang in southern Yunnan with salt, textiles, cooking utensils and rice from Thailand. These goods had been sold—and opium had been bought as return cargo.

The civil war in Burma had opened entirely new business opportunities for trader Ma. A rifle was five times less heavy than a sack of rice and worth seven times as much. So with a load of arms, bought on the black market in northern Thailand, Ma could obtain thirty-five times more opium than with a caravan carrying rice and consumer goods.[48] But his men had to move with extreme caution: guns were more likely to be coveted by rival bands than more peaceful items such as cooking utensils—hence the need for a well-equipped private army.

The Communist advance into Yunnan, however, had made Ma worried. The new regime in Lancang was still tolerating the opium trade, since so many local farmers there depended on poppy cultivation for their survival. But for how much longer? Ma was extremely pleased to have met his new friends—and they, in turn, had accomplished what they were looking for: a source of supplies and links with the outside world.

Contacts with Taiwan were established through the Chinese community across the border in northern Thailand: Chiang Kai-shek's headquarters in Taipei was delighted to hear that Professor Ting was still alive—and that he had brought with him a formidable KMT force. Through contacts in Thailand, supplies began to filter across the border into Möng Pong in this remote corner of easternmost Kengtung state.

After having disarmed the first KMT arrivals in January, the Burmese authorities had sent them to an army camp at Meiktila, south of Mandalay. Now there was another, sizeable KMT force in Kengtung, and they not only refused to surrender to the Burmese authorities but in June 1950, the KMT—which was now well established in eastern Kengtung—demanded the release of those already interned. The KMT generals even threatened to attack the Burma Army if it tried to disarm or detain any of their troops, knowing that Rangoon, already stretched on many other rebel fronts, would not have many soldiers to spare for a major campaign in the northeast.

Nevertheless, the War Office in Rangoon responded angrily to the KMT's demands, which they considered an outrageous violation of Burma's sovereignty. The same month, an ultimatum was issued to the KMT in eastern Kengtung: leave Burma immediately or face military action. To demonstrate its military prowess, the resupplied KMT then marched southwest from its base near the Mekong river and occupied Tachilek. The Burma Army went into action, and on 21 July, Tachilek was recaptured after fierce fighting.[49]

This was a high-priced victory, however. Casualties were extremely heavy on the Burmese side, and among those who died in related incidents was Wing-Commander Selwyn James Khin, the chief of the Burma Air Force. A Christian Burman and a former Battle of Britain pilot, Khin had replaced Samuel Shi Sho after the outbreak of the Karen rebellion in early 1949. His plane crashed while on an operational flight over the hills near Kengtung. He was succeeded as air force chief by Wing-Commander Tommy Clift, an Anglo-Shan.

Following their defeat at Tachilek, 200 KMT soldiers fled across the Mekong river to Laos, where most of them were disarmed by the French authorities. The main force retreated westwards, along the Thai-Burmese border mountains, and took over Möng Hsat, 60 kilometres north of the Thai border at Fang-Thaton. Möng Hsat was actually an overgrown village which had been officially designated as a "town": it originally consisted of no more than a few hundred bamboo huts by a river in a green and fertile valley surrounded by high mountains. This tiny settlement was of little strategic importance, but it boasted an airstrip which the Allied forces had built during World War II to receive supplies for the anti-Japanese resistance. The KMT forces decided to make it their main base after their retreat from Tachilek.

Meanwhile, the former commander of the Yunnan-based 8th Army, Gen. Li Mi, had continued from Hong Kong to Taiwan to receive instructions from Chiang Kai-shek.[50] His colleague, 26th Army commander Gen. Yu Chen-wan, had been killed in Kowloon Tong, Hong Kong, by an unidentified assassin during their exile in the crown colony. Li Mi's orders were to travel via Bangkok and Chiang Mai to rejoin his men in the Shan hills.[51] To further boost the strength and the influence of the KMT in the area, Ma's private band of border brigands was attached to the remnants of the 8th and 26th Armies: the trader himself obtained the presumptuous title "12th Divisional Commander".[52]

KMT soldiers upgraded the tiny airstrip in Möng Hsat and soon supply flights began to arrive from Bangkok and Taipei. A bamboo barracks was erected across the airfield, and a nearby paddy field was cleared and levelled into a parade ground, where soldiers performed daily drills against the backdrop of a gigantic portrait of Chiang Kai-shek. A wooden building with a concrete floor was constructed on a hilltop overlooking the camp and the airfield to serve as Gen. Li Mi's command headquarters.

It was becoming obvious to the Burmese authorities that a major military adventure was being planned: from these sanctuaries in the Shan hills, the KMT intended to reinfiltrate China from the Yunnan back door to reverse the red tide that had swept the mainland. Instead of a "liberated area" inside Yunnan, as professor Ting had planned initially, the resistance bases would have to be on the Burmese side of the frontier.

Since the end of World War II, many survivors of the 93rd Division had remained in the Thai-Burma border areas, where they were engaged in commerce. One of them was Gen. Liu Kuo Chwan (Lu Guoquan in *pinyin*). He was promptly summoned to the Taiwan embassy in Bangkok, which was becoming the nerve centre for the operations in the Shan states. Gen. Liu was appointed new commander of the 26th Army to replace the assassinated Gen. Yu.[53]

Meanwhile, the geopolitical scene in Asia in 1950 was undergoing some drastic changes which had severe repercussions even in Burma. At dawn on 25 June, Marshal Choe Yong Gun, the commander of the Communist army of the Democratic People's Republic of Korea, unleashed a carefully planned attack into the US-allied Republic of Korea to the south of the 38th parallel. The forces of the southern part of the Korean peninsula were completely taken by surprise, and fled in disarray. The United Nations Security Council was summoned to an emergency meeting the same day. The shocked delegates called for the immediate withdrawal of North Korean troops from South Korea. Pyongyang ignored the resolution and pushed even further south towards Seoul, the capital of the almost undefended South Korean republic.

The origin of this conflict lay in the final days of World War II. The Soviet Union had actually remained neutral in the war against Japan until 8 August 1945, two days after the US dropped an atomic bomb over Hiroshima and a day before the bombing of Nagasaki. Soviet troops quickly advanced down through Manchuria and Korea, while US forces entered the south of the peninsula from Japan. It was agreed that the Soviet Union would accept the surrender of the Japanese army in Korea north of the 38th parallel while US forces would accept the surrender south of that line.

UN-supervised elections were proposed, but the Soviet Union refused to cooperate. Nevertheless, elections were held south of the 38th parallel in May 1948 and three months later, the UN officially established the Republic of Korea with its capital at Seoul. The leader of the new republic was the staunch Korean nationalist and wartime anti-Japanese resistance leader Syngman Rhee. Moscow branded the move illegal and countered in September by setting up its own puppet state in the north: the Democratic People's Republic of Korea, with its capital at Pyongyang and headed by Communist leader Kim Il-Sung.

Underestimating the determination of the Communists to push on, the US withdrew most of its forces from South Korea. By June 1949, only a small military advisory group of 500 men remained to assist in the formation and training of Syngman Rhee's armed forces—and exactly a year later, the North Koreans attacked. On 27 June, shortly after the meeting with the UN Security Council, US President Harry S. Truman decided to send air and sea forces to assist the fledgling South Korean republic.

Hardly by coincidence, the UN on 7 July decided to dispatch additional ground troops from other countries, and it requested an American to head the unified command of these forces. Truman's choice was Gen. Douglas MacArthur, the commander of the US forces in the Far East. The US was now directly drawn into the battle against communism in Asia.

The conflict divided Asia and the rest of the world into opposing camps, for and against communism. Mao Zedong's China, not a member of the UN at this time, sent more than 400,000 "volunteers" to fight alongside North Korea's 130,000 men. Soviet land forces did not participate, but it was not forgotten that Mao had visited Moscow in December 1949 and January 1950, half a year before the invasion from the North. This was the Chinese Communist leader's first and only visit abroad, and it is widely believed that he discussed with Stalin the unification of the Korean peninsula under Communist control.[54]

The South Korean army numbered about 100,000 men, assisted by the same number of US troops, with additional contingents from a host of other members of the UN. Britain and Turkey sent two regiments each; Australia contributed two infantry battalions, New Zealand an artillery regiment; and one infantry battalion each came from Belgium, Colombia, Thailand, the Philippines, Ethiopia, France, Greece and the Netherlands; Luxembourg sent an infantry company, and South Africa and Canada an air unit each. Denmark, Sweden, Norway, Italy and India dispatched non-combat medical teams.

Burma reacted to the confrontation between the West and the Communist Bloc in its own way. Its delegates to the UN approved of sending UN troops to Korea—but they voted against a later General Assembly resolution which named China as the aggressor.[55] Instead, Burma joined other Asian and African countries in an effort to reach a cease-fire in Korea and to convene "an international conference to solve Asian disputes". When the CPB had gone underground in March 1948, Mao Zedong had not yet captured power in Beijing. But after the proclamation of the People's Republic of China, Burma suddenly shared a 2,170-kilometre border with the Communist giant and was eager to please it in order not to provoke Beijing into supporting its Burmese sister party.

For Chiang Kai-shek's government in Taipei, the so-called Republic of China that still represented China in the UN, the Korean War came as a gift from heaven. When Truman sent air and sea cover for South Korea in June, he also ordered the 7th Fleet to "prevent any attack on Formosa [Taiwan]" because "the occupation of [Taiwan] by Communist forces would be a direct threat to the security of the Pacific area and the US forces performing their lawful and necessary functions in that area."[56]

Taiwan became one of the most important strategic links in the US-sponsored anti-communist bloc that was emerging in Asia to counter China's increasingly aggressive designs. Gen. MacArthur even wanted forces from Taiwan to participate in the Korean War, but this was rejected by Truman, who thought such a move would widen the conflict with China.[57]

Although Taiwan did not send troops to participate in the Korean War, a fraternal relationship was established with Syngman Rhee's right-wing and staunchly anti-communist government in Seoul. Taiwan intelligence agents also closely monitored the war against the Communists in China and North Korea. Together with their South Korean counterparts, they began discussing the possibilities of opening a second front against China. Taiwan's troops were already there: south of the Yunnan frontier, China's soft underbelly.

Perhaps sensing what was about to happen, or just worried about the possibilities of a Communist Chinese intervention to wipe out the KMT menace in northeastern Burma, the official historian Dr. Maung Maung asked rhetorically in his account of the Nationalist Chinese operation in Burma: "The cold war of the rival big powers was then becoming more intense, and here and there localised hot wars were flaring up: Korea, Berlin . . . Would Burma be next?"[58]

On 24 March 1951 Gen. MacArthur issued a statement from Tokyo calling for a "decision by the United Nations to depart from its tolerant effort to contain the war to the area of Korea, through an expansion of our military operations to its coastal areas and interior bases [to] doom Red China to risk the imminent military collapse."[59]

Another hardline former US general and World War II veteran, Claire Chennault, had served as Chiang Kai-shek's main adviser for many years and now headed the unofficial 'China Lobby' in the US which advocated close ties with Taiwan and confrontation with Beijing. Hardly by coincidence, Chennault's airline, Civil Air Transport (CAT), had from the very beginning been responsible for air drops of arms and ammunition to the KMT at Möng Hsat.[60] He later admitted publicly that a plan did exist to implement MacArthur's idea of a broader war against China, using Burma as a springboard:

> It is reported—and I have reason to believe it is true—that the Nationalist [KMT] Government offered three full divisions . . . of troops to fight in Korea, but the great opportunity was not putting the Nationalists in Korea. It was a double envelopment operation. With the United Nations forces in Korea and the Nationalist Chinese in southern areas . . . . The Communists would have been caught in a giant pincers . . . this was a great opportunity—not to put the Nationalist Chinese in Korea, but to let them fight in the south.[61]

Since the beginning of 1951, the KMT generals in the Shan hills had been drafting more soldiers from the villages in the border areas: Lahus, Shans, Was, Palaungs and Sino-Shans. These fresh recruits were trained at the KMT's new base at Möng Hsat and armed with weapons that arrived on nightly flights from Taiwan. The planes carried an extra fuel tank to enable them to fly non-stop from Taipei; any landing en route could have been spotted by journalists and others. This was a secret operation, and Taiwan's direct involvement was never formally acknowledged.

By April, the KMT's force in the area had swollen to 4,000 men and by December it was 6,000 strong. Officers and cadres were flown in from Taiwan as well, and a strategy was mapped out. After leaving 1,000 heavily armed troops to defend Möng Hsat, the bulk of the fighting force then marched north to the Wa Hills and Kokang, closer to the Yunnan frontier.

Operations in the Shan states had become more secretive after 11 April, when Truman decided to relieve Gen. MacArthur as UN Commander and head of all US forces in the Far East. Truman, who wanted to limit the conflict in the Far East, had found himself at loggerheads with MacArthur, Chennault and others who openly advocated an all-out war with China.

The president argued that the hawks of the China Lobby did not bear in mind what he perceived as the greater threat to Europe posed by the Soviet Union. Officially, US involvement with the KMT then ceased. Unofficially, the China Lobby continued their activities in the Shan states, ignoring the president's orders. The covert KMT operation that followed was the first of many similar, "secret" wars that US security agencies carried out in Third World countries, among them Cuba, Laos, Nicaragua, Angola and Afghanistan.

All the "secret" KMT forces were now unified into a single command under Gen. Liu of the 26th Army. For strategic purposes, three military areas were demarcated. Liu was in direct command of the "Number Three Military Area" at Möng Hsat. The "Number One Military Area," commanded by Gen. Fu Cheng Yang, covered the Wa hills and had its headquarters at Pangyang. The "Number Two Military Area" was headquartered at Lunghtangchai, a large village of tumbledown mudbrick houses and cobbled alleyways in central Kokang, where Gen. Wang Yu Wai was in charge of operations.

The mountainous Kokang region in the far northeastern corner of the Shan states was of vital strategic as well as economic importance to the KMT. The district, 2,200 square kilometres or about the size of Luxembourg, was inhabited by ethnic Chinese who spoke a Yunnanese dialect. Kokang was famous for its fragrant tea—and its opium had for years been reputed to be the best in Southeast Asia.

Kokang's steep mountains and deep gorges were not suited for rice cultivation, so cash crops had to be raised and sold to merchants in Hsenwi and Lashio as well as across the border to China. Because of its isolation east of the turbulent Salween river, trade was conducted mostly with China across the border. Many Kokang families also had relatives on the Yunnanese side; the border was, after all, merely an artificial creation, decided upon by the governments in London and Beijing in the late nineteenth century.

Not surprisingly, many Yunnanese from across the frontier came over to join the KMT at Lunghtangchai, especially from the Keng Ma area adjacent to Kokang. One of them was Li Wenhuan, a junior administrator of Tseung-kan county, who later rose to become one of the most powerful of the KMT warlords in the Shan states. Inside Kokang, the KMT enlisted the support of Olive Yang, younger sister of the Kokang *saohpa*. This masculine young lady, still in her early twenties, built up her own armed units which, in effect, became an auxiliary force to the KMT.

Olive, known locally as "Miss Hairy Legs", had, like so many other scions of aristocratic Shan states families, attended the prestigious Guardian Angel's Convent in Lashio. Old classmates still remember how their parents used to warn them not to play with this singularly tough little girl: "Stay away from Olive!" they had said. "She's got a revolver in her schoolbag." Her formal education behind her, Olive no longer had to hide her guns. She was to be seen in the cobbled streets of Tashwehtang, the ramshackle hill capital of Kokang, in a grey uniform, with a Belgian army pistol on each hip. With the help of Olive, the KMT was getting ready to strike against Mao Zedong's Communists.

4

The Secret War

In May 1951, the KMT decided that the time was ripe to make a move. Two columns of heavily armed troops climbed the grassy, barren mountain range that separates Burma's Kokang district from China. They then entered Yunnan. The first unit, led by Li Mi himself, targeted Kengma, which was captured within a week.

The other column advanced from the Wa hills south of Kokang towards Teetang, another border town in Yunnan. Li Mi's men continued their advance, and headed for Mengsa, sixty kilometres northeast of Kengma. The aim was to capture the airfield in Mengsa—the closest to the Burmese border—and set up a base area there.

Following the first debacle at Kengma, the PLA had regrouped and counter-attacked. Li Mi was beaten, and within less than a month in Yunnan, he retreated to Möng Mau in the northern Wa hills. On hearing about the defeat, the second column also turned back and never even approached Teetang.

Undercover Burmese intelligence agents, who nervously monitored the fighting, reported that unidentified four-engine aircraft had dropped supplies on the KMT bases in Kokang and around Möng Mau throughout the campaign. It is not known where the planes came from, but they must presumably have taken off from airfields in northern Thailand, which were frequently used by Taiwan intelligence agencies for flying supplies to Möng Hsat, and to survey the Yunnan frontier.[1]

Following the first, abortive attempt to invade Yunnan, a second foray was mounted in July. This time a 2,000-strong force was mustered under the command of Gen. Liu Kuo Chwan, the Möng Hsat-based commander of the 26th Army. The area chosen this time was closer to the bases along the Thai border: Sipsongpanna in southern Yunnan, just across the frontier from Kengtung. Sipsongpanna, or Xishuangbanna as the Chinese call it, is one of Yunnan's remotest areas, a region of deep fertile valleys inhabited by Shans, and twisting mountain ranges, the home of Akhas, Palaungs, Was and other hill tribes.

Like the Shan hills in Burma, it was ideal guerrilla country. There were also rumours of scattered bands of local guerrillas still holding out in parts of Sipsongpanna, although it was impossible to determine whether they were politically motivated or just border bandits.

Using a newly established base at Möng Yang north of Kengtung as the staging point for the operation, Gen. Liu crossed into China with his massive, heavily armed column. They avoided Jinghong, the relatively well-defended administrative centre of Sipsongpanna, and made a push for Menghai, a much smaller town fifty-five kilometres to the west.

As had been the case in June, aeroplanes had dropped ammunition and other supplies during this second attempt to enter China, but the operation was equally disastrous this time. Within a week, they were beaten and returned to Möng Yang, carrying their many dead and wounded with them. The PLA was too tough and the local people did not welcome the KMT forces as "liberators", as they had expected: "When KMT agents went into their home villages in Yunnan their own families told them to leave immediately, and not come back because life was better than it ever had been under the KMT and 'they did not want trouble with the cadres'."[2]

In October, Li Mi left his jungle headquarters at Möng Hsat and travelled to Bangkok. After spending two months in the Thai capital, he continued on to Taipei to discuss the failures with his superiors. He had to fly via Hong Kong, where he ran into some unexpected problems. The Chinese language Hong Kong newsweekly *Sinwen Tienti* reported in its 29 December issue:

> The internationally popular ex-governor of Yunnan, Gen. Li Mi, quietly embarked on a civilian plane at Bangkok on Christmas Eve and landed at Hong Kong at 3:10 P.M. en route to Taipei. As he did not possess an entry visa for Hong Kong, he was detained at the airport immigration office for half an hour. However, he was permitted to meet and converse with his friends who came to greet him at the airport for a few minutes. Li Mi avoided answering questions regarding his present return and mission to Taiwan. "The main purpose of my present return to Taipei is to report to the President [Chiang Kai-shek] and to call on a few old high officials."[3]

Another Hong Kong publication, the *Observatory Review*, reported on 14 January 1952 under the headline "Li Mi returning to Yunnan within a month":

> The present return of Li Mi to Taiwan was to confer with the Chiefs-of-Staff regarding the instructions and tactics of guerrilla warfare. The conferences of Li Mi with Taiwan are being held very secretly. According to official circles, the most important request to be made by Li Mi to Taiwan is for more finan-

cial aid as the present allotment is insufficient. Secondly, Li Mi requests Taiwan to send some skilled hands to assist him in Yunnan as the previous batch of men who came from Taiwan created frictions amongst the others in the front line . . . . This time it is learnt the Political Bureau [of the KMT] will depute a group of about fifty men to assist Li Mi in Yunnan.[4]

During his brief stay in Taiwan, Li Mi was formally appointed "Governor of Yunnan Province" and also proclaimed Commander of the "Yunnan Province Anti-Communist National Salvation Army".[5] Anti-communist hardliners in Taipei were not very pleased with what was happening in Korea at this time. Truce talks had begun on 10 July 1951 at Kaesong in Korea, and the Communist side was confident that the UN forces would undertake no major offensive while the talks were in progress. The fighting subsided; only minor clashes took place throughout 1952.

The Communists took advantage of the lull in the fighting to strengthen their positions, rotate troops and bring in more heavy weaponry. The UN in South Korea was hardly in a position to do this—but Taiwan did not want to let the Communists get the upper hand. The answer was to intensify covert operations by the KMT on the southern flank of China, in effect rejecting UN diplomacy, which the hawks in Seoul and Taipei claimed only played into the hands of the Communists.

To undertake this massive, covert operation, more supplies for the KMT forces in northeastern Burma were obviously needed. Before long, two flights a week from Taipei to Möng Hsat brought in vast quantities of arms, ammunition, medical supplies—and reinforcements. In February 1952, the Burmese government reported that not 50 but 700 "instructors" had been flown in to Möng Hsat from Taiwan to oversee the campaign.[6] Including more local recruits, the total strength of the KMT in northeastern Burma had now increased to 13,000 well-equipped troops.[7] In February, Li Mi had also returned to Burma via Bangkok.

The direct Taiwan involvement in the KMT operation in Burma became evident when the Burmese side captured a strangely worded document dated 26 January 1952:

> To General Commander Li Ping Jen (Li Mi) and all the ranks and files of the whole army. You, under the guidance of the President have already accomplished many achievements. I take this opportunity of the spring festivity to express my deepest concern about you. The Communist bandits have not been exterminated as yet and our compatriots are awaiting for salvation . . . . Wishing you earlier victory and a happy new year.[8]

The letter was signed by Chiang Ching Kuo—the son of Taiwan's president, Chiang Kai-shek. Another captured document stated that "this Army is ... under direct command of President Chiang [Kai-shek]."[9] Chiang Ching Kuo also paid several visits to Möng Hsat to inspect the troops, underlining the direct connection between Taipei and the KMT in the Shan states.[10]

There were also strong rumours of the presence of US advisers. The *New York Times* had reported on 29 and 30 January 1952 that US engineers were assisting the KMT in improving the Möng Hsat airstrip. These activities were coordinated by a well-known US cinematographic company in Bangkok, the Far East Film Company. Headed by OSS veteran Robert North, it had since the end of World War II distributed anti-communist propaganda films throughout Thailand in close cooperation with the CIA as well as the Thai authorities. The Far East Film Company also served as a conduit for CIA money to the obscure South East Asia Supplies Corporation—or the "SEA Supplies", as North called it for short.[11]

The SEA Supplies Corporation had actually been in charge of sending American-made supplies to Möng Hsat by air since early 1951, when the secret war first began. The covert airlift began on 7 February that year as three C-46s and a C-47 flew into Möng Hsat carrying arms and ammunition that had been picked up from CIA stocks in Okinawa. The planes were piloted by Chief Pilot Robert E. Rousselot, and Captains Robert "Dutch" Brongersma, Charles E. Hayes, Robert C. Snoddy and Harold W. Wells—all veterans of the airlift in China during World War II, and, more recently, the Korean War.[12]

Like the Far East Film Company, SEA Supplies was a CIA front. It was formally headed by Sherman B. Joost, a Princeton graduate and one of the top combat commanders of OSS Detachment 101 in the Kachin Hills during World War II.[13] But its most colourful operative was Paul Helliwell, a well-known intelligence operative who had moved to Bangkok in 1951 to work with North.[14] Helliwell was no newcomer on the Southeast Asia scene: he had headed OSS intelligence in China during World War II. At that time, he had worked closely with the notorious Chinese secret police chief Tai Li, who a US observer described as "China's combination of Himmler and J. Edgar Hoover".[15]

During the war against the Japanese, T.V. Soong, the eldest son of Chinese Nationalist-Christian patriarch Charlie Soong, had built a Western-style residence for Gen. Joseph Stilwell on the edge of the Chialing near the command headquarters at Chungking. It had a roof terrace with flowers and a pool, and a magnificent view of the river. Tai Li supplied the servants who looked after Stilwell when he retreated to this odd edifice in the southern Chinese mountains.[16]

Tai Li was so ruthless, however, that even Stilwell began to have second thoughts about the regime he was relying on in the anti-Japanese war. He felt there was something fundamentally wrong about how the US had manoeuvred itself "into the position of having to support this rotten regime".[17]

According to Barbara Tuchman, Stilwell felt that his closest ally curiously mirrored what the US was fighting against in Germany: "a one-party government, supported by a Gestapo [Tai Li's organisation] and headed by an unbalanced man with little education".[18] Nevertheless, Stilwell did bring Chiang Kai-shek's army into Burma at a later stage in the war, the wisdom of which was seriously questioned by his British allies at the time.

Helliwell—and other, like-minded "cowboys" in the US army—were certainly less scrupulous about their connections, and thought more highly of the wily Nationalist Chinese leader. When Stilwell at one point in a discussion among US commanders said that Chiang was "a vacillating tricky undependable old scoundrel who never keeps his word", a fellow US general, Claire Chennault, retorted: "Sir, I think the Generalissimo is one of the two or three greatest military and political leaders in the world today. He has never broken a commitment or promise made to me."[19]

Chennault had raised the famous Flying Tigers in China during the war, and later set up the Civil Air Transport (CAT), his own airline which supplied Chiang's troops when they were fighting Mao Zedong's Communists. Old "Vinegar Joe" had died from cancer of the stomach in October 1946, and his namesake (but no relation), Col. Richard Stilwell, had become director of the Far East Division of the Office of Policy Coordination (OPC) in Washington, a strategic planning outfit which operated closely with the CIA.

When the war was going badly for Chiang, Chennault managed to persuade Richard Stilwell's boss, OPC director Frank Wisner, to support his fledgling airline in order to prop up the Nationalists. This failed badly, and CAT's last mission in China was to carry the last fleeing KMT warlord with his treasury of US$1.5 million in gold bars.[20]

When the secret war along the Sino-Burmese frontier was being organised, the old hands went to work again. The CIA had bought CAT when it was facing bankruptcy in 1950, and it was subsequently enlisted by Helliwell's SEA Supplies to carry munitions from Taiwan and Bangkok to Möng Hsat and the KMT forces in southern Burma—and to help the KMT carry opium out. Presumably, Helliwell had no qualms about this; during the campaign in China, he had paid his local informants with "sticky brown bars of opium".[21]

Chennault and Helliwell were prominent members of the informal "China Lobby" in US politics, a group of war veterans and right-wingers who had been supporters of Chiang Kai-shek during the war—and who became his strongest agents and partisans in the corridors of power in Washington after the Communist victory in China in 1949.

As it grew more powerful, the China Lobby came to include a broad spectrum of people, ranging from Helliwell and other shady intelligence operatives and drug runners to right-wing politicians, security planners and well-respected American patriots such as Henry Luce, the publisher of *Time* magazine. The son of a missionary couple, Luce had been born in China and to him Chiang Kai-shek, a Christian at least by name, was the symbol of faith, nationalism and anti-communism.

Already in 1937, "Generalissimo and Mme Chiang Kai-shek" had been made *Time's* "Man and Wife for the Year", and Luce never let his Chinese hero down.[22] *Time* became one of the staunchest supporters of the Nationalist Chinese cause during the Cold War.

The more pragmatic administration in Washington did not always agree with these ideologically motivated people, which had become evident during the rift between MacArthur and Truman in April 1951.[23] Truman's schism with MacArthur suggests that it was after the president had voiced concern over the confrontation with China that the KMT effort in Burma went even further into the obscurities of covert actions, which were led and organised by people who more or less conducted their own foreign policy.

The complexities of the US system, and the contradictions inherent in it, soon became obvious in Burma. As it turned out, not even the American ambassador to Rangoon, David M. Key, had been informed by his own government about the CIA's covert activities in the Shan states and along the Yunnan frontier. He finally resigned in disgust in April 1952 and returned to Washington, arguing that support for Li Mi's operations in Burma had "cost us heavily in terms of Burmese goodwill and trust".[24] According to one US newspaper report from March 1953:

> Officially, the United States never supplied or advised the Li Mi contingent. But up to a year ago Bangkok was full of cloak and dagger operatives and some American citizens unquestionably shuttled back and forth on mysterious missions between Bangkok and Li Mi's airstrip [near] Kengtung. The State Department always kept its skirts clear of these colourful folks.[25]

As a reflection of these contradictions, US agencies ironically ended up supporting people on both sides of the fence. At the same time as elements of the CIA were deeply involved with the KMT effort, US intelligence operatives had also helped set up the prestigious *The Nation* newspaper in Rangoon. Its founder, a remarkable character called Edward Law Yone, was born in the Kachin Hills. He impressed OSS officers at Myitkyina so much with his quick wits and knowledge of Burma that they had flown him out to Delhi for further training. In Delhi, however, the British had interned him at the Red Fort for "collaborating with the Japanese".

The OSS had re-recruited him, flown him to Colombo, where he had become one of the men under OSS playboy S. Dillon Ripley (later secretary of the Smithsonian Institution in the US) who were trained for operations behind Japanese lines. Law Yone had taken part in OSS forays into Arakan to prepare the way for a British tank assault from Chittagong.

Law Yone had emerged from World War II with lots of contacts within the OSS, some of whom had gone on to become CIA officers after the Agency had been created, while others had returned to the US to enlarge their family fortunes as lawyers and investment bankers. Some of these friends had helped Law Yone get started as a newspaperman in Rangoon after the war, chipping in to buy him an old printing press and to provide initial operating capital—exactly as other OSS/CIA operatives did in Thailand at the same time for Daniel Berrigan at the *Bangkok World* newspaper, for Alexander MacDonald of the *Bangkok Post*, for Robert North of the Far East Film Company (and later the Polaris drinking water company in Bangkok), and for Jim Thompson, the father of Thailand's silk export industry.

All these would-be entrepreneurs were willing to accept CIA help because they thought they were all on the side of the "good guys" in the Cold War that was emerging throughout the world, and in Asia in particular.[26] Several "pro-democracy" newspapers are said to have got their start in this way in other Asian countries at the same time.

Ironically, it was Law Yone's US-sponsored newspaper that went to extreme lengths to expose the KMT's activities in the Shan states. The well-respected Nation sent Dr. Maung Maung to the eastern hills to report on KMT activities there, which led to a series of devastating articles as well as a book, Grim War Against the KMT, which was published in Rangoon in 1953.

Dr. Maung Maung's articles outlined in detail US participation in covert operations in the Shan states. That elements of the CIA, backed by the China Lobby, would be on the side of their Nationalist Chinese allies in a war against the common enemy, the Chinese Communists, was hardly surprising. But the disclosures caused a diplomatic crisis between the US and Burma. Rangoon first turned to the US government requesting it to pressure Taiwan to withdraw its forces from Burma. The US had diplomatic relations with Taiwan, which Burma did not, as it recognised the People's Republic of China. But Washington appeared unable or unwilling to act. In late January, the Burmese government decided to raise the issue at the UN General Assembly meeting in Paris.

The Soviet Union and other socialist countries began openly accusing the US of supporting the KMT in Burma, without mentioning it in the context of the Korean War. In April, Sirdar J.J. Singh, president of the India League of America, stated publicly that former US air force pilots were flying some of the planes that dropped supplies in Burma and carried arms and ammunition to the new airstrip at Möng Hsat. Robert Taylor, a US Burma scholar, wrote in 1973:

He was undoubtedly referring to pilots for the Civil Air Transport (CAT), the airline founded by General Claire Chennault in 1946. CAT was closely connected with American intelligence operations in Asia throughout the 1950s and has since been absorbed by Air America, the official airline of the CIA in Laos.[27]

Stretched already on many fronts in battles against Communist and ethnic insurgents, the Burma Army had long hesitated to launch a major offensive against the well-armed, well-supplied and powerfully backed KMT. Fighting between the two forces had been limited to the counter-attack on Tachilek in July 1950 and a minor campaign, code-named "Operation Frost", in February 1951, during which the government's forces recaptured Tang-yan, a town in the northern Shan states under KMT occupation. But as the KMT continued to spread its area of operation, the Rangoon War Office became increasingly concerned.

It was also reported that the KMT was establishing links with the KNDO and other indigenous, ethnic rebel groups. In January 1952, KMT troops joined Karen and Karenni rebel forces and reoccupied the mining town of Mawchi in the Karenni Hills, which had served as the Karen rebel headquarters for a brief period in 1950.

The KMT had a grand scheme for establishing a foothold on the coast of the Andaman Sea, where vast quantities of supplies could be brought in by ship from Taiwan, supplementing the rather cumbersome airlifts with C-46 and C-47 transport planes to Möng Hsat. By strengthening the position of the ethnic rebels, the KMT would also benefit from the Burma Army's need to spread its forces on many different fronts across the eastern hills.

Shortly after the battle at Mawchi, a KMT officer, Li Bin-pu, came down to the Mese area opposite Khun Yuam in northwestern Thailand to escort a three-man KNU delegation to Möng Hsat. Mika Rolley set off for Möng Hsat together with Sgaw Ler Taw, Col. Ohn Pe, a section of troops and two elephants carrying supplies.

They marched north to Möng Hsat, where they were shown around the impressive military complex and promised arms and ammunition in exchange for letting the KMT pass through their territory in the mountains of eastern Burma down to the sea. They were received by Gen. Li Mi's personal assistant, the frail professor Ting, who made it clear that any assistance would be conditional. According to Mika Rolley: "Full support would be forthcoming only if we also joined a proposed 'anti-communist league' which he said was going to be set up in Asia. This was unacceptable to many of the Leftists in the KNU, so we left after about a month in Möng Hsat. But I posted a radio operator there so we could continue to liaise with the KMT."[28]

During his stay in Möng Hsat in April–May, Mika Rolley had observed the twice-weekly flight from Taiwan: "Inbound planes carried arms and ammunition—and opium when they left Möng Hsat. Several of the pilots were Americans. We had dinner together in Gen. Li Mi's house. They never introduced themselves but made no secret of their nationality."[29]

Col. Ohn Pe returned to Möng Hsat alone after some time and based himself there more or less permanently. Another ethnic rebel leader also made it to Li Mi's base and was given arms and ammunition: Zau Seng, a bow-legged Kachin veteran of World War II. He had fought together with Naw Seng during the Upper Burma Campaign but had decided to remain with the KNDO when his leader retreated into China.

A small group of Mon insurgents also benefited from KMT assistance. The Mons populated large tracts of territory along the Andaman sea, and this seemed to be the key to the success of the KMT's advance towards the south. A special agent was appointed: Francis Yap, a young Sino-Thai who had fought with the KMT against the Communists in China until he was wounded and hospitalised in Hong Kong in 1949.

Two years later, at the age of twenty-six, Yap was sent to Thailand to join Gen. Li Mi. Because of his local contacts and knowledge, he had been selected to liaise with ethnic rebel groups along the Thai border. His first attempt to contact the Karens had not been successful: he had been stranded in Myawadi at the border for days without getting any positive response from the KNU leaders.

Yap then turned his attention to the Mon rebels in the hills around Three Pagodas Pass on the Thai–Burma frontier. The Mons, sons and daughters of an ancient civilisation, had fought their rebellion in the shadow of the much mightier Karen army, and readily accepted the proffered aid from the KMT.[30] In 1952, the scattered Mon organisations were unified into the Mon People's Front (MPF), led by Nai Aung Tun, a veteran Mon politician whom Yap had summoned to Myawadi when the talks with the Karens had failed.

The Mon forces, previously organised as three battalions operating under Karen military command, were reorganised and properly trained by Yap at his so-called "Hongsa Military School" in the jungles near Pangga south of Moulmein. The *hongsa*, or Brahmin drake, was the national symbol of the Mon civilisation, and henceforth also became the emblem of the Mon rebellion.

Contrary to popular belief, the Karens never received any large amounts of weaponry from the KMT.[31] Li Mi and Prof. Ting clearly did not trust the leftist elements within the KNU who at this time were busy trying to organise a Marxist-style vanguard party, the Karen National United Party, which eventually came into being in November 1953.[32]

This, however, did not deter the KMT from sending down more forces to the Karen area. By August, 300 KMT troops arrived at the Karen base of Hlaingbwe in the eastern hills. Another batch of 400 KMT soldiers joined them in September and the combined force made contact with Yap's base in the Mon area further to the south. Guided by local Mon rebels, nearly 1,000 KMT troops marched on through the jungles down to Karokpi-Pangga south of Amherst. They had reached the sea.

Rangoon decided that it was time to move against the KMT. Brig.-Gen. Kyaw Zaw, then southern commander of the Burma Army based at Moulmein, was in charge of the operation: "While we were fighting the KMT forces south of Amherst, we spotted six foreign ships coming in towards the shore. I sent a spotter plane to reconnoitre. We realised it could not be a coincidence that the ships appeared at that particular time. But the crews on the ships had apparently lost contact with the KMT and we found out later that they had seized fishermen's boats and asked them where the KMT ground forces were. We managed to drive the KMT out of the area, but it was not until the following year that we solved the mystery with the ships. A Nationalist Chinese major-general defected to the Burmese embassy in Bangkok and we managed to smuggle him out to Rangoon. He told us the ships had been carrying 600 KMT officers and warrant officers, and more than 1,000 machine-guns. The plan was to arm and equip two divisions of KMT troops in Burma. The ships had come from Manila, the defector told us. It was not clear whether Taiwan or the US had arranged the shipment."[33]

Francis Yap confirms that the ships from Taiwan carried 900 military "instructors" and altogether 4,500 tons of munitions: "The ships were unable to get close to the shore because the place where they were supposed to dock, Ko Lagut, an island off the coast near Ye town, had already been occupied by the Burma Army. But if these ships had reached us, the outcome of Burma's civil war would have been different. The weapons were meant for the KMT, the Mons and even the Karens, if they were willing to join us."[34]

The cargo never reached the rebels, however, and no alternative to the Möng Hsat air route was established; some supplies were sent down to the Mons, but the Karens had to rely on the Thai black market and whatever they could buy from corrupt Burma Army personnel.[35]

The CPB reacted to the KMT intervention in its own way. In late 1951, the central committee met at Payathaung Botet near the Pegu Yoma mountains west of Pyinmana. According to Thakin Ba Thein Tin: "The Chinese revolution had succeeded and Yunnan, adjacent to Burma, had been liberated. We decided to contact our Chinese comrades for help. That was a correct decision. But a serious mistake was made at the same time: since Li Mi had occupied parts of the Shan states, we offered the government in Rangoon an alliance against the KMT, in the same way as the Communists in China had joined forces with the KMT against the Japanese invaders during World War II."[36]

The "Peace and Coalition Government (PCG) line", as it became known, turned out to be a complete failure. Rangoon did not need the CPB's troops to fight the KMT, and even if it had accepted the offer for political reasons, it would most certainly have provoked a massive US involvement with the KMT in Burma to prevent a Communist take-over in Rangoon.

U Nu was obviously aware of these dangers, and ignored the offer. The CPB, however, began unilaterally to show signs of "goodwill" and "reconciliation"—by handing back to the landowners land which had been distributed to poor, landless peasants in Pyinmana, Toungoo and Pegu districts. According to Thakin Ba Thein Tin: "The land distribution scheme was the main reason why we were so popular in the countryside at this time. Nearly all our soldiers came from the peasantry. Now, they left their guns and bullets with the party and went home, disillusioned."[37]

Some party hardliners, who disagreed with the new PCG line, began to leave secretly for China to ask for aid. The first batch of thirty Burmese Communists, led by *yebaw* Aung Gyi, trekked north shortly after the meeting at Payathaung Botet. Early the following year, Thakin Ba Thein Tin, then vice chairman of the party, set out on what was going to be a year-long, arduous journey by elephant and on foot towards Yunnan.

His party crossed the frontier near Laiza in Kachin State, and were escorted by local Chinese border guards to the town of Baoshan, where they boarded a plane for Kunming and, later, Beijing. One more group followed, bringing the total of CPB cadres in China to 143. Apart from Thakin Ba Thein Tin and *yebaw* Aung Gyi, the group also included Bo Zeya, the chief of staff of the CPB's People's Army, politburo member Thakin Than Myaing, and Thakin Baw, a senior member of the central committee.

They were well received by the Chinese and allowed to remain in Sichuan province, where they were given political training. But no military aid was forthcoming at this stage; China was not willing to sacrifice its friendly relations with the U Nu government for the sake of the CPB.

Much to their surprise, however, the newly arrived CPB members were introduced to an old comrade who had disappeared almost a decade earlier: Aye Ngwe, a Sino-Burman ex-student from Rangoon University. When it became clear that Aung San had failed to reach Communist-controlled areas in China in 1941, the CPB in Rangoon had sent Aye Ngwe overland to Yunnan.

He had walked across the border bridge at Kyuhkok-Wanting, where the Burma Road crosses the international frontier, in September 1941. It had taken five years for Aye Ngwe to make contact with the Communist Party of China (CPC)—by which time he had lost touch with the CPB. In 1947, he had become a member of the CPC and learned Chinese. When the CPB cadres began arriving from Burma in the early 1950s, Aye Ngwe was called in to act as interpreter.[38]

While the CPB was dwindling away, serious concerns were raised in governmental circles in Rangoon regarding the KMT, especially after the battle near Amherst. On 1 September 1952, the entire southern Shan states were placed under military administration in an attempt to block any further advances towards the sea. The KMT's interference in Burmese affairs became even more blatant in January, 1953 when they deposed the *saohpa* of Möng Hsu and installed their own puppet in his place.

Möng Hsu was located west of the Salween, well outside the KMT's main strongholds east of the river. A major offensive was mounted the same month and on 26 February, the Burma Air Force bombed the KMT's Möng Hsat garrison. But little headway was made against the well-fortified intruders. The KMT now had vast stocks of arms and ammunition plus new Dodge and Ford trucks. The concentration of equipment was "the largest Burma had ever seen", the *Nation* reported on 5 March. Three days before, U Nu had addressed the Chamber of Deputies in Rangoon:

> The Union Government has given serious thought to the problem since the beginning of 1950 when KMT forces encroached upon our territory, and three courses have been open to us:
> *One*: To take the matter up to the UN.
> *Two*: To negotiate with the Chinese Nationalist Government in Formosa through the good offices of those Governments which have diplomatic relations with it, with a view to the withdrawal of the KMT forces from the Union territory.
> *Three*: To counter-attack the KMT aggressors by the armed forces of the Union.[39]

All three options had been tried but with no success. On 25 March, the Burmese Government cabled the UN to request that the "Republic of China"—which was still representing China in the world body—be charged with aggression. To show its disapproval of Washington's participation in the KMT effort, Rangoon also declared that it did not want the US economic aid programme to Burma to continue beyond 30 June. The *New York Herald Tribune* described Burma's move as a "painful defeat" for American policy in Asia. Hectic diplomatic manoeuvring began behind the scenes. According to Robert Taylor:

> After conferring with the US Ambassador to Thailand, the Thai government offered to permit the KMT passage through Thailand to Formosa. The United States began a concerted effort to forestall a UN debate because it was stated that such a debate would serve only to the advantage of the Soviet Union and would drive a wedge between the United States and the governments of Asia.

The US also offered to pay for the removal of the KMT troops from Burma. Nationalist China also attempted to avoid a UN debate on the question. Possibly the more basic reason the US and Nationalist China desired to avoid a debate was that full disclosure of all the circumstances surrounding the KMT intervention would prove embarrassing to them.[40]

The final confirmation of active US participation in the KMT war came only two days after Rangoon's cable to the UN headquarters in New York. On the 27th, the Burma Army made its first advance against the KMT— and a few kilometres east of the Salween ferry at Wan Hsa-la, three white men were spotted fighting on the side of the KMT. The Burmese troops tried to capture them alive, but they resisted resolutely and were finally shot. Diaries and notebooks containing their home addresses in New York and Washington were found on their bodies.

Their pictures were displayed in the Rangoon *Nation* on 30 March; they were apparently small arms instructors for the KMT. The US embassy in Bangkok vehemently denied the report and suggested they were Germans. The Thai police 'confirmed' the claim a few days later: two were said to be "German deserters from the French Foreign Legion" and one an unidentified "German bandit".[41]

On 17 April, Justice Myint Thein, the chairman of Burma's delegation, addressed the UN General Assembly. In a lengthy speech, he outlined the history of the KMT invasion, their attempts to invade Yunnan and links between Möng Hsat and Taipei. The eloquent, well-respected Burmese diplomat did not mince his words:

> The question naturally arises—where have [all] these new arms come from? How is it possible for an original force of 1,500 comparatively lightly armed men to grow in the space of less than three years into a force of 12,000 well-armed men? Obviously this could not happen in the hinterland of Burma unless some outside power were furnishing the inspiration, leadership, direction and the equipment. Even if we had no other evidence, by a process of elimination we would inevitably arrive at the conclusion that the outside power was Formosa.[42]

Myint Thein went on to submit a strongly worded draft resolution, concluding that "aggression is aggression, irrespective of the identity of the aggressor and I venture to think that the United Nations will not draw a fine distinction in regard to the activities of the Kuomintang in Burma and say that aggression by Kuomintang on my country does not call for action. That, if I may say so, would make a mockery of the United Nations".

The Taiwan delegate to the UN, Dr. Tingfu F. Tsiang, responded to the accusations the same day:

The charge of aggression is related to an army led and commanded by General Li Mi. This army is called the Yunnan Anti-Communist and National Salvation Army. General Li Mi, the commander of this army, is a native son of the province of Yunnan. He was born in a village on the very border of China and Burma. The men under his command are banded together to fight communism. They are fighting for home and family because their homes and families have been ruined by the communist regime . . . they are regarded as heroes by all free Chinese everywhere. They receive financial aid from Chinese all over the world. They stand in the eyes of the Chinese people as Garibaldi and his comrades stood in the eyes of the Italian people when Italy struggled for sovereign independence and unity.[43]

Apart from these general statements, Tsiang went on to declare that his government did not exercise any control over this army of dedicated freedom fighters and, therefore, could not be held accountable for its actions. The Political Committee of the UN was not impressed. On 22 April, it adopted a Mexican draft resolution with fifty-seven votes against zero, with Burma and Taiwan abstaining. The following day, the General Assembly approved an amended resolution, following suggestions from Lebanon. The vote was unanimous except for Taiwan's abstention. It said:

> The General Assembly
> *Deplores* this situation and condemns the presence of these forces in Burma and their hostile acts against that country.
> *Declares* that these foreign forces must be disarmed and either agree to internment or leave the Union of Burma forthwith . . .
> *Recommends* that negotiations now in progress through the good offices of certain member states should be pursued . . .
> *Urges* all states to afford . . . Burma . . . all the assistance in their powers . . . to refrain from furnishing any assistance to these forces.[44]

The language of the finally adopted UN resolution was much weaker than what Burma had initially suggested. James Barrington, Burma's Anglo-Burmese ambassador to the UN, said a year later while addressing a gathering at Colby College in Maine, USA: "It seemed that the UN had two yardsticks for measuring aggression; that the shorter and more handy one is used when Communists are involved, and a longer one is used if self-proclaimed anti-communists are involved."[45]

In view of UN actions in Korea, the world body could not ignore or condone another invasion in another country such as Burma, but the fact that the West's interests and sympathies lay more with the KMT than the Burmese government contributed to the rather bland resolution that was finally adopted.

Thailand's role in the whole affair was mostly that of a conduit for supplies going to the KMT in Burma. Thai police and army officers were closely connected with the KMT network—and the CIA. North's Far East Film Company and Helliwell's dodgy SEA Supplies also helped build up the Thai police, then headed by the powerful Gen. Pao Sriyanonda, whom US researcher Alfred McCoy said resembled "a cherub with a Cheshire cat smile".[46]

Arms, armoured vehicles, aircraft and even naval patrol boats were supplied. Thailand's cooperation in the "secret" war against Communist China was crucial, and the country's military ruler, Gen. P. Pibulsongkram, was an ardent nationalist whose loyalties to the US and Taiwan could not be taken for granted. Pao, on the other hand, was easier to deal with, and he became the KMT's main backer in Thailand. Pao's influence far exceeded even that of the chief of the Thai army, Gen. Sarit Thanarat, who frequently complained to his American advisers that the SEA Supplies Company never gave him the same fancy equipment as Pao was receiving.

The wily police general also established close links with pro-KMT elements within Bangkok's Chinese business community. According to US scholar G. William Skinner, among them was an especially influential person who was described as "one of the richest and most pro-KMT Chinese in Bangkok . . . virtually a member of one of the most powerful cliques in the Thai ruling class. In a sense, he is the banker and business agent of the Police General, for whom he speaks in Chinese councils."[47]

The banker, who had arrived virtually penniless in Bangkok to look for a job in 1928, was Tan Piak Chin. He came from Chua Aw, a small, insignificant village in the impoverished Swatow district in southern China and later became better known under the name he assumed when he settled more or less permanently in Thailand a few years later: Chin Sophonpanich.

Chin had remained in Thailand during World War II and joined the Allied-sponsored resistance, the Free Thai movement, at the same time as his Asia Company had supplied the Japanese war machine with daily necessities. Using the income from these activities, Chin had gone on to speculate in war bonds and gold. In 1943, the Thai Ministry of Finance had issued thirty million Baht's worth of war bonds at 3% interest a year over an eight-year maturity period.

The most attractive feature of the issue was a redemption option in gold at eighty-six Baht cash per one *baht* (15.2 gram) weight. When the bonds finally matured in 1951, the value of gold was more than six times higher than stipulated. Chin invested his gold profits in a new company called Asia Trust which at the time became the centre of all foreign exchange dealings in Thailand.[48]

In 1952 Chin and some of his friends floated the Thai Financial Syndicate, which was involved in money-lending, discounting bills, foreign exchange transactions, dealing in stocks, bonds and precious metals, and importing gold. The board chairman of the new company was Gen. Pao himself.[49] This marriage of convenience between Bangkok's Chinese plutocrats and Thailand's men in uniform set the tune for many other, similar alliances in the future: the Chinese provided the money, and the police and the army secured protection and status in Thai society.

Gen. Pao's police also protected SEA Supplies' shipments of arms to the KMT in Burma—and in return, another commodity was coming out from the Shan hills in increasingly larger quantities: opium. The London *Times* gave a rare look into the Thai network in an article dated 6 April 1953. Its correspondent had travelled up to Chiang Mai in northern Thailand, then a small but rapidly growing provincial centre:

> This little town near the Burmese frontier is, in effect, a rear base for the Chinese Nationalist troops operating in the Shan state. In spite of denials in Bangkok, essential supplies are sent by road to the Nationalist headquarters at Möng Hsat and in return opium caravans escorted by Nationalist troops bring into Siam [Thailand] about 500 kilogrammes of drugs a week, according to conservative estimates . . . . Traffic across the border has been going on either from here or from Lampang [90 kilometres south of Chiang Mai] for two years, and it has become rather obvious as well as efficiently and ruthlessly run. Three attempts were made to assassinate a local newspaper editor who objected.[50]

Half a ton of opium every week for two years makes fifty-two tons. In addition, the Burmese government stated in its report to the UN: "A regular plane service of two flights a week between Taiwan and Möng Hsat was reported. These aircraft, C-46 and C-47 transport planes, were reported to have brought in arms and ammunition and medical supplies and carried opium on their outward flights."[51]

Justice Myint Thein declared in his address to the General Assembly on 17 April: "The Kuomintang troops have engaged in large-scale smuggling of opium, and in organised gambling, the profits of which have gone into their pockets."[52] In political terms, the KMT operation in Burma had accomplished little. There had been no general uprising in Yunnan, and Beijing had not diverted troops from Korea.[53] But the legacy of its impact on the local opium trade lingers to this day.

At Burma's independence in 1948, the country's opium production amounted to a mere thirty tons, or just enough to supply local addicts in the Shan states, where most of the poppies were grown. The KMT invasion changed that overnight. The territory they took over—Kokang, the Wa hills and the mountains north of Kengtung—was traditionally the best opium growing area in Burma. Gen. Li Mi persuaded the farmers to grow more opium, and introduced a hefty opium tax, which forced the farmers to grow even more in order to make ends meet.

By the mid-1950s, Burma's modest opium production had increased to a couple of hundred tons per year.[54] But opium was not an international problem at this time and, apart from the Burmese authorities in their reports to the UN, few paid any attention to the KMT's drug business. Ensuring Li Mi's loyalty to the "secret war" against China was a far more important consideration for some US security planners.[55] Besides, opium trading was not illegal in Thailand at this time.

In Thailand, opium had first arrived along with the massive influx of Chinese immigrants during the early nineteenth century. These immigrants soon came to dominate Thailand's (then Siam's) expanding commerce; they even became a majority in large cities, including the capital Bangkok. In 1822, King Rama II had promulgated Thailand's first formal ban on selling and consuming opium. In 1839, another king iterated the prohibition, and he introduced the death penalty for major opium traffickers.[56]

These efforts, however, were doomed to failure. Ethnic Chinese traffickers could be arrested and punished—but British merchants were virtually immune to prosecution. Large quantities of opium were brought to Bangkok by British ships from India. Even though it was nominally independent, Thailand did not escape the scourges that followed colonial rule in neighbouring countries.

Finally, in 1852, the legendary King Mongkut—played by Yul Brynner in the film *The King and I*—bowed to British pressures. He established a Royal Opium Monoply, to be leased to franchises managed by wealthy Chinese. Opium, lottery, gambling and alcohol permits were up for rent. By the end of the nineteenth century, taxes on these government monopolies provided 12–22% of Thailand's government revenues.[57] The government's hold on the trade was further strengthened in the early twentieth century, as US researcher Alfred McCoy explains:

> In 1907, the Thai government eliminated the Chinese middleman and assumed direct responsibility for the management of the opium trade. Royal administration did not impede progress, however; an all-time high of 147 tons of opium was imported from India in 1913; the number of dens and retail shops jumped from 1,200 in 1880 to 3,000 in 1917; the number of opium addicts reached 200,000 by 1921; and the opium profits continued to provide 15–20% of all government tax revenues.[58]

But because the royal monopoly had always marketed expensive drugs of Indian and Middle Eastern origin, cheaper opium had been smuggled overland from Yunnan and Sichuan since the mid-nineteenth century. According to McCoy: "There was actually so much smuggling that the royal

monopoly's prices throughout the country were determined by the availability of smuggled opium. The further an addict got from the northern
frontier, the more he had to pay for his opium."[59]

But despite this lucrative market for opium, poppy cultivation in Thailand itself remained negligble until World War II and the upheavals of the
1940s. Large number of Hmong and Yao hill tribes had started migrating
from southern China down to Laos and Thailand in the nineteenth century, but it was not until shortly after World War II—during the devastating civil wars first in China and later in Burma—that large numbers of
highland farmers started crossing into Thailand from the north.[60]

By the mid-1950s, the official state monopoly was becoming increasingly difficult to enforce as Hmong, Akha, Yao, Lisu and Lahu hilltribe
immigrants from China and Burma were planting poppies all over Thailand's mountainous northern provinces: Chiang Rai, Chiang Mai, Mae Hong
Son and Tak. State control was further undermined by the arrival of the
KMT on the scene, and the unofficial—but highly lucrative—deals the
Nationalist Chinese struck with corrupt, local Thai officials as well as high-
ranking police and army officers.

In this way, the booming opium trade of the mid-1950s not only helped
finance the KMT's war effort, but contributed to enhancing the wealth and
power of certain circles in Thailand. According to McCoy:

> Since SEA Supplies shipments to KMT troops in Burma were protected by
> the Thai police, Pao's alliance with the CIA also gave him extensive KMT
> contacts, through which he was able to build a virtual monopoly on Burmese
> opium exports . . . . Pao was recognised as the most powerful man in Thai-
> land.[61]

Relations between Thailand and Burma have always been tenuous, at
best. Still today, Thai schoolchildren learn little more about Burma than
that its invading armies destroyed the old royal capital of Ayutthaya in
1767. The Thais and the Burmese are no better neighbours than, let us say,
France and Britain, or Poland and Russia.

Traditional, atavistic Thai fears of the Burmese were reinforced in October 1953, when the Burma Army was trying to block the KMT's advance
south through Kayah State, which is right opposite Thailand's Mae Hong
Son province. A Burmese aircraft strayed across the border and accidentally
bombed a village on the Thai side, killing two people and injuring five.[62]

In response, Thai prime minister Pibulsongkram publicly threatened to
shoot down any aircraft that violated the country's airspace. Privately, however, he invited leaders of the Mon and Karen rebel armies to Bangkok,
where for the first time secret negotiations were held between ethnic minority groups from Burma and senior Thai officials.

In March 1954, they arrived in the Thai capital. The Mons were represented by Nai Shwe Kyin, one of the founders of the Mon movement, and Nai Hong Sa, who had a wide range of connections within Thailand's Mon community. Veteran Saw Thra Din—a member of the failed Karen Goodwill Mission to London in 1946—represented the KNU. Siddhi Savetsila, a young wing commander in the Royal Thai Air Force, along with police colonel Charoentit Charunjamratromran, received the confidential guests.[63]

For Thailand to police the porous, 2,100-kilometre border with its historical enemy would have been a difficult and extremely costly business. Instead, the Mon and Karen rebels, in meetings with Pibulsongkram and Gen. Pao, were encouraged to serve as buffers. While the Thai leaders pledged no direct support, the rebels were allowed to set up camps along the frontier, their families were permitted to stay in Thailand and they could buy arms and ammunition.[64]

But Thailand's new way of handling relations with its western neighbour had other objectives as well. It was no coincidence that Siddhi Savetsila was there to welcome the rebels from Burma: his sister had married Willis Bird, an OSS veteran of World War II, whose relative William Bird was the Bangkok representative of CAT.[65] All of them were deeply involved with the KMT in the secret war against the Chinese Communists—a war that certainly went much further than just providing Thailand with a convenient border buffer.

The actual command headquarters of this fight against Communist expansion was not Möng Hsat—but the Taiwanese embassy on Ploenchit Road in Bangkok. There, in defence attache Chen Tzeng Shi's private office, contingency plans were drawn up, air supplies organised, alliances forged with the Mons and others, and business deals made. Chen, a graduate of the 13th Class at China's prestigious Whampoa Military Academy, was, not surprisingly, closely connected with Helliwell of the SEA Supplies Corporation and Gen. Pao; the legendary Li Mi was, in fact, little more than their "boy in the hills" who carried out orders from Bangkok, Taipei and Washington.[66]

When US vice president Richard Nixon visited Rangoon in November 1953, angry crowds of anti-American demonstrators met him in the streets of Rangoon. Clearly realising the reason for the hostile reception, Nixon responded by feebly describing the KMT affair as "a major point of irritation in US relations with Burma", but expressed hope that the "fundamental understanding such as we know exists between our two countries will not give way to the passions of the moment".[67]

Nixon's mission to Burma was related to a statement his government had made, on 8 March of the same year, just before the UN debate began: the US had suggested a four power conference, including Taiwan, Thailand, Burma and the US, to discuss the repatriation to Taiwan of the KMT forces in Burma. For these four powers to meet was a sensitive issue, especially for the Burmese, who recognised the People's Republic of China and not Chiang Kai-shek's Taiwan-based Republic of China.

Burma at first refused to join such talks, but did dispatch a delegation to Bangkok to meet with Thai and US officials when the negotiations began on 22 May. It was not until 16 June, when an agreement seemed to be within reach, that the Burmese met all three delegations.[68] On the 22nd, the US ambassador to Thailand, Edwin F. Stanton, finally announced that an evacuation procedure had been agreed upon by all four parties.

The decision to repatriate the KMT forces in Burma happened at about the same time as the Korean War was brought to an end. On 27 June, an armistice was signed and the Korean peninsula was *de facto* partitioned along the cease-fire line that roughly followed the 38th parallel.

From Taiwan's point of view, the situation had returned to square one. If anything had changed it had been to Communist China's advantage: their troops, and especially their frequent use of human waves against well-fortified positions, had instilled fear among many of Beijing's opponents. The Communists had proven to be tough fighters who did not hesitate to lay down their lives to achieve their aims. The secret war against these "monsters" had to continue, repatriation or no repatriation.

The KMT leaders in the Shan hills declared that they refused to accept the repatriation scheme, arguing that they were defending Southeast Asia from an invasion of 150,000 Red Chinese troops.[69] The KMT claimed that their troops were "indigenous to northern Thailand and southern Yunnan and should not be sent to Taiwan".[70] The Burmese retorted by stating that they were going to the UN to have Nationalist China declared an aggressor and unseated from the world body.

Ne Win, the commander in chief of the Burma Army, summoned his most experienced commander to Rangoon: Brig. Kyaw Zaw, who had led the attack on the KMT near Amherst a year before. Kyaw Zaw, an ardently nationalistic, 34-year-old member of the Thirty Comrades, was promptly appointed northern commander of the Burma Army and told to lead the campaign against the KMT in the Shan states.

The aim was to put pressure on the KMT as the talks in Bangkok were dragging on without producing any result. They finally broke down in September when Burma withdrew from the talks because Taiwan had turned down its request that 5,000 KMT troops be evacuated in three months and the remaining 7,000 within six months. The same month, the Burma Air Force was sent up into the Shan hills to bomb Möng Hsat.

Kyaw Zaw moved his men up into the eastern Shan hills, to prepare for a major operation against the KMT. The first targets were KMT outposts west of the Salween river: the Mawchi mines area and Kadugyi in southern Shan states. According to Kyaw Zaw:

The KMT had about 12,000 troops while I had at my disposal only five battalions, an artillery unit and some engineers, or altogether 6,000 men. The main force of the Burma Army was busy fighting insurgents elsewhere in the country. Our main aim this time was to capture the ferry crossing at Wan Hsa-la on the Salween. Once we had cleared the areas west of the river of KMTs, we would in this way also be able to cross over to the eastern side and attack the main KMT bases there.[71]

The terrain in which the war was being fought was some of the most inhospitable in Southeast Asia. Dr. Maung Maung, who visited the battle-front in 1953, described it in this manner:

Major Thein Maung and his small staff of officers and men at camp NS . . . run the base supply depot, and it is their duty to keep the men in fighting lines fed and supplied. The task is no easy one. From [their] camp to Mongpan [Möng Pan in the southern Shan states], which is being built into a supply point, it is nearly a day's journey by truck; the roads are bad and there is a river crossing at Linkai [Burmese corruption of Langhkö]. Beyond Mongpan, there are no passable roads for trucks or even jeeps. The men must carry their rations with them. Local labour is engaged to carry other supplies and mules from the surrounding villages are hired to supplement the army animal transport. The labour force employed between Mongpan and the Wan Hsa-la front numbers more than 1,500. The men are not conscripts but volunteers, and after about a week of work, they want to return home, taking their pay.[72]

Only the question of army porters was incorrectly narrated in Dr. Maung Maung's report: they were certainly not volunteers, and few, if any, ever received any money for their labour. Since this time, the Burma Army has almost always relied on forcibly recruited villagers to carry its rations and ammunition, which has caused widespread loathing of the army in the frontier areas, and done little to win "the hearts and the minds" of the minority peoples who inhabit Burma's many war zones.

Kyaw Zaw pushed on after clearing the Mawchi mines and Kadugyi of KMTs. He reached Wan Hsa-la and the Salween river, where three KMT camps guarded the ferry crossing: "At first, we smashed the KMT at Wan Hsa-la itself. We had 1,200 mules, 20 elephants and 3,000 porters carrying supplies, but it was not possible to send the heavy artillery pieces across the turbulent Salween river. So we built a fire base on the west bank of the Salween and from there bombarded the KMT camps on the other side. We used every mortar bomb we had and shattered the KMT's defences."[73]

The officer in charge of the assault on Wan Hsa-la was Tin Oo, a young, bespectacled battalion commander who became known as the commander who slept in the jungle with his men and dug trenches together with them at the front-line.[74] This popular combat commander forced the KMT to evacuate their camps—and climb up the hillsides, where they became easy targets for his artillery. Infantry troops crossed the Salween, and the KMT fled in disarray.

Because of the bomb raids on Möng Hsat, the KMT had temporarily shifted their headquarters to Punghpakyem south of Möng Ton, or much closer to Wan Hsa-la and the Salween river. The Burma Army closed in on the new base, and the KMT was forced to yield. On 6 October, the bombing of Möng Hsat was halted to permit the KMT to withdraw. On the 29th, a joint US-Thai-Taiwan communique was issued in Bangkok stating that "2,000 KMTs, including their families, were to be withdrawn starting 7 November, that Nationalist China would no longer supply the KMT, and those who remained in Burma would be disavowed".[75]

The evacuation was to occur in three stages. The first began in November and continued into December; the second lasted from 14 February to 20 March 1954; and the third from 1 to 7 May. The KMT troops were brought by truck down to Chiang Mai, where they paraded through the streets, dressed up in smart uniforms and newly issued tennis shoes.

After this public display for the benefit of the media and foreign observers, they were flown out in C-46 and C-47 planes from Chiang Mai's airport. Other KMT units left via Chiang Rai, 180 kilometres north of Chiang Mai, and from Lampang to the south: "Many of us were sad to see them go. They were well-disciplined—and they were needed to fight Communism in the region."[76]

The aircraft were provided by CAT, and by coincidence, chief pilot Robert Rousselot, who had delivered the first load of arms and ammunition to the KMT at Möng Hsat in February 1951, was also at the controls of the first evacuation plane under Operation REPAT. He took off from the grass airstrip at Lampang on 9 November 1953. After nearly nine hours in the air, he landed with his uniformed passengers at Taipei's Sungshan airport, where a gala dinner awaited them.[77] In all, the CAT carried to Taiwan more than 6,000 people between November 1953 and May 1954.[78]

The evacuation no doubt weakened the KMT, but several thousand of its troops still remained in the hills of the Shan states. It was also becoming increasingly clear that not all the troops that were sent to Taiwan were genuine KMT soldiers. McCoy notes that many of the troops

carried rusting museum pieces as their arms. The Burmese observers, now allowed into the staging area, frequently protested that many of the supposed Chinese looked more like Lahus or Shans. Although other observers ridiculed these accusations, the Burmese were correct. Among them, there were large numbers of boys, Shans, and Lahus. Even by 1971 there were an estimated 300 Lahu tribesmen still living in Taiwan who had been evacuated during this period.[79]

All this time, fighting continued in the Shan hills. By March 1954, Kyaw Zaw's troops had overrun not only Punghpakyem but also the nearby Möng Hang valley and Wan Mekin, where the KMT had tried to build an alternative air base to Möng Hsat. Möng Hsat itself had been abandoned on 1 March, and on the 20th, the Burmese government re-established its administration there. With the strategic airfield under its control, Rangoon had gained the upper hand. The KMT retreated down to Loi Mak Angkhang right on the border, southwest of Fang in Thailand.

Kyaw Zaw, encouraged by this almost unexpected success, chased after the KMT right down to their new camp on the Thai border, which was also overrun without much difficulty. According to Kyaw Zaw, his troops captured at Loi Mak Angkhang one truckload of medical supplies, two truckloads of ammunition, 800 new, unused uniforms, two brand-new anti-aircraft guns and a wireless set—plus one huge barrel of raw opium. Kyaw Zaw remembers: "I ordered my men to burn the opium. One warrant officer almost cried when he saw the bonfire: 'Do you know how much this is worth?'"[80]

Even though Kyaw Zaw stood firm on his principles, the temptation for many other Burmese officers was there, and in the future many of them did not hesitate to take advantage of the lucrative trade that was now flourishing in the Shan states.

By reaching Loi Mak Angkhang, the Burma Army had pushed as far as it could at this stage. According to Kyaw Zaw: "Since we could not cross the Thai border, and we risked shooting into Thailand if we continued fighting KMT remnants in the hills around Loi Mak Angkhang, the operation was called off. Moreover, Ne Win arrived at Möng Ton and said nine Thai air force planes were hovering over Moulmein and Martaban. We could not continue fighting along the Thai border."[81]

The unexpected advances of the Burma Army in the Shan hills accelerated the diplomatic efforts to find a solution to the KMT problem by repatriating its forces to Taiwan. But reports vary widely as to how many KMT troops were actually sent to Taiwan. Out of a total of 12,000 KMTs in Burma, the government in Rangoon said that only 5,329 men with 1,142 dependants had been evacuated by September.[82]

The final report of the Joint Military Committee stated that the retreating KMT had turned in a total of 1,312 weapons, including 29 pistols, 588 carbines, 484 assorted rifles, 69 machine-guns and 22 mortars—in other words, only a small fraction of their impressive arsenal.[83] In late May, Li Mi announced from his Taiwan office that the Yunnan Anti-Communist and National Salvation Army had been dissolved.[84]

Despite the repatriation and Li Mi's departure, the KMT remained in Burma, somewhat "localised" in nature, but still fighting for the same ideals. A new reorganisation took place at the time of the "evacuation" in 1953–54, leading to the formation of a new set-up, commanded by Lieut.-Gen. Liu Yuanlin, a graduate of the fourth year of the Central Army Officers' Training School. Liu, a Fukkienese, came from Chiang Kai-shek's personal security force and was therefore trusted by the high command in Taipei to unofficially succeed the high-profile Li Mi.[85] Under Liu's command were five units, usually referred to as "armies" but which should more correctly be called "corps" (*chün* in Chinese, as opposed to *bingtuan*, army):

> The First *chün* led by Gen. Lu Renhao
> The Second *chün* led by Gen. Fu Jingyun
> The Third *chün* led by Gen. Li Wenhuan
> The Fourth *chün* led by Gen. Zhang Weicheng
> The Fifth *chün* led by Gen. Duan Xiwen.[86]

Rangoon decided to launch another offensive against the KMT during the 1954–55 dry season. But before the operation was mounted, Gen. Pao paid an unprecedented visit to Rangoon. He met Kyaw Zaw and the other officers in charge of fighting the KMT. He asked them what their difficulties had been during previous operations.

Kyaw Zaw, not mincing his words, replied that problems arose when his men got close to the Thai frontier: "The KMT always crossed into Thailand, while we had to remain on our side of the border."[87] Kyaw Zaw went on to ask for permission for his troops to cross three kilometres inside Thailand in hot pursuit of the KMT, five kilometres for aeroplanes and two kilometers for artillery shells. To Kyaw Zaw's great astonishment, Pao agreed: "It was only later that I found out that the KMT had cheated Pao in the opium business. He wanted to take revenge on the KMT and since his troops were not in a position to do this, mine had to attack them."[88]

The Thais even sent four senior army officers to liaise with the Burmese during the operation. Again, it was going to be an assault by a force that was numerically inferior, but tactically superior. Only two and a half battalions of government troops were allotted to Kyaw Zaw—for some inexplicable reason, all the other units of the Burma Army were gearing up for a major offensive against the dwindling CPB.[89]

With his vastly inferior force, Kyaw Zaw nevertheless managed to capture Loi Tum, right on the Thai border southeast of Möng Hsat. His advantage was air support, and the KMT was put on the defensive. Kyaw Zaw and his men marched into Li Mi's old headquarters of Möng Hsat, and sensing the influence that the Nationalist Chinese still wielded there, he realised that more troops were needed to defeat the KMT. According to Kyaw Zaw: "I asked the government to postpone the operation against the

CPB and send me reinforcements. If we could not deal a devastating blow to the KMT that year, our troops would lose hope and the KMT would become too confident. Rangoon agreed, and sent me four more battalions."[90]

The rainy season of 1955 was approaching, and both sides were in a hurry to get the fighting over and done with. Kyaw Zaw deployed his main force along the Möng Hang front—and captured the base. Other units detoured into Thailand and captured Loi Lang, a strategically located hill right on the border, from the rear. The next target was the KMT stronghold of Doi Tung, a steep mountain that straddles the Thai–Burma border a few kilometres west of Tachilek-Mae Sai. Kyaw Zaw first surveyed the area in a spotter plane, only to discover that the trees in the area were no thicker than his own thighs. His conclusion was that the KMT's bunkers would not withstand his artillery.

The Thais sent a liaison officer to talk to to Kyaw Zaw, asking him how long he thought it would take for him to capture the KMT stronghold. "If we attack at 8 A.M., our flag will fly over their base no later than 4 P.M.," he replied.[91] The KMT had assured the Thais—who maintained friendly contacts with both sides in the conflict—that they could hold on to their position for at least a month.

According to Kyaw Zaw: "Some Thai officers rushed back to the KMT after hearing our assurances to persuade them to sell their opium as quickly as possible—at the lowest price possible, of course. Ten thousand spectators gathered on the Thai side to watch the action. People were also gambling on the outcome of the battle."[92]

The assault began at eight in the morning, as planned, with a massive barrage of artillery shells. The KMT's bunkers were smashed and within three hours, the camp was overrun. At 4 P.M., following a few mopping-up raids, the Burmese flag was hoisted on the mountain top. Kyaw Zaw's troops had gained the respect of the Thais—and the back of the KMT had been broken. The Burmese built a pagoda on top of Doi Tung to commemorate their victory while the main KMT force moved north, to Keng Lap by the Mekong river opposite Laos.

The civil war, and especially the costly campaign against the KMT, had forced the government to spend nearly 30% of the budget on internal security.[93] The once tiny Burma Army—perhaps as few as 2,000 men in 1949—grew steadily in strength and importance. By 1955, Ne Win had more than 40,000 men under his command, equipped with modern weaponry acquired from mainly India and Britain.

Australia had also at an early stage recognised Burma's strategic importance. Under the Colombo Plan, it had become one of Burma's most generous aid donors. An Australian government report on "The Strategic Basis of Australia's Defence Policy" for 1953 had concluded that "under anti-communist regimes, Burma, Thailand and Indochina come under the category specified as countries 'whose defence will assist in the defence of Australia'."[94]

Australia's external affairs minister, R.G. Casey, saw Burma as especially important in this regard: "It is pretty clear that Burma is the weakest link in the Southeast Asian chain of countries . . . the Burmese Government has neither the political nor the military strength to clean up the mess and rule their own country."[95]

While some observers viewed this as an overly pessimistic view of Burma's situation, the Australians nevertheless decided that the defence of Burma was of utmost importance to Australia's own national security, and one place on the Australian Army Staff College's 1953 course was set aside for a Burmese officer.

In November, two senior Burma Army officers, Col. Maung Maung and Lieut.-Col. Tin Soe, visited Australia for consultations. They were met on their arrival in Melbourne by GSO1 in the Australian army's Directorate of Military Training, the legendary Lieut.-Col. F.P. "Ted" Serong. In August the following year no less than sixteen Burmese army officers were undergoing training in Australia.[96]

Australia was seen by the West as a more suitable military partner for neutral Burma than the old colonial power, Britain, or the United States. It also helped that Australia's governor-general at this time was Field-Marshal William Slim, who had commanded the 14th Army that drove the Japanese out of Burma in 1945. Although Slim was British, he was a popular speaker and broadcaster in Australia, and a personality with whom the Burmese could easily identify themselves.

But it was obvious that Burma wanted to diversify its sources of training as well as munitions, preferably to include smaller, non-aligned countries in order to maintain its professed neutrality. As early as June 1952, when the war against the KMT had begun in earnest, a combined military and political delegation, led by Home Minister Kyaw Nyein from the government and Brig. Kyaw Zaw from the army, had toured Europe in search of arms. They had visited Norway, Sweden, Switzerland, France, Britain and done a brief stop-over in Denmark. As a result of this tour, Sweden began delivering Bofors cannons for the Burma Navy.[97]

In June 1954, a Burmese military mission, led by Col. Aung Gyi and Commodore Than Pe, was dispatched to Israel to study that country's system of national service with a view to introducing it in Burma. Although the Burma Army remained a volunteer force, Rangoon began building up local militias, called *Pyu Saw Hti*, which borrowed features from the defence of collective settlements in Israel.

Another outcome of this visit was that Burma Army officers started to go to Israel for training, and the Israelis also sold Burma a number of reconditioned Spitfires.[98] Following a visit to Burma by Marshal Tito in January 1955, a close defence relationship was also established with Yugoslavia. A mountain battery of the Burma Artillery was supplied with 76 mm Yugoslav-made cannon, and Belgrade also pledged to equip an entire Burmese brigade with weapons.

For the Burmese government, another important agreement was reached in November 1954. Burma and Japan signed an official peace treaty, and Tokyo agreed to pay US$200 million in war reparations as well as an annual grant of US$5 million for technical assistance until 1964. Japan had complex motives for providing this level of assistance, which totalled about US$10 a person in the ten-year span.

Apart from the usual reasons such as the prospects for a lucrative market for Japanese products, there were also other factors involved. The underexploited and even unexplored natural resources of Burma were important attractions—and so were the emotional ties that had existed between Burma and Japan since Aung San and the Thirty Comrades went to Burma in the early 1940s.

Economic relations between Burma and Japan have long been based more on irrational emotions than on sound business practices. This helps explain why for so many years Tokyo tolerated the fact that Japanese money was being wasted on projects which benefited only a select few. These projects, meaningless for the population at large, later even included an astrological planetarium in Rangoon which was built to satisfy the whims of Lieut.-Gen. Ne Win.[99]

In September 1954, the increasingly powerful Ne Win led a high-powered military delegation to China, where they visited munitions factories and army training facilities. Ne Win was reported at the time to be interested in introducing Chinese equipment into the Burma Army. He announced upon his arrival in Beijing: "Friendship between Burma and China would be cemented by a closer link between the armed forces of the two countries."[100]

The purpose was obvious: China certainly did not fit into the category of small, non-aligned countries, but by courting the Chinese Ne Win evidently hoped to preempt any attempt by them to support the CPB. The Chinese remained non-committal, but, on the other hand, they also refrained from sending arms to the CPB. The 140 or so Burmese Communists who were in China at this time were busy studying at the party school in Chengdu, Sichuan. A few promising cadres were allowed to continue their Marxist-Leninist schooling at more advanced party institutes in Beijing.[101]

Although China did not agree to supply Burma with weapons, technical assistance to the Burmese to manufacture their own armaments had already come from an unexpected source.

A first attempt to make a deal with an Italian firm had not worked out at all. Money for the project had gone missing, and the Italian company had brought in a woman to stay with Ne Win, causing embarrassment for U Nu's government, which had gone as far as threatening to dismiss the army commander from service. This had been thwarted following an intervention by Socialist politician Ba Swe.[102] The Italian company never managed to produce more than a small quantity of crudely made Sten guns, which even today are nick-named "Ne Win's Sten."

But in West Germany, a small company was looking for a partner. Fritz Werner, an armaments engineering firm in Geisenheim had done good business during World War II by supplying the German troops fighting in the Soviet Union. When the war was over, the company went bankrupt and was taken over by the West German government.

In 1953—a year before West Germany recognised Burma and two years before the Germans established an embassy in Rangoon—Fritz Werner began assisting in setting up Burma's own defence industry. By 1957, with the assistance of the West German arms company Heckler & Koch, Fritz Werner had set up a factory on the outskirts of Rangoon to produce G-3 rifles.[103]

Meanwhile, the whole nation was facing hardship as a result of the civil war. Consumer goods, including staples like rice, oil and condensed milk, were in short supply. According to U Thaung, a Burmese journalist:

> The civilians faced their hardships boldly—but for the fighting forces it was different. Soldiers were giving their lives for the safety of civilians and they felt they should not suffer the same adversities together with the civilians . . . . There was a special shop, like a PX, run by a contracted firm for the army officers.[104]

But this was insufficient, and in 1951 the Ministry of Defence established the Defence Services Institute (DSI) as a non-profit organisation that could conduct business. The enterprise was controlled by twelve members, all military officers. A general store to distribute consumer goods to the members of the armed forces was opened in Sule Pagoda Road in downtown Rangoon. There, imported and locally produced goods were sold to soldiers and their families at low prices.

The start-up capital for the project was a loan of 600,000 Kyats which U Nu's government had provided to enhance the morale of the armed forces. Imported goods were exempt from port fees and import duties as well as domestic taxation. It became a success, and within a few years there were eighteen branches of the DSI shop across the country. The institute could repay the loan to the government and was soon running its projects independently with its own budget. According to U Thaung:

> The military leaders, happy and proud of their achievements, learned something wonderful from their business experience. They discovered that a busi-

ness enterprise without government taxes could yield a great fortune. And then the DSI expanded rapidly.[105]

The DSI's second venture was a publishing house whose original aim was to supply textbooks and writing material for the soldiers and their families. It was founded in 1951, but by 1955 it had been expanded into a major stationery store called Ava House. This time, the store was open also to civilians—the DSI's first venture into public trade.

Encouraged by its successes, the DSI went on to target civilians who worked as contractors for the army. In 1953 the International Trading House was formed to eliminate such contractors and make sure business opportunities, and profits, remained within the ranks of the armed forces. Civilian contractors still existed, but they had to go through the army firm, which acted as a kind of middle-man, reaping commissions and pay-offs. Later on, the International Trading House tendered for government contracts as well and so started to compete with private businessmen.

The army was becoming a state within the state, but few Burmese paid much attention to it. After all, the vast majority of the population had faith in the democratic system, the constitution and the rule of law.

The international community by and large shared this view—but a rare exception was a Central Intelligence Agency analyst who had predicted with remarkable foresight as early as in 1951: "[there is a] current struggle for control of the armed forces between the government and the army commander in chief, General Ne Win. For some time government leaders have been attempting to undermine Ne Win's dominant personal position within the army. Ne Win may retire completely from the struggle and leave the government in undisputed control. On the other hand, there is a continuing possibility that Ne Win might attempt a military coup, which could lead to protracted violence."[106]

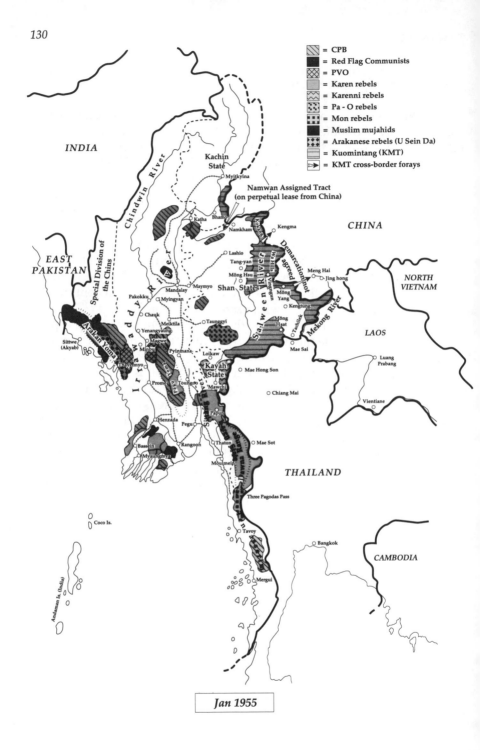

= CPB	
= Red Flag Communists	
= PVO	
= Karen rebels	
= Karenni rebels	
= Pa - O rebels	
= Mon rebels	
= Muslim mujahids	
= Arakanese rebels (U Sein Da)	
= Kuomintang (KMT)	
= KMT cross-border forays	

INDIA

Kachin
State

Myitkyina

Namwan Assigned Tract
(on perpetual lease from China)

Katha

Bhamo

Namkham   Kengma   CHINA

Lashio

EAST
PAKISTAN

Special Division of
the Chins

Chindwin River

Tang-yan   Möng   Meng Hai
Möng Hsu   Jing hong

Demarcation not
agreed

NORTH
VIETNAM

Mandalay   Maymyo   Shan States   Möng
Yang

Pakokku   Myingyan   Möng
Hsat

Salween River

Mekong River

Chauk

Meiktila

Taunggyi

Kengtung   LAOS

Sittwe
(Akyab)

Yenangyaung
Magwe

Tachilek

Arakan Yoma

Irrawaddy River

Minbu

Pyinmana   Mae Sai

Luang
Prabang

Loikaw

Prome   Toungoo   Kayah
                        State   Mae Hong Son

Pyapon   Chiang Mai   Vientiane

'Mawchi

Henzada   Pegu

Bassein   Thaton   Mae Sot

Myaungmya Rangoon

THAILAND

Moulmein

Three Pagodas Pass

Coco Is.

Tavoy

Bangkok

CAMBODIA

Andaman Is. (India)

Mergui

5

Retreat to the Jungle

The rise of right-wing authoritarianism in response to the Communist threat in the Far East was not confined to Burma. Although the backbone of the CPB insurgency had been broken after the early years of success, the party was still powerful, and throughout the region revolutionary movements were advancing steadily—as were the forces trying to stem the red tide which had overwhelmed China in 1949, threatened Korea a few years later and inspired Communist insurrections throughout the East.

The first serious test of strength between a Western power and local Communist rebel forces took place in a remote valley in the mountains of northwestern Vietnam. For fifty-five dramatic days at the beginning of 1954, Ho Chi Minh—once supported by the American OSS when he was fighting the Japanese—mobilised nearly 50,000 peasants, hill tribesmen and Communist guerrillas to besiege a French outpost called Dien Bien Phu.

Ho's commander, military master-strategist Vo Nguyen Giap, ringed the base with heavy artillery, including howitzers which had been hauled by manpower through almost impassable terrain along the mountainous border with Laos. Bicycle columns brought a steady supply of food to the guerrillas at the frontline.

Giap pinned down tens of thousands of colonial troops in the Dien Bien Phu valley and bombarded them daily with his artillery. On 7 May, the French commander, Gen. de Castries, finally surrendered. He had lost more than 1,600 men and many had fled or deserted.

The revolutionary Viet Minh army had suffered more than 10,000 casualties, but, like the Japanese fascists before them, Communist guerrillas had demonstrated that the White Man was not invincible. On 20 July, the warring parties signed an agreement in Geneva, Switzerland, according to which the French agreed to withdraw from Indochina. A provisional demarcation line, drawn at the 17th parallel, divided Vietnam into a Communist-held north and a non-communist south awaiting general elections.

The US, shattered by the French defeat at Dien Bien Phu but somewhat encouraged by the relative success in containing Communist expansion in Korea, stepped in to mobilise sympathetic regimes in Asia. In September, the US secretary of state, John Foster Dulles, summoned a meeting of his allies in the Philippine capital Manila. The Southeast Asia Collective Defence Treaty was signed on the 8th by the US, France, Britain, Australia, New Zealand, Pakistan, Thailand and the Philippines.

The Manila Treaty came into force on 19 February 1955 and the Southeast East Asia Treaty Organisation (SEATO) was born. It was headquartered in Bangkok with the Thai foreign minister, Prince Wan Waithayakon, as chairman of its supreme council.[1]

But SEATO's limitations were obvious: no other Southeast Asian countries apart from Thailand and the Philippines agreed to become full members of the pact. India, Burma and Indonesia expressed strong objection to the scheme, which to them appeared as an extension of the colonialism from which they had just freed themselves.

A military alliance with the Western powers could also prove counterproductive, they reasoned. It would lend credence to the Communist propaganda of "sham independence" and thus further fuel insurrections in the region. Only three months after the signing of the Manila Treaty, the idea of forming a neutral "third bloc" was conceived when some non-aligned countries met at the town of Bogor in Java.

In April 1955, twenty-five mostly newly independent countries from Africa and Asia met in Bandung, another town in the mountains of west Java. Amidst its fruit orchards, Dutch-built canals and colonial bungalows, Indonesian president Sukarno played host to an array of "Third World" leaders, including India's dignified statesman Jawaharlal Nehru, the mercurial Prince Sihanouk of Cambodia, Egypt's fire-brand prime minister Gamal Abdul Nasser, Sir John Kotelawala of Ceylon and Burma's U Nu. As the black limousines carrying the dignitaries arrived at the meeting hall in Bandung, many expressed greater fear of "colonialism" than of communism.[2]

China's Zhou Enlai was also present, but obviously with his own plans in mind. Prior to the Bandung Conference, India and China—the two rival giants of Asia—had endorsed the famous "five principles of peaceful coexistence": mutual respect for each other's territorial integrity and sovereignty; mutual non-aggression; mutual non-interference in each other's internal affairs; equality and mutual benefit; and peaceful co-existence.[3]

Nehru thought that after the Bandung Conference it would be impossible for China to flout these five principles. For Zhou, the agreement with India, and his subsequent participation in the Bandung Conference, were part of a scheme to encourage neutralist sentiment, weaken pro-Western influences, and to encourage the formation of governments likely to prepare the way for Communist take-overs.[4]

Few of the other participants realised this, however. The vast majority saw the conference as a means of securing peace in Asia, Africa and the rest of the world. During a private meeting, the Pakistani prime minister, Mohamed Ali, who attended the conference although his country had just joined SEATO, jokingly asked Zhou Enlai whether it would be difficult for China to make Chiang Kai-shek the viceroy of Taiwan in order to appreciably reduce world tension.

Zhou replied that it would not be difficult, and everybody laughed. U Nu listened eagerly to the conversation: a solution to the Taiwan issue would also solve the problem his government was facing along the Sino-Burmese frontier in the Shan states.[5]

A close, personal relationship between U Nu and Zhou was established, but Burma also realised that if it were to survive as an independent state—surrounded by India, China and SEATO member Thailand—it would have to adopt a strictly neutral foreign policy. In July, three months after returning from Bandung, U Nu went to the US, where he addressed the National Press Club in Washington:

> In the present circumstances of Burma, her membership in any alliance with a great-power military bloc is incompatible with her continued existence as an independent state. Our recent history is such, our experience with great powers is such, that in the minds of the people of Burma an alliance with a big power immediately means domination by that power.[6]

James Barrington, the eloquent Anglo-Burmese permanent secretary of Burma's foreign ministry, added:

> Unfortunately for Burma, she has had to live under the constant threat of war ever since her reemergence as an independent state . . . she has come to deplore the existence of military blocs because she firmly believes that the formation and growth of such blocs only add further to the tensions already existing in the world.[7]

From the US, U Nu went, hardly surprisingly in a Burmese context, to Moscow to avoid antagonising the Soviets. Western observers, however, raised eyebrows when, at a dinner speech for the Moscow ambassadors of countries that had attended the Bandung Conference countries, he concluded with a toast to "the participation of the Soviet Union in future Afro-Asian Conferences".[8]

Soviet leaders Nikita Khrushchev and Nikolai Bulganin paid a high-profile return visit to Burma in December. The Soviet leaders in public speeches castigated the colonial record of the British in Asia. Such statements were well received by some Burmese leaders—but more thoughtful

Burmese considered the whole visit rather distasteful, especially when Khrushchev began to point out faults in the construction of the sacred Great Cave of the Kaba Aye Pagoda, which the Burmese had erected the year before in preparation for the forthcoming Sixth Buddhist Synod in Rangoon.

Nevertheless, Khrushchev promised to build a hotel on the shores of the Inya Lake in the capital, a hospital in the Shan states' capital of Taunggyi, and to provide the prestigious Rangoon Institute of Technology with new premises. The Burmese reciprocated by donating a large quantity of rice to the Soviet Union.[9]

Burma was gaining respect in international circles, although its delicate situation was never fully understood by Western powers, who continued to view U Nu with suspicion because of his leftist rhetoric and links with the Eastern bloc. They were bewildered by U Nu's seemingly unpredictable policies and actions—which was a quality he shared with another non-aligned Asian leader, Cambodia's Prince Sihanouk. Far too few Westerners realised at that time that men such as U Nu and Sihanouk were not really leaning towards the Communist bloc. Skilful diplomacy was needed to maintain the independence and internal stability of their respective countries. Both U Nu's Burma and Sihanouk's Cambodia fell victim to Western penetration through proxies.

In April 1955, the same month as the Bandung Conference, a much less publicised—but for Burma not less important—meeting was held at Wayawngdaw Sakan, or "Bamboo Forest Camp", near Saytouttaya in Magwe Division in the forest of the northern fringes of the Arakan Yoma. It was a sombre meeting as CPB leaders gathered to assess seven years of armed struggle. Present were almost the entire political and military leadership of the Communist insurrection, including Thakin Than Tun, H.N. Ghoshal, Thakins Zin, Chit and Tin Tun, *yebaw* Htay, Dr. Nag, Myo Myint and Bo Ye Htut.[10] The delegates concluded that the CPB had become "divorced from the people of Burma" and, therefore, the armed struggle had to be abandoned. But there was one reservation: if the conversion of the CPB into a legal force was successful, the armed struggle should commence once again, with a broader support base.[11]

Following the first year's glorious advances, and promises of "victory within two years", the CPB's activities had dwindled from fighting regular battles and overrunning towns and cities to occasional skirmishes and ambushes. In late 1953, CPB guerrillas hiding out in the hills east of Mandalay ambushed the train to Lashio, killing fifteen people and wounding twenty-three, most of them civilians.

In March 1955, another train near Mandalay was blown up by CPB mines, resulting in the death of thirty people.[12] A month later, CPB insurgents stormed the jail in Nyaung-Oo, a small town near the Pagan temple complex in upper Burma, and released 134 prisoners, many of whom were party members. Even the worst pessimists of the day had to admit that the chances of the CPB's *pyithu tatmadaw*—or People's Army—marching into Rangoon were extremely remote.

By the mid-1950s, the CPB no longer held any towns; its headquarters had been forced out of the Pyinmana area and the entire party leadership had retreated into the jungles of the Pegu Yoma, the almost inaccessible, sparsely populated mountain range north of Rangoon where Saya San had raised the flag of rebellion in the 1930s. Other units were holding out in remote parts of the Irrawaddy delta, in the Arakan Yoma in the west, the Pokaung range between Minbu and Pakokku, in the remote jungles along the Thai border in the southeastern Tenasserim Division, in the hills north of Mandalay, and in the Kyawkku-Nawnglong-Nawng Wu area of the western Shan states.

By way of letter, the central government was informed in early 1956 that the CPB now wished to become a legal political party in exchange for a pledge that Burma would have to "stay away from the Anglo-American bloc".[13] The government was, perhaps understandably, not told of the CPB's more long-term plans. Information Minister Tun Win replied in a radio broadcast to the nation that his government was prepared to accept these conditions.

The CPB had not been formally outlawed until 1953, and if it was prepared to give up the armed struggle and join the democratic process, as the CPI in neighbouring India had indeed done, there were no objections from Rangoon. The "legal leftists" had already organised their own party, the Burma Workers' and Peasants' Party (BWPP), led by Thakin Chit Maung, Thakin Lwin and other well-known Marxists who had never joined the insurrection in 1948.

The CPB's statement about "the Anglo-American bloc" indicated clearly that they had missed the essence of Burmese foreign policy and why U Nu had participated in the Bandung Conference: but bottled up in remote jungle camps, many insurgents had begun to lose touch with reality. The Burma they knew was the Burma they had left to go underground in the late 1940s.

Soon afterwards, an emissary from the CPB headquarters arrived in Rangoon. The government was contacted through Bo Let Ya, one of the Thirty Comrades and an ex-party member. He first let the government know that the rebels were ready to surrender—only to inform Home Minister Khin Maung Gale shortly afterwards that he had acted on his own. The authorities suspected that this about-face had been caused by the legal leftists telling the CPB's emissary that the AFPFL government was about to fall, and that the rebels had only to support the opposition for them to win the upcoming election.[14]

Whatever really happened, the CPB had publicly announced its intention to lay down arms, and many cadres and soldiers in its army were confused. Then, later in 1956, came the twentieth congress of the Soviet Communist Party in Moscow in February. Nikita Khrushchev denounced Stalin, the hero of the Burmese revolutionaries, and declared his support for "peaceful coexistence," echoing the spirit of Bandung. A more conciliatory line towards the "capitalist bloc" was also put forth: Zhdanov's militant line from 1947 was giving way to strategies aimed at a "peaceful transition to socialism".[15]

News about the new tune from Moscow reached the Communists in Burma's forests through the BBC's Burmese language service. The fiery Thakin Soe of the Red Flag Communists responded angrily by sentencing Khrushchev to death from his jungle camp in the Arakan border area. He also vowed to shoot down any Soviet aeroplane that flew over his territory. But the main CPB took note of the new signals from Moscow and the old "Browder line" resurfaced within the party.

More and more cadres began supporting the attempts to negotiate with the government in Rangoon. Hundreds of CPB cadres simply surrendered, among them former student leader Chan Aye[16], *yebaw* Tin Aye—whom the CPB had sent to Rangoon after the 1955 meeting to contact the government—and *yebaw* Maung Maung, the chief of the Communist committee in Pyinmana. Maung Maung's defection in particular proved to be a devastating blow to the CPB's prestige; Pyinmana was its oldest and firmest stronghold in the central plains, and he took 200 men with him to attend a highly publicised surrender ceremony in his home town.[17]

U Nu and his ruling AFPFL began preparing for the 1956 general elections, even more confident of victory than they had been in 1951. The insurgencies had been contained, although the KMT especially still posed a significant problem. The *pyi daw tha* welfare programme was popular, and Burma enjoyed widespread respect internationally.

The Burmese went to the polls on 27 April, and the AFPFL won as everyone had predicted: it captured 145 out of 240 seats in the Chamber of Deputies while smaller parties associated with the league obtained another 28 seats. But the main surprise was the headway made by the National United Front (NUF), an alliance supported by the BWPP. The NUF also included the smaller Justice Party, headed by Dr. E Maung, a former Supreme Court justice, Thakin Thein Pe's (Thein Pe Myint) People's Unity Party and organisations representing the Arakanese and Pa-O national minorities. The NUF gained 36.9% of the vote and 48 seats.[18]

It has been assumed that the relationship between the BWPP and the CPB was in some ways similar to the present situation in the Philippines where the underground Communist Party of the Philippines has a legal arm, the *Bayan* or People's Party. Thakin Chit Maung, erstwhile leader of the BWPP, denies that his party ever had any direct links with the CPB, while admitting that the two parties had many similarities.[19]

The BWPP cadres had simply never agreed with the CPB's decision to resort to armed struggle in 1948. Nonetheless, there were frequent allegations that the BWPP received some clandestine support from the Soviet embassy in Rangoon.[20]

Such "gifts" probably served no other purpose than securing a pool of friendly locals who could be used for intelligence purposes. However, as former Rangoon-based Soviet diplomat Aleksandr Kaznacheev explains: "Our knowledge of local conditions was often superficial, and sometimes we were unable to understand properly the trends of political struggle and grasp incipient changes in time."[21] The "friends" the Soviets made in Burma were of questionable quality as intelligence assets. One of them, Ba Tin (no relation to *yebaw* Ba Tin alias H.N. Ghoshal), lived in a house full of a "weird blend of Buddhist and Communist bric-a-brac . . . a big golden image of Gautama on a fancy throne . . . opposite . . . two small Soviet-made busts of Stalin and Lenin."[22]

Ba Tin, having recently married an attractive young village girl, once showed a diplomat a poem he had written in praise of the Soviet Union. The poem lauded the sputniks as stars which were leading the Burmese to Communism. This theme was coupled with the idea of the man's own wedding; he likened his young wife to a sputnik, who would lead him to a similar paradise.[23]

Burmese leftists continued to attend international Soviet-sponsored peace, workers', youth and women's conferences. But these events had no more impact on the internal situation in Burma, nor the Soviet policy towards Rangoon, than, for instance, the first—and most misunderstood— such meeting: the 1948 Calcutta Youth Conference. Leftist trade unionist and BWPP leader Thakin Lwin attended the World Council of Peace in East Berlin in May 1954. He condemned the "US imperialists", was applauded by other delegates—and returned to Burma empty-handed.

Min Lat, a young CPB member and a bright representative of the Burmese student movement, had managed to get to Prague in the early 1950s through contacts with the International Union of Students. Some of his articles about Burma were published in newspapers such as the *Rude Pravo* and the *Lidove Noviny*, but his 192-page manuscript about the history of the CPB was gathering dust in his cupboard at home.

The reason was simple: Min Lat likened the U Nu government to Chiang Kai-shek's: "The people today stand confident and know that Chiang has fallen as Thakin Nu will surely meet his fate."[24] The policy of the Soviet Union and its East European allies was to support U Nu's government's efforts to remain outside the US-led bloc in Asia. Although Min Lat was allowed to remain in Prague, where he graduated from Charles University in 1953, his only book published in Czechoslovakia was a thesis on a new method of romanising the Burmese language.[25]

Beijing's Burma policy did not differ much from Moscow's. The 140 or so exiled Burmese Communists in Sichuan stayed in a separate compound in the provincial capital of Chengdu. As most of them had arrived in China as single men, many had married women who had more or less been provided by the Chinese authorities. "The family camp" in Chengdu soon boasted a kindergarten and a school for the children, and ideological training facilities for their parents. Some also attended courses in Marxism-Leninism at Beijing's higher party school—but no military instruction was offered.[26]

Three promising young cadres were selected to further their studies in Moscow in 1957. These were former student leader Khin Maung Gyi; San Thu, a party worker from Pyawbwe in central Burma; and Aung Win, a member of the Rangoon city party committee and former secretary of the Communist-led All-Burma Trade Union Congress.[27]

In Moscow, they were joined by two other young Burmese Communists: Kyaw Zaw (no relation to the army commander of the same name) and Thein Aung, who was also known as *yebaw* Lwin. Khin Maung Gyi was the most outstanding of the five. He attended the Academy of Social Sciences in Moscow and wrote a thesis on "Agrarian Problems in Burma".[28]

But the Burmese in Moscow were by and large lost and lonely. They lived isolated lives, and San Thu was the only one who really liked the Soviet Union. Years later, he still loves Russian food and even misses the weather: "We used to go skating in Gorky Park. It was lovely. And then there was New Year's Eve when we went walking in the streets until midnight. Sometimes we went skiing in the Caucasian mountains. That was great fun."[29] But no assistance was forthcoming for their armed struggle in the remote jungles of Burma.

Apart from obvious international and regional factors, there were also more down-to-earth reasons why the Burmese Left failed in the 1950s. According to US Burma scholar John Badgley:

> Perhaps the most obvious reason for the failure of the Communist movement and the entire radical Left of Burma has been the prevalence of a deeply-rooted factionalism which prevented the realisation of organisational and elite unity. Not only has factionalism persistently characterised the Burmese radical-leftist movements and parties throughout the entire period from 1946 up to the present, but it has been a factionalism in depth, from the top level of leadership down to the village cadres and student political groups. Even when they were fighting as allies in the insurrection, the White [the main CPB] and Red Flag [Thakin Soe's faction] Communists and the PCP could not overcome their differences—and developed new internal schisms of their own.[30]

By the mid-1950s, the Karens were also facing severe difficulties. In January 1955, thousands of government troops were mobilised for the first major offensive against remaining KNU strongholds in the eastern hills, adjacent to Thailand. The operation was code-named *Aungtheikdi*—"Final Victory"— and the government announced publicly that the "Karen insurgents are at the end of their tether".[31]

Heavily armed columns advanced up the dusty dirt-roads and jungle trails leading east from Pa-an and, despite fierce resistance from constantly ambushing Karen guerrilla squads, the rebel "capital" of Papun fell on 27 March. The capture of the last town held by Karen rebels coincided with Armed Forces Day in Burma. Papun had been in KNU hands for seven years; now, the Karens also had to retreat to the jungle like the CPB and all the other insurgents in the country.

A new, temporary headquarters was set up near Hlaingbwe to the south of Papun and, in June 1956, as the rains pelted down over the eastern hills, the Karens forged a loose alliance with fellow Karenni, Pa-O and Mon rebels, called "the Democratic Nationalities United Front" (DNUF). The KNU itself, regrouping and reconsidering previous tactics, met for three weeks in June and July for what was bombastically called "the Second National Congress"—a gathering of 70 rebel representatives in the hills near Papun.

Leftist ideology had spread throughout Burma in the wake of the Communist victories in China and Vietnam, and not even the Christian Karens had been unaffected by the new ideas. A Marxist-style vanguard party, the Karen National United Party (KNUP), had been set up in late 1953. Now the army was re-named "the Karen People's Liberation Army" (KPLA) with political commissars attached to all fighting units. The stated aim was to smash the "semi-colonial, semi-feudal" Burmese state.[32]

But although some of the top leaders of the Karen rebels revelled in Marxist rhetoric, most local commanders had begun to act as warlords in their respective areas, and central control of the movement was almost nonexistent. One of the most powerful military commanders was Saw Hunter Thamwe, a veteran of the campaign in the Irrawaddy delta, who had arrived in the eastern hills in 1954. He was a staunch anti-communist who frequently travelled to Bangkok to meet with Thai army officers, SEATO officials and reportedly also with representatives of the CIA.

Saw Hunter's official position was that of chairman of the Karen Revolutionary Council, the administrative body that replaced the old KGB in the wake of the 1956 congress. He had been elevated to that position most probably in an attempt to appease people like him, who were opposed to the Marxist policies of some of the leaders. The Thais also viewed the leftist drift of the Karen movement with deep suspicion: they wanted a border buffer, not a Marxist-oriented insurgency along their western frontier. Hence, Saw Hunter was favoured by Thai security officials, and he was allowed to set up an unofficial Karen "embassy" in Bangkok.[33]

The central authorities in Rangoon on their part decided to continue the rather successful counter-insurgency campaign as soon as the rainy season was over. As the new offensive was launched in October, the government appeared confident that the Karen insurgency would be wiped out "within six months".[34] But the Karens reverted to the hit-and-run tactics they had developed when they had fought alongside Maj. Seagrim and other British officers against the Japanese during World War II. The eastern hills were divided into three guerrilla zones: Toungoo-Nyaunglebin, Thaton, and Pa-an-Moulmein. Some successful counter-attacks were carried out, including a joint CPB-Karen raid on the town of Pegu on the Mandalay–Rangoon railway.

In the dense jungles of the eastern hills, a sturdy, 29-year-old local squad leader, Bo Mya, constantly ambushed and harassed the government forces. Born in 1927 in Hti Mu Khi village in the Papun hills, Bo Mya was educated up to 4th Standard and had served as a police constable during the Japanese occupation at the same time as he had passed on information to the Allied forces. He had openly joined Force 136 towards the end of the war and gone underground with the KNU in 1949. An animistic hill Karen by birth, Bo Mya did not convert to Christianity until 1961, a year after he had become zone commander of Pa-an-Moulmein.[35]

The offensive of 1956 failed to achieve its proclaimed aim—the Karen forces were battered but by no means defeated—though, on the whole, the insurgency was running out of steam. The badly fragmented groups in the western Arakan area had been mauled in November 1954 when Operation Monsoon had put an end to the *mujahid* rebellion in Maungdaw and Buthidaung near Burma's border with East Pakistan. Political concessions had also been applied: the Muslim fighters were promised rehabilitation and local autonomy in their area.[36] Elsewhere in the country, rebels were also surrendering or accepting government offers of equal rights and new land.

In one of his many unpredictable moves, U Nu had resigned from the premiership a few months after his party's victory in the April 1956 election. Socialist leader Ba Swe became the new prime minister. The army took full advantage of U Nu's absence from office to expand its influence even further. Ba Swe was a known army stooge, and he did not protest.

Ne Win was at this time busy building up his military intelligence apparatus, and political work was mostly in the hands of one of his lieutenants from the 4th Burma Rifles, Brig.-Gen. Aung Gyi, who was also a prominent member of Ba Swe's Socialist Party.

Through the Defence Services Institute, the army now owned and controlled Rowe & Co, which sold high quality foreign goods, the Ava Bank, which was set up after buying out A. Scott Bank, the Burma Asiatic Company formed after buying up the former East Asiatic Company, and, perhaps most important of all, the Burma Five Star Shipping Line, a freighter service company with a fleet of seven ships.[37]

With profits from its own businesses, the army had even funded a newspaper to convey its ideas to the public, the English-language *Guardian*, which had been founded in 1955 by Aung Gyi and the pro-military lawyer-historian Dr. Maung Maung. The paper's editor, however, was Sein Win, one of Burma's most prominent and respected journalists.

The rise of the Burma Army as a socio-economic institution coincided with a more active role for armies in countries elsewhere in Asia. As a direct result of the confrontation with their Communist adversaries, the armies of South Korea and Taiwan emerged as those countries' most powerful institutions. A new South Vietnamese army was being built with US assistance to resist the Communist threat from the North. In Indonesia, right-wing officers led by Gen. A.H. Nasution had in 1956 even formulated their own ideology, the *dwifungsi* ("dual function") doctrine which stated that the military has both a defence and a social-political role.[38] The rise of military power was supported by the USA, and not only in terms of arms aid and defence treaties.

A prominent US scholar, Samuel P. Huntington, gave political impetus to the militarisation of Asian societies by terming their armies "motors of development". He even condoned dictatorial practices by emphasising that a supposed Asian concept of "the divine right of the kings" legitimised the possibility of temporal authority changing the laws, thereby allowing authoritarian governments to design what he termed "rational policies based on a sense of utility".[39]

Huntington's contemporary, Lucien W. Pye, tried to explain the complexities of Asian politics in the context of an incoherent mix of Confucianism, narcissism, metaphysics and different methods of child-rearing. Huntington's and Pye's naive—but highly dangerous—gibberish became compulsory reading at staff colleges in the US, and for years to come clouded rational thinking in the political and military establishment in Washington.[40]

Certainly in Burma, the army's behaviour in the mid-1950s could be explained in far more mundane terms. According to Czech Burma scholar Jan Becka:

> Political and ideological work among the officers . . . was greatly expanded at that time, preparing the army to play the role of "saviour of the nation" . . . . The decisive criterion of the political and social prestige of any public figure in the Union of Burma was his participation in the resistance and/or service in the wartime national army.[41]

Consequently, those who headed the army considered themselves to be a part of the new post-war leadership and thereby implicitly claimed the right to participate in the decision-making process.

Democratic influence in the army was minimal, and almost exclusively confined to the ties which were still maintained with Australia. By 1957, Australia had provided training for about ninety Burma Army officers, while a Military Liaison Office had been established in Melbourne. The Burmese government requested several countries to send military instructors to Burma. Among them was Australia, and the Burmese requested specifically for Canberra to send Col. Ted Serong, an expert in counter-insurgent warfare and founder of Australia's Jungle Warfare Training Centre at Canungra in Queensland. Serong arrived in Rangoon in 1957, and became immensely popular. Unlike similar instructors from Yugoslavia and Israel, he lived with the Burmese and travelled widely across the country.[42]

At the same time, however, the army itself was also undergoing substantial changes—and these changes were not in the direction of a more professional, non-political army along Australian or other Western lines. Most of the original founders of the army, the Thirty Comrades, had gone into business or politics. One was an ambassador; some had died or faded into obscurity. Bo Let Ya suffered from tuberculosis. Bo Zeya, Bo Ye Htut and Bo Yan Aung had joined the CPB and gone underground.

A second generation of ex-commanders of the wartime resistance had taken over: Col. Aung Gyi, Col. Maung Maung, Col. Tin Pe and others, most of whom were close to Ba Swe's and Kyaw Nyein's Socialist Party. An entirely new Burma Army was emerging: a financially strong and ideologically motivated military machine over which the civilian government had virtually no control.

Only two from the first generation of officers—the legendary Thirty Comrades—were still serving with the army: Ne Win and his only serious contender for power over the armed forces, Kyaw Zaw, who was becoming increasingly popular because of his successful campaigns against the KMT. But then, in 1956, a mopping-up operation codenamed *Aung Marga* ("Victory Path") was mounted against the CPB in upper Burma and some secret defence documents were found in a captured communist camp. Without any evidence or any direct connection, Kyaw Zaw was accused of being guilty of the leak. The public was shocked, and many did not know what to believe.

On 13 February 1957, Kyaw Zaw was demoted to the rank of lieutenant-colonel, and on 7 June, he was eventually dismissed from the army altogether, although no evidence had surfaced to substantiate the allegations against him.[43] His career was ruined, and he settled down in Sanchaung in Rangoon with a modest pension from the army. Shortly after Kyaw Zaw's arrest, the army printed an information broadsheet about the campaign against the KMT. It did not even mention Kyaw Zaw. Instead, a smiling Ne Win in a bush hat was there inspecting the frontline troops "to personally direct operations against KMT aggressors".[44]

Eyebrows were raised. Ne Win had not even participated in combat against the KMT; he hardly ever ventured outside Rangoon. Every Sunday, he could be seen at the racecourse in the capital where he had his own private box.[45]

When U Nu resumed office on 1 March 1957, the situation had thus undergone fundamental changes. Ne Win was in undisputed control of the military, and the transformation of the army from being a defender of the government to an autonomous force with its own agenda had been completed.

The rise in prominence of the army was immediately felt in the AFPFL. U Nu, worried about the possible disintegration of the AFPFL, declared that it was no longer a front of various political parties and organisations, but a united political party. One faction, led by BSP leader Ba Swe and supported by deputy prime minister Kyaw Nyein—who had been pulled closer to the increasingly powerful military—favoured increased army participation in politics.

In May 1958, the situation became untenable and the AFPFL split despite U Nu's attempts to reorganise the party. The Ba Swe-Kyaw Nyein faction called themselves the "Stable" AFPFL, whereas U Nu's main faction was referred to as the "Clean" AFPFL. The "Stable" AFPFL even openly declared that they had the support of the army.[46]

The situation was further complicated by an amnesty offer which was issued on 15 August. More than 2,000 PVO insurgents, who had been up in arms since July 1948, surrendered. They almost immediately formed a legal organisation, the People's Comrade Party (PCP), and proposed to contest elections under a Communist-style programme.

Right-wing elements within the army (ironically called the "Socialists") disapproved, not trusting U Nu's assurances that this formed part of a scheme to solve Burma's internal problems by political means. The army's apprehension grew when other citizens, led by veteran nationalist Thakin Kodaw Hmaing, formed peace committees to woo the CPB into the legal fold.[47]

At 8 P.M. on 26 September, U Nu spoke to the nation over Radio Rangoon. He solemnly announced that he had invited Gen. Ne Win "to assume the reins of government . . . due to the prevailing situation regarding security and law and order".[48] The nation was stunned. Had a "parliamentary coup" taken place? The ruling party had split and the government had been further destabilised during a vote of no-confidence shortly before U Nu's announcement. He had won by seven votes, but only by accepting the support of the NUF and the regional parties; the majority Burmans had rallied behind his rivals in the "Stable" AFPFL.

It seemed that U Nu had turned to Ne Win and offered to resign in his favour because he was unwilling to face more trouble in the parliament, recognising that the budget and other crucial matters had to be settled.

Whatever the reason for U Nu's move, army officers from across the country met in Meiktila, a major garrison town south of Mandalay, on 21 October. For the first time, the army formulated its own policy. A document entitled the "National Ideology and the Role of the Defence Services" spoke of psychological regeneration which was the result of the "decisive leadership of the government and the clarity and conviction of the Defence Services".[49] In other words, it strongly resembled Nasution's *dwifungsi* concept of the Indonesian army. After having successfully entered business, the army had now begun to show a more direct interest also in politics and the running of the country.

On 28 October, Ne Win formed a military-dominated Caretaker Government, headed by himself—only a week after the crucial Defence Services Conference in Meiktila. The new administration also included Brig.-Gen. Aung Gyi, Brig.-Gen. Tin Pe, Col. Kyaw Soe and several other close associates of Ne Win, mainly from his own old unit, the 4th Burma Rifles.

In an attempt to explain the abrupt—and unforeseen—military takeover, Ne Win alleged in a speech before the parliament on 31 October that

> the rebels were increasing their activities, and the political pillar was collapsing. It was imperative that the Union should not drown in shallow waters as it nearly did in 1948–49. So it fell on the armed forces to perform their bounden duty to take all security measures to forestall and prevent a recurrence.[50]

A propaganda leaflet, produced by the Caretaker Government, claimed that the parliament had given him "the mandate to restore law and order in the country and also create the conditions that would be conducive to the holding of free and fair elections as soon as possible."[51]

These astounding statements contradicted the conclusion of the 21 October Meiktila conference, which Ne Win himself had organised. The main document from that meeting stated that

> the remnants of the Red Flag Communists are so small as to be hardly worth speaking about. Only a few leaders and a pocket here and a pocket there of the White Flag Communists [the main CPB] remain. With the exception of a very few, all the PCPs have surrendered. Of the KNDOs there are some left in the Papun area of the East Yomas and a little in the delta. The remnants of the MNDO are scarcely worth mentioning.[52]

To many observers, the army's unexpected moves and contradictory statements were even more confusing than the squabbles within the AFPFL at that time. But the army's new interpretation of the internal security situation was backed up by Sein Win, the journalist who was working for the military-funded newspaper, the *Guardian*. In a pamphlet called *The Split Story*, he alleged that U Nu had made remarkable

> appeasement and concessions to the rebels unprecedented in the history of any country. The multicoloured rebels [*sic*] who were on their last legs and suing for peace and leniency just before the two factions broke up the AFPFL, stiffened their attitude and changed their appeals to demands. They were tipped off to change their tone and stand by their allies, the crypto-Communists aboveground, on whose support Nu-Tin's survival depended.[53]

This imaginative interpretation of the mass-surrenders of the PVO rebels, and the formation of the PCP, was followed by an even more bewildering conclusion: "The AFPFL split was the biggest victory for the Communists since their insurrection [began] 11 years ago. It was an automatic victory without bloodshed, and the split paved the way for the Communist ascension to power."[54] The split in the ruling party was undeniable, but the insurgents hardly posed a threat any longer, and few were able to detect any serious decline in the overall law and order situation in the country.

Much later, U Nu in his autobiography *Saturday's Son* also claimed that he had heard about an imminent coup while travelling by steamer from Mandalay to Rangoon. It was not clear exactly who the plotters were—according to one rumour it was the paramilitary Union Military Police, according to another a faction of the army was preparing to rebel—but U Nu, in order to avoid a confrontation, said he had agreed to hand over power to the army on condition that a general election be held in six months.

U Nu, pondering what the effect of the changes would be, said:

> The army of course would rule over the country as a military establishment. At the moment the people regarded the soldiers as friends and protectors. After the takeover they would be looked upon with loathing. Politically, the party that had called in the army would suffer from the intervention. It was like putting a noose round one's own neck.[55]

Despite the promise to "restore law and order" in six months, the Caretaker Government did not hand back power to a civilian government until December 1960, after the promised elections had finally been held. In the meantime, the army had been active in a way which was unprecedented. After having claimed that "the insurgents were poised to take full advantage of the confused situation", the army soon began publishing lists and numbers of insurgents who had supposedly surrendered, of illicit arms that had been recovered, and reports of how the government machinery had been revitalised and the public's morale uplifted.

In November, in the first week the Caretaker Government was in power, the military estimated that there were about 9,000 insurgents in the country, less than a third the number of 1949. By 1960, the government claimed that out of these, 1,872 had been killed in action during operations since 1958, 1,959 had been wounded during the same period,1,238 captured alive and 3,618 had surrendered.[56] If these figures were correct, there would have been only 300 rebels left in the country by 1960.

While all these figures appear grossly inaccurate, some spectacular surrenders did take place during the reign of the new military government. Bo Hla Moe and Bo Kyaw Dun, CPB leaders in the Pegu area, with a platoon of Communist guerrillas laid down arms on 26 February 1959, as did Bo Ba Khin, commander of about 100 men, along with two local party organisers in central Burma, Lwin Maung and Bo Nyunt Maung, and 150 of their men.[57]

But rather than being a new development initiated by the Caretaker Government, this was more likely a continuation of the surrenders that had begun after the CPB's meeting at the Bamboo Forest Camp in April 1955. The Communist and Karen insurgencies were more or less over by the mid-1950s. After the relatively successful *Aung Marga* operation of 1956 and the surrenders of what remained of its forces in the Pyinmana area, the CPB had formally made the Pegu Yoma its new headquarters. From then on, the CPB— badly armed and poorly equipped—had been struggling to survive in the jungles, unable to pose any significant threat to the government.

After having taken credit for the surrenders—which, ironically, army-reporter Sein Win had claimed was one of the reasons why the military had to step in—the military-led Caretaker Government went on to assume more civilian duties. In a special notification, issued on 29 November 1958, it declared that Rangoon had to be "cleaned up".

Houses were ordered to be painted, and rubbish in the streets removed, as were about 165,000 squatters, mostly refugees who had streamed into Rangoon during the civil war and established ramshackle, ubiquitous kwetthis, or shanty-towns.[58] The slum dwellers were now relocated to a series of new "satellite towns", including North and South Okkalapa, and Thaketa across the Pazundaung Creek, a tributary of the Rangoon River.

As a result, all the poor people who had been living close to the city— where most of them had jobs in the docks, or as day labourers, rickshaw pullers or servants for rich families—now found themselves living far out in new suburbs. While this made downtown Rangoon more pleasant to look at for the urban middle class, and foreign visitors, the move created serious problems. Overnight it had become more expensive for those who had regular jobs to get to them; most of the day labourers found it almost impossible to survive. Hardly surprisingly, these new working class "satellite towns" soon became breeding grounds for anti-army discontent.[59]

Serious weaknesses in the administration were also becoming increasingly evident. A major problem was that independent Burma—again as a political move to thwart the CPB threat—had sent the British civil servants and all other foreign technicians packing. Many Anglo-Burman subordinates, who worked for the railways, customs and other services, were either replaced or had emigrated, mainly to Australia. A large number of Indians had also left the country in the wake of the Japanese occupation and more followed after Burma's—and India's—independence.

Although few were sad to see the *chettiars* go, this departure inevitably meant that Burma lost many skilled labourers, civil servants, small businessmen and experienced importers-exporters. As a result, Burma's national pride was boosted, but the economy suffered, since there were not enough educated and experienced Burmans to fill the posts when the "foreigners" had left.

Law Yone of the *Nation* wrote in an *Atlantic Monthly* supplement on Burma in 1958: "The loss in efficiency is incalculable, and Burma now finds herself obliged to bring in new and expensive Western technicians for positions which the earlier incumbents could have handled at far less cost."

Law Yone also critically scrutinised Burma's political system:

> Land allocations, crop loans, *pyi daw tha* development projects, welfare benefits, purchase of the harvests—all are controlled by AFPFL adherents. This is patronage. Intimidation sometimes occurs too, the small ones still wield enough power, they have guns, to make the opposition to them distinctly uncomfortable. Thus our political life, which we hope one day to make completely democratic, is in reality still a compromise between one-party rule, strong-arm tactics, and a fully documented system of courts, elected legislature, and individual freedom. The insurrection is largely to blame . . . yet it cannot be denied that the forms of democracy are maintained, and are sincerely acclaimed by the AFPFL leaders, who declare that they actively desire freedom of speech, a strong, free press, impeccable courts, and a democratic opposition.[60]

The general election in April 1960 was held in that spirit. The voters rejected the army-backed "Stable" AFPFL, led by Ba Swe and Kyaw Nyein, and U Nu's newly established *Pyidaungsu* (Union) party won with a landslide. It captured 52.7% of the vote and 157 out of 250 seats in the National Assembly, compared to 29.8% and 42 seats for the "Stable" AFPFL. The rest went to smaller, local parties mainly from the Shan and Arakan regions. The NUF suffered a severe setback, reducing its share of the votes from 36.9% in 1956 to 5.4%.[61]

Most significantly, U Nu's landslide was nationwide and included victories for allied parties in Shan State and the Chin Special Division, while its rival, the "Stable" AFPFL, had no areas of concentrated strength. The constituencies it won were scattered throughout central Burma and in the Karen and Shan states, while the voters in Karenni (Kayah) State voted for two independents.[62]

While democracy had returned to Burma and it was looking bright in the central parts of the country, the situation was less rosy in some of the frontier areas. The Shan minority in the northeast had remained by and large loyal to the Union after independence. After all, they had signed the Panglong Agreement with Aung San, and the new 1947 Constitution gave them the right to secede after a ten-year period of independence, should they be dissatisfied with the arrangement with Rangoon.

A Shan literary society had been set up at Rangoon University after World War II to promote Shan language and literature. It published the Tai Youth Magazine, and all its members also belonged to the Shan States Students' Union at the university.

Politics in the Shan States proper was dominated by a local alliance led by Sao Khun Hkio, the British-educated *saohpa* of Möng Mit, who was elected Chairman of the Shan States' Council at independence in 1948 and served as Burma's foreign minister from 1956 to 1958. The US-educated *saohpa* of Hsipaw, Sao Kya Seng, belonged to the same camp, as did many of the other princes. This alliance was close to U Nu and enjoyed support from local entrepreneurs and commercial interests.

The legal opposition consisted of a party led by U Tun Aye from Namkham, which was seen by the Shan public as pro-Burman and pro-military.[63] In the Yawnghwe area near Taunggyi, small groups of leftist Shans were active in an "anti-feudal movement" directed against the *saohpas*, but their influence was extremely limited.

The princess, or Mahadevi, of Yawnghwe, Sao Nang Hearn Kham (whose husband, Sao Shwe Thaike, had served as Burma's first president 1948–52), led a party which advocated independence for Shan State. She was elected to the Parliament in 1956, and served as an MP until the Caretaker Government took over two years later. This party was gaining support, especially from the Shan students in Rangoon.

Shan politics had become more intense because of the KMT invasion and the subsequent massive influx of the government's forces, which had upset the traditionally relatively peaceful scene in the northeast. When the southern Shan states had been placed under military administration in September 1952, the aim had been to suppress KMT activities there—but the outcome was also that the Shans saw their autonomy undermined. For many Shan peasants it was the first time in history that they had come into direct contact with any Burmese. Dr. Maung Maung, the official historian, commented on the military's relationship with the rural Shans:

Perhaps the last Burmese Army that came their way was the army that [11th century King] Anawrahta sent to subdue the Shans; pagodas still stand in Yawnghwe, Mong Nai, Linkai [Lankhö], Mong Pan and other villages, pagodas that Anawrahta built as symbols of his supremacy and Shan subjection. Now, the Army has returned as friends to fight a common foe.[64]

The Shans themselves viewed developments in their homeland in a completely different light. Sai Pan, a second year medical student in Rangoon, won the 1957 Rangoon University Shan Literary Society's essay competition by writing a melodramatic account of the fighting in the Shan hills:

Up in the Shan hills today nature still boasts her glory, the green forests and the blue mountains still remain as green and ever blue. Sun light flickers still make tiny ripples dance upon the blue Inle [Lake]. Under the roof of every home there is still the old hospitality which never turns strangers away . . . but beneath this beauty of nature's wonders something sinister is lurking; stealthily creeping and penetrating in, bringing endless pity-begging human tragedies. At one moment in the still woods, the engine of a car would be throbbing, its tyres crunching against the stony road. The next moment the KMT machine-guns would send echoes reverberating through the hills. Deep in the midst of the night blurred figures would crouch trembling together while KMT orders thunder through the stillness of the night. In a secluded corner of a barn a young dame would sob in hiding leaving the pursuing *yebaws* [Burma Army troops] furious with demands.

Clearly, the army presence in the Shan states was no more welcome than the KMT occupation. Sai Pan continued:

From the pine-clothed Kalaw hills to the outskirts of every major town army barracks have mushroomed, in every nook and corner khaki uniforms have become a routine sight . . . . On one hand the KMT are killing, looting and terrorising while on the other hand a great number of army bad heads are raping, menacing and creating racial prejudices . . . . Today beneath the boom of guns, the marching boots, rifle butts and harsh orders the Shans are reeling . . . . Full autonomy and equality are the phrases of the Panglong [Agreement] but for ten years they have been confined to paper and ink . . . . Independence has marked the end of British colonialism but army fascism has come to be the substitute.[65]

Sai Pan's thoughts reflected the thoughts of thousands of young Shan students like himself—and perhaps even more the feelings of the peasants in the Shan countryside. They had indeed not come into direct contact with any Burmese since the time of King Anawrahta—but the truth of the matter was that the new occupants were no better than the army that had tried to subdue them nine hundred years before. The only difference was that this time the Shans were squeezed between two forces, both of which were perceived as alien.

In late December 1956, more than 150 Shan nationalists met at Möng Yai in the northern Shan states. They included representatives sent by the *saohpas* as well as disgruntled students and peasants. Protests against the army's behaviour were heard and demands were raised for secession. The government in Rangoon was alarmed, especially since the Shans' constitutional right to secede was going to come into effect on 4 January 1958, when the ten years of independence would be up. On 7 February 1957, mass rallies were held in key Shan towns in support of the *saohpas'* right to uphold Shan autonomy.[66]

In April, while addressing a political gathering in Lashio, U Nu spelled out for the first time the government's attitude towards the controversial right of secession. Calling attention to the history of the US civil war, he continued: "The reason why the United States today is the strongest and most influential nation in the world is due to the fact that Abraham Lincoln prevented the southern states from seceding and thus consolidated the whole country. If only we are united our future is indeed bright. Therefore, it is my constant prayer that this remarkable episode from American history may serve as a very valuable lesson for all of us."[67]

"That was when we decided to go underground. To us, it sounded like a threat. We wanted to fight for complete independence from Burma," recalls Khun Kya Nu, who was a young Shan science student in Rangoon in the mid-1950s. His father, U Kya Bu, had served as chief officer of the Shan State Agricultural Department and was one of the signatories of the Panglong Agreement. The Shan students in the capital were becoming increasingly restive, and many spoke of joining the Karens, the Karennis, the Mons and the Pa-Os in fighting U Nu's central government.

But no armed Shan force existed at this time, and the initiative to form one did not actually come from the student activists in Rangoon. The first to begin serious preparations for the formation of a Shan rebel army was Saw Yanda, alias Sao Noi, a Shan adventurer from Yunnan who had moved to Burma in the early 1950s. Although he had only very basic monastic education, he had been active in the literary movement in the Shan-inhabited Bhamo area of Kachin State and he had also participated in the 1956 Möng Yai conference. In 1957, Sao Noi was an ardent nationalist in his mid-30s who wore his hair shoulder-length: he had vowed not to cut it until Shan State had become independent.

In early 1958, Sao Noi travelled to Kengtung to meet the *saohpa* there, Sao Sai Long. An influential Shan leader, Sao Sai Long attended school in Australia during World War II and spoke English mixed with peppery

Australian slang. He was also affectionately known as "Shorty" by his fellow *saohpas* and English-speaking leaders in Rangoon. Two American travellers wrote about "Shorty": "He is both anti-Communist and anti-Chinese, for his . . . state suffered more cruelly than any other from invasion by the rag-tag of Chiang Kai-shek's army in 1951 and 1953."[68]

The situation in Kengtung was especially precarious not only because of the large presence of KMT troops, but also because of the large numbers of government forces which had been sent into the area to fight the intruders. This had caused resentment as well, but Sao Sai Long, wary of any violent backlash from Rangoon, discreetly told Sao Noi to continue to Möng Pan, a smaller state to the southwest. The *saohpa* of Möng Pan received Sao Noi in his *haw*, or "palace", which was little more than an elaborate wooden building overlooking the local market. Möng Pan state was one of the smaller principalities, with a population of about 20,000 people, nearly all of them peasants. The *saohpa* was sympathetic to Sao Noi's ideas. Like all the Shan princes, he had a small private police force, and he ordered some of his constables to join Sao Noi.

Prior to the KMT invasion, these police forces had been of a mostly decorative nature: dressed up in red and blue tunics and with silver swords slung over their shoulders, they stood guard outside the *haws*, or patrolled local markets to keep an eye on drinkers and gamblers. But after martial law was declared in the southern Shan states, they had become local militia forces, trained, armed and equipped by the Burma Army to resist the KMT.

Their weapons were not new, however. Being Shans and not Burmese, they obviously had little or no loyalty to the central authorities in Rangoon and, perhaps sensing their lack of commitment to Rangoon's cause, the central authorities had issued them only with surplus material and arms that were no longer used by the regular forces.

A local trader from the southern Shan states with connections in Thailand, Pu Ling Gung Na, happened to be in Möng Pan at the time and he joined Sao Noi's band. Together they set out from Möng Pan, leading the ex-*saophpa* policemen into the jungle near Thailand. Pu Ling Gung Na came along to forge ties with the authorities on the other side of the frontier, which was essential for the survival of any effort to start a Shan insurrection. Gung Na was an athletically built man in his early forties, polite and well-mannered despite his shady business connections. He did not drink and smoked cheroots only rarely.

Sao Noi had got what he wanted: the nucleus of an armed force—even if it consisted only of a handful of men with old muskets and Lee Enfield rifles—a financier for his revolution, and prospects of outside contacts in Thailand. In May, the ragtag band set out from Möng Pan. They marched east, along mule tracks which took them over steep mountains and dense forest, towards the Thai border. On the 21st, the party reached the small village of Möng Kyawt southwest of Möng Ton. A meeting was held and Sao Noi proclaimed the formation of *Noom Suk Harn*, the "Young Brave Warriors". Pu Ling Gung Na was appointed "president" and Sao Noi himself became "military commander" of the dedicated but tiny force.

In June, as the rainy season set in, they finally arrived at Loi Mak Angkhang, a mountain on the Thai border. A small, temporary camp was built, but when the rains were over in November, Sao Noi, Gung Na and their men moved to Pangtawng, a well-sheltered plateau between two high ridges just a few hundred metres from the actual frontier.

It was an ideal place for a camp: a parade ground was cleared, a flagpole raised and bamboo barracks built on the surrounding slopes. Gung Na made contact with his Thai friends, who introduced him to some police officers in Chiang Mai. Their cooperation, or at least acquiescence, was necessary to maintain the base at Pangtawng.[69] A tax gate was soon established there to levy revenue on the opium convoys that passed through Pangtawng on their way to the nearby KMT base at Tam Ngob, also on the Thai border. The nearest Thai town, Fang, was only eighteen kilometres away, and supplies could be bought there and sent up to the camp on the mountain.

Before long, word spread that Sao Noi and Gung Na had set up base on the Thai border. This coincided with the formation of Ne Win's Caretaker Government, and the Shan literary movement was facing severe difficulties under this new regime: students, secondary-school pupils and others were frequently arrested and interrogated by military intelligence.

It was becoming increasingly difficult to talk publicly about matters which previously could be discussed in the open. Shan students and monks in Rangoon began to meet secretly in the monastery of U Na King, a revered Shan monk from Möng Nawng who had been in the capital for a number of years. The monks had organised their own movement to revive Shan identity, and U Na King was their undisputed *sayadaw*, or great teacher.

One night shortly after the formation of Ne Win's Caretaker Government, forty young Shans met in U Na King's monastery to swear an oath. They cut their wrists, dripped the blood into a glass, mixed it with rice liquor and drank it. The young Shans pledged to fight for an independent Shan State and declared themselves ready to sacrifice their lives if necessary. U Na King bestowed on the young radicals new *noms de guerre*, all beginning with "Hsö"—"tiger" in Shan—to demonstrate their bravery and determination. The Tiger was also the Shan national symbol.

In the end, however, only ten of them trekked up to the Thai border to join what they believed was a major military undertaking. Some of the others who went underground were village school teachers from the Shan states, or village headmen, or they came from the *saohpa* police forces. But the vast majority consisted of young peasant boys who wanted to fight what they perceived as their hated enemy, the Burmese. Traders also joined in for various reasons. Some thought that an independent Shan country would be in a better position to do business with the outside world while others just wanted to take advantage of the booming opium trade along the border.

The first university students from Rangoon arrived at Pangtawng in late 1958. They were led by the athletically built Sai Kyaw Tun, an outstanding sportsman at Rangoon University and an amateur boxer whom U Na King had given the name Hsö Wan; the "Solar Tiger". He was the nephew of the *saohpa* of Möng Yai and a natural leader, despite his tender age: he was only twenty when he left Rangoon for the jungle.

A group of eight Shan students had travelled from the capital to the border town of Tachilek, where they had crossed the frontier to Mae Sai in Thailand and then gone via Chiang Mai and Fang up to Pangtawng. The best-known of the eight included Sai Tun Aye, a student from Möng Nang who had just obtained his Bachelor of Commerce at Rangoon University; Sai Kyaw Sein (Hsö Hten; the "Ace Tiger"), a good swimmer from Hsipaw; Sai Myint Aung (Hsö Khan; the "Striking Tiger"), a science student who had been active in the literary movement in Rangoon; Sai Pan, the author of the award-winning article in the Tai Youth Magazine; and Sai Hla Aung (Hsö Lane; the "Striped Tiger"), a geology student who had campaigned for the Yawnghwe Mahadevi in the 1956 election.

While in Chiang Mai, Sai Kyaw Tun had run into a young British adventurer who today is remembered only as "Harry". He was in his early twenties, a kind of early-day hippie traveller, and had enthusiastically joined the Shan students when they proceeded up to Pangtawng.[70]

In early 1959, they were joined by Khun Kya Nu and his relative Khun Thawda, who, like his uncle, the Hsipaw *saohpa* Sao Kya Seng, had been educated in the US. Thawda, who was also known as Pi Sai Long, gave up his teaching post at the Kambawza Shan Chiefs' College in Taunggyi to join the resistance.

"We left Taunggyi on 9 March," recalls Khun Kya Nu, then a handsome and youthful 24-year-old science student. "We travelled by jeep a roundabout way via Loi-Lem and Panglong to avoid being detected, and finally reached Pang Phon, a small village near Möng Küng. There, we managed to make contact with my cousin, Khin Maung Win from Kehsi Mansam, who was already in the underground. After waiting for nine days, he arrived with thirty-six fully armed men. We got into their jeeps and trucks and drove at night along small jungle roads towards the south. The vehicles took us as far as Kengtawng, north of Möng Pan. From there we had to walk over the mountains down to Pangtawng."

The young intellectuals were not used to rough jungle life and it took them more than three weeks to reach the camp on the border, where they met up with the motley crew that composed the *Noom Suk Harn*. "Most of them thought that it would take a few months or so to achieve independence. But we students were prepared for a long, protracted struggle. We knew it was not going to be easy," Khun Kya Nu says. A look around the camp at Pangtawng was enough to convince the students that they were in for a long wait before their country could become independent. There were only a few hundred ragtag "soldiers" armed with the few weapons that the *saohpa* police and the village headmen had brought with them: muskets, flintlocks and some Japanese and American rifles left over from World War II.

But regardless of the intentions and ideals of the young Shan nationalists at Pangtawng, other interests too were at work. Pu Ling Gung Na's opium business was doing well, and his partners in Chiang Mai were investing their profits in perfectly legitimate enterprises such as jewellery shops, silk factories and a new department store.

The smugglers inside Burma were also becoming cleverer and bolder as the trade via Thailand flourished. In the summer of 1960, Chinese opium traders in Shan State were brazen enough to charter three DC-3s belonging to the state-owned Burma Airways to transport opium southward. They had transported the opium by mule from northeastern Shan State, over forest and mountain trails, down to the airport in Lashio which is located about fifteen kilometres from the town. The chartered planes then flew several tons of opium to Kengtung, from where it was sent overland down to the Thai border.

The *Guardian* newspaper in Rangoon, which exposed the story, criticised the government for having let its own civilian aircraft be used for such shipments. The *saohpa* of Kengtung had his own interpretation of the affair: he reproached the editor of the *Guardian* for printing the news, not denying that the incident had taken place, but simply arguing that such publicity would affect the livelihood of the thousands of hill-tribe farmers in Shan State, for whom the opium poppy had become the only source of income.[71]

Gradually, the opium trade was generating money for virtually everyone in the area, albeit in vastly disparate proportions: the farmers who grew the poppies and earned a pittance from months of laborious work in the fields; the merchants who bought opium from the farmers and carried it to the markets, earning enough to buy houses and open shops in Burmese towns all over the north; the Shan rebels who taxed the growers and the caravans to raise money for arms and ammunition; the KMT warlords who reaped fortunes off the trade and invested it in legitimate businesses in Thailand; and corrupt government officials, who, for a fee, were prepared even to hire out state-owned aircraft to assist the traders.

At the receiving end, millions of opium addicts in Thailand, Hong Kong, Malaya and Singapore consumed the drug in dark, smelly opium dens—

and it was their money that ultimately paid for the whole trade, filtering up and down to various levels of the opium hierarchy.

In this complex system, there were no fixed patterns, or firm alliances, and there was certainly no "spider in the web", who controlled the entire trade—a common Western misperception of the drug trade which still dominates the thinking of European and American drug enforcement officials. Rivalry, betrayal, conflicting interests, and lack of trust have always characterised Southeast Asia's drug trade.

On the Thai border, the Shan rebels and the KMT actually depised each other, but they had to co-exist. An accomodation of sorts was therefore reached between the two groups. Initially, the KMT had deeply resented Shan taxation of their opium convoys at Pangtawng, but gradually they came to accept it. On a broader political scale, the fledgling Shan insurrection came in some ways as a godsend for the forces that wanted to continue the "secret war" against China, which was still continuing despite the "evacuation" in 1952–53. The US and Taiwan had no strategic interest in the Shan cause as such, but turmoil in the Shan states suited the KMT. Apart from the alliance with Olive Yang of Kokang, the KMT had also failed to establish any noteworthy links with other local chieftains in the Shan states. A Shan rebel army would provide the KMT with what it needed: a front behind which it could hide to deflect international criticism—and thwart the possibility of further UN action. More importantly, an indigenous ally would help them gain local support, or at least acceptance, which had been lacking ever since the first Nationalist Chinese units first entered the Shan states in 1950.

Since the very beginning, there had been many players in this covert operation, and they continued to be involved in it for diverse and often contradictory reasons. The hawks within the CIA and Taiwan's Intelligence Bureau of the Ministry of National Defence had not given up hope of "liberating" the Chinese mainland from sanctuaries in the Shan hills, even though that by now seemed an impossible dream.

It is plausible to assume that higher-ups in the US intelligence community realised this, but they nevertheless saw the KMT remnants as useful intelligence assets for espionage against China. After all, they still maintained a string of bases in northern and northeastern Burma, stretching from Na Hpaw, Pa Jau and Loije southwest of Myitkyina in Kachin State, and all along the Yunnan frontier down to the Mekong river and the border with Laos.

The Thais no doubt perceived the KMT as a useful buffer between themselves and their traditional enemy, the Burmese—this was apart from the very obvious economic benefits Thailand derived from the KMT operation in Burma. The latter was perhaps the most important factor in a Thai context. Since the early 1950s, the opium trade had corrupted and destabilised

Thailand's military and paramilitary establishment. Paul Helliwell's SEA Supply Company had made police general Pao Sriyanonda not only rich but also turned him into the most powerful man in the country.

With CIA support, Pao's police force grew steadily. By 1956, he had some 48,000 policemen stationed throughout Thailand, with more than 10,000 in Bangkok alone. The police even had its own air force and navy, and outnumbered Gen. Sarit Thanarat's regular army, which consisted of 45,000 men. According to Thai researcher Surachart Bamrungsuk: "Pao and the CIA had a mutual interest: Pao used the CIA to his advantage, while the CIA exploited his willingness to perform operations that served US interests."[72]

Pao had accumulated not only political power through his powerful police force, but also economic influence through banking and corporate ownership, which owed much to money derived from the opium trade with the KMT.[73] The opium trade had become especially important since traditional sources in other parts of the world had dried up. Iran had agreed, in April 1946, to ban poppy cultivation; Chinese supplies had also ceased after the 1949 revolution, when Mao Zedong's Communists wiped out virtually all opium production in Sichuan and Yunnan. According to Surachart Bamrungsuk:

> While the Iranian and Chinese opium supplies were gradually disappearing in the early 1950s, the Kuomintang began to fill the void by expanding opium production in the areas they occupied in the Shan states. In 1954, British customs in Singapore stated that Bangkok had become a major centre for international opium trafficking in Southeast Asia .... By 1955 the Thai police under General Pao Sriyanonda had become the largest opium-trafficking syndicate in Thailand, and were involved in every phase of the narcotics traffic.[74]

This business was well worth fighting for, and it resulted in an open conflict between Pao and Sarit. The tenuous political and military balance between the two contenders for power and influence was finally upset in September 1957. Army tanks and infantry moved into Bangkok. They encircled the police headquarters in the Thai capital and proclaimed martial law. Pao fled the country to look after his bank accounts in Switzerland, where he later died as one of the richest men in the world.

His local banker, Chin Sophonpanich of the Bangkok Bank, was also forced into exile, and spent most of his time in Hong Kong until he eventually returned in 1964. Thailand's prime minister, P. Pibulsongkram, escaped to Cambodia and later fled to Japan, where he died in 1964. Sarit and the army had seized power. For the coming sixteen years, Thailand was to be ruled by a single group of men: military officers who rose to power when Sarit decided to make his move. The power of the police had been effectively broken and a new elite was emerging.[75]

The handsome, silver-haired Gen. Thanom Kittikachorn soon became the most public of these new powerholders. His charming appearance earned him the nickname "Siamese Smile" in the foreign media. But the most powerful of Sarit's underlings was the plump Gen. Prapass "Porky" Charusathiara, whose "sunglasses, tiny moustache, and coarse features in a heavy face gave [him] a sinister appearance, especially next to Thanom. Whereas Thanom was able to interact easily with visiting foreign leaders, Prapass shied away from such contacts."[76]

Sarit's rise to omnipotence was not smooth, however. Unruly civilian politicians were still around, and parties opposed to Sarit won the election on 15 December 1957. A second coup then had to be staged on 20 October 1958 before he could consolidate his grip on power. In the interim, Sarit had been admitted to Walter Reed Military Hospital in Washington, where he was visited by US Secretary of State Dulles and President Eisenhower. They discussed a "free world defence against Communist pressure", and Sarit promised to turn Thailand into the bulwark that the US needed to halt the Communist advance in East Asia.[77]

For obvious reasons, the new pact SEATO took great interest in the new order in Thailand. The SEATO secretary-general, Pote Sarasin, had even headed a pro-Sarit caretaker government shortly after the first coup. He returned to his old post in SEATO when Sarit was firmly back in the saddle after the second military takeover. Significantly, immediately after this second coup, all political parties were abolished and a large number of arrests were made for alleged breaches of the Anti-Communism Law.[78]

Neutral foreign observers, however, reported that there was no communist danger, and the real reason for the coup was that the government was facing bankruptcy. Gen. Pao had plundered the country, and its foreign exchange reserves were shrinking. Despite the close relationship between Pao and Chin of the Bangkok Bank, anti-Chinese rhetoric under the fiercely nationalistic Prime Minister Pibulsongkram had alienated most of the Sino-Thai business community. Chin had fled the country together with Pao, but Sarit promised to restore the confidence of the Sino-Thai plutocracy in the government when he himself took over as prime minister on 9 February 1959.[79]

With the economic arrangement in order and the army ("the Motor of Development", to quote security scholar Huntington) firmly in charge, the US pledged to take care of Thailand's military needs.[80] It was in this new, much more favourable environment that various cloak-and-dagger types also went to work again—in the Golden Triangle. The equilibrium that had been upset by the removal of Gen. Pao had not only been stabilised, but the murky world of secret agents found themselves with a new, much better organised set-up.

Prapass was their new man. At the time of Sarit's coup, he had been commanding general of the First Division, deputy commanding general of the First Army as well as deputy minister of interior under Gen. Pao. But Prapass had supported Sarit in his power struggle with Pao, and was later awarded the Interior Ministry for his loyalty. In that capacity, Prapass took over the role previously played by Gen. Pao—and added a powerful new security apparatus which was built up under his command in the early 1960s: the CSOC, or the Communist Suppression Operational Command, which later became known as the Internal Security Operational Command (ISOC). Naturally, this new outfit was in charge of border security, which included liaison with the KMT as well as ethnic minority groups along the Thai–Burma frontier.

Gen. Sarit's new government decreed shortly after assuming power in 1959 that the 52-year-old Royal Thai Opium Monopoly was abolished. But narcotics-related corruption, and private business activities, were already rampant in Thailand; no serious attempts were made to stop the enormous traffic from the poppy fields of Burma and northern Thailand down to the sea lanes. Thailand remained the most important transhipment centre for Burmese opium, and Bangkok remained the major Asian drug capital.

Along Thailand's northern frontier, a crucial role in cementing a relationship between the Shan rebels and the local authorities was played by Sao Khunsuk, the uncle of the Kengtung *saohpa*, Sao Sai Long. Sao Khunsuk had served in the Burma Frontier Force with the rank of captain before World War II and retreated with the British to India when the Japanese invaded Burma. During the war, he served as British consul in Chiang Mai and entered Burma with the Allied forces in 1945.

When the Japanese had been driven out, he administered Kengtung state after independence on behalf of his nephew, Sao Sai Long, who was a minor. He was imprisoned for two months during Ne Win's Caretaker Government, but left for Thailand after his release and took part in the formation of the early Shan resistance movement. Through police and army contacts in Chiang Mai, Sao Khunsuk had indirect access to Gen. Sarit and other high-ranking Thai military officers. He was also connected with Taiwan, the CIA and SEATO.[81] Supplies from Thailand posed no problem: only money was needed.

And money was what the Shans were expecting from contacts which were being established with SEATO. The pact's involvement with the Shans was in line with US/KMT policies, and therefore not surprising: the hawks did not trust the Burmese government, and the Thais, although they had no sympathy for Shan independence, still saw a sturdy border buffer as essential for their national security.

Meetings between Shan rebels and KMT officers were held in Chiang Mai in northern Thailand to discuss how the two groups should co-exist. A young Thai newspaper man, M.R. Kukrit Pramoj, was sent by Bangkok as a special envoy to the Shans. In early 1959, he introduced three young Shans from Pangtawng—Khun Thawda, Boon Tai and Sai Tun Aye—to SEATO secretary-general Pote Sarasin. A secret meeting was held in Bangkok, but very little came out of it. The Shans were allowed to remain along the Thai border, but no outside monetary assistance ever reached the rebels in the border mountains northwest of Fang.[82]

So despite all these plans and efforts, the Shan "army" on the Thai border remained a pathetically small force. It consisted in early 1959 of less than 450 men: 200 had come down from Möng Yai, 40 from Kehsi Mansam and 100 from Möng Nawng. In addition, there was Sao Noi's initial force of about 100 ex-*saohpa* policemen and Gung Na's assorted outlaws. Some basic military training was provided when a few Karens and Kachins from the Burma Army defected to the rebels in 1959. One of them, an ethnic Karen lieutenant called Bo Hla Khin had come over from the nearby Möng Ton garrison, and he held daily drills with the new recruits. But, as Khun Kya Nu recalls: "It was not a proper army and no one had any real idea of political organisation or military strategy."[83]

The students were also becoming increasingly dissatisfied with Sao Noi's authoritarian ways and the shady business activities of Gung Na. They wanted to see action, and Sai Kyaw Tun asked Sao Noi for permission to return to his home state, Möng Yai, to organise the people there. Reluctantly, Sao Noi agreed, and Kyaw Tun marched off together with commerce graduate Sai Tun Aye, and Bo Dewing, a 38-year-old local warlord from the Möng Yai area. Bo Dewing had been the leader of the 200-strong group from his native state that had joined the insurrection in early 1959.

Their target was Tang-yan, a town of 6,000–7,000 people on a broad, grassy plain 100 kilometres southeast of Lashio. Tang-yan had been held by the KMT for more than a year in the early 1950s. After its recapture by government forces, a major garrison was established in the town for its defence and also to serve as a nerve-centre for the Burma Army units that confronted the KMT in eastern Shan State.

From the Shan nationalists' point of view, Tang-yan was an important centre in the north, located not far from Möng Yai, where the meetings had been held in 1956 and 1957. As a result, the Shan rebels enjoyed widespread support in the area, and the first to link up with the unlikely duo, the student Sai Kyaw Tun and warlord Bo Dewing, was an equally unlikely ally: Bo Maung, the Wa commander of a paramilitary Union Military Police (UMP) unit that had distinguished itself fighting the KMT.

On 15 November—the full moon of the twelfth month according to the Shan calendar—the unusual gathering of allies met at Pang Tet-diao village in the Loi Maw area of Möng Yai state to discuss the operation. Bo Maung had about fifty Wa UMPs with him, and a rumour had already spread across the area that they were about to turn their guns against the government, or "the Burmese", as the locals said. It was not enough, but soon about 300 to 400 village youths had been recruited for the campaign. Long Khun Maha, a 47-year-old writer and poet who had served as "chief minister" of Möng Yai state, also joined the meeting at Pang Tet-diao.

The idea was to attack several targets in the north simultaneously. Bo Dewing and Kyaw Tun were assigned to capture Tang-yan. Sao Tao was sent north to ambush the train to Lashio, Hsö Lane (the geology student) headed with a few hundred boys for Nampong closer to Lashio, and Long Khun Maha volunteered to go to Hsenwi to raise more men and funds. Bo Maung, a deeply superstitious man, laid out chicken bones on the ground by the campfire that night to predict the outcome of the campaign. The signs looked good.[84]

But already the next day, fighting broke out prematurely. At Soon Gwei ("Banana Plantation") village not far from Loi Maw, Bo Maung's men ran into a government truck with armed guards carrying salaries to the garrison at Tang-yan. A firefight broke out, and the Burma Army was both taken aback and alerted: who were these rebels? Only the KMT was known to operate in the area, but they always sought to avoid confrontation with government forces.

An urgent message was sent to Tang-yan, and the Shan rebels retreated temporarily into a forested area near the town. But then, on 22 November, they emerged from their hiding-place to launch a surprise attack. Hundreds of Shans and Was stormed into the town, shouting as they fired their weapons The local UMP, the Immigration Police and the badly undermanned local army fled headlong; despite the skirmish at Soon Gwei no one had expected Tang-yan to be the target for these hitherto unknown rebels. Attacks were also carried out at Nampong, and the train to Lashio was ambushed by the rebels.

In Tang-yan, the rebels emptied the armoury, the treasury—and all the liquor stores. "It was like the Wild West," one of the veterans remembers.[85] The government launched a massive counter-offensive within days of the shock of losing Tang-yan. Five aeroplanes bombed and strafed the town, and on the 30th—a week after the capture—the rebels retreated. But their morale had been boosted: the Shan rebels had scored their first battle victory, and word spread across the north that Bo Maung and the students were about to "drive the Burmese out of Shan State". Although based on exaggerated reports and wishful thinking, this was how the news was received in the villages, and more youths took to the jungle.

When the battle of Tang-yan was over, Sai Kyaw Tun returned to Pangtawng with Bo Maung and his force of ex-UMP Wa tribesmen, and the poet Long Khun Maha. Among the young Shan school students who had also joined the "heroes of Tang-yan" was a chubby, eighteen-year-old schoolboy from Kyaukme called Sai Kyaw Khin. He was later, under the name Sao Sam Möng, to become one of the ablest guerrilla commanders that the Shan insurgency ever produced.

The students had demonstrated to Sao Noi that they could not only fight but also organise the people. They presented their increasingly authoritarian leader with an ultimatum: the movement had to adopt some discipline, a charter to work from and a political organisation to match the army—or they would break away and set up their own organisation.

Sao Noi was not interested in their suggestions, and in March 1960 the students moved away from Pangtawng. On 24 April, they set up the Shan State Independence Army (SSIA) at Möng Yawn, a fertile Shan valley across the border from Thaton in Thailand. Long Khun Maha was appointed "president" and Bo Maung became chief of the army, which consisted mostly of Bo Maung's force of former UMP Was.

Rangoon viewed these developments with deep concern, and sent Khun Kya Nu's father, the well-respected U Kya Bu, down to the Thai border to persuade the students there to return home. The message he had to convey was that "bloodshed was not necessary", assuring them that "you won't be arrested if you come back".

Most Shan students were apprehensive of the offer, but Long Khun Maha decided to travel with U Kya Bu to Rangoon for talks. As soon as he arrived at Mingaladon, he was apprehended by Military Intelligence agents waiting in the airport lounge. It was only after U Kya Bu had made strong representations to the foreign minister, Sao Khun Hkio, a Shan, that Long Khun Maha was released. But he was not allowed to rejoin his followers in the jungle; he was sent to Taunggyi, where he was employed as announcer for the Shan language service of Burma's official radio.[86]

For many Shans, this was the end of any attempt to solve the conflict between them and the authorities in Rangoon by peaceful means. Since it was now much riskier to remain along the border, the young Shan rebels also decided to march north to Möng Leün in the Wa hills—one of the remotest corners of Shan State, which had never been under any central control from Rangoon. Only the former school teacher from Taunggyi, Khun Thawda (who had been appointed new president of the SSIA), Sai Pan and a few others were left behind in Fang to maintain at least some kind of contact with the outside world.

In July, while the move away from the Thai border was taking place, the first Shan student died in action. The hero of the battle of Tang-yan, the prize-winning boxer and athlete Sai Kyaw Tun, was killed by government forces in a firefight near Möng Hpayak in eastern Kengtung state. He had been marching north from the Thai border with a small group of men when they were ambushed by the Burma Army. Sai Kyaw Tun was only twenty-one when he died, and his memory is still revered among many Shan war veterans.[87] The situation was becoming tense—and British adventurer "Harry" left for home never to be heard of again.

The way to Möng Leün led through the remote and isolated Mawhpa area east of the Salween river, a hilly tract inhabited by Lahu tribesmen. The government had organised them into a local militia force, initially to fight the KMT, but they also resisted the arrival of the Shan nationalists. Ironically, the SSIA's first battle was not with the Burma Army, but a five-month long campaign against the Lahus. But despite these unexpected clashes, the students began organising themselves in a way that had been impossible under Sao Noi's leadership. Hsö Lane, the geology student, was sent to Hsenwi with seven men and the same number of rifles to initiate an uprising there. Another batch was dispatched to Hsipaw, the nerve centre of Shan nationalism. They returned after a few months, bringing with them some village circle headmen and other new recruits, among them Bo Kang Yom alias Sao Tao, a middle-aged *bomong* (headman) of a village in the Hsipaw area.

The students held a new meeting at Pingyawng village in the Mawhpa area and concluded, rather optimistically, that the time was ripe for an offensive against the Burma Army. Bo Maung was put in charge of the operation, which was to include concerted attacks in as many different areas as possible. Small-scale guerrilla attacks did then occur, including an ambush of the train to Lashio.

But the problem of Sao Noi's *Noom Suk Harn* remained. The existence of two different Shan groups made local people confused and hampered popular support. On the other hand, the business interests, which were intertwined with intelligence interests, were not pleased to see the emergence of the SSIA.

The new group appeared to be a more genuine Shan political movement than *Noom Suk Harn*, and was therefore viewed with suspicion by business and intelligence circles in Thailand. Sao Noi was easy to control; he could be used by the KMT and others whose main interest lay in securing parts of Shan State for cross-border intelligence gathering into Yunnan. The Thais were not interested in any "independence" for the area, which the SSIA was fighting for.

Acutely aware of this, the SSIA decided to send Khun Kya Nu to neutralise the most powerful *Noom Suk Harn* commander inside Shan State: Moh Heng, an erstwhile commander of the CPB who had surrendered in May 1958. In November of the same year, Moh Heng had rejoined the underground, this time with the *Noom Suk Harn*, and he had rebuilt his old base area in his native Lai Hka-Möng Küng region north of Taunggyi, well away from Sao Noi's camp on the Thai border.

The idea was simple: since Moh Heng was unlikely to join the SSIA, a third "group" had to be formed to "unite" the two forces. In January 1962, the plan was accepted. Moh Heng agreed to become the chairman of the Shan National United Front (SNUF) with Khun Kya Nu as his deputy. The SNUF, in effect, became the political arm of the SSIA. Sao Noi's influence was diminishing, and a Shan movement led by students was gathering momentum.

In Rangoon, meanwhile, the Shan student movement had almost become defunct following the crackdown launched by the Caretaker Government and the flight to the border of several of its most prominent organisers. It was not until the 1960 general elections that overt political activities again became possible. The main organiser of the Shan students this time was Sai Tzang, the son of Burma's first president, Sao Shwe Thaike. As a student, Sai Tzang had been active in the Shan cultural revival movement of the mid-1950s; now he had become a university tutor in history and English literature. Contacts between the students in the hills of Shan State and those studying in Rangoon were re-established. Sai Tzang himself secretly went to Lai-Hka in late 1960 to meet his old friend from the university, Khun Kya Nu and other Shan students who were already in the jungle.[88]

The resurgence of a militant Shan nationalist movement had been parallelled by a similar development among the Kachins. Since Naw Seng's retreat into China in May 1950, the Kachins had remained loyal to the central government. Only a few of Naw Seng's men, among them the short, bow-legged Zau Seng and a few other World War II veterans, had remained with the Karen rebels, and never given up the thought of continuing the fight for an independent Kachin country.

However, dissent began to surface up in Kachin State in the late 1950s. The area was poor and neglected. The Kachins had fought tenaciously against the Japanese, but, apart from a few jeeps for the state ministers, no other "war reparations" from Tokyo ever reached this remote border state. Many Kachins had turned angry and bitter.[89]

In early 1958, seven young Kachins met secretly at night near Inya Lake in Rangoon. The meeting was organised by Zau Seng, who had reached the capital clandestinely. He came together with Phungshwi Zau Seng, a Rangoon University graduate who now worked as a civil servant in the Kachin-inhabited area of northeastern Shan State.

The other five were Kachins from Rangoon University, and the most striking of them was a six-foot-tall student of history, political science and psychology: Zau Mai, the great-grandson of the *duwa*, or local ruler, of Malizup, the area where the Mali Hka and the Nmai Hka merge in the north to become the mighty Irrawaddy: "We called our group the 'Seven Stars' as we always met at midnight when the seven stars of Orion rose in the dark sky. We decided to follow the Karens and other minorities and take up arms against the government in Rangoon."[90]

Soon after this first night-time meeting in Rangoon, Zau Seng left together with four Kachin students for northeastern Shan State. In Lashio, Zau Seng re-established contact with his younger brother Zau Tu, who was still studying at Rangoon University. He was sent, along with Zau Mai, to the Karen headquarters along the Thai border to request assistance for their plans. But the Karens had hardly enough weapons to arm their own troops, let alone to share with the Kachins. The disappointed Kachins travelled north again—but found on their return that there was fertile ground for a rebel movement.

In early 1960, the Sino–Burmese border had at last been demarcated after years of negotiations between Rangoon and Beijing. As part of the deal, a few Kachin villages had been handed over to the Chinese in exchange for Burmese sovereignty over an area northwest of Namkham known as the Namwan Assigned Tract, which the British had originally leased from China in the 19th century.[91] The deal was not unfair by international standards, but rumours soon spread across Kachin State to the effect that vast tracts of Kachin territory had been ceded to China. Even today, it is not unusual for many Kachins to point across the border at a piece of land and claim that it was given to China by Rangoon. The failure of the central government to clarify the nature of the border agreement was at the root of misunderstandings which were soon to drive hundreds of young Kachins underground.[92]

To add fuel to the fire, one of U Nu's promises before the April 1960 election had been to make Buddhism the state religion of Burma, a move seen by the predominantly Christian Kachins as an open provocation. On 5 February 1961, the Kachin Independence Army (KIA) with Zau Seng as its commander was set up in the Kachin-inhabited hills near Lashio. The goal was to fulfil Naw Seng's dream of establishing "a free republic of Kachinland".[93] The army had in its possession thirty rifles of World War II vintage with five to fifteen rounds of ammunition each. It was not much to challenge the might of the Burma Army, but the young Kachins were enthusiastic and ready to fight.

Two days later, Zau Seng's younger brother Zau Tu and eight young Kachins, guns in hand, stormed the treasury in Lashio. It was eight in the morning, and the guards were caught unawares as they were having breakfast. Zau Tu made away with 90,000 Kyats in cash, which provided the financial basis for the rebellion that they were planning.

Lax security played to the advantage of the Kachins: at the same time, all the attention of the Burma Army was focused on the eastern border near Laos and China. Relations with Beijing had improved considerably after the signing of the border agreement in 1960. Zhou Enlai had visited Burma for a week in the beginning of January 1961 to ratify the demarcation of the frontier. China also pledged to afford Burma an interest-free loan of £30 million. What was not announced, however, was that Burma had agreed secretly to allow Chinese forces to enter Burma and attack the KMT.

On 26 January, a combined force of three divisions of regulars from the Chinese People's Liberation Army (PLA), a total of 20,000 men, crossed the frontier between Sipsongpanna and Kengtung state. In human waves, they swept down across the hills surrounding Möng Yang, Möng Wa and Möng Yawng. The campaign, code-named "the Mekong River Operation", broke the back of the KMT in northeastern Burma. Beaten Nationalist Chinese forces retreated towards Möng Pa Liao on the Mekong river, where 5,000 Burmese troops launched an attack. Their base was captured without much resistance—but when the Burmese troops marched in, they found large quantities of US-made arms and ammunition.

When the news hit the papers in Rangoon, violent demonstrations were held outside the US embassy on Merchant Street. Neither the Burmese nor the Chinese, however, have ever acknowledged that the PLA formed the core of the force that drove the KMT out of the eastern border areas.[94]

Soon after the Mekong River Operation, the CIA reported that Taiwan had evacuated 3,371 soldiers and 825 dependants from the Burma–Thai–Laos border area to Taiwan between 17 March and 12 April.[95] But even so, the agency estimated that approximately 3,000 KMT "irregulars" remained in the border areas. 1,500–2,000 of them had reportedly based themselves in northern Thailand, and the remainder in Burma and in Laos.

Four or five hundred KMT troops were said to have been recruited by the Laotian army to patrol the area between Luang Prabang and Ban Houei Sai—and the government in Vientiane was attempting to enlist more to garrison Nam Tha province further to the north.[96] The interests that supported the KMT were determined not to let it disappear: the KMT was simply too useful for intelligence gathering, economic benefits and outright mercenary activities.

While these violent activities were going on in remote frontier areas, ex-president Sao Shwe Thaike initiated a legal movement to preserve the Union by strengthening its federal character. On 24 April 1959—during the reign of Ne Win's Caretaker Government—all the thirty-four *saohpas* had formally given up their positions at a ceremony held at Taunggyi. The Shan states had become Shan State, administered by an elected state government. Rangoon probably viewed this as a victory over the "feudal chiefs" who had "surrendered their powers", while the Shans saw it as the formal finalisation of a movement that had begun several years before: the *saohpas* did not hand over power to Rangoon, but to the elected Shan State government.[97]

But the war, and the massive concentration of government troops in the eastern border areas as a direct outcome of the KMT intervention, had effectively undermined the efforts to create a more democratic system in Shan State. The Shan insurrection, small and insignificant as it might be, was another concern. Sao Shwe Thaike's initiative was supported by the former foreign minister, the Möng Mit *saohpa* Sao Khun Hkio, and most other princes and politicians in Shan State. They reasoned that by restructuring the federal system, the Union could be preserved, and the fledgling insurgency undermined.[98]

On 8–16 June, Shan leaders meet in Taunggyi to initiate a federal movement to find a political solution to Burma's ethnic crisis. A broad spectrum of Shan State leaders, including the *saohpas*, and Shan and Pa-O politicians, rallied behind the move to implement a more genuine federal structure. Even Prime Minister U Nu was sympathetic to the demands:

> There was nothing sinister about this Federal Principle, which was an adaptation of the constitution of the United States. It had three main features: 1. Burma proper would be turned into a constituent state of the Union, bringing it into parity with all other existing states; 2. The two chambers of Parliament, namely, the House of Nationalities and the House of Deputies, would be invested with equal powers; 3. All constituent states of the Union (regardless of size and population) would have equal representation in the House of Nationalities.[99]

In order to discuss these issues, U Nu decided to convene a "Nationalities' Seminar" in Rangoon to be attended by Shan and Karenni leaders whose respective states enjoyed the constitutional—but highly controversial—right to secede from the Union.

It was obvious that the resentment of the minorities was directed not towards the government in Rangoon but the fast-growing, increasingly arrogant military machine that in effect had become a state within the state. According to the last Mahadevi of Hsipaw: "Ne Win considered the frontier areas worthy recipients of one thing only: his army, which had spread like cancer into all corners of the Union. Things would have turned out differently if General Aung San, the founder of the Union of Burma and its army, had lived instead of falling victim to an assassin's bullet. The Shan *saohpas* had trusted him, as had so many other Kachin and Kayah leaders. It was the main reason why they had agreed to join Burma Proper to form the Union, with the right to secede after ten years."[100]

But soon after the transformation which the army had undergone during the 1950s, its unscrupulous treatment of the hill peoples had started. The *saohpas* found themselves powerless to protect their people from the atrocities committed by the army, who "behaved like ruthless occupation forces rather than protectors of the land", to quote the Hsipaw Mahadevi. Her US-educated husband, *saohpa* Sao Kya Seng, had been outraged when the district headmen of Namlan, Möng Hkö and Kalagwe reported lootings, rapes and unprovoked killings committed by the military.

Once, when he had been touring the area near Namlan, Sao Kya Seng had arrived at the site of a torched village where the burnt-out homes were still smouldering. Families had lost their possessions and knew nothing of the fate of their brothers and husbands who had been abducted to act as porters and forced labourers for the troops. According to the Mahadevi: "Sao felt horrified and frustrated to witness the aftermath of this unnecessary rampage by the military, knowing that he was unable to promise that this outrage would not happen again."

U Nu travelled north in the late 1950s to visit Sao Kya Seng. While being driven in a car together with Sao Kya Seng through the lush, green countryside of the Hsipaw valley, the *saohpa* told him how disenchanted the Shans had become with Burmese domination of the federation. U Nu listened carefully, and responded: "We must preserve the Union of Burma. Otherwise we're doomed." "In that case you'd better control the military," Sao Kya Seng replied. "I will, believe me, I will," U Nu said with great emphasis before getting out of the car to offer his prayers at the white pagoda at Bawgyo.

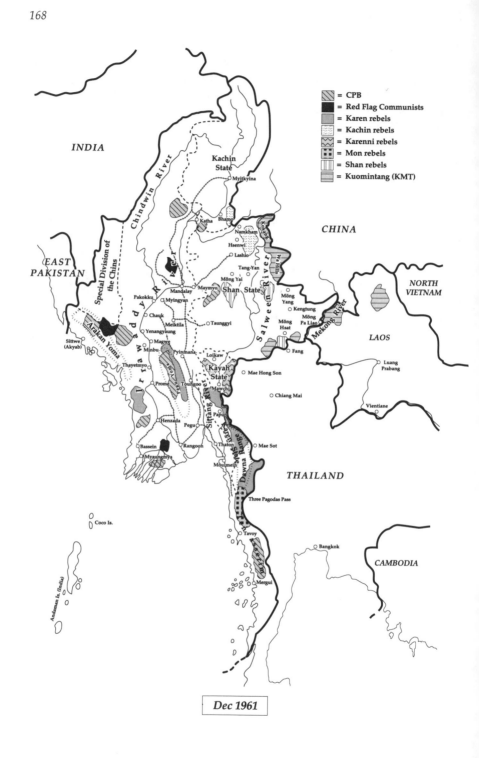

INDIA

Kachin
State

• Myitkyina

EAST
PAKISTAN

CHINA

Special Division of
the Chins

Katha   Bhamo

Namkham

Hsenwi

• Lashio

Tang-Yan

Möng Yai

Shan State

NORTH
VIETNAM

Pakokku   Mandalay
Myingyan

Maymyo

Möng
Yang

Kengtung

Möng
Pa Liao

Chauk

Meiktila

Taunggyi

Möng
Hsat

LAOS

Yenangyaung

Sittwe
(Akyab)

Arakan Yoma

Magwe
Minbu

Pyinmana

Loikaw

Fang

Luang
Prabang

Thayetmyo

Kayah
State

• Mae Hong Son

Prome   Toungoo
Mawchi

• Chiang Mai

Vientiane

Henzada

Papun

Pegu

Bassein   Rangoon
Myaungmya

Thaton   • Mae Sot

Moulmein

THAILAND

Three Pagodas Pass

Coco Is.

Tavoy

• Bangkok

CAMBODIA

Mergui

Andaman Is. (India)

= CPB
= Red Flag Communists
= Karen rebels
= Kachin rebels
= Karenni rebels
= Mon rebels
= Shan rebels
= Kuomintang (KMT)

Chindwin River

Irrawaddy River

Salween River

Mekong River

Sittang River

Dawna Range

Tenasserim

Dec 1961

Aung San and Daw Khin Kyi at their wedding on September 6, 1942.

General Aung San and his children, 1947. *Left to right:* Aung San Suu Kyi, Aung San Oo and Aung San Lin.

Ne Win and Aung San.

KMT base in the Shan Hills of Burma, 1960s.

KMT troops at Möng Hsat, early 1950s.

KMT village in northern Thailand; portraits of the king and queen of Thailand flanked by portraits of Chiang Kai-shek, Sun Yat-sen and Chiang Ching-huo (Taiwan's president) (photo by Hseng Noung Lintner).

Chinese schoolgirls in Ban Mai Nong Bua, a Kuomintang settlement in northern Thailand (photo by Hseng Noung Lintner).

Ban Mai Nong Bua: A KMT settlement in northern Thailand (photo by Hseng Noung Lintner).

Three Americans killed in action with the KMT in Burma, 1953.

Left: Olive Yang, the ruler of Kokang and KMT ally (photo from the private collection of Jackie Yang). *Right:* Naw Louisa Benson (Karen, ex-Miss Burma) with Francis Yang, Kokang officer.

Left: Opium poppy (photo by Bertil Lintner). *Right:* Opium packets on display in Shan State, Burma (photo by Hseng Noung Lintner).

Opium market, northern Burma, 1987 (photo by Hseng Noung Lintner).

Mule convoy crosses the border between Thailand and Burma's Shan State (photo by Bertil Lintner, 1983).

Opium smoker, Golden Triangle (photo by Bertil Lintner).

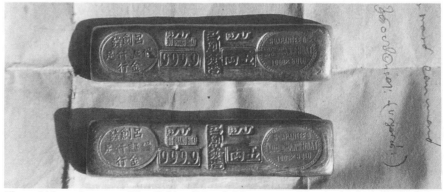

The gold bars that gave "The Golden Triangle" its name: exchange for opium (photo by Bertil Lintner, 1982).

Shan lady and child (photo by Hseng Noung Lintner).

Old Kachin warrior (photo by Hseng Noung Lintner).

The Naga Hills, northwestern Burma: Villagers of the Naga Hills tribes in the remote Paktai Range along the Burmese-Indian border (photo by Hseng Noung Lintner).

Sao Kya Hseng and his Austrian bride (photo by Bertil Lintner).

Typical Ka Kweye home guard unit in southern Shan State, early 1970s.

SNA Kengtung, early 1960s.

Shan rebels in the Kengtung area, 1960s.

SSA (Shan State Army) jungle rally, 1979.

SSA, Salween River, Shan State, Burma (photo by Bertil Lintner).

Top: Young recruits, KNLA (Karen National Liberation Army) (photo by Bertil Lintner). *Bottom:* Karen children dancing in rebel camp (photo by Hseng Noung Lintner).

6

The Military Takes Over

On 1 March 1962, a visiting Chinese ballet troupe staged a performance in Rangoon. It attracted a large audience, among whom could be seen the increasingly powerful Gen. Ne Win. The show went on until late in the evening. When it was over, the general shook hands with the leading Chinese ballerina, and then quietly left. The audience assumed that he too was going home to sleep after watching the show.

Burma's prime minister, U Nu, had meanwhile been continuing his meetings with Shan and Karenni leaders at his official Windermere residence. The Federal Seminar had been convened in Rangoon at last, and a political solution to the ethnic crisis seemed to be in sight.

The armed forces had other plans, however. In the early hours of 2 March, troops moved in to take over strategic positions in the capital. At about two o'clock in the morning, U Nu was arrested at his home in Pyidaungsu Lane. Five other ministers, the chief justice and over thirty Shan and Karenni leaders were also taken into custody. Among them was ex-president Sao Shwe Thaike, who was led away by armed guards, never to be seen again.[1]

There was no bloodshed in Rangoon, apart from a shoot-out at Sao Shwe Thaike's house on Kokine Road. His seventeen-year-old son Sai Myee was gunned down by the raiding soldiers on the night of the coup when Sao Shwe Thaike "resisted arrest", as the official report said. Sai Myee's elder brother, Sai Tzang, recalls: "When I examined my brother, I found two wounds. A rifle bullet had ripped into his ankle and there was another hole, from a small calibre round, in the back of his head. It was evidently cold-blooded killing. He was, it can be said, the first of the many thousands of unarmed young citizens of Burma killed with calculated coldness by the military regime."[2]

At 8:50 A.M., Gen. Ne Win went on the air and announced: "I have to inform you, citizens of the Union, that the armed forces have taken over responsibility and the task of keeping the country's safety, owing to the greatly deteriorating conditions of the Union." In a special message to the country's traditionally militant students, he added: "I urge the education authorities and the students who are in the midst of their examinations to carry on their work."[3]

On the following day, the federal 1947 Constitution was suspended and the bicameral parliament dissolved. At a press conference on 5 March, a Revolutionary Council, chaired by Ne Win, declared that the army believed in democracy, socialism and "healthy politics".[4] In principle, this meant a strong, central government controlled by the military. The army had developed from being a state within the state to becoming the state itself.

Burma's fourteen-year-long experiment with federalism and parliamentary democracy was over.

There was little immediate opposition to the coup: few people seemed to believe that this take-over would be different from the Caretaker period of 1958–60. But the arrest and subsequent disappearance of the first president, Sao Shwe Thaike, suggested that this time the army had plans for remaining in power indefinitely.

Another prominent Shan leader, Sao Kya Seng, the *saohpa* of Hsipaw, also disappeared within days of the coup d'etat. He had attended the Parliament in Rangoon the day before the military take-over and then flown to Taunggyi to visit his sister. Early in the morning of 2 March, soldiers came to the house where he was staying—only to find that he had just left for Heho airport by car to catch the plane to Lashio on his way home to Hsipaw. Sao Kya Seng was still unaware of what had taken place in Rangoon only hours before.

But at Taunggyi gate on the road to Heho, the military had already put up a roadblock. Sao Kya Seng's car was stopped—and eye-witnesses saw him being taken to a small nearby guard-house, where he was detained together with U Win, the Principal Land Records' Officer of the Shan State Government and two other government officials. Sao Kya Seng was last seen being driven away to Ba Htoo Myo military camp, north of Taunggyi, where he was most probably executed.[5]

With the most prominent leaders of the country—and especially of the Shan minority—either murdered or imprisoned, the army was able to get down to business. Within less than a month of the coup, Ne Win had achieved a power over the state machinery that nobody had enjoyed since the monarchy was abolished in 1885. In sharp contrast to the legalistic approach of the 1958–60 Caretaker Government—when Ne Win had frequently appeared in parliament to answer questions and had even petitioned it to allow him to rule for more than six months—this time the military ruled by decree. It also introduced its own set of laws to formalise, rather than legalise, its omnipotence.

Burma's new power structure consisted of Ne Win at the top of the pyramid, and under him the stratum of loyal, second generation officers who had also participated in the 1958–60 Caretaker Government: Aung Gyi, Tin Pe and Kyaw Soe, all formerly of Ne Win's old regiment, the 4th Burma Rifles, plus some officers from the 3rd Burma Rifles and others who had served under Ne Win in the high command in Rangoon.

Among the few civilians in the council were Dr. Maung Maung—the lawyer and writer who had always been close to the military—and Ba Nyein, a dedicated Marxist who had left the Burma Socialist Party in 1950 and helped set up the leftist Burma Workers' and Peasants' Party. He now became Ne Win's main economic adviser.[6]

Almost immediately, five "State Supreme Councils" were also formed to take over the state governments. The limited autonomy they had previously enjoyed was done away with by a single military decree. A Burma press council was set up on 30 April to control the hitherto outspoken media. "To uplift the morals" of the people, the Revolutionary Council banned horse-racing, beauty contests and popular dance competitions. The US Ford and Asia Foundations as well as the Fulbright programme were suspended along with US and British language training centres.

The state control of the administration and the exclusion of outside influences seemed to be in line with the policy of any military dictatorship asserting its power. But the ban on racing and similar activities raised eyebrows throughout Rangoon: the general himself was not exactly renowned for an austere, puritanical lifestyle. This was the first example of the hypocrisy which came to characterise Burma's unique version of socialism. While the old racecourse at the Kyaikkasan grounds in Rangoon was converted into a parade and meeting field, Ne Win was to be seen betting avidly at the Ascot races on his first trip to Britain after the coup.

The "ideology" of the new military regime was published on the same day in a document entitled the "Burmese Way to Socialism". This was followed later by the "System of Correlation of Man and his Environment", which again was an effort to provide philosophical underpinnings for the military government. These documents were written by a team of leftist ideologues, including Ba Nyein.[7]

Another staunch supporter of the new order was the old Communist leader Thakin Thein Pe, who now called himself Thein Pe Myint, having left the CPB to publish the *Vanguard* newspaper in Rangoon. Basically, the "Burmese Way to Socialism" was a hodgepodge of Marxism, Buddhist thinking and humanism which reflected an attempt by the military regime to be seen as belonging to Burma's specific political traditions. On 4 July, the military announced the formation of the new Burma Socialist Programme Party (BSPP), which at first was a cadre party comprised only of the members of the Revolutionary Council.

The inclusion of the rabid ideologue Ba Nyein—and the clear drift towards totalitarianism draped in Marxist rhetoric that followed—made most foreign businessmen, who had initially welcomed the coup, change their minds about military rule. The stability the army envisaged was clearly not for them. The reaction among the public at large to the coup, and the resulting transformation of Burma's political and economic system, became one of shock and anger when the freedoms they had previously enjoyed were severely restricted.

The students, always at the forefront of any protest movement in Burma, were the first to demonstrate openly against the military take-over. Sao Shwe Thaike's son Sai Tzang was on the campus in Rangoon on 7 July: "The evening was cool and balmy, the atmosphere charged with excitement. In the past two or three days, there had been a series of confrontations with the police but these were largely indecisive until a student was shot and wounded. This infuriated and galvanised the student body and by the morning of the 7th, the police were finally evicted from the campus. Students had shut the main gate and declared the campus a 'fortress of democracy'. All day, speeches were held, condemning the coup and calling for the restoration of democracy. The Students' Union building, which had been an important symbol of Burmese nationalism since the 1930s, was alive with activities and filled with youthful laughter and cheerful bantering as students came and went."[8]

The festive atmosphere changed later that evening when the students saw soldiers being deployed along the leafy University Avenue, armed with newly issued West German G-3 assault rifles. Soon, a small Fiat arrived and three officers stepped out to confer with their colleagues in charge of the troops facing the campus. The students booed and whistled. After a short while, the Fiat drove away. One of the remaining officers turned around to face the students, raised his arms and waved them above his head in a circular motion three times.

"We looked at each other, wondering what it all meant," Sai Tzang recalls. "Our questions were answered immediately and violently by gunfire. I dropped into a ditch and lay there not knowing what to do next. Then, the firing stopped. But when some students started running, gunfire resumed. There was a lull, soon followed by a volley as students started running again. While I myself was running, I tripped on a body lying on the ground and fell. There was a red flag of the Students' Union lying by the lifeless open palm of the dead student. Without thinking, I grabbed the flag and ran as fast as I could, praying frantically that I would not be hit. Finally, I reached the safety of the hostel building. Then, the soldiers began firing into the buildings and we heard bullets thudding into walls and the tinkling of glass as windowpanes shattered. It was clear that the soldiers were firing not merely to disperse the crowds, but were under orders to shoot to kill."

Officially, fifteen were killed and twenty-seven wounded.[9] But both neutral observers and students who were present during the shooting say that the university looked like a slaughterhouse where not fifteen but hundreds of potential leaders of society in many fields lay sprawled in death. The man in charge of the operation was Sein Lwin, one of Ne Win's closest lieutenants, and the orders to kill had come directly from the strongman himself.[10]

In the early hours of 8 July, Rangoon residents were awakened by an explosion that reverberated through the city. The army had dynamited the historic Students' Union building, reducing it to rubble. David Steinberg, a US Burma scholar, described the act as

> gratuitous and unnecessary: . . . [The building] had been as familiar a symbol in the secular sphere as the Shwe Dagon Pagoda was a symbol of Buddhism. . . . The student demonstrations and their tragic aftermath were harbingers of the continuous trouble the military experienced from the volatile student community.[11]

Josef Silverstein and Julian Wohl commented:

> The General [Ne Win] defended the actions of his government on that occasion by declaring that the students had been prompted in their actions by certain political organisations (identified in an earlier communique as Communists) and said: "I have no alternative but to meet *dah* [sword] with *dah* and spear with spear."[12]

Burmese totalitarianism had returned with an unprecedented ferocity, and provoked an unexpected response from the country's young intellectuals. The army had clearly wanted to show just who was in charge—but the massacre on the campus in Rangoon also prompted hundreds of students to join the underground.

Sai Tzang, a Shan, went to the guerrillas of his ethnic group in the northeast, where the insurgency flared anew, especially in reaction to the "disappearances"—or, as most people suspected, executions—of popular leaders such as Sao Kya Seng and Sao Shwe Thaike. Hsipaw, the former domain of Sao Kya Seng, probably supplied more youths to the Shan rebel army than any other Shan state.

The cruelty and the abolition of the federal system had upset other minorities as well, and hundreds of young Kachin students filtered into the hills of the north, where a formidable rebel army was being organised by the three brothers, Zau Seng, Zau Tu and Zau Dan. Karen students went to the eastern hills, and even among the Muslims along the East Pakistan border in the western Arakan area, a new rebel movement sprang up. Many Burmans joined the until then almost depleted ranks of the Communists in the Pegu Yoma mountains north of Rangoon.

Even more importantly, the CPB began receiving open support from China for the first time. The military take-over had upset the regional stability provided by Burma's neutral democratic government; furthermore, China had long been wary of the ambitious and sometimes unpredictable Ne Win. A number of important events took place immediately after the coup in Rangoon.

The CPB exiles in Sichuan were for the first time allowed to print propaganda leaflets and other material in China. On 1 August, the Burmese communists in China published a document titled: *Some Facts about Ne Win's Military Government*. It denounced the new regime and lashed out against the recent killings at the campus in Rangoon:

> On 7 July, the government shot down the innocent mass of university students. . . . Altogether 107 university students were killed and over 300 wounded as a result of the massacre. Never in the history of the world student movements have so many students been killed or wounded in a single incident. . . . If the government continues to carry on its activities of annihilation [it] should be held responsible for all the consequences.[13]

The most urgent task for the Sichuan exiles—or Sichuan *laopings* ("veterans"), as they came to be known—was to find a way to contact the CPB units in the forests of the Pegu Yoma and other places in central Burma. There had been no contact between them and the group of more than 140 Burmese communists in Sichuan since the latter trekked to Yunnan in the early 1950s.

By a strange twist of historical events, it was the new military regime in Rangoon that unwittingly provided an opportunity for the Sichuan *laopings* to re-establish these links. Probably hoping that the insurgents would give up when faced with the massive force of the new military government, it called for peace talks after about a year in power.

From 14 July 1963, the CPB, Thakin Soe's much smaller Red Flag Communist Party, the Karen, Mon, Shan, Kachin rebel armies, and some smaller groups attended negotiations in Rangoon and elsewhere, with guarantees of free and safe passage to and from the peace parley, regardless of the outcome.

The colourful Thakin Soe probably attracted the most attention when he arrived in the capital on 11 August, accompanied by a team of attractive young girls in khaki uniforms. Apart from alleged mistresses, one of them was actually his seventeen-year-old daughter, Ni Ni Soe. She was asked by the *Nation* whether she would like to visit her elder sister, Yi Yi Soe, who had been so anxious to meet her after years of separation. The well-drilled Stalinist girl retorted that Yi Yi Soe was a "traitor" to the cause.[14] When the talks began on the 14th, Thakin Soe placed a portrait of Stalin in front of him on the negotiating table and then began attacking the revisionism of Khrushchev and the opportunism of Mao Zedong's China. Thakin Soe was soon excluded from the talks.

The CPB's delegation to the talks was headed by *yebaw* Htay, a rotund, moon-faced veteran party organiser from Sagaing. He had already joined the CPB during World War II and become a member of the Central Committee at the second congress in July 1945. *Yebaw* Htay had initiated the "Peace and Coalition Government" line in the 1950s.

Meanwhile, twenty-nine Sichuan *laopings* arrived by special planes from Beijing, purportedly to participate in the talks in Rangoon. In the eyes of the China-trained Marxist-Leninists, people like *yebaw* Htay were revisionist traitors—but it was too early to start an inner-party struggle at this time. The talks provided an excellent opportunity for the Sichuan *laopings* to return home.

The best-known of them was Bo Zeya, one of the Thirty Comrades who had joined the Communist insurrection in 1948. He was pictured in the Rangoon press hugging his sick seventeen-year-old daughter, who had been born in a jungle hideout, hence her name Taw Taw which means "the Jungle". She had been sent to Rangoon as a child, and her father was now seeing her for the first time in years.[15]

But behind the facade of sentimental family reunions, the CPB had other plans. Among the returnees were also *yebaw* Aung Gyi, who had participated in the Calcutta youth conference in 1948, and *yebaw* Taik Aung, a hardened peasant boy from Pegu who had joined the party as a teenager. And while *yebaw* Htay was putting forth a number of fairly moderate demands in Rangoon, Thakin Ba Thein Tin—who had returned from Beijing not to participate in the talks but as an "observer"—slipped out of Rangoon and made it to the Pegu Yoma. He brought with him radio transmitters and other aid from China. During a secret meeting, some leading, trustworthy cadres were briefed about a grand plan to revive the CPB insurrection—with the help of Beijing.[16]

In Rangoon, the talks were leading nowhere. The Shans wanted to reinstate the old federal system. Kachins, led by Zau Dan, demanded an autonomous Kachin State with the right to secede from the Union. A local communist party in Arakan, led by Kyaw Zan Rhee, demanded a separate "Arakan Republic".[17]

The military, on their part, were no less intransigent. While ignoring the proposals of the minorities, they demanded that the strongest group, the CPB, should concentrate all its troops inside an area stipulated by the authorities, inform the government if there were any remaining guerrillas or cadres elsewhere, stop all organisational activities of the party, and cease fund-raising.[18]

The government's demand for outright surrender, without any real concessions, was a blessing in disguise for the CPB. No one could agree, and the talks broke down on 14 November. The various rebel groups were allowed to return to their respective jungle camps, as the government had promised. But only two of the 29 Sichuan *laopings* went back to Beijing: Thakin Ba Thein Tin and another CPB cadre. The other twenty-seven went to the Pegu Yoma. Known as "the Beijing Returnees", they assumed *de facto* leadership of the party at home—and Thakin Ba Thein Tin had already assured a safe radio link through which orders could be conveyed directly from Beijing.

Beijing, not the Pegu Yoma, from now on became the real brain centre of the CPB. Following the split within the international Communist movement at about the same time, Khin Maung Gyi, San Thu and Thein Aung returned to Beijing in November while the talks where still going on in Rangoon. Aung Win and Kyaw Zaw, the other two CPB cadres in Moscow, had married Russian women and decided to stay behind.

A "leading group of five" was established in Beijing shortly after Thakin Ba Thein Tin's return from the peace talks in Rangoon. This group, which emerged as the nucleus of the new leadership of the CPB, consisted of Thakin Ba Thein Tin as "leader"; Khin Maug Gyi as his personal secretary; Thakin Than Myaing, an old *Dohbama Asiayone* hand from Kyaukse in the central plains who had been in charge of radio propaganda for Dr. Ba Maw's puppet government during the Japanese occupation; Than Shwe, a BIA veteran from Henzada who had been trained by the Imperial Japanese Army during the war; and Tin Yee, a former student activist from Pegu who had taken part in the "1300 Movement" of 1938.

At their first meeting in Beijing following the breakdown of the peace talks, a master plan was drawn up. The CPB needed a new base area along the Chinese frontier, where supplies could be brought in easily from Yunnan. After establishing a "liberated zone" in the northeast, the CPB, with Chinese assistance, would push down from the hills to Burma proper and link up with the Beijing Returnees and the rest of the "old" CPB in the Pegu Yoma. Just as Mao Zedong's partisans had built up a "red base" in Yan'an during the Chinese civil war, the Pegu Yoma mountain range just north of Rangoon was going to become the place from which the Burmese communists would prepare for their final victory.

In December, San Thu, one of the Moscow returnees, was put in charge of a team that began surveying possible infiltration routes from Yunnan into northeastern Burma. China lent its first help by building a network of asphalted highways leading from Yunnan's provincial capital of Kunming to various points along the borders with Burma and with Laos, where another Communist movement was active.[19]

The problem was that apart from Than Shwe and Tin Yee, most of the Sichuan *laopings* were simply well-read Marxist intellectuals with little or no experience in military matters. The nucleus of a new "People's Army" had to be found—but in fact that had already been taken care of. Naw Seng and his 300 Kachin warriors had been living as ordinary citizens in Guizhou province since they had retreated to China in 1950. They were therefore known as Guizhou *laopings*, or veterans. In early 1963, even before the peace talks in Rangoon, Naw Seng was brought to Sichuan. He was introduced to Thakin Ba Thein Tin. Among the Kachin delegates was Zau Mai, who had joined Naw Seng as a seventeen-year-old during the "Upper Burma Campaign" in northeastern Shan State: "We were told that the time had come to go back to Burma and fight. It was not a difficult choice. We were eager to leave our people's commune in Guizhou. All of us left for a training camp in Yunnan, where our military skills were rehearsed."[20]

Aye Ngwe, the first Burmese Communist to reach China, was sent there to give Naw Seng's Guizhou *laopings* political lectures in Marxism-Leninism. The entire well-planned venture was the brainchild of China's powerful intelligence chief, Kang Sheng, the godfather of the Cultural Revolution that was about to break out in China.[21]

A slender, bespectacled man with a thin moustache, the chain-smoking Kang emanated the aura of a fanatical Communist for whom ideology was all that mattered: people and their lives came second, if at all. He had headed the Communist assassination corps in Shanghai as a young man and then gone to Moscow for training by the Comintern.

Following the Communist take-over in China, Kang had brought with him from Stalin's Soviet Union the personality cult, the use of terror and the invention of imaginary enemies. When Khrushchev denounced Stalin in 1956, Kang had reacted in a way similar to Thakin Soe by a vehement denunciation of the "traitor and revisionist" who had dared criticise the father of the first workers' republic.

The haphazard meetings in Calcutta in 1948 had barely produced a "conspiracy", let alone a common strategy for the Communist movements in East Asia. Kang, however, was extremely ambitious. As head of the Chinese Communist Party's International Liaison Department, it was his duty to coordinate contacts with Communist organisations in other countries. And he had a firm vision of what he wanted East Asia to be.

Arranging for the Sichuan and Guizhou *laopings* to meet was the first step in his plans for Burma. Through Kang's agents at the Chinese embassy in Rangoon, the small cells of ethnic Chinese Communists were also for the first time put in touch with the CPB. They were few in number, but embassy officials in Rangoon arranged for ethnic Chinese from the capital and from some small towns in the Irrawaddy delta to go to the Communist guerrilla zone along the Shweli river—the closest to the planned new base area along the Yunnan frontier that the CPB's influence reached at this time.[22]

Developments in Rangoon seemed to favour the Communist plan to subvert the new regime: Burma was plunged into a severe economic and political crisis in the wake of the introduction of the "Burmese Way to Socialism". Some had resisted the new line, and rifts had already become evident within the ruling Revolutionary Council in early 1963.

Aung Gyi, whom most people considered Ne Win's heir apparent, had voiced criticism of the officially announced economic policies and suggested a much more pragmatic approach. On 8 February, he was dismissed. Within a week, Ne Win announced a state take-over of production, distribution, import and export of commodities. No new private enterprises would be allowed and on 23 February all banks were nationalised.

A new Enterprises Nationalisation Act was promulgated on 26 February, according to which all major industries had to be government-run. Aung Gyi's dismissal was followed by the rise to power of Brig.-Gen. Tin Pe, an orthodox Marxist like Ba Nyein.

Prior to these moves, Rangoon had been a booming and bustling international trade centre where a number of foreign banks were represented: the Hongkong and Shanghai Bank, the Chartered Bank, Grindlay's Bank, the State Bank of India, the Habib Bank and others. Several international airlines had Rangoon as a major destination in Southeast Asia, and Mingaladon Airport was then considered one of the most modern in the region.

Before long, all this seemed to belong to a dim and distant past. The nationalisations wrecked the economy, and measures were taken to root out private funds and deprive the old elite of power. On 17 May 1964, all 50 and 100 Kyat banknotes were demonetised, basically wiping out private savings. This, and the nationalisations, forced about 200,000 Burmese of South Asian origin—many of whom had lived in Burma for generations—to emigrate to India and Pakistan.

Among them was Omar Farouk, whose family had for decades run a major Indo-Burmese enterprise in Rangoon. He arrived in Karachi in 1967, a city he had not even visited before: "It was a tragic blunder. We felt—and still feel!—as Burmese as anybody else. We had been living in Burma for at least 200 years, and although some of our forefathers came from the Subcontinent, we are basically of mixed blood. Then, one day, somebody taps you on the shoulder and says: 'Hey! You are not Burmese. When are you going back home?' So we used to reply: 'This is home!' But the ordinary Burmese were not prejudiced. They couldn't understand why we had to leave. It was all a government trick to confiscate our property. We were accused of sending money abroad, but when the currency had been demonetised, we had nothing left. We arrived in Pakistan almost broke."[23]

Aye Saung, a former student activist from Toungoo, recalls how the new economic policies affected life in his home town in central Burma:

"In 1963 all the shops were nationalised. I remember one morning some soldiers coming to the medicine shop next to our house. They came with green sign-

boards, bearing the words "People's Shop No.-" For the next few days the soldiers stayed in the shop. They seemed to be making a list of the goods. After a
week, there was nothing on the shelves, and the shop was closed down. Our
family was issued with a ration book, and for the first time we experienced
shortages. When visitors came to our house we had to report them to the headman of the quarter. People travelling to other parts of the country found themselves being stopped at checkpoints, as the government attempted to curb the
smuggling that had become rampant.[24]

The infamous "People's Shops" soon became a national joke. Initially,
they were meant to function along the efficient lines of the Defence Services Institute enterprises of the 1950s. By the time of the Caretaker Government, these had become the largest in the country and with the return of
the civilian government in 1960 were renamed the Burma Economic Development Corporation. But without private competition and with more
pseudo-Marxist ideas being introduced by Ba Nyein and others, the entire
system almost collapsed.

Distribution now became so badly organised that the few consumer
goods which were now produced in the country reached outlying areas
months after they had left the factories. Umbrellas appeared when the hot
season set in and blankets when the rains began—if anything at all was
available. But by adding the word "people" in front of the new enterprises,
and organs of state control, the military tried to give its rule an air of socialism, which they hoped would appeal to "the masses".

Beer and alcoholic drinks came from the "People's Brewery and Distill-
ery". Fashion-conscious ladies had their hair done at the "People's Pride
Hairdressing Salon". The public was supposedly protected by the "People's Police Force" and ruled by a number of "People's Councils" on different levels, while the judiciary was renamed the "Council of People's Jus-
tices". And, neatest of them all, pastries were sold by the "People's Patisse-
ries" while toothpaste came from the "People's Toilet Industry".

Burma's previously lively press was effectively brought under state control within a few years of the coup. Prior to the military take-over, Burma
had had more than thirty newspapers. Apart from the leading ones in Burmese and English, there were also five in Chinese, two in Hindi and one
each in Urdu, Tamil, Telugu and Gujarati.

The prestigious *Nation* had already been closed in May 1963, and its editor, Edward Law Yone, was arrested shortly afterwards for "hindering the
implementation of internal peace". In September, the government set up the
Loktha Pyithu Nezin to compete with the still existing private newspapers.
An English-language version, the *Working People's Daily*, soon followed. At
the same time, Thein Pe Myint's *Vanguard* was nationalised along with the
Guardian, but the latter was already being secretly financed by the military.[25]

Discontent was brewing throughout Burma; the country was ripe for revolution. While the CPB was making careful preparations in China, the various ethnic rebel armies were making significant progress all over the frontier areas. The Karen insurgents were the first to benefit from the new order in Rangoon. Following the collapse of Burma's own production of consumer goods and strangled imports in the wake of the introduction of the "Burmese Way to Socialism" after the coup, enterprising black marketeers and smugglers soon made up for the shortcomings.

Most of the contraband was brought in from Thailand—and the Karen units along the Thai border, led by Bo Mya, the local hill-tribe commander in the eastern Dawna Range, set up a series of "toll gates" through which the goods were funnelled. The first was at Phalu south of the Thai border town of Mae Sot, which was set up in 1965. This was followed a few years later by Wangkha, north of Mae Sot.

In the early days, it took three days for a mule convoy carrying contraband to reach the main highway at Tak, eighty kilometres distant in the central Thai plain. But in the late 1960s, the Australian government financed the construction of a new, metalled road that wound its way from Tak over the hills up to Mae Sot on the Moei river, which formed the border. It was all part of the so-called "Asian Highway Programme"—a pipedream which would connect Istanbul with Saigon. But hermetically sealed Burma allowed no roads to be built through its territory; the fine, Australian-financed road ended on the banks of the Moei. For the border traders, however, it was a boon.

The Karen rebels established links with Thai merchants and military authorities, whose interests were often intertwined. After a few years, at Wangkha alone, the sum of 100,000 Thai Baht was being collected by the Karen rebels per day in taxes—at the rate of 5–10% of incoming and outgoing merchandise. In other words, between one million and two million Baht was in circulation every day at Wangkha alone.[26]

Along the entire 2,100-kilometre Thai–Burmese border, dozens of similar gates were set up, by the Karen, the Mon, the Karenni and the Shan rebels. Consumer goods, textiles, machinery, spare parts for vehicles and medicine went from Thailand to Burma and teak, minerals, jade, precious stones and opium in the opposite direction.

The total value of these unofficial transactions has never been thoroughly researched, but it is fair to assume that Thailand owes much of its rapid economic growth and development to the thriving cross-border trade with Burma. The Burmese government had to turn a blind eye to these smuggling activities along the border, since no goods at all would have resulted in political and social unrest.

For the Karen rebels under Bo Mya in the eastern hills, it meant that they could use the tax they collected on the trade to buy new US-made arms and ammunition and other supplies on what is usually euphemistically referred to as "the Thai black market". The ragtag Karen guerrillas started to look almost like a regular army with smart uniforms, steel helmets and officers' insignia. Bo Mya emerged as the most important Karen field commander; the old commander in chief of the Karen forces, World War II veteran Gen. Min Maung, had died in action in 1961, so there were few rivals around.

The Karens had suffered a minor setback shortly after the peace talks in 1963 when the chairman of their rebel "government", Saw Hunter Thamwe, and the commander of the Karen's 5th Brigade, Brig. Lin Tin, had surrendered with 400 followers. Saw Hunter had disagreed with the leftist Karens in the interior, the Karen National United Party, and the rift led to his eventual surrender. Lin Tin, a warlord type, had got into trouble with the Thai authorities across the border. Karen sources allege that he had been cheated by Thai merchants, and decided to teach them a lesson. He sent a whole company of troops into Mae Sot and sacked the local police station, the town's only defence.[27]

Saw Hunter settled peacefully in Rangoon—but Lin Tin was in no mood to give up the struggle. His men stayed in a camp near Thaton, waiting to move, if ordered. Then, to the surprise of many, he married Naw Louisa Benson, a famous Karen-Jewish film star and twice crowned Miss Burma. Naw Louisa had at one stage been close to Ne Win, and it is said that Lin Tin intended to use her film actress friends to get close to the strongman and have him assassinated. News about the plot may have leaked out, for Lin Tin was gunned down by unknown assassins outside a cinema hall in Thaton in September 1965. Naw Louisa led his men back into the jungle, where they rejoined Bo Mya's forces in the hills opposite Mae Sot.[28]

In the Shan State, the government soon controlled little more than major towns and, occasionally, the roads between them. Two British film-makers, Adrian Cowell and Chris Menges, spent five months with a local resistance group in the Kengtung area, the Shan National Army (SNA). They entered Shan State from northern Thailand in October 1964, and trekked north over the hills to the Möng Yang area close to the Chinese frontier. In March 1965, they emerged in Thailand again, and reported that

> when listening to informants outside Shan State it is difficult to appreciate how completely the people of Kengtung state support the SNA. During the whole journey, we slept in 56 villages and passed through roughly 200 more, and the news of two visiting foreigners spread rapidly throughout the area. Headmen from villages in which Burmese troops were stationed (often only 30 minutes to 1 hour away) would arrive with gifts and all the people in their villages knew they were coming to see us. At no time were we betrayed.[29]

The SNA fielded about 5,000 well-armed men and controlled most of Kengtung's 32,000 square kilometres. But Cowell also noted that SNA officers in the camps along the Thai border sold opium brought from Kengtung—and bought guns smuggled from Laos to Chiang Khong on the Mekong river.

Local Thai authorities had intelligence agents attached to the units of the SNA, as they had with all other border-based rebel groups. The rebels provided the Thais with useful information about next-to-inaccessible areas along the Yunnan frontier as well as with a substantial income from the opium and gun trade. Further, many rebels from Burma, and especially from the SNA, were hired as mercenaries by the Thais and the CIA to fight Communist rebels in Laos, where a new "secret" war was being fought.

Following the French defeat at Dien Bien Phu, the US had begun to take a keener interest in the defence of Indochina. The first American ground troops had arrived in Vietnam in late 1961, where a Communist insurgency was gaining momentum. But Laos was a neutral country according to the Geneva Accords of July 1962, so no regular foreign forces were permitted to fight there. Instead, the CIA built up a "secret" army of indigenous Hmong hill tribesmen, supported by forces from Burma's frontier areas.[30]

The old Civil Air Transport, which had supplied the KMT in Möng Hsat in the early 1950s, had been succeeded by Air America, the CIA's own airline. This new company supplied the secret forces in Laos, but many of the pilots were still the same as those who had flown to Möng Hsat ten years before.[31]

The SNA was one of the offshoots of the original *Noom Suk Harn*, but it had followed a different development. Its founder, Sao Ngar Kham, alias U Gondara, had been the abbot of Yang Kham Buddhist monastery and orphanage in Kengtung. When the Shan rebellion had broken out in 1958, he had made the mistake of openly supporting the dissidents. He had been arrested and tortured, but had managed to escape into the hills, where he had first joined the Shan State Independence Army. Later, he had broken away and set up the SNA. Its main base in Thailand, Huei Nam Khun, was a small village in the hills near the frontier northwest of Chiang Rai. Less than a kilometre away, at Huei Krai, the Kuomintang ran a major caravan station, where mules laden with raw opium from Burma trotted past huge portraits of Chiang Kai-shek.[32]

Sao Ngar Kham and his deputy, a Christian Shan called Sara Ba Thein, usually dressed up in ornate parade uniforms, complete with epaulettes, service ribbons and and ceremonial swords. They ran their own administration in Kengtung and even issued their own banknotes, which were accepted as legal tender throughout the area. Following a business dispute, Sao Ngar Kham was assassinated at Huei Krai in 1964. Sara Ba Thein took over the army, and continued to smuggle opium down to Thailand—and to send mercenaries to fight in Laos.

But the SNA was far from the strongest of several Shan rebel armies. At the end of 1963, Sao Shwe Thaike's widow, Sao Nang Hearn Kham, had miraculously managed to escape from Rangoon. A senior Shan monk and a young medical student, Sai Nyan Win (later known as Hseng Harn), had accompanied the Mahadevi of Yawnghwe and three of her children, her youngest surviving son, Harn, and two daughters, Leün and Sita, via Kawkareik in Karen State to Myawadi opposite Mae Sot.

The escape had been planned by a group of sympathetic politicians in Rangoon, including some Burmans. Ne Win's Military Intelligence heard of the escape a few days after they had slipped out of Rangoon, and search teams were promptly dispatched in pursuit. But all that they could lay their hands on was an unknown woman travelling with three children near Myawadi. The real Mahadevi had already crossed the border to Thailand, where the local authorities in Tak had quickly whisked her up to Chiang Mai.

In Chiang Mai, a prominent banker and upholder of local culture, Kraisri Nimmanhaeminda, took the Mahadevi and her family under his wing. "Khun Kraisri", as he was known, was a pan-Thai-ist with a keen interest in all Tai peoples, including the Shans. He took care of the Mahadevi's immediate needs: a house, and schools for the children. The governor of Chiang Mai provided police protection and warned the Burmese consulate in the city not to interfere.[33]

The escape of the Mahadevi was something of a political coup. Intelligence operatives, Thai as well as American, immediately became involved. Wichitr Jayawann, officially editor of a local Chiang Mai newspaper, *Kon Muang News*, had been involved with the Shans from the very beginning, and he introduced the Mahadevi to several CIA people in northern Thailand: former missionaries and staff at the USIS office in Chiang Mai. It was decided to convene a meeting of all Shan factions in Chiang Mai in November. It was attended by the Mahadevi, Sao Noi of *Noom Suk Harn*, some of the SSIA students and Sao Ngar Kham and Sara Ba Thein from the SNA.[34]

No unity could be reached, however. The Kengtung representatives refused to accept the Mahadevi's leadership; republican sentiments were strong among some of the SNA commanders, and they already had in any case what they thought was comfortable backing from CIA-connected Americans in Bangkok, who were also connected with the KMT network. Quarrelling over money which had been used to pursue these American contacts was said to be one factor that eventually led to Sao Ngar Kham's assassination a year later.[35]

Li Wenhuan, the powerful KMT general who commuted between his mountain-top fortress at Tam Ngob on the border and his newly built, fortified mansion on the tree-shaded Faham Road in Chiang Mai, also tried to move towards closer relations with the Mahadevi. He offered to place all his troops under her command in exchange for a monopoly on Shan State opium. His aim was obviously to control all Shan armies through the Mahadevi, who bluntly refused the proposal.[36]

The KMT—and the CIA—subsequently lost interest in the Mahadevi, and liaison with the Thai authorities was maintained only through local officers of the Border Patrol Police (BPP), which Gen. Sarit had built up with American backing. A Thai intelligence unit, led by Pi Kob, a relative of the exiled Shan leader Sao Khunsuk, was loosely attached to the Mahadevi. As had been the case with the SSIA a few years before, the Thais viewed with apprehension the emergence of a politically conscious Shan movement: the Thais wanted a border buffer, a source of information and money—but not a political force that they might not be able to control.

While these new developments were in progress, Sarit, the old Thai strongman and the architect of Thailand's Burma border policy, died suddenly on 8 December 1963. His death caused some confusion in the Thai political scene—especially when it was revealed that he had misappropriated state funds totalling more than 600 million Baht. Sarit's total wealth was estimated at nearly three billion Baht—an astronomical sum at the time.[37]

It was soon "discovered" that the old strongman had used government funds to maintain more than a hundred mistresses and to invest in business. A fair portion of his wealth also came from the drug trade: throughout his reign, the army had maintained its own opium warehouses in Lampang in northern Thailand, where merchants and distributors stored and picked up the drug.[38]

After having defeated police general Pao Sriyanonda and his inner circle in 1957, the army had simply taken over the role previously played by Gen. Pao. But actual trade remained in the hands of wealthy ethnic Chinese businessmen; the military provided protection and often ensured the safe passage of the goods.

High-ranking officers never dirtied their own hands, but a pyramidical system had emerged, in which money passed up the chain of command to the top, "where authoritarian leaders enjoy an ostentatious life style vaguely reminiscent of the old god-kings", to quote Alfred McCoy.[39]

Sarit had been a ruthless and corrupt dictator, but his reign had also been characterised by a degree of efficiency that was not entirely frowned upon. According to Thai academic Thak Chaloemtiarana, "he was remembered as a doer and not a talker, whose firmness reduced the frequency of arson, got roads repaired, cleaned up cities, improved communications and advanced the economy". While in other countries, a corruption scandal of the magnitude that was unearthed after Sarit's death would have ruined a man's reputation, "Sarit's image has weathered criticism well. It is still possible to find people making remarks such as 'We need a person like

Sarit to make the streets safe again', or 'If only Sarit was alive, he could solve this problem'."[40]

Sarit's former underlings, Thanom Kittikachorn and Prapass Charusthiara, now took over. Thanom became prime minister and Prapass his deputy as well as commander in chief of the army and ultimately responsible for the CSOC (the Communist Suppression Operations Command; later ISOC, the Internal Security Operations Command), which, among other things, oversaw liaison with all the various buffer groups along the border with Burma.

According to Thai researcher Chai-anan Samudavanija:

> Of all senior military leaders, Prapass was the most heavily involved in financial and commercial interests . . . a strong personality and a decisive leader, Prapass was willing to use his personal wealth to achieve his political objectives.[41]

At first, it was doubted whether Thanom and Prapass would be able to provide the same decisive leadership as Sarit had done. But the Thanom-Prapass alliance benefited both men, according to Chai-anan:

> Prapass was the ultimate in a strong, decisive character; his keen perceptions of the realities of domestic political dynamics and his vast resources of authority and wealth allowed him to operate successfully within the networks of military/politicos and their factional groups. But where he was weak— reputation, relations with the palace, international contacts and expertise in dealing with representatives of foreign governments, and physical appearance—Thanom was strong.[42]

One of the first steps to ensure a solid economic power base for the new politico-military elite in Thailand was to invite back Chin Sophonpanich, the estranged founder of the Bangkok Bank. He returned on 6 January 1964 from his exile in Hong Kong, where he had spent most of the time since being forced out by Sarit five years before. To ensure a smooth relationship with the new military leaders, he offered Prapass the post of chairman of the Bangkok Bank's board of directors, which the general gladly accepted.[43]

Although the Thai financial and security establishment, for understandable reasons, maintained its firmest ties inside Burma with remnants of the KMT, the Shans were permitted to go ahead with their political plans without Gen. Li Wenhuan's participation. On 25 March 1964, representatives of several Shan rebel groups met in Chiang Mai to form the unified Shan State Army (SSA) with the Yawnghwe Mahadevi as its paramount leader.

The new army was a merger of the old SSIA, its offshoot the Shan National United Front, and the Kokang Revolutionary Force led by Jimmy Yang, the elder brother of "the opium warlady" Olive Yang. However, the Kengtung group, the SNA, refused to join—as did an SSIA splinter group in Möng Yai in the north headed by the local warlord there, Bo Dewing, who had taken part in the Tang-yan battle of 1959.

But it was a major step forward for the Shans. For the first time, they had a unified command of sorts, and their status in Thailand had been strengthened by the arrival of the Mahadevi, even if the degree of Thai sympathy and support had fallen somewhat short of Shan expectations. The armed forces were reorganised along more modern lines. Five brigades were formed.

The first was commanded by Sai Hla Aung, alias Sao Hsö Lane, the geology student who had arrived at the Thai border in 1958. His second in command was Sai Tzang, the Mahadevi's son, who had now assumed the nom de guerre Sao Hsö Wai ("the Tiger who looks over his shoulder"). Sai Hla Aung was half-Palaung, from Tawngpeng state in the north, and his brigade included two battalions of Palaung fighters. Their area of operation included most of northern Shan State: Hsenwi, Namhsan, Möng Mit, Möng Kut (the ruby mine area in the north which the Burmans called "Mogok"), and part of Hsipaw.[44]

The second brigade was led by Bo Maung, the Wa "hero of Tang-yan". It consisted of three battalions, two Wa and one Shan, and operated in the northern Wa Hills as well as in the Möng Yai area west of the Salween river.

Moh Heng, the ex-CPB, *Noom Suk Harn* veteran, commanded the third brigade with former student activist Khun Kya Nu as his deputy. This brigade was formed of the old SNUF, hence the unlikely combination. The rustic peasant warlord Moh Heng had lost his left arm in a battle with government forces near Punghpakyem in 1960, while Khun Kya Nu was a young, handsome charmer. Educated in Rangoon, he spoke better Burmese than Shan. But his cunning and knowledge of the bitter realities of Shan politics had already been recognised.

The fourth brigade was led by Bo Ngar Möng, whose 1,000 troops controlled most of the Hsipaw area. Ngar Möng was originally an itinerant herbal medicine vendor, faith healer and master tattooist who had headed a small band of brigands near Hsipaw since the late 1950s. But his military skills had been noted by the Shan students and he was promoted to brigade commander following the formation of the SSA.

The fifth brigade of the new army consisted of Jimmy Yang's Kokang forces. Jimmy had served as MP for Kokang under the U Nu government; he had founded the East Burma Bank and been a member of good standing of both the Rotary Club and the Turf Club in Rangoon. But his fortunes had turned after the military take-over in 1962, and by linking up with the

SSA, Jimmy apparently hoped to regain some of the influence he had lost. In his native Kokang, Jimmy's sister Olive had been detained in 1963 along with other ethnic leaders in the aftermath of the coup.

Olive was kept in detention together with the disgraced member of the Revolutionary Council, Brig.-Gen. Aung Gyi, and was reportedly sexually humiliated by the male prison guards because of her lesbian tendencies. Most of the fortune which she had earned from the opium trade and other businesses had been swindled away, reportedly by Wa Wa Win Shwe, a famous Burmese film actress, who had been her not-so-secret lover.[45]

In Kokang, Jimmy had led the remnants of Olive's old army into the underground in October 1963. The Rangoon government struck back by using one of Olive's old lieutenants, a young, moon-faced man with curiously friendly eyes called Lo Hsing-han. Lo had failed to distinguish himself at school, finishing his studies at the equivalent of 4th grade in the US system. "About the only activity he excelled in was the military service, which was compulsory," recalls a boyhood acquaintance quoted by Anthony Paul.[46]

By the time Lo was twenty-one he had become a wild drifter with a taste for guns and girls. This he financed by peddling in opium—his elder brother, Lo Hsing-ko, was chief inspector of police in Kokang, so there was no interference when he wanted to earn some pocket money.[47] The young Lo also attached himself to Olive's private army. "He always used to follow two or three steps behind Olive, cradling a tin of 555 cigarettes. Whenever he thought Olive would like to smoke, he'd open the tin and with a flourish give her a cigarette."[48]

Following Jimmy's mini-rebellion in Kokang, the government in Rangoon badly needed a puppet in the area, and Lo seemed to fit the bill. Rangoon was floating the idea of forming local home guard units to fight the insurgents in areas which the government's forces had difficulty in reaching. These local militias were to be called *Ka Kwe Ye* (KKY), literally "defence", and were part of a new counter-insurgency strategy that the government was about to launch.

The plan was to rally as many local warlords as possible, mostly non-political brigands and private army commanders, behind the Burma Army in exchange for the right to use all government-controlled roads and towns in Shan State for opium smuggling. By trading in opium, the Ne Win government hoped, the KKY militia would be self-supporting. Indeed, there was hardly any money in the central coffer to support a sustained counter-insurgency campaign at this stage.[49] But Rangoon was also hoping to undermine the financial basis of the rebels in Shan State who depended on opium tax to maintain their troops. In theory, the KKY plan seemed a master stroke.

The authorities had just seized a large consignment of opium from one of Lo's convoys. Lo was told: "If you form a KKY for the central government, we'll return the opium."[50] Lo readily agreed. He got his opium back and placed his troops—the majority of Olive's old Kokang force—under the command of the Burma Army garrison in Lashio. Two brothers in the Kokang army, Pheung Kya-shin and Pheung Kya-fu, disagreed, however, and retreated with a few followers across the frontier to China, where they were looked after by the local Communist security authorities.

Lo was far from the only local warlord to accept such an offer from Rangoon. At Loi Maw, a spectacular poppy mountain overlooking the west bank of the Salween river near the market town of Nawngleng, a young half-Shan, half-Chinese warlord had been active for years, trading in opium and fighting whoever came in his way. His name was Chang Chifu and he was the stepson of the *myosa*, or local tax collector, of the small town of Möng Tawm under the Möng Yai *saohpa*. His real father, a local Chinese, had died when Chang was a child. His mother, a Shan, then married the Möng Tawm *myosa*.[51]

Chang was a neglected child. While his three half-brothers went to missionary schools and were given the Christian names Oscar, Billy and Morgan, the young Chang grew up with his Chinese grandfather, who was the headman of Loi Maw. Chang never went to school, but he gained his first military experience in skirmishes with the KMT forces who had set up base at Loi Maw in the early 1950s. The enterprising young man had formed his own band—which was subsequently converted into the Loi May KKY, a government militia. Chang was later to assume the Shan name "Khun Sa" and become the best-known warlord the Golden Triangle has ever produced.

Other KKY commanders included Bo Lai Oo, an ethnic Wa. He had initially joined Bo Maung's insurgents, who fought alongside the Shans. But Bo Lai Oo had surrendered in 1966 to become a KKY commander in the garrison town of Tang-yan—which his former commander had captured in 1959. There was also Win Tin, alias Wu Chung-tin, a Chinese warlord with KMT connections who was based at Loi Sae, a poppy mountain south of Tang-yan, and various Wa commanders from the eastern hills. These warlords, who were supposed to fight the insurgents, built up their own private armies and purchased with opium money all the military equipment available on the black market in Thailand and Laos, including M-16 and Browning automatic rifles, M-70 grenade launchers and 57mm recoilless rifles.[52]

The KMT invasion, the government's attempts to dislodge the intruders, and the Shan rebellion that followed were all factors that had contributed to the devastation of the Shan countryside. The traditional, rice-based economy had been severely damaged. Farmers had to become porters for the government troops during their offensives against the insurgents. Many of them left their paddy fields and took to the hills, where the opium poppy was the only viable cash crop. This trend was reinforced by the steady rise in demand for the drug. As a Shan analyst explained, the economic policies of the new military government also contributed to a rapid increase in opium production during the 1960s:

> The fast rolling opium bandwagon was further oiled by the introduction of the Burmese Way to Socialism following General Ne Win's coup in 1961. All businesses and banks . . . were nationalised. . . . In such an economic vacuum there arose a black market economy which for opium traffickers was a boon . . . Opium was bought by them at very low prices from ragged cultivators, transported in armed caravans to the border and refined into heroin. And on the return trip to get more opium, Thai goods and commodities were taken back and sold in Shan State. . . . Rather than creating socialism, the Burmese Way to Socialism delivered the economy into the hands of the opium traffickers. As such, opium became the only viable crop and medium of exchange. Thus, cultivation of opium, limited to the east of the Salween prior to 1963, not only spread all over Shan State, but to Kachin, Karenni and Chin states as well.[53]

There was certainly no shortage of rebels to fight for the KKY, if they so wished. The Kachin Independence Army of Zau Seng, the bow-legged World War II veteran and ex-intelligence officer of OSS Detachment 101, was in almost full control of Kachin State, and the Kachin-inhabited areas of northeastern Shan State. There, he clashed with the SSA in what could be seen as a continuation of the historical rivalry between the advancing Kachins, and the Shans trying to defend their rich ricelands from the fierce tribesmen from the north. Burma's civil war was by no means a clear-cut battle between government forces and the rebels: the insurgents clashed frequently with each other, and sometimes even with units from the same group.

The KIA had expanded rapidly since the coup of 1962. The following year, a number of well-known Kachin personalities joined the army. Among them were Brang Seng, the headmaster of the Baptist High School in Myitkyina, and two former government officials, Malizup Zau Mai from Sinlumkaba and Zawng Hra from Sumprabum.

But to break the land-locked isolation in the north, Zau Seng needed foreign contacts and secure supply lines from neighbouring countries. The first attempt was made in 1964, when Zau Seng and a few other officers set off along elephant trails through uninhabited territory and over the mountains to India. They crossed the border near the Chaukan Pass and reached Vijaynagar, a small garrison town in the nose-shaped piece of Indian territory that juts into Burma southwest of Putao.

"We were quite well received," remembers N'Chyaw Tang, another World War II veteran who accompanied Zau Seng to the Indian border.[54]

"An Indian military intelligence officer, Major Sinha, promised us aid and signals training."

N'Chyaw Tang was posted as liaison officer at Chaukan Pass "with proper credentials: a section of troops, two bolt-action British .303 Lee-Enfield rifles, two shotguns, a transistor radio and a pistol." He erected a log cabin in the high mountains, which were covered by snow and ice in winter. But nothing came out of the mission: on 14 October 1964, N'Chyaw Tang sat by the oven in his log cabin, and sadly drafted a letter to his headquarters, recommending that the KIA give up the attempts to get aid from India.

Zau Seng already had other plans. He had set off for the Thai border, where through his old intelligence connections he had managed to establish a good working relationship with KMT general Li Wenhuan. In 1965, the Kachins were allowed to set up a base near Gen. Li's mountaintop base at Tam Ngob. Soon, hundreds of Kachin troops were given military drills by Nationalist Chinese officers and were trained in the use of modern radio equipment.

Jade and opium from Kachin State were carried by KIA troops to Tam Ngob, where they were used in bartering for guns, ammunition, medicine and other necessities.[55] Kachin State was the world's only source of top quality jadeite. For centuries, the jade had gone across the border to China, but the Communist revolution in 1949 had brought that trade to a standstill. Now, a new route was opened: down to northern Thailand, and on to Hong Kong, which emerged as the world's leading jade centre.[56]

The KMT connection also resulted in the formation of a Kachin chapter of the World Anti-Communist League (WACL), an obscure organisation that tried to organise various groups that could be used in encircling China. The idea of an alliance of such rightist groups had been mentioned by Gen. Li Mi and Prof. Ting when ethnic minority leaders had visited the KMT base at Möng Hsat in the early 1950s.

With assistance from the intelligence services of Taiwan and South Korea, the Asian Peoples' Anti-Communist League (APACL) had been formed in 1954 to unite "conservatives from all over the continent to battle the 'Red hordes' that threatened them all."[57] The APACL and some like-minded groups merged in 1966 to form the WACL. Zau Seng, carrying his Kachin flag with a red and green field with two superimposed *dahs*, or swords, attended several APACL and WACL meetings in Saigon and Manila.

The chaos that ensued in the frontier areas following the 1962 coup d'etat had contributed greatly to the KMT's recovery from the PLA's devastating "Mekong River Operation" of 1961. The Thai government extended no official recognition to the KMT along the northern border, but they could come and go as they pleased, and Gen. Li was allowed to build an impressive residence in Chiang Mai. Their main contact with the Thai authorities was Prapass, who reportedly encouraged the KMT to increase the volume of opium they brought down to the Thai border to finance their activities. This benefited the Thai authorities as well, as it infused millions of dollars into the local economy.[58]

Li's 3rd KMT army at Tam Ngob was the best-organised drug trafficking group in the region. The other main unit, the 5th KMT under Duan Xiwen was based at Mae Salong in the hills northwest of Chiang Rai, but most of its troops were active along the Mekong river in Laos, guided by the CIA and assigned to collect intelligence from across the border in Yunnan. As the Vietnam War was escalating, it was becoming of utmost importance to find out about, and, if possible, to disrupt, the flow of Chinese weapons and other supplies to North Vietnam.

Apart from Gen. Duan's troops, there was also a little-known elite unit which was called by its French name "Bataillon Spécial 111". Commanded by the highly competent Li Teng, it was manned mainly by ex-POWs from the Korean War. The Allied forces had captured more than 20,000 Chinese PLA troops from the human waves of young conscripts which the Communists had sent down across the 38th parallel.

More than two-thirds of the Chinese POWs were violently opposed to the idea of returning to their Communist homeland, and after careful vetting by Taiwanese intelligence agents, a fair number of them were resettled on the Nationalist Chinese island. The most trustworthy were given special training and had slogans like "Death to Communism!" tattooed on their arms to prevent defection. They were sent to the Chinese frontier in northern Laos, where they remained for years as the most secretive of all the mercenary groups that were deployed there during the so-called "Secret War".[59]

The most important KMT contingent in northeastern Burma was the 1st Independent Unit, led by a Yunnan-born Chinese, Ma Ching-ko. Directly controlled by the Intelligence Mainland Operation Bureau of the Ministry of Defence in Taipei, Ma built up an impressive espionage network along the Yunnan frontier. From a string of eight bases in the Thai–Lao–Burma–China quadrangle, Ma's 1,500 specially trained KMT troops used an even wider web of informants in towns and villages on all sides of the borders in the area to collect vital intelligence for both Taipei and Washington.[60]

Modern radio equipment was installed in Vingngün and other remote, mountainous areas adjacent to China, and at the base of KKY commander Win Tin (alias Wu Chung-tin) at Loi Sae south of Tang-yan. The green, fertile valley of Möng Wa in eastern Shan State, close to the Mekong river, served as a third major staging point.

The Vingngün base, however, was perhaps the most important because of its proximity to an area of Yunnan where even the central Chinese government exercised little control. The base was led by Col. Sao Tuen-sung, a high-ranking intelligence operative. His three main assistants were three enterprising brothers who had fled Yunnan shortly after the Communist take-over in 1949: Wei Hsueh-long, Wei Hsueh-kang and Wei Hsueh-yin. Popularly known as "the Wei Brothers", they were engaged in both espionage and opium trading.[61]

Ma reported directly to the CIA base at Nam Yu in northwestern Laos, passing on vital intelligence on the movement of Chinese supplies to Hanoi and to the Pathet Lao guerrillas in Laos. He was also able to verify in the field information from aerial photography and satellite images. Observed French researcher Catherine Lamour: "Ma Ching-ko had built up the grandest infiltration operation of secret agents that ever took place in any country after World War II."[62]

The co-existence of drug trafficking networks and espionage rings with US connections has led many authors and journalists to jump to the conclusion that drug money was used to finance covert operations, and that the CIA was somehow behind the traffic. People with years in the field deny such allegations. US covert operations, they say, were financed by secret funds from Washington. Drug money provided extra income, or "pocket money", for some of the people who were involved in these operations. In the case of the KMT, drug money was also undoubtedly used to buy equipment and rations, and to pay soldiers. In a surprisingly candid interview with a British newspaper in 1967, Gen. Duan of the 5th KMT declaimed: "We have to continue to fight the evil of communism and to fight you must have an army, and an army must have guns, and to buy guns you must have money. In these mountains the only money is opium."[63]

In this truly entangled imbroglio, it soon became impossible to say where drug running ended, and insurgency, counter-insurgency and espionage began. By the late 1960s, the components of the emerging opium hierarchy could be described in this way:

The farmers who grew the poppies earned a pittance for months of laborious work. They were mostly hill tribes, such as Kachin, Lahu, Wa, Lisu, Palaung and Akha, but there were also poor, ethnic Chinese peasants from Kokang and other areas in the hills east of Kutkai and Hsenwi in northeastern Shan State. Despite living at subsistence level, they had to pay "taxes" to various rebel groups claiming their areas, and bribes to various government officials who were supposed to enforce the law. By this time, an estimated 40% of all poppy fields in Shan State were located in Kokang and Hsenwi states, 15% in the Wa Hills, nearly 15% in Möng Yai state, 10% in Kengtung, and the remaining 20% in Möng Pan, Möng Hsu, Möng Nawng, Möng Nai, and Hsi-Hseng in south and central Shan State.[64]

The rebels who operated in the poppy growing areas collected tax from the farmers. The distribution of poppy fields in Shan State explains why some of the groups were more dependent on opium than others. Jimmy

Yang soon drifted away from the SSA and allied himself with Gen. Li's 3rd KMT, which enabled him to continue the trade from his native Kokang. The SNA controlled the opium-rich hills north of Kengtung and conducted their own convoys both to the Thai border and across the Mekong to Laos.

The most politically motivated of the groups, the SSA, was on the other hand never involved to any appreciable extent in the opium business. No more than 1,000 *viss* , or a little over 1.5 tons, was grown in the SSA area south of the Hsenwi-Lashio road and north of Kehsi Mansam. This harvest was less than 0.2% of all the opium produced in Shan State at that time. The SSA nevertheless levied a 10% opium tax on the growers, another 10% on the buyers, and an additional tax for traders and caravans passing through their territory.[65] Opium tax paid for the rebels' arms purchases in Thailand and Laos.

The merchants who bought the opium from the farmers and paid tax to the rebels were—and still are—respectable, local businessmen who live quite openly in government-controlled market towns. They sent their agents to the hills to purchase opium, and then used various armed bands to transport the drugs to the refineries along the Thai border or in Laos. The front for a middle-man operation like this could be an ordinary trading house, doubling as a wholesaler of potatoes, pork or consumer goods.

The KKY units were often hired by the merchants to convoy the drugs. Many KKY commanders were also merchants themselves. If Lo Hsing-han or Khun Sa, for instance, conducted a convoy down to the Thai border, they would be carrying their own opium as well as drugs belonging to other merchants, most of whom did not have their own private armies. A fair number of them were Panthay Muslims, who remained quietly in the background despite all the turmoil, trading in opium through proxies.

The KKY commanders usually carried their opium to the market town of Tachilek, near the border junction of Burma, Laos and Thailand. There, the opium was exchanged for bars of pure gold, hence the area's nickname, the "Golden Triangle". Opium money was also used to finance the purchase of the consumer goods which they brought back as return cargo in their lorries and mule trains.

The Burmese government was supposed to enforce the law, which officially prohibited drug trafficking. But lacking the power and the political will to do so, government officials were usually content with receiving "tea money" from private merchants and various KKY commanders. Some of the return cargo brought back by the KKY, especially fancy furniture, was given to civilian officials as well as military officers to lessen their possible irritation with the trade.[66]

Government troops sometimes provided security for the KKY's convoys. They also often cooperated with the KKY in the battlefield, which was the actual purpose of the programme. The Burma Army garrison town of

Tang-yan, strategically located between Loi Maw, Loi Sao, Loi Tao and other, main opium growing areas in northern Shan State, developed into the most important centre for the trade.

The KMT acted as a buffer and unofficial "border police force" for Thailand, and it collected intelligence for Taiwan, the US and Thailand—in that order. In return, the Thai authorities turned a blind eye to the KMT's smuggling activities along the border.[67]

Intelligence agencies from various countries maintained liaison with the KKY, the KMT and some of the Shan rebel groups, either as pure money-making operations, or because many of the drug traders proved to be valuable intelligence assets. For historical reasons, Taiwan agents were especially active, working together with not only the remnants of the KMT but also some of the KKY forces. Since some of these were led by ethnic Chinese from Burma, a relationship was not difficult to establish. Lo Hsing-han of the Kokang KKY was closely connected with Taiwanese intelligence.[68]

Taiwan's links with Khun Sa's Loi Maw KKY were maintained through Chang Shu-chuan, alias Sao Hpalang, a former KMT officer of Manchurian origin who had come to Shan State from Laos in the 1960s. The CIA used as many of the KMT's contacts as possible as their own intelligence assets, and recruited mercenaries to fight their "Secret War" in Laos.

International narcotics syndicates inevitably became involved by supplying chemists to the heroin refineries along the Thai–Burmese border, and by taking care of regional and international distribution of the drugs. The syndicates operated independently, but since most of them were dominated by ethnic Chinese often connected with the so-called Secret Societies, or Triads, in Taiwan, Hong Kong and Macau, links with the KMT and some of the KKY forces were easily established.

These crime gangs remain one of the main obstacles to a solution to the conflict in Shan State since it is in their interest to perpetuate the state of anarchy that makes the drug trade possible. Given the vast amounts of money they possess, their power and influence—as well as their ability to manipulate local rebel leaders, government officials and drug enforcement agencies—are considerable.

Perhaps significantly, international law enforcement agencies seldom turn in their direction, but tend to concentrate their efforts on the armed bands inside Shan State, as if they had contacts in Hong Kong, New York and Amsterdam.

The couriers were perhaps the most visible links in the narcotics chain since they were often caught and exposed by the media. A courier could be anyone who was hired by the syndicates to carry drugs from one place to another. The couriers were often conveniently—but incorrectly—referred to by the media as well as law enforcement agencies as "drug traffickers"—

perhaps to deflect attention from the syndicates, which seemed to be above the law.

The addicts, the consumers of the drugs, and their families were without doubt the most pitiful victims of the opium business next to the impoverished farmers who grew the poppies. Although most of the narcotics from the Golden Triangle were destined for foreign markets, it is often forgotten that drug abuse was—and still is—widespread in tribal villages in the Golden Triangle, causing enormous social problems locally. In the 1960s, in some opium growing villages in the Golden Triangle, the addiction rate was already as high as 70–80% of all male inhabitants.[69]

In China, the master-strategist Kang Sheng was soon to launch a strike into this cockpit of anarchy. Preparations were underway for a Chinese-sponsored CPB attack on northeastern Shan State. In a wider perspective, Kang Sheng was aiming at spreading Communist revolution as far south as Australia. One of Thakin Ba Thein Tin's closest associates in Beijing was a Queen's Counsel and leading Communist from Australia, Edward F. Hill. A former secretary of the committee for Victoria, he had left the main party in 1964 to set up the Communist Party of Australia (Marxist-Leninist), and then been assigned by Kang Sheng to watch other Maoist parties in the region and to encourage them to draft anti-Soviet polemics.[70] Thakin Ba Thein Tin remembers: "Ted Hill and I were together in Beijing. We wrote appeals against Soviet revisionism and for world revolution. He was a fine, cultured kind of man."[71]

Australia had not been entirely wrong in viewing military cooperation with Burma as being of utmost importance for its own security. The connection which Ted Serong had so successfully built up in the 1950s had come to a halt after the 1962 military take-over. His presence in Burma had been of some concern to the Chinese, who had pressed for his removal. He had finally left in April 1962. According to Australian scholar Andrew Selth: "Despite the impact he made in Burma at the time, Serong felt that much of his later work was in fact undone by General Ne Win who, in the wake of his successful coup, reorganised the entire defence force structure to consolidate his domestic political position."[72]

Kang Sheng might have grossly overestimated the importance of Hill's tiny Australian party—but Burma was an entirely different story. There was indeed fertile ground for a Communist take-over. Following the split between Moscow and Beijing, Burma fell within the China's sphere of influence. Both Communist superpowers supported North Vietnam against the Americans, but Beijing could for historical reasons not count on Hanoi being an ally for much longer than the war lasted.

Most probably, Vietnam would then lean towards the Soviet Union to counter-balance the influence from its centuries-old foe, China. But there was no such competition in Burma, where the Soviets had only a few, inconsequential admirers like Ba Tin the sputnik man. It was all Kang Sheng's. If Burma could be won, China's influence would extend down to the Malayan Peninsula. Singapore, Indonesia and even Australia would be within reach. Or, at least, that was what Kang Sheng thought.[73]

First, however, the CPB "at home" had to be shaped up. As a direct outcome of Thakin Ba Thein Tin's clandestine visit to the Pegu Yoma in 1963, his old comrade Thakin Pe Tint, a prominent Central Committee member, had secretly left the mountain range north of Rangoon and managed to reach China to cement ties between the exiles in Sichuan and Beijing, and the units in the Pegu Yoma and elsewhere in Burma. Together with Khin Maung Gyi, he was flown to Tirana in 1967 to attend the 5th Congress of the Albanian Party of Labour. They were received by Enver Hoxha and other Albanian leaders, and returned to Beijing impressed by the firm commitment to "pure" Marxism-Leninism which they had seen.[74]

The Beijing-based CPB declared: "The CPB is struggling against revisionism or right-wing opportunism as the main danger in the international Communist movement inside our party."[75] Internationally, the CPB stance was reflected in the fierce attacks on the "Khrushchev revisionists"; at home by bloody purges in the Pegu Yoma. The Beijing returnees, inspired by the Cultural Revolution that had broken out in China and assigned the task of cleansing the party in preparation for the momentous events that were being planned in Beijing, staged grisly mass trials in the Pegu Yoma. They enlisted the support of militant young *tat ni lunge*, or "Red Guards," many of whom were orphans raised by the party and led to regard it as their "parent", and hence were immensely loyal to their new masters.

The first victims were *yebaw* Htay, who had headed the CPB's delegation to the 1963 peace talks, and the veteran H.N. Ghoshal, one of the founders of the party. On 18 June 1967, the party leadership led them out onto an open field in the headquarters area in the Pegu Yoma. Htay and Ghoshal were both tied up with coarse ropes amidst the cheers of dozens of screaming *tat ni lunge*.

Regular CPB soldiers dressed in *longyis* and armed with semi-automatic rifles were positioned at regular intervals, while a high-ranking party cadre read out the sentence: death for treason and betrayal of the proletarian cause. Htay was branded "Burma's Deng Xiaoping", while Ghoshal was denounced as "Burma's Liu Shaoqi". Party chairman Thakin Than Tun announced to the young militants that they should be ready to execute the order. Among them was Htay's own son, Po Tu.

The *tat ni lunge*, young boys and girls in their teens, started beating the two prisoners with clubs until blood began streaming down their faces. Po Tu shouted at his father, who was lying on the ground: "I'll kill this traitor!". Ghoshal was especially humiliated because of his Indian origin. When they were led to the graves that had already been dug for them in the jungle, Ghoshal began singing the Internationale. Htay shouted:"Long live the Communist Party of Burma!" The youngsters stabbed them repeatedly with rusty knives. Both party veterans died a slow, painful death.[76]

Many of the intellectuals who had joined the CPB in the wake of the 1962 coup were purged and killed in a similar manner as well. This policy, officially referred to by the grim staccato *pyouk-touk-htak*, has been translated into English as "the Three Ds", namely "Dismissed from office; Dispelled from the party; and Disposed of (i.e. executed)."

Dozens of young and old Communists were brutally slaughtered by their own comrades. One of the most hardline of the Beijing Returnees was Taik Aung, whom many people considered a ruthless fanatic. Among the exiles in China, the old *Dohbama* veteran Thakin Than Myaing was also purged in a similar campaign and sent to a Chinese labour camp.[77]

Elsewhere in Burma, the situation seemed to favour the CPB. In 1967, there were acute shortages of rice and basic foodstuffs in Rangoon. At the same time, the Chinese community in the capital had also been influenced by the Cultural Revolution, and many young Sino-Burmese began wearing red Mao badges. This violated an official Burmese regulation, so the young "Red Guards" in Rangoon were ordered to take off their badges. When some of them refused, anti-Chinese riots broke out in June and July.

Chinese shops and homes were ransacked and looted, and many Sino-Burmese were killed. The authorities did not intervene until the mobs stormed the Chinese embassy in Rangoon: the riots were clearly orchestrated by the authorities to deflect attention from the food crisis, but the mob violence had got out of hand.[78]

The Chinese responded by branding the Ne Win government as "contra-revolutionary, fascist and reactionary" over Radio Beijing.[79] Secretly, many Sino-Burmese from Rangoon and elsewhere were helped by the Chinese embassy to reach the CPB's base area along the Shweli river in the north, to join some of their comrades who had fled some years before.

A few months later, Radio Beijing began accusing the Burma Army of "border violations", saying that Burmese forces had intruded into Yunnan and that Burmese aircraft had violated Chinese airspace. Foreign observers in Rangoon were somewhat disconcerted, but no one was able to predict what it all would amount to. Finding excuses for a Chinese invasion of Burma? That seemed highly unlikely . . . .

As part of the preparations for the CPB's thrust into northeastern Burma, some minority armies were also encouraged to join in the fight, even though they were not necessarily Communists. On 27 January 1967, a group of 132 Naga rebels from India reached Pangwa Pass on the Yunnan frontier after an arduous, three-month trek through northern Sagaing Division and Kachin State.

The Nagas were a small tribal group in northeastern India who had been up in arms against New Delhi since the early 1950s. Initially supported by Pakistan, they had been introduced to a Chinese agent in Karachi as early as 1962. He had recommended that they to go to China and ask for assistance, despite the fact that nearly all Nagas were ardent Baptist Christians.[80]

The group was led by Thuingaleng Muivah, a well-educated Naga intellectual of the Tangkhul tribe from Manipur. He was escorted to Kunming, where heavy gunfire was to be heard at night. The Cultural Revolution was raging across China, and the Yunnanese capital was a virtual battleground where Red Guards and "counter-revolutionaries" fought it out against each other after sunset. Even the panes in the windows of their guest house were shattered. After spending the night there, Muivah and his military officer, Gen. Thinoselie M. Keyho, were flown to Beijing, where red carpet treatment awaited the two guests from India. They were met at the airport by deputy foreign minister Han Nienlong.

According to Muivah: "We arrived during the heat of the Cultural Revolution. The morale of the Chinese was high and they were very hospitable. They sincerely supported all revolutionary groups and liberation movements, including ours. We were taken to see the old base at Yan'an, to Shanghai, Nanking, Canton and other important places."[81]

Their soldiers received military and political training in Tengchong in western Yunnan, where they remained for a year. The Nagas, the Chinese reasoned, could prove useful for many purposes: to irritate Beijing's archenemy India, but also to fight against Rangoon. There were hundreds of thousands of Nagas on both sides of the border. Muivah and Thinoselie met Zhou Enlai and Kang Sheng himself—who requested that they accept the leadership of the CPB.

Perhaps inspired by the Nagas, the Kachins—who had escorted and guided Muivah's group across Kachin State—also decided to contact the Chinese. The decision was taken at a meeting in May 1967, and the anti-Chinese riots in June and July encouraged the Kachins to believe that China would be willing to support them. In September, a group led by Brang Seng, the former headmaster of Myitkyina's Baptist High School, crossed the border at Pangwa. They were taken to Beijing and Shanghai, and the Chinese promised that aid would be forthcoming.[82]

A second delegation left in November. They were treated to a banquet in Beijing, hosted by Zhou Enlai and, almost inevitably, Kang Sheng. During the course of the lavish dinner party, the Kachins were introduced to both Thakin Ba Thein Tin and Naw Seng. A military alliance was agreed upon.[83] Warehouses for Chinese weapons destined for the KIA were already being built at the foot of the high mountain passes along the Kachin–Yunnan frontier.

In the Pegu Yoma, the Beijing returnees continued their purges to the last minute: they had been informed that a major event was going to take place "at about New Year's".[84] On 26 December, Bo Yan Aung, one of the Thirty Comrades who had accompanied Aung San to Amoy in 1940, was executed. He was suffering from pneumonia, but the party did not want him to die without an appropriate punishment. The *tat ni lunge* threw him to the ground and spat on the old hero. They screamed that he had been trained by "Japanese fascists"—and a teenage girl began stamping her feet on his throat while her equally young comrades beat him to death with bamboo clubs.

Bo Yan Aung's "crime" was that he had refused to condemn his old comrades, *yebaw* Htay and Ghoshal.[85] The CPB experienced an extremely bloody year before their master plan was put into action.

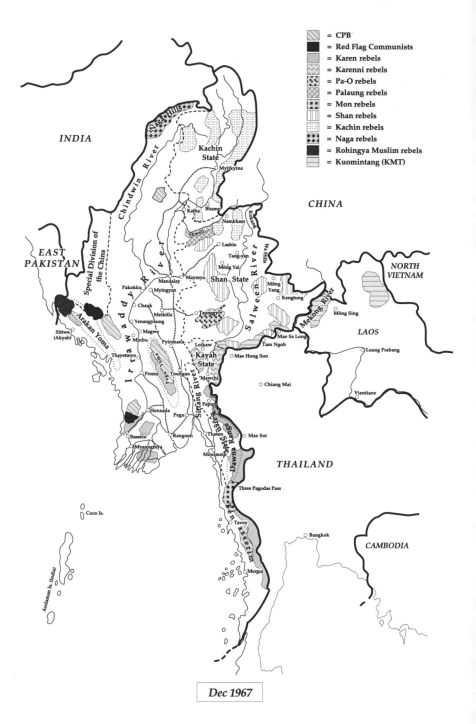

	= CPB
	= Red Flag Communists
	= Karen rebels
	= Karenni rebels
	= Pa-O rebels
	= Palaung rebels
	= Mon rebels
	= Shan rebels
	= Kachin rebels
	= Naga rebels
	= Rohingya Muslim rebels
	= Kuomintang (KMT)

INDIA

EAST PAKISTAN

CHINA

NORTH VIETNAM

LAOS

THAILAND

CAMBODIA

Naga Hills

Kachin State

Myitkyina

Katha   Bhamo

Namkham

Shweli

Lashio

Tang-yan

Mong Yai

Shan State

Mong Yang

Kengtung

Mong Sing

Luang Prabang

Vientiane

Chiang Mai

Mae Hong Son

Mae Sa Long

Tam Ngob

Loikaw

Kayah State

Mawchi

Papun

Pegu

Three Pagodas Pass

Mae Sot

Thaton

Moulmein

Tavoy

Bangkok

Mergui

Coco Is.

Andaman Is. (India)

Special Division of the Chins

Chindwin River

Irrawaddy River

Arakan Yoma

Sittwe (Akyab)

Thayetmyo

Minbu

Prome

Toungoo

Pyinmana

Meiktila

Yenangyaung

Magwe

Chauk

Myingyan

Mandalay

Pakokku

Maymyo

Taunggyi

Henzada

Bassein

Myaungmya

Rangoon

Pegu Yoma

Sittang River

Salween River

Wa Hills

Kodaung

Karen State

Dawna Range

Tenasserim

Mekong River

Dec 1967

7

The Communist Juggernaut

In the early hours of 1 January 1968, New Year's celebrations were still going on in the market village of Möng Ko on the Sino–Burmese border in northeastern Shan State. Most of the local villagers were Kachins, but they lived side by side with sizeable communities of Shans and Palaungs. Merchants—mostly of Chinese extraction but also a few Indians—were keeping their stores and teashops open. Music and songs in different languages and dialects filled the crisp, chilly winter night. Here and there groups of men sat playing cards and drinking clear, potent rice liquor.

At 4 A.M. there was a sudden burst of rapid automatic rifle-fire near the local garrison. People ducked for cover under the tables in the liquor shops. Those who were asleep in their homes leapt to their feet in astonishment. "It's Naw Seng coming back!" one villager exclaimed, remembering the World War II hero and Kachin nationalist, who had retreated into China from the very same place eighteen years earlier. "No! It's a Chinese invasion!" shouted another excited villager.[1]

Neither of the perplexed villagers was entirely wrong. Three hundred CPB troops had set out shortly after midnight from Man Hai, a small Chinese village just north of the stream that divides the Möng Ko valley into Burmese and Chinese sectors. They had forded the shallow waters early in the morning, undetected under cover of darkness.

Möng Ko was defended by only a platoon of thirty-seven government soldiers—no match for the far superior, heavily armed Communist force. CPB gunners bombarded the tiny garrison with Chinese-made bazookas and machine-gun fire. The garrison was overrun in thirty minutes and its commander lay dead. At 5:20 A.M., the local people were summoned to a public meeting in the centre of the village—and there was indeed Naw Seng, rifle in hand. But he had not come back to fight for a "Pawngyawng Republic" this time: he was the military commander of the CPB unit that had crossed the border at night.

The villagers gaped at the heavily armed and well-equipped troops which were milling around in the village. Naw Seng was a local hero, and the people greeted him as such, caring little about the ultimate aim of his operation.

His political commissar, Moscow-educated Khin Maung Gyi, had given "political guidance" to the operation, and he certainly had no sympathy for the separatist aspirations of some of the ethnic minorities in northeastern Burma. He kept well in the background as Naw Seng went around, shaking hands with old friends and telling them that the time had come to rise up against the government in Rangoon.

Rice, salt, condensed milk and other goods, which had been captured from the Burma Army outpost that morning, were distributed to the villagers. It was still dark, and people groped around, flashing torches into the military's godowns. What had been the nightmare-scenario of Burma's security planners since the outbreak of the insurgency in the late 1940s had now materialised: the CPB, with Chinese backing, had established a foothold on the Sino–Burmese border.[2]

Four days after the attack on Möng Ko, a second Communist column, led by the Pheung brothers, crossed the frontier from Yunnan and entered Kokang in the northeasternmost corner of Shan State. The Pheungs' training in China had been completed, but most of their troops were "volunteers" from China: Red Guards of the Cultural Revolution that was raging there at the time. Although Naw Seng's force was made up mostly of his old followers of Guizhuo *laopings*, Chinese Red Guards and instructors from the regular People's Liberation Army had been included in his unit as well.

Lo Hsing-han's local *Ka Kwe Ye* home guard unit put up stiff resistance, but his men were defeated as the CPB's forces advanced over the rugged mountains of Kokang, effectively and ruthlessly eliminating all obstacles in their way. Bridges were blown, roads were mined and the poorly armed troops at the few government garrisons in the area fled in disarray.

In February, a third Communist column entered Burma from the Chinese side. This time the targets were the flat, fertile ricelands of Khun Hai and Man Hio, two Shan-inhabited enclaves of Burmese territory located north of the Shweli river, opposite Namkham. Even here, local chieftains and warlords had been contacted before the CPB decided to strike. Since the area was dominated by ethnic Shans, the Shan State Army (SSA) had been operating there for several years. But the local unit, led by Sara Mong and Kang Yoi, hardly ever listened to the SSA high command in the Hsipaw area—or, for that matter, to the Yawnghwe Mahadevi in Thailand. The two warlords readily accepted CPB offers of arms and ammunition. Ohn Kyi, a Sichuan *laoping* who had been a dedicated Marxist-Leninist since his teens, became their political commissar.[3]

The following month, the CPB pushed east from Möng Ko and captured Phong Hseng (Paunghsaing in Burmese), another large market village on the Chinese frontier. Fighting was spreading quickly right across the Sino–

Burmese border areas north, east and northeast of Kutkai. By May, Kokang's township centre at Lao Khai had fallen to the CPB. All remaining government forces from Kokang retreated and regrouped at Kunlong, where the road from Hsenwi to the Chinese frontier crosses the Salween river.

The central authorities were taken aback by the sudden surge of violence, and although many local units had tried to resist the CPB avalanche with discipline and determination, no large numbers of reinforcements could be sent up to the new war front in the northeast for several months. When a substantial attacking force was at last dispatched from the garrisons at Kutkai, Hsenwi and Lashio in late July, it was ambushed by heavily armed Communist soldiers.

The bridges along the Burma Road—the old World War II supply line to China—were blown. Rangoon's columns were stuck, unable to either retreat or advance. On 22 July, an entire company of government troops was wiped out by a far superior Communist force at Tao Long on the Burma Road south of Möng Yu. The CPB captured all their weapons, and set the trucks ablaze before they retreated into the hills, carrying the booty with them.[4]

The last government forces withdrew from Khun Hai and Man Hio in August, by which time nearly all of Kokang was also firmly in the hands of the CPB. The CPB was now in control of a 3,000-square-kilometre area, encompassing Khun Hai, Man Hio, Kokang, the Möng Ko area, and and the hills surrounding Phong Hseng. The roads from Lashio to Kutkai, Namhpakka, Namkham and Kyuhkok-Panghsai had become insecure, and only heavily guarded truck convoys could make the journey north, towards the Chinese frontier.

The plan, which had been mapped out in Beijing and Sichuan years before, was now being put into action; the anti-Chinese riots in Rangoon in June 1967 had provided the Chinese with a convenient excuse to openly support an all-out CPB offensive in northern Burma. An entirely new era in Burmese insurgency had been ushered in.

The new CPB columns which entered northeastern Shan State in early 1968 were better trained, better organised and certainly much better equipped than any of the old units that were still holding out in central Burma—with which the new northeastern forces hoped to link up. To achieve this goal, a firmly controlled base area had to be established in northeastern Burma, where supplies from across the frontier could be sent in without much difficulty. The immediate plan was to divide the new battle front into a number of "War Zones", which eventually would be brought under CPB control:

303: The Möng Ko region west of the Salween river. This was the CPB's first new base area in the northeast.

404: Kokang, which was occupied by the end of 1968.

202: The old guerrilla zone along the southern bank of the Shweli river, southwest of Namkham. If reinforced and resupplied from China, this strategically important area would provide the CPB with a springboard to penetrate the Mandalay area and Burma proper. Kyi Pyang, a CPB veteran and a native of Monywa, was sent down to organise and rebuild the scattered units at Möng Wei near the Shweli into "War Zone 202".

101: Kachin State. According to the agreement which Thakin Ba Thein Tin and representatives of the Kachin Independence Army had reached in Beijing in November 1967, the Kachin rebels had been promised arms and ammunition if they joined forces with the CPB. This was going to be "War Zone 101".

But during Naw Seng's exile in Guizhuo, the KIA had been formed, and established strongholds in the Möng Ko region. The CPB assault on Möng Ko—which took place while the KIA leaders were still in China—was seen by the Kachin rebels as a betrayal of the military alliance which the two groups were supposed to have forged. Fierce fighting broke out between the CPB and the KIA near Möng Ko within weeks of Naw Seng's dramatic return to Burma. To his chagrin, he found himself fighting his own people.

In Kachin State proper, however, Ting Ying and Zalum, two local KIA commanders in the Kambaiti area, defected to the CPB in early 1968 along with 400 of their men. Ting Ying's and Zalum's area became "War Zone 101". At the same time, fighting with KIA guerrillas continued in the Möng Ko area—and this, not the government's counter offensive, proved to be the main stumbling block for the CPB's advance in northeastern Shan State.[5]

Despite the unexpected fighting with the KIA in the northeast, the CPB's tactics were obvious: the predominantly Burman CPB wanted to implement the grand plan of building up a new revolutionary base area along the Chinese frontier by forging alliances with local warlords and chieftains in the northeastern mountains. It was hoped that if they were offered unlimited supplies of guns and ammunition, they would adopt the Marxist-Leninist policies of the Burmese Communists, or, at least, pay lip-service to those ideals, which was all that the CPB really needed.

So far, this had been going according to plan. But would the CPB be able to use the new War Zones in the northeast as springboards to push down to Burma proper—the Pegu Yoma, the Irrawaddy delta, the Pinlebu area north of Mandalay and other traditional base areas—where their old comrades in arms were still holding out, and struggling to survive?

At the War Office in Rangoon, meanwhile, military planners were stunned and shocked. An entirely new front had been opened in the northeast and the obvious Chinese involvement was alarming, to say the least. The official media said it was "a Chinese invasion"[6]— which was not entirely untrue. While the CPB's political commissars were all ethnic Burman Communists who had spent years in exile in Sichuan, the vast majority of the troops were actually Chinese Red Guards and other "volunteers" from across the northeastern frontier. Only a few of the military commanders were natives of Burma, and of these nearly all came from Naw Seng's group of Guizhou *laopings*. The Sichuan *laopings* were almost exclusively political commissars.

The government's forces had had to admit defeat in the Möng Ko area and in Kokang, and news was equally depressing from all other fronts in the northeast. The China-sponsored CPB thrust into northeastern Burma also occurred at the same time as the Communist Tet offensive in Vietnam, which shook Asia and the world.

Given the remoteness of northeastern Burma, and the absence of foreign media in the country as a whole, the re-emergence of the CPB did not attract nearly as much publicity as the almost simultaneous fighting in Vietnam.

But at the War Office in Rangoon, the Burmese commanders were no less worried about the future than their American and South Vietnamese counterparts in Saigon. Even if the CPB's offensive may have been a coincidence, Communist forces were from Rangoon's perspective on the march not only in Burma but throughout the region. There was cause for acute alarm.

Ne Win convened an emergency Commanding Officers' Conference in Rangoon on 12–22 September to discuss the mounting crisis. In his long, emotional speech, Ne Win stressed a "people's war" had to be launched against the insurgents.[7] But the Burma Army also realised that it was not strong enough to push the CPB back in northeastern Shan State. Instead, Rangoon turned its attention to the much weaker CPB areas in central Burma, which the forces along the Sino–Burmese border were attempting to reach with Chinese arms and supplies.

On 16 April 1968—only four months after the initial attack on Möng Ko—a Burma Army unit patrolling the foothills of the Pegu Yoma had managed to encircle and kill Bo Zeya, the official chief of staff of the CPB's *pyithu tatmadaw*, one of the legendary Thirty Comrades and the most prominent of the Beijing Returnees.

On 24 September—a few days after Ne Win's speech before the commanding officers' conference in Rangoon—another blow was dealt to the CPB in central Burma. Party chairman Thakin Than Tun was assassinated in his camp in the Pegu Yoma by an infiltrator sent by the Military Intelligence Service (MIS) in the capital.[8] Aung Sein was staying in the hut next to Thakin Than Tun's in the jungles of the Pegu Yoma at that time:

"It was afternoon twilight and we could hear fighting in the distance. The 77th Light Infantry Division was closing in, so all our troops were at the front facing the onslaught. Only families and a few leaders remained at the camp. Maung Mya, the infiltrator, was waiting for his chance. It came when Thakin Than Tun left his hut to go to the latrine. Maung Mya rushed up and shot him with a .303 rifle. The bullet entered through the chairman's right ribs, went through the heart and exited just below his left shoulder. Within minutes, he was dead. We were all shocked, and Maung Mya took advantage of the confusion to slip out. We learned later that he had spent the night in the jungle and reached the enemy camp the next day."[9]

Aung Sein and his comrades left their camp immediately after the assassination, carrying the dead chairman's body with them. They marched all night through the jungle. At daybreak, they reached a glade in the forest, where they buried Thakin Than Tun, his corpse wrapped up in plastic sheets. A defector from the CPB later guided government forces to the burial place, and his almost decomposed body was taken out for identification. Photographs were taken and the body was then reburied and left to rot in this unmarked grave in the jungle. The authorities were satisfied: the fiery former school teacher, who had led the Burmese Communists since the 1940s, was indeed dead.

The Pegu Yoma cadres, who by now had learned about the fighting in the northeast, decided to establish contact with their much better equipped, Chinese-supported comrades along the Yunnan frontier. In early 1969, a group of ten CPB members from the Pegu Yoma left central Burma and began a long march to the northeast. It was almost a year before they reached Möng Ko. Their leader, Taik Aung, had been one of the party's most active inquisitors during the *pyouk-touk-htak* purges a few years before. He was greeted as a hero when he arrived at the new main base in the northeast to be received by the *de facto* leader of the CPB, Thakin Ba Thein Tin.

To establish a bridgehead between the new base area and the Pegu Yoma, a veteran cadre who had accompanied Taik Aung on the trek to the northeast, Myo Myint, was sent to organise the Pa-Os in the hills south of Taunggyi, east of Pyinmana. If the CPB was ever to push down to central Burma, this would be the most likely route.

Shortly after the assassination of Thakin Than Tun, the CPB in the Pegu Yoma had elected as their new chairman Thakin Zin, a Sino-Burmese, former timber merchant from Daik-U who had been a party member since the anti-Japanese struggle during World War II. Officially, the northeastern forces recognised Thakin Zin as their new chairman as well. But, in reality, a "new" CPB, led by Thakin Ba Thein Tin, was emerging in the northeast. Following the setbacks in the Pegu Yoma and the assassination of Thakin Than Tun, it was also becoming increasingly uncertain whether they would be able to link up with the old forces in the Yoma and elsewhere in Burma proper.

Life in the forests of the Pegu Yoma was tough. Than Maung, an orphan who had been "adopted" by the party and become one of the *tat ni lunge* Red Guards who had carried out the executions of the old leaders in 1967, remembers: "There were about 1,000 Communist soldiers in the Pegu Yoma in the late 1960s, armed with .303 Lee-Enfield rifles, the odd Sten gun left over from World War II and a few automatic weapons we had captured from the enemy. We were always hungry and sometimes went without food for several days. There were only a few villages in the Yoma, and they were very poor. Most of them were ethnic Karens. And it was dangerous to go down to the plains to collect rice from the farmers."[10]

Pegu Yoma veteran Aung Sein fills in: "Every time we went, we had to fight our way down and up again. Mostly, we had to eat boiled trunks of wild banana trees, but our stomachs were never full. It was all right when we lay down. But we got dizzy when we stood up. But no matter how poor we were and what hardships we had to face, the comrades never wavered. Their morale was high and all of us firmly believed in a red future."[11]

Aung Sein had gone to China in 1953 as a soldier in Thakin Ba Thein Tin's escort, but was sent back to the Pegu Yoma in 1967 to inform his old comrades-in-arms about the imminent attack on Möng Ko. Shortly afterwards, the purges had begun.

As part of the "People's War" to fight the CPB in the northeast, Ne Win had suggested during the September 1968 conference in Rangoon the formation of a People's Militia in remote areas which could not be defended by regular troops.[12] The nucleus of these local forces already existed in the KKY home guards; the vice chief of staff and finance minister, Brig.-Gen. San Yu, was now given the task of upgrading them to acceptable standards. San Yu was one of Ne Win's most trusted lieutenants; he had served under the general since the days of the 4th Burma Rifles in the 1940s, and now not only held several vital government positions, but was also general secretary of the ruling BSPP.[13]

It was noted by Rangoon that many of the local militias were already well-equipped with modern weapons which had been bought with opium profits on the "black" arms market in Thailand. Khun Sa of Loi Maw KKY, and Lo Hsing-han from Kokang were still the most powerful of the local militia commanders. Khun Sa's troops guarded Loi Maw mountain overlooking the Salween at a point where the CPB's forces could try to cross the river.

Khun Sa had made his headquarters at the nearby garrison town of Tang-yan: by the end of 1968, CPB troops were already penetrating the Wa Hills opposite Loi Maw, threatening not only Tang-yan but also the much more strategic town of Lashio. Following the defeat of his forces in Kokang, Lo Hsing-han had moved his headquarters to Lashio, where he attached his home guard unit to the Northeastern Command of the Burma Army.[14]

In January 1969, Mahasang, a young warlord from Vingngün in the Wa Hills was invited to join the new counter-insurgency campaign that was about to be mounted against the CPB. He marched into Tang-yan with 850 heavily armed Wa troops to pledge their loyalty to the Union. Mahasang was only twenty-four, but already a veteran soldier. He was the second son of Sao Maha, the last *saohpa* of Vingngün (who died later in 1969), and the heir to the tiny principality in the wild Sino–Burmese border mountains. Mahasang's elder brother, Mahakhong, had been recruited by the KMT, which maintained a considerable presence in Vingngün throughout the 1960s, and he had even been sent to Taiwan for training.[15]

The authorities across the border in China had long been wary of these developments, and especially of the local support base that Ma Ching-ko and the KMT had been building up in the Vingngün area. Mahakhong had been assassinated in 1967 by one of his men, a young stable boy who looked after the mules that were used to convoy opium out of Vingngün, one of northeastern Burma's most important poppy growing areas.

The boy had been apprehended and interrogated. It was revealed that he had been paid by Red Chinese intelligence agencies to get rid of Mahakhong. The assassin was promptly executed.[16] Command of the Vingngün army was taken over by Mahasang, who had considerable experience mainly in planning security for opium convoys but also in fighting rival gangs.

In Tang-yan, Mahasang teamed up with his fellow Wa warlord, Bo Lai Oo, who worked closely together with Lo Hsing-han and through him was connected with the KMT opium network. Next to Khun Sa, Bo Lai Oo was in fact one of the most prominent traders in the garrison town, which was becoming notorious for drug trafficking in the late 1960s.[17]

An abundance of other warlords operated in the immediate vicinity of Tang-yan, and most of them had accepted the offer to covert their private armies into KKY home guard units. Ironically, several of them, such as Win Min, alias Wu Chung-tin, of Loi Sae, belonged to KMT general Ma Ching-ko's Taiwan-directed intelligence network.[18]

Although there is nothing to suggest that the Burma Army's cooperation with Taipei's agents went beyond business and local security concerns, the presence of these agents in the hills of northeastern Burma— and Rangoon's inability to get rid of them—had been a long-standing irritant in relations between China and Burma. While there is no reason to doubt the ideological commitment of the Chinese, it is plausible to assume that Kang Sheng's decision to give all-out support to the CPB in northeastern Burma was not motivated solely by a desire to export "proletarian revolution": the wily Chinese intelligence chief was obsessed with real and imaginary conspiracies against the Communist regime in Beijing.[19]

Hardly by coincidence, the first targets of the Burmese Communists— which had been designated by their Chinese instructors before they streamed across the border to Burma into 1968—were well-known bases for the powerful intelligence operation that Ma Ching-ko had established in the 1960s: Möng Ko itself, Hwe Möng Long to the west, Phong Hseng to the east, and Lunghtangchai in Kokang.

Hwe Möng Long, especially, was a centre for KMT activities in northeastern Shan State, located just inside the frontier with Yunnan. The CPB found radio transmitters, code books and other secret documents from Taiwan when the base was captured in July 1968. More than twenty "Taiwan agents" were also apprehended and handed over to the Chinese Communist authorities across the border, where they were most probably summarily executed.[20] Most of them came from the Baoshan area in western Yunnan, a long-time stronghold of various KMT warlords.[21]

It was obvious that Rangoon's concern was directed towards its own internal security and little else, which the acceptance of the KKY's opium trading in exchange for fighting the CPB very clearly indicated. This was also the reason why steps were taken in the capital itself to solidify the nation in the wake of the "Communist invasion". In November 1968—two months after the crisis meeting at the War Office in Rangoon—Ne Win decided to invite a number of recently released political prisoners and others to form an "Internal Unity Advisory Body", a "think-tank" designed to "get opinions on the future political and administrative organisation of the nation".

The new think-tank included former prime minister U Nu (who had been released in October 1966), Kyaw Nyein (released in January 1968), and other elder statesmen. For six months, they deliberated on problems related to the constitution, socialism and the one-party system, and in May 1969 the majority of them suggested a return to democracy and a constitutional government. To the dismay of many, Ne Win rejected the requests.[22]

U Nu himself, who had initially placed some hope in the negotiations, had already left the country in April, when it was becoming clear that the ruling military was not really interested in any power-sharing agreement. He travelled on a pilgrimage to India, but continued to London where on 29 August he announced at a press conference the formation of the Parliamentary Democracy Party (PDP) to overthrow Ne Win by force.[23]

Although it was U Nu who made the official declaration of war against Ne Win's government, the brain behind the move was Edward Law Yone, the well-respected editor of the *Nation*, who had been arrested shortly after Ne Win's coup in 1962. He had been released together with Kyaw Nyein and some other former state leaders in January 1968, and Law Yone had left for Bangkok, Thailand, almost immediately to contact other opponents of the military government.

At his rented villa in Soi Lang Suan around the corner from Bangkok's central Lumpini Park, Law Yone met with former commanders of the Burma Army who had also fled Burma, with leaders of various ethnic rebel forces, and a scattering of younger characters. Among them were no less than four of the Thirty Comrades: Bo Setkya, Bo Yan Naing, Bohmu Aung and Aung San's close friend Bo Let Ya.

Other prominent personalities included erstwhile chief of operations, Brig.-Gen. Henson Kya Doe (an ethnic Karen, who had been dismissed from service in 1949 when the Karen insurrection broke out); ex-chief of the Air Force, Air Commodore Tommy Clift (an Anglo-Shan former Air Force commander who had been included in the initial 17-member Revolutionary Council after the 1962 coup); Jimmy Yang of the exiled ruling family of Kokang; representatives of the Yawnghwe Mahadevi's SSA; and Karen rebel leader Mahn Ba Zan.

Law Yone was "a short, hard-driving and acutely intelligent man, egocentric, solidly built with a square face and steel grey hair, speaking English with a distinct British colonial accent. He could spit out bits of Horace and Shakespeare, then tell a Chinese muleteer's joke—all while simultaneously playing a clarinet, marimba and church organ."[24]

He had spent nearly six years in jail hatching a plot to overthrow Ne Win's military government, whose incompetence he saw as the main reason why the country had gone down the drain since 1962. The plan seemed simple when it was being discussed over endless glasses of sweet Burmese tea at Law Yone's Soi Lang Suan residence: the ethnic minorities—the only non-communist, armed opposition to the regime—were not in a position to topple Ne Win for reasons of geography, distance, distrust, poor communication and different political attitudes. And so long as Ne Win held Rangoon and Mandalay, no foreign government would recognise a Burmese government in exile, even if it was pro-Western and inclined towards democracy.

The traditionally militant Buddhist *sangha*, or clergy, in Mandalay, on the other hand, if properly inspired, might rise up against the regime, bringing with them large numbers of ordinary people—or so Law Yone had worked out in jail. A coordinated attack by the ethnic rebels—and the Burman resistance army which he intended to raise with help from the army veterans around him—might bring down the government in Rangoon. In order to influence the *sangha*, Law Yone needed U Nu, who was considered a devout Buddhist.[25]

U Nu flew into Bangkok in October 1969, and was granted political asylum by the Thai government: Law Yone had established close connections with Prapass Charusathiara through the Internal Security Operational Command, which also liaised with the Karens, the Mons and other "buffers" along the Thai–Burma border. The PDP would be equipped with its own armed force—called the Patriotic Liberation Army (PLA).

By expanding the resistance to include U Nu, who was believed to be enjoying widespread support inside the country, Law Yone hoped there would be a chance to persuade foreign governments, primarily West Germany, Japan, Britain and the USA, to support his policy of "parliamentary democracy" and "federalism". Law Yone banked especially on his World War II contacts in the OSS and the CIA—but he was slow to recognise that nearly all of his old friends in Washington's security agencies had retired. The few who remained had little influence. All the support he could get, after months of tedious and frustrating efforts, was a few million dollars from Asmara, a Canadian oil company, which had been promised exclusive exploration rights "once Rangoon had been captured".[26]

Although the West most probably found Law Yone's modern political ideals more attractive than Ne Win's atavistic military dictatorship, the timing of the launching of his campaign could not have been more unfortunate. Communist forces were advancing in Vietnam, fighting with Communist insurgents was continuing in the newly formed federation of Malaysia—and now Burma had been added to the list of countries threatened by Chinese designs for Southeast Asia.

Military analysts in Washington and London saw little viability in Law Yone's "Third Alternative" to Rangoon's "Burmese Way to Socialism" and the renewed threat from the CPB. On the contrary, it could weaken the government in Rangoon and thus, indirectly, play into the hands of the CPB. The CIA maintained liaison with Law Yone and his group through some of their agents in Thailand so as not to antagonise them—but no assistance of any consequence was forthcoming.[27]

Attempts to enlist the support of some of the hopefully more independent-minded warlords in Shan State were equally unsuccessful. In September 1969, two delegates from the SSA travelled in disguise up to Tang-yan to meet with Khun Sa and persuade him to switch sides. Unlike most other powerful home guard commanders, who were ethnic Chinese, Khun Sa was at least half-Shan.

Khun Sa, perhaps sensing that firmer ties with Thailand would benefit his business, expressed interest in collaborating with the new, anti-communist resistance that was being organised in Bangkok. But news of the meeting leaked out: on 29 October, Khun Sa was arrested at Heho airport near Taunggyi as he was returning from a business trip to Tachilek on the Thai border. He was imprisoned in Mandalay and charged with high treason for his contacts with the rebels.[28]

Meanwhile, in October 1969 the CPB had formally announced the formation of the "Northeastern Military Area", combining Kokang with the Möng Ko-Möng Hom-Möng Ya areas west of the Salween. Than Shwe, a CPB veteran, had been appointed political commissar and Naw Seng had become the overall military commander of the CPB's northeastern forces. Than Shwe was actually one of the few CPB cadres from Sichuan who had any previous military experience. He had joined the BIA in 1942 and attended the Officers' Training School in Rangoon during the Japanese occupation. In 1950, he had joined *yebaw* Aung Gyi on the first trek to China and he was, of course, a member of the "leading group of five" that had been set up in Beijing in November 1963.[29]

The KKY home guards were put to the test in the battlefield against this new, effective Communist military machine in January 1970. Government forces had mounted an offensive to dislodge a force of several thousand CPB troops who had ensconced themselves on a grassy plateau overlooking the town of Panglong in the northern Wa Hills. This Panglong—not to be confused with the town of the same name in which the famous agreement was signed in 1947—is located in a narrow valley which stretches up to Hopang near the Ting river further to the north. It was the seat of a local *saohpa*, Khun Saw, who had his own KKY force of 500 men.

Khun Saw's private army was commanded by his son, Khun Tun Lu or Bo Kyaw, a swashbuckling young man in his mid-twenties. Khun Tun Lu had attended missionary school in Maymyo and therefore had an English name: Richard. At home in Panglong, however, he was called "Dickie". He led his men with a firm hand, always carrying two Colt revolvers in his belt, one on each hip.

"If the KKY turned out to be good fighters, we planned to convert them into a full-fledged, regular People's Militia which would fight together with us against the insurgents in the field," recalls Col. Khin Maung Soe, the commander of the government's artillery unit at Panglong in early 1970.[30]

Rangoon had reason to believe that the Panglong KKY would fight with determination against the Communists on the mountain range above the valley. CPB troops had taken over the main village in the hills near the Chinese frontier, a ramshackle settlement called Kyinshan, which despite its poor appearance was the centre for the opium trade in the region. The entire border range formed one gigantic poppy field, and the Panglong *saohpa* had lost his most lucrative income when the CPB had marched into Kyinshan in late 1969.

Although the *saohpa* himself was a Shan, many of his subjects were Panthay Muslims—and taxes paid by the Panthay merchants and muleteers, who had dominated the opium trade in the Panglong-Hopang area for more than a century, provided Khun Saw with substantial sums of money every year.

The mountain range was ideal poppy country. The air was cool, there was always a fresh breeze, and morning dew nourished the plants. And now it was January and the poppies were already in flower, ready to yield precious opium resin within a month or so. To the Panthay opium merchants, victory for the CPB would mean that they would have to look elsewhere for business. They threw in their lot with Dickie's KKY and the Burma Army in the fight against the Communists.

Khun Sa's once powerful Loi Maw KKY had vanished into the jungle after the arrest of their leader, so his force could not be reckoned on. But a few hundred militiamen from Kokang KKY came down to join the campaign. They were commanded by Lo Hsing-han, who was already big in the drug business, and closely connected with the Panthay traders of Panglong. With the arrest of Khun Sa, Lo's importance had grown.

From his new base in Lashio, Lo had sent several massive convoys down to Tachilek on the Thai border, and his unit was now equipped with the best weapons purchased on the so-called "black" arms market in Thailand: US-made M-16 rifles, M-60 rocket launchers, and 57mm and 75mm recoilless rifles. Lo's convoys, each protected by hundreds of heavily armed troops, carried his own opium and, for a fee, cargo which belonged to the Panthays of Panglong and other merchants.

The combined government force—regular troops and various KKY militias—numbered approximately 2,000 men. Their overall commander, Lieut.-Col. Tun Yi, was a short, rotund and bald-headed man in his 40s.[31] A tough, able warrior, he was nick-named "Napoleon" by his fellow officers.

But against his forces stood more than 3,000 Communist troops, heavily armed with Chinese-supplied weapons. Some of the village chieftains in Kyinshan, who resented the Panglong *saohpa's* collection of revenue on the local opium crop, had already joined forces with the CPB. The best-known of them was Lo Shing-ko, an ethnic Chinese opium trader from nearby Ywinching, whom the CPB had already approached in 1968 with promises of arms and ammunition if he lent his support to the anti-government struggle.[32]

The government's tactics focused on harassing the CPB on the mountain range with artillery bombardment, which would force them to come down and face the combined force in the valley. But it was not an easy task: the mountain range was almost denuded of forest. In between the poppy fields grew tall elephant grass, which provided ideal hiding places for the Communist guerrillas. It was almost impossible to spot them and even harder to find a target for the artillery barrages.

Col. Khin Maung Soe and his men tried to fire upwards with their four 76mm Yugoslav-made mountain guns, but to no avail. He wanted to bring his artillery pieces closer to the CPB positions and fire high-angle up the mountain. This was tried with some success, but he also knew that if he came too close to the enemy, and if they happened to capture one of his guns, he would have to face court martial in Rangoon on his return from the front. The mountain guns had to be pulled back.

Attempts to storm the range with infantry forces proved disastrous. Col. Kyaw Sein, the commanding officer of the 3rd Kachin Rifles, was cut down by a hail of Communist bullets as he tried to advance up the mountain with his battalion and several hundred KKY militias. He died instantly, and the supporting KKY forces fled in disarray. They had, after all the expectations of Rangoon, turned out to be useless as fighters in regular warfare: their discipline was abysmal and it became apparent that their martial skills extended to protecting opium convoys, not to attacking fortified positions in difficult terrain.

The only KKY commander who fought well was Lee Pa-mi, a local opium trader from the hills east of the Salween. A hardy ethnic Chinese, he commanded a force of about 100 men who fought bravely alongside "Napoleon" Tun Yi's troops. Dickie's Panglong troops, however, soon found themselves doing little more than cooking food for the government forces.

Eventually, Tun Yi asked for air support. Six warplanes were promptly dispatched from Lashio and Meiktila Air Base south of Mandalay: a British-made Vampire fighter-bomber, a Shipmag spotter plane, a Dakota and three T-33 trainers. But because of the proximity to the border, and the very likely possibility of an angry Chinese response if bombs hit territory across the frontier, the planes had to fly in a south-north fashion.

It was almost impossible to spot the CPB troops in the high grass on the Kyinshan plateau. As a last resort, napalm was dropped from the T-33s. The pilots were all young and daring—and acutely aware of the CPB's 12.5 mm anti-aircraft machine-guns on the mountain. Nevertheless, they nosedived towards the CPB's invisible hilltop positions and dropped their napalm. The government forces in the valley were jubilant as they saw the dry grasslands above them go up in flames.[33]

The euphoria was short-lived. The air raids did indeed force the CPB troops out of Kyinshan—but only to come charging down the mountain towards the Panglong valley, spraying automatic rifle-fire from their Chinese-made AK-47s. Dozens of government troops and KKY militiamen were killed as waves of almost suicidal Communist soldiers emerged from the Kyinshan range.

The attack on the Communist stronghold above Panglong ended in a catastrophe. Casualties were extremely heavy on the government side, the KKY had turned out to be useless—and the CPB was greatly encouraged by the debacle of the Burma Army. Kyinshan was never recaptured by Rangoon's forces—and Khun Saw was assassinated in Lashio shortly after the debacle by disgruntled opium merchants.[34]

Apart from the CPB, Lo Hsing-han also emerged as a winner of the battle for Kyinshan, not in military terms but economically. He bought raw opium from the fields in eastern Shan State (even from the CPB, it was alleged) at 450 Kyats a *viss* (1.6 kilograms). By the time the opium reached Lashio, its value had increased more than threefold to 1,500 Kyats. From Lashio, his convoys of 2,500–3,000 mules carried a fortune's worth of drugs down to Tachilek on the Thai border. Some of the opium belonged to him and his men, while any private muleteer could join his convoy and carry his own opium under Lo's protection for a fee of 3,000 Kyats a mule.[35]

Other opium merchants, mostly Panthays, used Lo's KKY army as a private transport company: they paid him to convoy their opium to the heroin refineries on the Thai border. There, the going price for a *viss* at this time was 3,500–4,000 Kyats, or nearly ten times as much as the grower in northern Shan State got for the same amount of raw opium.

A quarter of Lo Hsing-han's profit was spent on procuring arms and ammunition in Thailand, another quarter went to buying gold bars, and the rest was invested in textiles, electronics and other consumer goods which were brought back to Lashio and other urban centres in Shan State; thus a killing was made both ways.[36]

The refineries in Tachilek and near Pieng Luang, run by KMT Chinese with powerful connections in Hong Kong, Macau and Taiwan, put out vast quantities of heroin—the new drug which was being successfully marketed locally in Southeast Asia as well as, increasingly, internationally.

To conceal his embarrassment over the poor performance of his men at the battle for Kyinshan, Lo arranged a lavish dinner party at Kunlong for the government soldiers who had taken part in the fighting. Col. Khin Maung Soe remembers delicacies being served from sukiyaki-style hot pots, and Red Label and Black Label Johnny Walker whisky flowing all night. The officers got a sweater and a pair of trousers each, while the privates enjoyed themselves with food and drinks. An unusual competition was also arranged between two men who were both named Khin Maung.

The first Khin Maung was a Sino-Burmese from Mandalay who acted as the Burma Army's liaison officer with the Kokang KKY. He was also Lo Hsing-han's interpreter. The other Khin Maung, an ethnic Chin, was a lieutenant of the 3rd Kachin Rifles who was based at a forward position called the "11th Mile Camp." It overlooked the CPB's forward position near Chinsweho in southern Kokang and was designed as a *san pya sakan*, a camp that could not be abandoned. Its defenders had to stay and fight till death if attacked. Such camps were always manned by ruffians and outright criminals who had no other prospects of obtaining an honourable position in Burmese society. Khin Maung was no exception.

First, the two Khin Maungs had to lie down in the army barrack, face to face. An oil lamp was lit and thirty balls of opium were kept for each of them. Khin Maung from Mandalay was unable to smoke as much as Khin Maung of the 3rd Kachins, despite noisy encouragements from the Burma Army officers who were there. The next phase was a Black Label competition. Khin Maung of the 3rd Kachins consumed two bottles and emerged as the winner, to the applause of everybody present. The party ended in a drunken brawl.[37]

The battle of Kyinshan in early 1970 had encouraged the CPB to push on. They had discovered the weaknesses of the Burma Army's tactics and its limitations when it came to planning and logistics. In March, heavy fighting broke out west of Möng Ko as CPB forces tried to expand the area under their control. Möng Paw, a market village of more than 1,000 households twenty kilometres west of Möng Ko, was overrun on 21 March. On the 27th, Communist forces attacked Panghsai, a border town located where the Burma Road crosses the international frontier.

Thakin Ba Thein Tin himself arrived in Wanting on the Chinese side to direct the battle, assisted by Chinese military advisers. The aim was to capture Panghsai on the 28th, the 22nd anniversary of the CPB's armed struggle. Communist gunners pounded the government's garrison on a hilltop overlooking the border crossing with recoilless rifles and 120mm mortars. It was blown to pieces and, on the 28th as planned, CPB troops in green fatigues and with red stars on their caps, marched into Panghsai. With a population of several thousand people, it was the largest place to fall into Communist hands thus far.

The following month, the CPB began penetrating deep towards Lashio and other urban centres in northeastern Shan State. Commanded by Zau Mai, one of Naw Seng's Kachin veterans, and with ideologue Khin Maung Gyi as political commissar, 1,500 Communist troops set out from Möng Ko on 12 April. One detachment led by Tun Tin—another of Naw Seng's veterans—stormed into Lashio town and attacked the railway station. A bridge was blown on the Hsenwi-Lashio road, and an entire company of government troops was wiped out near Hsenwi.[38]

"We were the mouse and the CPB was the cat in those days," says artillery officer Col. Khin Maung Soe. Khin Maung Gyi of the CPB remembers that "1970 was the best year for us. We fought many battles of annihilation."

The situation was also becoming serious in the Wa Hills. In October 1969, the CPB had already sent party veteran Mya Thaung to the Wa Hills to enlist the support of local chieftains. Mya Thaung came from Bassein and had been trained by the British army in Dehra Dun in India after World War II. After returning to Burma, he had served with the 3rd Burma Rifles, who mutinied in July 1948. In October, he had joined the CPB and had gone to China in 1952. Now he was back fighting in Burma, his British training augmented by political indoctrination during China's Cultural Revolution.

He had never seen any Was before, though: "In China, PLA instructors told us about the Was: how they at first had to fight the Was on their side of the border when the liberation army pushed south from Kunming in late 1949. But later, the PLA had managed to win the confidence of the Was in China. We learned from the PLA that they had in 1949–50 supported Wa bands which were opposed to the KMT in Yunnan. We decided to support any Wa chieftain who was waging guerrilla war against the KKY militias in the Wa Hills."[39]

Taking advantage of tribal rivalries, the CPB managed to win over three prominent Wa warlords: Chao Ngi Lai alias Ta Lai from Saohin-Saohpa opposite Cangyuan in Yunnan, Pao Yo-chang alias Ta Pang from Khun Ma, and

Ai Kalong from Ai Kyin in the wildest and most remote sector of the Wa Hills where the people were still head-hunters when the CPB moved in. All three led small bands of poorly armed local forces; they now received Chinese-made automatic rifles, mortars and grenade launchers from the CPB.

In December 1969, Chao Ngi Lai and CPB commissar Kyaw Htin, one of Mya Thaung's lieutenants, launched their first attack. The target was the township centre of Saohpa (or Pangwei) in the easternmost corner of the Wa Hills. The town was defended by a small garrison of government troops, supported by a local KKY force led by Saw Lu, a 27-year-old Wa who had been educated by missionaries at the Karen Baptist School in Myaungmya in the Irrawaddy delta. Chao Ngi Lai's better-equipped forces overran Saohpa without much difficulty, and the Burma Army and its home guard unit regrouped at Möng Mau further to the w~st.

But the advance from this first foothold in the Wa Hills was slow. Saw Lu was not the only Wa who resisted the newcomers, as throughout history these fierce and proud tribesmen had resented any outsiders who had tried to subdue them. Fighting between the CPB and local bands broke out across the Wa Hills. According to Mya Thaung: "In the Khun Ma area, an entire village, including women and children, put up a last stand, barricading themselves inside a longhouse. We fired a B-40 rocket through the door at the end of the longhouse. That finished them all off."[40]

Within a year or so, local resistance had subsided and the Was came to accept the CPB's dominance through their superior firepower. Many Was were recruited into the CPB's "People's Army", and they turned out to be excellent fighters. Wa became one of the major languages in which news and fighting bulletins were broadcast when on 28 March 1971 the CPB inaugurated its own radio station, the *People's Voice of Burma*. It began transmitting in early April from Mangshi in Yunnan, north of Möng Ko, and even if the revolutionary rhetoric was alien to most Was, listening to the exciting news of major battles and victories—in their own language—became popular among local people, who gathered by the fireplace at night with their Chinese-made transistor radios which the CPB had distributed in villages across the Wa Hills.

In late April, the Was were put to the test against a major concentration of Burmese government forces—up till then, they had only been fighting rival Wa bands. Mya Thaung and Chao Ngi Lai targeted Möng Mau, the township centre of the northern Wa Hills and one of the few places in the area where there was any significant government presence. Five battalions of Wa troops, supported by some Chinese "volunteers", encircled the town which is located on a grassy plateau just below Loi Mo mountain. To prevent government reinforcements from reaching the battle zone, other Communist units cut the route to Panglong to the north, the only motor road into the Wa Hills.

Communist mortar and artillery fire pelted down on Möng Mau, and the overpowered government garrison was abandoned after a day's heavy fighting. It was 1 May—Labour Day—when the victorious CPB marched in, a date especially chosen by the CPB's Burman political commissars, but presumably of little significance for the Wa troops, who had little or no notion of the ideology they were supposed to be fighting for. For them, it was a battle against the central authorities, which all of them despised regardless of political inclination.

The CPB was spreading its influence all along the Yunnan frontier. In October, an entirely new unit crossed the border from Sipsongpanna into the hills north of Kengtung. Led by Pe Thaung, who had served as political commissar of the unit that had escorted Thakin Ba Thein Tin to China in 1953, they decided to support another local tribe: the Akhas, who had suffered tremendously under the KMT since the early 1950s.

In 1967, some local Akhas in the Pa Lu-Pa Le area near the Burma–Laos–China triborder junction northeast of Kengtung had risen in rebellion against the KMT in reaction to heavy tax collection and general abuse. Led by Lao Er Ji Pyao, and armed with home-made flintlocks, spears and knives, they had ambushed and harassed the KMT incessantly, without any outside support. In 1970, Lao Er Ji Pyao and a few of his men had been invited to China: "We were told that we would get modern arms—if we joined hands with the CPB."[41] Hardly surprisingly, they agreed and on 5 October 1971, Pe Thaung proclaimed the formation of "War Zone 815", named after the founding date of the CPB (15 August 1939).

In November, another announcement was made: the CPB forces in the Kyawkku-Nawnglong-Nawng Lu area near the Zawgyi river in western Shan State—the domain of party veteran Kyin Maung—had become "War Zone 108". This choice of number was of less revolutionary significance than 815, though: 9 was Thakin Ba Thein Tin's lucky number, and 1+0+8 equals 9. This bizarre belief in numerology is common to Burma: by coincidence, Ne Win's lucky number is also 9.[42] More importantly in the context of the war, the Kyawkku-Nawnglong-Nawng Lu area north of Lawksawk was sufficiently close to the northeastern base area, and unlike other "old areas", it was resupplied with Chinese arms and ammunition.

The Communist juggernaut rolled on, and on 28 November, Communist forces launched a surprise attack on a forward base at 7171 mountain a few kilometres east of the town of Kunlong on the Salween river. The company defending the hilltop position was annihilated in a savage, eight-hour long battle. The commander, Lt. Shwe Kyu, was killed, as were all three platoon commanders and nearly eighty soldiers.

The CPB forces marched on to take up position on Shan Tele mountain, overlooking the Salween river. Their aim was obvious: one of only two bridges spanning the swift-flowing Salween river is at Kunlong. Ironically, the bridge was built by the Chinese during U Nu's reign in Rangoon to cement friendship between the two countries.[43]

There are very few places where it is possible to cross the Salween, so if the CPB had captured the Kunlong with its impressive suspension bridge, it would have been an easy task to send thousands of troops to the west bank of the river. From Kunlong, it is only seventy-five kilometres by road to Hsenwi, and another fifty to Lashio. A victory for the communists at Kunlong would have left the entire northern Shan State open to them.

Ne Win was away in England when the fighting at Kunlong began, and San Yu had to rush up to Lashio and the forward headquarters at Na-ti on the Hsenwi-Kunlong road to boost the flagging morale of the troops. "The whole area became a war zone," remembers Aung Myint, a Burma Army officer who took part in the campaign. "Convoys of army trucks rumbled along the road from Hsenwi to the river carrying reinforcements and ammunition to the front. Command posts were established everywhere and daily weapons drills were conducted by the roadside."[44]

"Napoleon" Tun Yi was in charge of the troops at this battle as well. His first tactic was to charge Shan Tele peak with infantry forces. With fixed bayonets, they ran uphill, shooting as they advanced through the forest. But the well-entrenched CPB troops on the mountain repelled more than forty such attacks, inflicting heavy casualties.

The firepower of the Communists seemed inexhaustible—as was their logistical advantage. It was close to the Chinese border, and fresh supplies of bullets and even rations for the CPB soldiers were sent in daily. Wounded CPB soldiers were treated in Chinese hospitals across the frontier. It also became obvious that most of the troops were actually Chinese regulars from the PLA. "We found tell-tale bodies in the forest on the hillsides," recalls Aung Myint.

When they resorted to Chinese-style human wave tactics, the situation at Kunlong became desperate. Some defenders of the bridge fled in disarray, others deserted and were never found again. "Napoleon" Tun Yi ordered his engineers to mine the bridge with dynamite sticks: if Hai Kham Ba on the outer defence line fell, the bridge would be blown. Each battalion commander was ordered to keep one bullet for himself to commit suicide rather than be captured alive by the CPB—or have to return in disgrace to Rangoon, where court martial was awaiting everyone who abandoned his post. It was a do-or-die battle, the biggest the Burma Army had ever fought in the northeast.

At the battle for Kyinshan, the KKY had turned out to be more of a liability than an asset as a fighting force, but despite this Lo Hsing-han's men were also present at Kunlong. This time, however, they were there as local guides to help direct infantry assaults and artillery barrages rather than as conventional soldiers. Their knowledge of the local terrain was still far superior to the Burma Army's, whose commanders all came from central Burma and did not even speak the local languages.

In return, Lo was permitted to use army vehicles to transport his opium out of the area. Government forces would sometimes even go along to assist in protecting his convoys of mules or lorries from Lashio down to the Thai border.[45]

It was the artillery that finally turned the tide at Kunlong. In the 1950s the US had given the U Nu government 105mm howitzers as a token gesture of appreciation of his neutralistic foreign policy, but they could not be used without the express approval of Ne Win himself. San Yu in Rangoon called Ne Win, who had not yet returned from London, to ask for permission to send them up to Kunlong. He agreed.

The howitzers were positioned around Shan Tele, and as the CPB forces came charging down the mountain in human waves, air-burst shells were fired. They were effective even against enemy troops inside bunkers: the concussion when the shells exploded in the air caused bleeding from the nose and mouth. Hundreds of Communist soldiers died—but the waves never seemed to end.

On 7 January 1972, eventually, after forty-one days of continuous heavy fighting, the Communists pulled back from Shan Tele. The Kunlong bridge was safe, and so was the road to Hsenwi. It was the Burma Army's first major victory against the CPB in the northeast, and the morale of the troops was boosted tremendously.

Having failed to cross the Salween, the CPB realised that it had to turn its attention to less well-defended positions. The Communist forces moved south from Möng Mau and Ai Kyin in the northern Wa Hills, east of the river. An attack was launched on Kalong Pa-Ma Tat, a government outpost in the Sino–Burmese border mountains, and the position was overrun.

The Communists marched on, across the wild Wa Hills, encountering little or no resistance along their way south. The aim was to link up with Pe Thaung's newly established War Zone 815, and thus seize control over the entire border from Panghsai on the Burma Road in the north down to the Mekong river and the Laotian frontier.

In rapid sequence in June–July 1972, the CPB took over three more township centres east of the Salween: Na Hpan, Man Hpang and Pangyang, bringing the total of township centres under CPB control to five: Kokang had already fallen under CPB domination in 1968 and Saohpa (Pangwei) in December 1969. At the same time, the market towns of Vingngün and Loi Leün were captured, and, finally, the border town of Panghsang on the Nam Hka river, which separates Burma and China.

Some of these places were lightly defended only by KKY units, for instance Mahasang's domain at Vingngün. His troops were no match for the well-equipped CPB. The survivors had to flee to their commander's base at Tang-yan, east of the Salween, where they joined the combined forces of Mahasang, Bo Lai Oo and Lo Hsing-han.

What seemed to be a steady march forward for the CPB was not without obstacles. The disaster of Kunlong was perhaps the most important defeat, but there were also other serious setbacks. Internally, the party was shattered on 9 March 1971 when the overall military commander of the northeastern forces, war hero Naw Seng, died under mysterious circumstances near Möng Mau.

The first internal announcement from the CPB said he had died when falling off a horse "on the way to the frontline". Almost immediately, the official CPB version was changed. Now he was killed in a fall from a cliff while hunting in the Wa Hills. Many Kachins, however, believe that he was murdered by the CPB because he refused to fight his own kin in the KIA: by 1972, the two rebel forces were still engaged in heavy battles in the hills south of Möng Ko.[46]

In central Burma, the situation for the revolutionary forces was becoming desperate. The leader of the Red Flags, Thakin Soe, had continued to surround himself with a harem of pretty girls in khaki uniforms at his base camp at Than Chaung on the northern edge of the Arakan Yoma—but he had done little fighting since the break-down of the peace talks in 1963.

The Burma Army attacked him in any case, and on 13 November 1970, the now 65-year-old firebrand commander of Burma's most militant Communist revolutionaries was captured by government troops. Thakin Soe's remaining armed force was not significant—only about 200 men scattered in small units around Than Chaung, near Pakokku and Htichaink in the north, and in the countryside around Twante in the Irrawaddy delta—but his capture was a severe psychological blow to committed leftists in Burma's urban areas, who still revered the old leader.

Indirectly, it affected the morale of many Communist sympathisers in central Burma, including those who constituted the CPB's potential support base.

While the campaign against the communists in central Burma was continuing quite successfully, the authorities had also cracked down heavily on leftist movements in Rangoon, Mandalay and other cities. Scores of suspected Communist sympathisers had been rounded up, and sent to the Coco Islands, a Burmese territory in the Gulf of Bengal. Originally established as a penal colony by Ne Win's Caretaker Government in 1959, it was enlarged and expanded in 1969 to house thousands of political detainees. Aung Htet, a leftist student activist from Mandalay, was among the first batch of more than 200 prisoners who were sent to the Coco Islands on 13 February 1969:

"On the 11th, about 100 prisoners, including myself, were assembled in one hall in Insein Jail. We were all CPB and Red Flag sympathisers. At first, we thought we'd be released as it was the day before Union Day. But at 11

P.M. on 13 February, all of us were taken out. Prison warders with clubs lined our way out to a row of Hino buses outside the jail compound.

"The windows of the buses were covered with white sheets. We were herded aboard and driven to Botataung jetty where a Five Star liner, the *Pyi Daw Nyunt*, was waiting for us. There were searchlights everywhere, focusing on our way up to the ship. I saw lines of soldiers; their steel helmets and bayonets glistened eerily in the searchlight. We were joined by detainees from other prisons and all of us, 233 political prisoners, were brought in chains to the ship's cargo room.

"It took two days to reach the Coco Islands. When we arrived, an army colonel, Tun Yin Law, gave a speech: This is the Coco Islands, which you may have heard of. Try to escape if you dare. The waters around here are full of sharks. This is also a different kind of prison. You have to work and to grow your own food. If you don't work, you'll have nothing to eat.'

"It was clearly modelled after Indonesia's penal colony on the Boro Islands. After the CPB's push into the northeast in 1968, Ne Win obviously wanted to isolate us physically from any contacts we may have in the towns or elsewhere."[47]

Only three prisoners managed to escape from the island: a Burman Communist, and two Karens who had been arrested for working for the KNU in Rangoon. They secretly built a boat from coconut trees and made a sail from bedsheets sewn together. They set sail at night, and voyaged across the open, shark-infested sea for fourteen days before reaching the coast near Ye in Tenasserim Division. They had barely managed to survive on dried biscuits, tortoise flesh and rainwater.

Almost dead from starvation, they staggered ashore. But when they reached the first village, the local headman became suspicious of the strange-looking men. He informed the army—and two of them were promptly arrested. Only Mahn Aung Gyi, one of the Karens, managed to escape and made it to a Karen base camp in the Pegu Yoma. He died from malaria a year later.[48]

The miscalculation on the part of the authorities was that they had instructed the prisoners to till the soil on the island, and in order to do so, they had to be issued with spades, shovels and other tools. That was why these three prisoners had managed to build their own boat. Other prisoners also collected scrap-metal from a shipwrecked Greek ocean liner, and after five months or so, many had managed to arm themselves with crude, home-made weapons, with which they kept the guards at bay.

The CPB sympathisers sewed their own party flags with the hammer and the sickle, and began to openly celebrate May Day and important party days, and they held regular meetings in the camp on the island. The prison authorities had given them radios which were fixed on the frequency of Radio Rangoon, but the prisoners managed to manipulate them and were soon able to tune in to the CPB's clandestine *People's Voice of Burma*.

The confrontation between the prison authorities and the uncontrollable inmates came to a head in late 1969. The entire camp went on a hunger-strike for better food. The authorities gave in after seven days, but this only encouraged the prisoners to press on. In March 1970, a second hunger-strike broke out. It lasted for forty days. In September, the prisoners kept up their hunger-strike for forty-seven days.

The most serious strike came in May 1971, when the prisoners took turns to protest against the entire concept of isolation on a remote island in the Gulf of Bengal. They committed themselves to fast until death. As soon as one hunger-striker had died, he was put in a home-made, wooden coffin draped in CPB flags. The other prisoners clenched their fists and sang the Internationale as the coffins piled up outside the prison barracks.

On the fifty-third day of the hunger strike, when eight prisoners had died, the authorities finally gave in. The prisoners would be allowed to return to the mainland. In December 1971, a ship was dispatched from Rangoon to pick up the deportees on the Coco Islands. They were transferred to Insein Jail in the capital.

The armed Communist rebels, who were still holding out in pockets of central Burma, could do little more than listen to revolutionary appeals broadcast over the *People's Voice of Burma*, and hope that the seemingly powerful forces in the northeast would come down and rescue them from what otherwise seemed to be unavoidable collapse. In 1971, almost the entire CPB unit in Henzada in the Irrawaddy delta region eventually gave up and surrendered to the government.

The remnants of the delta forces regrouped in the Pegu Yoma, which by now had also become the major retreat base also for the Karen rebels after the Burma Army had cleared almost the whole of the Irrawaddy delta of all insurgents by the end of 1971.[49]

For other revolutionaries the situation was even worse as they did not even have the hope of outside support to cling to. U Nu's and Law Yone's non-communist resistance had managed to link up with units of the Karen and the Mon insurgent armies along the Thai border, and on 25 May 1970 the three had set up a united front to fight the Rangoon government. But they soon fell out with each other on the issue on the right of secession, which the ethnic minority armies demanded and U Nu rejected.

The former prime minister spent most of his time in Bangkok meditating, feeling increasingly isolated and disillusioned. Law Yone soon left for America, realising that the West would not lend him more than token support. Although he kept in touch with the resistance along the Thai–Burma border for some time, he soon retired to Washington. He then began writing his memoirs, which, however, never found a publisher.

The Karens along the Thai frontier, led by ex-Force 136 runner Bo Mya, were making a handsome income from taxing the cross-border trade in contraband. They were tolerated by the Thais, who viewed them as "a 'Foreign Legion', guarding their borders and preventing links between the Burmese and the Thai Communists."[50]

But the less fortunate units that remained deeper inside Burma were finding it more and more difficult to survive. In the Pegu Yoma, the Karen National United Party (KNUP), in effect a leftist organisation separate from the right-wing Karen rebels along the Thai border, cooperated closely with the CPB. In October 1969 the KNUP had already officially announced its adherence to "Marxism-Leninism, Mao Zedong Thought".[51]

In December 1971, the KNUP also decided to send a 37-man delegation to the CPB's new base area in the northeast to request assistance from China. It was to take them two years to reach the Yunnan frontier, guided along the way by Shan rebels from the SSA.[52]

Following the CPB's territorial gains in the Wa Hills throughout 1972, the civil war took a new turn in 1973. The first reason for this was that the KKY programme had been a complete failure. The KKY commanders had become more and more involved in the opium trade, and instead of fighting the insurgents, the home guards had to negotiate tax agreements with them since they controlled the countryside and could block the movement of opium convoys down to the Thai border.

On Independence Day 1973—4 January—Ne Win finally sent orders to the Shan State capital of Taunggyi to cancel the programme by which the KKY home guard armies had been built up by the Burmese intelligence office. Some smaller groups gave up and surrendered their weapons. Others sold their guns to the rebels and then returned home. But the most powerful armies simply went underground.

The immediate outcome was a rebellion among the Lahu tribe of southern Shan State. On 10 January, a powerful Lahu ex-KKY force attacked the town of Möng Hsat in southern Shan State. The following day, several hundred Lahus, armed with flintlocks, shotguns, daggers and clubs, stormed into Möng Ton sixty-seven kilometres to the east.

There was no army unit defending Möng Ton at the time, only a section of poorly armed policemen. The enraged Lahus shot up the local BSPP office, and then beat a retreat. Neither attack was a military success, or especially spectacular, but they shook the local authorities in southern Shan State. Schools and offices were closed down for a few days, and army reinforcements were dispatched from nearby garrisons.[53]

By a strange twist of circumstances, the sudden outburst of violence in the Möng Hsat-Möng Ton area could also be seen as an after-effect of Edward Law Yone and U Nu's abortive attempts at forming a non-communist resistance along the Thai border. When little was achieved on the southern front in the Mon and Karen areas, they had appointed as their "northern commander" Jimmy Yang, who had originally joined the SSA in 1964.

The ex-banker and erstwhile MP from Kokang had been entrusted with most of the limited funds Law Yone and U Nu had managed to raise in the US. Jimmy had managed to sell them the idea of a large, tribal force made up of Kokang Chinese, Was and Lahus; if properly organised, it would undermine the support base of the CPB and the scheme would therefore, hopefully, attract more foreign sympathy and support.

Word spread across the border areas opposite Chiang Mai and Chiang Rai in northern Thailand that Jimmy "with powerful foreign backing" was planning a revolt in Shan State. The Lahus were ready to join—but Jimmy made the mistake of spending all the money on his own Kokang force, which was based near KMT Gen. Li Wenhuan's camp at Tam Ngob. The scheme was unsuccessful, and instead of becoming the leader of the pan-tribal, anti-communist resistance in Shan State, Jimmy ended up working for the Rincome Hotel in Chiang Mai.[54]

The Lahus went ahead with their revolt in any case—and the trigger was not simply that Rangoon had ordered them to disband their KKY force in southern Shan State. The leader of the tribal force was a remarkable man called Pu Kyaung Long ("the Old Man of the Monastery"), who was re-puted to be nearly 100 years old. He was the *payah*, or politico-religious leader of the Lahus, their equivalent of the Dalai Lama, and usually stayed at Loi Kham near Möng Ton. He lived in a big bamboo house built on stilts, which looked like a pagoda, hence his name.[55]

As a KKY commander, Pu Kyaung Long had like all the others received unofficial permission to trade in opium in exchange for fighting Shan in-surgents in southern Shan State. But their opium had been confiscated by government troops and was allegedly later sold by local commanders to buyers along the Thai–Burma border.[56]

The outcome was predictable. Pu Kyaung Long declared war on Ran-goon. His "soldiers" were dressed in tribal garments and wore sacred threads and talismans for protection against bullets. Following the raids on Möng Hsat and Möng Ton, Pu Kyaung Long and his tribal force with-drew to a mountain on the Thai–Burma border called Loi Lang (Doi Lang in Thai), where they set up base. It was soon to become a major centre for the drug traffic in the region.

Disgruntlement over the opium business—but on a much larger scale—was also the reason why one of the most powerful KKY com-manders went underground in 1973: Lo Hsing-han. With his large, well-equipped private army, Lo had no intention of giving up his power and influence. Shortly after the order to disband the KKY, Lo began secret negotiations with the SSA. When contact had been established, he slipped out of Lashio, where he had lived for years in a fortified villa under the aegis of Burma's military intelligence—and where he had cultivated a close relationship with the then Northeastern Commander of the Burma Army, Col. Aye Ko, who was later to become a prominent BSPP leader.

It was also obvious that Lo Hsing-han's open activities in the garrison town had become a major embarrassment for the Burmese authorities. In 1972, senior US narcotics adviser Nelson Gross had proclaimed him "kingpin of the heroin traffic in Southeast Asia . . . Lo Hsing-han is an international bandit and responsible for a growing proportion of Asia's and America's drug-caused miseries."[57]

Statements like these were surprising news in Shan State. But there had been a dramatic change in official US narcotics policy. By directly and indirectly supporting various players in the Golden Triangle opium trade, notably the KMT, the US had made a grave mistake. The refined and much more addictive product heroin had become extremely popular, and a large clientele was developing among the American soldiers in Vietnam. When the GIs gradually returned home, the narcotics problem went from Saigon's army barracks to the middle-class suburbs in the United States. The public became alarmed, and the authorities started taking measures aimed at solving the drug problem.

Washington's first step was to build up its powerful Drug Enforcement Administration. But already involved in a controversial war in Vietnam, Washington quickly realised that aid and assistance in the new "war on drugs" had to be subtle. Some of the aid was more conveniently channelled through a newly established UN agency. According to an official US document:

> Through the initiative of the United States, the United Nations Fund for Drug Abuse Control (UNFDAC) was established to provide voluntary contributions to enable the United Nations and its narcotics organisations to increase their narcotics control assistance to member governments. Moreover, the Fund has served as an essential supplement to US efforts in those countries which prefer to receive assistance from multilateral rather than bilateral sources.[58]

Even so, it was obvious that Washington's "war on drugs" started on the wrong footing from the very beginning. Gross's statement about Lo Hsing-han was dismissed by most astute observers as a media-directed exaggeration.

While the drug authorities were trying to focus the world's attention on one single trafficker—who in any case was actually little more than a middle-man between the opium merchants of northern Burma and KMT refinery operators along the Thai border—two relatively unknown traders in Kengtung, Chi Kya Shui and Yang Sang, a.k.a. Yang Shih-li, were, in fact, trading in much larger quantities than the "kingpin" himself.

From his base in Lashio in northern Shan State, Lo Hsing-han was only able to organise three or four convoys a year carrying opium, jade and other contraband down to the border at Tachilek, the apex of the Golden Triangle. Shi Kya Chui and Yang Shih-li, on the other hand, were more conveniently based at Kengtung, only 170 kilometres north of Tachilek, making it possible for them to make up to ten trips a year.[59]

But Lo Hsing-han was easy to pinpoint since he had a large and powerful army, needed for convoying opium from Lashio across rebel-held territory down to Thailand. He matched the classic stereotype of a gun-brandishing opium warlord. Moreover, to go after the politically much more influential and powerful profiteers in Bangkok or Taipei would most certainly have upset regional alliances and possibly also destabilised governments whose loyalty were of utmost importance to the US. Despite all the bravado in Washington, national and regional security, not drug suppression, continued to be the most important objective of US policy in East Asia.

For the Shan rebels, Lo Hsing-han's escape from Lashio and the new tune from Washington nevertheless seemed to be the rescue from what appeared an unavoidable fate: to be crushed between the Burma Army and the CPB. To counter the CPB politically, the SSA had summoned a meeting in the jungle near Loi Hkö south of Hsipaw on 16 August 1971 and set up its own party, the Shan State Progress Party (SSPP).

The youthful, former science student Khun Kya Nu had been elected president. The Mahadevi of Yawnghwe had left Thailand for Canada in 1969, but her son, Sai Tzang (now known as Hsö Wai or Khun Loum Hpa) remained behind in the jungle. He had been become SSPP general secretary and the Shan movement's main theoretician.

But this was clearly not enough to resist the Communist avalanche in Shan State. The Shan rebels had little money and no foreign backing. An alliance with Lo Hsing-han seemed to be the answer. The Shans agreed to assist Lo—if he agreed to sell all his opium to the US narcotics bureau. In this way, the Shans hoped to get both money and international recognition for their cause.[60]

On 24 May 1973, an agreement was signed between the "opium king" and the Shan rebels. It contained five points: first of all, the SSA invited the US Narcotics Bureau to visit the poppy growing areas of Shan State and to transmit information about opium convoys on their own wireless transmitters; the SSA and Lo Hsing-han pledged to collect as much opium as possible from Shan State and sell it to the US authorities to be destroyed; the SSA also pledged to attack all opium convoys which were not subject to this agreement; in return, the SSA expected the US to help find a "permanent solution to the problems of Shan State; and, finally, if assistance was forthcoming, the elected government of Shan State would, after an agreed transition period, allow helicopters under international supervision to search out and destroy any opium fields that still remained.[61]

After signing the agreement at the SSA stronghold of Loi Hkö in northern Shan State, Lo Hsing-han and a veteran SSA officer, Sao Hsö Hten, set off with an armed force for Tang-yan to persuade other former KKY commanders to support the proposal. Several of them did, including the powerful Wa warlord, Mahasang, and the former Loi Maw KKY of the imprisoned Khun Sa, which was now led by his deputy, Chang Shu-chuan, alias Sao Hpalang ("General Thunder"), a KMT veteran. Between them, the various armies hoped to produce 300 tons of raw opium.

The SSPP president, Khun Kya Nu, and Adrian Cowell, a British filmmaker who had spent sixteen months with the Shan guerrillas and also helped draft the proposal, left for Thailand to contact the Americans.

The proposal was unique in that it was the first time parties directly involved in the drug trade agreed not only to give up the business, but also to cooperate with international narcotics agencies to prevent a recurrence. It was a proposal which indirectly undermined the credibility of official, government-to-government cooperation, which both the US and UN agencies at the time were trying to promote.

But perhaps more importantly, if implemented, it would put scores of opium merchants out of business, as well as substantially reduce the income of virtually every policeman posted in the opium growing areas, or along major trading routes. It was doomed to failure.

On the morning of 17 July, Adrian Cowell went to deliver the proposal, along with a detailed report on the Golden Triangle opium trade, to the US Embassy on Wireless Road in Bangkok: a third of the world's heroin for approximately US$12 million. He left the embassy at 1 P.M. Three hours later, in the mountains, Lo Hsing-han was arrested.

Lo Hsing-han had crossed the frontier into a remote corner of Thailand's northwestern Mae Hong Son province to escape a Burma Army attack on his temporary camp in the border areas. A Thai helicopter had landed at Ban Toom village where Lo was staying—and he had been persuaded to enter. Sai Tu, a junior SSA officer who had been assigned to watch on Lo Hsing-han, was also helicoptered away from Ban Toom: "The Thai officers told Lo Hsing-han that we would be taken to the next village to discuss the proposal. Then they would send us back. Lo really thought that he was going to negotiate with the Americans. But the helicopters didn't land until we reached Mae Rim army camp near Chiang Mai. We understood that we had been double-crossed."[62]

The US ambassador in Bangkok praised the arrest, and the Thais published a heroic account of their accomplishment. Lo was dispatched to Bangkok in triumph and ceremoniously displayed for the international press and its photographers. A month later, Lo was extradited to Burma to stand trial, fetched by government officials and flown by a special plane to Rangoon. He was later to stand trial and be sentenced to death, not charged with opium trafficking—which he in any case had carried out with the tacit agreement of Burma's military intelligence— but "insurrection against the state", a reference to his brief alliance with the SSA.[63]

In fact, Lo's arrest had no impact on the overall flow of drugs from the Golden Triangle. In a daring raid on 16 April, Charlie Win, a young Sino-Burmese, had entered Taunggyi in broad daylight with a section of soldiers from the ex-Loi Maw KKY, but with no flashes on their uniforms. They were looking for a foreign ambassador who was reputed to be visiting the Shan capital. Unable to find him, they spotted two Caucasians—and their wives—who were out for a morning stroll.

To the horror of the two screaming women, the rebels raised their pistols at the two foreigners. They quickly, and perhaps also wisely, obeyed orders. The rebels half-ran, pushing their Caucasian captives in front of them, until they reached the outskirts of Taunggyi, where a car was waiting.

Two hostages had been kidnapped—and Charlie Win's demand was the release of the imprisoned Loi Maw commander, Khun Sa. The two accidental captives turned out to be two Russian doctors who were inspecting the Soviet-built hospital in Taunggyi.

An entire division of government troops was thrown in to rescue the Russians. The operation was unsuccessful. It was not until August 1974 that the captives were eventually released—through Thailand. The Loi Maw rebels agreed to set them free, supposedly unconditionally, but by strange coincidence, Khun Sa was released from jail in Mandalay on 9 September. What actually happened is hardly any secret: Gen. Kriangsak Chomanan, the commander of the northern Thai forces, had been called in by Rangoon to negotiate with Ronald Chang or Khun Hseng, Khun Sa's uncle, for an exchange of prisoners.[64]

After Khun Sa was released, he was kept under surveillance in Mandalay for a while, but managed to slip away in early 1976 and return to his men in the jungle. They had already set up a new camp at Ban Hin Taek northwest of Chiang Rai, actually inside Thailand, where a powerful new armed force emerged: the Shan United Army (SUA).

The force was dominated by ethnic Chinese opium merchants, but by adding "Shan" to the name of their army, they evidently hoped to gain favours from the closely-related Thais. It was now that Chang Chifu assumed the Shan name "Khun Sa".[65] His group simply took over the trade from Lo Hsing-han. The heroin business especially was booming, with thousands of addicts all over Southeast Asia. Most American soldiers had returned home after the Paris Accord of 1973, but the pushers simply crossed the Pacific. The trade routes became international, and complex networks were established via Bangkok, Hong Kong, Taipei, Honolulu and the US West Coast.

The real impact of Lo's arrest was felt within the SSA. According to Chao Tzang Yawnghwe: "Politically, the 'Lo Hsing-han affair' dealt the non-communist leaders of the SSA and the SSPP a severe setback from which they never recovered. They could offer no defence against Communist-inspired attacks accusing the West and the United States in particular of perfidy and travesty of justice."[66]

A few months after Lo's arrest, in December 1973, the first SSA unit, accompanied by the thirty-seven Karens who had left the Pegu Yoma two years before, reached the CPB area along the Yunnan frontier. The Shans were led by Sao Hsö Hten, one of the first students who had joined the *Noom Suk Harn* in 1958, and the youthful Sao Hsö Noom (the "Young Tiger"), a Wa-Shan whose father had been the last *saohpa* of Möng Leün.

The Shans were given red-carpet treatment in the CPB's new regional headquarters at Panghsang. They were shown around the impressive military complex, which included army barracks, training facilities and cinemas featuring films about the Chinese civil war.

The CPB's base area formed a *de facto* buffer state between China and the government-held areas of Burma. It had its own administration and tax system, police force and prisons, schools, hospitals, markets and roads where trucks and jeeps displaying number plates issued by the CPB plied. Hydroelectric power stations were built with Chinese assistance at Möng Ko and Panghsang, and the party's radio station continued to beam out daily broadcasts in a number of local languages. Burma had become a divided nation, not just a country with a guerrilla civil war.

A bridge had been built from Panghsang, across the Nam Hka border river to the Chinese side, and supplies were transported daily into the CPB's area: arms and ammunition, uniforms, radio transmitters, army jeeps, petrol, military maps, and even rice, other foodstuffs, cooking oil and kitchen utensils.

Overlooking the Nam Hka— and off-limits to all but the most trustworthy among the inner circle of top party leaders—was the secluded residence of Thakin Ba Thein Tin, the *de facto* leader of the "new" CPB in the northeastern border mountains. Hsö Hten, Hsö Noom and the Karen leader Sgaw Ler Taw were received there with a lavish dinner party. They were promised everything they needed—provided they accepted the political leadership of the CPB. They were then taken on a tour of a people's commune in Yunnan across the border, and on to Kunming where a Chinese motorcade drove them around to see all the sights of the capital of Yunnan.[67]

The Karens returned home after a while, having refused to accept the CPB's leadership. For the Shans, it was far more tempting to accept the offer, especially after the so-called "Lo Hsing-han affair". As a first step, Shan troops were sent to Panghsang for training; the seeds of discord had been sown and the Shan movement was soon to split over the question of an alliance with the CPB.

The War Office in Rangoon viewed these new alliances with some concern, but its strategy was still to eliminate the old base areas in central Burma in order to isolate the CPB along the Yunnan frontier. In early 1975, a major operation was launched in the Pegu Yoma, still officially the CPB's headquarters. The Burmese Army's crack 77th Light Infantry Division—the first in a new series of special units set up to combat the Communists and other insurgents—encircled the CPB's old bases in the Yoma.

The Communists were running out of ammunition and food; starving, they straggled through the dense forest of the Yoma. Party chairman Thakin Zin and his secretary, Thakin Chit, were hiding out in an abandoned jungle farm when a government patrol suddenly appeared. A little boy, one of the party leaders' bodyguards, was apprehended and he revealed the identity of the two Communist leaders who were in a nearby glade.

The officer, 2nd Lieut. Myint Swe of the 107th Regiment, gasped in astonishment—and pushed his soldiers on. A minute later, he spotted the two old men and ordered his men to fire. Thakin Zin and Thakin Chit died in a hail of bullets. It was 1:50 P.M. on 15 March—and the Burma Army had scored its most important success since the assassination of Thakin Than Tun more than six years before.[68]

The morale of the Burma Army was boosted: the scheme to link up the northeastern base areas with the old strongholds in central Burma had failed decisively. In the end, Chinese arms reached only "War Zone 108" in western Shan State.

While the CPB was failing in central Burma in the turbulent mid-1970s, unrelated anti-government protests swept Rangoon, Mandalay and other urban areas, aggravating the situation and, in the end, strengthening the military's grip on power. A new, "civilian" constitution had been promulgated on 3 January 1974, following an Albanian-style referendum in which over 90% had voted in favour of the government's proposal.

Officially, Burma was now the "Socialist Republic of the Union of Burma" ruled by the BSPP. But, in reality, nothing had really changed. According to US Burma scholar David I. Steinberg:

> The BSPP was the alter ego of the Revolutionary Council. . . . About 60 percent of all members belonged to the military or police, or were retired officials of these services. . . . The *tatmadaw* (armed forces) control the BSPP and its subsidiary organisations; and the *tatmadaw*, the BSPP and the administration are under the control of Ne Win.[69]

If anything, the "referendum" and the new constitution had legitimised army rule in Burma.

This did not satisfy the population at large, and on 13 May, the oil workers at Chauk went on strike demanding higher wages. The unrest spread from the oil fields—the origin of the historic anti-British movement of the 1930s—to Rangoon. Railway workers and labourers at a spinning mill in the capital went on strike on 6 June. The government responded by sending in troops who fired indiscriminately on the workers.

More unrest erupted towards the end of the year, when the body of former UN secretary general U Thant was flown back to Burma for burial. Rangoon's traditionally militant students seized the opportunity to launch massive anti-government demonstrations. The army were called in again, and scores of students were killed when the troops sprayed automatic rifle fire into the crowds. Martial law was clamped on Rangoon, but the unrest continued for more than a year until the government had forced the opposition into submission.

The authorities blamed the protests on "unscrupulous elements from the outside who had created disturbances", and made vague references to the Communists.[70]

But unlike in 1962, this time there was no exodus of intellectuals to the CPB's base area, despite the fact that the Communists were now militarily much stronger than ever before. This was not only because the Communists had managed to alienate themselves from the urban population as a result of the *pyouk-touk-htak* purges in the 1960s.

It was also because encouraging unrest among them ran contrary to the CPB's Maoist strategy, the essence of which was still to establish strongholds in the rural areas in order to surround the towns and the cities. Significantly, the CPB only assigned one not very senior cadre, Zaw Win, to liaise with the students in Rangoon.[71] Although he managed to woo a few over to the CPB side, the number was insignificant compared to the many Burmese intellectuals who flocked to the Thai border to join U Nu's resistance.

Instead, the CPB was busy reorganising itself and remapping its military tactics following the loss of the central base areas. After the death of Thakin Zin and Thakin Chit, a new, extended Central Committee was formed. From 1975 onwards, the "northeastern group" became the official, rather than only the *de facto* , leadership of the CPB. Thakin Ba Thein Tin was elected new chairman and Khin Maung Gyi became party secretary. Then, in October 1975 a new plan, codenamed "7510" (after the year and month) was drawn up. The aim was to extend the northeastern base area, east of the Salween, to the areas west of the river, and then to try to re-enter central Burma and rebuild the lost strongholds there.

But in order to do this, alliances with the non-communist, ethnic rebel groups west of the Salween were imperative. The newly established ties with the northern forces of the SSA proved crucial, as did similar alliances which were being forged with smaller bands of Pa-O, Padaung (Kayans) and Kayah (Karenni) rebels. These groups benefited from arms supplies from the CPB in return for allowing the Communists to operate in their respective areas.

A new brigade, 683, was set up for the westward push. It was commanded by Li Ziru, one of the many Chinese Red Guard volunteers who had joined the CPB in 1968: "We crossed the Salween towards the end of 1975 and fought our way through Shan State together with the SSA for more than a year. It was not until February 1977 that we reached the Loi Tsang [Elephant Mountain] range in western Shan State, overlooking the party's old stronghold in the Kyawkku-Nawng Long-Nawng Wu area."[72]

But the new 683 Brigade was unable to push further west than Loi Tsang, and even to stay there they had to depend on the SSA's local contacts and support base. The Shans and other minority peoples in the area clearly favoured the non-communist rebel groups and viewed the arrival of the CPB with suspicion. As a result, the SSA was also forced to distance itself from the CPB in order not to lose the support it was still enjoying. Not only had Plan 7510 failed—the alliance with the SSA was also in jeopardy.

In northern Kachin State, the rebels had little hope of success despite widespread popular support for their cause. The KIA had been fighting a two-front war since 1968 with extremely heavy casualties. On 1 March 1975, the KIA's ablest field commander, Zau Dan (one of the three brothers who had founded the movement in 1961), was killed in battle with the CPB in northeastern Shan State. The other two brothers—Gen. Zau Seng and vice chief of staff Zau Tu—were based at the Tam Ngob headquarters of Gen. Li Wen-huan, where they were busy trading in jade and opium.

At the front in the north, the soldiers were almost starving, and in a desperate attempt to raise funds, a German mining engineer was kidnapped at the Namtu silver mine in northern Shan State on 4 March. He was released on 8 May after the West German government had paid a US$250,000 ransom through its embassy in Bangkok. The money, however, went to Tam Ngob, and did not alleviate the situation in the north.

The word spread that both Zau Tu and the ideologue, Pungshwi Zau Seng, had taken minor wives despite protests from the Baptist church. The third leader on the Thai border, Gen. Zau Seng, seemed to care little about the welfare of his soldiers: he spent most of his time in Chiang Mai and Bangkok, meeting officials from Taiwan and Thailand, and pursuing his jade business.

On 12 August, a mysterious radio message arrived at the KIA's jungle headquarters in the Triangle area between the Mali Hka and Nmai Hka rivers. It came from Tam Ngob and simply said that "the old leaders can no longer fulfil their duties". Maj. N'Chyaw Tang, who received the strange message, handed it over to Brang Seng, the highest-ranking Kachin official in the north. He replied the following day by requesting a clarification. The reply this time was more explicit: it outlined how the old leaders had deposited the organisation's money in their own bank accounts in Bangkok. Therefore, Zau Seng, Zau Tu and Pungshwi Zau Seng had been executed on the 6th.

The Kachin movement was plunged into a deep crisis. For several months, the remaining leaders in the north tried to keep it secret, but the official media in Rangoon made the news public, saying that there had been infighting within the KIA. The CPB sent a cryptic congratulatory message to the KIA: "All officers, cadres, rank and file of the KIA! Dear Comrades! Greetings: we do wish you all well, do have strong spirits and courage."[73]

An emergency meeting was called at Pa Jau, a camp on the Yunnan frontier, on 15 January 1976. It lasted for almost a month, until a new leadership had been elected. Brang Seng became chairman of the political wing, the Kachin Independence Organisation (KIO), and Brig. Tu Jai chief of staff of the KIA with Malizup Zau Mai as his deputy.

Four months later, the KIO and the CPB signed an alliance, ending the war between the two groups. The agreement was written in pure Maoist language:

> Today, throughout the world the two superpowers—the Soviet social-imperialists and American imperialists—are trying to divide and rule the world between them. . . . It is necessary to decisively stand on the side of the world's peoples headed by the socialist People's Republic of China. . . . Both parties totally agree that the common enemy of the people of all nationalities—the Ne Win-San Yu military government—is the chief representative of the three main enemies: imperialism, feudalism-landlordism and bureaucrat capitalism.[74]

Had the ardent Christian KIA become Communist? Despite the Maoist rhetoric—and invitations to all Kachin rebel leaders to visit China—little actually changed in an ideological sense inside the rebel held areas of Kachin State. But Chinese-made assault rifles, machine-guns, mortars and ammunition began flowing in.

The KIA withdrew its last men from the Thai frontier, only to unleash a vicious campaign against Burma Army outposts in the north with their newly acquired weaponry. The road between Myitkyina and Bhamo was cut and a secure base area set up along the Chinese border. A new headquarters was established at Pa Jau, a collection of grassy hills only a few kilometres from the frontier which the Kachins turned into a sprawling community of rebel officers, jade traders and a few civilians.

The Kachins were now, like the CPB before them, able to establish their own "buffer state" with its own administrative system, schools, hospitals and infrastructure. But the KIO's territory was not confined to any specific border area: it stretched from Chaukan Pass on the Indian frontier, across Kachin State to Pa Jau adjacent to China; from the hills south of Putao to the Kachin-inhabited areas of northeastern Shan State. The area under the KIO's influence encompassed nearly 40,000 square kilometres.

The Kachins were now also able to deal directly with the Chinese authorities across the Yunnan frontier—but not on the same level as the CPB. Connections with the KIA were maintained through the foreign relations branch of the Chinese Foreign Ministry, which maintained branch offices not only in the Yunnanese provincial capital of Kunming but also in remote border towns such as Yinjiang and Tengchong.

The CPB, which was recognised as a "fraternal communist party", dealt with Kang Sheng's security apparatus and his International Liaison Department (ILD) of the Communist Party of China. The ILD reported directly to the Central Committee and, as John Byron and Robert Pack put it, "[it] had an almost unlimited charter in external affairs during the 1950s and 1960s, wielding far greater infuence than its government counterpart, the Foreign Ministry."[75]

During the 1970s, Panghsang was not only the CPB's main base; there were also about a dozen representatives of the Communist Party of Thailand and more than twenty cadres from the PKI, the Indonesian party, including two daughters of its once powerful chairman, D.N. Aidit.[76] The Communist Party of Malaya's *Suara Revolusi Malaya* ("Voice of the Malayan Revolution") broadcast from Hengyang south of Changsha in Hunan province.

All "fraternal communist parties" also had offices in Kunming as well as in the diplomatic quarter of Beijing.[77] Kang Sheng had grand plans, and the CPB's base area along the Yunnan frontier was the springboard from which he hoped to spread Communism down to Southeast Asia.

The alliances with the Kachins—and the Shans—strengthened the CPB's position all over northern Burma. But its policy towards the power struggle which at this time was raging in China had a less favourable impact on the party's future. Kang Sheng, the CPB's mentor, died in Beijing on 16 December 1975 at the age of seventy-seven.

On 8 January 1976, less than a month later, Zhou Enlai died of cancer of the bladder. It was widely believed that Zhou had intended to position the more pragmatic Deng Xiaoping to take over the government. With Kang out of the picture, the hardliners felt that their influence was in danger of being curbed. Mao's wife, the voluptuous former film actress Jiang Qing, launched a vicious campaign aimed at ousting Deng and other moderates.[78]

The power struggle raged until April 1976, when China's radical Left managed to reassert itself and oust Deng. The CPB—unlike other communist parties in the region—made the crucial mistake of speaking out loudly in favour of the hardliners: "The revisionist clique [with which Deng was linked] headed by Liu Shaoqi has been defeated," the CPB stated in a congratulatory message on the 55th anniversary of the CPC in June 1976. It went on: "The movement to repulse the Right deviationist attempt at reversing correct verdicts, and the decision of the Central Committee of the CPC on measures taken against rightist chieftain Deng Xiaoping are in full accord with Marxism-Leninism, Mao Zedong thought".[79]

Then Mao Zedong himself died on 9 September. The CPB stated in a message, mourning the old chairman's death:

> Guided by Chairman Mao Zedong's proletarian revolutionary line, the Chinese people seized great victories in the socialist revolution and socialist construction in the Great Proletarian Cultural Revolution, in criticising Liu Shaoqi's counter-revolutionary revisionist line, in criticising Lin Biao and Confucius and in criticising Deng Xiaoping and repulsing the Right deviationist attempt at reversing correct verdicts and consolidating the dictatorship of the proletariat, thus, consolidating the People's Republic of China—the reliable bulwark of the world proletarian revolution.[80]

The CPB had reason to re-evaluate the reliability of that bulwark when Deng reassumed power at a Central Committee meeting in Beijing in July 1977. The CPB, which once had branded its own "revisionists" *yebaw* Htay and Ghoshal as "Burma's Deng Xiaoping" and "Burma's Liu Shaoqi" respectively, fell silent. Kang was gone, and so was Mao.

The *Beijing Review* and other official Chinese publications, which had previously published battle news and CPB documents, stopped printing anything about the "revolutionary struggle in Burma". The CPB had been mentioned for the last time in November 1976 when Thakin Ba Thein Tin and Thakin Pe Tint went to Beijing to call on Mao's successor as chairman, Hua Guofeng, who was soon to lose power to Deng.[81]

The Burmese military quickly and shrewdly exploited the rift by lending its good offices to China in Cambodia, by then forming the focus of Chinese interest as concern in Beijing increased over Vietnam's designs on its Indochinese neighbour. Communist forces had emerged victorious in all three Indochinese countries, only to fall out with each other, with China supporting the Khmer Rouge regime in Cambodia, and the Soviet Union backing Vietnam and Laos.

On 26 November 1977, Ne Win became the first foreign head of state to visit Phnom Penh after the Khmer Rouge take-over. The Chinese were no doubt behind the unusual visit, hoping to draw the Khmer Rouge out of its diplomatic isolation. Ne Win played along, for his part hoping that Beijing would further reduce its support for the CPB.

He was not disappointed. In 1978, the CPB's entire China-based central office, including the broadcasting station, the *People's Voice of Burma*, was forced to return to Panghsang, the official general headquarters since the fall of Pegu Yoma in 1975. The Chinese "volunteers" were also recalled.

The shift in China's policy was clearly demonstrated on 26 January 1978 when China's paramount leader, the twice-disgraced and now resurrected Deng Xiaoping, flew into Rangoon for a six-day visit. The diminutive but extremely shrewd Chinese leader was greeted by Ne Win as an honoured guest.

Relations between Beijing and Rangoon were showing signs of serious improvement for the first time since the anti-Chinese riots in 1967. Admittedly, Deng had at about the same time declared in Malaysia that "government-to-government" relations were different from "party-to-party" relations, thus implying that Chinese support for the CPB and similar Communist rebellions in the region would continue.

But the writing was on the wall: all the erstwhile Chinese patrons of Thakin Ba Thein Tin and the CPB, were either dead or out of power—and Deng, the old "capitalist roader", to use the pejorative of the Red Guards, was back at the helm in Beijing. He had other plans for spreading China's influence in Southeast Asia than arming Communist revolutionaries.

Faced with this new situation, the CPB central committee met, first at Möng Ko and later at Panghsang, for a marathon meeting that lasted from November 1978 to June 1979. The party's fortieth anniversary on 15 August 1979 was subdued. In a lengthy speech to his sullen comrades, Thakin Ba Thein Tin emphasised that the party must be "self-reliant" and, without being specific, said that the CPB "had made many mistakes" during its forty-year-long history.

In other announcements, "non-interference" was declared as a major aspect of the CPB's relations with "fraternal communist parties".[82] The "CPB decade" was over, eleven and a half years after Naw Seng's spectacular push into Möng Ko early on New Year's Eve 1968.

8

Guns, Drugs, and Ethnic Resistance

The rainy season of 1976 had not yet started when the non-communist ethnic rebel leaders began assembling near the Thai frontier. Escorted by their personal security guards, many of them arrived at the new headquarters of the Karen rebels suffering from malaria and dengue fever. The camp was called Manerplaw ("Victory Field"), and it had been established the year before right on the bank of the Moei border river.

Sheltered to the north, west and south by steep, rugged mountains, Manerplaw was virtually impregnable. It was an ideal place for a camp, but it also showed how far east the Karen rebels had been pushed. Their first headquarters had been located in Insein, a Rangoon suburb. Then they had moved to the town of Toungoo on the main Rangoon–Mandalay railway line, before being forced to retreat to Papun in March 1950. When Papun fell five years later, the Karens moved to the hills around Hlaingbwe, an even smaller town in the eastern hills. Since the late 1960s, a string of new camps right on the Thai border were the only permanent bases the Karens maintained inside Burma.

The Dawna range, parallel to the Thai border, was all that remained of the vast territory the Karens had once controlled, having been forced out of the delta in 1970–71 and out of the Pegu Yoma in 1975. But the eastern hills were ideal guerrilla country; Bo Mya and others had sniped at and ambushed the Japanese there during World War II. After independence, the Rangoon government never managed to fully control the area; it became the Karen "rebel state" of Kawthoolei, and Bo Mya intended to make it the base for the entire non-communist, ethnic resistance against Rangoon.

By the time the delegates began their session in a bamboo barrack on 26 April 1976, the situation in the region seemed grim for the non-communist resistance. Communist forces had emerged victorious from the wars in all the countries of Indochina: Vietnam, Laos and Cambodia. The CPB was still strong and posed a significant threat to Burma's stability.

Thailand's three military rulers for many years, Thanom, Prapass and Thanom's son, Narong Kittikachorn, had been driven into exile in Taiwan by a massive, popularly supported student uprising in October 1973. Thailand's fragile democratic government was having to face both the volatile student community and Communist guerrillas, who were active throughout the country, and the former were showing clear signs of sympathy for the latter.

Thailand's domestic security service, the Communist Suppression Operations Command (CSOC, later known as the Internal Security Operations Command or ISOC), was created by Prapass, but since its inception in 1965 it had been headed by Gen. Saiyud Kerdphol, one of Thailand's most professional soldiers.

Border issues and "special operations", however, were in the hands of Sudsai Hasdin, a controversial, maverick colonel with a crew cut and a quirky smile. In the aftermath of the 1973 uprising, he had founded what in effect amounted to a private army, named the *Krathing Daeng*, or the Red Gaurs. It consisted of vocational students and assorted hoodlums from the Thai countryside who had been mobilised to counter leftist trends at the universities in Bangkok. Many of his men were also mercenaries recruited from among Burma's many ethnic minorities.

The Border Patrol Police (BPP), founded by Sarit and partly funded by the CIA, had always paid particular attention to remote areas inhabited by hill tribes.[1] There had been for many years a clear interaction between CSOC, Col. Sudsai, the BPP and the minority armies from Burma that were based along the Thai border.

Sudsai himself had been working for CSOC since 1968. The following year, he had been assigned to set up a special operations centre to "assist the hill tribes" in northern Thailand. Officially designated Centre 113, the unit had been set up by SEATO in cooperation with CSOC.[2]

The hill tribes, with their uncertain loyalty to Thailand, were considered soft targets for the Communists, and SEATO also sponsored the formation of the Hill Tribe Research Centre at Chiang Mai University, where well-qualified scholars, sometimes unwittingly, provided the Thai and US security agencies with useful research on the hill peoples of the Golden Triangle. Lieut.-Gen. Jesus M. Vargas wrote in the SEATO report for 1967–68:

> The Hill Tribe Research Centre . . . continues to make significant progress in its primary task of producing worthy studies on the tribal peoples in Thailand. Such studies are becoming increasingly important as the Communists have concentrated much effort to subvert the hill peoples of the country. To counteract Communist subversion, it is important to have a wide knowledge of these people.[3]

Liaison with the ethnic rebels from Burma formed part of this policy: apart from the fact that they functioned as a buffer in the hilly areas of northern Thailand, where many tribes were to be found on both sides of the border, some of them served with the *Krathing Daeng*. They also provided vital cross-border intelligence. In return, the agreement which had been reached during P. Pibulsongkram's time in the early 1950s had not been altered; if anything, it had become even more pronounced as the Communist threat grew.

The rebels continued to be allowed to let their families live on Thai soil, and to buy arms, ammunition and other supplies in Thailand—and now the Thais also attached special agents to Karen and Mon units, who served as observers and advisers. They also issued travel permits for rebel leaders who wanted to go to Chiang Mai or Bangkok—and helped them procure munitions in Thailand.

But some order had to be established among the plethora of minority rebels that were roaming the Burmese jungle. The aim of the Manerplaw meeting was to form a third alternative to the Communists and the government in Rangoon. This new front had to be made up of ethnic minorities only, as U Nu and Law Yone's non-communist resistance had all but collapsed. Bo Let Ya of the Thirty Comrades still had some men under his command in the Three Pagodas Pass area and further to the south, but they were becoming inconsequential. All their attempts to initiate an uprising among the Burmans had failed, and their relationship with the Mons and the Karens was strained.

Representatives from thirteen ethnic groups attended the Manerplaw meeting, which lasted for more than two weeks. The outcome was declared on 10 May: ten of these groups decided to form the National Democratic Front (NDF).[4] It was far from the first attempt to coordinate the activities of Burma's many ethnic rebel armies, but it was much better organised than any of its predecessors. It was to become the only front which did not die a sudden death after a few years. Crucial for its survival was, of course, the tacit support it received from Thailand's security agencies.

Bo Mya had with astonishing efficiency, accompanied by sometimes rather ruthless methods, purged the Karen National Union of all leftist influences. First, he had distanced himself from the radical Karen National United Party and formed his own Karen National United Front (KNUF) in 1968.

The Karens in the Pegu Yoma had then decided to send an old veteran, KNUP vice chairman Mahn Ba Zan, to negotiate with Bo Mya. But Mahn Ba Zan had subsequently defected to Bo Mya and become chairman of his KNU faction. The confusion had not been sorted out until after the arrival of the Pegu Yoma survivors in the eastern hills in 1974–75. They had been forced to surrender to Bo Mya. A few KNUP leftists had been executed; the others had met for a last meeting of the party at Sawtha on the banks of the Salween in September 1975.

In December, the KNUP had been dissolved and amalgamated with Bo Mya's faction. A reunited KNU emerged, with Mahn Ba Zan as its official leader but dominated by Bo Mya.

The leftists had not had much to offer by way of an alternative to Bo Mya's well-oiled set-up along the Thai border; Sgaw Ler Taw and the others, who had left the Pegu Yoma for Panghsang and China a few years before, had returned in June 1975 to find the Pegu Yoma gone—and to report to the Karens along the Thai border that the Chinese would not offer any aid unless it was channelled through the CPB.[5]

In the north, however, there was no choice but to join up with the powerful Communists. The Kachins formed a military alliance with the CPB shortly after the Manerplaw meeting. The Kachin Independence Army was subsequently strengthened, but it almost immediately withdrew from the Thai border and closed down its old liaison post at Gen. Li Wenhuan's KMT base at Tam Ngob.

Meanwhile the Shan State Army was also moving closer to the CPB militarily as well as politically. Sao Hsö Khan, or Sao On Paung, one of the first Shan students to go underground, began openly to advocate communist ideology, and Shan commanders held meetings in the jungle under huge portraits of Marx, Engels, Lenin, Stalin and Mao Zedong.

In March 1976, a month before the Manerplaw meeting, the two most prominent politicians in the SSA's political wing, the Shan State Progress Party, president Khun Kya Nu and general secretary Sao Hsö Wai (Chao Tzang Yawnghwe) were ousted in a mini coup: they settled in Chiang Mai and did not attend the Manerplaw meeting. The SSPP was represented by Hseng Harn, the young medical student from Hsipaw who had accompanied the Yawnghwe Mahadevi to Thailand in 1964. Unlike the Kachins, the SSA never left the NDF, despite the alliance with the CPB.

The anti-communist element in Thailand's security policy reached a new height in October 1976. The old dictator, Thanom, had quietly returned from Taiwan as an ordained monk, which sparked a new round of student unrest in Bangkok. His comrade-in-arms, Prapass, had turned up earlier, only to be forced to leave Thailand again amid violent student protests.

The political climate was becoming as hot as the weather in the Thai capital. Deepening the crisis were vociferous allegations by the Right that certain ministers in the government of Seni Pramoj, a respected civilian, were "Communists". While the Left was demanding that Thanom leave the country; the Right just as strenuously sought the removal of the alleged "Communist" ministers.

A climax was reached on 6 October. By then, several hundred hard-core *Krathing Daeng*, motivated by longstanding association, faith and loyalty, had formed an elite force around the "godfather of the Right", Col. Sudsai.

Sudsai himself checked into a suite in the Royal Hotel, overlooking an open field outside Thammasat University called Sanam Luang. From there, he directed a force of 100 *Krathing Daeng* daredevil volunteers, who entered the campus undetected at six in the morning of 6 October: "Our mission was to break into the campus first so that the police would follow. As soon as our mission was accomplished, we all withdrew from the campus at around 7:10 A.M. The rest was the duty of the police officers."[6]

Police units, supported by BPP contingents and with helicopters hovering ahead, then stormed the campus. According to the government, they killed only forty-six students, while unofficial sources say the number of victims was in the hundreds. Young students were hung from the tamarind trees which surround Sanam Luang, and their bodies thrown on fires that had been lit on the field. Many more were wounded and at least 1,300 arrested.[7]

That same day, the official radio announced the seizure of power by the "National Administrative Reform Council", which became known by the sinister acronym NARC. It was headed by military strongman Adm. Sa-ngad Chaloryu, but it appointed a right-wing civilian, Thanin Kraivixien, as prime minister.

In direct response to the carnage in Bangkok, more than 4,000 students and other activists fled to the jungle to swell the ranks of the Communist Party of Thailand (CPT). They boosted the morale of the revolutionaries and brought with them new, fresh ideas to the guerrilla hide-outs in the isolated mountains and forests in the south, north and, especially, the northeast. The influx ranged from three of Thailand's most popular music bands (including Gammachon and Caravan), famous student leaders, teachers and professors, intellectuals, labour unionists and leftist politicians.

A *Krathing Daeng* leader commented: "After 6 October . . . the Red Gaurs . . . also went underground to watch leftist activities while others went into the jungles and took up arms to help protect road construction crews and fight the Communists."[8]

While no ethnic insurgents from Burma had taken part in the storming of Thammasat University, hundreds were recruited by Sudsai for duties in the jungle, where his vocational students found life too tough. Was, Lahus and Pa-Os from Burma willingly joined in the fight, as did large numbers of ex-KMT soldiers from Tam Ngob and Mae Salong in northern Thailand— and many fighters from the latest addition to Burma's list of insurgent groups: the Shan United Army (SUA), formerly known as Loi Maw *Ka Kwe Ye* (KKY).

Khun Sa's new base at Ban Hin Taek, inside Thailand northwest of Chiang Rai, was developing fast. With Lo Hsing-han out of the way, Khun Sa had taken over much of the cross-border trade in opium. Heroin refineries were established in the mountains north of Ban Hin Taek, where uniformed SUA soldiers mingled with BPP policemen and Thai paramilitary forces.

The only connection with the rest of Thailand consisted of a rutted dirt-track over the hills, but this served to conceal what was at the end of the road: a booming settlement of two-storey, concrete merchant houses, sprawling market places, cinemas, brothels, army barracks, a Chinese temple, and a Shan pagoda.

For a man like Khun Sa, virtually uneducated and raised by foster parents, this was quite an achievement. He proudly invited his stepbrothers to join him, and both Khun Aung Tun (Oscar) and Khun Ywat Möng (Billy) came; Khun Aye (Morgan) was already well-established as a legitimate businessman in Burma.

Despite its name and the presence of a few Shan field commanders, the SUA remained dominated by ethnic Chinese opium merchants and ex-KMT officers. His chief of staff, Chang Shu-chuan, was actually a Manchurian who had fought with the legendary Bataillon Spécial 111 in Laos before joining Khun Sa in the mid-1960s.[9] In the SUA, he assumed the Shan name Sao Hpalang ("General Thunder").

The second in command, Leng Chong-ying, was also an ex-KMT officer who had served in Laos, but had been born in the Beijing area. He was given the Shan name Leng Seün.

The Shan element of the organisation had to be emphasised in order to maintain a good relationship with the Thais. To strengthen the facade even further, Khun Sa invited Long Khun Maha, the Shan writer and poet who had been the first president of the Shan State Independence Army in 1960, to settle in Ban Hin Taek, where Khun Sa bought a printing press for him.

Khun Sa and his well-equipped SUA emerged as Gen. Li Wenhuan's most important rival in the drug trade. Gen. Li's own troops were dwindling; the old soldiers had settled in the border areas as merchants and farmers, and the younger generation had less incentive to fight on in the hills and jungles of Shan State.

Gen. Li needed a proxy inside Burma. Having failed to forge an alliance with the SSA, he had contacted one of its best-known commanders, Moh Heng, the one-armed, Shan ex-CPB officer. Already disgruntled with the subordinate position he had been forced to occupy following the arrival of the Mahadevi in Thailand, Moh Heng had accepted Li's offers of support. In 1968, he had taken over the Thai border village of Pieng Luang from a smaller, rival group. With backing from Gen. Li's 3rd KMT, the Shan United Revolutionary Army (SURA) had been set up at Pieng Luang in January 1969.

By the mid-1970s, Pieng Luang had become a booming border town that rivalled Ban Hin Taek in wealth, prosperity, and importance for the cross-border trade as well as cross-border intelligence gathering. It soon boasted well-stocked shops, three brothels, four gambling dens, schools, a thirty-bed hospital, and, on a hill overlooking the settlement, the secluded residence of Moh Heng himself. The town was divided into two parts: to the east of the main road lived the Shans in wooden houses and bamboo shacks, and to the east were concrete Chinese merchant houses and a temple dedicated to the goddess of prosperity.

Khun Sa had reason to despise the KMT. In 1967, when he was a young and upcoming warlord, he had set out from Vingngün in the Wa Hills with a massive, sixteen-ton opium convoy, destined for Ban Khwan, a small Laotian lumber town across the Mekong river. He had announced that he was not going to pay any tax to the KMT for his opium, which at that time was compulsory for all convoys passing through the areas bordering Thailand and Laos. More traders had joined his convoy, so by the time it reached Kengtung, "its single-file column of five hundred men and three hundred mules stretched along the ridgelines for over a mile".[10]

The convoy had crossed the Mekong on 14 and 15 July, and the KMT had rushed to intercept it. Hundreds of fighters had come down from Tam Ngob and Mae Salong. On the 29th, they had attacked. Fierce fighting raged for several days, and wounded soldiers from both sides were treated at hospitals in Chiang Rai, where they often ended up in the same wards, chatting with each other and sharing cigarettes.

The outcome of the battle is still somewhat obscure. Gen. Ouane Rattikone, the commander in chief of the Royal Lao Army, ran several heroin refineries in the Ban Houey Sai area at this time, and he sent the Lao air force to bomb the battle site. Officially, he had cheated both Khun Sa and the KMT, and made off with the opium. Other sources say the opium had already been sold, and that Khun Sa had subsequently made his first significant investment in Thailand.

Whatever the case, the rivalry between Khun Sa and Gen. Li persisted, and this was obvious inside Thailand as well. Charlie Win, the young Sino-Burmese who had kidnapped the two Soviet doctors in Taunggyi in April 1973, had been rewarded by Khun Sa with a trading house in Chiang Mai. The company, Saha Charoenmit, officially dealt in jade and other precious stones, but it also served as an SUA warehouse in the city. Located around the corner from Moon Muang Road, Chiang Mai's main tourist strip, where foreigners gathered for fruit shakes and cheap Thai food, it was conspicuous for its solid iron gate and the high wall that surrounded it.[11]

Gen. Li's presence in Thailand was even more blatant. He continued to live in his fortified villa on Faham Road in Chiang Mai, and had even acquired Thai citizenship after a "resettlement deal" in early 1972. Washington had contributed US$1 million to the deal which had included a drug burning show in which twenty-six tons of opium had been publicly burnt. Gen. Li had stated that he was washing his hands of the trade. Some observers, however, were not so convinced:

> These 26 tons of what was said to be opium was burnt, although witnesses have privately testified the smell was that of burning soya-beans and banana, and not the unmistakable pungent, sticky odour of burning opium; the ex-KMT then, not surprisingly, proceeded to demand additional payment for their destruction of another ton, the 27th ton.[12]

The 3rd and the 5th KMT were renamed "Chinese Irregular Forces" (CIF) and permitted to remain on Thai territory. The CIF was also placed directly under the control of the Supreme Command in Bangkok; a special task force, code-named "04", was set up to supervise the ex-KMT in Mae Salong, Pieng Luang and Tam Ngob.

The status of the new CIF was further enhanced in October 1977, when the military deposed the civilian figurehead, Thanin, and Gen. Kriangsak Chomanan became prime minister. A former commander of the 3rd Thai Army Region, which encompasses the entire north of the country, Kriangsak had been the one to negotiate Khun Sa's release from jail in Mandalay in 1974. His relationship with the ex-KMT forces was even stronger: to express their gratitude for all the sympathy Kriangsak had shown them, Gen. Duan Xiwen's men had built a vacation house for the Thai general in Mae Salong.[13]

Following the massacre of students the year before, the Thanin government had tried desperately to improve its image by using the internationally popular "anti-drug" issue. A "total war" on narcotics had been declared, and it had been widely accepted as real.

"This is the first time a Thai prime minister has put an anti-narcotics drive at the top of the government's priorities," declaimed Peter Law, the head of the drug suppression unit at the British embassy in Bangkok. "The present atmosphere is the best yet to conduct all aspects of anti-narcotics operations."[14]

Thanin's dismissal and the ascent to power of Gen. Kriangsak dispelled such pretences: the Thai government had by then already achieved the international respectability it had so badly needed in October 1976, and it was time to get down to *realpolitik*.

The Thais were actually caught in a dilemma. They needed support from the nations concerned about communism and drugs, but many drug trafficking bands were closely connected to Thailand's security agencies, and the Thais benefited economically from the trade.

There was rampant corruption, but laundered drug money was rein-vested in the local economy. In 1977, several names of prominent drug traf-fickers who were living in "palatial splendour" in Thailand were mentioned in a testimony given by congressman Lester Wolff before the Select Com-mittee on Narcotics Abuse and Control of the US Congress. One of them was Chang Kai-cheng, or Thawee Sakulthanapanich, who resided in Bang-kok, Chiang Mai and Mae Sai, opposite Tachilek. He moved in high busi-ness circles, and owned or co-owned the Broadway Hotel and the Bai Cha-Hom Tea Company in Bangkok, a trucking and a hardware company in Chiang Rai—and he had excellent narcotics connections in Hong Kong, Singapore, Malaysia, the Netherlands and the United States.

Another was Chang Chen-ch'eng, a.k.a. Suthep Banjapokee, who lived

> in Bangkok in a beautiful modern home which has an underground room used for gambling and smoking opium. . . . He owns the Victory Hotel in Bangkok and a jewelry store at the rear of the hotel called Beauty Thai Silk. . . . He began to make considerable amounts of money in 1968 when Thailand's armed forces participated in the Vietnam war. This effort gave him the op-portunity to smuggle large quantities of heroin to Saigon for sale to Ameri-can soldiers.[15]

Sha Ming, who ran a big heroin refinery near Chiang Rai and who had enjoyed a good relationship with Kokang KKY commander Lo Hsing-han before his arrest, was mentioned as another prime mover of narcotics from the Golden Triangle to the world market. Sha Ming had moved to Thai-land from Burma in 1961. He ran a heroin refinery near Ban Houey Sai in Laos, and in Tachilek in Shan State, where he operated closely together with Lo Hsing-han, Yang Shih-li and other KKY home guard commanders.

Following Rangoon's order to disband the KKY, Sha converted his re-finery into several mobile laboratories before establishing a new facility near Chiang Rai in Thailand. He was a kind of superintendent for Chang Chen-ch'eng's operation, managing the refineries, hiring chemists and or-ganising distribution of the drugs.

Still another was Ma Hseuh-fu, a Yunnanese who had fled to Burma after the Communist take-over in China. He made his first fortune as an opium merchant in Shan State, and moved to Bangkok in 1964, where he ran the June Hotel and several tea companies. The June Hotel was popular with American Peace Corp volunteers in the 1960s. Many of them stayed there, and its coffee shop was a popular meeting place for the young Ameri-cans while on leave from their upcountry stations.[16]

Ma's Cha Mon Tea Company in Bangkok served as a front for the tran-shipment of large quantities of heroin into international markets. A member of the Triads, the Chinese secret societies, he was closely connected with Gen. Li.

Li's rival Khun Sa was connected with other networks. Heroin, which had been refined in laboratories under Khun Sa's control, was marketed in northern Thailand by Ma Cheng-wen, a Yunnanese Muslim (Panthay) born in Burma. He arrived in Thailand as early as 1963 and later became head of the SUA's office in the border town of Mae Sai, opposite Tachilek in Burma, where one of his duties was to procure and distribute chemicals for the heroin refineries along the border. He operated behind the front of the I-Chin Mining Company in Chiang Mai.[17]

An important connection with Bangkok's Chiu Chao Chinese was Lu Hsu-shui, better known by his Thai name, Vichien Vajirakaphan. He owed the Lung Feng goldshop in the heart of Bangkok's bustling Chinatown. The shop, which was opened in 1971, was used to finance Lu's narcotics trafficking. Lu was born of a poor Chinese family in Bangkok, and made his start in the narcotics business by trading opium for gold with the KMT in northern Thailand. Some of Lu's profits were invested in the popular Chiang Inn Hotel next to the night bazaar in Chiang Mai.[18]

An anonymous "American living in Thailand" wrote in a letter to Wolff in July 1977:

> There are several strong reasons for the Thais to unofficially countenance the presence of these groups [the SUA and the ex-KMT forces] along the northern border. Of practical importance is the valuable intelligence the Thais receive from them about communist activity in northeastern Burma. The Communist Party of Burma has control of around half the opium harvest, and it disposes of the raw opium by selling it to traders. . . . The volume has become such that the northwestern Thai towns' economy has become an appendage of it. Profits from the sale of opium and heroin are generally reinvested in another illegal trade: basic dry goods and things like radios are bought from northern Thai merchants for shipment across the border and illegal sale in Burma. If the narcotics traffic is forcibly stopped, the economy in the area will be wrecked.[19]

The drug networks had by the 1970s obviously come a long way since the modest beginnings of Tachilek trader Ma Shou-I and his band of brigands in the early 1950s. It should be noted, however, that many local people did not—and still do not—regard the traffickers as criminals. In a Chinese context—and nearly all opium and heroin merchants in the Golden Triangle are ethnic Chinese—these were wealthy men who often made lavish donations to charities and religious institutions.

Bo Yang, a well-known author from Taiwan, wrote after a visit to the Golden Triangle, where he had met ex-KMT officials and Khun Sa's representatives:

> On one point we do share a common understanding: the people of the north Thailand region, including ethnic Chinese and other minority peoples, all revere Luo Xinghan [Lo Hsing-han] despite his past involvement in the narcotics trade. I have heard it said that the bulk of his income from narcotics trafficking was spent on the construction of Chinese schools and the relief of poverty.[20]

While Lo may not have spent "the bulk" of his narcotics fortunes on such projects, he did finance the construction of a grand Chinese temple in Lashio, and generously supported the local Chinese community there, as did Khun Sa and all the other kingpins, which inevitably meant that they built up a network of clan members, followers and underlings. These could be called upon at any time and the "godfathers" knew that any assignment they ordered, no matter how risky, would be carried out to the letter.

All of them were also well-connected with military circles and politicians in Thailand as well as in Burma. They never forgot the wedding of a certain general's daughter, or a politician's birthday, or if a political party needed campaign funds or a police officer a new house. In return, these indigenous elites provided the feudally structured Chinese underworld with status and protection.

In this tangled web of personal allegiances and patron-client relationships, the "law" was of little or no relevance. And even if the law was to be used, there was in a legal sense little proof against the kingpins as they seldom dirtied their own hands: they had scores of loyal followers who handled the murkier sides of their enterprises. After all, Al Capone, the crime lord of Chicago in the 1920s, had also lived openly in his city. When the authorities finally managed to nail him, they had solid proof of only one charge against him: tax evasion.

Even the main masterminds of the narcotics trade in East Asia could claim some kind of legitimacy in a Chinese context. They were the Triads, which had been set up originally to overthrow the Manchu Ching Dynasty and to restore the more indigenous Mings. The first such group documented was the White Lotus Society, which could trace its origin to pre-Manchu days but only became powerful in the seventeenth century.

Another powerful group was the Hung Society, which evolved into the "Triad Society": to these tightly knit brotherhoods, bound together by almost religious rituals in order to avoid betrayal by fellow members of the group, the number 3 was of central significance. Numerologically, it was a magic number.: 3 multiplied by 3 equals 9, and any number whose digits add up to 9 is divisible by 9. To the Chinese, 3 was also the mystical number denoting the balance between Heaven, Earth and Man.[21]

Their ardent desire for self-preservation kept the anti-Manchu cause, and the Triads, alive for centuries, in China itself and especially among the overseas Chinese, who had emigrated mainly from the southern provinces where pro-Ming sentiments were strong.

The Mings were never restored, but the Ching dynasty was at last overthrown in 1912 and replaced by a republic. The Triads emerged as powerful groups which many Chinese ambitious for advancement found it prudent to join. Many KMT leaders were also Triad members, including Sun Yat-sen of the Society of Three Harmonies. Chiang Kai-shek relied heavily on the Green Gang in Shanghai during the civil war with the Communists, but many Triad societies had by then degenerated into street gangs involved with drug peddling, assassinations and extortion.

The Green Gang leader, Tu Yueh-sheng, nick-named "Big-eared Tu" because of his enormous ears, was a notorious gangster, and hardly a patriotic visionary. He dominated the opium and heroin trade in Shanghai during the freewheeling 1930s, and secretly sponsored Chiang Kai-shek's political career.[22] To express their gratitude, the Taiwan authorities later erected a statue in honour of "Big-eared Tu" in Xizhi village near Taipei. The four-character inscription on the momument praises the dead man's "loyalty" and "personal integrity".[23]

In the 1940s, new Triads had been set up by KMT officers and the Nationalist Government's secret police to fight the Communists more effectively. The best known was the 14K Society, founded in 1947 by a KMT general, Kot Siu Wong. The gang's name came from its first headquarters, which had been located at No. 14, Po Wah Road in Canton.[24]

When the Communists had won, Gen. Kot fled to Hong Kong with hundreds of his followers. Many of them settled in Rennie's Mill, a run-down village on Junk Bay east of Kai Tak airport, where Taiwanese flags are still flying over shabby-looking houses.

The 14K soon spread its tentacles throughout the Crown Colony, and to Chinatowns all over the world. "If Chinese restaurants are one feature of Chinatown, Chinese secret societies are another," wrote Chinese author Lynn Pan.[25] A 1986 report of the Hong Kong government Fight Crime Committee's working group on gangs and organised crime estimated that there were fifty different Triad societies in Hong Kong varying in size from a hundred members to several thousand.

One of the most powerful drug rings in Hong Kong was for many years headed by the Ma brothers, who were closely connected with the 14K Triad and another influential crime gang, the Sun Yee On syndicate. Natives of the Chiu Chao region of southern China, they had arrived in Hong Kong in 1949 virtually penniless.

After years working as street thugs in the vicinity of the notorious "Walled City" of Kowloon, they had started as petty heroin pushers in 1967. The elder brother, Ma Sik-yu, travelled to Burma's Golden Triangle to procure pure, No. 4 heroin. The younger brother, Ma Sik-chun, remained in Hong Kong in charge of streets gangs and distribution.

Ma Sik-yu had during his trips to the Burmese border in northern Thailand become acquainted with Gen. Li of the 3rd KMT. Li arranged for Taiwan intelligence operatives to meet Ma. Local representatives of Taiwan's well-established spy network in the Golden Triangle concluded that the Ma brothers would turn out to be financially solid as well as useful in intelligence gathering.[26]

The Ma network had by the mid-1970s become the largest drug empire in Hong Kong's history. Ma Sik-chun established a pro-Taiwan newspaper, the *Oriental Daily News*, while the elder Ma continued to run drugs from the Golden Triangle—and to provide Taiwan with vital intelligence from the Sino–Burmese border areas.

Ma Sik-yu, whose US$750 million-a-year business gave the two brothers respectability in the British Crown Colony, was commonly known as "White Powder Ma". Soon, another member of the family, a nephew called Ma Woon-yin, was brought into the multi-billion-dollar business.

The Hong Kong police were powerless. Finally, all that they could do was to arrest a central, but still rather insignificant, underling of the Ma drug empire: Ng Sik-ho, who was nick-named "Limpy" because of an injured leg that had resulted from a Triad fight in his youth. Ma Sik-yu slipped out of Hong Kong in February 1977 and fled to Taiwan, where he remains, protected by KMT intelligence for his valuable contributions to the Nationalist Chinese security services.

Ma Sik-chun and Ma Woon-yin were also arrested in connection with this scandal, only to find themselves offered US$ 200,000 bail each. This was easily paid—and they managed mysteriously to creep out of their houses at midnight. Taking advantage of the confusion surrounding the Chinese Moon Festival, they stepped aboard a freighter, registered in Panama, and steamed towards Taiwan.[27] Their subsequent fates are unknown.

In Taiwan, the notorious Bamboo Union Gang operated closely with the intelligence services of the Nationalist Chinese regime on the island, and on more than one occasion the gang's hitmen were sent abroad to carry out assassinations on behalf of the government.[28] Without exception, the Triads financed their various nefarious activities with "black money" earned from extortion and drug trafficking.

Among all the Southeast Asian countries, Thailand was about the only one where the influence of the Triads remained limited. They were certainly present there, but during the reign of Field Marshal P. Pibulsongkram and Police General Pao Sriyanonda in the 1950s the powerful Thai police had crippled the political clout of the Triads among Bangkok's huge Chinese business community.

The question of organised crime was especially sensitive in Thailand as the vast majority of its urban Chinese population consisted of Tewchou, or Chiu Chao Chinese from the Swatow area 270 kilometres up the Chinese coast from Canton. The Chiu Chaos had been deeply involved in the pro-Ming resistance to the Manchu rulers in Beijing from the seventeenth century.

When the Chiu Chaos failed to oppose the Imperial Court effectively, they had dispersed and migrated to a few selected places in Southeast Asia, of which Bangkok was the most important. Even today, the vast majority of Bangkok's ethnic Chinese are of Chiu Chao origin.

Their trading networks were more closely knit than those of other overseas Chinese, and their secret societies by far the strongest. Before long, they had come to dominate smuggling and opium traffic along the South China coast through their powerful exile community in Hong Kong—and their access through Thailand to the Golden Triangle opium trade was worrying indeed for Bangkok's traditional rulers.

While Yunnanese traffickers with direct access to people such as Khun Sa and Gen. Li were responsible for smuggling opium from northern Burma to the heroin refineries along the Thai border, it was the Chiu Chao syndicates who financed and controlled the major heroin shipments destined for the international market.

According to an official US document:

> These men are the bankers of the narcotics trade. Operating behind legitimate business covers and using Thai names, the major Chao Chou [Chiu Chao] financiers in Thailand are regarded as respectable businessmen, and have been immune from arrest and prosecution, largely because they rarely, if ever, personally touch narcotics. Only fellow members of a Chao Chou secret society know when and how a narcotics deal is being put together and who is involved.[29]

Journalist Melinda Liu summed up the new drug pecking order in a few words: "Hill tribes in Burma grow the opium. Insurgents in Shan State transport it. Yunnan Chinese tax it. And Chaozhou [Chiu Chao] Chinese buy and export it."[30]

The symbiotic relationship that had developed between the Yunnanese and the Chiu Chao—and the different roles which the two Chinese communities came to play—had its roots in the recent history of northern Thailand.

The socio-economic structure of northern Thailand had first been altered by the arrival of the railway in the 1920s. After more than ten years of hard work, blasting through the hills, the first train steamed into Chiang Mai, and the King in Bangkok could expect to control his northern Thai subjects more effectively.

But with the railway came, not exactly surprisingly, thousands of Chiu Chao-speaking Chinese from Bangkok. With trading partners already well-established in the capital, they swiftly took over most of the commercial activities in the north as well. They could soon be seen in shops and company offices all over Chiang Mai, though bearing Thai names and being just as assimilated as their cousins in Bangkok.

The next major change came with the influx of the Yunnanese, who had first arrived in the wake of the Communist victory in China. With them came also the opium; they were the muleteers, the local traders and the people with business links stretching as far north as Yunnan. But their role in the drug trade ended in Chiang Mai and, to a lesser extent, in Bangkok. The big business, and the regional and the international networks, were firmly in the hands of the Chiu Chao.

A working relationship had to be established with the immensely powerful Chiu Chao underworld in order to neutralise what could have amounted to subversion, and possible destabilisation of Thailand—and to make sure a fair share of their profits were reinvested in the Thai economy.[31]

When this had been accomplished, all that Thailand could actually afford to do to limit its role in the international drug traffic was to allow foreign interests to rid its own territory of poppies. Ambitious crop substitution projects were launched in the hills of northern Thailand, supported by the United Nations Fund for Drug Abuse Control and a host of foreign governments.

Coffee, kidney beans, potatoes, cabbages, thyme, marjoram, strawberries and orchids were introduced as new cash crops in the northern hills to woo the local hilltribe farmers away from poppy cultivation. Many did, and Thailand's own opium production was substantially reduced.

But Thailand had in any case never been a significant opium growing country; it was a transit country for narcotics from Burma as well as the nerve-centre of the trade, where deals were organised, couriers were hired and money was laundered. These activities continued unhampered, despite the massive foreign assistance to Thailand's opium eradication programme.[32]

Almost no foreigners had even tried to come to grips with the profound complexities of the Golden Triangle drug trade before US congressman Lester Wolff and Joseph Nellis, chief counsel of the Select Committee on Narcotics

Abuse and Control, proposed a radically new approach to the problem in the late 1970s. The Shan armies had decided to repeat their offer of 1973 to sell as much as possible of the opium harvest in the Golden Triangle to the US government. Lo was in jail, but Khun Sa agreed to support the proposal.

In April 1977, Wolff and Nellis travelled together to northern Thailand. While Wolff was following developments from Chiang Mai, Nellis and three of his aides boarded a helicopter and took off for Ban Hin Taek. They had decided to negotiate directly with the opium warlord to see whether it would be possible to cut the trade at the crucial stage along the border.

Although Khun Sa, contrary to popular beliefs and myths spread by many Western narcotics agencies, was not the mastermind of the international drug trade, his troops did control an area along the Thai border where raw opium was being refined into heroin. The actual owners of these refineries were Bangkok, Hong Kong and Taiwan-based syndicates who paid tax to Khun Sa in exchange for enjoying the protection of his army. If he decided to throw the syndicates out, they would have nowhere to go; the refineries had been forced to move from Hong Kong to the safer havens in the Golden Triangle in the 1960s, when it became impossible to carry out such activities in the British Crown Colony.

A number of heavily armed Thai BPP policemen greeted the American visitors on their arrival, and they were escorted to Khun Sa's residence in the hills. As the warlord spoke no English, one of his men acted as the interpreter. Ironically, he was Sai Joe, a young Shan who had learnt English while serving as a mercenary with the CIA in Laos.[33] The interview was full of Khun Sa platitudes—as usual, he emphasised his role as a "Shan freedom fighter", but the Americans were nevertheless impressed. Nellis later testified:

> [Khun Sa] is a very tough, aggressive and fearlessly ambitious man who has spent his lifetime escaping from efforts to capture him and coping with military problems. He would very much like to become a recognised political leader as well. He enjoys a joke, does not seem to mind his evil reputation as the biggest dope pusher in the world, and is an extremely pleasant and hospitable host.[34]

Referring to his discussions with Thai officials, Nellis concluded:

> The affinity between the opium warlords and the Thai government has been explained in terms of the over-powering corruption prevalent in the Thai military and civilian society. . . . [But] when one considers that Thailand is completely surrounded by radical left-wing military dictatorships and has a major insurgent problem of its own, it does not take long to conclude that if I were responsible for Thai security, I would be very happy to have well-trained,

armed men at my northwest borders who act as a buffer between me and
those who seek to subvert my country.

Increased tools for enforcement of narcotics laws already breached by corruption and the doing of nothing more is not going to make any difference
whatever, in my opinion. We must find a way to destroy this pestilence at the
source.

After a heated debate in the US Congress, the proposal was rejected.
Instead, the US authorities declared:

> The narcotics trade has long fostered a state of lawlessness over wide areas
> of Burma and northern Thailand. The rule of law in these areas has been
> replaced by depredations of warlord armies and bandits such as Chan
> Shee-fu's [Chang Chifu; Khun Sa] so-called Shan United Army. We have, there-
> fore, stressed the need for law enforcement.[35]

Dr. Peter Bourne, Director of the Office of Drug Abuse Policy, declared:

> It is unthinkable that any representative of this administration [that is,
> of then President Jimmy Carter] would negotiate with representatives of
> insurgent groups opposed to the legitimate government of Burma, much
> less use the American taxpayers' dollars for a programme that would, in
> effect, provide a subsidy for narcotics traffickers and arms for an insur-
> rection.[36]

The US decided to step up its support for Rangoon's "anti-narcotics campaign", which had been initiated in the wake of the arrest of Lo Hsing-han
in 1973. On 29 June 1974, the US and the Burmese government had signed
an agreement to cooperate in narcotics matters. As part of the deal, the US
also promised to supply Rangoon with

> six commercial Bell 205 utility helicopters together with initial spare parts,
> auxiliary equipment, and funds for related expenses, at a cost of up to S\$4.8
> million. . . . The United States Government is prepared subsequently to pro-
> vide an additional twelve helicopters, together with spare parts . . . to be de-
> livered during fiscal years 1976–1977.[37]

American assistance to Burma had actually begun shortly after the battle against the CPB at Kunlong in early 1973, although it was never officially acknowledged at the time. US-made M-1 carbines, recoilless rifles,
M-79 grenade throwers and 3.5-inch rocket launchers had been shipped to
Rangoon in an effort to stem the Communist tide—and also for the Americans to show their admiration for the fighting ability that the Burma Army

had displayed at Kunlong.[38] The helicopters were meant "for narcotics suppression purposes",[39] but the Americans apparently had no objections to their being used in ordinary counter-insurgency operations, even against rebels such as the Karens who were not involved in the trade.[40]

Many observers suspected that the US was playing the heroin card in order to break into Ne Win's hermetically sealed Burma. But it was a scheme which ran into severe problems immediately. The gross and well-documented human rights violations of the military regime in Burma had already become a controversy during the congressional hearings which were held shortly after Wolff and Nellis's visit to Ban Hin Taek.

An outspoken critic, Robert Schwab, stated:

> We are encouraging and supplying material for military operations against ethnic minorities by a government without any sustainable pretence to legal authority in the region. . . . This policy and aid would be questionable under any administration. Under the Carter administration they are clearly irreconcilable with explicit and reiterated human rights declarations.
>
> We have refused aid to several countries on the basis of their lack of concern for human rights; yet, in Burma, we provide the very equipment that makes deprivation of human rights more efficient, coupled with a policy that urges this deprivation to the utmost. . . . According to the great laxitude of the terms under which the helicopters [and presumably the fixed-wing aircraft] are given to the Burmese, they could conceivably be used even for strafing women and children in the poppy fields and still not violate the agreement.[41]

In any event, the US went ahead with its assistance, and the UNFDAC began a programme to substitute the opium poppy with other cash crops also in Burma. Bankrolled by the Norwegian government, the US$5 million project differed considerably from the Thai model. First of all, UN officials were only allowed in the administrative side of the 5-year project.[42] Secondly, most of it was spent on "preventative" crop substitution, i.e. new plants and crops were distributed in any area where poppies could potentially be grown.

The rationale for this was that "any limitation of the target population to the opium producing areas . . . would be counterproductive and a discrimination against the law abiding non-poppy growing farmers."[43] With this liberal interpretation of the concept "crop substitution" it was hardly surprising that the annual production in Burma had increased from 350 at the beginning of the programme to 1,280 tons when Norway eventually terminated its assistance in 1988.

The US and the UN's delicate—and potentially scandalous—involvement with the Burmese government had been in danger of becoming a major embarrassment long before that. In early 1978 forgotten Burma suddenly hit the headlines of the international media. More than 200,000 Muslim refugees streamed into Bangladesh from Burma's western Arakan State. Destitute and starving, they streamed up the muddy road to Teknaf across the Naaf border river, claiming that they had been driven from their land by Burmese government troops.

The refugees reported that government officials had first moved into Akyab, the Arakan state capital, and then in one night's sweep arrested more than 1,000 Muslims. A house-to-house search had been carried out forcefully and systematically, spreading panic through the local Muslim community. A demonstration against the drive was put down by the army, which killed several people.[44]

The unusual operation was code-named *Naga Min*, or King of Dragons, and was supposedly aimed at "properly registering every inhabitant of this country, citizen or foreigner. . . . However, 19,457 Bengalis fled to escape examination because they did not have proper registration papers."[45] The actual number of refugees was more than ten times the official figure, and the vast majority of them were not "Bengalis" but Rohingyas, a Muslim minority which had been living in Arakan for centuries. To counter charges of illegal residence in Burma, many refugees produced yellowed identification cards, issued as far back as the mid-1950s.

The Rohingya refugee crisis came at a time when Burma was facing severe political and economic difficulties. Rangoon and other cities had been rocked by student demonstrations against the regime, and discontent was still simmering throughout the country.

Economically, the situation was worse than ever, despite some attempts at liberalisation. When faced with a similar situation in 1967, the authorities had managed to divert the population's anger so that it was directed against the Chinese in Rangoon, thereby causing the violent Chinatown riots in June of that year.

The Muslim Rohingya minority was even more vulnerable than the Chinese in the capital. Many Burmese insisted they were Bengalis, and the government could expect support from even its most vocal opponents at home, despite the orgy of rape, arson and murder that the Burma Army had unleashed in Arakan, and which had been well-documented by journalists and relief workers visiting the Teknaf area of southeastern Bangladesh.

William Mattern of the *Far Eastern Economic Review* travelled to Rangoon and concluded: "Even President Ne Win's most bitter domestic critics vigorously deny the allegations of religious persecution, racial discrimination and systematic apartheid."[46]

In Arakan, the insurgency among the local Buddhists, which the "King of Arakan" U Sein Da had initiated in the late 1940s, had never really taken off. Although certainly no less nationalistic than other minority peoples in

Burma, the Buddhist Arakanese seemed to prefer a strong army presence in their state to a regional uprising that could destabilise Arakan and lead to a real influx of Muslims from neighbouring, overpopulated Bangladesh.

As a domestic ploy, the campaign against the Rohingyas was working— but it provoked a stream of protests mainly from Islamic countries, leading to intervention by the United Nations. The international media was full of headlines such as "Burmese Muslims machine-gunned", "Crime against humanity", "Burma carrying out genocide," and "The world's greatest unreported tragedy". It was acutely embarrassing for the United States: if politicians in Washington linked human rights violations to further assistance to Burma's military government, its fledgling anti-narcotics programme in Burma would be in jeopardy.

Then, by a strange coincidence, Asia's two rival political weeklies, the *Far Eastern Economic Review* and *Asiaweek*, published in the same week conspicuously similar stories which linked the Rohingya refugees to drug trafficking and Communism. The *Review*, which almost always bylines its stories, ran a piece by "A Correspondent". It made some astonishing claims:

> Some of [the] most militant refugees allege that they had made agreements with the BCP [i.e. the CPB] to allow the party freedom of operation within Arakan. . . . On this analysis, the Rohingyas are a far cry from the innocent victims of government repression that the Bangladesh press makes them out to be.[47]

Asiaweek went a step further and headlined its article "Drugs, Rebels and Refugees." It went on to quote "observers" as saying that

> it looks like some sort of an emerging alliance between Burmese communists and Bangladeshi and Indian border insurgents. No less ominous for government leaders in the region is another theory that centres on the drying-up of the traditional opium route through Laos and Thailand. According to this view, the Arakanese, in collaboration with the Shans and the Karens of Burma, are attempting to open a route through Bangladesh.[48]

It was, of course, nonsense that the routes through Thailand were "drying up", and the attempt to drag the Karen rebels into the picture discredited the story. But it was obvious that the misinformation had been leaked simultaneously to the two magazines in order to discredit the refugees and save what could be saved of the reputation of the government in Rangoon. The source of this disinformation was traced to the US embassy in Bangkok.[49] In any event, the UN intervention eventually forced Rangoon to let the Rohingyas return home.

There were no further references in the press to links between the Rohingyas and Communists and drug smugglers. But Western officials continued, rather absurdly, to blame the Golden Triangle drug trade on the ethnic rebels in the area, not making any distinction between them and groups such as the KMT and the SUA—and ignoring the most crucial issues: official complicity and the pivotal role of the Triads.

While some of the ethnic rebels collected tax on opium passing through their respective areas, not a single insurgent group in the jungles of Burma had the international contacts that were needed to distribute tons of heroin world-wide, to launder millions of dollars in banks in Singapore and the Cayman Islands, and to hire couriers in Amsterdam, London and Lagos.

But Western drug enforcement officials never looked in the direction of the main culprits of the trade. It was far more convenient to arrest a few couriers, and to attend the drug burning shows which were orchestrated regularly by the governments in the drug producing countries.

A Southeast Asian source with connections in the intelligence community commented: "The [US] Drug Enforcement Administration earns its budget by making poor Shan farmers seem guilty, and otherwise doing nothing except occasionally bust some careless scavenger. In this way, the DEA ironically ends up serving only to police the narcotics trade for the greater benefit of the drug kingpins."[50]

The symbiotic but complex relationship that existed between the druglords and some Thai politicians became apparent in early 1980. Kriangsak's power base was being undermined by political rivals scrambling for power in Bangkok. A strike broke out at the Thai Tobacco Monopoly, and outside elements—among them the controversial Sudsai Hasdin—joined in and instigated state enterprise unions to threaten a general strike. Kriangsak finally resigned on 28 February, and his defence minister, Gen. Prem Tinsulanonda, became the new prime minister.

In August the following year, Kriangsak used a bitterly fought by-election in Thailand's northeastern Roi-et province to stage a comeback as head of a newly formed political party, the National Democratic Party, which was emerging as the only real alternative to Prem. But given the political stature of Prem's backers—who included the palace—Kriangsak fell short of challenging effectively the new leadership. But Kriangsak's old allies had not forgotten him: Gen. Li Wenhuan and Khun Sa each secretly contributed US$50,000 to his election campaign in Roi-et.[51]

The importance of the drug armies for Thailand's national security was also demonstrated in 1981. The old Gen. Duan Xiwen of the 5th KMT had died in a Bangkok hospital on 18 June 1980, and was put to rest in a grand tomb built on a hillock on the outskirts of Mae Salong, the prosperous community he had founded in the mountains northwest of Chiang Rai. His chief of staff, Col. Lei Yutian, succeeded him as commander of the 5th KMT.

Lei had hardly settled in as new chief of Mae Salong when the local 04 command post there relayed an important message from the Thai Army's Supreme Command in Bangkok: help was urgently needed to dislodge CPT guerrillas from a strategically located peak overlooking Phitsanulok on the main railway from Bangkok to Chiang Mai.

The hilltop position, Khao Ya, belonged to a larger complex of CPT strongholds in the Khao Khor mountains, which rose to the east over Thailand's central plain. To the far west, bordering Burma, were the CPT strongholds south of Mae Sot. The Supreme Command in Bangkok had received reliable intelligence that the Thai Communists were planning to launch a major offensive aimed at cutting the railway and linking up with their comrades near Mae Sot. If this scheme succeeded, Thailand would be cut in two.[52] Khao Ya had its own school, hospital, a small munitions factory, training camp, ammunition warehouses and administrative offices.

The Thais had lost large numbers of their own troops trying to penetrate the base, so the KMT—or "CIF" as they were called officially, although almost no one used that name—were requested to muster 250 men each, divided into two sections: Unit 31 (the 3rd KMT) and Unit 51 (the 5th KMT). A young KMT officer from Mae Salong, Yang Weigang, was appointed frontline commander. The plan was endorsed by Prime Minister Prem himself.

The Chinese irregulars were airlifted by C-130 planes to Phitsanulok, where they were joined by Thai Black Panther rangers. The main attack was mounted on 16 February 1981. The Thai rangers formed the advance force, but were driven back by a heavy barrage of 57mm recoilless rifles and 60mm mortars.

The KMT officers concluded that they had failed because they had tried to launch a direct assault on the CPT's well-fortified positions. They recommended other tactics: Yang Weigang was ordered to lead his troops in a flanking manoeuvre around Khao Ya. After trekking through the dense forest, hiding by day and marching at night, his troops finally reached the rear of the mountain.

On 6 March, they attacked. According to Bo Yang: "Carrying his rifle and stripped to the waist, Yang continually exposed himself to fire in the most dangerous sectors of the combat zone and made repeated charges towards the most heavily armed blockhouses."[53] On the 8th, after three days of bitter and heavy fighting, the young KMT officer finally reached the CPT encampment on the top of the mountain. By nightfall, the CPT had retreated and the KMT cleared the area. The threat to Phitsanulok—and indeed to Thailand as a whole—had been averted. When the heroes of Khao Ya later arrived at Chiang Mai airport, they were given a rousing welcome directed personally by the Thai overall commander of 04, Gen. Parkom.

Disabled veterans were given a modest pension and certificates which enabled them to stay legally in Thailand.

Despite such occasional services for their Thai hosts, the KMT and the SUA continued their fight for control of the cross-border trade, which meant enormous income from taxes. But rivalry, betrayal and assassinations have always been the very essence of opium politics, and both factions never hesitated to deploy brutal and devious methods. The three Wei brothers, who had fled Vingngün after the CPB take-over of the Wa Hills, were for instance first allied with Khun Sa. The middle brother, Wei Hsueh-kang, was even employed by Khun Sa as his treasurer. He was arrested when it was discovered that he had cheated Khun Sa, and put in prison in Ban Hin Taek.

The wily Wei managed to bribe the guards—and escaped to Bangkok, from where he continued to Taiwan. Meanwhile, his brothers Wei Hsueh-long and Wei Hsueh-yin established contact with Gen. Li, and helped recruit a new army made up of Wa tribesmen who had not joined the CPB. Most of them were followers of Mahasang, the son of the last *saohpa* of Vingngün, and Ai Chau Hsö, an erstwhile Wa KKY commander from Yonglin in the Wa Hills, where he had grown up in a family of slave owners. Wei Hsueh-kang soon returned from his exile in Taiwan, and the brothers built up a third major syndicate in northern Thailand.

The situation was getting out of hand, and the US authorities were becoming especially concerned. They began to pressure the Thais to do something about the drug problem in the north. It was hardly possible to move against the well-connected Gen. Li—whose tentacles reached all the way to Langley, Virginia—but Khun Sa seemed an easier target. Like Lo Hsing-han before him, he fitted the stereotype of a gun-wielding jungle warlord. He was proclaimed "the spider in the web" and the "kingpin of the Golden Triangle heroin trade".

In July 1981, the Thai authorities announced that a Baht 50,000 price had been put on Khun Sa's head.[54] The sum was in itself laughable—the equivalent of US$2,000—and Khun Sa himself must also have sniggered at the announcement, as he was staying in Thailand, partly protected by Border Patrol Policemen and other paramilitary units.

In August, a new campaign was mounted. The reward was raised to Baht 500,000.[55] Leaflets announcing the reward were air-dropped in the Ban Hin Taek area. To the amusement of many, the leaflets said that the offer was "valid until 30 Sept. 1982".[56]

It all seemed like just another theatrical show—until fighting broke out in the Ban Hin Taek area in October. A 39-man assassination squad had trekked from the border town of Mae Sai, into Burma, and attacked what they thought was Khun Sa's residence from the rear.[57] As the commandos had come from the Burmese side of the frontier, Khun Sa's troops apparently believed that the attackers were either Burmese government troops or CPB forces. They returned fire, and almost the entire unit was wiped out.

It was only when they searched the dead bodies that the mystery was resolved. The troops were all dressed in uniforms bearing the insignia "TIA", which stood for the Tai Independence Army. The TIA had been set up some years before by a Shan princeling, Priwat Kasemsri, who dreamt of unifying all the Tai peoples in the region.

The attempt never got off the ground, but some remnants of the TIA remained as border bandits in the hills near Tachilek. Others were recruited into the Thai paramilitary forces, which had a special training camp at Pak Thong Chai near Nakhon Ratchasima in the northeast. The Pak Thong Chai training facility was an off-shoot of Col. Sudsai Hasdin's activities in the 1970s, and the vast majority of the paramilitary forces there were either hill tribes from northern Thailand, or Pa-O, Karen, Shan, Lahu and Wa mercenaries from Burma.

Discovering that he had killed a number of commandos under the command of the Thais, Khun Sa was alarmed. In Chiang Mai at the time there were also persistent rumours—vigorously denied by the US consulate in the town—that a Caucasian had led the attack, and died in the ensuing gun battle.[58] Whether true or not, the writing was on the wall: the Americans meant business. They were putting pressure on the Thais to do something about Khun Sa's blatant presence on Thai soil.

On 21 January 1982, the attack was launched. About a thousand paramilitary forces, mainly from the border police in Tak but also including rangers from Pak Thong Chai, suddenly appeared in Ban Hin Taek. Supported by aeroplanes and helicopter gunships, they started shooting into the village. Fierce fighting raged for several days before Khun Sa retreated across the border to Burma.

Casualties were heavy on both sides, and the media was full of heroic reports from the battle against the "drug kingpin". Western law enforcement agencies lauded the attack, and Thailand's international image was considerably enhanced. To crown their victory, the Thais bestowed the more auspicious name Ban Therd Thai ("the village upholding Thai spirit") on Ban Hin Taek ("cracked stone village").

However, within a year of the battle for Ban Hin Taek, the SUA had not only rebuilt its shattered forces; it had also extended its influence right along almost the entire border between Thailand and Burma's Shan State.[59]

In July 1982, Khun Sa's forces had attacked the mountain of Doi Lang, home of a rival band of Lahu rebels and freelancing Chinese heroin traffickers. Doi Lang probably more than anything else epitomised the anarchy along the border. It had been the stronghold for Pu Kyaung Long's Lahu rebels after the attacks on Möng Hsat and Möng Ton in

1976. He had died there in 1979, reputedly at the age of ninety, and been succeeded as *payah* of the Lahus by his son, Char Ui. He began to encourage ethnic Chinese opium merchants and heroin manufacturers to operate under his protection. During Char Ui's heyday in 1980–81, Doi Lang was described as a mountain of "moonshine, gambling and heroin".[60] There were five heroin refineries, each protected by the Lahus for a fee of Baht 50,000 a month.

Doi Lang (Loi Lang in Shan) is strategically located where the mule trails from Burma meet up with the Thai highway system, and it thus soon became the most important gateway from the Golden Triangle to the outside world. Lao Su, an ethnic Chinese drug trader who had escaped from jail in Thailand in 1977, was one of the first to set up a refinery under Char Ui's protection. This pot-bellied former KMT officer stayed at Doi Lang for many years. Perhaps missing the glitzy, urban life he had left behind, Lao Su set up a ramshackle casino at Doi Lang, which attracted gambling-loving Chinese from all over northern Thailand and even Bangkok.

Then A Bi, a young ethnic Lahu officer showed up. A Bi, the black sheep of Pu Kyaung Long's family, had gone to the CPB headquarters at Panghsang in 1974 and returned four years later. The Chinese aid to the CPB was drying up, and even the Communists—who controlled most of the poppy fields—were beginning to show considerable interest in the opium trade.

Lao Su needed a stronger force than Char Ui's to protect his interests, as by August 1982 Khun Sa's forces had seized most of Doi Lang. He linked up with A Bi's CPB unit, which was penetrating the Doi Lang area. This sealed Lao Su's fate with the Lahus. In February 1983, they shot him and carried his bullet-ridden body over to Thailand. The Bangkok media reported that Lao Su had been shot in a "Thai Border Patrol Police ambush".[61]

The Wei brothers had moved into the Doi Lang area shortly after their break with Khun Sa in the early 1980s. They began to cement a most unlikely alliance between their own syndicate, the Wa National Army of Prince Mahasang and Ai Chau Hsö—and the CPB.

Khun Sa, on his part, enlisted the support of Yang Weigang, the hero of Khao Ya. After the battle against the CPT, Yang had returned in triumph to Mae Salong. Fame and prestige had gone to his head, and he tried to seize power from Gen. Duan's successor, Col. Lei Yutian. His attempt failed, and Yang escaped to Doi Lang with a band of Khao Ya veterans to fight alongside the SUA.[62]

The Thais were not entirely unhappy with Khun Sa's clearing up of the mess in the border areas. They certainly did not want his troops to maintain barracks and munition depots on Thai soil—which had been the case at Ban Hin Taek—but his usefulness as an unofficial "border police guard" and intelligence asset was still widely recognised.

In February 1983, Khun Sa moved on to take over the entire area opposite Mae Hong Son in northwestern Thailand. First of all, he had to get rid of the SSA, whose main border base was at Möng Mai–Homöng across the border from Mae Hong Son. Following a meeting near Möng Mai in August 1981, the SSA's political arm, the SSPP, had decided to sever ties with the CPB, and its relations with the Thais had subsequently improved. Khun Sa wanted no competition: his group was to be the only representative of the Shans.

A heavily armed, 300-strong force led by Leng Chong-yin marched into Möng Mai. The intimidation worked: without firing a single shot, the SSA retreated across the Salween river to the north.[63] At the same time, gunmen carried out a string of assassinations in Chiang Mai and Mae Hong Son. About half a dozen SSA leaders—including Hseng Harn, the chief liaison officer with the Thais, and Sao Boon Tai, one of the founders of the Shan movement—were gunned down by hired assassins.

Khun Sa built his new headquarters at Homöng, until then a small village a few kilometres north of Möng Mai. This was turned into a "new Ban Hin Taek" with parade grounds, concrete houses, schools, hospitals and pagodas. Supplies, weapons and ammunition flowed from south of the borderline.

But Khun Sa also needed a firmer deal with the Burmese authorities. On 7 March 1984, SUA representatives reportedly met the Eastern Commander of the Burma Army, Brig.-Gen. Aye San, at the garrison town of Möng Ton to finalise the details of a joint-cooperation agreement. According to French researchers André and Louis Boucaud: "The Burmese military offered Khun Sa free trade in opium and its derivates if he undertook to use his troops trained for jungle warfare, against the minorities' insurgent groups and the communist guerrillas."[64]

Within weeks of that meeting, the SUA overran a number of ethnic insurgent camps in the Mae Hong Son area—including the Koung Neing headquarters of the Pa-O rebels—and more assassinations of ethnic leaders based in Thailand followed. This, and the absence of any fighting at all between the SUA and the Burma Army, lent credence to the suggestion that the original idea behind the KKY home guard programme of the 1960s and early 1970s was never fully abandoned, simply reshaped.

Aye San himself more or less confirmed this publicly while addressing a gathering of foreign diplomats and UN drug enforcement officials in Taunggyi on 19 May 1984. He vehemently refuted reports that the Burma Army had reached an understanding with Khun Sa.

The proof, he said, was that he could now reveal that his forces had "attacked and seized Khun Sa's temporary headquarters" in the Lao Lo Chai area opposite Ban Hin Taek. Nine government soldiers were killed during the action, Aye San claimed, adding that the ground troops had been supported by airstrikes. The attack on Khun Sa's base was said to have taken place between 7 and 10 May.[65]

It did not take long for foreign intelligence agencies to discover that no such attack had taken place at all in the vicinity of Lao Lo Chai, where Khun Sa was indeed staying at the time, as he had not yet moved to the new headquarters at Homöng.

The operation Aye San was referring to, *Mohein* ("Thunderbolt") Phase 8, belonged to a series of yearly campaigns officially aimed at drug traffickers in the Golden Triangle—but in 1984 it had taken place in April, and the target had not been any of Khun Sa's camps. The fighting had occurred at the Sankang mountain range north of Moh Heng's base at Pieng Luang, more than a hundred kilometres away from Lao Lo Chai.

On 1 April, Moh Heng's Shan United Revolutionary Army had merged with the 2nd Brigade of the SSA—which had been in disarray since the loss of Möng Mai the year before—to become the Tai Revolutionary Council (TRC). The new group was not without political credentials, despite the fact that the alliance with Gen. Li's 3rd KMT was still in force, and Rangoon perceived it as a threat.

Aye San's doctored report at Taunggyi dispelled all doubts about the existence of an understanding between Khun Sa and Rangoon. The very fact that he was allowed to make these claims in the presence of the diplomatic and UN community from Rangoon indicated that the understanding was not just a local deal but approved by the highest authorities.[66]

Although narcotics-related corruption never reached the same heights in Burma as it did in Thailand—where there was far more money in circulation—it was by no means uncommon. Connections between the drug traffickers and the military authorities went back to the days of the KKY programme. Then, it was political expediency. But as the trade—and the friendship—grew, so did the amounts of money changing hands.

A report compiled in 1985 by the *Gonganbu*, China's Public Security Bureau, details the activities of a drug trafficking ring in northern Burma led by Liu Binghong, the former KMT governor of Longling county in Yunnan. It says: "In 1982 Liu Binghong through connections with the head of Burma's Ministry for Home and Religious Affairs, Bo Ni, used Kyats 2 million . . . to move the centre of their activities to Rangoon."[67] Col. Bo Ni was also chief of Burma's National Intelligence Bureau.

Burma also had the same patronage system as Thailand, with money constantly moving upwards in the hierarchy. Low-ranking officers had to curry favour with their superiors, who in turn had to curry favour with the top at the War Office in Rangoon.

According to one Burmese researcher: "Even the wives of officers are required to answer to the needs of the wives of commanding officers. For example, one Shan officer was assigned to combat or other unpleasant duties and passed up for promotion, much to his bewilderment. This went on until one day he was told by a friend that in order to be upwardly mobile, his wife would have to curry favour with the battalion commander's wife. Hence, his wife from then on went regularly to the commander's wife, and helped with cooking and social events. As a result, the officer's life improved considerably and he became, as it were, 'one of the boys'."[68]

This anecdote illustrated a simple axiom in many Asian cultures: officers, out of necessity, have to become "clients" of their superiors. While a wife is expected to help the senior officer's wife with cooking, the husband would have to engage in more expensive ways of showing his respect for his patrons. Western analysts are often quick to assert that there is no evidence of "high-level" involvement in drug trafficking in countries such as Burma and Thailand, while they do not rule out the possibility of "involvement by some local officers in the field".

Asians usually argue that this reflects a complete lack of understanding of how their societies function. A high-ranking officer may never dirty his own hands—but he can certainly still benefit roundly from the drug trade and other illegal activities. The officer in the field, eager to be promoted out of a dangerous and unpleasant posting, can only do so by currying favour with his superiors. And in most remote areas of Burma, the only source of quick and easy money is narcotics.

While the drug trade began dominating the economy of the Golden Triangle, the ethnic rebels were fighting for survival. The situation in the region had changed dramatically since the Vietnamese had invaded Cambodia in early 1979. The Khmer Rouge was ousted and Pol Pot fled with his men to the Thai border. The balance of power was upset once again.

China, which had been the Khmer Rouge's principal foreign ally and Vietnam's main enemy, now needed Thailand's cooperation in order to support the Khmer Rouge. Astonishingly, Thailand agreed. But the conditions were firm: China had to end its support for the CPT. A seemingly unlikely alliance was formed between Pol Pot's Khmer Rouge, the anti-communist Thai government, and Beijing. The common enemy was Vietnam.

At one stroke, the CPT lost its backing from China, its former bases in Cambodia, which had been taken over by Vietnam, and its bases in and supply routes through Laos; the staunchly Maoist CPT had denounced the Vietnamese occupation of Cambodia, and Hanoi's ally Vientiane ordered them out.[69] Then came the losses of Khao Ya and other bases in the Khao Khor mountains. The CPT fell into disarray. Thousands of intellectuals who had joined the Communist guerrilla army in 1976 gave themselves up. Some of the most confused, like Boonsong Chalaythorn, former student activist and one of the heroes of the October 1973 uprising, even joined Sudsai Hasdin's *Krathing Daeng*.

The Thai government issued a general amnesty decree, which was honoured. Few, if any, of the former CPT fighters and cadres were harassed after being allowed to surrender with a certain amount of dignity. In the Mae Sot area, where ethnic Hmong tribesmen had filled the ranks of the CPT's army, several hundred surrendered on 27 December 1982. They were welcomed back as "national joint developers".[70]

The Communist threat to Thailand was over—and the crucial role that the Karens, the Mons and other ethnic rebel groups from Burma had played in Thailand's security was soon to belong to the past. There was hardly any CPT left with which the CPB could link up—and even if it did, China would not break its assurances to the Thai government and allow Chinese-made munitions to reach Thailand's fast disappearing Communist insurgents.

Taking advantage of the new situation, Burmese government troops launched their most determined offensive thus far against Karen camps in early 1984. Mae Tha Waw, a Karen stronghold along the Moei river, fell on 28 January after several days of fierce fighting. Maw Pokay, Klerday, Wangkha, Phalu and other camps came under daily bombardment.

The Thais still supported their old Karen allies, but the writing was on the wall. "Burma's success or failure may hinge largely on whether or not they can obtain food supplies from the Thai side of the Moei River borderline," a *Bangkok Post* correspondent commented on 10 April 1984. He went on to quote a senior diplomat as saying that "all the evidence points to the fact that they are there to stay. It's not just a hit-and-run situation. This time the Burmese are determined to do some long-term damage to the Karen cause." But the Karens dug in and resolutely defended their fixed positions along the Moei river.

In the far north of the country, the Kachins were adopting a different strategy. In 1980 Rangoon had announced a general amnesty for political prisoners and rebels. Officially, 1,431 rebels surrendered. The figure was probably grossly exaggerated, but most of the exiled Burman dissidents in Thailand, remnants of U Nu's resistance, returned to Burma—and so did U Nu himself from his exile in Bhopal, India.

Jimmy Yang returned to Rangoon from France, where he had spent a few years after having failed to reorganise the Kokang force. Lo Hsing-han was released from jail in Rangoon, as was Gen. Tin Oo, a popular former army chief who had been arrested in 1976 in connection with an abortive coup attempt against Ne Win.

In August 1980, peace talks also began between Rangoon and the two strongest groups in the north: the KIA and the CPB. Kachin rebel officers came down from their mountains to attend negotiations in the old school house in Dabak Yang by the Dabak river in the valley below their headquarters on the Chinese frontier—and later in the state capital of Myitkyina. Kachin soldiers came out of the jungle to the towns to be with their families and friends—and to play soccer with Rangoon's troops.

The Kachin rebel leader, Brang Seng, and a few of his colleagues were later flown to Rangoon for talks with Gen. Ne Win himself. While in the capital, Brang Seng and his colleagues appeared one Sunday at Judson Baptist Church. Startled Kachin friends from the capital, who were attending the service, asked what he was doing in Rangoon. The Kachin leader revealed to the entire church that he and other rebel officers had come to Rangoon to negotiate peace and that the KIA was willing to lay down arms if the government granted autonomy to Kachin State.[71]

Sullen agents from Burma's military intelligence service could only stand by helplessly and watch the church service turn into a prayer meeting for Brang Seng and his mission in the capital. Rangoon had intended to keep the talks secret, but had failed miserably.

The peace talks broke down in May 1981 as the government did not offer anything more than "rehabilitation" for the rebels; no political concessions were even considered. But the KIA had scored a significant political victory, winning the respect and admiration of Beijing—which had been the guarantor of the talks—and of many ordinary Kachins who were appalled at Rangoon's intransigence.

"But we realised that we had been negotiating from a position of weakness. Only if we were united with all the other ethnic groups would we succeed," concluded Brang Seng after the talks.[72]

In contrast, talks in May 1981 between the CPB and government officials lasted only one day. A three-man CPB delegation, led by vice chairman Thakin Pe Tint, met government representatives in Lashio and demanded recognition of the CPB as a political party and the right to maintain its army and its control over the "liberated area" along the Chinese border.[73] Apparently finding no room to negotiate, the government's officials ended the talks without further discussion.

In late 1982, a KIA delegation was dispatched to the Thai border. Led by Gauri Zau Seng, a short, soft-spoken former university student who had been in the underground since 1964, they trekked through Shan State, guided along the way by troops from the SSA. They arrived at the Thai border in early 1983—just after the SSA had lost Möng Mai to Khun Sa's SUA. They set up a temporary camp at the Pa-O headquarters at Koung Neing—which was occupied by the SUA after less than a year. Finally, the Kachins established a border liaison post in the area of the Karenni rebels on the Pai river opposite Mae Hong Son. They rejoined the NDF—and invited the front to send delegates to the north.

A 26-man team, which included representatives from all the members of the NDF—Mons, Karens, Arakanese, Karennis, Pa-Os, Shans, Was, Palaungs, Kachins and Shans—finally set off from the Thai border in April 1985. Escorted by more than a hundred Shan, Palaung and Kachin guerrillas—and chased by government troops—they finally reached Kachin State in November to a rousing welcome from dancing villagers and Kachin bagpipers and salutes from 12.5mm anti-aircraft guns.

A conference was held at the Kachin rebel headquarters of Pa Jau from 16 December to 20 January 1986. The delegates admitted that the NDF had been a front in name only, with little or no coordination of the activities of its various members. As a first step towards closer military cooperation, it was decided to divide the NDF into three regional command areas. The northern command included the Kachins, the Palaungs and the Shans. The central command was comprised of the Was, the Pa-Os and the Karennis, and in the south, the Mons, the Karens and the Arakanese were supposed to form one single command.[74]

When that had been agreed, the NDF delegation marched south, through CPB territory down to Panghsang. A second meeting was held in the premises of the CPB's old broadcasting station on a hillock overlooking the Nam Hka border river. Thakin Ba Thein Tin, at seventy-three and in failing health, shook hands with the non-communist delegates of Burma's ethnic rebels. On 24 March, the CPB and the NDF agreed to coordinate military operations against the Rangoon government. The purpose of the exercise was to step up the military pressure on Rangoon, so that the next time peace talks were held, the government would have to face a unified, militarily powerful opposition.[75]

The staunchly anti-communist Karens, led by Bo Mya, denounced the alliance with the CPB, causing a split within the NDF from which the front never fully recovered. But in the north, a joint Kachin-Shan-Palaung battalion was formed in mid-1986, which operated closely together with the CPB forces in the Möng Ko area of northeastern Shan State.

The new alliance was put to the test on the battlefield in mid-November. On the 15th, hundreds of heavily armed Communist troops began to take up positions around a barren mountain west of Möng Ko called Hsi-Hsinwan. Olive green, Chinese-made army trucks groaned their way along dusty jungle roads, carrying ammunition from the nearby CPB garrisons at Möng Paw and Möng Ko. Troops then marched quietly in the dark to well-hidden outposts on the mountain.

More than 1,000 CPB troops had been mobilised for the carefully planned assault. Kachin, Shan and Palaung guerrillas were enlisted to ambush and harass reinforcements, which were bound to be sent up to the battle zone as soon as the attack began: there were only about 100 government soldiers on the top of Hsi-Hsinwan. For the CPB especially, it was an important battle. The Communists were losing momentum in the armed resistance, and they had to demonstrate to their weaker, ethnic allies that they were still a force to be reckoned with.

The attack began at dawn on the 16th with a massive rocket bombardment. The CPB's operational commander, Zhang Zhiming, was a tough commander in his late 30s. He liked to style himself as "Kyi Myint" (which "Zhiming" sounded as in Burmese); he was actually born in Yunnan and had belonged to a Red Guard-style organisation during the Cultural Revolution. In 1968, at the age of eighteen, he had joined the CPB as a volunteer. When all the other Chinese volunteers were recalled ten years later, Zhang Zhiming and a few others had stayed on in Burma.

Most people suspected that he was working for China's intelligence services, and that was the reason why he had been requested to remain with the CPB. Apart from speaking his native Chinese, Zhang was fluent in Burmese, Shan and Kachin.[76]

The battle continued all day—and the government outpost was blown to pieces by the heavy bombardment. Victorious CPB troops stormed into the abandoned camp, where they hoisted their red flag with its hammer and sickle. The following day, reinforcements arrived. Truck convoys fought their way up the old Burma Road towards the Chinese frontier.

The bridges had been blown, but the trucks roared through the shallow water of the rivers. Aeroplanes were dispatched from Meiktila air base south of Mandalay. Howitzers were positioned all around the battle site. Almost mimicking the CPB's human wave tactics, government troops launched one assault after the other, paying little attention to the extremely heavy casualties they suffered. Rangoon was determined to recapture the mountain.

On 7 December, the CPB was forced to retreat from Hsi-Hsinwan. Four weeks later, government forces pushed down from the mountain and captured Möng Paw, a bustling market village of more than 500 houses which the CPB had captured in March 1970. The advance continued, and on 6 January, government forces marched into Panghsai.

Located where the Burma Road crosses the international frontier, with a population of 7,000 people, Panghsai was the biggest settlement within the CPB's base area in the northeast—and its commercial centre. It had several video halls, beauty parlours, hotels, a big market place with plenty of contraband goods and excellent Chinese food.[77]

When the threat posed by the CPB forces in this strategic border town had been removed, government forces also crossed the Shweli river from Namkham on 13 January and recaptured the two enclaves of Khun Hai and Man Hio, which had been in Communist hands since 1968.

In terms of territory it was not a big loss—the areas which the government retook in December 1986 and January 1987 totalled about 500 square kilometres out of the CPB's total of 20,000 square kilometres in the northeast—but it was a devastating blow to the morale of the CPB's army. The loss of Panghsai deeply affected the CPB's finances: tax on the cross-border trade with China was the party's single most important source of income, and it was now gone.

Shortly before the battle of Hsi-Hsinwan began, Brang Seng had left his Pa Jau headquarters to embark on a long and strenuous trek down through Shan State to the Thai border, where he arrived in March 1987. When Rangoon discovered that the most important leader of the non-communist resistance was down in Manerplaw to strengthen the ethnic alliance, a major offensive was launched against KIA strongholds in the far north.

Thousands of troops were thrown into a war zone once again, and the targets this time were the KIA's general headquarters at Na Hpaw and Pa Jau, the site of its political wing, the Kachin Independence Organisation.

Yet again, the Burma Army demonstrated its superiority on the battlefield. On 26 May, as the NDF was meeting at Manerplaw, a radio message reached Brang Seng: Na Hpaw had fallen. The government's forces continued their advance over the grassy mountains along the Sino-Kachin frontier, and Pa Jau was captured four days later. The Burma Army appeared invincible; exactly eleven years after the formation of the NDF, the ethnic rebels were no closer to achieving the autonomy or the federation they were fighting for.

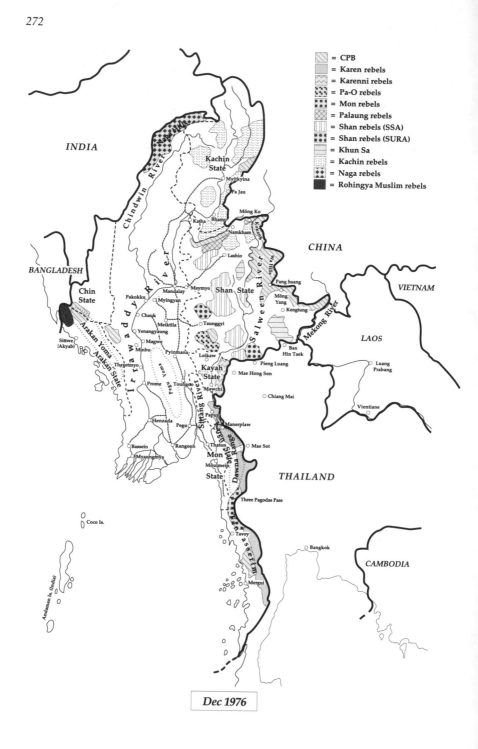

INDIA

BANGLADESH

Chin
State

Kachin
State

Myitkyina

Pa Jau

Möng Ko

Katha   Bhamo

Namkham

Lashio

CHINA

VIETNAM

Mandalay

Maymyo

Pang hsang

Pakokku

Myingyan

Shan State

Möng
Yang

Kengtung

LAOS

Chauk

Meiktila

Yenangyaung

Taunggyi

Magwe

Minbu

Pyinmana

Ban
Hin Taek

Luang
Prabang

Sittwe
(Akyab)

Loikaw

Pieng Luang

Thayetmyo

Kayah
State

Mae Hong Son

Vientiane

Prome   Toungoo

Mawchi

Chiang Mai

Henzada

Papun

Pegu

Manerplaw

Bassein

Rangoon

Thaton

Mae Sot

Myaungmya

Mon

Moulmein

State

THAILAND

Three Pagodas Pass

Coco Is.

Tavoy

Bangkok

CAMBODIA

Mergui

Andaman Is. (India)

Chindwin River

Irrawaddy River

Arakan Yoma

Arakan State

Pegu Yoma

Sittang River

Salween River

Mekong River

Ma Hpai

Kokang

Dawna Range

Tenasserim

Dec 1976

= CPB
= Karen rebels
= Karenni rebels
= Pa-O rebels
= Mon rebels
= Palaung rebels
= Shan rebels (SSA)
= Shan rebels (SURA)
= Khun Sa
= Kachin rebels
= Naga rebels
= Rohingya Muslim rebels

9

Burma in Upheaval

On 5 September 1987, the announcer of Burma's official radio read out a brief message:

> The State Council proclaims the following ordinance to have the same force as law. Ordinance No. 1 of 1987: the 25, 35 and 75 Kyat currency notes issued by the Union of Burma Bank will cease to be legal tender as of 11 A.M. on Saturday 5 September 1987, the 13th day of the waxing moon of Tawthalin, year 1349 of the Burmese calendar.[1]

No reason was given. In one sweep, 60 to 80% of all money in circulation in Burma had become worthless. The announcement came at a time when the final exams were approaching for the students in Rangoon. This was also when they had to pay their yearly fees and, suddenly, they found that most of their money was valueless.

At the prestigious Rangoon Institute of Technology (RIT) in the northern suburb of Gyogon, there was a spontaneous outburst of violence minutes after the announcement had been made. Three hundred enraged students stormed out of the campus on to Insein Road, where they smashed traffic lights and burnt government vehicles.

It was all over in a few hours—but the government nevertheless was shaken. Not since 1976 had Burma's students demonstrated against the government. Its response was to close down the universities and colleges in Rangoon. The students who came from upcountry were bused back to their home towns—where they were received as heroes by the local people, who had heard the news.

After the brief September riots, the government declared that the demonetisation had been aimed at "insurgents and black marketeers", an explanation which few found satisfactory. Burma's insurgents were chiefly based in border areas and kept most of their funds in Thai or Chinese currency.

The black marketeers might have suffered temporarily, but they were able to make up for the loss after a few more trade deals. The ones who suffered the most were the ordinary people, who lost their savings.

The existence of banknotes in such strange denominations as 35 and 75 Kyat had been one outcome of Ne Win's superstition, which he had permitted to overshadow rational government planning; they had been introduced in 1985 and 1986 to replace the old 100 Kyat note.

But more was to come. Later that month two new denominations were issued: 45 and 90 Kyats. The rationale behind the move was that both numbers added up to 9: 4+5=9 and 9+0=9. Ne Win's lucky number was 9, according to his chief astrologer.

The schools and universities had barely reopened on 26 October before underground student groups began activities in Rangoon, Mandalay and other towns. At the beginning of November, students in the Arakan State capital of Sittwe went on a rampage and shouted anti-government slogans.

On the 7th, students at the Ye Zin Agricultural College in Pyinmana in the central plains demonstrated against the government, pulling down portraits of Ne Win from the walls in their institution, and smashing them on the floor. Sporadic bomb blasts were heard in Rangoon, the targets including a cinema and, curiously, the Czech embassy on Prome Road.

Discontent was brewing throughout Burma towards the end of 1987. In December, Burma was forced to apply for Least Developed Country status with the UN, a move that many proud Burmese perceived as a national insult and a final confirmation of the total failure of twenty-six years of the Burmese Way to Socialism. Burma was a potentially rich country, not a basket-case like Bangladesh, or a tiny island nation like the Republic of Kiribati—other nations in the region who had won the dubious distinction of being an LDC.

Years of frustrations with the inept regime were beginning to surface everywhere. In January 1988, a Burmese commented to a visiting foreigner: "The play is over, but the audience is forced to remain in their seats, and the actors refuse to leave the stage."[2] The situation was so tense that even a small incident had the potential to develop into a mass movement.

On 12 March 1988, a Saturday night, three young RIT students strolled down to a small teashop near their institute in Gyogon. It was a simple, country-style bamboo structure with an earthen floor. The walls were decorated with Burmese calendars and posters of Thai filmstars, purchased on the ubiquitous black market in the capital. The teashop, though not fancy, was popular with the RIT students. It was cheap and it had a tape recorder with a collection of the latest cassettes of popular Burmese music.[3]

As the three students entered the bamboo hut, a love song by the famous Burmese crooner Kaizar filled the sparse premises. A group of local people, speaking in loud drunken voices, were seated at a crude wooden table.

The students ordered a cup of tea and had some cakes. They had brought with them a tape of their favourite singer, Sai Hti Hseng, a Shan whose songs slightly resemble Bob Dylan's.

Kaizar's romantic gush never seemed to end, and the students became increasingly impatient. They called the owner of the teashop over and asked him to play their tape. One of the drunkards protested loudly. "Sai Hti Hseng? That intellectual bullshit!" A brawl broke out, and one of the students was badly injured. His friends reported the incident to the local police station, and after recording the details, the police went to the teashop and arrested the culprits. The case seemed to be under control.

The next day, the accused were released. As it happened, one of the drunkards was the son of the chairman of the local People's Council, one of the hand-picked administrative units which formed the local power base of Gen. Ne Win's authoritarian one-party state.

When the news reached the RIT students, they were infuriated. What had begun as a fight between students and local youths—not an uncommon feature in many university towns— had become a political issue. The students marched down to the People's Council office to protest. The council chairman refused to listen to their grievances. Then, 500 men of the dreaded *Lon Htein*, or riot police, appeared, armed with clubs and G-3 automatic rifles.

Anger blossomed into reckless fury, and stones were thrown in the direction of the riot police. Suddenly, the sound of rifle-fire rang out and bullets shredded the air. Several students fell to the ground, bleeding profusely. One of them was Maung Phone Maw, a 23-year-old RIT student. His friends carried him back to their hostel, where he died shortly afterwards in the arms of one of his teachers. At least two more wounded students died in hospital—having been shackled to their beds. Armed guards had been placed outside their wards.

The Burmese public decided they had had enough. The teashop incident was the spark that finally ignited a massive pro-democracy movement across the country. On 18 March, thousands of people marched down the streets of central Rangoon. The police and the army responded fiercely. Both male and female students were clubbed to death. Arrested students were crammed into a police van, which sat for hours in the heat; forty-two young people died of suffocation.

The brutality did not stop the protests. After all, the Burmese public was forty million strong and the ruling elite only a handful. People reasoned that Ne Win and his inner circle of cronies had remained in power only because they controlled the armed forces, which by early 1988 had grown to 200,000 men. But the public counted on the fact that the average soldier was just an ordinary village boy. Surely, the troops would eventually realise there was no point in defending a government that had lost all popular support.[4]

Following a new bout of street demonstrations in June, the ruling Burma Socialist Programme Party convened an emergency congress in late July. On the 23rd, the delegates met in the Saya San Hall, next to the old British racecourse at the Kyaikkasan grounds in Rangoon. Right behind the 77-year-old strongman Ne Win came a much younger, stoney-faced man, his confidant Col. Khin Nyunt, the chief of the Directorate of the Defence Services Intelligence (DDSI), Burma's dreaded secret police.

Ne Win rose to the podium—to announce that he was stepping down as BSPP chairman. San Yu, who had served as figurehead president since 1981, also resigned. But it was obvious that Ne Win was not giving up power. Towards the end of that dramatic week in July 1988, a new successor to the post of president and BSPP chairman was announced. The choice was Sein Lwin, Ne Win's trusted lieutenant from the 4th Burma Rifles, who had tracked down and killed the Karen leader, Saw Ba U Gyi, in August 1950.

Sein Lwin had also carried out the massacre at Rangoon University on 7 July 1962, and he had been in charge of suppressing the demonstrations in March and June 1988.

Ne Win had concluded his resignation speech with a stern warning: "In continuing to maintain control, I want the entire nation, the people, to know that if in the future there are mob disturbances, if the army shoots, it hits—there is no firing in the air to scare."[5]

The public was shocked but also infuriated. On 1 August, underground student organisations began distributing leaflets, calling for a general strike. Students suddenly appeared in teashops and at bus stops, distributed the leaflets—and quickly vanished into crowds of people. Some leaflets were mimeographed on rough, brownish paper while others were hand-written.

On 2 August, Buddhist monks joined the students outside the Shwe Dagon, and fiery appeals were made for a strike against the BSPP regime. There was also a widespread awareness that this marked the 50th anniversary of the mighty 1300 Movement of 1938, the beginning of the end of British rule in Burma.

The strike began on 8 August. It was an auspicious date: 8-8-88. At 8:08 A.M., dockworkers in Rangoon walked out. When word spread, people began marching towards the city centre, brandishing flags, banners and placards. Many carried portraits of the assassinated national hero, General Aung San, the architect of Burma's independence. Aung San still symbolised everything that Burma was not but should have been: peaceful, democratic and prosperous.

Peter Conard, a Bangkok-based Buddhist scholar, happened to be in Rangoon that week in August: "I was standing on the balcony of my hotel room just before 9 A.M. when I spotted some masked youths on bicycles racing down the almost empty road outside, calling out something in Burmese. Apparently they were announcing that the demonstrators were coming. A few minutes later, some students came and formed human chains around the soldiers who were posted at the main intersections. I was told that the students intended to protect the troops from possible, violent attacks from the demonstrators. And then the first marchers arrived. I saw them coming in a massive column across the railway bridge on Sule Pagoda Road with flags and banners, heading for the city centre. There were thousands of them, clenching their fists and chanting anti-government slogans. People came out of their houses, applauding and cheering the demonstrators on."[6]

Hundreds of thousands came. Among them was a disciplined column of Buddhist monks, who carried their alms bowls upside down to symbolise that the whole nation was on strike. Within an hour, the entire area around the Sule Pagoda and the nearby Bandoola Park in downtown Rangoon was packed with cheering people. "You couldn't see the end of it," said Georgina Allen, a 22-year-old British student.

House balconies were crammed with spectators; some were even on the rooftops. About ten makeshift podiums were erected outside the City Hall, and one speaker after another went up to denounce the government—and to demand a restoration of the democracy that had existed prior to the 1962 coup d'etat.

Street vendors handed out cheroots, sweets, bread and snacks to the demonstrators. People stuck wads of banknotes into the hands of those who seemed to be the organisers. The few foreign journalists who had made it into Burma were cheered when they raised their cameras to take pictures of the marchers. Some young demonstrators even walked up to the lines of troops, unbuttoned their shirts and shouted: "Shoot me if you dare!"

The massive demonstrations were by no means confined to Rangoon. In nearly every town and major village across Burma—Mandalay, Sagaing and Shwebo in the north, Bassein in the Irrawaddy delta, Pegu, Toungoo, Pyinmana and Minbu in the central plains, the oil towns of Yenangyaung and Chauk along the Irrawaddy river, Moulmein, Mergui and Tavoy in the southeast, Taunggyi in Shan State and even as far as the Kachin State capital of Myitkyina—millions of people took to the streets to give vent to twenty-six years of pent-up frustrations with the inept BSPP regime.

In Rangoon, the euphoric atmosphere prevailed all day. In the evening, thousands of people moved to the grassy field behind the Shwe Dagon Pagoda where a picnic-like meeting was held. Even though bren-gun carriers and trucks full of armed soldiers were parked in the compound of the City Hall and in nearby Barr Street, nobody really thought that the troops would be called out. "We almost thought we'd won and that the government had given up," said Ko Lin, a 21-year-old medical student from Rangoon's Yankin township.[7]

At 11 P.M. there were still thousands of people outside the Sule Pagoda. Thirty minutes later, trucks loaded with troops roared out from behind the City Hall. Bren-gun carriers with their machine-guns pointed straight in front of them followed closely behind. Spontaneously, the demonstrators began singing the national anthem.

Two pistol shots rang out—and then the sound of machine-gun fire reverberated in the dark between the old, colonial buildings of central Rangoon. People fell in droves. They scattered, screaming, into alleys and doorways, stumbling over open gutters, crouching by walls. Then, in a new wave of panic, they began running again. Richard Gourley, who was in Rangoon on that fateful day, wrote in the *Financial Times*:

> Eye-witnesses saw armoured cars driving up to groups of demonstrators and opening fire indiscriminately, challenging official claims that they were using only moderate force. Some witnesses reported seeing demonstrators carrying bodies of dead protesters over their heads as they marched through the streets.[8]

The shooting continued until early the following morning. Two days later, the US Senate unanimously condemned the bloodbath in Burma. This news reached Rangoon by radio on the Voice of America's Burmese service. People cheered in their homes even as the killings continued outside. A State Department human-rights report later described what happened in Rangoon between 8 and 13 August:

> Numerous eyewitnesses confirm that troops clashed with and killed fleeing demonstrators and fired indiscriminately at onlookers and into houses. On 10 August, troops fired into a group of doctors, nurses, and others in front of Rangoon General Hospital . . . who were pleading with the troops to stop shooting. . . . Four separate eyewitness accounts of a 10 August incident in North Okkalapa, a working-class suburb of Rangoon, describe how soldiers knelt in formation and fired repeatedly at demonstrators in response to an army captain's orders. The first casualties were five or six teen-age girls who carried flags and portraits of Burma's assassinated founding father, Aung San. All four eyewitnesses reported large numbers of dead and wounded and estimated several hundred casualties at the scene. Eyewitnesses reported similar incidents throughout Rangoon during the 8 to 13 August period. Deaths probably numbered over two thousand, but actual numbers can never be known. In many cases as soon as they finished firing, troops carted off victims for surreptitious mass disposal in order to mask the extent of the carnage.[9]

The killings came to a halt on 13 August when the official radio announced that Sein Lwin had resigned. Hardline tactics having failed, a "soft" approach was adopted. The army withdrew from Rangoon and Dr. Maung Maung, Burma's official historian, was appointed new figurehead leader. But the public was not impressed. A new general strike was proclaimed and the country ground to a halt.

In every city, town and major village from Myitkyina in the north down to Kawthaung, or Victoria Point, at the southernmost tip of Burma, millions of people marched in daily mass demonstrations on a scale which had never been seen in Southeast Asia before.

During the night of 25 August, an unusually large crowd gathered at the foot of the Shwe Dagon. Some had brought their bed rolls, and entire families squatted in circles around their evening meals. By mid-morning the next day, several hundred thousand people of all ages, and national and social groups in Burmese society had come together for what would be the biggest rally in the fledgling movement for democracy in Burma. They were all there well in time to get a good viewpoint for the meeting that had been announced for the 26th: Aung San Suu Kyi, Aung San's 43-year-old daughter, was going to address the crowd.

The slim, professorial woman had returned to Burma from her home in Oxford, England, in April to nurse her sick mother, Daw Khin Kyi. Aung San Suu Kyi had left her home country in 1960, at the age of fifteen, when Daw Khin Kyi had been appointed Burma's ambassador to India.

She later moved to England, where she married Michael Aris, a British Tibetologist. But despite her many years abroad, Aung San Suu Kyi had never lost her love for her home country, which she visited almost every year. And she had never forgotten whose daughter she was. Now, Aung San Suu Kyi was pushed to the fore by the tidal wave of events.

A huge portrait of her father, and a resistance flag from World War II stood above the stage as reminders of the struggle for independence from Britain half a century before. Loudspeakers were directed towards the enormous crowd. Eventually, she arrived. There were so many people that her car had to stop outside the meeting ground, and she walked the remaining stretch up to the stage amidst deafening applause and cheers.

Aung San Suu Kyi's first public speech was confident:

The present crisis is the concern of the entire nation. I could not, as my father's daughter, remain indifferent to all that was going on. This national crisis could, in fact, be called the second struggle for independence.[10]

She then spoke on a more personal note:

A number of people are saying that since I've spent most of my life abroad and am married to a foreigner, I could not be familiar with the ramifications of this country's politics. I wish to speak very frankly and openly. It's true that I've lived abroad. It's also true that I'm married to a foreigner. But these facts have never, and will never, interfere with or lessen my love and devotion for my country by any measure or degree. People have been saying that I know nothing of Burmese politics. The trouble is, I know too much. My family knows better than any how devious Burmese politics can be and how much my father had to suffer on this account.

Most of the people who had come to see and hear her outside the Shwe Dagon had probably done so out of curiosity. But during her speech, the daughter of Burma's foremost hero won the hearts of her audience. She emerged as the leading voice for the movement that demanded an end to decades of dictatorial rule. "We were all surprised," a participant in the meeting commented much later. "Not only did she look like her father, she spoke like him also: short, concise and right to the point."[11]

Burma's democratic movement continued with renewed vigour. A popular leader had emerged at last; Aung San Suu Kyi was seen as a female reincarnation of Burma's independence hero. Even more importantly, she shattered the myth that Ne Win, being one of the legendary Thirty Comrades, had inherited the mantle of leadership from Aung San—which had been a recurrent theme in official rhetoric since the military take-over in 1962.

What remained of that myth finally collapsed on 6 September, when nine out of the eleven survivors of the Thirty Comrades denounced their erstwhile comrade, Ne Win, and called on the army to join the pro-democracy uprising.[12]

The notion about the unbroken continuity of Burma's armed forces—from the days of the Japanese occupation to the post-1962 military-dominated government—had been backed up with many writings by Western academics.[13]

This argument failed to take into account the fact that there had actually been more World War II veterans in the various insurgent organisations than in the Burma Army since independence. Almost the entire PVO, the People's Volunteer Organisation—which was made up of thousands of veterans from the Burma Independence Army and other wartime resistance forces—had gone underground in 1948, including two of the Thirty Comrades: Bo La Yaung and Bo Taya. Another three had joined the CPB when the Communist insurrection broke out shortly after independence: Bo Zeya, Bo Ye Htut and Bo Yan Aung. A further four of the Thirty Comrades had rallied behind U Nu's resistance in the late 1960s: Bo Let Ya, Bo Yan Naing, Bohmu Aung and Bo Setkya.

By the mid-1950s, only two of the Thirty Comrades remained in the Burma Army: Ne Win and Kyaw Zaw. The latter was outmanoeuvred in 1956, and went underground twenty years later—to join the "new" CPB in the northeast.[14] He was the only survivor, apart from Ne Win himself, not to join the protest in 1988 as he was at Panghsang on the Chinese frontier.

Ne Win had given favour to his old regiment, the 4th Burma Rifles, and nearly all officers to rise to positions of authority during the 1950s as well as after 1962 came from this rather narrow power base. When the Revolutionary Council (RC) was set up in 1962, it was popularly referred to as the "Fourth Burifs government".[15] RC member, Brig.-Gen. Aung Gyi came from this regiment, as did the two other most powerful members of the junta, brigadiers Tin Pe and Kyaw Soe.

While other officers were gradually weeded out of the top military leadership, more ex-4th Burma riflemen rose to power: Sein Lwin, "the Butcher of Rangoon"; BSPP stalwart Col. Aye Ko, who had been close to Lo Hsing-han in the early 1970s; Gen. Kyaw Htin, who served as chief of staff of the army from 1976 to 1985, and defence minister from 1976 to the BSPP's emergency congress in July 1988; and Tun Tin, deputy prime minister and finance minister from 1981 to 1988.

The economically and politically powerful military machine that emerged in the 1950s and, especially, after 1962, was in terms of organisation as well as personalities entirely different from the army that Aung San had founded during World War II.

Many Western scholars carried the rather thin argument about "continuity" in Burma a bit further and argued it had always been an authoritarian state with a strong centre, gradually expanding its authority over the peripheral areas in an inevitable process of assimilation of the non-Burman nationalities.

Therefore, the colonial era with its nineteenth century liberalism, and the extension of the institutions this system had created during the democratic period immediately after independence, amounted to little more than a brief, alien interlude in the country's history.

Following the military take-over in 1962, Burma "reasserted" the continuity which the colonialists and the liberals had upset.[16] A Burma-born American scholar even went as far as implying that Ne Win could be a "reincarnation of the Buddha".[17]

For many years, this distorted image of Burma and its political heritage dominated Western perceptions—which was probably the main reason why the rest of the world was taken completely unawares when the country exploded in 1988. The Burmese themselves had repeatedly told foreign friends that everyone despised the government and desperately wanted change—but this was usually ignored and the sycophantic Western academics were generally believed.

The Burmese government had also managed to create a peaceful and comfortable environment for diplomats and UN personnel in Rangoon—which was no mean achievement considering the decades-long turmoil of

Burma's frontier areas. Most foreigners in the Burmese capital spent their sleepy days going between their homes, their embassies or UN offices, the tennis court and the clubs for beer at night.

In between, they changed money on the black market, which enabled them to live as kings. Many supplemented this by smuggling antiques in diplomatic bags, a practice which was actually encouraged by the government to make even the foreigners part of the rotten system in Burma.[18]

It was a fool's paradise where few bothered to find out the bitter realities of the repression. When Amnesty International in May 1988 released a detailed report on human-rights abuses in the country, titled "Burma: Extrajudicial Execution and Torture of members of Ethnic Minorities", most foreign diplomats in Rangoon dismissed it as "exaggerated". The UN people in the Burmese capital did not even react.

The isolation of the foreigners in Burma was part of the tragedy. Even contacts between government officials and foreign diplomats were kept to an absolute minimum. Burton Levin, then US ambassador in Burma, commented in a speech at the Asia Society in New York on 29 November 1988: "We had no meaningful contact with any element of the Burmese government. They had a designated group of foreign ministry types who would come to our dinners and talk about golf and tennis, the weather and what fruits were in season . . . during my first three months in Burma, my backhand improved immensely, and I even took up the game of golf, which I had thought was just a waste of time. But I had time to waste."

In August and September 1988, the traditional image of Burma collapsed like the fragile house of cards it had always been. Millions of people from all walks of life joined marches against the old regime, demanding a new, democratic future.

Among the millions who marched in the capital were lawyers in their court robes, doctors and nurses in hospital white, bankers, businessmen, labourers, writers, artists, film actors, civil servants from various ministries, housewives banging pots and pans to voice their demands, long processions of trishaw drivers, Buddhist monks in saffron robes, Muslims brandishing green banners, Christian clergymen chanting "Jesus loves democracy"—and even columns of blind people and transvestites demanding equal rights.

In the Shan State capital of Taunggyi, policemen, doctors, local merchants, government employees and farmers with bullock carts joined the demonstrations, which attracted nearly 100,000 people and resembled a lively country fair. Strike centres were established in more than 200 of Burma's 314 townships. Rice farmers from the countryside around nearly every town arrived in lorries, bullock carts and on foot to participate; it was an entire population, urban as well as rural, who in unison demanded an end to the military-dominated one-party rule that had held the country in its suffocating grip for more than two decades.

Communal friction and old grudges were forgotten and, maybe for the first time ever, all national and political groups across the country joined together for a common cause. In Rangoon, Chins and Kachins showed up at the demonstrations dressed in their traditional, tribal costumes—and were cheered by onlookers. In Arakan State in the west, where tension between Buddhists and Muslims had long been prevalent, these two religious groups now marched hand in hand chanting anti-government slogans. The yellow banner of Buddhism fluttered beside Islam's green flag with the crescent moon.

One by one, several ex-politicians also began issuing statements in support of the movement. Aung Gyi, the ex-brigadier who had been Ne Win's heir apparent in the early 1960s and was later dismissed from the army, had been involved since the very beginning by writing a series of open letters to the old strongman, criticising human-rights abuses and calling for economic reforms.

Now, the octogenarian U Nu—who had returned home during the 1980 amnesty—also became active again. On 28 August, he defied the one-party constitution and set up Burma's first independent political organisation in twenty-six years, the League for Democracy and Peace. Several of his old comrades from the democratic period of the 1950s—and the resistance in the 1960s—declared their support for the ex-prime minister.

Tin Oo, the former army chief who had been imprisoned in 1976 and released during the 1980 amnesty, spoke to an enthusiastic crowd outside Rangoon General Hospital in late August. Cho Cho Kyaw Nyein, the daughter of socialist stalwart Kyaw Nyein, who had ordered the crackdown on the CPB in 1948, resurrected the old Anti-Fascist People's Freedom League.

At the same time, Thakin Chit Maung, Thakin Lwin, Thakin Tin Mya, Bo Ye Htut and other leftist leaders, some of whom had spent time in the Communist underground in the 1950s, also re-emerged from oblivion and obscurity. The fighting spirit of the once fiery Thakin Soe was reborn as well. From his hospital bed, the ailing 83-year-old former Red Flag Communist leader issued a flaming appeal in support of the uprising.

But the government still refused to step down. By strange coincidence, nearly 9,000 criminals "escaped" or were released—without food or money—from prisons in widely dispersed towns throughout the country on virtually the same day: 25 August. In Rangoon, this caused virtual panic. The local citizens' committees, which had been set up by the population to run day-to-day affairs when the old administration had broken down, worked overtime to try to feed the newly released prisoners. But crime began to increase, with lootings of government depots becoming an almost daily occurrence.

In some cases, it was obvious that the army even encouraged the lootings. Early in the morning of 6 September, looters were seen carrying construction material, papers and office furniture from the compound of a German-sponsored rodent control project in Gyogon-Insein. At the same time, two army trucks were parked in the yard of the nearby People's Land Settlement Department.

The soldiers did not even attempt to stop the looting—instead, they were loading their own trucks with goods from the warehouses. Two hours later, after the army lorries had left with their loot, about 200 people invaded the offices and the godowns and took almost everything that the soldiers had left behind. Later, in a strongly worded Note Verbale, the German Embassy in Rangoon stated: " . . . Army units . . . did actively participate in the looting and did encourage it by their obvious passivity."[19]

It also became clear that the DDSI—the powerful military intelligence apparatus—was still active even if the regular army had evacuated Rangoon in the wake of the August massacre. A most remarkable incident had taken place at four o'clock in the morning on 26 August, before Aung San Suu Kyi was going to give her speech outside the Shwe Dagon.

Two Toyota pick-up trucks carrying between them six people had been stopped for a routine check in 29th Street in central Rangoon by local vigilantes belonging to the citizens' committees. While searching the vehicles, the vigilantes found, to their astonishment, a whole stack of leaflets defaming Aung San Suu Kyi and her British husband, Michael Aris.

The hand-written leaflets contained crude drawings of the couple and slogans such as "Call your bastard foreigner and buzz off now!" and "Genocidal Prostitute!" Some of the slogans and drawings were startlingly obscene.[20]

The vigilantes immediately apprehended the six and tied them up. A pistol was found in one of the pick-up trucks together with ID cards of two of the men. One was corporal San Lwin and the other private Soe Naing, both from the DDSI. The six were taken to Thayettaw monastery in central Rangoon, where the monks had set up a court and a temporary prison.

The interrogation was filmed and the identities of the other DDSI agents were also established. The leader of the team was a DDSI captain, Si Thu, a trusted officer who was close to both Ne Win and his intelligence chief, Khin Nyunt. Pictures of the apprehended DDSI agents were displayed on notice boards all over Rangoon before they were released.[21]

The initial euphoria over the new and unprecedented freedom which the people of Rangoon had enjoyed since the army had withdrawn from the city soon became mixed with fear, paranoia—and anger. Suspected DDSI agents were no longer released—like Capt. Si Thu and his men—but hacked to death in the streets. About fifty people altogether were publicly executed, most of them by beheading.

What had begun as a carnival-like, Philippine-style "people's power" uprising was beginning to turn nasty and coming more to resemble the hunt for the *tonton macoutes* in Haiti after the fall of "Baby Doc" Duvalier in 1986.

Aung San Suu Kyi, who had emerged as the unofficial leader of the pro-democracy uprising, constantly sent her people, mostly young students who were camping in her compound on University Avenue, to try and intervene in the beheadings. In some cases they were successful in saving the lives of suspected agents, but public anger with the military intelligence was so intense that it was almost impossible to prevent the lynchings.

Finlly, on 18 September, after more than a month of daily protests, the army stepped in again. Trucks full of troops and armoured cars with machine-guns rolled into Rangoon in an operation entirely different from the August massacre. This time, the forces were impeccably organised and the operation carried out with cold-blooded efficiency. Any crowd in sight was mowed down systematically as the army vehicles rumbled down the streets in perfect formation.

The carnage continued for two days, while the State Law and Order Restoration Council (SLORC), a new junta headed by army chief Gen. Saw Maung, announced that it had to "prevent the disintegration of the Union"—and that no more than fifteen demonstrators were killed.[22]

Diplomatic sources in Rangoon thought otherwise: they reported back to their capitals that at least 1,000 people had been killed. Even the wounded were carted away in trucks to be disposed of. Melinda Liu wrote in her cover story for *Newsweek* after the massacre: "Witnesses at the cemetery said they heard the cries of shooting victims who had been brought to Kyandaw [crematorium] while they were still alive—and were cremated along with the corpses."

At Rangoon General Hospital she saw

> victims with mangled limbs, chest wounds and legs in blood-stained casts. In the emergency ward, gunshot victims writhed on rusting gurneys, dripping blood onto the grimy floor. Undersupplied at the best of times, the hospital was running desperately low on blood and plasma. It was also running short of morgue space. I saw 30 bodies piled helter-skelter in the refrigerated vault. . . . One man was missing the top of his head; a 10-year-old boy had a bullet hole in the middle of his forehead.[23]

The senseless massacre was condemned immediately by all Western democracies, and by Japan and India. A Western ambassador in Rangoon lashed out at the new junta: "It's so shameful what's happening. I have no words for it. It's just a small group of people who want to consolidate their power and are willing to shoot down school children and unarmed demonstrators to do so." Rangoon, he said was "like a city occupied by a foreign army".[24]

Foreign aid to Burma was cut off by the US, Australia, Britain, Germany and Japan. The aid from the US had consisted mostly of anti-narcotics assistance amounting to US$12.3 million a year. By terminating its support, Washington obviously wanted to make a point.

The programme was in any case already in trouble following a very critical report from the US General Accounting Office, which stated: "In Burma, corruption facilitates illicit trafficking and makes effective action against narcotics difficult to sustain . . . [and] a political settlement with the insurgents may be needed before long-term narcotics reduction can be achieved."[25]

In Rangoon, the new junta quickly consolidated its grip on power. But the military take-over immediately triggered a mass exodus to Burma's border areas, where the ethnic insurgents were active. Thousands of students and other activists boarded cars and buses, bound for Moulmein and Kawkareik and from there trekked through the jungles and over the hills to the Thai border near Mae Sot or the rugged Three Pagodas Pass northwest of Kanchanaburi; many jumped on fishing boats headed for Victoria Point in the far southeast, and crossed over to the small fishing and smuggling town of Ranong, on the Thai side of the wide river estuary that separates the two countries. They ended up in areas controlled by Mon and Karen rebels.

From the Shan State capital of Taunggyi, hundreds of people took refuge in the hills east of Inle Lake, where ethnic Pa-O guerrillas were active. Some of them remained there, while hundreds continued their trek down through the jungles to the Karenni insurgent area opposite Mae Hong Son. From Mandalay and Sagaing, students fled north to the Kachin Hills.

Others headed west, towards India, and crossed into Manipur and Mizoram. Activists from Arakan State filtered into the Cox's Bazar area of southeastern Bangladesh. A total of approximately 8,000 to 10,000 people left the cities, towns and villages of central Burma for the border during the last weeks of September 1988.[26]

Only two groups in the jungles and hills of Burma did not receive any significant number of refugees from the urban areas: the Communist Party of Burma (CPB) in the northeast and Khun Sa's Tai Revolutionary Council (TRC) along the Thai border. The movement of 1988 had been an uprising against totalitarianism, so there was little sympathy for communist ideology. The orthodox CPB had in any case paid only scant interest to the pro-democracy movement, which seemed to go against the Maoist doctrine of "capturing the countryside first, then surrounding the cities and moving into urban areas later".[27]

The policy of the CPB's leadership towards the pro-democracy uprising was, however, discussed at a politburo meeting at Möng Ko on 10 September. Apparently, some of the younger cadres were encouraged by the uprising and wanted to link up with it.

But after discussing in general terms the movement's demands, Chairman Thakin Ba Thein Tin, the most senior of the ageing Burman Maoists concluded: "The No. 1 point I would like to say is not to let them [the younger cadres] lose sight of the fact that we are fighting a longterm war. It is impossible for us to make attacks in the towns taking months and years. That is possible only in our rural areas."[28]

Khun Sa's attitude was even more remarkable. In an interview with a British journalist, the opium warlord expressed little sympathy for the pro-democracy demonstrators: "The disturbances occurred not only because of the ruler's intractability but also because of the instigation from the outside powers especially the West who have been in an impatient mood to grab a bite of our natural resources. The poor students and monks died without knowing for whom they actually died."

He went on to tell the interviewer how worried he had been during the demonstrations: "I had been losing sleep and appetite over the disturbances, fearing US arms imports for the anti-government protesters. And then came the 18 September coup. I was much relieved and able to eat and sleep again."[29]

While Khun Sa may have been relieved when the military reasserted power, the CPB—from its limited Maoist perspective—went on the warpath to "capture the countryside". The target was Möng Yang, a small town close to the Chinese border north of Kengtung in eastern Shan State. The CPB unit in that area, the 768 Brigade led by Sai Noom Pan and Michael Davies, were remnants of Sao Ngar Kham's old Shan National Army who had linked up with the CPB in 1976.

Hence, they enjoyed considerable support from the local population, who tended to value ethnic affinity higher than ideology. Sai Noom Pan's own father, for instance, was the local headman of Möng Yang. Michael Davies was a Shan-Welsh insurgent leader who was well-known in the mountains north of Kengtung.

Several hundred heavily armed CPB troops launched an all-out attack on Möng Yang on 23 September. The following day, they marched into the town. The commanding officer of the Burma Army's 11th Battalion, Maj. Soe Lwin, was killed in the battle along with 130 of his men.[30] More than thirty automatic weapons were confiscated by the rebels as well as about 15,000 rounds of ammunition.

The government forces immediately launched a counter-offensive. For two consecutive days, aeroplanes strafed and bombed Möng Yang, reducing parts of it to rubble. Other units pounded the town with mortars and artillery. The orders apparently were to recapture the lost position at any cost; diplomatic observers in Rangoon at the time estimated government losses, dead and wounded, at nearly a full battalion.

After a few days of heavy fighting, the CPB withdrew from Möng Yang—and the government took revenge on the local population. Many villagers were summarily executed and the chief monk at Parliang monastery was taken away and severely beaten. The headman, Sai Noom Pan's 72-year-old father Shan Lan Pang, was made to kneel in front of a Burma Army officer who pumped nine bullets into the old man's body before he died.[31]

While the CPB's interest in the uprising of 1988 had been minimal, the ethnic insurgents had missed the bus from the very beginning. In late July, when Ne Win resigned and the political temperature in the Burmese capital was reaching boiling point, Karen guerrillas launched a dawn attack on Mon rebel positions at Three Pagodas Pass in an attempt to wrest control over the toll gates on the lucrative black-market route across the pass.

Heavy fighting raged in the area for several weeks with dozens of casualties on both sides, until a peacekeeping team from the National Democratic Front managed to negotiate a cease-fire between the two rival rebel forces.

Throughout the August–September uprising, there was almost no fighting between the rebels and the government forces, which was part of the reason why several units were able to be withdrawn from the border areas and be posted in Rangoon and other urban centres. Brang Seng, the leader of the Kachin rebels, who was now based on the Thai border, said in an interview in *Newsweek*, which was made before the SLORC's take-over but published in the 26 September issue of the magazine: "Before the present crisis there were preparations for a countrywide coordinated offensive, but we had to put that on hold. . . . We did not want to . . . appear opportunistic by going on the offensive at this point."

Gen. Saw Maung's take-over changed all that and the ethnic rebels did, at last, go on the offensive. Following heavy fighting in the eastern foothills of the rugged Dawna range, Karen guerrillas on 12 October managed to recapture their old base at Mae Tha Waw on the western bank of the Moei border river, which had been overrun by government forces in January 1984. Again, government casualties were extremely heavy, but again—as had been the case at Möng Yang—orders were to recapture the position at any cost. Eventually, on 21 December, the Karens were forced out.

In the north, a combined CPB-Kachin force on 13 December launched an unusually savage ambush on a government column at Kongsa in the hills east of Kutkai. An entire column, comprising two companies, was wiped out. The rebels claimed they had killed 106 government soldiers, including two captains, two lieutenants and two warrant officers. Seventeen were wounded and fifteen captured alive, including the column commander

Maj. Hla Myint. One hundred and fifteen pieces of assorted arms—automatic rifles, pistols, grenade launchers, machine-guns and mortars—were seized along with nearly 200,000 rounds of ammunition.[32]

The official Burmese media, which until then had hardly ever mentioned fighting with the insurgents, was suddenly full of detailed battle reports, with the obvious aim of demonstrating to its domestic audience as well as the international community that the Burma Army was also "defending the country", not only gunning down unarmed school-children in the streets of Rangoon. Fighting would also give the demoralised—and in the eyes of the public, widely despised—privates in the army a sense of purpose.[33]

The government's ferocity was not only directed towards the indigenous rebels. Perhaps in an attempt to "punish" the US government for its stern condemnation of the massacres in Rangoon, on 19 September—the day after the military take-over—the Burma Army ambushed a group of US-based, right-wing Laotian resistance fighters, who were on their way from the Thai border through eastern Shan State to Yunnan.

The *Working People's Daily* displayed pictures of American and Royalist Laotian flags, documents from the US-based Southeast Asian Freedom Organisation, and other paraphernalia captured from Savutdi Kyaunkvongsup, one of the dead Laotians—including his green card, Illinois driving licence and social security documents.[34]

After the stick came the carrot: the Burmese military knew only too well that it had a potential constituency within various US drug agencies, who paid only scant interest to human rights. Already in November and December, the *Working People's Daily* began publishing pictures of "apprehended drug traffickers" with hands tied behind their backs and the captured heroin laid out in front of them.

The Rangoon office of the Drug Enforcement Administration began sending favourable reports back to Washington about the new military government in Burma.[35] The DDSI had already years before that assigned one of its most experienced operatives, John Htin Aung, to infiltrate the US Embassy in Rangoon, where he had managed to get hired by the DEA. Thus, it was not too difficult a task to manipulate the agency.[36]

The thousands of young pro-democracy activists who had fled to the Thai border, had gone there believing that foreign assistance would be waiting for them. They were aware of the forceful condemnations of the new junta, the SLORC, by the US, the European Community and even usually apolitical Japan. If the outside world was on their side, surely they would now supply the opposition with arms and ammunition! Many of them had also believed the government's propaganda that the insurgents were supported by "foreign interests"—and they had, at least, hoped to get their share of that aid.

But frustrations and disappointment soon became apparent when they discovered that there was no foreign aid at the Thai border. The students also discovered that the ethnic insurgents had to struggle to feed and equip their own troops, and they could provide the dissidents with only a handful of weapons. The immediate concern of the pro-democracy activists became sickness and malnutrition.

Some students died of malaria shortly after their arrival in the Thai border areas. Others suffered from skin diseases and eye infections. Food had been a problem all along since they had left the towns, and the remote camps at Three Pagodas Pass and other bases on the Thai–Burma frontier were hardly havens for gourmets. The urban youths in their new environment soon found themselves eating snakes, lizards, dogs, trunks of banana trees and whatever they could forage for in the jungle.

Meanwhile, the SLORC's financial situation was becoming critical. Burma's foreign exchange reserves stood at probably less than US$15 million after the military take-over, foreign aid had been cut off, and exports were down to a minimum. The SLORC desperately needed foreign exchange. The easiest way out was to put Burma's vast natural resources up for sale to neighbouring countries.

The first to respond were the Thais. On 14 December 1988, Gen. Chavalit Yongchaiyudh, Thailand's acting supreme commander, flew into Rangoon accompanied by an entourage of 86 people, including army officers, Thai pressmen, businessmen and staff from the Burmese embassy in Bangkok. Gen. Chavalit, embracing SLORC chairman Gen. Saw Maung on the tarmac of Mingaladon airport and addressing him as "my dear brother", became the first foreign dignitary to visit Burma after the September coup.

Hardly by coincidence, some unprecedented business deals were signed between Burma's military authorities and several Thai companies shortly after Gen. Chavalit's highly-publicised one-day visit to Rangoon. By early 1989, a stampede of logging concerns, most of whom had close connections with business-oriented Thai army officers, were entering deals with the SLORC.

A document written by Rangoon's Timber Corporation in February said that twenty concession areas had been granted along the Thai–Burma border, with total exports of 160,000 tons of teak logs and 500,000 tons of other hardwood logs authorised. The state corporation estimated revenues of US$112 million annually from the logging, a bonanza by the scale of Burma's trade.[37]

Two Thai fishery companies, the Atlantis Corporation and Mars & Co., each received permission to catch 250,000 tons of fish in Burmese waters. A small firm, the Thip Tharn Thong, signed a contract on 17 December 1988 to barter used cars and machinery in exchange for Burmese gems, jade and pearls.[38]

The logging deals were especially timely for Thai interests; following a mudslide caused by deforestation in southern Thailand in late November 1988, the government in Bangkok had introduced a ban on logging throughout the country. The deals with Burma helped the Thai wood and furniture industry out of an imminent crisis.

The importance of the ethnic rebels as a border buffer had also declined following the virtual collapse of the Communist Party of Thailand in early 1980, and owing to the fact that the former supplier of the Communists, China, had now become the Thais' ally over Cambodia. Thailand could afford to drop the ethnic rebels, especially in view of the immense profits that were offered.

As part of the deal, a reception centre for students who wanted to return to Burma "voluntarily" was also set up at the provincial airport at Tak on 21 December, and a similar centre was attached to the 11th Infantry Regiment's camp at Bang Khen, a northern Bangkok suburb. The first batch of 50 Burmese students from the border areas was repatriated five days later.

More than 300 students were sent back before the entire repatriation programme was terminated in March 1989 amidst stern international criticism and a strongly worded protest note from the United Nations High Commissioner for Refugees in Geneva.[39]

But the SLORC had managed to kill two birds with one stone: by early 1989, Burma's foreign exchange reserves were building up again—and the student resistance along the Thai border had been dealt a severe blow. A third, long-term objective was also inherent in the move: by offering Thai companies logging concessions along the border, the SLORC evidently hoped to undermine the financial basis of the rebels, who depended on taxation of all kinds of cross-border trade, including hitherto limited quantities of timber.

In the northeast, the CPB was also facing problems. The Chinese decision to drastically reduce aid to the CPB had had a devastating effect on the party's activities. The party's annual budget had totalled Kyats 56 million in the late 1970s.[40] An official CPB breakdown showed that 67% of this amount came from trade (i.e. taxation of the cross-border trade with China), 25% from "the centre" (Chinese aid); 4% from "the districts" (house tax on people living in the base area); 1% from contributions made by army personnel; and 2% from other unspecified sources.[41]

When the Chinese had decided that the CPB had to be "self-reliant", they had directed all cross-border trade through Communist-controlled toll gates along the Sino–Burmese frontier. The most important was Panghsai (or Kyu-hkok), where the Burma Road crosses the international frontier into the Chinese town of Wanting.

Tax levied by the CPB at Panghsai amounted to Kyats 27 million, or nearly 50% of the CPB's budget in the late 1970s. Black-marketeers from government-controlled areas, as well as other rebel groups (for instance the KIA, which at this time also traded in Chinese-made consumer goods), had no choice but to trade through the CPB.

In 1980, however, China announced a new open-door trade policy and soon there were about seventy unofficially approved "gates" along the border through which Chinese goods entered Burma. The Kachin Independence Army (KIA) could now also trade directly with China; in addition some goods crossed the frontier at the only point then controlled by the government before the fighting of late 1986 and early 1987: a narrow corridor from Nongkhang in Burma to Man Khun in China, between the two CPB-controlled enclaves of Khun Hai and Man Hio opposite Namkham on the Shweli river.

The government had access to a small stretch of the border opposite Muse as well, but that area was considered too insecure because of the proximity of the CPB garrison at Panghsai only a few kilometres to the east.

The Communists found it increasingly difficult to practise this new policy of "self-reliance", and with the reduction of revenue on the cross-border trade, they turned their attention to the few resources available to them in the northeastern base area. Unlike the KIA's territory in Kachin State, where the soil is rich with jade, rubies and sapphires, there are almost no minerals in Kokang, the Wa Hills and other CPB areas. The only cash crops are some tea in Kokang—and plenty of opium in Kokang, the Wa Hills and the 815 region near Laos.

An estimated 80% of all poppy fields in Burma were already under the CPB's control, but party policy until the late 1970s had been to curb production. With Chinese assistance, new varieties of wheat had been introduced, but few among the hill-tribe population knew how to prepare these new crops. The CPB's crop-substitution efforts ended in 1976, after an invasion of rats in the southern Wa Hills which wiped out much of the area's crops. The CPB assisted the famine victims by distributing 60,000 Indian silver rupees—still the most commonly used hard currency in the Wa Hills—and 1,600 kilograms of opium.

When the crisis was over, many families had reverted to growing poppies, which are less vulnerable to pests than the substitute crops. With the reduction of Chinese aid in 1978–79, there was naturally even less incentive for the CPB to pursue its crop-substitution programme.

The CPB now began showing increased interest in the potentially lucrative drug trade—certainly an unorthodox alternative for a party claiming to be Communist. Some leaders objected, but they were overruled by hardliner Taik Aung, who at that time pulled the strings from behind the old leadership. Devious and sinister, Taik Aung was the Rasputin of the CPB. From inquisitor of the Pegu Yoma in the 1960s he had risen to commander of the central security force in Panghsang.

Taik Aung was, in effect, the real ruler of the CPB in very much the same way as Kang Sheng had been the ruthless strongman behind the official leadership of the Chinese party.

Taik Aung had no qualms about trading in narcotics, and he was determined to expand the CPB's influence over the Golden Triangle opium business. Thousands of *viss* (1.6 kilograms) of opium were stockpiled at Panghsang. From there the party transported the drugs via Möng Pawk in the CPB's Northern Kengtung District to the bank of the Nam Hka river, then on by bamboo raft down to the junction of the Salween and downriver to Ta-Kaw.

There it was loaded onto mules and porters and carried to the Thai border via Möng Pu-awn and Möng Hkok. Thus, the CPB became directly involved with remnants of the Kuomintang—and drug warlord Khun Sa—along the Thai–Burmese border, where they refined the opium into heroin.

The CPB also allowed increasing numbers of heroin refineries to operate within its own base area. These refineries were run by the same syndicates as the ones along the Thai border, and they had to pay "protection fees" and other taxes to the CPB. The first refinery in the CPB area had actually already been established in Kokang in the mid-1970s. Its manager, Pheung Kya-shin, was the officer who had led the CPB forces into Kokang in January 1968. In charge of the territory, he became involved in the drug business. At that time, the CPB paid Pheung 400,000 Kyats to close down his refinery.[42]

He was subsequently transferred to the party headquarters at Panghsang, but he soon set up a new refinery at Wan Ho-tao in Northern Kengtung District. With the CPB's entry into the drug trade in the mid-1980s, he was simply told to pay taxes to the party.

The CPB's official policy was confined to collecting 20% of the opium harvested in its base area. This opium was stockpiled at local district offices, where the CPB's "trade and commerce departments" sold it to traders from Tang-yan, Nawng Leng, Lashio and other opium-trading centres in the government-controlled area west of the Salween.

In addition, there was a 10% "trade tax" on opium that was sold in the local markets and a 5% tax on any quantity leaving the CPB's area for other destinations.[43] The funds derived from these sources were viewed as legitimate—but several local commanders became increasingly involved in other private trading activities including the production of heroin.

At the same time the CPB's once rather efficient civil administration began to break down. Schools and clinics had to close because of lack of funds, and party cadres showed less motivation in their work. The main preoccupation of the civil administrators out in the districts became tax collection for the party; they also engaged in trade in order to support themselves and their families.

Paradoxically, the area controlled by the orthodox Marxist-Leninists of the CPB became a haven for free trade in then socialist Burma. The economy remained thoroughly capitalistic and the CPB never even tried to implement land reform in the northeast—in sharp contrast to the dramatic land-distribution schemes which the party had carried out in central Burma in the early 1950s. Communist ideology became a hollow concept without any real meaning to the people in the northeastern base areas.

The disillusionment with the old leadership increased after the battles of Hsi-Hsinwan—and the subsequent loss of the important trading town of Panghsai as well as Möng Paw, Man Hio and Khun Hai. The Möng Yang battle had also ended in defeat. Even the successful ambush at Khonsa did little to enhance the flagging morale of the CPB.

The CPB had used disastrous, Chinese-inspired human-wave tactics, resulting in huge numbers of deaths. The readiness of the almost exclusively Burman leadership of the CPB to sacrifice its hill-tribe cannon fodder without hesitation reflected its long-standing insensitivity towards the ethnic minorities in the area it controlled along the Chinese border. Resentment of the old leadership became even more intense than before.

The CPB's failure to link up with the biggest popular uprising in modern Burmese history—no more than fifty or sixty students had fled to the CPB area—annoyed the few younger intellectuals within the party as well as some of the better educated, Burmese-speaking minority cadres who had heard about the uprising in central Burma on the VOA's and the BBC's Burmese services. The vast majority of the CPB's hill-tribe rank-and-file was, however, unaware of the fact that there had even been a mass uprising in the first place.

The contradictions within the CPB intensified, and all factors combined to reach a climax by the beginning of 1989. To make matters even worse for the local units, the CPB had shortly after its third congress in 1985 decided to launch a "rectification campaign" with the aim of "improving discipline and political as well as military training of soldiers and cadres, rebuilding the civil administration, improving relations with other rebel armies and punish cadres involved in illegal activities".[44]

In directives related to the last item, the CPB said that any party member found to be involved in private opium trading would face severe punishment and anyone caught with more than two kilograms or more of heroin would face execution. The CPB's involvement in the drug trade had become an embarrassment to the party's ageing, ideologically motivated leadership; furthermore, Taik Aung had suffered a stroke in 1983 after drinking badly distilled, home-made liquor. He had been sent to China for hospitalisation, much to the relief of many CPB soldiers and younger cadres.

It is also plausible to assume that the "campaign" had been launched under Chinese pressure. The spillover of drugs from the CPB's area into

China was becoming a problem, and increasing amounts were also being smuggled via Kunming to Hong Kong. Subsequent to the decision in 1985 to clamp down on the drug trade, party agents were sent out to check up on local cadres and report any wrong-doing to the centre at Panghsang.

While this did not affect the illiterate rank-and-file of the CPB, it nevertheless put a final end to any further cooperation between the top party leadership and several local commanders who had begun to act as the warlords they had once been in their respective areas. The CPB's early policy of acting through them in order to take over the border areas had backfired severely; the only reason why they had not rebelled against the leadership was the fact that they thought the Burman Maoists enjoyed the support and protection of "Big Brother" China across the frontier.[45]

But times were changing, and China's policy was no longer to give all-out support to Communist rebel movements in Southeast Asia. By early 1989, the Chinese had signed several trade agreements with the Burmese authorities, and Chinese pressure on the CPB to reconsider its old policies was becoming more persistent. Already in 1981, the Chinese had begun offering asylum to party leaders and high-ranking cadres. This offer included a modest government pension (Rmb 250 a month for a Politburo member; Rmb 200 for a member of the Central Committee; Rmb 180 for any other leading cadre; and Rmb 100 for ordinary party members), a house and a plot of land, on the condition that the retired CPB cadres refrained from political activity of any kind in China.

The old guard, especially the *Sichuan laopings* who had lived in China during the days of the Cultural Revolution and been close to Mao Zedong, saw the offer as treachery, although they never criticised China openly. The offer was repeated in 1985 and again in 1988. Some of the younger, lower-ranking CPB cadres accepted the offer, but none of the top party leadership did so with the exception of Than Shwe who went to China in 1985.

In early 1989, the Chinese once again approached the CPB and tried to persuade the leadership to give up and retire in China. A crisis meeting was convened on 20 February at Panghsang. For the first time, the still staunchly Maoist Thakin Ba Thein Tin lashed out against the Chinese. In an address to the secret meeting he referred to "misunderstandings in our relations with a sister party. Even if there are differences between us, we have to co-exist and adhere to the principle of non-interference in each other's affairs. This is the same as in 1981, 1985 and 1988. We have no desire to become revisionists."[46]

The minutes of the secret meeting were leaked, however, and this may have encouraged the disgruntled rank-and-file to rise up against the old leadership. On 12 March, Kokang Chinese units led by Pheung Kya-shin took the first step and openly challenged the CPB's central leadership. Two days later, his forces captured Möng Ko. The mutiny quickly spread to all other CPB base areas in the northeast. Then, late at night on 16 April, troops from the predominantly Wa 12th brigade stormed Panghsang.

The rebellious troops seized the well-stocked central armoury, the army general headquarters and other buildings. While they were smashing portraits of Communist icons Marx, Engels, Lenin, Stalin and Mao Zedong and destroying party literature in a fierce outburst of anti-party feeling, the CPB's ageing leaders fled headlong across the Nam Hka border river into China. For the first time in history, a Communist insurgency had been defeated from within its own ranks.

The CPB's radio station was also taken over and on 18 April the mutineers broadcast the first denouncement of what they termed "the narrow racial policies of the Communist Party of Burma".[47]

An even stronger broadcast followed on 28 April. The mutineers declaimed:

> Conditions were good before 1979. But what has the situation come to now? No progress whatsoever is being made. Why? In our opinion, it is because some leaders are clinging to power and are obstinately pursuing an erroneous line. They are divorced from reality, practising individualism and sectarianism, failing to study and analyse local and foreign conditions, and ignoring actual material conditions. . . . They have cheated the people of the Wa region, and through lies and propaganda have dragged us into their sham revolution. . . . How can an enemy armed with modern weapons be defeated by an empty ideology and through military methods that do not integrate theory with practice? We, the people of the Wa region, never kowtow before an aggressor army whether it be local or foreign. Although we are very poor and backward in terms of culture and literature, we are very strong in our determination. What became of the lives of people in the Wa region following the wrestling of power by an evil-minded individual within the CPB at a certain time in the past? It was a hard life for the people. The burden on the people became heavier with more taxes being levied. We faced grave hardships. Can the people avoid staging an uprising under such a condition?[48]

It is uncertain who that "evil-minded individual" was. But while all of the most important CPB leaders escaped to China unharmed, two especially disliked figures were captured alive: Mya Thaung, the political commissar of Northern Wa District, and Soe Thein, the overall political commissar of the Northeastern Region, who was notorious for manipulating the ethnic minorities.

A third high-ranking CPB member who was ear-marked for arrest—and possible execution—was the chief of staff of the army, Tin Yee, who in the past had been responsible for sending many young Was to die in human-wave attacks on government positions. But Tin Yee swam across the Nam Hka river the night the 12th Brigade attacked, and escaped to China with the other top leaders from Panghsang.

Within a month of the initial uprising in Kokang, the CPB ceased to exist—almost fifty years after its formation in the flat in Rangoon's Barr Street, and forty-one years after it had decided to resort to armed struggle against the government. More than 300 leaders and their families ended up exiled in disgrace in China.

The CPB mutiny in March and April 1989 altered dramatically the military map of Burma and resulted in a number of new, seemingly unlikely alliances. Many had initially expected that the CPB mutineers—who were all from the ethnic minorities in the northeastern border mountains—would link up with the NDF and the other ethnic rebels on the Thai border. The NDF did indeed send a delegation to Panghsang after the mutiny, but they were overtaken by the SLORC who were determined to neutralise the still powerful army of the former CPB.[49]

A cease-fire with the CPB would also free thousands of troops from combat duties in the frontier areas and make it possible to redeploy them in the Burmese heartland to control a population which had so vehemently rejected the government in Rangoon.

The first surprise came when the SLORC called in the old warlord Lo Hsing-han to act as an intermediary with the mutineers. Following his release during the 1980 amnesty, Lo Hsing-han had been given two million Kyats by the government to build a new military camp at the so-called "Salween Village" in the Nampawng area southeast of Lashio.

Lo also set up another home guard unit, this time under the government's new *Pyi Thu Sit* (People's Militia) programme, started after the disbanding of the KKY seven years before. The new agreement was effectively the same as the former accord between Rangoon and the KKY: fight the rebels and gain, in return, access to government-controlled roads for smuggling.[50]

But it was several years before Lo Hsing-han was able to regain any of his former strength and prominence. The 1989 mutiny within the CPB came at the right time. On 20–21 March, only a week after the first uprising in the CPB's Northern Bureau headquarters at Möng Ko, Lo Hsing-han paid his first visit to Kokang since being driven out by the Communists in 1968. But this time, the Pheung brothers arranged a dinner party for their former enemy.

Lo's visit was followed by a trip to the north by the ex-brigadier-turned-politician Aung Gyi and Olive Yang, the former opium warlady of Kokang. They met Pheung Kya-shin's younger brother, Pheung Kya-fu, and other former CPB commanders in Lashio.[51]

In late April, shortly after the fall of Panghsang and Aung Gyi and Olive Yang's journey up to Lashio, Khin Nyunt, the head of the DDSI, and Col.

Maung Tint, then chief of the Burma Army's northeastern command in Lashio, helicoptered to the town of Kunlong on the Salween river bridge opposite Kokang, the site of the bitter battle in 1971–72. They met with Pheung Kya-fu and agreed upon a temporary cease-fire.[52] After this initial meeting in Kunlong, Khin Nyunt paid several highly publicised visits to Kokang.[53]

On 11 November, Wa chieftain Chao Ngi Lai, who controlled the bulk of the former CPB army—nearly 80% of the rank-and-file were Wa hilltribesmen—and some of his officers were taken by helicopter from the Wa Hills to Lashio to meet Khin Nyunt, Maung Tint and several other SLORC leaders. A "border development programme" had already been launched by the SLORC and, according to official figures, seventy million Kyats were to be spent on building roads, bridges, schools and hospitals in these previously neglected frontier areas. Diesel, petrol, kerosene and rice were distributed in the former CPB areas.[54]

Lo Hsing-han's importance grew as an intermediary in negotiating with the mutineers, especially those from his native Kokang. Lucrative business opportunities overshadowed old animosity between him and the Pheungs. The former CPB commanders, who only months before had been denounced in the official Burmese media as "drug traffickers", "drunkards", "womanisers" and "bandits", suddenly became respectable citizens, and were now described as "village elders" and "leaders of the national races".[55]

The former CPB army, meanwhile, had split up into four different forces, along ethnic lines. The northernmost CPB territory, the former "101 War Zone" around Kambaiti, Panwa and Hpimaw passes in Kachin State, became the New Democratic Army (NDA), led by Ting Ying and Zalum, who had defected from the KIA in 1968.

The units in Möng Ko and Kokang were transformed into the Myanmar National Democratic Alliance Army (MNDAA), led by the Pheung brothers. The Wa units merged with some non-communist Wa forces along the Thai border to become the United Wa States Army (UWSA), headed by Chao Ngi Lai.

In the east, north of Kengtung, the CPB's former 815 War Zone became the National Democratic Alliance Army Military and Local Administration Committee (Eastern Shan State), led by Lin Mingxian ("U Sai Lin" or "Sai Leün" in the official media) and Zhang Zhiming ("U Kyi Myint"). Both were former Red Guards from Yunnan who had joined the CPB as volunteers in 1968. Lin had married Pheung Kya-shin's daughter and had close connections with the Kokang commanders.

Zhang, the commander of the forces at the battle of Hsi-Hsinwan, had come down to the former 815 War Zone shortly after the mutiny. He had travelled through Yunnan, escorted by agents from China's Public Security Bureau—and carrying fifty kilograms of pure No. 4 heroin in his vehicle.[56]

To placate these groups, and to make sure that they did not turn their guns against the government, the old KKY accord was revived once again. This time, the general political situation in the country was also much more serious from the government's point of view than it had been in the 1960s; although more than 300 students had been forcibly repatriated by the Thais, and more had given up the harsh life in the jungle to become refugees in Bangkok, there were still thousands of dissidents desperately looking for a source of arms and military training.

With communist ideology gone from the CPB, a link-up was a possibility, and the former CPB forces now controlled the vast stockpiles of arms and ammunition in Panghsang, which were left from the decade of massive Chinese support from 1968 to 1978. It was of utmost importance to the SLORC to neutralise as many of the border insurgencies as possible—especially the former CPB—no matter the consequences.

Chemicals, mainly acetic anhydride, which is needed to convert raw opium into heroin, were brought in by truck from India and within a year of the CPB mutiny, intelligence sources claimed that there were at least seventeen heroin refineries in Kokang and the adjacent former CPB territory west of the Salween: four near the former CPB's Northern Bureau headquarters at Möng Ko; six at Möng Hom, about twenty kilometres to the south; two at Nam Kyaun; one at Loi Kang Möng south of the Hsenwi-Kunlong road; and four inside Kokang proper, east of the Salween.[57]

In the Wa Hills, six refineries were located, and their processing rate doubled during the first half of 1990.[58] In Lin Mingxian's area in eastern Shan State, new heroin refineries went into operation near the Man Hpai headquarters of the former 815 War Zone, and at Loi Mi mountain near the border town of Möng La inside the former CPB area.[59]

Not everybody within the former CPB agreed with the new alliances which were being forged with the SLORC, however. In the Möng Yang area, both Sai Noom Pan and Michael Davies objected. Michael was assassinated by Lin Mingxian's gunmen in May 1989. A year later, Sai Noom Pan—whose father had been brutally murdered by the Burma Army—committed suicide, unable to accept the new order.

With such well-respected, local community leaders out of the way, Chinese gangster syndicates led by Lo Hsing-han and his younger brother Lo Hsing-minh, the Pheung brothers, Lin Mingxian and Zhang Zhiming took over the former CPB and turned it into the most heavily armed drug trafficking organisation in Southeast Asia, outnumbering and outgunning even the hitherto most powerful opium warlord in Burma, Khun Sa. Narcotics quickly emerged as Burma's major, although illegal, export.

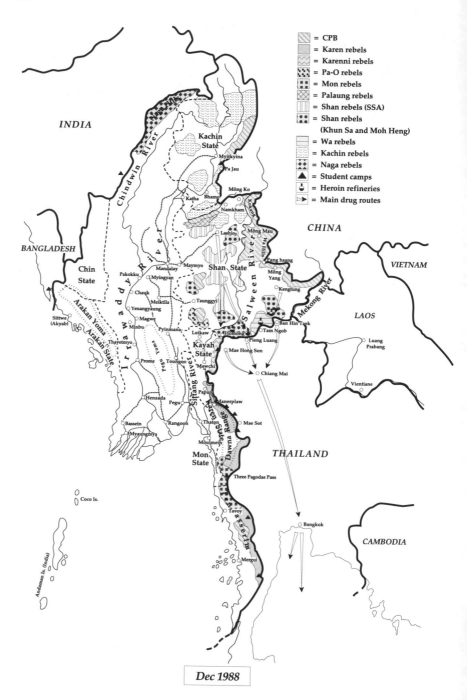

▨	= CPB
▦	= Karen rebels
◇	= Karenni rebels
⬚	= Pa-O rebels
▦	= Mon rebels
⬚	= Palaung rebels
⬚	= Shan rebels (SSA)
⬚	= Shan rebels
	(Khun Sa and Moh Heng)
▤	= Wa rebels
⬚	= Kachin rebels
◆	= Naga rebels
▲	= Student camps
☗	= Heroin refineries
⇒	= Main drug routes

INDIA

Kachin State

Myitkyina

Pa Jau

Mong Ko

Katha Bhamo

Namkham

Chindwin River

CHINA

BANGLADESH

Chin State

Mandalay

Maymyo

Lashio

Mong Mau

Pang hsang

Shan State

Mong Yang

Kengtung

VIETNAM

Pakokku

Myingyan

Chauk

Meiktila

Yenangyaung

Magwe

Minbu

Taunggyi

Salween River

Mekong River

LAOS

Sittwe (Akyab)

Arakan Yoma

Irrawaddy River

Fyinmana

Loikaw

Homong

Tam Ngob

Ban Hin Taek

Luang Prabang

Thayetmyo

Arakan State

Pegu Yoma

Kayah State

Mawchi

Pieng Luang

Mae Hong Son

Vientiane

Prome

Toungoo

Chiang Mai

Henzada

Sittang River

Pegu

Papun

Manerplaw

Bassein

Rangoon

Thaton

Mae Sot

THAILAND

Myaungmya

Moulmein

Dawna Range

Karen State

Mon State

Three Pagodas Pass

Coco Is.

Tavoy

Bangkok

CAMBODIA

Andaman Is. (India)

Tenasserim

Mergui

Dec 1988

CPB soldier (Wa Ethnic), 1986 (photo by Hseng Noung Lintner).

CPB Chairman Thakin Ba Thein Tin (photo by Hseng Noung Lintner).

Communist Party of Burma (CPB) cadres at the Panghsang headquarters on the Sino-Burmese border in Shan State (photo by Hseng Noung Lintner).

Wa Village, the Wa Hills (photo by Bertil Lintner).

Lahu New Year 1987: Lahu hill tribesmen in the CPB's territory (photo by Bertil Lintner).

Wa girls dancing, Vingngun, December 1986. "Wa are plucking flowers and sending the prettiest ones to Chairman Mao" (photo by Bertil Lintner).

CPB troops at Hsi Hsinwan, November 1986 (photo by Bertil Lintner).

The new Central Committee at the Third Party Congress, Panghsang, September–October 1985. *Front row, left to right:* Pe Htaung, Ye Tun, Tin Yee, Khin Maung Gyi, Thakin Ba Thein Tin, Myo Myint, Kyaw Mya, Kyin Maung, Mya Min. *Back row, left to right:* Aye Ngwe, Kyaw Myint, Li Ziru, Tint Hlaing, Chao Ngi Lai, Kyaw Zaw, Sai Aung Win, San Thu, Tun Lwin, unknown, Zau Mai, Soe Thein.

Wa children attending CPB school at Panghsang.

KIO Chairman Brang Seng at jungle meeting, 1986; behind him is Zau Mai, KIA chief of staff (photo by Hseng Noung Lintner).

Pan Jan Church, KIA girls (photo by Hseng Noung Lintner).

KIA (Kachin Independence Army) training (photo by Hseng Noung Lintner).

KIA troops marching through the Triangle (photo by Hseng Noung Lintner).

Three Pagodas Pass (Thai-Burmese border) (photo by Hseng Noung Lintner).

University students demonstrate for democracy in Rangoon, August 1988.

Monks joined the pro-democracy demonstrations in August-September 1988.

Victims of the army's firing into crowds of demonstrators, Rangoon, 1988.

Even children demanded democracy in 1988.

Demonstrations in Kawthaung, September 1988 (photo by Conard-Swan).

Aung San Suu Kyi, 1989.

The Democratic Alliance of Burma, Klerday November 19, 1988. *Front row, left to right:* Brang Seng (Kachin), Bo Mya (Karen), Nai Shwe Kyin (Mon); *Back row, fifth from left:* Ye Kyaw Thu, CRDB; *eighth from left:* Tin Maung Win, CRDB. *Others:* Karens, Shans, Was and Burmese students (photo by Heldurjaan Netocny, Sweden).

Khun Sa, December 1993 (photo by Hseng Noung Lintner).

Soldier from Khun Sa's private opium army guarding a border check gate on the Thai-Burmese frontier (photo by Bertil Lintner).

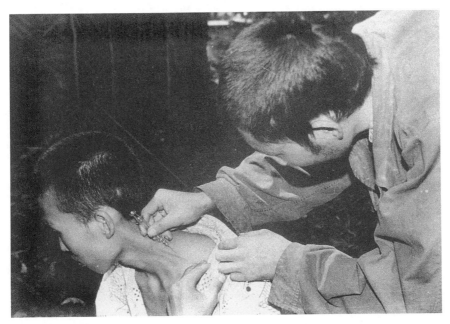

Drug addicts, Yunnan, 1991.

Training near Three Pagodas Pass, Mon rebel area, December 1988 (photo by Heldurjaan Netocny, Sweden).

Bruce Stubbs of the DEA (in camouflage fatigues) posing for the camera together with Kokang officers and Lo Hsing-han (in black leather jacket). *In the background:* U.S.-supplied Bell helicopter, donated to help Rangoon suppress narcotics (photo by Yindee Lertcharoenchok).

10

The Strife Continues

In Burma, no day is merrier than *Thingyan*, which falls in mid-April and marks the Burmese New Year. This is the height of the hot season, and it is celebrated in the most sensible manner: by throwing buckets of cold water at anyone who dares venture into the streets. The old year must be washed away and the new anointed with fresh water.

It is also a time when it is allowed to ridicule the powers that be: in rhythmic chants and with clear twists of meaning, satirists point out the shortcomings of the rulers. This practice was tolerated even during the most repressive years of BSPP rule.

But *Thingyan* 1989 turned out to be different. Ne Win had not been seen in public since his resignation in July 1988. However, somewhat unexpectedly, his picture had appeared on the front page of the *Working People's Daily* of 27 March, Armed Forces Day. Dressed in a crisp white uniform, he was seated at a big table, surrounded by Gen. Saw Maung and other officers. They were all roaring with laughter

Hardly surprisingly, Ne Win's reappearance was ridiculed by the students of Rangoon, who staged a traditional slogan competition on University Avenue. It was held outside the office of the National League for Democracy, a political party which had been set up a week after the SLORC's take-over. The chairman of the party was Tin Oo, the former army chief, but the league's most popular figure and unifying factor was undoubtedly general secretary Aung San Suu Kyi.

In theory, Burma's one-party system had been abolished when the State Law and Order Restoration Council assumed power, but although new parties were being formed at an astonishing rate—within months more than 200 parties had registered with the authorities—it soon became obvious that this did not mean a democratic environment.

The star performers at the NLD slogan competition were all rounded up and arrested shortly after the event. At about the same time, arrests began of grassroot organisers from the NLD and another organisation, the student-led Democratic Party for a New Society (DPNS), especially in Pakokku, Taunggyi, Kyaukpadaung, Monywa, Myinmu and other upcountry towns.

In Rangoon, the DPNS leader, 27-year-old Moe Thi Zon, went underground and soon showed up at the Thai border, where he joined the underground student organisation, the All-Burma Students Democratic Front (ABSDF), which was allied with the ethnic rebels. In an interview with a TV team from Australia's Special Broadcasting Service shortly before his disappearance from Rangoon, Moe Thi Zon had declared: "The final victory must come through armed struggle. If you see how the military is treating us, we've got no other choice."

But the NLD and other mainstream political parties continued their peaceful activities unabated despite the repression. Leaflets, bulletins, unofficial newspapers, audio cassettes and video tapes were circulated all over Burma and meetings were held in defiance of martial law decrees. In response, a draconian new printing law was promulgated, aimed at preventing the political parties from issuing "unauthorised publications". In effect, it ensured a monopoly on information for the official, state-run *Working People's Daily*—the only legally permitted newspaper since the SLORC's take-over.

Responding to these moves, Aung San Suu Kyi became increasingly outspoken in her criticism of the military regime. For the first time, she openly attacked Ne Win, accusing him of being responsible for Burma's economic and political misery and implying that nothing would fundamentally change as long as the old strongman was still there, pretending that he had retired—but still pulling the strings from behind the scenes. She began travelling upcountry, giving speeches in remote places, even in the frontier areas.

"The movement of 1989", as it became known, was in many ways more significant than the upheaval of 1988. The spectacle of massive, restive crowds dancing down the streets, shouting slogans and waving banners, now belonged to the past. Instead, tens of thousands stood in silence, listening attentively for hours on end to an entirely new message: democracy through discipline, responsibility and non-violent struggle.[1]

Aung San Suu Kyi's stamina and courage infused her massive audiences across the country with hope and self-confidence. Perhaps even more importantly, the troops that were sent out to disperse the crowds began to get down from their army lorries—to listen to her message.

It was obvious that this new movement posed a much more serious challenge to the old regime than the street demonstrations of 1988: a new power centre was emerging, offering a viable alternative to the SLORC. Among all the politicians who had emerged or re-emerged on the Burmese scene since August 1988, Aung San Suu Kyi stood out as the only one who could unify all segments of Burmese society: the urban as well as the rural population, the young student radicals and the older, much more moderate pro-democracy activists.

More importantly, by virtue of being the daughter of the founder of the Burma Army, she was in a position to rally even the armed forces behind her. It was also not forgotten that her father had signed the historic Panglong Agreement with the ethnic minorities, and that he had been one of the few Burman politicians they had ever trusted.

The old rulers were becoming redundant and they would soon belong to history—if this young woman was allowed to continue her country-wide campaign for a new Burma.

The situation became even more tense in the weeks before the forty-second anniversary of Aung San's assassination on 19 July 1989. Aung San Suu Kyi had declared that she would march—in a peaceful and disciplined manner—with thousands of her followers to pay respect to her fallen father, and not take part in the SLORC-organised ceremony.

But on 18 July, before anything could happen, army trucks with loudspeakers criss-crossed Rangoon to announce the SLORC's latest decree, under which anyone opposing the regime could be tried by military tribunal. Those found guilty would receive one of three sentences: three years imprisonment with hard labour, life imprisonment or execution.[2] Early in the morning of the 19th, an estimated 10,000 soldiers, including artillery and armoured car units, moved into Rangoon to reinforce the numerous troops already stationed there.

Roadblocks were erected at strategic points in the city, all major hospitals were told to expect casualties and all telephone and telex lines between Burma and the outside world were cut. To avoid what would clearly turn out to be a bloodbath, Aung San Suu Kyi called off the march.

On 20 July, troops surrounded her residence on University Avenue. The hundreds of students who had been camping there virtually non-stop since the 1988 uprising, were arrested. Aung San Suu Kyi was placed under house arrest. The NLD chairman, Tin Oo, was led away to Insein Jail, as were all the other prominent NLD organisers. In sweeps all over the country, thousands of NLD workers were arrested and party offices closed down.

In order to defend the crackdown, the chief of Burma's secret police and first secretary of the SLORC, DDSI chief Khin Nyunt, gave a lengthy speech on 5 August. He accused the CPB of manipulating the NLD and plotting to destabilise the government—news about the dramatic events in the northeast and the collapse of the CPB as a Communist insurgency was not yet common knowledge in Rangoon. On 9 September, Khin Nyunt spoke out again, this time claiming that his intelligence outfit had unearthed "a rightist conspiracy" involving some unnamed foreign embassies in Rangoon.

The speech was printed and distributed in a book which bore the archaically fanciful title "The Conspiracy of Treasonous Minions within the Myanmar naing-ngan [Burma] and Traitorous Cohorts Abroad". Among the cohorts "exposed" in the book were Burmese exiles, foreign journalists, Senator Daniel Moynihan, congressmen Stephen Solarz and Dana Rohrabacher—and even Burmese state leaders who had been dead for years.[3]

Neither of Khin Nyunt's speeches offered much in terms of evidence. Most observers dismissed the CPB conspiracy claim as an attempt to discredit the NLD in the eyes of the rank and file of the army, whose loyalty was essential for the survival of the SLORC. Having fought the CPB insurgency virtually since independence, the army had strong feelings about the Communists.

The speech was later turned into a booklet, which contained pictures of all major CPB leaders in the underground, as well as people such as Daw Kyi Kyi, the 69-year-old widow of the late chairman, Thakin Zin. She had been arrested—along with her two sons and two daughters—although it was not clear what her offence had been. The charge, in any case, was "high treason".[4]

Khin Nyunt's second speech appeared to be meant as a warning to the international community—which had almost unanimously condemned the SLORC regime and its brutality—to refrain from "interfering in Burma's internal affairs", and to intimidate local Rangoon residents who were known to have contacts with foreigners in the capital. Khin Nyunt's imaginative speeches came at a time when most democratic countries—including the United States, the twelve members of the European Community, India, Canada and Sweden—had expressed serious concern over human-rights abuses in Burma.[5]

Isolated diplomatically and condemned by most Western powers, the SLORC was desperate to be re-admitted into the international community. Given the deals it had just struck with the traffickers along the Sino–Burmese border, it may seem ironic that it decided to do this by exploiting the drug issue. But the DEA's local office in Rangoon had already been infiltrated, and the SLORC knew that narcotics was a highly emotional issue in the United States.

In late February 1990—seven months after the crackdown in Rangoon—a Burmese government delegation, led by Foreign Ministry director general Ohn Gyaw, visited Washington to lobby for resumption of US anti-narcotics assistance. The US State Department refused to see the SLORC delegation, but it did manage to speak to Rep. Charles B. Rangel, chairman of the Committee on Narcotics of the House of Representatives, and DEA officials.

The meeting embarrassed the State Department because the delegation included Brig.-Gen. Tin Hla, the commander of the Burma Army's 22nd

Light Infantry Division, which had never been involved in any "anti-narcotics efforts"—but which had carried out the August 1988 massacre in Rangoon.[6]

The administration in Washington remained firm in its decision to bar all assistance to the generals in Rangoon as long as they violated human rights and tolerated the drug traffic from the Golden Triangle. The DEA, however, seemed equally determined to push US law-makers into accepting a resumption of aid to Rangoon.

One of the first US politicians to be encouraged by the DEA to undertake a "fact-finding mission" to the Far East was Rep. William Hughes of New Jersey. On his return, Hughes declaimed: "The US policy towards Burma is seriously flawed. It is a mistake on our part not to act on this drug trafficking because we are not satisfied with the government's human rights record."[7]

Statements like these failed to impress the administration in Washington, which argued that it was precisely the SLORC's human rights record, and its desire to cling on to power at any cost, that had caused the narcotics explosion in northeastern Burma after 1988. But the SLORC apparently discovered an opening when on 15 March 1990, the US attorney-general Richard Thornburgh announced that Khun Sa had been indicted by a New York federal grand jury.

A shipment of heroin, confiscated in the US, had been "traced back" to the kingpin in the hills of the Golden Triangle, according to law enforcement agencies in New York. DEA chief John Lawn stated publicly that Burma's military government "is as determined as we are to deal with the problem".[8]

Lawn conveniently ignored Brig.-Gen. Aye San's phantom war of 1984, which clearly proved that there was a collusion between Rangoon and the wily warlord. Lawn's own, rather simplistic attitude to the complexities of the Golden Triangle drug trade had also become obvious as early as 1987, when, addressing a gathering of anti-narcotics agencies in Kuala Lumpur, he called for "no mercy" in the war on drugs. Southeast Asian governments, Lawn growled, must "take on hostile opium growers in armed confrontations".[9]

At the time, the local media in the region had quickly exploited Lawn's remarks to make some propaganda gains for themselves. The Bangkok press, for instance, soon reported that Burmese government forces had attacked Khun Sa's stronghold in Burma. Casualties were high, the newspapers said. The *Bangkok Post* announced that Burma had allowed Thai troops to cross the border into Burma "in hot pursuit" of Khun Sa's forces.[10]

The Nation reported on 3 March 1987 that "F-5E jets may be used in bombing Khun Sa's bases". By mid-March, Thai army commander, Gen. Chavalit Yongchaiyudh, touring the battlefront, declared that the campaign against Khun Sa had been "a success".[11]

But in April, only a few weeks later, the infamous US PoW hunter James "Bo" Gritz paid a clandestine visit to Khun Sa's new headquarters at Homöng. He was astonished to find no damage in the camp: "I did not see a bullet hole, a shell mark or a bomb crater anywhere. There was no smell of cordite in the air. There was not so much as a burnt leaf to mark what was supposed to have been a war with thousands of Burmese and Thai troops fighting against the drug kingpin, Khun Sa."[12]

When asked about the recent fighting, the warlord laughed heartily: "Oh that. That was a newspaper war."[13] Gritz became curious: "When I questioned Khun Sa about the matter, he said that Thai and Burmese officials had both come to him early in January [1987], and said that they stood to lose millions of dollars in US drug-supression funds unless they made it look like they were doing something. So they worked out a deal. Khun Sa agreed to let them come up to the border and fire off their guns and a few rockets into the air, so that they could claim that they were doing their part in fighting this 'monster', whom [US] Ambassador Brown [in Bangkok] had described as 'the worst enemy the world has'."[14]

Khun Sa agreed to the charade if he would be allowed to build a new road from Mae Hong Son in northeastern Thailand up to his Homöng headquarters across the border in Shan State. Bulldozers and earthmoving machines soon roared through the jungle. Hundreds of Thai construction workers mingled with uniformed Khun Sa troops as the road was carved out of the border mountains.

By April 1987, trucks, cars and jeeps began travelling this new road, carrying arms, ammunition and rations for Khun Sa's troops. Dignitaries visited Khun Sa; a flow of foreign journalists even filmed the road. But, officially, the road did not exist.

This unusual new road was mentioned before the Committee on Foreign Affairs at the US House of Representatives in July 1987. Asked why the Thais had helped Khun Sa build this road, Ann B. Wrobleski, assistant secretary of state of International Narcotics Matters, replied:

> Well, we are as curious as everybody else. We queried our embassy in Bangkok and asked them for their response. The road was built for the specific purpose of allowing easy access by Thai security forces into the area to control the illegal cross-border trade in arms as well as narcotics.[15]

In reality, the much-publicised opium war of 1987 produced only one casualty. A young soldier in Khun Sa's army was hurt when he fell off a large truck while travelling along the new road to his headquarters.

Inevitably, this famous road became an international embarrassment, despite attempts to cover up the whole affair. The Thais moved in and dynamited it. Yet a few days later, the bulldozers were back and the road was rebuilt. A year later, a network of four roads connected Khun Sa's headquarters with the highway system of northern Thailand. It all strikingly resembled the 1950s, when Thai police general Pao Sriyanonda staged his theatrical operations against the KMT. In the end, little had really changed.

The indictment of Khun Sa in early 1990 was supposed to pressure the Thais and the Burmese into taking the situation more seriously. The DEA, however, overlooked the fact that with the emergence of Lo Hsing-han's new heroin empire in the former CPB area of northeastern Shan State, Khun Sa had outlived his usefulness—and the Rangoon government was in a position to sacrifice him, if that would mean improved relations with Washington. But Rangoon was not willing to commit its own forces to the fight. Instead, the central authorities decided to support the Was of the former CPB.

Throughout 1989, Khun Sa's forces and the United Wa State Army fought pitched battles with Khun Sa's forces, officially called the Möng Tai Army— "Möng Tai" being the indigenous name for Shan State. This time the fighting was real: it was not just another phantom war.

The fighters, however, were Was, not regular Burmese troops, although the SLORC actively assisted the former CPB forces. Wa soldiers arrived at the Thai border in Burma Army trucks, and frequent reports also indicated that the Rangoon government provided ammunition and air support for the UWSA.[16]

The Was, once again, found themselves being used as cannon fodder for other people's interests. This time, they were not forced to fight for communist ideology, but to help improve Rangoon's international image— and to protect opium routes and heroin refineries belonging to the new heroin empire in Kokang and, closer to the Thai border, the notorious Wei brothers, who were also using the Was for their own ends.

The DEA willingly played along with this cynical alliance, perhaps hoping that the effort would result in the capture of Khun Sa. Rangoon, on its part, pushed ahead with its PR campaign to announce that the general election which it had promised to hold when it had assumed power in September 1988 was, at last, going to be held in May 1990.

The DEA office in Rangoon, already a tool for SLORC propaganda, did not miss the opportunity to try to further improve the international standing of the Burmese generals. In late April, a few weeks before the general election, the DEA's new country attache in Rangoon, Angelo Saladino, went into action. He had decided to mastermind a media blitz by arranging for an international TV crew to film a drug-burning ceremony organised by the military authorities in the Burmese capital.[17]

It had to be done in total secrecy, without the knowledge of the US embassy in Rangoon. The ambassador, Burton Levin, was one of the most outspoken critics of the SLORC, for which he had earned the respect and admiration of most ordinary Burmese.[18] Finally, Saladino managed to persuade the Burmese authorities to issue visas for a four-man team from CBS and a *Time* photographer. They were all qualified professionals—but they were also unaware of the manipulations which were going on behind the scenes in Rangoon and at the DEA headquarters in Washington.[19]

On their arrival in Rangoon, the foreign journalists were met by officials from Khin Nyunt's secret police, the Directorate of the Defence Services Intelligence, who took care of them throughout their stay. But it did not take long before the embassy staff found out what was going on behind their backs. Inevitably, the differences which existed between the DEA and the State Department surfaced in a way which embarrassed everybody concerned.

The TV footage—which despite the DEA's manipulations turned out to be very professional in its presentation—had Saladino and the deputy chief of mission, Chris Szymanski, publicly contradicting each other before the camera. Saladino assured his audience that the SLORC was sincere in its anti-narcotics drive; Szymanski pointed out that drugs were pouring across Burma's borders in all directions and that nothing substantial was being done about it.

Levin had been out of the country when the foreign newsmen arrived. He returned a few days later, infuriated by Saladino's unauthorised manoeuvres. Saladino was called in to see the ambassador, who roundly reprimanded him for disobeying the orders of DCM Szymanski.[20]

In Washington, the State Department dismissed the bonfire as a "publicity stunt".[21] But Congressman Rangel, who was close to the DEA, said in an interview which was included in the CBS report from Rangoon: "They're saying that the Burmese army is brutal. Hey! Of course they have to be brutal; they're fighting a war on drugs."[22]

The much-awaited election was held shortly after Saladino's ill-fated attempt at a PR coup. Probably believing that its year-long propaganda campaign in the *Working People's Daily* against the NLD had been effective— and evidently underestimating the degree of hatred towards the military that still existed—the SLORC decided to allow an astonishing degree of openness.

After months of repression, severely restricted campaigning and harassment of candidates and political activists during the election itself, even foreign journalists were invited to cover the event, and there were no reports of tampering with the voting registers.

On election day, there was a massive turn-out of voters. Entire families lined up outside the polling booths early in the morning of 27 May 1990 to make sure they would be able to cast their votes.

The outcome was an astounding victory for the NLD. It captured 392 of the 485 seats contested in the 492-member assembly—elections were postponed in seven constituencies for security reasons. The rest went to

NLD allies from the various minority areas, while the military-backed National Unity Party (the new name for the BSPP since 26 September 1988) captured a mere 10 seats.

One of the few NUP candidates to be elected was old Commander "Dickie" who had fought alongside the Burma Army against the CPB at Kyinshan in early 1970. He secured 3,336 votes in the small constituency of Panglong-Hopang, his old bailiwick. The only other candidate in Hopang was Saw Philip of the pro-democracy Wa National Development Party, who got 2,324 votes.[23]

The NLD's overwhelming majority was a clear indication that Aung San Suu Kyi's year-long campaign, from August 1988 to July 1989, had produced remarkable results, and not only in terms of support for her party. There was not a single reported incident of violence or misbehaviour on the part of the public on election day. The Burmese went to the polls with unity and dignity.

The SLORC was probably as taken aback as almost everybody else; it was totally unprepared for an NLD victory of this magnitude. The NLD won even in Rangoon's Dagon township, which includes the capital's cantonment area and the SLORC's headquarters. The leader of the NUP, Tha Kyaw, a former BSPP minister, was also defeated by the NLD in his constituency in Hmawbi, near a major army camp and an air force base. For this reason, political observers noted after the election that whatever the military decided to do to counter its outcome, it would have to tread carefully so as not to provoke a backlash from its own rank and file, who had apparently also voted for the NLD.

Many Burmese at the time pointed out that the election—in which more than ninety different political parties had participated—should not be viewed as a Western-type poll with different parties competing for seats. Rather, it was a referendum in which the NLD represented the democratic aspirations of the vast majority of the Burmese people, while the NUP stood for the old system.

The SLORC, however, once again demonstrated its lack of political acumen—and its belief that it is possible to control people with threats and brute force alone. The DDSI chief Khin Nyunt appeared again on 27 July, claiming that a "constituent assembly", vested only with the task of drafting a new constitution, had been elected, not a parliament.

He added: "It should not be necessary to explain that a political organisation does not automatically obtain the three sovereign powers of the legislative, administrative and judicial powers by the emergence of a *Pyithu Hluttaw* [parliament] .... Only the SLORC has the right to legislative power .... Drafting an interim constitution to obtain state power and to form a government will not be accepted in any way and if it is done effective action will be taken according to the law."[24]

Since its inception, the SLORC had always justified its human-rights abuses by referring to "the law"—a meaningless concept in the existing Burmese context since the SLORC, claiming sole legislative powers, made its own laws without consulting anybody. The statement was also a retraction of earlier promises made by Khin Nyunt; at a meeting with foreign military attaches in Rangoon on 22 September 1988, shortly after the formation of the SLORC, he had declared that "elections will be held as soon as law and order have been restored and the *tatmadaw* will then hand over state power to the party which wins".[25]

On 28 July, the NLD members who had been elected to the assembly met at the Gandhi Hall in Rangoon's Kyauktada township and adopted a resolution calling on the SLORC to stand down and hand over power to a democratically elected government. During the interim period "the people shall, as a minimum, enjoy the freedom of publication and expression. It is against political nature that the NLD, which has overwhelmingly won enough seats in the *Pyithu Hluttaw* to form a government, itself has been prohibited from the minimum of democratic rights," the widely distributed Gandhi Hall Declaration said.[26] It also called for "frank and sincere discussions with good faith and with the object of national reconciliation".

All this echoed the thoughts of Aung San Suu Kyi—but there was nothing to indicate that the SLORC intended to release her from house arrest, not even after the massive election victory of the NLD. The NLD in a separate resolution at the Gandhi Hall meeting called for the release of Aung San Suu Kyi and all other political prisoners; the SLORC, however, was as non-committal as usual. By holding the elections and then refusing to honour the outcome, the military government had also clearly undermined whatever legitimacy it could once claim to have had.

In effect, the election had pitted the pro-democracy forces directly against the pillar of the old regime, Ne Win and his private police force, the DDSI, headed by Khin Nyunt—or, in a historical context, it had been a peaceful but head-on collision between Burma's increasingly anachronistic authoritarian tradition and an explicit desire to continue the democratic development which had been interrupted by Ne Win's coup in 1962. Despite her absence from public life for more than a year, Aung San Suu Kyi and her ideals were still very much alive.

When it became obvious that the SLORC was not going to honour the outcome of the election—and that the NLD and the ordinary people were in no position to alter the military's stance—Burma's *sangha*, the order of monks, took the initiative. On 8 August 1990, the second anniversary of the 1988 uprising, thousands of Buddhist monks marched through the streets of Mandalay.

It was not officially a demonstration—the monks were out on their morning alms round—but the choice of date and the vast number of monks who took part in the ceremony made the intention obvious enough. Tens of thousands of people showed up in the streets to offer food to the monks, while nervous soldiers looked on. At one point along the route, some students hoisted a peacock flag, the symbol of Burmese nationalism and now also of the NLD and the pro-democracy movement.

Some soldiers apparently over-reacted. They opened up with their automatic G-3 rifles and bullets ripped through the crowd. Shi Ah Sein Na, a seventeen-year-old novice from Mogaung monastery in Mandalay was wounded as bullets punctured one of his lungs and shattered his shoulder. He fell to the ground, bleeding profusely.

Nine more monks and at least two onlookers were also hit. Alms bowls broken by bullets lay in the street while the soldiers charged the crowd. Fourteen monks were badly beaten and at least five were arrested. Several of the wounded went missing after the incident. Some were presumed dead.[27]

The brutality against the monks appalled everyone. To add insult to injury, the authorities in Rangoon flatly denied that any shooting had occurred in Mandalay on 8 August. The state-run radio claimed that the students and the monks had attacked the security forces and that one novice had been slightly injured in the commotion.[28]

The official white-wash of the incident was not accepted by the monks in Mandalay. On 27 August, more than 7,000 monks gathered in the city. They decided to refuse to accept offerings from soldiers and their families, or to perform religious rites for them, in effect excommunicating anyone associated with the military. The boycott soon spread all over Mandalay, the home of some 80,000 monks, and other towns in upper Burma: Sagaing, Monywa, Pakokku, Myingyan, Meiktila, Shwebo and Ye-U.

In Rangoon 2,000 monks met at the Buddhist study centre of Ngar Htat Gyi to join the campaign against the military. The conflict with the monks was one of the most serious challenges to the military thus far: the boycott severely affected the ordinary soldiers and their families, and the loyalty of the rank and file was crucial for the survival of the SLORC.

Again, the SLORC decided to use force to quell the opposition. In the early hours of 7 September, Kyi Maung, acting head of the NLD since the incarceration of Aung San Suu Kyi and Tin Oo, was arrested on trumped up charges along with what remained of the party's top leadership. In the weeks that followed, more than sixty-five MPs-elect were arrested.[29]

Yet, few people really believed that the army would dare move against the Buddhist monks. But it did. On 20 October, SLORC chairman Gen. Saw Maung ordered the dissolution of all Buddhist organisations involved in anti-government activities. "Those who refuse will not be allowed to remain monks," he stated.[30] Local military commanders were also vested with martial law powers, enabling them to disrobe monks and have them imprisoned or executed if they did not comply with the government order.

Two days later, leaflets ordering the monks to give up the boycott were dropped from army helicopters over several Mandalay monasteries. Then the army moved into action. One hundred and thirty-three monasteries were raided by heavily armed troops and scores of monks led away into captivity.[31] Gen. Saw Maung, who had travelled to Mandalay to conduct the action against the monks, returned to Rangoon on 24 October after ending the operation successfully. Among those arrested were some of Burma's best-respected, senior abbots, including U Thumingala, head of a renowned teaching monastery in Rangoon.

In many ways, the last hope for the democratic opposition had been pinned on the monks. When the army demonstrated that it did not hesitate to move against even the most respected segment of Burmese society, most people lost heart. The pro-democracy movement crumbled and all overt opposition to the SLORC ceased.

The international response to the crackdown was one of anger and condemnation. Virtually every democratic country issued statements demanding the release of those arrested and that the SLORC should respect the outcome of the election. The SLORC countered these moves in its own inimitable way. The economy had been opened for foreign investment since late 1988, but now the SLORC embarked on a relentless campaign to attract businessmen from overseas. The aim was to attract "customers whose only motives are instant achievements and profits".[32]

Department stores, video and television showrooms were opened in Rangoon and soon billboard-size advertisements for Japanese radios and American soft drinks could be seen at major intersections in the capital. For many foreigners, who had seen Burma during the days of the austere, pre-1988 BSPP government, it seemed as if something substantial was happening to the economy.

The reforms, however, had been implemented not to initiate any fundamental change of Burma's political structure, but rather to maintain the military's grip on power. Socialism was a non-goer with the international community, and, like the northern neighbour China, economic reforms were also aimed at diverting the attention of the population at large from politics to making money—and in SLORC's Burma, many businessmen flourished, especially the drug traffickers.

In February 1990, the government in Rangoon even announced a four-month "tax amnesty", which allowed private businessmen to declare and pay a 25% profits tax on assets they could not show were obtained legally. While designed to generate income for a financially strapped regime, Western observers viewed the programme as a means whereby narcotics traffickers could launder their proceeds. The entire programme netted over six billion Kyats (US$900 million at the official rate, US$100 on the black market), of which a substantial sum was suspected to have been drug money.[33]

But the SLORC took no chances. The massive build-up of the army which had been initiated after the 1988 events was further accelerated. The strength of the three services of Burma's armed forces increased from an estimated 180,000–190,000 before 1988 to close to 300,000. Assistance for this build-up came from the SLORC's newest and most trustworthy ally: China.

A seemingly insignificant event in the midst of the political turmoil that had engulfed Burma during the summer of 1988 had later turned out to be an extremely important watershed in Sino–Burmese relations: on 6 August 1988, amid almost daily mass demonstrations in Rangoon and only two days before a general strike crippled the entire country, most observers were probably amused to read in the official media in Rangoon that China and Burma had signed an agreement allowing official cross-border trade to take place between the two countries.

The timing appeared to be most unfortunate; the rest of the world was watching what they thought were the last days of the old regime. Almost the entire, 2,170-kilometre Sino–Burmese frontier was in any case controlled by the CPB and other rebel forces. Following the border agreement in 1960, the frontier had been marked with border stones which were erected by a joint Sino-Burmese team that literally walked the entire length of the common border.

When these had crumbled more than two decades later, new stones were erected in 1985 in accordance with a new agreement. But this time, the Burmese border inspection team had to come from the Chinese side. The new border stones, the location of which the Chinese had decided, were conveniently located in open paddy fields and glades in the jungle —far away from major rebel bases along the frontier.

But the Chinese, who have always been renowned for their ability to plan far ahead of everybody else, had expressed their intentions, almost unnoticed, in an article in the official *Beijing Review* as early as 2 September 1985. Titled "Opening to the Southwest: An Expert Opinion", the article, which was written by a former vice-minister of communications, Pan Qi, outlined the possibilities of finding an outlet for trade from China, through Burma, to the Indian Ocean.

He mentioned the Burmese railheads of Myitkyina and Lashio in northern and northeastern Burma as possible conduits for the export of Chinese goods—but he conveniently refrained from mentioning that all relevant border areas, at that time, were not under central Burmese governmental control.

This situation changed in early 1987, when the Burmese government managed to dislodge the CPB from Panghsai. The Chinese, whose policies had changed dramatically since the days of Kang Sheng and the Cultural Revolution, began to penetrate the Burmese market through an extensive economic intelligence reporting system within Burma. This network monitored the availability of domestically manufactured Burmese products, as well as the nature and volume of illegal trade from other neighbouring countries such as Thailand, Malaysia, Singapore and India.

China could then respond to market conditions by producing similar goods in its state sector factories. More than 2,000 carefully selected items were reported to be flooding the Burmese market. Chinese-made consumer goods were not only made deliberately cheaper than those from other neighbouring countries, but also less expensive than local Burmese products.[34]

But the main change came after the 1989 CPB mutiny, when the border trade began to boom. Ties between Burma and China were gradually strengthening. In October 1989, half a year after the CPB mutiny and three months after Aung San Suu Kyi had been placed under house arrest, a 24-man Burmese military team, headed by Lieut.-Gen. Than Shwe, vice chairman of the SLORC, was invited to China.

The high-profile nature of the visit was evident in Beijing, where the Burmese guests posed for a photograph with Prime Minister Li Peng, the butcher of Tiananmen Square. Intelligence chief Khin Nyunt, who was included in the delegation, had in a reference to the killings in the Chinese capital declared on 30 September that "we sympathise with the People's Republic of China as disturbances similar to those last year broke out in the People's Republic [this year]".[35]

By 1990, Burma had become China's principal political and military ally in Southeast Asia: the first shipment of Chinese arms arrived in mid-August as the monks of Mandalay were launching their boycott of the SLORC. A Chinese freighter docked in the port of Rangoon and for two consecutive nights convoys of army trucks rumbled through the Burmese capital to the military area near Mingaladon immediately north of the city.[36]

This was to be followed by F-7 jet fighters, Hainan-class naval patrol boats, 100 light and medium tanks, including T69IIs and the Chinese version of the Soviet PT76 light amphibious tanks (T83), APCs and Infantry Fighting Vehicles, 37mm twin-barrel anti-aircraft guns, 57mm single-barrel anti-aircraft guns, radio sets for military use, radar equipment for the F-7, and enough light arms and ammunition to equip seventy-four new battalions.

Some of the hardware was delivered in Rangoon, while substantial quantities went by road from Ruili in Yunnan to Muse and Kutkai in northeastern Shan State.[37]

Taking into account the Rangoon massacres of 1988, and China's Tiananmen Square massacre the following year, it was hardly surprising that the two isolated, internationally condemned neighbours would move closer to each other. Burma's strategic importance to China was also evident: China soon became involved in upgrading Burma's badly maintained roads and railways. Chinese experts began to work on a series of infrastructural projects in Burma.

Chinese military advisers also arrived, the first foreign military personnel to be stationed in Burma since the 1950s. Burma was, in effect, becoming a Chinese client state; what the CPB failed to achieve for the Chinese on the battlefield had been accomplished by shrewd diplomacy and flourishing bilateral trade.

It was also urgent for the SLORC to improve its international standing after the crackdown of 1990. And again, narcotics became the lure. In November, as the initial outrage over the campaign against the monks and the arrests of the winners of the May election had cooled down, Rangoon staged a drug burning ceremony in Kokang itself. Khin Nyunt himself flew up to the event with two DEA officials from Rangoon and some UN personnel.[38]

Eyebrows were raised in many quarters when the Myanmar National Democratic Alliance Army (MNDAA) overlord and long-time heroin trafficker Pheung Kya-shin was featured as "leader of the Kokang nationals"—officiating at the drug burning ceremony! In his speech, Pheung asked for support for his "programme for the destruction and suppression of narcotics drugs".[39] Then, two supposed heroin refineries were put to the torch.

Pheung's speech, which was reproduced in the state-run *Working People's Daily* a few days after the event, contained some remarkable statements. He said, for instance, that "there was only buying and selling of opium in the area before the arrival of the CPB. Buying and selling of morphine base and heroin did not exist."[40]

Pheung failed to mention, however, that he was the military commander of the CPB unit that took over Kokang in 1968, or that it was he who established the first heroin refinery in the area in the mid-1970s. At the time of his speech, Pheung himself was the owner of several heroin refineries in the Nam Kyaun area immediately west of the Salween river as well as at Si-Aw, his headquarters in Kokang proper.[41]

A second, similar charade was organised in January 1991 in Möng Ko, and a few Thai journalists were also invited. This time, Pheung Kya-shin again pledged to fight narcotics. He went on to destroy a further three supposed heroin refineries and burn about 100 kilograms of drugs. Don MacIntosh of the United Nations Fund for Drug Abuse Control declared after the ceremony: "I am pleased to be in Shan State and have the opportunity to [attend] this important drug eradication exercise."[42]

The attitude of the US embassy in Rangoon was also changing following the departure of Burton Levin and his experienced staff. A new batch of diplomats, who had neither witnessed the 1988 massacres, nor seen the 1990 election, had arrived in Rangoon. They seemed determined to sacrifice whatever Levin had accomplished in terms of public goodwill in favour of "improving relations" with the SLORC.

Donald Jameson, the new counsellor for political and economic affairs, delivered a speech shortly after Pheung Kya-shin's show in Kokang: "We are impressed by the efforts which the Government of Myanmar is making to promote development in the border regions and to eradicate opium production."[43]

Sources from the area, however, were much less impressed: they claimed that the drugs that had been burnt had actually been bought from Pheung Kya-shin and other heroin traffickers in the area for 80,000 Kyats a kilogram, or approximately the local price for good quality, No. 4 heroin. They also said the number of heroin refineries in the area had increased from seventeen in mid-1990 to twenty-three in early 1991.[44]

Hardly surprisingly, the local organiser of the trip to Möng Ko was John Htin Aung, the DDSI agent who had managed to infiltrate the DEA office in Rangoon.[45]

Present at the ceremony at Möng Ko was also Ai Chau Hsö, a notorious heroin trafficker from the Thai–Burmese frontier and Khun Sa's foremost rival for control of the border trade in the south. In an interview with one of the Thai journalists invited, he confirmed his commitment to fight Khun Sa.[46] Sen. Daniel Moynihan stated at the time: "The Burmese regime has done nothing more than change business partners: turn on Khun Sa and get the public relations advantage that the DEA is giving them, and use the former CPB, and turn them into a willing drug-trafficking partner."[47]

Critics were also quick to point out that official Burmese complicity in the drug trade was nothing new. The old KKY programme of the 1960s and 1970s had also been based on semi-institutionalised drug trafficking agreements, and narcotics-related corruption had always been widespread in Burma. But all information about past and present official involvement with drug traffickers was conveniently erased from the collective memory of US narcotics officials and UN agency personnel.

The gross misrepresentation of the situation in Burma was also enhanced by Daniel O'Donahue, a former US ambassador to Thailand (and Burma), who stated: "Many Burma Army troops, previously dedicated to anti-narcotics operations, were withdrawn from the field and redeployed to enforce martial law."[48]

In reality, there had been no such troop rotations. The forces which were used to quell the demonstrations in 1988 came mainly from the 22nd and the 44th Light Infantry Divisions from Karen State, an area where no poppies are grown.

No troops were pulled out of northeastern Shan State until well after the cease-fire agreement had been reached with the ex-CPB forces in late 1989. These troops were subsequently redeployed in Kayah (Karenni) and Kachin states, where they were engaged in fighting ethnic rebels. What seemed to have happened since 1988, however, was a much more blatant and more thinly disguised involvement with drug trafficking groups than before.

The way in which various UN agencies dealt with the problem was scarecely more enlightened. The UNFDAC (now renamed the United Nations International Drug Control Programme, the UNDCP) initiated a crop substitution programme in Burma in the mid-1970s, totalling US$6.5 million for the "first phase" 1976–81, and about the same sum for two subsequent phases. The scheme was temporarily halted in the wake of the upheaval of 1988.

The UN's counter-productive "preventative crop substitution programme" had been followed by an even more dramatic narcotics boom. The area under poppy cultivation rose from 103,200 hectares in 1988 to 161,012 in 1991. During the same period, the annual heroin production skyrocketed from 68 tons to 185 tons, of which 181.5 was meant for export.[49] The UNDCP resumed assistance to the government in Rangoon in 1990, basically continuing the same counter-productive policies as it had implemented before the upheaval of 1988.

The rapid increase during the late 1980s was also due to a number of factors. Near-perfect weather conditions during several growing seasons was one important element—as was the Rangoon government's decision in September 1987 to demonetise without compensation all 25, 35 and 75 Kyat bank notes in circulation.[50] After that, most Burmese lost confidence in paper money and turned to traditional hard currencies: gold and real estate in the towns—and opium in the frontier areas.

Paradoxically, a US aid programme, suspended after the bloodbath in Rangoon in September 1988, may also have been a contributing factor. The US$18 million a year project financed the aerial spraying of opium crops otherwise inaccessible to Rangoon. But instead of curbing production, narcotics officials believe the programme only inspired farmers in the poppy growing areas to increase their planting in the hope of compensating for expected spraying losses. "We sprayed them into over-production," said a narcotics expert in Bangkok.[51]

After the CPB mutiny in 1989 put an end to fighting in the northeast, thousands of former Communist combatants, mostly young tribesmen, returned home to their villages in the hills, providing many new labourers in the poppy fields. Hence, there was no shortage of raw opium to supply the heroin refineries which had been established by former CPB commanders in the northeast.

In his speech in Kokang in November 1990, Pheung Kya-shin requested assistance for a "crop substitution programme" in his home area to be introduced in Lao Khai and Chinsweho—two villages which are located in Kokang's only valley, and, therefore, areas where it would be virtually impossible to cultivate poppies on a commercial scale in any case.[52]

A similar programme was initiated in a similar, non-poppy growing area in the rice producing valley of Hsaleü near Möng Yang in the hills north of Kengtung. In March 1991, a team of UN experts, headed by D.H. Rector, even visited the area and, probably without knowing who they were introduced to, held talks with the two most prominent heroin traffickers in eastern Burma: the notorious former Red Guard volunteers Lin Mingxian and Zhang Zhiming.[53] In July, the United Nations Development Programme announced that it would provide US$1.3 million to support the SLORC's "border development programme".[54]

The manipulation of UN agencies and, to some extent, the administration in Washington was not by coincidence. John Htin Aung had managed to influence the office in Rangoon into adopting the official SLORC line—until he was dismissed by Washington for failing a polygraph examination regarding his affiliation to the DDSI.

But the main brain behind the manipulations was DEA country attache, Angelo Saladino. In March 1991, he authored a memorandum addressed to DDSI chief Khin Nyunt in which he listed, item by item, ways to deceive the US government and UN agencies.

The highly controversial document not only effectively undermined official US government policy towards Burma, but provided specific details on ways to "deprive many of Myanmar's most vocal critics of some of their shopworn, yet effective, weapons in the campaign to discredit [Myanmar's] narcotics programme". Saladino continued to recommend ways for SLORC to "silence even its most biased critics".[55]

It took some time before Washington discovered Saladino's incredible memorandum. When noises were made, Saladino hurriedly flew back to the DEA headquarters in the US at his own expense. He managed to convince his superiors that he had not, after all, actually sent the memorandum to Khin Nyunt. This was a blatant lie—but it bought Saladino an additional three months' time in Burma. Only when it became clear that Saladino was not presenting a complete picture of his activities in Rangoon, was he recalled to the US and subjected to an investigation for professional misconduct. But the damage to the once favourable image of the US in Burma had been done, and his successor as Burma country attache, Richard Horn, did not alter the DEA's role as apologist for the SLORC.[56]

Against the backdrop of all these manipulations and international manoeuvres, there was little room for the ethnic resistance. In the wake of the crackdown after the May 1990 election, about a dozen MPs-elect fled to the Thai border, where they linked up with the Karens and other ethnic insurgents.

Shortly after the first flight to the border following the September 1988 massacre, the National Democratic Front had initiated a broader front, the Democratic Alliance of Burma (DAB), which included all the members of the NDF, minus the Karennis who insisted on their "independent" status, plus about ten smaller Burman dissident groups. Of these only the All-Burma Students Democratic Front (ABSDF), now led by Moe Thi Zon, and the Committee for Restoration of Democracy in Burma (CRDB) were of any significance, and the DAB had been by and large unable to affect the situation inside the country.

With the arrival of the MPs-elect and a few dozen NLD cadres from the towns, this was supposed to change. At a grand ceremony at the Manerplaw headquarters of the Karen rebels, on 18 December 1990, six MPs-elect proclaimed "the National Coalition Government of the Union of Burma". It was headed by Sein Win, a first cousin of Aung San Suu Kyi. His father, Aung San's elder brother Ba Win, had been gunned down together with the independence hero in the Secretariat in Rangoon on 19 July 1947.

But it soon became obvious that no foreign country was going to recognise the jungle-based "cabinet"—and the desperate move also reflected the dire straits into which the once mighty NLD had fallen.

The NLD had been decapitated for the first time in July 1989, when Aung San Suu Kyi, Tin Oo and all the other top leaders of the league had been incarcerated. A second-rung leadership, headed by Kyi Maung, had taken over. He was hardly of the same calibre as his arrested colleagues, but proved to be strong enough to carry the NLD through its election victory in May 1990.

Then, four months later, Kyi Maung and other second-rung leaders were also arrested. The NLD had been decapitated a second time, and third-rung leaders took over: Sein Win and his colleagues on the Thai border—and, in Rangoon, the NLD announced that its new official chairman was Aung Shwe, a former army officer who had served as ambassador to Australia in the early 1980s. A meek, colourless figure, he and the rest of the internal third-rung NLD leadership were soon cowed into submission by the SLORC. Burma's pro-democracy movement was effectively crushed.

Even in the border areas, the SLORC was having its way. Following the collapse of the CPB, other smaller armies—which had depended on the Communists for arms and ammunition—also gave in. The first to break up were the Shans of the Shan State Army. In September 1989, about 2,000 SSA troops led by Hsö Hten, one of the original student activists from Pangtawng in the late 1950s, struck a deal with Rangoon.

This agreement was followed by the defection of Mahtu Naw, a local Kachin rebel commander from the Kachin-inhabited areas of northeastern Shan State, who had also been heavily dependent on the CPB. His 4th Brigade of the Kachin Independence Army (KIA) made peace with Rangoon in January 1991. Although Mahtu Naw did not have more than a few hundred men under his command, his defection shattered the battle-hardened and well-organised KIA, which until then had been the only ethnic insurgent army in the area that had not suffered any splits or internal divisions.[57]

The demise of the KIA's 4th Brigade—and the publicity the event was given in the state-run Rangoon media—could hardly have come at a worse time. As Radio Rangoon and the *Working People's Daily* announced the news, a high-powered Kachin rebel delegation was clandestinely visiting New Delhi at the invitation of the Indian security authorities. India had become concerned about the rapidly growing Chinese influence in Burma, especially in the north.

India was also facing problems with its own ethnic insurgents in the northeast—Nagas, Manipuris and Assamese—who were using bases in northwestern Burma as sanctuaries for their cross-border raids into India. Earlier attempts to persuade Rangoon to assist India in combating this menace had produced no results, and the Indian authorities obviously thought that by supporting the KIA, they would be able to police the other side of the border as well as counter-balance China's influence in Burma.

The KIA established a base near Pinawng Zup opposite the Indian army base at Vijaynagar in northeastern Arunachal Pradesh, and some supplies could be brought in from Dibrugarh and other towns in Assam. The KIA was also permitted to post a liaison officer in New Delhi, and the Kachins, with Indian assistance, helped train and equip small armies of Kuki and Chin tribesmen in the jungles opposite Manipur to counter Naga rebels in the area. But the defection of Mahtu Naw shook the Indian confidence in the KIA: the massive assistance which the Kachins had expected to receive to make up for the loss of the CPB as a source of arms and ammunition never materialised.

On 27 March, the Pa-O rebels in the vicinity of the Shan State capital of Taunggyi followed suit, and on 21 April, the Palaungs in the hills north of Namhsan in northern Shan State signed a ceasefire agreement with the SLORC. Ironically, thousands of former insurgents in the frontier areas were rallying behind the ruling military just when almost the entire population of the central plains had turned against the regime following the pro-democracy movement that had swept Burma.

The conflict was far from over, however, and towards the end of 1991, the pressure that some foreign countries had put on the SLORC also seemed to be working. In December, Aung San Suu Kyi, still under house arrest in Rangoon, was awarded the most prestigious of international honours: the Nobel Peace Prize. The announcement caused euphoria in Burma: a few thousand students gathered on the Rangoon University campus and began shouting anti-SLORC slogans. The official response was the same, however. Troops cordoned off the entire university area and 900 youngsters were arrested.[58]

But the strain was taking its toll on the SLORC chairman, Gen. Saw Maung. He was becoming increasingly erratic and his public speeches incoherent and rambling, covering subjects such as dying tomorrow and Jesus in Tibet.[59] At last, he suffered a nervous breakdown and collapsed.

The deterioration of his health became obvious on 21 December 1991, when he was going to be the first to tee-off at a tournament at the military golf course in Rangoon. In front of the Burma Army's top brass and government officials, Saw Maung began screaming: "I am King Kyansittha!" Patting his holstered pistol, he warned onlookers to be "careful" or "I will personally kill you".[60]

His reference to one of the kings of the ancient Pagan empire was especially eccentric. Kyansittha, a powerful king whose name means "the remaining soldier" or "the one who was left behind", was the main character in a Moses-like story of a man who survived attempts on his life to become king. Saw Maung may have seen himself as the only SLORC member who also served with the pre-1988 regime.

An astonished Burmese public witnessed a repeat of Saw Maung's erratic performance exactly a month later when the state television showed him addressing a meeting of local SLORC officials. Apart from references to Kyansittha, the old regime and various Buddhist scriptures, Saw Maung exclaimed in the middle of his speech: "Today our country is being ruled by martial law. Martial law means no law at all." He concluded by telling the bewildered audience that "I always work with caution, perseverance and wisdom. Wisdom does not mean black magic."[61]

In the region, the SLORC was also facing severe difficulties. On 21 December 1991, a Burma Army unit crossed the border into Bangladesh and attacked an outpost of the Bangladesh Rifles, killing one soldier and injuring three. The incident proved to be diplomatically disastrous; it came less than a month after Bangladeshi foreign minister Mustafizur Rahman had visited Rangoon to settle a number of bilateral issues, including a massive influx of Muslim Rohingyas into Bangladesh.

As had been the case in the aftermath of the turmoil of the mid-1970s, the military had again tried to divert attention from the country's economic and political woes to the vulnerable Muslim minority in the northwestern corner of Arakan State. Already in early 1991, the first few thousand refugees from Burma had come streaming up the muddy road from Teknaf, bringing with them tales of forcible eviction from their homes, and the destruction of mosques and Islamic schools.[62]

By December, the number had risen to 50,000. The military escalation that followed the cross-border raid caused the situation to deteriorate to the extent that thousands of Rohingyas poured across the border every day. By early 1992, more than 200,000 refugees were living in makeshift camps along the Burma–Bangladesh border south of Cox's Bazar.

The rapid build-up of the Burma Army, the ceasefires with several insurgent groups in the traditionally rebellious north of the country, and the fact that almost all overt opposition to the SLORC had ceased had all meant that the army was in danger of becoming idle. The militarisation of the Arakan border was an outcome of this syndrome; there was no insurgency in the area apart from a handful of Rohingya guerrillas who actually spent most of their time in Bangladesh. Burma was becoming a threat to regional security.

Burma's problems also spilled over the Thai border in the east when in early 1991 a major offensive was launched against the Karens, one of the few remaining noteworthy rebel groups in the south. Orders were to capture Manerplaw before 27 March, Armed Forces' Day.[63]

More than ten thousand government soldiers were mobilised for the campaign, and thousands of civilians were rounded up and forced to become porters for the troops. Almost the entire Bangkok press corps flocked to Manerplaw to watch the comparatively small rebel group resist the onslaught of the mighty Burma Army—with all its new Chinese equipment.

The battle was fought amidst spectacular limestone crags bearing colourful names, which provided the press with attractive datelines. The Burma Army was closing in on a mountain called Chipawi Cho—or "Sleeping Dog Hill"—northwest of Manerplaw, across the deep gorge of the Salween river. From there, they apparently hoped to shell Manerplaw on the Moei river.

Heavy fighting raged for more than two months around Sleeping Dog Hill. The mountain eventually fell on 14 March—but this did not help the extremely costly advance of the Burma Army. The most effective artillery that could be placed on top of the mountain were 120mm Israel-made Soltam mortars, with a range of nine kilometres. Manerplaw was twelve kilometres away.

Air strikes had little effect: the planes could not hit the well-sheltered rebel base with their bombs. Armed Forces Day passed without the fall of Manerplaw being celebrated. The fighting died down with the SLORC having suffered a major international propaganda defeat. The world media was full of stories of the heroic Karen rebels defending their base, interviews with female porters who had been raped, and pictures of burning villages.

In mid-April, Prince Khaled Sultan Abdul Aziz, commander of the Saudi contingent in the 1991 Gulf War, visited Dhaka and lashed out against the SLORC for its persecution of the Rohingya Muslims. He publicly recommended a Desert Storm-like action against Burma—"just what [the UN] did to liberate Kuwait".[64] Even some of Burma's closest allies in the ASEAN block of countries began to distance themselves from the SLORC. Singapore, Brunei, Malaysia and Indonesia all condemned Burma's military regime for the exodus of the Rohingyas.

Faced with an increasingly embarrassing situation internationally, the SLORC made a radical decision. On 23 April, Radio Rangoon announced that Gen. Saw Maung had stepped down in favour of his deputy, Gen. Than Shwe.

When the shift in leadership was first announced, few anticipated any major changes. No one had any illusions that sullen, taciturn Than Shwe was a closet liberal with any grand schemes up his sleeve. But then, unexpectedly, the SLORC began releasing political prisoners, including the old statesman U Nu who had been under house arrest since 29 December 1989.

The SLORC continued to take a number of steps aimed at improving its international image. On 27 April, an agreement was reached with Bangladesh on the repatriation of the Rohingya refugees. The same day, the SLORC announced that it had suspended its operations against the Karen rebels in the name of "national solidarity". Troops were withdrawn from the Manerplaw front, although Sleeping Dog Hill and other forward positions which had been captured during the offensive earlier in the year were not abandoned.

The SLORC also announced that Aung San Suu Kyi's British husband, Michael Aris, and their two sons, were allowed to visit her in Rangoon. On 23 June, talks were held for the first time between the SLORC and representatives of some political parties, including the shattered remains of the NLD. All universities were reopened on 24 August, and journalists were once again allowed in to visit Burma.

What was really happening? It soon became obvious that apart from a slight economic revival, including a mini-boom in free enterprise primarily in Mandalay (because of the cross-border trade with China) but also in pockets of Rangoon itself, very little had actually changed. On the contrary, it seemed that the SLORC was now so secure in its position of power that it could afford a few concessions. Organised opposition was dead, the politicians silenced and the population at large too weary to continue any suicidal protests.

The SLORC had demonstrated time and again that it would rather shoot and arrest people than give in to any popular demands. The reforms initiated after Than Shwe's ascension to power were not aimed at introducing any structural changes, but to create what a Rangoon-based diplomat aptly described as "dictatorship with a human face".

That Burma remained a cancer on the body of otherwise comparatively healthy Southeast Asian nations was evident in the northeast, in spite of the cease-fires and "border development schemes". The heroin trade was flourishing as never before, and new routes and markets were being opened. With the setting up of new refineries along the Yunnan frontier, Khun Sa's role as a middleman along the Thai border was substantially reduced. New trading routes were developed across the border into Yunnan—and on to ports along the coast of southern China.

Officially, the former CPB commanders were barred from entering China because of their known involvement in the drug trade. But the fact that all of them had been operating for years along the Sino–Burmese border meant that they had long-standing working relationships with Chinese security authorities.

A well-placed source from Möng Ko insisted in an interview in early 1991 that this personal friendship enabled them to visit China regularly and own property across the border, including hotels and private houses. "Sometimes they are even escorted by Chinese security officials and driven around in their cars," the source alleged.[65]

Within a year of the CPB mutiny, China had become a major transshipment route for Golden Triangle heroin destined for the West. According to narcotics officials, trafficking in such large quantities meant that official complicity must have reached much higher levels than just local security officials along the Sino–Burmese border. The degree to which the influx of drug money had affected politics and society in Yunnan became clear in late 1992 when thousands of Chinese troops supported by tanks were forced to besiege a border town which had been taken over by drug smugglers.

The Chinese journal *People's Armed Police News* in its 13 December 1992 issue reported that a major military operation had been carried out against drug traffickers in southern China for "over two months beginning 31 August". The target was Pingyuan, a town near the Vietnamese border, which served as a major smuggling centre for Chinese contraband entering Vietnam before that border was open to legal trade in late 1991.

The economy of the area was in the hands of the ethnic Yunnanese Muslims—Panthays or "Hui" as they are called in China—who had dominated the caravan trade in Burma for more than a century. Through their contacts throughout the Golden Triangle, and especially in the Panglong-Hopang area between Kokang and the Wa Hills, Panthay drug smuggling rings had built up an extensive network of routes from Burma through southern China, and on to the world market.

By 1992, Pingyuan had become a "country within the country", giving safe haven to outlaws and bandits from across China, the unusual report in the *People's Armed Police News* stated. Thousands of heavily armed troops, supported by armour, eventually moved in.

When the fighting, which lasted for eighty days, was over, the Chinese commanders found luxury villas, bars and dance halls run by the traffickers. Among them was Ma Siling (Ma is a common Panthay name), who was found living in a fortified villa in Pingyuan despite having been officially sentenced to death by a local court for drug trafficking.

Significantly, knowledge of the operation in Pingyuan was kept from the low-level officials in Yunnan. The net haul after the operation: 854 people arrested and 981 kilograms of drugs seized along with 353 assorted weapons. Over 1,000 Chinese officers and privates received awards for "meritorious service in the operation", according to the *People's Armed Police News.*

As of late 1991 and early 1992, the traffickers were also looking elsewhere for outlets for their drugs. Rather than heading up to the Chinese border, trucks loaded with raw opium and heroin began heading down towards the central plain to the south, around Mandalay, a town which was quickly emerging as a hub of the drug traffic in northern Burma—its many new restaurants, hotels and luxury cars were ample evidence of this fact.

From Mandalay, some trucks headed south to Rangoon—while a new drug route was also opened to the northwest. In early 1992, a string of six new refineries was identified along the Chindwin river, close to the Indian border: north of Singkaling Hkamti, near Tamanthi, Homalin, Moreh, Kalemyo, Tiddim and Paletwa on the western edge of Chin and Arakan states.[66] For the first time, refineries were established in traditionally "white", or insurgent-free, areas, close to major Burma Army installations.

As a result, drug addiction became rife in the northeastern Indian states of Nagaland and Manipur. The latter state had 600 drug addicts in 1988. Two years later, there were at least 15,000—and the state also turned up more than 900 AIDS carriers, identified as heron addicts who used common needles to inject the drug. Manipur, a state of only 1.2 million people, by 1992 had the highest incidence of drug-related AIDS infections in India.[67]

While the drug trade in the Möng Ko area and in Kokang was "free", with many private traffickers and pedlars, Lin Mingxian and Zhang Zhiming—the old Red Guards in the former 815 area near Laos—had established the best organised drug syndicate in northern Burma. The trade in the hills north of Kengtung became strictly controlled by a committee of thirteen people, headed by Lin.

A major refinery complex was set up near China–Burma border stone number 250 opposite Man Tsang Shan village in Chin. They collected raw opium from their own area as well as from Luong Nam Tha province in Laos across the Mekong border river, and their refinery was soon capable of turning out 1,000 to 2,000 kilograms of pure No. 4 heroin a year.[68]

Through Laos, a new route was opened down to Cambodia, where the island of Koh Kong emerged as a major drug trafficking centre. Lin had a wide network of contacts in Laos, dating back to the late 1970s and 1980s when right-wing Laotian guerrillas and Hmong hill-tribe fighters transited his area en route to training camps in Yunnan.

The first documented case of Burmese heroin turning up in Laos occurred in August 1991, when Laotian security forces pursuing a group of unidentified rebels who had crossed the border from Burma captured two of them and seized fifteen kilograms of pure heroin.[69] After this abortive attempt to open a route through Laos, Lin and his group were said to have approached corrupt elements within the Laotian military instead.

In Cambodia, drugs passed through Khmer Rouge as well as government-controlled areas, sometimes literally right under the noses of the UN police personnel who were stationed in the country in 1992–93 to supervise general elections.[70]

Along the Thai border, Khun Sa was desperately trying to consolidate his forces, and to retain as much of the trade as possible. His front man as chairman of the "Tai-land Revolutionary Council", Moh Heng, had died from cancer on 12 July 1991. A grand funeral for the Shan veteran was held at his base at Pieng Luang in the mountains northwest of Chiang Dao.

Thousands of Shans filed past the coffin, and among the guests at the funeral were several high-ranking Thai army and police officers. Sudsai Hasdin, the old mentor of the ethnic armies along the Thai–Burma border, travelled up from Bangkok to pay his last respects to Moh Heng.

Following Moh Heng's death, Khun Sa had also in name become the overall leader of his organisation. But in order to retain the smooth relaionship with the Thais, a new Shan front man was needed. The choice was Bo Dewing, a veteran guerrilla commander who had actually fought against Khun Sa in the mid-1960s.

The appointment of Bo Dewing, an elderly, relatively well-respected figure, helped reinforce Khun Sa's Shan image. Following the virtual surrender of the SSA, many Shan fighters who disagreed with the cease-fire agreement with the SLORC had also joined his Möng Tai Army (MTA)—which quickly expanded its territorial influence towards the north of Shan State.

Mahtu Naw's Kachin force was also disintegrating, and Kan Chit, Moh Heng's right-hand man, who had become Khun Sa's northern commander, moved in to take over the areas east of Lashio and Hsenwi where the KIA's former 4th Brigade had been active until early 1991. Many soldiers of the erstwhile SSA had also defected to the MTA following the cease-fire agreement which was concluded in 1989: in many ways, Khun Sa benefited roundly from the cease-fire agreements between some of the ethnic rebels and the SLORC.

But in terms of control over the actual traffic, Khun Sa's influence was dwindling fast. In a desperate—and exceedingly brutal—attempt to reassert control over the trade, MTA troops butchered several hundred villagers in southern Shan State in early 1993. The first massacre took place on 9 February in the Pangtawee village tract north of Khun Sa's Homöng headquarters. The villagers had sold their opium to another, KMT-connected buyer along the Thai border. On 20 March, 123 villagers were gunned down by MTA troops near the town of Möng Hsat for defying an order not to mine for precious stones in a "disputed area".[71]

With new routes being opened to the northwest through India, southeast into Laos and Cambodia and, most dramatically, northeast into Yunnan, Thailand was also feeling the pinch economically. Revenues in Thailand from the Golden Triangle drug trade totalled a staggering 80.5 billion Baht (US$3.2 billion) in 1989.[72] Revenues have subsequently declined somewhat, and other commodities in the fast-developing Thai economy have become at least equally important. But drug money continues to play a vital role in Thailand's economy, as it has done for almost a century.

The Golden Triangle heroin boom inevitably led to rivalries and fights over the spoils of the trade. The first serious infighting within the new heroin empire in the northeast broke out in December 1992 in Kokang—and it almost escalated into a full-scale war in the Golden Triangle.

When Khin Nyunt struck a deal with the former CPB forces in Kokang, he had favoured the Pheung clan over the traditional rulers of the area, the Yangs. This turned out to be a serious tactical error, and the Yangs eventually rebelled against Pheung Kya-shin and his brother Pheung Kya-fu. Gunfire once again rumbled between the steep mountains of Kokang as the two rival gangs engaged in fierce clashes.

The Was rushed to the support of the Yangs, while Khun Sa decided to reinforce the Pheungs. MTA troops in trucks drove through Lashio at night, whisked through the town by military intelligence officers, but were ambushed by the Was near Nam Jarap on the Hsenwi-Kunlong road before they could reach Kokang. The Pheungs were defeated; the elder brother retreated across the border into China and later went down to the former 815 area to join his son-in-law, Lin Mingxian. Yang Mo An and Yang Mo Lian took over Kokang—and its abundance of refineries.

The opium war of 1992 was over—but tension in the area prevailed. Next it was the Was, whose relationship with the SLORC was deteriorating rapidly. The turning point had come in January 1992, when the military authorities in Lashio arrested Saw Lu, a prominent Wa community leader.

Saw Lu had never been in the underground; on the contrary, he had fought as a home guard commander with the government forces against the his fellow Wa CPB commander Chao Ngi Lai at Saohin-Saohpa in December 1969. Having served loyally as a BSPP official throughout the 1970s and most of the 1980s, Saw Lu had during the 1988 pro-democracy uprising founded both the Wa National Development Party and the Lahu National Development Party (his wife Mary is a Lahu).

Unbeknown to most people, however, Saw Lu was also an informant for the DEA in Rangoon. His arrest was prompted by a detailed report he had compiled about the involvement in the drug trade of Maj. Than Aye, chief of military intelligence in Lashio. The report was intercepted as it was being sent down to Rangoon. Saw Lu, his wife, their two sons and two adopted sons were all thrown in jail in Lashio. Saw Lu himself was hung upside down and given electric shock treatment in the presence of Maj. Than Aye himself.[73]

On hearing about the arrest, Chao Ngi Lai and his United Wa State Army issued an ultimatum: if Saw Lu was not released before 26 March, the cease-fire with Rangoon would be over. On the 16th, Saw Lu was set free. He almost immediately escaped to the Wa Hills, where the UWSA appointed him "official spokesman for international affairs".

Saw Lu's first initiative was to persuade the Was to accept an opium eradication programme that he had worked out while still in Lashio. The SLORC's "Border Development Programme" had not produced any tangible improvements in the Wa area, and the USWA now appealed to the international community for direct assistance. A proposal, drafted by Saw Lu in early 1993, also spelled out some very specific political demands: the establishment of an autonomous Wa State within the Union of Burma, and genuine democratic reforms.[74]

The Wa initiative came at a crucial time for the struggle in Burma. The armed non-communist resistance was falling apart, a development which had been accelerated by a series of secret peace talks between the SLORC and the KIA. The cease-fires with the CPB and the SSA had placed the Kachin rebels in a quandary: the Communists had supplied them with ammunition in the past, and the Shans had provided the link between their territory in the north and the Thai border in the south.

Cut off from both former allies, the KIA was facing a severe crisis. To add to the confusion, the Chinese were putting heavy pressure on the Kachins to strike a deal with Rangoon: private merchants and state corporations in Yunnan were eagerly waiting to exploit the vast resources of timber and jade in Kachin State.

In April 1993, Kachin rebel representatives came down from their mountains along the Chinese frontier to meet SLORC officials in Myitkyina. A cease-fire agreement was agreed upon in principle, but the Kachins insisted that a military cease-fire must include other main, armed resistance groups as well for the truce to be workable. Hardly surprisingly, the Karens in the south—the most persistent of all ethnic rebels in Burma—resisted such moves to find an accomodation with the present regime in Rangoon.

The deteriorating relations between the Was and the central authorities in Rangoon also indicated that Burma's ethnic strife had not been not solved by any means despite the cease-fires. A superficial calm had returned to Rangoon and other urban areas—very much like the deceptive atmosphere that had prevailed before the upheaval of 1988—but the ethnic issue remained, unaddressed and unsolved, as did the question of meaningful democractic reforms.

Aung San had been assassinated half a year before the civil war broke out shortly after independence, and it was then that the disintegration of Burma had begun. In 1993, his daughter—who was the first person capable of unifying the entire nation to emerge on the political scene in Burma in decades—remained under house arrest. Where Burma was heading in the summer of 1993 was no clearer that it had been when the first shots were fired at Paukkongyi in April 1948. It remained a country in deep distress— and it had become, unrivalled, the world's biggest producer of heroin.

330

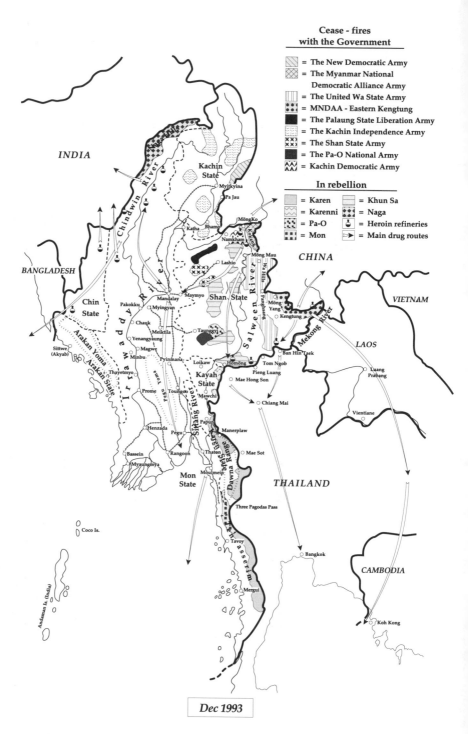

Cease - fires
with the Government

◩ = The New Democratic Army
⬚ = The Myanmar National
     Democratic Alliance Army
▥ = The United Wa State Army
⠿ = MNDAA - Eastern Kengtung
■ = The Palaung State Liberation Army
⠂ = The Kachin Independence Army
⤬ = The Shan State Army
◼ = The Pa-O National Army
⋀⋀ = Kachin Democratic Army

In rebellion

▨ = Karen   ▤ = Khun Sa
⩗ = Karenni   ⣿ = Naga
▧ = Pa-O   ⚱ = Heroin refineries
▦ = Mon   ⇒ = Main drug routes

INDIA

Kachin
State

Myitkyina

Pa Jau

MöngKo

Katha Bhamo

Namkham

BANGLADESH

Lashio

Möng Mau

CHINA

Chin
State

Pakokku   Mandalay   Maymyo

Myingyan

Shan State

Möng
Yang

Kengtung

VIETNAM

Chauk

Meiktila

Yenangyaung

Taunggyi

Ban Hin Taek

LAOS

Sittwe
(Akyab)

Magwe

Minbu

Pyinmana

Loikaw   Homöng

Tom Ngob

Pieng Luang

Luang
Prabang

Thayetmyo

Kayah
State

Mae Hong Son

Chiang Mai

Prome   Toungoo

Mawchi

Vientiane

Henzada

Pegu

Papun

Manerplaw

Bassein   Rangoon

Thaton   Mae Sot

Myaungmya

Moulmein

Mon
State

THAILAND

Three Pagodas Pass

Coco Is.

Tavoy

Bangkok

CAMBODIA

Mergui

Koh Kong

Andaman Is. (India)

Arakan Yoma

Arakan State

Irrawaddy River

Chindwin River

Naga Hills

Sittang River

Salween River

Shweli

Mekong River

Dawna Range

Tenasserim

Pegu Yoma

Dec 1993

Epilogue:
Is There Any Solution to the Problem?

The explosion of the drug trade in the Golden Triangle is not the outcome of any evil conspiracy by tribal warlords and "hostile opium growers", to quote former DEA chief John Lawn. Nor is it the result of the nefarious activities of sinister CIA agents. Rather, it is the inevitable consequence of the decades-long Burmese tragedy: the inability of successive governments in Rangoon to come to terms with the country's ethnic minorities and the refusal of post-1962 military-dominated regimes to permit an open, pluralistic society.

Short-sightedness on the part of the security agencies of the US and Taiwan in the early 1950s—and the Chinese policy towards Burma since the late 1960s—have also played their roles. But there is little point in moralising over the intricacies of a complex network which over the years has included players ranging from armed bandits in the hills to Chinese gangsters, from bankers in the big cities to politicians, army commanders, police chiefs and even well-respected foreign magazine publishers.

It is obvious that past and present approaches by the DEA as well as various UN agencies to Burma's drug problem have been not only ineffective but downright counter-productive. The UN has been constrained by the limitations of its mandate—to deal with and through governments only—and by the incompetence and inexperience of most of its anti-drug personnel in Asia.

The narcotics policies of nearly all post-World War II US administrations have been crippled by security concerns. In the 1950s, alliances of convenience between various intelligence agencies and well-organised crime organisations became important during the Cold War, when the end seemed to justify any means.

Much later, in the late 1980s, former DEA undercover agent Michael Levine concluded after quitting the agency in disgust that "we gave up the drug war in favour of a war against communism. In fact, we made a conscious choice. . . . The war on drugs is a fraud," full of "mistakes, false promises, and ineptitude".[1]

The Golden Triangle provides several examples of this phenomenon. Western powers turned a blind eye to the drug trafficking activities of the secret KMT army in Shan State and corrupt elements within the Laotian, Thai and Burmese armies, as long as all these remained useful allies in the war against the Communist advance in Southeast Asia.

To cover up these activities, the US even went to the extent of disseminating deliberate disinformation. Throughout the 1950s Harry Anslinger, the chief of the US Federal Bureau of Narcotics, published lengthy and seemingly meticulously detailed reports claiming that the US and the West were being flooded by "Yunnan opium" and heroin manufactured in mainland China.[2] It was all part of a Communist plot to subvert the morals of Western youths, a kind of psychological warfare.

This bizarre theory was expressed most vividly in China lobbyist Stanton Candlin's *Psycho-chemical Warfare: the Chinese Drug Offensive against the West*, which was published by the Conservative Book Club in New Rochelle in 1973. The "proof" of China's involvement, Candlin stated, was that drugs entering Hong Kong arrived via Lamma Island, which he asserted was "under Chinese Communist jurisdiction".[3]

Certainly, the expatriate, Bohemian community of artists, writers and young businessmen who populate this island—a part of Hong Kong and under British jurisdiction—would have been amused to hear that they were under Chinese Communist control. Other "proof" include "revealing photographs"— such as paper boxes containing prepared opium which had been seized in Vietnam during the war.

The photo caption pointed out the existence of Chinese characters on the boxes—but failed to mention that all overseas Chinese communities in Southeast Asia naturally use Chinese characters. Candlin also overlooked the fact that these particular boxes also bore Thai writing: "Boonrawd Brewery", the biggest beer manufacturer in Bangkok.[4]

It was only later, after the United States normalised relations with Beijing, that US narcotics agents admitted that "there was no evidence for Anslinger's accusations".[5] It had all been part of Cold War propaganda. In fact, there was no proven movement of narcotics in, out or through Yunnan and southern China before the former CPB forces established their refineries along the Sino–Burmese frontier in the wake of the 1989 mutiny.

Burmese heroin—popularly but erroneously referred to as "China White" because it transits Yunnan—began to flood the US drug market in 1990. By late 1991, 56% of the heroin reaching the United States originated in the Golden Triangle, up from a mere 14% four or five years before.[6] Drug abuse of all kinds cost the United States US$76 billion in the same year.[7]

In Australia, a country with 30,000 addicts—approximately the same proportion of addicts to the total the population as in the United States— 75% of all heroin comes from the Burmese sector of the Golden Triangle, with 5% from Laos and Thailand.[8]

Against this background, the DEA's present Burma policy seems all the more erratic and inappropriate; if there had still been a Communist threat in Burma, their being apologists for the SLORC would have been easier to understand.

But given the surge in drug production and the present geopolitical situation in Southeast Asia, there seems to be no justification for the DEA, or the UN, to continue their see-no-evil, hear-no-evil approach. A plausible explanation could be that these agencies are more concerned about self-preservation, and their own budgets and personal careers, than actually fighting the scourge of drugs.

This aspect became obvious in 1993 when the SLORC decided to hire a PR agent to represent their interests in the United States. To the astonishment of many, the man was Lester Wolff, the human-rights and alternative drug policy advocate of the 1970s. For US$10,000 a month, Wolff agreed to "help improve relations between our two peoples and our two governments . . . to the better understanding of the views and policies of the Union of Myanmar in the United States".[9]

Along with assorted American businessmen, several former congressmen and politicians went on all-expenses-paid "fact-finding" tours of Burma under the care and guidance of the SLORC. The trips differed little from the well-orchestrated propaganda trips which, for instance, the Soviet Union organised for Western intellectuals in the 1930s. While thousands of political prisoners languished in jail, playwright George Bernard Shaw and others had praised Stalin for "blessing the Soviet people with plenty".[10]

In a similar vein, the US "Honest Ballot Association" submitted a report on 6 May 1993 following a trip to Burma, stating that

> Myanmar believes that it is being treated unfairly and is anxious to tell and show its side of the issue. . . . We also found a government that seems to be trying to make real economic and social progress while at the same time maintaining sufficient control to keep its many divergent ethnic and national forces from causing a complete disintegration.[11]

The delegation seemed deeply impressed by the SLORC's "anti-drug activities", and on 28 March they "had the opportunity to meet with the leaders of Myanmar's National Races". A list of these "leaders", however, revealed that all of them were former CPB commanders and other drug warlords, plus ex-KIA commander Mahtu Naw and Hsö Hten of the SSA. One of the "national leaders" who received the American visitors was "U Kyi Myint", in other words Zhang Zhiming, the Yunnanese heroin smuggler from the CPB's former 815 War Zone.[12]

The "Honest Ballot Association" concluded that Aung San Suu Kyi was a divisive force in Burmese politics, and recommended a resumption of US assistance to Burma. The dossier presented by the delegation on its return also contained a letter from the DEA's Burma country attache, Richard Horn, in which he listed "recent Government of Burma achievements in narcotics law enforcement" and praised the participants for coming to Burma to "acquire first-hand knowledge of the drug trafficking problem".

A more enlightened approach can be detected in recent announcements from the the State Department. In March 1990, US assistant secretary of state for narcotics matters, Melvin Levitsky, stated quite bluntly with regard to Thailand that "the problem [in Thailand] now is . . . increasing reports of corruption. . . . It is very clear that, particularly along the Burma border, there is collusion between some high-level and some low-level officials and traffickers."[13]

Predictably, Thai military spokesmen reacted fiercely to the frank statement. Lieut.-Gen. Naruedol Dejpradiyuth shot back: "This sort of accusation is unacceptable. We need evidence in order to investigate this."[14] He went on to assure the world that the SLORC was also "making efforts to fight opium-growing", and stressed the need for cooperation between the governments of Thailand and Burma.

That Thailand came under fire from the US at this juncture was hardly by coincidence: the country had played out its role as a "frontline" state in the war against Communism, and there was no longer any need to take national security concerns into consideration: for the first time, the *drug* issue was addressed by US officials.

Sherman Funk, the US State Department's inspector-general, went on to criticise the US embassy in Bangkok: "[Its] reporting on the narcotics situation in Thailand did not accurately reflect more candid reporting by other US officials. . . . Thailand's excellent infrastructure provides convenient routes for Golden Triangle drugs en route via sea and air transit terminals to the US and other international markets. . . . On previous occasions US dignitaries have been advised to praise Thai efforts to control narcotics. What has been lacking is a candid approach, seeking Thai cooperation with a meaningful interdiction programme that would disrupt drug-trafficking through Thailand."[15]

Such a fundamental change in approach is needed. But in the case of Burma, it is not only a question of corruption. The crucial issue of the country's national minorities and ethnic insurgencies was addressed in the official programme of the National League for Democracy in 1989:

> The forty-year history of [ethnic] relations has been a chapter of misfortune verging on the tragic. Along Burma's extended borders from the extreme north to the far south there are no less than thirteen groups of insurgents—a situation which is sapping the strength and resources of the nation. The development of the country has suffered greatly since approximately 40 per-

cent of the national budget has to be devoted to defence requirements. For these reasons we must seek a lasting solution to the problems of the ethnic minorities. . . . It is the aim of the League to secure the highest degree of autonomy consonant with the inherent rights of the minorities and the well-being of the Union as a whole.[16]

With the demise of the Cold War, it should not be too difficult to undertake a thorough, objective study of the Burmese civil war, free from narrow security concerns, and with the aim of finding a lasting solution to the problem. The shaky business deals which the SLORC has reached with some rebel groups in the north hardly serve as models for such a solution: these agreements have not addressed the underlying issues which caused the minorities to take up arms in the first place.

No anti-drug policy in Burma has any chance of success unless it is linked to a real political solution to the civil war and a meaningful democratic process in Rangoon. The alternative is a continuing strife—which will keep the heroin flowing.

Appendix 1:
Burma's Civil Strife—A Chronology

1945

27 March: The Burmese nationalists turn against the Japanese.

1 May: Rangoon is recaptured by the resistance. The Japanese forces begin to withdraw from Burma.

17 May: The British government issues a White Paper accepting eventual independence for Burma with Dominion status within the British Commonwealth.

1 June: The All-Burma Trades Union Congress is formed in Rangoon with Thakin Ba Hein, a prominent Communist, as its first leader.

15 June: The official victory parade is held in Rangoon; the flag of the Burmese resistance flies beside the Union Jack.

20–21 July: The Communist Party of Burma (CPB) holds its second congress in Rangoon.

19 August: The Anti-Fascist People's Freedom League (AFPFL), Burma's main political front (which includes non-communist nationalists, Communists and some ethnic minorities), holds a mass meeting at the *Nethurein* Cinema Hall in Rangoon. Demands are raised for full independence for Burma, outside of the Commonwealth.

5–9 September: A meeting is held in Kandy, Ceylon (now Sri Lanka), between Lord Mountbatten representing the British, and ten Burmese military leaders (among them Aung San, Bo Let Ya, Ne Win, Kyaw Zaw, Bo Zeya and Thakin Than Tun) plus Saw Ba U Gyi representing the Karens. A regular Burma Army is formed. There will be four Burman infantry battalions; two each from the Chins, Karens and Kachins; one field artillery regiment; an armoured car regiment; and various reserve and ancillary units such as the engineers. Of a total of 12,000 men, 5,000 soldiers with 300 reserves and 200 officers with 200 reserves will be taken from the wartime resistance forces.

16 October: The British governor, Sir Reginald Dorman-Smith, returns to Burma after a 3^1/$_2$-year absence to oversee Burma's transition to independence.

November: U Sein Da sets up the Arakan People's Liberation Party (APLP) and starts to collect recruits, arms and ammunition in the Arakan area.

1 December: The People's Volunteer Organisation (PVO) is formed as an association for wartime veterans not included in the new Burma Army. In effect, it becomes a militia force loyal to AFPFL leader Aung San.

1946

17–19 January: Mass meetings are organised by the AFPFL outside the Shwe Dagon Pagoda in Rangoon. Several hundred thousand people attend.

3 February: Karen politicians and community leaders meet in Rangoon to discuss their stand towards the expected British withdrawal from Burma.

22 February: Thakin Soe's radical faction of the CPB breaks away from the main party and in March sets up the Communist Party (Burma), more commonly known as the Communist Party (Red Flag) [CP(RF)]. Seven of the 31 members of the central committee join the new party.

March: Shan *saohpas* meet Burman politicians at Panglong in the Shan states to discuss the future of the frontier areas. Kachins, Karens and Chins participate as observers.

18 May: The CPB organises a mass rally at Tantabin. The police open fire and three demonstrators are killed.

10 July: The British government outlaws Thakin Soe's CP(RF) following a series of violent incidents in the countryside.

August: CPB-inspired peasant uprisings take place in Yamethin and Toungoo districts.

31 August: Sir Hubert Rance takes over as governor of Burma.

August–December: The Karens send a Goodwill Mission to Britain to negotiate for a separate Karen state that includes a seaport. The mission is unsuccessful.

5 September: The Rangoon City Police go on strike and appeal to other groups to assist their efforts to win higher pay and better conditions. Civil servants, students and oil field workers join in.

September: The CPB meets in Rangoon to elect a new three-man politburo following Thakin Soe's expulsion: Thakin Than Tun (general secretary), Thakin Ba Hein (member) and Thakin Thein Pe (member).

23 September: The AFPFL calls a general strike to press demands for independence.

27 September: While the strikes are in progress, a new eleven-member Governor's Executive Council is appointed, including six representatives of the AFPFL. Aung San becomes deputy chairman (in effect prime minister), Thakin Thein Pe councillor for agriculture and rural economy (the highest post ever held by a Communist in the British Empire). Karen leader Saw Ba U Gyi becomes information councillor.

2 October: The strikes are called off.

10 October: The Executive Council of the AFPFL votes to expel the CPB from the front.

12 October: The communist-led All-Burma Trades Union Congress calls for a general strike, but the response from the workers is cool.

16 October: The Governor's Executive Council lifts the ban on CP(RF) and the Red Flag Cultivators' Union so "they would content themselves with normal political activity".

22 October: Thakin Thein Pe resigns from the Governor's Executive Council.

31 October: Thakin Soe is arrested. Strikes and demonstrations break out.

1 November: The Supreme Council of the AFPFL confirms the order to expel the CPB from the front.

3 November: The CPB finally leaves the AFPFL following a long, stormy meeting which had begun in October. Communist militiamen who had served with the PVO form their own force: the People's Democratic Youth League, better known as the Red Guards.

4 November: The AFPFL passes a number of resolutions demanding that the tribal areas under the direct jurisdiction of the governor be incorporated in Burma proper.

11 November: Thakin Soe is released and disappears underground.

20 November: CPB leader Thakin Ba Hein dies from malaria. He is replaced as politburo member by Thakin Ba Thein Tin.

1947

24 January: The CP(RF) is banned for a second time as it had not confined its activities to legal political work.

27 January: Aung San and British prime minister Clement Attlee sign an agreement in London promising an interim government for Burma in preparation for independence "within or without the British Commonwealth".

5 February: The Karen National Union (KNU) is set up when 700 representatives from all Karen-inhabited areas of Burma meet in Rangoon. Voices are raised for a separate Karen state, outside of the Union of Burma but remaining a member of the Commonwealth. The KNU also decides to boycott the upcoming general election.

12 February: Leaders of the Shan, Kachin and Chin peoples sign an agreement with Burmese nationalist leader Aung San at Panglong in the Shan states. They agree to join the proposed Union of Burma in exchange for some degree of autonomy for their respective areas.

28 February: KNU leaders meet Aung San. The negotiations are inconclusive.

February: Thakin Ba Thein Tin and *yebaw* Aung Gyi represent the CPB at the British Empire Conference of Communist Parties in London.

4 March: The KNU leader, Saw Ba U Gyi, resigns from the Governor's Executive Council. A faction led by Saw San Po Thin breaks away from the KNU and links up with the AFPFL.

10 March: San Po Thin joins the government; his Karen Youth Organisation becomes a member of the AFPFL.

March: The Frontier Areas Committee of Enquiry is set up to ascertain the views of the minorities on Burma's forthcoming independence. The Burma Army mounts "Operation Flush" to quell a peasant rebellion in the Pyinmana area in Burma's first counter-insurgency operation. The leader of the campaign is the commander of the 4th Burma Rifles, Col. Ne Win.

9 April: Elections to the Constituent Assembly are held. The AFPFL captures 60% of the vote and 171 seats in the Lower House (of its 255 seats 182 were non-communal, 24 were reserved for the Karens, 4 for the Anglo-Burmans and 45 were chosen from the Frontier Areas). The CPB does not participate as an organisation but fields twenty-eight independents, of whom seven are elected. The KNU stands firm on its boycott.

23 May: The Frontier Areas Committee of Enquiry reports to the central authorities in Rangoon. The concept of federalism is universally accepted.

9 June: The Constituent Assembly meets in Rangoon to discuss a new constitution.

17 July: The Karen National Defence Organisation (KNDO) is established officially as the KNU's militia.

19 July: Aung San and six cabinet ministers are assassinated in Rangoon. U Nu becomes new AFPFL leader and chief of the cabinet.

20 August: The *Mujahid* Party, Burma's first Muslim resistance army, is formed in Buthidaung, Arakan, by Jafar Hussain (a.k.a.) Jafar Kawwal, a popular singer.

29 August: Burma's defence minister, Bo Let Ya, signs an agreement with John Freeman, MP and head of the British defence delegation to Burma. Known as the Let Ya-Freeman Agreement, the pact stipulates that the British are to withdraw their forces from Burma but they promise advisers and to provide military training for Burmese officers in Britain. In return, Burma agrees not to accept any other military mission from outside of the Commonwealth.

22 September: The Cominform is established at Wiliza Gora in Poland. Soviet spokesman Andrei Zhdanov advocates a much more confrontational line than the world Communist movement has followed since World War II.

24 September: The Constituent Assembly approves of a new constitution, guaranteeing a democratic system and limited federalism. The Shan and Karenni states get the right to secede from the proposed Union of Burma after a ten-year period of independence. A Kachin State with no right to secede is established. There is no provision for a Karen state.

3–4 October: Karen delegates from all over Burma meet at Moulmein and reiterate their demand for a separate Karen state including Tenasserim Division, Irrawaddy Division, Insein and Hanthawaddy districts, and Nyaunglebin subdivision of Pegu District.

17 October: U Nu and Clement Attlee sign an agreement in London, recognising Burma's desire to become an independent republic.

November: Small-scale fighting breaks out in Arakan, where U Sein Da's APLP begins to attack urban centres.

December: Muslims in Arakan, led by Jafar Kawwal, launch the *Mujahid* rebellion to fight for an Islamic state in their territory. CPB politburo member H.N. Ghoshal attends a Communist Party of India (CPI) conference in Bombay.

1948

4 January: Burma becomes an independent republic outside of the Commonwealth.

11 February: Karens demonstrate in several towns for a separate state.

19–25 February: Burmese Communists and nationalists attend a meeting of the Southeast Asian Youth Conference in Calcutta.

28 February–6 March: Six CPB leaders, including Thakin Than Tun and Thakin Ba Thein Tin, attend the second congress of the CPI also held in Calcutta.

February–March: CPB-instigated strikes shake Rangoon.

18 March: A CPB-organised mass rally of peasants is held in Pyinmana, attended by 75,000 people. Thakin Than Tun and Ghoshal address the crowds and resoluions are passed in support of the strikers in Rangoon.

10 March: KNU and AFPFL leaders meet; the negotiations are again inconclusive.

25 March: U Nu orders the arrest of CPB leader Thakin Than Tun.

27 March: Thakin Than Tun speaks to a crowd of 3,000 workers in Rangoon.

28 March: The CPB goes underground and resorts to armed struggle.

March: Mon nationalists set up the Mon National Defence Organisation (MNDO), modelled after the KNDO.

2 April: The first battle between the CPB and government forces takes place at Paukkongyi, Pegu District. The fighting soon spreads throughout central and upper Burma.

3 April: The CPB occupies Kyeintali police station in Arakan and Talokmyo, Myingyan District.

4 April: The CPB occupies Sinma police station, Bassein District.

5 April: Communist rebels concentrate their forces at Pyaungthe Chaung, Kyitshar and Bombadi Chaung in Toungoo District.

6 April: The CPB occupies Yitkangyi, Pegu District. Government forces retake Myitkyo police station, Pegu District.

7 April: The CPB occupies Kamase, Pegu District.

8 April: The CPB occupies Yitkangale and Kadatsein, Pegu District.

9 April: Civil police forces raid and burn Padaung village, regional headquarters for the CPB's administration in the Myingyan area.

10 April: Government forces reoccupy Kamase, Pegu District.

11 April: Government forces reoccupy Yitkangyi, Paukkongyi and Ohnne in Pegu District. Government forces raid and occupy the CPB's stronghold at Myingaseik village, Bassein District.

15 April: Government forces reoccupy Yitkangale, Pegu District.

17 April: Government forces reoccupy Myitkyo, Pegu District.

April: Government forces raid and occupy Kyidaw village, a CPB stronghold in Bassein District. The CPB establishes a parallel administration at Legyamyaung near Daik-U, Pegu District.

May: Heavy fighting rages between government forces and CPB insurgents in central Burma. Seven members of the CPB's central committee meet at Kyaukkyipauk, Toungoo District, to endorse the decision to take up arms. Only Ghoshal disagrees. The CPB leaders move to the Pyinmana area, where a temporary headquarters is established.

25 May: U Nu announces a "Leftist Unity" programme to appease the leftists and counter the insurrection by political means.

15 June: Twenty-one privates of the 1st Burma Rifles (Burifs) defect at Waw, Pegu District, and join the CPB. Thirty-one soldiers at Abya Buda, Pegu District, kill their officer and join the CPB.

16 June: The 1st Burifs stationed at Myitkyo, Pegu District, join the CPB insurrection. The areas around Waw, Daik-U and Thanatpin in Pegu District are in the hands of the CPB. Elements of the 6th Burifs also join the mutiny.

July: A parallel administration run by the CPB is established at Myitkyo, Pegu District.

24 July: Government forces reoccupy Myitkyo, Pegu District, but the CPB still controls the railway line between Abyu Buda and Nyaungkhashe.

28 July: Bo Po Kun and Bo La Yaung order their "White Band" People's Volunteer Organisation (PVO) to go underground.

29 July: The PVO insurrection begins. Htantawgyi police station, Pegu District, falls to the PVO.

31 July: Three hundred Special Police Reservists of Bassein District go underground and take nine police stations.

4 August: Two platoons of the 16th Battalion of the paramilitary Union Military Police (UMP), stationed at Kayan, Hanthawaddy District, mutiny, occupy the town and join the PVO insurrection.

8 August: Elements of the 1st Burifs stationed at Thayetmyo mutiny and take over the administration of the town.

9 August: Army mutineers take Prome and march down towards Rangoon as far as Kyaungale village, where their advance is halted by government forces. In the Karenni states, Bee Tu Reh (who had declared in mid-1947 that Burma's independence did not concern the Karennis as they had always been independent), is arrested by the authorities and murdered shortly afterwards. As a result, a rebellion breaks out in the Karenni states.

10 August: Three hundred and fifty officers and soldiers of the 3rd Burifs (led by Bo Ye Htut) and No. 3 General Transport Company desert from Mingaladon and proceed in thirty-two army trucks towards the north of the Rangoon-Prome road but are halted near Wanetchaung. The combined army mutineers form the Revolutionary Burma Army (RBA) and ally themselves with the CPB.

14 August: Karen Union Military Police (UMP) take over the town of Twante.

Mid-August: PVO and Burman UMP deserters occupy Thongwa and Kyauktan, Hanthawaddy District, and also Yandoon and Danubyu, Maubin District. KNDOs and MNDOs in Thaton District begin attacks and collection of firearms. The Mawchi mines area and Bawlake in the Karenni states are occupied by Karen militants.

21 August: The Karen UMP in Thaton and Kyaikkami rebel.

29 August: Government forces reoccupy Allanmyo.

30 August: Government forces reoccupy Thayetmyo. The KNDO takes over Thaton.

31 August: A combined KNDO-MNDO force assisted by Karen UMP mutineers takes over Moulmein.

September: Shwegyin and Kyaukkyi are also captured by the KNDO. The rebels hand Moulmein and Thaton back to the Rangoon government. Bawlake is recaptured by government forces. There are battles between the Burma Army and PVO deserters at Pantanaw and Yandoon in Maubin District. The PVOs still occupy Yegyi, Athok, Kyaunggon and Nathainggyaung, Bassein District.

9 September: Government forces reoccupy Prome and clear all strategic towns on the Rangoon-Prome trunk road.

11 September: Burma's military intelligence reveals that a British journalist in Rangoon, Alexander Campbell of the *Daily Mail*, and Col. John Cromarty-Tulloch (who was believed to be in Calcutta at the time), were in contact with the KNU. Campbell is subsequently expelled from Burma.

October: Fighting between the PVO and government forces in Pegu and Hanthawaddy districts. Government forces reoccupy Tantabin, Insein District. A Regional Autonomy Enquiry Commission is appointed in Rangoon. The central committee of the CPB meets near Pyinmana to assess six months of fighting. The armed struggle is approved of and the CPB also decides to confiscate land from major landowners and distribute it to poor farmers.

November: Government forces reoccupy Pantanaw from the PVO and some places in Thayetmyo, Myaungmya and Thatin districts.

December: The 1st Karen and the 1st Kachin Rifles of the Burma Army conduct a massive offensive against CPB rebels in the Pyinmana area, where the Communists have begun their land redistribution scheme. U Nu's government invites CPB leaders Bo Zeya, Bo Ye Htut, Bo Thein Dan and Bo Thet Tun for peace talks in Rangoon. The rebels promise to send a reply by 15 March.

23–25 December: At least eighty Karen villagers are killed by government forces while celebrating Christmas in villages near Palaw in Tavoy District.

1949

1 January: The KNDO takes over Twante opposite Rangoon.

24–28 January: The 1st Karen Rifles in the Toungoo area mutiny and join the KNDO. They raid Zayatgyi and capture the towns of Tanatbin, Pyu and Toungoo in quick succession.

25–29 January: The KNDO occupies parts of the port city of Bassein.

30 January: The KNDO is outlawed.

31 January: Fighting between government forces and the KNDO begins in Insein immediately north of Rangoon.

1 February: Lieut.-Gen. Smith-Dun, the Karen commander in chief of the Burma Army, resigns and is replaced by Lieut.-Gen. Ne Win. Prome is once again in the hands of army mutineers, the PVO and the CPB. The KNDO occupies Einme in the Irrawaddy delta.

2 February: The whole of Insein is under KNDO control.

5 February: The 2nd Karen Rifles at Prome mutiny and travel down towards Rangoon in twenty buses, taking Hattalin and Zigon on their way, but are halted at Wetkaw Bridge in Tharrawaddy District. Mutineers from the 1st Karen Rifles at Toungoo advance towards Rangoon but are stopped at Payagyi. The Regional Autonomy Enquiry Commission releases its report: it is rejected by the KNU.

7 February: Civil servants in Rangoon go on strike.

16 February: The Railway Workers' Union joins the strike. The 1st Kachin Rifles, commanded by Naw Seng, are ordered to retake Toungoo from the Karens. Instead, he defects with his entire battalion and joins the Karens.

20 February: Karen insurgents and Naw Seng's Kachins occupy Meiktila. The CPB takes over Yamethin and Pyinmana.

21 February: Naw Seng and his men capture two aeroplanes in Meiktila and proceed to Ani Sakhan. They also occupy Maymyo town and the nearby army camp of Ani Sakhan. The KNDO and the CPB take over Kyaukse.

23 February: The CPB takes over Myingyan and the oil field area of Yenangyaung and Chauk.

24 February: Government forces reoccupy Ani Sakhan and Maymyo.

25 February: Minbu and Magwe are occupied by army mutineers and PVOs.

February: The KNDO takes over Loikaw in the Karenni states.

1–3 March: Karen insurgents attack Nyaunglebin, Pegu District.

12–13 March: Combined KNDO and CPB units occupy Mandalay and also Myitnge and Kume. Government forces reoccupy Thazi on the main railway line from Rangoon to Mandalay.

12 March: Leftist insurgents of various groups meet in CPB-held Prome to discuss political and military cooperation.

17 March: PVO deserters and other insurgents reoccupy Thayetmyo.

22 March: Government forces retake Meiktila.

24 March: The formation of the People's Democratic Front (PDF) is announced in Prome by the CPB, the CP(RF), the PVO, the APLP and the RBA. The combined force takes over Henzada and Pakokku. The CPB issues an official reply to U Nu's invitation for peace talks: U Nu will be arrested and arraigned before a "People's Court", it says.

1 April: Lieut.-Gen. Ne Win becomes deputy prime minister with charge of the Home and Defence ministries, in addition to his post as supreme commander of the armed forces.

3–6 April: Government forces reoccupy parts of Mandalay.

6–8 April: Peace talks are held in Rangoon between U Nu and Lieut.-Gen. Ne Win representing the government and Saw Ba U Gyi from the KNU. The talks are inconclusive.

9 April: The CPB takes over Tharrawaddy. The PDF front seizes the administration of the entire Henzada and Tharrawaddy districts. The KNDO takes over the delta town of Pantanaw.

17 April: Karen insurgents at Maymyo surrender to government forces.

20 April: There are battles between Karen insurgents and government forces at Nyaunglebin and Daik-U. Nyaunglebin is captured by the KNDO and Naw Seng. His forces march towards Rangoon.

21 April: Government forces retake Meiktila.

24 April: The whole of Mandalay is once again in government hands.

1 May: Naw Seng's forces are stopped at Pegu, eighty kilometres north of Rangoon. They retreat north towards Toungoo.

May: There are battles between Karen insurgents and government forces at Pyinmalwin and Letkokkwin, Pegu District. Government forces reoccupy Daik-U and Phaungdawthi. The KNDO retreats to Nyaunglebin. Government forces reoccupy Tada-U in Sagaing Division, and Pyawbwe, Yamethin and Tatkon in central Burma from the CPB. Battles occur between government forces and insurgents near Hmawbi north of Rangoon.

22 May: The KNDO evacuates its troops from Insein after a 112-day siege. The Karen rebels withdraw to Thaton, Toungoo and the Irrawaddy delta region. A new headquarters, including a broadcasting station, is established at Toungoo.

June: Arms shipments from India begin to arrive in Rangoon.

10 June: Government forces recapture the oil field area of Yenangyaung and Chauk. The 26th UMP at Kyaukpyu and Sandoway, Arakan, mutiny and take over the towns.

13 June: Government forces retake Twante and Thaton from the KNDO. The CPB attacks Ye-U, Shwebo District.

14 June: The Karens set up their own "Government of Kawthoolei" in Toungoo. All Karen forces (KNDO, Karen Rifles mutineers, UMP) are reorganised into the Kawthoolei Armed Forces (KAF).

26 June: Government forces retake Kyaukse from the KNDO and the CPB and Kyauktan, Hanthawaddy District.

10 July: Government forces retake Myingyan southwest of Mandalay and Myinmu in Sagaing Division from the CPB and Phaungdawthi police station, Pegu District, from the KNDO. Karen insurgents occupy Mongpai in the Karenni states.

19 July: U Nu promises to restore "peace within one year".

22 July: Government forces retake Ponnangyun (Arakan) but insurgents still hold Myohaung.

25 July: Heavy fighting between the Burma Army and ethnic insurgent forces is reported in the Karenni states.

13 August: Karen and Kachin rebels led by Naw Seng occupy Taunggyi in the Shan states. Ethnic Pa-O rebels take part in the fighting.

25 August: The CPB's general headquarters announces that its "liberated area" embraces 184,000 square kilometres with a population of over six million.

27 August: Government forces retake Tharrawaddy and Henzada from the CPB. Naw Seng's forces occupy Lashio and hold it for a day.

31 August: Naw Seng's forces occupy Namkham in the northern Shan States.

8 September: Naw Seng leaves Namkham.

20 September: The "Kawthoolei Government" is dissolved and replaced by military administration in KNU-held areas.

1 October: Mao Zedong proclaims the People's Republic of China in Beijing.

15 November: Naw Seng and his mutineers from the 1st Kachin Rifles set up the Pawngyawng National Defence Force (PNDF), the first Kachin rebel organisation.

November: New government units are raised, armed with more weapons from India. The army feels confident enough to retake towns and villages under rebel occupation.

23 November: The KNDO withdraws from Taunggyi. Small bands of Pa-O insurgents remain in the hills surrounding Hsi-Hseng.

17 December: Burma recognises the People's Republic of China.

1950

1 January: Muslim *mujahids* in Arakan capture the towns of Rathedaung and Buthidaung. The CPB also takes part in the capture of Rathedaung.

12 January: Government forces recapture Loikaw in the Karenni states from the KNDO.

January–March: More than 2,000 Kuomintang (KMT) forces in Yunnan cross the border into the eastern Shan state of Kengtung following the Communist victory in China. They set up base in the hills of Kengtung state.

25 February: Government forces retake Nyaunglebin from the Karen rebels.

12 March: Disagreements within the PDF erupt between the CPB and the PVO during a meeting in CPB-held Prome. The PVO drives the CPB out of Thayetmyo.

19 March: Government forces retake Toungoo from the Karen rebels. The Karens move their headquarters to Mawchi in the Karenni states.

29 March: Government forces retake Pyinmana from the CPB.

8 April: Government forces retake Magwe from the PVO.

15 April: Government forces retake Minbu from the PVO.

29 April: Government forces retake Pakokku from the CPB.

5 May: Naw Seng and 300 of his men from the PNDF are cornered in northeastern Shan State and retreat across the border to China.

19 May: Government forces reoccupy Prome from the CPB.

25 June: The Korean War begins.

June: Renegade KMT forces in Kengtung state capture Tachilek on the Thai border opposite Mae Sai.

17 July: Saw Ba U Gyi calls a KNU congress in Papun, the first since the armed struggle began. Mon and Karenni delegates also attend. The Kawthoolei Governing Body (KGB) is set up to coordinate civil administration in KNU-held areas. Papun becomes the new Karen rebel headquarters.

19 July: The PVO is officially disbanded.

21 July: Government forces recapture Tachilek from the KMT.

August: The KMT regroups at Möng Hsat, southern Shan states, where a major base is established, including an air strip.

12 August: Saw Ba U Gyi, Saw Sankey and one "Mr. Baker" are killed at To Kaw Koe village near Kawkareik, opposite the Thai border town of Mae Sot.

1 September: The CPB's "People's Liberation Army of Burma" and the RBA merge to become the CPB's "People's Army" (*pyithu tatmadaw*). Thakin Than Tun says: "If we continue to fight with industriousness and determination . . . we will surely defeat the enemy within two years."

13 September: Burma and the US sign a friendship treaty.

21–24 September: KNU leaders meet at Mawchi to choose a successor to Saw Ba U Gyi. U Hla Pe (a Pa-O) is offered the post but is unable to accept it because of his work among the Pa-Os. Joshua Poo Nyo is appointed as an interim choice.

11 October: *Mujahid* leader Jafar Kawwal is assassinated in Arakan by a rival. He is succeeded by Cassim. Fighting continues in Arakan.

15 October: Government forces reoccupy Thayetmyo from the PVO and army mutineers.

17 October: The US pledges to give US$21 million worth of military assistance to Burma.

27 October: Government forces retake Sandoway in Arakan from UMP deserters.

11 November: Government forces retake the delta town of Einme from the KNDO.

10 December: Government forces retake the delta town of Pantanaw from the KNDO.

1951

19 January: The KNU holds a congress at Lumbu village near Toungoo. Saw Hunter Thamwe is elected new chairman, but he in turn appoints Sgaw Ler Taw to be acting chairman in his absence (Saw Hunter is based in the Irrawaddy delta region).

February: Rangoon launches "Operation Frost" against the KMT in the eastern Shan states.

7 February: The first aeroplanes carrying supplies from Taiwan land at the KMT-controlled air strip at Möng Hsat.

May: KMT forces based in Kokang and the Wa Hills launch their first cross-border raid into Yunnan. The town of Kengma is captured, but the KMT is forced to retreat back to Burma after a week of heavy fighting.

June: General elections begin, the first under the 1947 constitution.

7 July: Burma and India sign a treaty of friendship and mutual co-operation.

10 July: Truce talks begin between the UN and the Pyongyang government at the town of Kaesong in Korea.

July: KMT forces enter Sipsongpanna, southern Yunnan, but are driven back into Burma.

15 August: The US ambassador in Rangoon, David M. Key, who had not been briefed about the covert KMT operation in the Shan states, cables a protest to Washington.

October: KMT Gen. Li Mi leaves Möng Hsat and travels to Bangkok.

November: CPB leaders gather for a central committee meeting in the Pyinmana area and decide to adopt a policy of "Peace and Coalition Government" (the "PCG Line") to counter the KMT invasion of northeastern Burma. Land confiscated from big landlords in 1949–50 is handed back to them by the CPB.

December: Li Mi continues to Taiwan via Hong Kong.

1952

January: The general election is completed. AFPFL gets 60% of the vote and 147 seats (including affiliates: about 200 seats). The opposition (mainly ethnic parties) gets 33 seats and the rest goes to independents. The KMT and the KNDO join forces and occupy Mawchi in the Karenni states.

March: More than 2,000 KMT troops begin pushing south from the Karenni states and into the northern Karen Hills.

April: US ambassador David McKey resigns as he has not been informed about clandestine CIA support for the KMT in Buma.

30 April: Burma and Japan sign a friendship treaty, finally ending the state of belligerency between the two countries.

August: Three hundred KMT troops reach the KNDO base of Hlaingbwe in Karen State.

1 September: The Shan states are placed under martial law following fierce fighting between government forces and Pa-O rebels and KMT intruders.

September: A Karen State is finally set up, comprising hilly areas in eastern Burma. The KNU rejects it on the grounds that the main Karen-inhabited areas in the Irrawaddy delta are excluded. More KMT troops reach Hlaingbwe and almost 1,000 soldiers march down to Karokpi-Pangga, south of Amherst on the Andaman coast. Fierce battles are fought with the Burma Army. The KMT is driven back from the coast.

1 October: Thakin Than Tun of the CPB, Thakin Soe of CP(RF) and Bo Po Kun of the PVO sign an agreement, known as the Tripartite Alliance Pact, near Monywa, northwest of Mandalay.

November: Thakin Zin of the CPB and Mahn Ba Zan of the KNU agree on a cease-fire. The truce becomes known as the Zin-Zan Agreement.

1953

4 January: The KMT occupies Möng Hsu and deposes its *saohpa*. The Burma Army mounts a major offensive against the KMT in the Karokpi-Pangga area south of Moulmein.

8 February: A combined KNU-KMT force attacks the Karenni state capital of Loikaw.

27 February: A combined KNU-KMT force attacks Loipuk, Bawlake and Nam Hpe in the Karenni area.

25 March: The Burmese government formally complains to the UN about the KMT invasion of the northeastern Shan states.

17 April: Justice Myint Thein addresses the UN General Assembly in New York.

22 April: The UN General Assembly adopts a resolution demanding the evacuation of the KMT troops in northeastern Burma.

22 May: Thai, Burmese, Taiwanese and US officials meet in Bangkok to discuss the repatriation of the KMT forces in Burma.

May: CPB politburo member Thakin Ba Thein Tin reaches Yunnan, China, after an arduous one-year journey by elephant and on foot. Hlaingbwe is recaptured by government forces from the Karen rebels.

9 June: Karen leaders meet in Waythaung village near Wakema in the Irrawaddy delta and decide to set up a Marxist-style vanguard party, the Karen National United Party (KNUP).

16 June: A second meeting is held in Bangkok to discuss the repatriation of the KMT.

22 June: The US ambassador to Thailand, Edwin F. Stanton, announces that a procedure to evacuate the KMT has been agreed upon by all four parties: Burma, Thailand, Taiwan and the US.

27 June: An armistice is reached in Korea, in effect ending the war.

30 July: Defence Minister Ba Swe says that Burma is going to the UN to have Nationalist China declared an aggressor and unseated from the world body.

August: The entire oil field area around Yenangyaung and Chauk is cleared of CPB and PVO forces.

17 September: Burma withdraws from the four-power talks in Bangkok because Taiwan does not agree to withdraw 5,000 troops from Burma within three months and the remaining 7,000 within six months.

September: The KNUP is established officially at a ceremony at Gayetau village in Maubin, the Irrawaddy delta.

Late September: The Burma Air Force begins bombing the KMT base at Möng Hsat.

6 October: Bombings of Möng Hsat are halted to permit the KMT to withdraw.

20 October: The government formally declares the CPB an unlawful organisation.

21 October: The government outlaws the PVO.

October: The Burma Air Force accidentally bombs a village near Mae Hong Son in northwestern Thailand.

29 October: A joint US-Thai-Taiwan communique is issued in Bangkok stating that 2,000 KMT troops, including their families, are to be withdrawn.

9 November–8 December: The first batch of KMT troops from Burma is repatriated to Taiwan via Chiang Mai and Lampang in northern Thailand.

20 November: CPB insurgents ambush the Mandalay-Maymyo train, killing fifteen passengers and injuring twenty-three.

22 November: The Mawchi mines in the Karenni states are recaptured by government forces from the Karen rebels.

23 November: US vice president Richard Nixon arrives in Rangoon and is met by anti-American demonstrations.

28 November: The UN passes a resolution, calling upon the US to work for the removal of the remaining KMT troops in Burma.

November: The KNU holds its First National Congress in the Papun hills. The establishment of the KNUP is approved.

1954

4 January: The Let Ya-Freeman Agreement, signed on 29 August 1947 between Burma and Britain, is terminated.

February: The PVO and the *Mujahids* in Arakan sign a "non-aggression pact".

14 February–20 March: The second batch of KMT troops from Burma is evacuated via Chiang Mai and Chiang Rai in northern Thailand.

March: Karen and Mon rebels visit Bangkok for talks with Thai military authorities. They are allowed to set up camps along the Thai border and to buy supplies from Thailand.

20 March: Möng Hsat is recaptured from the KMT as the Burma Army launches Operation *Bayinnaung*, led by Brig.–Gen. Kyaw Zaw. Heavy fighting rages between the KMT and government forces in the eastern Shan states.

April: A major offensive is launched against Karen rebels in the Papun area and KMT forces in Tenasserim ("Operation *Sinbyushin*"). The campaign fails to recapture Papun town but much of the new Karen State is brought under government control.

1–7 May: The third batch of KMT troops from Burma is evacuated via Chiang Mai in northern Thailand.

7 May: French forces led by Gen. de Castries surrender to the Communist Vietminh at Dien Bien Phu, northern Vietnam, following a 55-day siege.

May: The *Mujahid* leader Cassim is arrested by East Pakistani authorities and imprisoned in Chittagong jail.

May–June: "Operation Bandoola" is launched against CPB strongholds near Pakokku.

June: A Burmese military mission, led by Col. Aung Gyi and Commodore Than Pe, visits Israel.

26–27 June: Government forces, led by Brig. Kyaw Zaw, battle KMT forces at Möng Hang in the Shan states.

28–29 June: Chinese foreign minister Zhou Enlai visits Rangoon.

28 June–9 July: Government forces repel a KMT attack on Möng Hkak north of Kengtung.

31 July: The military administration of the southern Shan states comes to an end.

8 September: The US, Britain, France, Australia, New Zealand, Pakistan, the Philippines and Thailand sign the Manila Treaty, paving the way for the formation of the Southeast Asia Treaty Organisation (SEATO).

22 October: The government outlaws the Muslim *Mujahid* Party.

5 November: Japan and Burma sign a peace treaty, officially ending hostilities which began in 1945.

November: "Operation *Mote-thone*" ("Monsoon") is launched against the *Mujahids* in northern Arakan. The Muslim insurrection crumbles.

December: Saw Hunter Thamwe leaves the Irrawaddy delta and arrives in the eastern mountains to take up his post as KNU chairman. He replaces the KGB with a new governing body called the Karen Revolutionary Council (KRC).

1–16 December: U Nu visits China. Talks are held about the border question and the question of nationality of Chinese residents in Burma.

1955

21 January: The government launches "Operation *Aungtheikdi*" ("Final Victory") against the Karen rebels in the eastern hills.

19 February: SEATO comes officially into being. India, Indonesia and Burma express strong concern about the scheme.

26 March: CPB guerrillas mine a train near Mandalay. Thirty people are killed.

27 March: Papun is recaptured by government forces from the Karens after seven years of rebel control.

April: Burma attends the Bandung Conference in Indonesia and becomes one of the founders of the Non-Aligned Movement.

April: The CPB's central committee meets at Wayawngdaw Sakan, or "Bamboo Forest Camp", near Saytouttaya in Magwe Division. The delegates conclude that the CPB has become "divorced from the people of Burma" and, therefore, the armed struggle has to be abandoned.

April–May: The government launches "Operation *Yangyiaung*" against the KMT. Operational commander is Brig.-Gen. Kyaw Zaw.

May: A 200-strong Karen rebel force attacks Khalaukchaik near Rangoon.

The CPB declares a policy of "Peace and Unity".

30 May: Gen. Li Mi publicly declares in Taipei that the National Salvation Army for Yunnan has been dissolved. In reality, more than 1,000 KMT troops remain in the Möng Pa Liao-Kenglap area on the Mekong river in eastern Kengtung state.

15 August: CPB guerrillas dynamite a bus near Tavoy, killing thirty-seven passengers.

September: Lieut.-Gen. Ne Win leads a high-powered military delegation to China. They visit munitions factories and army training establishments.

16 September: CPB guerrillas storm Nyaung-Oo jail in central Burma and free 134 prisoners.

1 October: The government launches the *Pyu Saw Hti* town and village defence scheme to build up local militias.

8 November: The CPB declares officially the "1955 line" to attain "cessation of civil war and attainment of peace within the country".

November: Thirty Chinese soldiers enter the Wa Hills and clash with the same number of troops from the Burma Army.

December: Soviet leaders Nikita Khrushchev and Nikolai Bulganin visit Rangoon.

1956

20 January: Thakin Than Tun writes to Prime Minister U Nu expressing his wish to discuss peace with the government.

February: The twentieth Congress of the Communist Party of the Soviet Union is held in Moscow. Khrushchev denounces Stalin and declares his support for "peaceful coexistence".

27 April: General elections are held. The AFPFL captures 55% of the vote and 173 seats (including allied parties and independents). The National Unity Front (NUF) gets 36.9% and 48 seats.

April: The Democratic Nationalities Democratic Front (DNUF) is formed in the hills near Papun by Karen, Karenni, Pa-O and Mon rebels. Another Chinese army unit enters the Wa Hills and clashes with the Burma Army.

June: U Nu resigns as prime minister and hands over the post to Socialist leader Ba Swe.

26 June–11 July: The KNU holds its second National Congress in the hills near Papun. A left-leaning policy is adopted. The Kawthoolei Armed Forces are renamed the Karen People's Liberation Army (KPLA) and political commissars are appointed to each military unit.

24 October–7 November: U Nu (in his capacity as AFPFL president) visits China and holds talks with Zhou Enlai. China agrees to withdraw all its forces from disputed border areas in Kachin State.

10–20 December: Zhou Enlai visits Burma. A joint Burma-China statement is issued on the 20th by the prime ministers of the two countries.

27–28 December: Shan *saohpas* and more than 100 other delegates meet in Möng Yai, northern Shan states. Demands are raised for secession from the Union.

November–December: The army launches "Operation *Aung Marga*" ("Victory Path") against the CPB in upper Burma. It is claimed that documents are found linking the northern commander, Brig.-Gen. Kyaw Zaw, to the insurgents.

1957

7 February: Rallies are held all over the Shan states to press demands for secession.

13 February: Brig.-Gen. Kyaw Zaw is relieved of his post as northern commander.

1 March: U Nu returns to office as prime minister.

2 March–2 April: U Nu visits Kunming.

April: CPB cadres begin to surrender to the government. The most prominent of them is *yebaw* Tin Aye, who delivered Thakin Than Tun's letter to the government in January 1956.

20 April: The leaders of the Shan Buddhist community hold a meeting at Möng Yai, attended by elected representatives from all over the Shan states. They advocate secession from the Union.

27 April: U Nu addresses a crowd in Lashio and questions the right of secession that the Shan states enjoy under the 1947 constitution.

16–19 May: Another conference is held at Möng Yai. The delegates call for "democracy" and "Shan unity".

7 June: Brig.-Gen. Kyaw Zaw is dismissed from the army.

5 July: Shan Buddhist leaders move their centre of activities from Möng Yai to Hsipaw. Many Shans say they are ready to go underground.

29 July: The Karenni National Progressive Party (KNPP) is formed with the backing of the KNU to replace the former Karenni National Organisation.

October: Two hundred CPB guerrillas surrender to the government. Among them is Maung Maung, chairman of the Pyinmana district committee.

November: Sixty-eight communist parties from all over the world meet in Moscow. The CPB is represented by Thakin Ba Thein Tin. Khin Maung Gyi, San Thu and Aung Win are posted in Moscow as CPB representatives. They are joined by two other young CPB members, Kyaw Zaw and Thein Aung (*yebaw* Lwin).

1958

4 January: Ten years of independence have elapsed. The constitutional right of the Shan and Karenni states to secede from the Union comes into effect.

January: U Sein Da surrenders with 1,000 of his APLP followers.

5 May: One thousand three hundred Pa-O rebels led by U Hla Pe surrender in Taunggyi.

10 May: Moh Heng and 400 of his Shan rebels surrender in Hsipaw, northern Shan State.

21 May: Sao Noi (Saw Yanda) and Pu Ling Gung Na form a Shan rebel army, *Noom Suk Harn* ("The Young Brave Warriors"), at Möng Kyawt village near the Thai border opposite Chiang Dao.

27 April–5 May: The ruling AFPFL splits into two factions: the "Stable" AFPFL led by Socialists Ba Swe and Kyaw Nyein, and the "Clean" AFPFL led by U Nu and Thakin Tin. By 9 June; the split is irrevocable.

23 June: The military, led by Gen. Ne Win, holds a conference in Mingaladon and reaffirms its "neutral role" and its "complete faith in democracy". The military promises to "stand by the constitution".

19 July: Nai Aung Tun surrenders with more than 1,000 Mon rebels.

20 July: Nai Shwe Kyin, the only Mon rebel leader who did not surrender, forms the New Mon State Party (NMSP).

15 August: PVO insurgents, led by Bo Po Kun, begin to surrender. By October, more than than 2,000 have turned themselves in. Many of them set up the People's Comrade Party (PCP) to contest general elections.

26 September: U Nu announces in a radio broadcast that he has invited Gen. Ne Win to form a military-led Caretaker Government.

14 October: The composition of the proposed Caretaker Government is announced. It will consist of nine ministers, including the prime minister.

21 October: A military conference in Meiktila adopts a policy declaration entitled "The National Ideology and the Role of the Defence Services".

28 October: U Nu resigns and the military, led by Gen. Ne Win, forms a new government.

November: Moh Heng and some of his followers rejoin the Shan rebel movement. Combined Karen-CPB forces attack Daik-U and Nyaunglebin on the Rangoon-Mandalay railway and some other places in central Burma.

1959

24 April: All thirty-four Shan *saohpas* formally give up their positions at a ceremony held at Taunggyi. The Shan states become Shan State, administered by an elected state government.

April: The CPB moves its headquarters to the Pegu Yoma mountains north of Rangoon.

16–25 May: The CPB, the NMSP and the KNUP meet and form the National Democratic United Front (NDUF; the Chin National Vanguard Party and the KNPP joined later in 1959, and the Pa-O dominated Shan State Nationalities Liberation Organisation joined on 25 July 1974).

22 November: The garrison town of Tang-yan is captured by Shan rebels led by Bo Maung, a former Union Military Police officer who has gone underground; Bo

Dewing, a local warlord from the Möng Yai area; and Shan students led by Sai Kyaw Tun (Sao Hsö Wan).

30 November: Airstrikes and ground attacks force the Shan rebels to evacuate Tang-yan.

1960

10 January: A Karen rebel unit ambushes a train north of Moulmein, killing seventeen passengers including several police officers and government officials.

24–29 January: Gen. Ne Win (prime minister of the Caretaker Government) visits China and holds talks with Zhou Enlai. A treaty of friendship and mutual non-aggression and a Sino-Burmese agreement on the boundary question are signed on 28 January.

April: General elections are held. U Nu's *Pyidaungsu* (Union) Party captures 52% of the vote and 157 seats in the Lower House, compared to 30% and 42 seats for the military-backed "Stable" AFPFL led by Ba Swe and Kyaw Nyein.

4 April: U Nu forms a new government and becomes prime minister once again.

15–19 April: Zhou Enlai visits Burma.

24 April: Shan students break with Sao Noi and his *Noom Suk Harn*. The Shan State Independence Army (SSIA) is set up, led by Long Khun Maha, a Shan writer and poet.

29 April: The Nationalities Liberation Alliance (NLA) is formed by the Karen rebels, the Karennis and Sao Noi's *Noom Suk Harn*. The Kachins join when they resort to armed struggle in February 1961.

May: The CPB reiterates its call for peace through negotiations.

June: Some of U Sein Da's followers, led by Maung Sein Nyunt, rejoin the underground and set up the Arakan National Liberation Party (ANLP).

28 September–4 October: U Nu visits China and attends China's National Day celebrations.

1 October: A boundary treaty between China and Burma is signed in Beijing.

December: The legal Chin Affairs Council raises demands for a Chin State within the Union of Burma.

December: CPB leaders attend a conference of eighty-one communist parties in Moscow. The conference puts forward the concept of "national democracy" — a transitional form of government between bourgeois nationalism and socialism.

20 December: The National Liberation Front is established in South Vietnam and gets support from the Communist North.

1961

2–9 January: Zhou Enlai visits Burma. The border agreement is ratified. An economic and technical cooperation agreement is signed on 9 January, according to which the Chinese pledge to give Burma an interest-free loan of £30 million to be disbursed during the period 1 October 1961 to 30 September 1967.

24 January: The Constitution Revision Steering Committee of Shan State passes a resolution in Taunggyi, calling for a more genuine federal structure of government.

26 January: A combined force of three divisions (20,000 men) of regulars from the Chinese People's Liberation Army (PLA) and 5,000 Burmese troops attack KMT bases north of Kengtung in eastern Shan State. The campaign is codenamed the "Mekong River Operation".

27 January: A Sino-Burmese trade agreement is signed in Beijing.

February: The KMT base at Möng Pa Liao is captured by the PLA supported by Burmese government forces. US-made arms and ammunition are found, leading to violent demonstrations outside the US embassy in Rangoon.

5 February: The Kachin Independence Army (KIA) is set up in the Kachin-inhabited areas of northeastern Shan State.

7 March: Kachin rebel Zau Tu launches an attack on Lashio and robs the local treasury of 90,000 Kyats. The rebellion soon spreads to Kachin State proper and vast areas of the state are taken over by the KIA.

March: The town of Penwagon on the Rangoon-Mandalay railway is occupied by Karen rebels for three days.

5 April: The government of Taiwan announces that all KMT troops in Burma were repatriated in the early 1950s.

11 April: A joint US-Taiwan communique says that "the 6,000 KMT soldiers remaining in Burma's Shan State are not in any way connected or concerned with the US government or the Republic of China".

13 April: Gen. Min Maung, the military commander of the Karen rebel forces, is killed in combat in the Karen Hills.

8–16 June: Shan leaders, among them Burma's first president, Sao Shwe Thaike and former foreign minister Sao Khun Hkio, meet in Taunggyi to initiate a federal movement to find a political solution to Burma's ethnic crisis.

26 August: Buddhism is adopted as the state religion of Burma, which leads to discontent among the predominantly Christian Kachins.

10–15 October: U Nu visits China.

22 November: US President John Kennedy decides to send combat troops to assist the non-Communist government in South Vietnam. SEATO also gets involved in the Indochina conflict.

1962

24 February: China issues a protest against US intervention in Vietnam, saying that this action is not only a "direct threat" to North Vietnam but also places in jeopardy "the security of China and the peace in Asia".

25 February: A Federal Seminar is convened in Rangoon to find ways to amend the constitution to allow more rights for the minorities.

28 February: The *Hanthawaddy* daily publishes a note which pro-military opposition leader Ba Swe had sent to U Nu, protesting against the demands of the Shans and other ethnic minorities to amend the constitution.

2 March: The Burma Army, led by Gen. Ne Win, overthrows U Nu's democratic government and seizes power in Rangoon. U Nu and his ministers are jailed along with over thirty Shan and Karenni (Kayah) leaders.

3 March: The 1947 constitution is suspended and the Parliament is dissolved.

8 March: Five centrally appointed State Supreme Councils are formed to take over the state governments.

9 March: The new junta, the Revolutionary Council, invests Gen. Ne Win with full executive, legislative and judicial powers (these remain in force until 1974).

11 March: The formation of the underground Communist Party of Arakan (CPA) is announced by left-wing rebels in Arakan.

3 April: The "Burmese Way to Socialism" is published to be the guiding ideological basis of the new regime.

4 July: The Burma Socialist Programme Party (BSPP) is formed by the new military rulers.

7 July: Troops open fire on students at Rangoon University. Officially, fifteen are killed and twenty-seven wounded, but independent observers place the number of casualties in the hundreds.

8 July: The army dynamites the Students' Union building in Rangoon. Universities and colleges are closed.

23 July: The Geneva accords on Laos are signed. The thirteen attendant nations agree to respect the neutrality of Laos and to withdraw all foreign military personnel. The CIA begins its "secret war" in Laos, using indigenous Hmong hill tribesmen as well as KMT forces and Shan, Lahu and Wa guerrillas from Burma to fight the Communist Pathet Lao.

1 August: The CPB exiles in China are allowed to issue their first public statement, condemning the new military regime.

1963

17 January: The BSPP publishes a document entitled the "System of Correlation of Man and his Environment", which provides philosophical underpinnings for the "Burmese Way to Socialism".

8 February: Brig. Aung Gyi is dismissed from the Revolutionary Council and as minister of trade and industries for his moderate approach.

15 February: Ne Win announces state take-over of production, distribution, import, and export of all commodities. No new private industry will be allowed; the private sector is limited to retail trade. A rapid decline of the economy follows.

23 February: All banks (public, private, foreign, domestic) are nationalised.

3 March: Kachin rebels raid the police station in Mohnyin town in Kachin State and make off with more than 150 pieces of arms.

26 March: Mohammed Jafar Habib sets up the Rohingya Independence Force (RIF) on the East Pakistan (now Bangladesh) border.

1 April: The ruling Revolutionary Council announces a general amnesty for insurgents. All arms are to be turned in by 1 July.

20 April: Liu Shaoqi visits Burma.

18 May: *The Nation* is closed down.

6 June: News Agency Burma is established by the military government to take over all private news wire services.

11 July: Negotiations between the military government and insurgents begin in Rangoon.

12 July: The first group of CPB members, led by *yebaw* Aung Gyi, returns from China to Rangoon to participate in the peace talks.

23 July: The second group of CPB members, led by Bo Zeya, returns from China to Rangoon to participate in the peace talks.

9 August: Thakin Tin, Bohmu Aung and Thakin Tin Maung are released from custody. Ba Swe, Kyaw Nyein and Law Yone are arrested.

3 September: The third group of CPB members, led by Thakin Ba Thein Tin, returns from China to Rangoon to participate in the peace talks.

28 September: The *Working People's Daily*, a premier government organ, is founded. The *Vanguard* and *Guardian* newspapers are nationalised.

15 November: Negotiations with Mon, Chin and Karenni insurgents end in failure. Over 700 leftists and Communists are arrested. Students demonstrate; universities and colleges are closed once again.

November: Thakin Ba Thein Tin returns to Beijing from Rangoon. CPB members Khin Maung Gyi, San Thu and Thein Aung return from Moscow to Beijing where they rejoin Thakin Ba Thein Tin and the others. Thakin Ba Thein Tin, Khin Maung Gyi, Thakin Than Myaing, Than Shwe and Tin Yee set up a "leading group of five" in Beijing to prepare for a China-sponsored push into Burma. San Thu begins to survey the Sino-Burmese border areas for possible infiltration routes into northeastern Burma. Naw Seng's Kachins, who have been staying in Guizhou, go to Sichuan for talks with Thakin Ba Thein Tin and other CPB leaders.

12 December: Brig. T. Clift resigns as vice chief of staff (air). Col. Thaung Dan replaces him.

18 December: Talks with the Shan rebels are terminated.

1964

28 January: The ruling Revolutionary Council announces a new set of laws for all states, eliminating the limited autonomy some of them had enjoyed previously.

31 January: The general amnesty, which was declared on 1 April 1963, expires.

14 February: Zhou Enlai arrives in Rangoon. A communique is issued on 18 February.

12 March: Karen rebel leader Saw Hunter Thamwe signs an agreement with the Revolutionary Council in Rangoon. The agreement does not cover other factions of the Karen rebel movement.

25 March: Three rebel groups in Shan State (the Shan State Independence Army, the Shan National United Front and the Kokang Revolutionary Force) merge to become the Shan State Army (SSA), headed by Sao Nang Hearn Kham, the widow of Burma's first president, Sao Shwe Thaike.

28 March: All political parties except the BSPP are banned.

18 April: The Revolutionary Council decrees that all Buddhist organisations must register with the government.

April: The 5th Brigade of the Karen rebel army, led by Lin Tin, surrenders to the government.

3 May: The Revolutionary Council rescinds the order to register after demonstrations by Buddhist monks.

17 May: All 100 and 50 Kyat banknotes are demonetised without compensation.

10 July: Zhou Enlai visits Burma.

8 August: The Kayan New Land Party (KNLP) is formed in the Pekon-Möng Pai area of southwestern Shan State by Bo Pyan, a World War II veteran, and Kayan (Padaung) university students led by Shwe Aye as a result of discontent among several tribal groups, including the Padaungs, caused by the demonetisation.

1 September: The *Kyemon* newspaper is nationalised.

11 September: The *Botataung* newspaper is nationalised.

16 September: The *Guardian* magazine is nationalised.

2 November: Universities and colleges are reopened after having been closed for ten months.

1965

6 January: The *Washington Post* reports that a *Pravda* editorial has noted that Burma is pursuing the "correct path" to socialism.

1 April: One hundred and twenty-nine private schools are nationalised.

3–4 April: Zhou Enlai visits Burma.

26–27 April: Zhou Enlai again visits Burma.

30 April: Ninety-two Buddhist monks are arrested for protesting against a constitution for a government-sponsored All Buddha Sasana Sangha organisation and the issuance of identity cards for monks.

15 June: Brig. Aung Gyi is arrested and imprisoned.

5 July: Christian hospitals in Rangoon and Namkham (Shan State) are nationalised.

24 July–1 Aug: Ne Win visits China. A joint communique is issued, reaffirming the 1961 treaty and five principles of peaceful coexistence.

9 September: The Karen National United Party, the Karenni National Progressive Party and the Shan State War Council of the Shan State Army meet and form the Revolutionary Nationalities Alliance (RNA).

14–25 September: Ne Win visits the Soviet Union. A joint communique is issued, reaffirming mutual friendship.

6 December: All private newspapers are formally banned.

6–10 December: The first BSPP seminar is held.

1966

4 January: Bo Mya, the leader of the eastern units of the Karen rebels, expels left-wing Karens from his area. He begins to establish a rightist Karen movement based along the Thai border.

February: One hundred Communists are arrested when cells are said to be found in the military.

4 April: Six hundred and eighty-five private schools throughout the country are nationalised.

17–19 April: Liu Shaoqi and Marshal Chen Yi visit Burma.

7–11 May: Ne Win visits Pakistan. A boundary agreement with Pakistan is signed on 9 May.

16 May: Mao Zedong issues a circular which calls for the cleansing of the Chinese Communist Party. The Cultural Revolution begins.

18 August: Mao Zedong takes the salutes of hundreds of thousands of young Red Guards in Beijing's Tiananmen Square. China becomes the centre for "world revolution".

8–10 September: Ne Win goes to the US on a state visit.

18 October: U Nu and Ba Swe are released from custody.

1967

27 January: One hundred and thirty-two Naga rebels from northeastern India reach the Yunnan frontier, having been trekking through northern Burma since 24

October 1966. Led by Thuingaleng Muivah and Thinoselie M. Keyho, they are received by the Chinese, who provide them with political and military training.

10 March: Burma signs a border agreement with India.

13 May: Communist and Karen insurgents seize Gyobingauk, 160 kilometres north of Rangoon, and hold it for several hours.

18 June: Inspired by the Cultural Revolution in China, the CPB launches its *pyouk-thouk-tak* ("dismissed from office; dispelled from the party; disposed of") purges in the Pegu Yoma. Party leaders H.N. Ghoshal and *yebaw* Htay are executed.

19 June: The Ministry of Education bans the wearing of all "unauthorised badges" by students. The order is aimed at the wearing of Mao badges primarily by students of ethnic Chinese origin in Rangoon.

26 June: Two thousand Burmese gather outside two Chinese schools in Rangoon.

27 June: Martial law is declared in parts of Rangoon as 5,000 rioters gather.

28 June: One thousand three hundred and twenty-eight Chinese in Rangoon are detained. The Chinese embassy protests officially against the incident.

29 June: The Chinese embassy in Rangoon is attacked by demonstrators. Beijing announces that its ambassador will not return to Rangoon. Official Burmese sources say over fifty Chinese were killed during the period 22–29 June; the Chinese say that several hundred were killed.

30 June: Radio Beijing begins to attack the Ne Win government as "contra-revolutionary, fascist and reactionary".

5–9 July: Heavy fighting rages near the Burma-Laos-Thailand triborder junction as KMT forces attack an opium convoy belonging to Chang Chifu (Khun Sa). The Laotian Air Force intervenes and takes off with the opium.

7 July: China's aid programme to Burma is suspended.

16 July: A correspondent for the New China News Agency is expelled from Burma.

29 July: KMT troops from Tam Ngob and Mae Salong in Thailand attack Khun Sa's Loi Maw *Ka Kwe Ye* home guards near Ban Khwan in Laos, close to the Thai border, after they have conducted a sixteen-ton opium convoy across the Mekong river.

1 August: Martial law ends in Rangoon.

11 August: The Chinese foreign ministry delivers a protest to the Burmese embassy in Beijing, accusing Burmese aircraft of intruding into Yunnan. The Chinese also claim that there have been two cases of Burmese troops firing across the Chinese boundary and twenty cases of Burmese armed forces crossing the border.

13 August: The military in Sittwe, Arakan, fires on a crowd of people demonstrating to demand sufficient rice rations. More than 100 demonstrators are killed.

19 August: KMT troops retreat into Thailand from Laos; their "opium war" with Khun Sa is over. The Laotian air force and Laotian infantry have intervened and made off with Khun Sa's opium.

21 August: All Burmese students studying in China are recalled. Critical Burmese sources claim that the anti-Chinese riots were stirred up by the government to deflect attention from acute rice shortages.

25 August: The *Beijing Review* publishes a long article hailing the 28th anniversary of the CPB (15 August) and stressing the need for a "people's army" waging a "people's war".

August–September: The Kachin rebels send their first delegation to China, led by Brang Seng. They visit Beijing and Shanghai.

6 October: All Chinese technicians are ordered to leave Burma.

12 October: Win Maung, a former president, is released from custody.

October–November: More than 1,000 Shan rebels in northern Shan State switch sides and become government *Ka Kwe Ye* home guards.

November: A second Kachin rebel delegation from the KIO, led by Zau Tu, visits China. They meet Zhou Enlai and Kang Sheng as well as CPB leaders (Thakin Ba Thein Tin, Naw Seng and others) in Beijing.

26 December: Bo Yan Aung, a leading member of the CPB (and once one of Aung San's closest associates) is executed in the Pegu Yoma.

1968

1 January: Several hundred heavily armed CPB troops, led by Kachin wartime hero Naw Seng, cross the border from China and capture Möng Ko in northeastern Shan State. All-out Chinese support for the CPB insurgency begins.

5 January: CPB troops led by Pheung Kya-shin and Pheung Kya-fu cross the border from China into the Kokang area in northeastern Shan State.

15 January: CPB and KIO leaders meet in Beijing and agree on military cooperation. But fighting between the two groups break out when Communist forces enter Kachin-rebel held territory in the hills south of Möng Ko.

21 January: One of the bloodiest and most protracted battles of the Vietnam War begins at the US marine fire base at Khe Sanh, situated ten kilometres east of the Lao border.

27 January: 127 political prisoners are released, including Dr. Ba Maw, Law Yone, former foreign minister Sao Khun Hkio, Kyaw Nyein, Brig. Aung Gyi and former chief justice Myint Thein.

January: Four hundred KIA troops from its 5th and 6th columns led by Ting Ying and Zalum in the Kambaiti-Pangwa area defect to the CPB and set up the 101 War Zone on the Chinese border in Kachin State.

31 January: Communist forces in South Vietnam launch a country-wide Tet offensive against urban centres.

February: CPB troops enter Khun Hai and Man Hio, two enclaves of Burmese territory north of the Shweli river, opposite Namkham.

25 February: The Khmer Rouge launch a widespread guerrilla campaign in western Cambodia.

March: A second group of Naga rebels from northeastern India, 330 strong and led by Isak Chishi Swu and Mowu Gwizan, reaches the Chinese frontier after having trekked through Kachin State. They are given shelter and training in Tengchong, Yunnan.

6 April: The Chinese protest against "unwarranted arrests" of ethnic Chinese in Burma.

16 April: Bo Zeya, chief of staff of the CPB's People's Army since 1950, is killed in action near the Pegu Yoma.

May: Lao Khai market town in Kokang is occupied by Pheung Kya-shin's pro-CPB forces.

21 June: Bo Mya, a Karen leader in the eastern hills, breaks with the rest of the left-leaning Karen rebel movement and sets up the Karen National United Front (KNUF) near the Thai border.

22 July: A heavy battle rages between government forces and CPB troops at Tao Long on the Burma Road north of Kutkai. The Nam Tao bridge is blown up.

August: The last government forces withdraw from Khun Hai and Man Hio. Nearly all of Kokang is also in CPB hands. Hpaunghsaing (Pong Hseng) east of Möng Ko and the Möng Hom-Möng Ya area south of Möng Ko are taken over by the CPB.

19–22 September: A Commanding Officers' Conference is held. Ne Win discusses the formation of a people's militia and the launching of a "people's war" against the insurgents.

24 September: The CPB chairman, Thakin Than Tun, is assassinated in the Pegu Yoma.

29 November: The Revolutionary Council invites thirty-three political leaders to form a "think-tank" designed to find a solution to Burma's political and constitutional crisis.

4 December: An Internal Unity Advisory Body of thirty-three civilians is appointed by the government to "get opinions on the future political and administrative organisation of the nation." It includes U Nu, Kyaw Nyein and several other former state leaders.

December: CPB forces led by Aung Gyi (Yang Ko-san) begin to penetrate the northern Wa Hills.

1969

20 January: Moh Heng breaks with the SSA, joins forces with the 3rd Kuomintang of Gen. Li Wenhuan and establishes the Shan United Revolutionary Army (SURA) at Pieng Luang on the Thai border.

31 January: The *Hanthawaddy* and *Myanma Alin* newspapers are nationalised.

3 April: *Yebaw* Aung Gyi, a leading CPB member, is killed in action near Nyaunglebin.

11 April: U Nu leaves for India, ostensibly on a pilgrimage.

1 June: The Internal Unity Advisory Body submits its report, recommending a national coalition government, peace talks with the rebels, and the decentralisation of the economy. Twenty-two members want a multi-party system while eleven recommend a socialist system. U Nu submits a separate report in absentia.

2 June: Ne Win rejects the proposals of the advisory board.

29 August: At a press conference in London, U Nu announces the formation of the Parliamentary Democracy Party (PDP) to overthrow Ne Win by force; it begins to raise funds for arms.

8 September: CPB units in Kokang set up a "People's Government" to formalise its control over the area.

October: The CPB formally sets up its Northeastern Military Area, combining Kokang with the Möng Ko-Möng Hom-Möng Ya areas west of the Salween in northeastern Shan State. Than Shwe is appointed its political commissar and Naw Seng its military commander.

20 October: Khun Sa is arrested in Taunggyi.

29 October: U Nu is granted political asylum in Thailand and tacitly allowed to form a government in exile.

December: Students riot in Mandalay, ostensibly over tickets to a sporting event but the real cause is believed to be dissatisfaction with the regime. Schools and colleges are closed. CPB units occupy Pangwei (Saohpa) township centre in the Wa Hills.

1970
January: School and colleges are reopened.

February: Heavy fighting breaks out between government forces and the CPB in Kyinshan near the Chinese border east of Panglong-Hopang. The government side is supported by local *Ka Kwe Ye* forces led by Lo Hsing-han. The CPB takes over the entire Kyinshan area.

21 March: The CPB captures Möng Paw in northeastern Shan State.

28 March: The CPB takes over the town of Panghsai-Kyuhkok on the Chinese border after a heavy, two-day battle.

April: Heavy fighting west of the Salween river. CPB forces attack the railway station in Lashio and destroys a bridge on the Lashio-Hsenwi road.

29 April–1 May: In the largest US military operation since 1968 US and South Vietnamese forces invade eastern Cambodia.

5 May: Prince Sihanouk and the Khmer Rouge form a government in exile in Beijing. China steps up its support to armed Communist movements in Southeast Asia.

25 May: The Nationalities United Liberation Front (NULF) is established by Mon and Karen rebels, and U Nu's PDP at a meeting in Bangkok attended by U Nu, Mahn Ba Zan and Nai Shwe Kyin.

13 November: Government forces capture Thakin Soe, the Red Flag Communist leader, at his Than Chaung camp near the Arakan Yoma.

14 November: The Burmese ambassador, absent since the anti-Chinese riots in June 1967, returns to Beijing.

1971
Jan–April: The CPB and Karen rebels are driven out of the Irrawddy delta region. They retreat to the Pegu Yoma.

28 March: The *People's Voice of Burma*, the CPB's clandestine radio station, is officially inaugurated. It begins transmitting from Yunnan in early April.

1 May: The CPB captures the township centre of Möng Mau in the Wa Hills after a heavy battle with government forces.

6–12 August: Ne Win goes to Beijing for a six-day visit to try to mend fences with the Chinese leaders.

16 August: The SSA sets up a political wing, the Shan State Progress Party (SSPP) during a meeting at Wan Ping village, Khum Pang area, northern Shan State. Khun Kya Nu is elected president and Sao Hsö Wai general secretary.

25 September: A 99-member (34 from the military and 63 civilians) committee is set up to draft a new constitution.

5 October: CPB units led by CC member Pe Thaung enter the hills northeast of Kengtung from China and begin organising the local people. The area is later named the 815 War Zone after the founding date of the CPB, 15 August (1939). Following heavy fighting in the Irrawaddy delta region, the CPB and the Karens withdraw to the Pegu Yoma.

November: The CPB establishes the 108 War Zone in the Kyawkku-Nawnglong-Nawng Wu area of western Shan State, which has been under CPB influence since 1948–49.

28 November: The CPB overruns a Burma Army outpost near the town of Kunlong on the Salween river. Government reinforcements are brought in to prevent the CPB from capturing the Kunlong bridge on the Salween.

1972

7 January: The battle for Kunlong bridge ends after forty-one days of continuous heavy fighting. The CPB fails to capture Kunlong, and its push west is halted.

16 February: The Chinese ambassador, absent since the anti-Chinese riots in June 1967, returns to Rangoon.

6 March: The KMT burns twenty-six tons of opium at Mae Rim, north of Chiang Mai, to demonstrate that it is "washing its hands of the drug traffic".

9 March: Naw Seng dies under mysterious circumstances: the CPB says he fell off a cliff while hunting in the Wa Hills.

20 April: Ne Win and twenty other military officers resign from the service.

5–6 June: The CPB pushes south from Kokang and the northern Wa Hills. Its forces capture the market village of Manghseng and a nearby government garrison in the southern Wa Hills.

June–July: The CPB captures Vingngun, Na Hpan, Loi Leün, Pangyang, Man Hpang and Panghsang (a small town in the southern Wa area adjacent to the Chinese border which later becomes Communist headquarters).

7–8 July: Students distribute leaflets in Rangoon condemning the destruction of the Students' Union building in July 1962.

17 November: Aung Gyi, Ba Swe and Kyaw Nyein are arrested, allegedly in connection with a plot to assassinate the cabinet.

1973

January: Ne Win sends orders to Taunggyi to disband the *Ka Kwe Ye* home guards. They are asked to surrender their weapons.

10 January: Lahu rebels in southern Shan State occupy the town of Möng Hsat.

11 January: The Lahus occupy Möng Ton in southern Shan State.

27 January: The peace agreement officially ending the war in Vietnam is signed in Paris.

February: The Lahu National United Party (LNUP) is set up at Doi Lang on the Thai-Burma border to coordinate the Lahu rebel movement.

February: The CPB occupies the Mawhpa area east of the Salween river, southwest of Panghsang.

21 February: A cease-fire agreement is signed in Laos, and the US halts its bombing of the country.

16 April: Followers of Khun Sa kidnap two Soviet doctors in Taunggyi. The kidnappers announce that they will be released in exchange for Khun Sa who is in Mandalay Jail.

April: Panghsang in the Wa Hills becomes the headquarters of the CPB's "Northeastern War Zone" while the Pegu Yoma remains official GHQ.

10 May: Ne Win visits Thailand.

24 May: Lo Hsing-han goes underground and links up with the Shan State Army. The Shan rebels persuade Lo Hsing-han to sign a proposal offering to sell the entire opium harvest in Shan State to the US government.

17 July: Lo Hsing-han is arrested at Wan Tung village northwest of Mae Hong Son after crossing the border to Thailand to escape a Burma Army attack. He is later extradited to Burma.

27 July: U Nu leaves Thailand at the Thais' request. He goes into exile in Bhopal, India.

September: Khun Myint's Shan forces in the hills north of Kengtung ally themselves with the CPB, linking up CPB territories in eastern Shan State with those in the Wa Hills. The CPB thus controls a 20,000-square-kilometre base area in northeastern Shan State.

14 October: A student uprising in Bangkok topples the government of Thanom Kittikachorn and Prapass Charusathiara.

October: A 37-strong Karen (KNUP) delegation reaches CPB headquarters at Panghsang, escorted by 96 troops from the SSA led by Hsö Hten and Hsö Noom.

November: The CPB and Khun Myint's forces occupy the town of Möng Yang in eastern Shan State and hold it for several weeks.

15–18 December: SSA leaders Hsö Hten and Hsö Noom appeal for help from the CPB during a meeting at Panghsang. The first links between the SSA and the CPB are estblished. The Shan and Karen rebel delegations to Panghsang are invited to visit China. They travel to Simao and Kunming.

15–31 December: A nationwide referendum is held for the new constitution. According to official figures, 90.19% vote in favour of it.

1974

3 January: The new constitution is adopted. Separate Chin, Mon and Arakan states are established, but without the limited autonomy which the ethnic states were guaranteed under the 1947 constitution.

2 March: The 12th anniversary of the 1962 coup; the new constitution comes into effect.

18 March: Karen rebels and the PDP seize the border town of Myawaddy (opposite Mae Sot in Thailand) for a short period.

19 March: Ne Win signs an amnesty for insurgents which was authorised the previous day by the National Assembly. There is no response to the offer.

13 May: Demonstrations and strikes rock Rangoon and other places, caused by food shortages.

6 June: The army moves in to quell the labour unrest. Troops and police fire on textile and dockyard workers, killing twenty-two and wounding eighty according to official sources. Unofficially, more than a hundred were killed.

29 June: The US and Burmese governments sign an agreement for "suppressing the illegal cultivation, processing, production, and trafficking of narcotic drugs". The US government agrees to supply Rangoon with Bell 205 helicopers for this purpose.

7 September: Khun Sa is released from Mandalay Jail. The two Soviet doctors were released shortly before, ostensibly "unconditionally". The deal has been negotiated through Thai general Kriangsak Chomanan.

October: The PDP initiates several grenade attacks in Rangoon and other cities.

11 November: Gen. Ne Win arrives in China for an official visit.

18 November: A three-man tribunal in Rangoon sentences Htwe Myint, a pro-democracy activist and former third secretary of the Burmese embassy in Indonesia, to death for treason.

25 November: U Thant, former secretary-general of the United Nations, dies in New York.

1–2 December: Communists seize power in Vientiane, abolish the 600-year-old monarchy and proclaim the Lao People's Democratic Republic.

5 December: Students and monks demonstrate over U Thant's burial site and seize his body. Slogans shouted: "Down with the one-party dictatorship" and "Down with the fascist government". This is the first significant activity by the monks in a decade.

11 December: The government declares martial law.

12 December: Renewed demonstrations in Rangoon. Officially, nine people are killed, seventy-four wounded and 1,800 arrested. Unofficially, the casualties are in the hundreds. Schools are closed.

1975

4 March: KIA rebels kidnap a West German drilling expert from the state-owned lead and silver mines at Namtu in northern Shan State.

15 March: CPB chairman Thakin Zin and secretary Thakin Chit are killed during a government offensive in the Pegu Yoma. Panghsang becomes the CPB's GHQ officially.

March: KIA rebels raid the towns of Banmauk and Mansi in Kachin State and escape with firearms and 960,000 Kyats in cash.

March: A second SSA delegation, led by Sam Möng, Khun On Paung (Hsö Khan) and Hsö Hten, arrives in Panghsang.

17 April: Victorious Khmer Rouge forces enter Phnom Penh.

18–23 April: Hearings are held at the House of Representatives in Washington regarding the proposals by the Shan rebels to sell the opium crop to the US government. The proposals are rejected.

30 April: Saigon falls to Communist forces.

8 May: The West German mining engineer is released by the KIA after the West German government has paid a US$250,000 ransom through its embassy in Bangkok.

13 May: Universities and colleges, closed since 1974, are reopened.

16–26 May: The CPB's central committee meet in China and elect a new leadership. Thakin Ba Thein Tin becomes new chairman, Thakin Pe Tint first vice chairman and Khin Maung Gyi second vice chairman.

3 June: The CPB's clandestine radio announces that the party's chairmanship has been taken over by Thakin Ba Thein Tin.

6 June: Student demonstrations begin again on the anniversary of the 1974 workers strike, lasting five days. Schools and colleges are closed again.

8 June: A 35-second earth tremor shatters 900-year-old temples and monuments of culture at Pagan.

11 June: Troops move into the strikers' camp near the Shwe Dagon Pagoda and arrest 213 students and others. Later, 203 of these are tried by special tribunal and given four- and five-year jail sentences, and another 80 striking workers from the Burma Pharmaceutical Corporation and the Jute Mill are sentenced to ten to sixteen years in prison for "obstructing the socialist economy".

August: US Senate majority leader Mike Mansfield makes an unofficial "fact-finding" visit to Burma.

6 August: Kachin rebel leaders Zau Seng, Zau Tu and Phungshwi Zau Seng are assassinated near Tam Ngob on the Thai border.

27 September: Rebels attack Bhamo airport in Kachin State.

October: The CPB draws up the "7510 Plan" (October, 1975) to spread its influence to areas west of the Salween river.

11–15 November: Ne Win visits China for four days, and reaches an agreement that there will be no "aggressive acts" between the two nations.

2 December: The Pathet Lao complete their "peaceful revolution" and form the Lao People's Democratic Republic.

16 December: China's security chief Kang Sheng dies in Beijing.

24 December: Ne Win storms into Inya Lake Hotel and stops the music as a noisy Christmas party is going on.

1976

5 January: Universities and colleges, closed since June 1975, are reopened.

8 January: Zhou Enlai dies in Beijing.

February: Khun Sa slips out of Mandalay and makes it to Ban Hin Taek on the Thai-Burma border where he rejoins his men.

2 March: Universities and colleges are closed again following student unrest in Rangoon.

6 March: Gen. Tin Oo resigns as defence minister.

21 March: A large force of Karen rebels seizes Thaton for a few hours.

March: The SSPP/SSA splits. The old leaders, Sao Hsö Wai and Khun Kya Nu, are ousted and settle in Thailand. A pro-CPB faction, led by Sao On Paung, takes over.

April: Deng Xiaoping is ousted from power following demonstrations held in Beijing after Zhou Enlai's death.

26 April–10 May: Ethnic rebel leaders from about a dozen different groups meet at the Manerplaw headquarters of the KNU and set up the National Democratic Front (NDF).

4 July: Kachin rebels attack Myitkyina airport.

5–6 July: CPB and KIO leaders meet and form a military alliance ending eight years of war between the two groups. The Kachin rebels begin to receive Chinese arms through the CPB.

July: The authorities say they have unearthed a coup attempt by young officers opposed to the socialist system.

20 July: Kyaw Zaw, the famous former brigadier-general of the Burma Army, arrives in CPB-held territory near the Chinese border to join the communist insurgency.

30 July: The CPB sends a message to the 55th anniversary of the Communist Party of China, condemning the "revisionist clique" headed by Liu Shaoqi and Deng Xiaoping.

2 August: Kokang Chinese remnants on the Thai border, led by Donald Yang and Lo Hsing-han's younger brother Lo Hsing-minh, set up the Shan State Revolutionary Army (SSRA) at Mae Aw opposite Mae Hong Son.

31 August: Martial law is lifted in Rangoon Division.

August: Khun Myint's forces in northern Kengtung formally join the CPB to become its 768 Brigade (named after August 1976).

9 September: Mao Zedong dies in Beijing.

10 September: The trial of the accused coup plotters begins. Former army chief and defence minister Tin Oo is implicated.

30 September: The CPB reiterates its condemnation of Liu Shaoqi and Deng Xiaoping.

6 October: Scores of students are massacred at Thammasat University in Bangkok as the Thai right wing reasserts power.

November: The CPB's 683 Brigade leaves Panghsang and crosses the Salween river.

1977

11 January: The accused coup plotters are sentenced. Some students demonstrate against the sentences.

16 January: The CPB and the SSPP issue a joint communique declaring the formation of a united front of the two parties.

February: The CPB's 683 Brigade reaches Loi Tsang mountain near Möng Küng in western Shan State.

11 April: CPB forces, led by Zhang Zhiming (Kyi Myint) occupy the town of Möng Mit in northern Shan State and hold it for a day.

16 April: Joseph Nellis visits Khan Sa's Ban Hin Taek headquarters in northern Thailand.

12–13 July: Hearings are held in Washington before a select committee on narcotics abuse and control of the House of Representatives. A second Shan proposal to sell the opum crop to the US government is rejected.

August: The Communist Party of China holds its 11th congress in Beijing and officially declares an end to the Cultural Revolution. Deng Xiaoping returns to power.

1 October: Universities and colleges, closed since 2 March 1976, reopen.

20 October: Kachin rebels capture Namsan Yang on the Bhamo-Myiktyina road. The road is cut by the rebels, who establish a permanent presence in the Namsan Yang valley.

26 November: Ne Win arrives in Phnom Penh as the first foreign head of state to visit Cambodia after the Khmer Rouge take-over in April 1975.

1978

26 January: Deng Xiaoping arrives in Rangoon on a six-day visit. In Malaysia, he had said that government-to-government relations were different from party-to-party relations, implying that the Chinese would continue to support the CPB and similar Communist rebellions in other countries.

11 February: The government launches the *Naga Min* (Dragon King) operation in Arakan State, ostensibly to "check illegal immigrants". Hundreds of heavily armed troops raid Muslim neighbourhoods in Sittwe; 5,000 people are arrested.

3 March: Operation *Naga Min* reaches Kyauktaw township in Arakan; 200 people are arrested. Incidents of rape, looting and arson are reported.

5 March: Army columns reach Maungdaw and Buthidaung in northern Arakan.

15 March: Four naval gunboats arrive in Buthidaung from Sittwe. Villages are burned and thousands of civilians begin to flee across the border to Bangladesh.

15 April: Kachin rebels raid Shwegu town in Kachin State and capture sixty pieces of arms and more than 600,000 Kyats in cash.

16 April: Saw Mun Na, chief of staff of the Karenni rebel army, is killed in southern Shan State. His team of Karennis are on their way to Panghsang to request assistance from the CPB. The majority of the troops return to Kayah State after the incident; thirteen soldiers led by Than Nyunt slip out and make it to Panghsang.

mid-May: Some 2,000 to 3,000 Rohingyas a day arrive in southeastern Bangladesh. Relief agencies in Bangladesh say more than 70,000 Rohingyas have fled; the Burmese government says that "19,457 Bengalis [have] absconded and abandoned their homes".

6 June: Bangladesh foreign secretary Tabarak Husain arrives in Rangoon to discuss the refugee crisis. The number of Rohingya refugees in Bangladesh has risen to 150,000.

30 June: Some 200,000 Rohingyas have fled to Bangladesh.

9 July: Burma and Bangladesh reach an agreement on the repatriation of the Rohingyas.

31 August: The repatriation of Rohingyas begins.

17 November: Following a five-year trial, a court in Rangoon sentences Lo Hsing-han to death for "rebellion against the state".

28 November: PPP/PLA leader Bo Let Ya is killed by Karen rebels near the Thai border. The non-communist Burman resistance against the government collapses.

25 December: Vietnamese forces invade Cambodia.

1979

7 January: Vietnamese forces topple Pol Pot's Khmer Rouge regime in Cambodia. China begins massive support to the Thai border-based Khmer resistance.

31 January–1 February: Heavy fighting rages on the road to the Hpakan jade mines in Kachin State. Kachin rebels wipe out an entire column of government troops and capture 144 pieces of arms.

17 February: Chinese troops launch attacks across the Vietnamese border.

9 March: Kachin rebels attack Nga Nga Yang near Nalung in Kachin State, kill thirty-four government soldiers and capture 122 pieces of arms.

12 July: Rangoon announces a new US$63 million aid agreement with China for unspecified projects.

7 September: Burma leaves the Non-Aligned Movement at its meeting in Havana, Cuba. San Yu criticises the Vietnamese invasion of Cambodia.

19 November: Thousands of government forces are mobilised in the biggest offensive so far against the CPB in the Northeast, codenamed *Min Yan Aung*. Twenty-five battalions are engaged, and the aim is to capture Panghsang "before Christmas". The Chinese support the CPB, but at a much reduced rate.

28 November: China's foreign minister, Huang Hua, arrives in Burma.

1980

6 January: The *Min Yan Aung* operation is called off. The government's forces fail to reach Panghsang but manage to recapture the Mawhpa area and to establish a forward base on Loi Hisao-kao mountain, twenty-five kilometres to the west of CPB headquarters.

April: The CPB captures Muse (northern Shan State) for two days, and Möng Yawng (eastern Shan State) for four days.

24 May: The government announces a ninety-day general amnesty for insurgents.

10 July: The government announces that the Chinese aid programme signed in Beijing on 12 July 1979 will consist of eight projects: the building of the Rangoon-Syriam bridge, 40,000 spindle yarn-making machines, three rice mills with a 150-ton per day capacity, the supply of water to Moulmein city, and three million renminbi-yuan for machinery and tools.

16 July: Bo Thet Tun, military commander of the CPB's "Northwestern Forces" (northern Arakan and Magwe Division) surrenders to the government.

29 July: U Nu returns from his exile in Bhopal, India, to Burma under the amnesty offer.

16 August: The government announces that 1,431 rebels have surrendered under the amnesty. The total number at the end of the amnesty period is said to be 2,189. Independent estimates put the figure at 300 to 400 surrenders. Among the ones who accepted the amnesty offer are CPA chairman Kyaw Zan Rhee and Thet Tun, the commander of the CPB's northwestern forces in the Minbu area. Bo Yan Naing, Bohmu Aung, Kya Doe and other ex-PDP/PPP leaders return from Thailand, and U Nu returns from India. Lo Hsing-han and Thakin Soe are released from jail.

23 September: CPB chairman Thakin Ba Thein Tin sends a letter to Ne Win proposing peace talks. He has waited deliberately until after the amnesty period to show that "we do not recognise the amnesty offer".

13 October: The Burmese representative is absent during the UN vote to seat a representative from Cambodia.

17 October: Kachin rebel leader Brang Seng arrives in Rangoon as head of a KIO delegation that has been invited for talks with the government.

18 October: Brang Seng and the KIO delegation meet Ne Win in Rangoon. Negotiations begin.

23 October: The KIO delegation returns to Kachin State. The two parties agree to hold peace talks.

17–24 November: The first round of peace talks is held in Myitkyina between the government and Kachin rebels of the KIO.

18–21 December: A second round of peace talks is held in Myitkyina.

1981

January–February: The CPB forms "Force 180", led by Bo Kyaw Moe, tries to penetrate the Pinlebu area north of Mandalay, using KIA territory in Kachin State as a springboard. The force is wiped out by government troops before it manages to re-enter Burma proper.

3–4 March: A third round of talks is held in Myitkyina between the government and the KIO.

10 April: The fourth round of talks is held in Myitkyina between the government and the KIO. The KIO insists on autonomy within the Union of Burma. The government reiterates its suggestion that the KIA be transformed into a local militia force recognised by Rangoon. The talks break down.

5 May: Peace talks begin in Lashio between the government and the CPB. The delegation from Rangoon is led by Aye Ko; the CPB is represented by central committee members Thakin Pe Tint, Ye Tun and Hpalang Kam Di (Pe Tint's personal physician, Kyaw Zwa, is also present, which leads some foreign observers in Rangoon to erroneously believe that ex-brigadier Kyaw Zaw led the CPB delegation).

9 May: The government calls off the talks with the CPB. The CPB delegates return to Panghsang.

14 June: Thakin Ba Thein Tin announces over the CPB's clandestine radio that "though the Ne Win-San Yu military regime has unilaterally broken up the negotiations, the CPB remains prepared to sit down at the table again if the conditions are favourable".

July: Shan leaders meet at Kiu-Hok on the Thai border for the SSPP's second congress. Hsö Lane is elected president on the 23rd. The SSPP decides to break with the CPB.

8 August: The BSPP's fourth congress concludes in Rangoon. Ne Win announces that he intends to retire from his position as president of Burma, but remain chairman of the BSPP.

9 November: San Yu becomes new president.

1982

April: The New Mon State Party at Three Pagodas Pass splits into two factions, one led by Nai Shwe Kyin and the other by Nai Nol Lar.

June: The NDF holds its first congress at Manerplaw KNU headquarters. Nai Nol Lar's NMSP joins the front.

1 July: US assistant secretary of state for Asia and the Pacific visits Rangoon and assures the government of continued support for Burma's anti-narcotics programme.

August: Khun Sa's forces capture Doi Lang from the Lahu rebels.

28 September: Karen rebels attack the radio station in Rangoon and a nearby police station. Two rebels are killed and three captured alive.

December: The *Min Yan Aung-II* operation is launched against the CPB. Fighting rages for about a month, mainly in the 815 War Zone.

1983

January: *Min Yan Aung-II* is called off. No significant gains are made against the CPB. An offensive is launched against Karen rebel bases along the Thai border.

February: A new CPB force, codenamed "102", is formed to try to re-enter Pinlebu in Burma proper. It is wiped out by the Burma Army and the survivors flee across the Chindwin river into the Naga Hills near the Indian border.

Mid-February: Some 200 or 300 Karen rebels cross the Rangoon-Mandalay railway line, heading for Pegu Yoma. They clash with government forces at Nyaunglebin on the 18th. Six government battalions supported by armour pursue the rebel column, which is wiped out.

17 May: Burma's intelligence chief, Brig.-Gen. Tin Oo, long considered Ne Win's heir apparent, is ousted from the government along with Col. Bo Ni, head of the National Intelligence Bureau.

June: An unexpected rainy season offensive is launched against KNU strongholds north of Mae Sot. Government forces capture the strategic Naw Taya peak overlooking KNU bases along the Moei border river.

18 July: Ousted SSPP/SSA leader Hsö Lane surrenders to the government at Kengtawng, southern Shan State. Khun Sa's troops take over the SSA's former base at Möng Mai-Homöng on the Thai border opposite Mae Hong Son and establish a new headquarters there.

8 August: The trial of Tin Oo begins.

23 August: Bo Ni is charged with misuse of state funds.

9 October: Ninteen people, including four visiting South Korean cabinet ministers, are killed by a bomb at Aung San Martyr's Mausoleum in Rangoon.

11 October: Burmese security forces kill one North Korean agent, accused of planting the bomb on the 9th, and arrest a second suspect.

12 October: Another North Korean agent is captured in Rangoon.

18 October: A French technician and his wife are captured by Karen guerrillas at a construction project near the Karen state capital of Pa-an.

4 November: Burma severs diplomatic ties with North Korea.

14 November: Tin Oo is sentenced to five life terms for "misuse of property and state funds."

11–16 November: Government forces launch attacks near the Thai border on Karen rebels who kidnapped the French couple.

22 November: The two captured North Korean agents are put on trial in Rangoon.

24 November: The Karen rebels hand the French couple over to the Red Cross in Thailand.

9 December: The two North Korean agents are sentenced to death.

1984

January: Government forces push down from Naw Taya peak, captured in June 1983; a major offensive is mounted against the KNU along the Thai border. The Lahus, led by Char Ui, surrender to the authorities.

28 January: Government forces overrun the Karen rebel base of Mae Tha Waw after a fierce battle.

February: Heavy fighting continues along the Thai border. Maw Pokay comes under fierce attack but does not fall to the government's forces.

28 February: Kachin rebels capture Singkaling Hkamti in northern Sagaing Division, rob the local treasury and armoury, release all prisoners in the town and lock up government officials in their place.

7 March: The eastern commander of the Burma Army, Brig.-Gen. Aye San, meets secretly at Möng Tom in southern Shan State with representatives of Khun Sa's organisation. Khun Sa's representatives agree to attack rebel groups along the Thai-Burma border in exchange for a free hand in the opium trade.

11 March: Khun Sa's men blow up KMT Gen. Li Wenhuan's house in Chiang Mai. The blast also damages 40 nearby buildings.

12 March: Burmese troops cross into Thailand in an attempt to capture the Karen rebel base of Maw Pokay from the rear.

21 March: Khun Sa's forces attack and occupy the Pa-O rebel headquarters at Koung Neing near the Thai border opposite Mae Hong Son.

1 April: The 2nd Brigade of the SSA and Moh Heng's SURA join forces to become the Tai Revolutionary Council/Army (TRC/TRA) at a meeting at Pieng Luang near the Thai border west of Chiang Dao. Moh Heng is elected chairman of the combined group. Government forces attack Loi Sanklang north of Pieng Luang.

19 May: Brig.-Gen. Aye San tells foreign diplomats and UN officials at a briefing in Taunggyi that his forces have overrun the headquarters of opium warlord Khun Sa. The claim is dismissed by intelligence sources: fighting has been reported only from the TRC's area opposite Pieng Luang and nowhere near Khun Sa's headquarters.

2 June: Thousands of government troops, supported by artillery and air strikes, attack the 2nd Brigade headquarters of the Kachin Independence Army at Gauri Bum in western Kachin State.

22 June: Gauri Bum falls after twenty days of heavy fighting.

4 July: Moh Heng's Shan rebels of the TRC burn forty-seven kilograms of raw opium and twenty-one kilograms of heroin base at a ceremony at their base at Maisung, across the border from Pieng Luang near the Thai-Burma border.

1985

1 February: Thai special forces raid Pieng Luang and apprehend a large number of ex-KMT officials. Twenty-four corpses are found in the forest near Pieng Luang.

3 March: Khun Sa's SUA joins Moh Heng's TRC.

29 May: KNU troops shell the town of Myawadi on the Thai border opposite Mae Sot.

16 June: Myawadi is bombarded again by Karen guerrillas.

August: Char Ui's Lahus go underground again and set up the Lahu National Organisation/Army (LNO/LNA).

9 September–2 October: The CPB holds its third congress at Panghsang. A new 29-member Central Committee is elected (21 full members and 7 alternates). The CPB advocates a united front with ethnic rebel groups but holds firm on Marxism-Leninism Mao Zedong thought.

3 November: All 100-Kyat banknotes are demonetised.

19 November: A 26-man NDF delegation reaches the Kachin rebel headquarters at Pa Jau after an arduous, eight-month trek from the Thai border.

16 December: The NDF begins its meeting at Pa Jau.

1986

21 January: The NDF meeting at Pa Jau is over. The delegates decide to coordinate political and military activities and to seek a military alliance with the CPB. The delegation leaves for Panghsang.

17–24 March: The NDF delegation holds talks at Panghsang with CPB leaders and signs an agreement (on the 24th) to coordinate military activities.

15 August: The KNU on the Thai border denounces the Panghsang agreement between the NDF and the CPB.

October: The new central committee of the CPB meets at Panghsang. The CPB decides to launch a "rectification" campaign against "bourgeois" tendencies within the party, including opium trading by local commanders.

16 November: More than 1,000 heavily armed CPB troops attack government positions on Hsi-Hsinwan mountain in northeastern Shan State. The position is overrun after a bloody, day-long battle.

7 December: The CPB withdraws from Hsi-Hsinwan after three weeks of airstrikes and artillery bombardment from the government's side.

16 December: Government forces open a second front against the CPB near Pangyang in the south. Heavy fighting rages east of the Salween river, opposite Panghsang.

1987

3 January: Government forces push down from Hsi-Hsinwan and capture Möng Paw from the CPB.

4 January: Burmese exiles in the US announce the formation of the Committee for Restoration of Democracy in Burma (CRDB).

6 January: Government forces advance along the Burma Road and capture Panghsai-Kyu Hkok from the CPB.

13 January: Government forces cross the Shweli river opposite Namkham and recapture Khun Hai and Man Hio from the CPB.

31 January: Government forces capture Man Pi camp (south of Möng Paw), the headquarters of the NDF's combined Kachin-Shan-Palaung brigade.

22 May: An offensive is launched against Kachin rebel strongholds near the Chinese border southeast of Myitkyina.

25 May–8 July: The NDF holds its second congress at Manerplaw on the Thai-Burma border. Differences surface between the Karen and the Kachin rebels. Bo Mya is replaced as NDF chairman by Karenni leader Saw Maw Reh.

26 May: Government forces capture Na Hpaw, the headquarters of the Kachin Independence Army.

30 May: Government forces capture Pa Jau, the headquarters of the KIA's political wing, the Kachin Independence Organisation.

10 August: Ne Win admits in a nine-and-a-half minute TV speech that mistakes have been made during his twenty-five years in power, adding that even constitutional changes must be made "in order to keep abreast with the times".

5 September: The government demonetises the Kyats 25, 35 and 75 banknotes without compensation, making 75% of the country's money in circulation worthless. Some 500 to 1,000 students go on a rampage in Rangoon.

26 October: The government reopens schools and universities (closed since 6 September) without incident.

November: Students demonstrate against the government in Pyinmana, Mandalay Division, and Sittwe, Arakan State.

9 December: The two factions of the NMSP (led by Nai Nol Lar and Nai Shwe Kyin respectively) reunite with Nai Shwe Kyin as chairman.

1988

20 January: US congressman and chairman of the House Committee on Narcotics, Charles B. Rangel, visits Rangoon and praises the Burmese government's "anti-drug efforts". He says that the Burma Army's "war on drugs" is a war not only for the Burmese people but also for the international community.

12–18 March: Student unrest rocks Rangoon. It begins with a brawl in a teashop on the 12th and escalates to massive, anti-government street demonstrations on the 18th. Scores of people are killed and at least 1,000 demonstrators are arrested. Universities, colleges and schools are closed.

10 May: Amnesty International publishes a 71-page report saying that the Burma Army is responsible for summary executions, torture and rape in the frontier areas, and for forcing villagers to act as porters and walk ahead of troops as human mine-detectors during campaigns against the insurgents.

30 May: Schools and universities reopen with an attendance rate of about 30%.

15–21 June: Renewed student protests in Rangoon and elsewhere. The riot police, or *Lon Htein*, brutally crush the demonstrations. A curfew is introduced; universities, colleges and all schools are closed again.

July: Anti-government riots are reported from Prome, Pegu Division, and Taunggyi, Shan State.

23 July: Ne Win resigns as BSPP chairman, his last official post. San Yu resigns as president. Sein Lwin becomes new president and BSPP chairman. Karen and Mon rebels battle for control over the important black market gate at Three Pagodas Pass.

8 August: Anti-government demonstrations, involving millions of people, break out simultaneously in towns and cities all over the country. Hundreds of people are killed as the army opens fire on demonstrators in Rangoon.

9 August: Hundreds of people are killed when police and army units open fire on demonstrators in Sagaing.

12 August: Sein Lwin resigns.

19 August: Dr Maung Maung is appointed new president and BSPP chairman.

26 August: Aung San Suu Kyi addresses several hundred thousand people in her public appearance (outside the Shwe Dagon Pagoda in Rangoon).

August–September: All cities, towns and major villages throughout the country are shaken by daily mass demonstrations for democracy. A general strike cripples the country.

8 September: Five small groups in Arakan State (the Arakan Independence Organisation, the Arakan Liberation Party, the Arakan National Liberation Party, the Communist Party of Arakan and the Tribal Nationality Party of Arakan) unite under the banner of the National United Front of Arakan (NUFA).

10 September: The CPB's politburo meets at Möng Ko. Younger cadres, who support the uprising in the towns, are criticised by party chairman Thakin Ba Thein Tin: "The No. 1 point I would like to say is not to let them [i.e. the younger cadres] lose sight of the fact that we are fighting a longterm war. It is impossible for us to make attacks in the towns taking months and years. That is possible only in our rural areas."

18 September: The military, led by Gen. Saw Maung, steps in to shore up the regime, overwhelmed by popular protests, and sets up the State Law and Order

Restoration Council (SLORC). At least 1,000 people are killed as troops spray automatic rifle fire into crowds of angry demonstrators. Thousands of young dissidents begin to flee to the Thai border areas and to the KIA area in the north. The 1974 constitution is abolished.

24 September: The pro-democracy movement forms the National League for Democracy (NLD) with Aung Gyi as its chairman, Tin Oo as vice chairman and Aug San Suu Kyi as general secretary.

September: CPB captures Möng Yang, a garrison town in eastern Shan State, and holds it for a few days. Heavy fighting rages in the area for several weeks.

12 October: Karen rebels recapture their old Mae Tha Waw stronghold near the Thai border which was overrun by government forces in January 1984.

5 November: Dissident students in the Thai border areas form the All-Burma Students' Democratic Front (ABSDF) and vow to take up arms against Gen. Saw Maung's regime.

15 November: US congressman-elect Dana Rohrabacher visits the Thay Baw Bo student camp near the Thai border and promises moral and political support.

18 November: The ten ethnic resistance armies of the NDF plus twelve underground student groups and Burmese opposition parties form the Democratic Alliance of Burma (DAB) at Klerday near the Thai border. Karen rebel leader Bo Mya is elected chairman and Kachin rebel leader Brang Seng vice chairman.

22 November: The Thai government grants temporary asylum to Burmese students who fled after Gen. Saw Maung's takeover.

3 December: Aung Gyi quits the NLD.

10 December: Tin Oo becomes new NLD chairman.

13 December: A combined CPB-KIA force wipes out an entire Burma Army column in Khonsa, east of Kutkai in northeastern Shan State; 106 government soldiers are killed, 17 wounded and 15 captured alive including the column commander. All their weapons and nearly 200,000 rounds of ammunition are seized by the rebels.

14 December: Thai army commander Gen. Chavalit Yongchaiyudh visits Burma and returns with generous logging and fishing deals in return for assisting in the repatriation of Burmese dissident students now staying in the Thai-Burmese border areas.

21 December: As a part of the deal reached between Gen. Chavalit and Gen. Saw Maung in Rangoon on 14 December, a reception centre is set up near Tak airport in Thailand for the repatriation of Burmese dissident students staying in the border areas. The Burma Army recaptures Mae Tha Waw from Karen rebels.

26 December: The first batch of eighty Burmese students are flown back to Rangoon from Tak, Thailand.

27 December: The Thai government allows Burmese aircraft in Thai airspace to take aerial pictures of border areas until 31 March 1989.

1989

5 January: US State Department spokesperson Phyllis Oakley accuses the Burmese military of arresting and killing students who have returned from the Thai border areas.

7 January: Twenty-six Burmese students, who had staged a hunger strike at the repatriation centre at Tak to protest their deportation, are flown back to Rangoon.

10 January: Amnesty International alleges that the Thai military is forcing Burmese students to return to Rangoon from Tak. The Thai government declares that the Burmese students along the border have to return before 31 March, or face charges of illegal entry.

18–20 January: Forty-six Bangkok-based Thai and foreign correspondents are invited to visit Rangoon, Loikaw, Taunggyi, Meiktila and Pagan to meet students who have returned from the Thai border.

19 January: Burmese government troops capture Klerday, the DAB and ABSDF headquarters near the Thai border. U Nu's son, U Aung, sets up the Alliance for Democratic Solidarity (Union of Burma) on the Thai border.

28 January: Bo Yan Naing, one of the Thirty Comrades and a former member of U Nu's resistance, dies in Rangoon at the age of 71.

5 February: Posters begin to appear in several townships in Rangoon urging people to boycott Thai merchandise to protest the logging and fishing deals between Gen. Chavalit and Gen. Saw Maung as well as the forced repatriation of Burmese students from Tak in Thailand.

7 February: A US State Department report on human rights in Asia accuses the Burmese regime of resorting to indiscriminate killings, arbitrary arrests and torture of political prisoners. Karen rebels along the Thai border declare that they will obstruct any logging operations between Thailand and Burma that do not benefit them economically.

20 February: The CPB's politburo holds a crisis meeting at Panghsang. It is revealed that the Chinese have approached the CPB and offered the leaders retirement in China. The CPB leadership reacts angrily to the suggestion, saying: "*We* have no desire to become revisionists."

12 March: A mutiny breaks out in the CPB in the Kokang area.

14 March: The Kokang mutineers capture the CPB's Northern Bureau headquarters at Möng Ko.

20 March: Lo Hsing-han arrives in Kokang for discussions with the CPB mutineers. It is believed that the Rangoon government has given its approval to his mission.

26 March: The Burma Army captures the Karen rebel stronghold of Maw Pokay near the Thai border after fierce fighting.

27 March: Armed Forces Day. Ne Win attends a dinner party in Rangoon, making his first public appearance since relinquishing the chairmanship of the BSPP in July 1988. Sporadic gunfire is heard in Rangoon as groups of students demonstrate against the military. Several thousand people demonstrate in Mandalay and shout anti-government slogans.

1 April: The Thai authorities close down the Tak reception centre for Burmese students.

5 April: Capt. Myint Oo threatens to kill Aung San Suu Kyi in Danubyu during an NLD campaign trip in the Irrawaddy delta region.

11–13 April: Thai deputy foreign minister Prapas Limpabandhu pays a four-day visit to Rangoon. Gen. Saw Maung offers a "priority trade reward" to Thailand.

13–16 April: The Buddhist New Year, *Thingyan*, is celebrated in Rangoon with an anti-government slogan competition at the NLD's headquarters on University Avenue. Heavily armed troops cruise the streets of Rangoon.

17 April: Rebellious Wa troops capture the CPB's Panghsang headquarters near the Chinese border, ending the 41-year-long Communist insurgency in Burma. The CPB's ageing leadership flees to Meng Lien in China.

20 April: Leaders of the CPB mutiny come to Lashio to meet (former brigadier-general turned politician) Aung Gyi and (former Kokang *saohpa*) Olive Yang.

22 April: Khin Nyunt, the head of Burma's military intelligence, travels up to Kunlong on the Salween river, opposite Kokang, to meet with Pheung Kya-fu and other CPB mutineers.

23 April: Arrests begin of students who participated in the NLD New Year slogan competition. Student leader Moe Thi Zon, the chairman of the Democratic Party for a New Society, leaves Rangoon for the Thai border.

4 May: Thakin Soe, the veteran Red Flag Communist leader, dies in Rangoon at the age of 84.

20 May: Four hundred Burmese troops cross into Thailand in an attempt to attack the Karen rebel base at Wangkha from the rear and burn down Ban Wang Kaew on the Thai side.

27 May: The SLORC announces that it has changed the formal name of the country from Burma to Myanmar. It also rejects Thai-proposed peace talks with the country's ethnic rebels.

19 June: The primary schools reopen after having been closed since 9 August 1988.

21 June: Thousands of people commemorate the first anniversary of the massacre in Myenigone market in Rangoon. Troops open fire and kill one person. Aung San Suu Kyi is briefly detained.

23 June: The *Working People's Daily* publishes fierce attacks on the NLD and Aung San Suu Kyi, who responds by beginning to criticise Ne Win openly at mass meetings in Rangoon.

7 July: A bomb explodes at the Syriam oil refinery near Rangoon.

10 July: A bomb explodes at Rangoon City Hall.

18 July: The confrontation between the NLD and the SLORC reaches its climax as the former announces its own plans for commemorating Martyrs' Day, the 42nd anniversary of the assassination of Aung San. The SLORC responds by sending several battalions of heavily armed troops into Rangoon.

19 July: Martyrs' Day. Thousands of soldiers patrol the streets of Rangoon to prevent the NLD's march from taking place. The NLD cancels its plans to hold a separate ceremony.

20 July: The SLORC places Aung San Suu Kyi and Tin Oo under house arrest for one year. Scores of NLD workers are arrested nationwide.

23 July: The SLORC announces the formation of three-man military tribunals to "try those who have committed offences". Sentences range from three years' jail with hard labour, to death. Arrests of oppositionists continue. At the same time, thousands of criminal prisoners are released.

5 August: Brig.-Gen. Khin Nyunt holds a six-hour press conference in Rangoon and accuses the NLD of being manipulated by the CPB. He also claims he has unearthed a CPB conspiracy to seize power.

14 August: The middle schools reopen. Widespread arrests of political activists are reported.

15 August: A spokesman for the KNU says that a Karen rebel carried out the bombing at the Syriam oil refinery on 7 July, and not the three people who were sentenced to death.

21 August: Teachers' training institutes reopen.

26 August: The US embassy in Rangoon says it has credible reports that the government is beating and torturing political prisoners.

29 August: A military tribunal in Shwebo sentences eleven people to death for alleged involvement in an attack on a police station in Taze, Mandalay Division, in September 1988. "So few students were killed during last year's uprising in Burma that it is not even worth mentioning," the health and education minister, Dr Pe Thein, says.

30 August: Munitions arrive in Rangoon by ship from Israel and Belgium via Singapore.

2 September: The SSA enters into a cease-fire agreement with the SLORC similar to those reached between Rangoon and forces of the former CPB.

9 September: Brig.-Gen. Khin Nyunt gives a seven-hour-long speech, claiming he has discovered a rightist conspiracy to seize power, allegedly involving some foreign embassies in Rangoon.

25 September: The secondary schools reopen.

6 October: A Burmese airliner en route from Mergui to Rangoon is hijacked to Thailand.

18–29 October: A 24-man senior Burmese military delegation, led by Lieut.-Gen. Than Shwe, visits China.

11 November: Chao Ngi Lai and some ex-CPB Wa officers are taken by helicopter to Lashio to meet Khin Nyunt and other high-ranking SLORC officials.

15 November: Amnesty International publishes a report, estimating that 6,000 people have been arrested for political reasons since September 1988, 3,000 of them since July 1989. Other estimates put the total higher. Amnesty International also says that 100 people have been sentenced to death by the newly established military tribunals.

16 November–6 December: Secret peace talks are held in Rangoon between the SLORC and insurgent leaders who in March–April led a mutiny against the political leadership of the now defunct CPB.

5 December: The former 101 War Zone of the CPB in Kachin State join the other mutineers to enter into peace talks with Rangoon.

11 December: About 100 political parties have announced that they are going to participate in the May 1990 elections. Demonstrations continue in Mandalay.

15 December: The forces of the former CPB's 101 War Zone in Kachin State make peace with the government, the last of the ex-CPB units to do so.

22 December: The NLD chairman, Tin Oo, is sentenced to three years imprisonment with hard labour by a military tribunal in Rangoon.

29 December: The SLORC places U Nu under house arrest along with twelve of his associates. Government forces, using Thai territory as a springboard, capture the Karen rebel base at Phalu on the Thai border.

1990

16 January: Rangoon's Elections Commission bars Aung San Suu Kyi from contesting the elections. Troops move into Rangoon as hundreds of people protest against the decision.

24 January: The Karen rebel base of Thay Baw Bo, which also houses several hundred dissident Burmese students, falls to government forces.

31 January: Walay, another Karen rebel base on the Thai border, is captured by government forces; 6,000 villagers and dissident students have fled to Thailand since the fighting began at Palu in December.

January: The KIA's 4th Brigade in northeastern Shan State makes peace with Rangoon and becomes a government-recognised militia force.

5–11 February: Heavy fighting rages at Three Pagodas Pass on the Thai-Burmese border. Burmese troops cross into Thailand and capture the headquarters of the Mon insurgents on the 11th. Some 6,000 to 10,000 Karen and Mon villagers plus 700 dissident students flee to Thailand.

13 February: The United Nations' Commission on Human Rights decides at its 46th Session in Geneva to appoint a special envoy to investigate human-rights abuses in Burma. It also calls on the SLORC to allow "all political parties and personalities . . . to participate in the electoral process and the elections".

Late February: A Burmese delegation visits Washington to lobby for resumption of US aid to Burma. The State Department refuses to see them, but they speak to the DEA and Congressman Charles B. Rangel, the Chairman of the House Commmittee on Narcotics.

13 March: Thai army chief, Gen. Chavalit Yongchaiyudh, pays a "goodwill visit" to Burma. His second since the September 1988 take-over.

21 March: Ye Thiha and Ye Yint, the two students who hijacked a Burmese airliner to Thailand on 6 October 1989, are sentenced to six years in jail by a court in Bangkok.

22 March: Troops from the NMSP and the ABSDF enter Ye town in Mon State. The town is bombed by the Burmese air force, killing several civilians.

27 March: Pa-O rebels of the PNO/PNA decide to make peace with Rangoon and become a government-recognised militia force.

10 April: Burmese aeroplanes bomb positions near the Karen rebel headquarters of Manerplaw. Hundreds of refugees flee to Thailand.

21 April: Palaung rebels of the PSLP/PSLA make peace with Rangoon and become a government-recognised militia force.

30 April: The SLORC stages a drug burning show in Rangoon. The DEA in Rangoon arranges for a CBS television crew to film the event.

2 May: Amnesty International releases a report saying that torture of political prisoners is widespread in Burmese prisons. It also charges that the army has "almost unrestricted authority to carry out arbitrary arrests, to detain prisoners incommunicado for months without charge or trial and to interrogate them using torture".

27 May: More than 70% of the people vote in Burma's first multi-party general elections since 1960. The NLD wins a landslide victory and captures about 60% of the vote—and 392 out of 485 seats in the *Pyithu Hluttaw.*

30 May: Gen. Saw Maung says that the SLORC will "lawfully hand over power but threatens to national security may disrupt the process".

8 June: The SLORC says that the assembly can be convened only after election expenses and candidates' objections to the poll result have been settled.

19 June: Gen. Saw Maung rules out "quick power transfer" and declares that "a new constitution must be drafted". He emphasises that this will be a complicated and lengthy process.

20 June: The NLD calls for a dialogue between the political parties and the SLORC.

29 July: The NLD candidates who have been elected to the assembly meet at the Gandhi Hall in Rangoon and adopt a resolution calling for "frank and sincere discussions with good faith and with the object of national reconciliation" and "a speedy transformation into a democratic system." The delegates also urge the SLORC to release Tin Oo, Aung San Suu Kyi and all other political prisoners. Heavily armed troops patrol Rangoon.

7 August: The Rangoon commander, Maj.-Gen. Myo Nyunt, denies that the SLORC is delaying the handing over of power.

8 August: The second anniversary of the 8.8.88 uprising. Troops fire on demonstrators in Mandalay, killing two monks and two students.

10 August: A SLORC spokesman, Col. Than Tun, denies that anyone was killed during the shooting in Mandalay. He also accuses the NLD of "inciting unrest". Soldiers carrying rifles and machine-guns drive around Rangoon in military trucks. Scores of people are arrested nationwide. The first major shipment of arms and ammunition from China arrives in Rangoon.

27 August: The monks in Mandalay declare that they will not accept offerings from military personnel, or take part in military organised ceremonies, in effect excommunicating the SLORC.

2 September: The Rangoon commander, Maj.-Gen. Myo Nyunt, states that the "NLD is not ready to rule".

7 September: The SLORC arrests the NLD's acting leader, Kyi Maung, and acting party secretary Chit Khaing along with four NLD leaders in Mandalay. People in Mandalay rally against the arrests.

28 September: Arrests continue all over Burma. The US, Britain and other countries protest against arrests of their local embassy staff in Rangoon.

22 October: Troops raid 133 monasteries in Mandalay. Scores of monks are arrested in Mandalay and Rangoon.

22 November: The first drug burning show is held in the former CPB area as Kokang heroin trader Pheung Kya-shin acts as master of ceremonies and sets fire to opium and heroin at Lao Khai in Kokang. SLORC officials, UN personnel, DEA agents and a TV crew from Hong Kong attend the ceremony.

18 December: Eight NLD MPs who have fled to the Thai border set up the National Coalition Government of the Union of Burma (NCGUB) at a meeting at Manerplaw. "prime minister" is Sein Win, Aung San Suu Kyi's cousin.

December: The 4th Brigade of the KIA in northeastern Shan State makes peace with the SLORC.

1991

11 January: The former 4th Brigade of the KIA is legalised and becomes the Kachin Democratic Army (KDA).

28 January: A second drug burning ceremoy is held in the northeast, this time at Möng Ko as local drug traffickers burn some of their opium and heroin. SLORC officials, UN personnel, DEA agents and Thai journalists attend the ceremony.

14 February: The National League for Democracy (Liberated Area) is set up at the KNU's Manerplaw headquarters by MPs and other NLD activists who have fled to the Thai border.

22 February: The Democatic Front of Burma becomes the Anti-Military Dictatorship National Solidarity Committee with Gen. Bo Mya (KNU) as chairman and Win Khet (NLD) as general secretary.

27 March: The rebel Pa-O National Organisation decides to make peace with Rangoon.

11 April: Pa-O rebels of the PNO sign a cease-fire agreement with the SLORC in Taunggyi.

21 April: Palaung rebels of the PSLP sign a cease-fire agreement with the SLORC.

5 May: Heroin trader Lin Mingxian stages a drug burning ceremony at his Möng La headquarters north of Kengtung. SLORC officials, UN personnel, DEA agents and Chinese embassy officials attend the ceremony.

Early May: Eleven Chinese-made F7 jet fighters are delivered to Burma as part of a US$1 billion arms deal between Beijing and Rangoon which also includes naval patrol boats, tanks, armoured personnel carriers, light arms, anti-aircraft guns and missiles, ammunition and other military equipment.

14 August–24 October: The ABSDF holds a marathon meeting on the Thai border. The front splits into two factions, one led by Moe Thi Zun and the other by Dr. Naing Aung.

21–26 August: Gen. Saw Maung visits China. He meets Prime Minister Li Peng and President Yang Shangkun, who promise more political and military aid to Rangoon.

29 August: Thirteen dissidents are arrested in Rangoon and accused of having links with ethnic rebels in the border areas.

30 August: Sixteen more dissidents are arrested on similar charges.

6 September: UN secretary general Javier Perez de Cuellar appeals for the release of Aung San Suu Kyi.

8 September: SLORC member Lieut.-Gen. Aung Ye Gyaw says that the junta may stay in power for another ten years.

3 October: The NCGUB and other dissidents call for UN sanctions against Burma.

4 October: Intelligence chief Maj.-Gen. Khin Nyunt says in a radio speech that 10,516 civil servants have been dismissed from their jobs since the SLORC assumed power.

8 October: Fighting breaks out between Karen rebels and government forces near the town of Bogale in the Irrawaddy delta southwest of Rangoon.

10 October: Heavy fighting continues in the Irrawaddy delta. The government uses airstrikes and gunboats to fight the rebels.

14 October: The Nobel Peace Prize Committee in Oslo, Norway, announces that this year's prize will be awarded to Aung San Suu Kyi. She provides "one of the most extraordinary examples of civil courage in Asia in recent decades".

17 October: The Bangkok-based Polish ambassador to Burma is refused a visa to go to Rangoon and congratulate Aung San Suu Kyi.

22–26 October: A team from the United Nations Commission on Human Rights visits Rangoon to continue human-rights investigations.

23 October: The Singapore-based Norwegian ambassador to Burma is refused a visa to go to Rangoon and congratulate Aung San Suu Kyi.

29 November: The UN General Assembly adopts a resolution condemning human-rights abuses in Burma and urging the release of Aung San Suu Kyi and other political prisoners.

2–6 December: Philippine foreign minister Raul Manglapus pays an official visit to Rangoon to discuss human rights issues on behalf of the Association of Southeast Asian Nations (ASEAN). The SLORC reportedly tell him that they fear "Nuremberg-style trials" if they give up power to a civilian government. They also vow not to release Aung San Suu Kyi.

10 December: Aung San Suu Kyi's eldest son, Alexander, accepts the Nobel Peace Prize in Oslo. Groups of students demonstrate in Rangoon for her release and democratic reform.

11 December: Heavily armed soldiers clear all the students from the dormitories at Rangoon University. Several hundred students are arrested. All universities are closed "indefinitely".

12 December: More troops are deployed around Aung San Suu Kyi's house in Rangoon. The state-run radio says a bomb has exploded in Mandalay, killing two bystanders.

15 December: The NLD remaining in Rangoon expels Aung San Suu Kyi from the party. The NLD along the Thai border condemns the decision, branding it illegal. Ne Win summons SLORC leaders and berates them for failing to win over the people.

17–19 December: Japanese deputy foreign minister Kunihiko Saito visits Rangoon to try to persuade the SLORC to implement democratic reforms. He meets Foreign Minister Ohn Gyaw.

18 December: Rangoon-based sources say 900 students have been arrested since the 11th.

19 December: It is reported that Gen. Saw Maung suffered a nervous breakdown on the 17th. Saw Maung was hospitalised during Saito's visit which explains why he was unable to see the SLORC chairman.

21 December: Burmese forces cross the border into Bangladesh and attack an army outpost. One border guard and three civilians are killed.

22 December: The Inter-Parliamentary Union, an organisation of parliamentarians worldwide, says that sixty-four elected Burmese MPs have been arrested since the May 1990 election and urges their release.

28 December: Intelligence chief Maj.-Gen. Khin Nyunt says that the SLORC will "never accept" Aung San Suu Kyi.

31 December: The EC countries state that they will withdraw their defence attaches from Rangoon.

December: More Muslim Rohingyas from Arakan State flee across the border, bringing the number of refugees in Bangladesh to nearly 20,000. The situation along the frontier is tense as Burma denies it ever carried out any cross-border attack. Both the Burmese and the Bangladeshis beef up their troop presence along the common border.

1992
January: Heavy fighting breaks out between Karen rebels and government forces along the Thai-Burma border. The government forces begin a push to capture

the Karen rebel headquarters of Manerplaw, which is also the base for the NCGUB and other dissidents.

9 January: Two more NLD MPs are disqualified, bringing the number up to seventy-one. At least 100 school children are arrested in the latest crackdown in Rangoon.

21 January: The Committee for Islamic Solidarity in Indonesia likens the SLORC to the Nazis and urges the UN to intervene to stop atrocities against the Rohingyas. The number of Rohingya refugees in Bangladesh reaches 30,000.

25 January: The NLD expels its jailed chairman, Tin Oo, from the party. Shortly afterwards, a military tribunal extends his jail term from three to ten years.

28 January: Eight NLD politicians, including four MPs, flee to Kachin rebel-held territory in northern Burma.

29 January: The SLORC appoints three more ministers to the cabinet, in effect making its government permanent and nullifying the outcome of the May 1990 election. One of them is Brig.-Gen. Myo Thant, new minister for information, who until then had been involved with "development work" with the ex-CPB mutineers in the northeast.

Late January: The six states of ASEAN meet in Singapore, reject Western pressure for a tougher stand against the SLORC and instead advocate a policy of "constructive engagement".

31 January: UN personnel, DEA agents and diplomats attend an opium eradication show in Kokang, headed by heroin trader Pheung Kya-shin.

Late January–early February: Two thousand and eighty-six university teachers have to attend a four-week "re-education course". They are blamed for the student unrest in December.

7 February: The SLORC appoints new chiefs of the air force and navy. Rear Adm. Than Nyunt replaces Vice Adm. Maung Maung Khin, and Maj.-Gen. Thein Win replaces Lieut.-Gen. Tin Tun.

11 February: Singapore condemns the SLORC for the exodus of Rohingyas to Bangladesh.

19 February: Brig.-Gen. Thaung Myint is appointed new minister for social welfare and resettlement. He has until now been one of the most powerful officers involved with "development work" with the ex-CPB mutineers in the northeast.

22 February: The European Community donates US$670,000 to the Rohingya refugees in Bangladesh.

23–26 February: Lao prime minister Khamtai Siphandone visits Burma. He is the first head of foreign government to arrive in Rangoon since the massacres of 1988.

25 February: A helicopter crashes into two jet fighters, ready to take off from Hmawbi Air Base north of Rangoon to bomb Karen rebel camps along the Thai border. Seven people die in the accident. Fighting continues along the border as the SLORC throws hundreds of ill-trained teenagers into the battle for Manerplaw. The number of Rohingya refugees in Bangladesh reaches 100,000.

4 March: The United Nations Human Rights Commission in Geneva condemns the SLORC for widespread human-rights abuses. It also decides to nominate a "special rapporteur" to investigate the situation in Burma.

14 March: Sleeping Dog Hill, a strategic mountain ten kilometres west of Manerplaw, is captured by government forces after two months of heavy fighting.

18 March: Brunei joins other ASEAN states in condemning the SLORC for the exodus of Rohingyas to Bangladesh.

20 March: SLORC vice chairman Gen. Than Shwe takes over the post of defence minister from the ailing Gen. Saw Maung. A further nine political parties are banned, bringing the number of legal political parties down from 235 at the time of the election in May 1990 to ten.

26 March: The SLORC blames the candidates for the delay in convening the national assembly which was elected in May 1990. "They have given inaccurate accounts of their campaign expenses," the statement says.

27 March: Armed Forces Day, the deadline for capturing Manerplaw, passes without any major advances along the Karen front despite airstrikes and heavy artillery fire from nearby government positions.

30 March: A Western diplomat says that the SLORC has fired hundreds of teachers and administrators who failed the four-week "re-education course" in January–February.

Early April: The UN under-secretary general for Humanitarian Affairs, Jan Eliasson, visits Burma and Bangladesh in an attempt to find a solution to the Rohingya refugee crisis. He tours the Arakan border areas in Burma as well as the refugee camps in Bangladesh. The number of Rohingya refugees in Bangladesh has increased to more than 250,000.

Mid-April: Prince Khaled Sultan Abdul Aziz, commander of the Saudi contingent in the 1991 Gulf War, visits Dhaka, Bangladesh, and recommends a Desert Storm-like action against Burma; "just what [the UN] did to liberate Kuwait".

23 April: Gen. Saw Maung steps down as SLORC chairman in favour of Gen. Than Shwe.

24 April: Than Shwe is appointed prime minister and defence minister. The SLORC announces that it will convene a National Convention to draft a new constitution. Eight more NLD MPs are disqualified.

25 April: The same NLD MPs are released from jail in Rangoon. U Nu, Bohmu Aung and three other political prisoners are also released. Japan congratulates Gen. Than Shwe on his appointment.

27 April: Maj.-Gen. Maung Hla, overall commander of the offensive against the Karens, announces that he has suspended operations along the Thai border. Some students who were arrested with Aung San Suu Kyi in July 1990 are released from jail.

28 April: In Dhaka, the Burmese and Bangladesh foreign ministers announce that they have agreed to repatriate the Rohingya refugees to Burma.

1 May: Cho Cho Kyaw Nyein, Khin Maung Swe and nine other political prisoners are released.

3–16 May: A lavish sports festival is held in Rangoon. "Myanmar athletes—a world to conquer" is the motto. Some foreign journalists are allowed in to cover the event.

7 May: More political prisoners as well as 190 criminal convicts, who had served as porters in the operations against the Karens are released.

10 May: Two hundred and fifty-three convicts are released from jail.

13 May: Fourteen political prisoners, including some NLD activists, are released from jail.

14 May: Two hundred and twelve convicts who had served as porters in the operations against the Karens are released.

28 May: The SLORC sets up a steering committee to discuss the forthcoming National Convention which will be held "in accordance with Decree 1/90 of 27 July 1990". It consists of twenty-eight representatives from seven political parties and fifteen SLORC officials led by Maj.-Gen. Myo Nyunt.

23 June: The steering committee for the National Convention holds its first meeting in Rangoon. Western diplomats dismiss the event as mere "window dressing".

1 September: The Karenni rebels recapture their old headquarters at Hweponglaung near the Thai border opposite Mae Hong Son.

2 November: The Burma Army launches a counter-offensive against the Karenni rebels and retakes Hweponglaung.

29 November: Fighting breaks out between the Pheungs and the Yang clan in Kokang. The SLORC remains neutral in the conflict.

December: The drug war in Kokang continues. The Yangs win and drive Pheung Kya-shin and Pheung Kya-fu out of the area.

1993

9 January: The National Convention meets in Rangoon but is suspended after two days.

22–24 January: The SLORC and the KIA hold peace talks in Myitkyina.

1 February: The National Convention is reconvened.

9 February: Forces belonging to Khun Sa's Möng Tai Army kill sixty-one villagers near Langkhö in southern Shan State.

16–20 February: Eight Nobel Peace Prize laureates, including the Dalai Lama and South African archbishop Desmond Tutu, visit Thailand and call for the release of Aung San Suu Kyi. All of them, except the Dalai Lama, also visit Karen refugee camps along the Thai-Burma border.

17–19 February: Karen, Kachin and Mon rebels participate in a peace seminar at the Carter Centre in Atlanta, Georgia.

28 February: Win Ko, NCGUB minister for finance, is found murdered in his hotel room in Kunming, Yunnan.

4–6 March: The SLORC and the KIA meet again in Myitkyina.

16 March: Three hundred and seventy-four members of the Japanese Diet appeal to UN secretary-general Dr. Boutros Boutros-Ghali to pressure the SLORC to release Aung San Suu Kyi and to hand over power to the MPs who were elected in May 1990.

20 March: Forces belonging to Khun Sa's Möng Tai Army massacre more than 100 villagers near Möng Hsat.

7 April: The National Convention is suspended amidst opposition from national minority representatives who disagree with the military's demand for a highly centralised political structure.

6–8 April: The KIA holds a third round of talks with Burma Army representatives in Myiktyina. The two parties agree on a cease-fire.

24 April: Lieut.-Gen. Khin Nyunt pays his first visit to Panghsang (now renamed Pangkham) since the CPB leadership was driven out on 17 April 1989.

7 June: The National Convention meets again in Rangoon. Lieut.-Gen. Myo Nyunt says that the new constitution must guarantee a leading role for the army in "national politics".

July: KNU and DAB leader Bo Mya visits the United States, where he meets State Department officials.

August: US Congressman Charles Rangel and some other American politicians visit Burma. On the 29th they meet heroin trader Lin Mingxian at Möng La.

16 September: The National Convention is adjourned once again because of continued opposition mainly from national minority parties which advocate a federal system.

28–29 September: The KIA holds a third round of talks with Burma Army representatives in Myiktyina. KIA commander Maj.-Gen. Zau Mai meets intelligence chief Lieut.-Gen. Khin Nyunt.

15 October: Twelve political activists are sentenced to long prison terms for criticising the SLORC's National Convention. The DAB and the NDF suspend the membership of the KIO because of its unilateral peace agreement with Rangoon.

23 October: KNU leader Bo Mya arrives in London. He openly criticises the Kachin cease-fire with Rangoon.

3 December: The UN General Assembly passes a resolution condemning human rights abuses in Burma and calling for the release of Aung San Suu Kyi and other political prisoners. It also urges the SLORC to restore democracy in Burma.

6 December: The DAB and the NDF announce that they would be prepared to send a delegation to Rangoon for peace talks, but that any agreement would have to be reached with the two front organisations, not with any individual member.

December: The Burma Army launches an offensive against Khun Sa's Möng Tai Army along the Thai border.

Appendix 2:
Men and Women of Burma's Insurgency

A BI

Lahu. Born around 1953 in the Möng Hsat area of southern Shan State. The nephew of Lahu *payah* (politico-religious leader) Char Ui. Joined the Lahu uprising in Möng Hsat-Möng Tun in January 1973. Went to Panghsang in 1974 to contact the Communist Party of Burma. Returned in 1978 as military commander of the CPB forces in the Möng Hsat area. Fought with Khun Sa at Doi Lang mountain over the control of opium routes across the Thai border in the early 1980s. Killed in action with the Burma Army near Möng Hsat in 1985.

AUNG, Bohmu

Burman. Born in 1910 in Kyauktaga near Pegu. One of the Thirty Comrades and leader of the People's Volunteer Organisation in the late 1940s. Member of the Constituent Assembly and Speaker of the Chamber of Deputies. Minister of Defence and a prominent member of U Nu's *Pyidaungsu* (Union) Party before the 1962 coup. In jail 1962–63 and 1963–68. Joined U Nu's Thai-border based resistance in 1972 and later took refuge in Chiang Rai, Thailand. Returned to Burma during the 1980 amnesty and participated in the 1988 uprising for democracy. Arrested along with U Nu in December 1989 and released in April 1992.

AUNG GYI, *yebaw*

Burman. Born in 1922 in Rangoon. Obtained a BA in history from Rangoon University in 1940. Active member of the student movement and the Communist Party of Burma. Participated in the 1947 British Empire Communist Parties Conference in London together with Thakin Ba Thein Tin and, in February 1948, went to India to attend the Calcutta Youth Conference. Went to China with Than Shwe in 1950. In Sichuan, China 1950–68. Participated in party congresses in the Soviet Union and Bulgaria. One of the Beijing Returnees who participated in the 1963 peace talks. Played a leading role in the purges in the Pegu Yoma in 1967–68. Killed in action near Nyaunglebin on 3 April 1969.

AUNG KHAM HTI

Pa-O. Born in 1931 in Kyauktalong in the hills south of Taunggyi, the Shan State capital. Buddhist monk and Pa-O community leader in southern Shan State; joined the Pa-O movement in 1966. Disrobed in 1969 to take a more active part in underground politics. Became chairman of the Pa-O National Organisation in December 1977. Based himself at Kyauktalong with a few hundred men. Signed a peace treaty with the Rangoon government in March 1991. The PNO was legalised shortly afterwards and subsequently withdrew from the National Democratic Front and the Democratic Alliance of Burma. Its armed wing now is a government-recognised militia force.

AUNG TUN, Nai

Mon. Born in 1913 in Thanbyuzayat. Headman of Pa-nga village near Thanbyuzayat before he went underground in August 1948. Chairman of the Mon People's Front 1952–58, Surrendered in July 1958 and was elected to parliament in 1960. Minister for Mon affairs and rehabilitation in U Nu's government 1960–62. Imprisoned when Gen. Ne Win seized power in March 1962. Released in 1968 to become a member of the 33-man Internal Unity Advisory Board; died on 29 April 1970 in Moulmein. His son, Nai Tin Aung, now heads the Mon refugee committee in Sangkhlaburi, Thailand.

AUNG WIN, Sai

Shan. Born in 1937 in Loi-Lem, Shan State. Vice chairman of the Rangoon University Students' Union 1961–62. Participated in the 1962 student movement against the military. Joined the Communist Party of Burma in January 1964 in Henzada district. Served in the Pegu Yoma and went to Shan State in 1969. Became a member of the CPB's central committee in 1975. Tried to persuade the Shan State Army to join the CPB, but failed. In charge of the Shan language programme of the CPB's clandestine broadcasting station and later head of the economic department at Mong Ko, the CPB's northern bureau headquarters. Moved to Panghsang in April 1987 and joined the CPB mutiny in 1989. Surrendered in June 1990. Now fronting for prominent businessmen in Taunggyi.

BA HEIN, Thakin

Burman. Born in 1913 in Mandalay. President of the All-Burma Students' Union in 1938. Translated Marxist literature for the *Nagani* Book Club in Rangoon. Leader of the *Dohbama Asiayone* and the leftist Freedom Bloc; organised the oil workers in Yenangyaung. One of the first *thakins* to join the CPB in 1939. Imprisoned by the British in Mandalay, 1940–42. Served in the wartime government of Dr. Ba Maw but went underground in 1945 as a resistance leader in the Toungoo area. Became member of the All-Burma Trade Union Congress, 1945–46. Editor of the *People's Power* or *Pyithu Ana* magazine. Died from malaria on 20 November 1946. Married to Daw Khin Gyi, who attended the second congress of the Communist Party of India in February 1948 in Calcutta. Considered the father of "true communism" in Burma by the CPB.

BA THEIN, Sara

Shan. Born around 1920 in Möng Nai. Christian. Became deputy commander of the Kengtung-based Shan National Army in 1961. Succeeded Sao Ngar Kham as SNA commander in 1964. Closely connected with the CIA; sent soldiers to fight in Laos. Ousted in 1967 and settled in Hat Wai near Chiang Khong, northern Thailand. Surrendered along with thirty of his remaining followers on 16 May 1976. Imprisoned on his return. Died in Kengtung in 1990.

BA THEIN TIN, Thakin

Born in 1914 in Tavoy; son of a Chinese petty trader and an ethnic Burman mother. Attended primary and secondary school at Tavoy, passing his matriculation exam in 1931 and gaining admittance to Rangoon University. Unable to further his studies because his debt-ridden father could not afford university fees. Became full-time worker for the *Dohbama Asiayone* in 1938 and joined the Communist Party of Burma in October 1939.

District party committee organiser in Tavoy; fought against the Japanese in Tavoy in 1945. Became a member of the central committee at the second congress in 1945; became a member of the politburo in 1946. Participated in the 1947 British Empire Communist Parties Conference in London and, in February 1948, went to Calcutta together with then CPB chairman Thakin Than Tun to attend the second congress of the Communist Party of India.

Went underground in March 1948 and was elected vice chairman of the CPB in 1950. Left for China in 1953. Attended several party congresses in Moscow and Beijing, and visited Hanoi in 1963. *De facto* leader of the CPB from the mid-1960s onwards, but did not become official party chairman until the death of Thakin Zin on 15 March 1975. Resided in China until 1978. Re-elected chairman at the CPB's third congress in 1985. Fled to China during the mutiny in April 1989.

BA THIN, Saw

Karen. Born in 1927 in Henzada. Educated at the American Baptist Mission Karen High School in Henzada. Clerk at the War Office in Rangoon in 1946; joined the Karen uprising in January 1949. Fought in Insein and later in the Toungoo-Kawkareik-Hlaingbwe area in the east with 2nd Division commander, Gen. Thakarbaw. Member of the central committee of the Karen National Union since 1963; head of the KNU's educational department in the 1970s and 1980s. KNU general secretary and prime minister of the rebel Karen state of Kawthoolei since 1984.

BA U GYI, Saw

Karen. Born in 1905 in Bassein. Son of a wealthy landlord; graduated from Rangoon University in 1925. Called to the English bar in 1927; a lawyer by profession. Minister of revenue in 1937. Achieved prominence in the immediate post-World War II era when frictions between the Burmans and the Karens escalated. Information councillor in the pre-independence cabinet 1946–February 1947 and councillor for transport and communications February–April 1947; advocated a separate dominion for the Karens within the Commonwealth. Formed the Karen National Union in February 1946. Led the Karen uprising in January 1949. Killed near Kawkareik close to the Thai border on 12 August 1950.

BA ZAN, Mahn

Karen. Born in 1916 in Maubin. School teacher at Ma-ubin before joining the Karen National Union in early 1947. Became the first commander of the Karen National Defence Organisation on 16 July 1947. Negotiated an alliance with the Communist Party of Burma in the Pegu Yoma in 1952, which led to the formation of the National Democratic United Front. Vice chairman of the Karen National United Party in 1956. Was sent over to the Thai border to negotiate with Bo Mya in

1968. Chairman of the KNU from 1969 until 10 August 1976. Died at the KNU's Manerplaw headquarters on the Thai border in May 1982.

BENSON, Naw Louisa

Karen. Born in 1941 in Rangoon. The daughter of Saw Benson, a Jew of Portuguese origin, and his Karen wife, Chit Khin. Miss Burma (1956 and 1958) and film star. Educated in Rangoon and in Boston, USA. In 1964 married Lin Tin, a Karen rebel leader who had surrendered. She led his former 5th Brigade back into the jungle when he was killed near Thaton in September 1965. Married Glenn Craig, an American, in 1967 and now lives in California. Active in overseas Karen associations and in the movement for democracy in Burma.

BOON TAI, Sao (a.k.a.) Sai Pan

Shan. Born in 1935 in Kengtung. Studied medicine in Rangoon; student leader in the 1950s and active in the Shan literary society. Joined the *Noom Suk Harn* in 1958 and the Shan State Independence Army SSIA in 1960. Participated in the 1963 peace talks in Rangoon. Colonel in the Shan State Army. Succeeded Khun Kya Nu as the president of the Shan State Progress Party in 1976. Resigned in 1979. Assassinated in Chiang Mai, northern Thailand, on 21 August 1983.

BRANG SENG

Kachin. Born in 1930 in Hpakan, Kachin State. Educated at the Kachin Baptist School, Myitkyina; entered Rangoon University in 1952 and obtained a BA and a BEd in 1955. Burma's delegate to the YMCA in Singapore in 1957; headmaster of Myitkyina Baptist School 1957–60 and its principal 1961–63. Went underground with the Kachin Independence Army/Organisation in 1963. Led the first Kachin rebel delegation to China in 1967. Chairman of the KIO since 1975. Made peace with the Communist Party of Burma in 1976 and led a delegation of the National Democratic Front to the CPB's Panghsang headquarters in March 1986. Left Kachin State in late 1986 to travel abroad. Became vice chairman of the Democratic Alliance of Burma on 18 November 1988 and was attached to its headquarters at Manerplaw on the Thai-Burma border until the KIO made peace with Rangoon in April 1993. Suffered a stroke on 21 October 1993 in Kunming, where he is now in hospital.

CHANG CHIFU (a.k.a.) Khun Sa

Sino-Shan. Born in 1934 in Hpa-perng village in the Loi Maw area of Möng Yai, northern Shan State, of a Chinese father and a Shan mother. His father died when he was a child, and his mother remarried the Shan *myosa* of Möng Tawm (tax collector under the Möng Yai *saohpa*). Chang grew up with his Chinese grandfather who was the headman of Loi Maw. Joined an armed band in the Loi Maw area in the early 1950s and frequently shifted sides between the government and the rebels. In 1963 his private army was converted into a government-recognised *Ka Kwe Ye* (home guard) force under the northeastern command of the Burmese Army in Lashio.

His forces attacked Shan rebel forces in the area and in return he was allowed to trade in opium and heroin. Became one of Burma's most prominent drug traffickers in the 1960s, but lost to KMT rivals in a famous battle at the Lao-Thai-Burma border junction in July 1967. His fortunes dwindled and he was arrested by the Burmese authorities on 20 October 1969.

His men subsequently went underground and on 16 April 1973 kidnapped two Soviet doctors from the hospital in Taunggyi. In exchange for their freedom, Chang was released from Mandalay jail on 7 September 1974. He joined his men underground in February 1976 and moved to Ban Hin Taek near the Burmese border in northern Thailand.

He then assumed the Shan name Khun Sa and his former home guard unit was renamed the Shan United Army, ostensibly a rebel army. He was forced out of Thailand in January 1982 but quickly built new bases on the Burmese side of the border, where he established a new working relationship with Burma's military authorities. He merged his SUA with Moh Heng's Tai Revolutionary Council on 25 March 1985.

Khun Sa became chairman of the TRC (renamed the Shan State Restoration Council in1991) in September 1991 following Moh Heng's death in July. "Resigned" in July 1992 and Bo Dewing was appointed figurehead leader of the SSRC. Re-elected SSRC president on 12 December 1993.

CHANG SHU-CHUAN (a.k.a.) Sao Hpalang

Chinese. Born in 1927 in Liaoning, Manchuria. Joined the KMT during World War II; based at Chungking and Whampoa. Fled to Burma following the communist victory in China. Evacuated to Taiwan in 1952. Served briefly as an intelligence officer in Korea in the early 1950s and with Bataillon Spécial in Laos 1960–63. Returned to Shan State in the mid-1960s; Khun Sa's chief of staff and main military strategist ever since. Now based at the Möng Tai Army's general headquarters at Homöng, southern Shan State.

CHAO NGI LAI (Kyauk Ni Laing) (a.k.a.) Ta Lai

Wa. Born in 1939 in Kyauk Chung village, northern Wa Hills. Local warlord in the Saohin-Saohpa area, northern Wa Hills. Contacted by the Communist Party of Burma in 1968; captured Saohpa together with Kyaw Htin from the CPB in December 1969. Appointed commander of the 2nd Battalion of the CPB's army and became an alternate member of the central committee at the third congress in 1985. One of the most important leaders of the March–April 1989 mutiny; elected general secretary of the new Burma National United Party in May 1989 and leader of its successor, the United Wa State Party, on 3 November 1989. The party was legalised shortly afterwards and its armed wing, the United Wa States Army, was recognised as a government militia force.

CHAR UI (Kya U)

Lahu. Born around 1935 in the Loi Kham Long area near Möng Tun in southern Shan State. The third son of the *payah* of the Lahu, Pu Kyaung Long. Joined the Lahu rebellion in southern Shan State, led by his father, in January 1973. In February, the rebels set up the Lahu National United Party and the Lahu State Liberation Army which joined the National Democratic Front in 1976. Was based at Doi Lang and inherited the title of *payah* when his father died on 7 July 1980. Driven out of Doi Lang by Khun Sa in August 1982. Surrendered to the Burmese government in

January 1984. Went underground again a year later and set up the Lahu National Organisation/Army on 3 August 1985. Based at Muang Na on the Thai-Burma border west of Chiang Dao.

CHISHI SWU, Isaac

Naga of the Sema tribe (from India). Born in 1929 in Chishilimi village near Kohima in the Naga Hills of India. Educated at missionary school at Kohima and at Barapani Christian College near Shillong. Obtained a BA degree in political science and philosophy from St. Anthony's College, Shillong, in 1958. Went underground with the Naga National Council in 1959. "Foreign secretary" of the "federal government of Nagaland" 1960–67. Underwent political and military training in East Pakistan in 1963. Attended peace talks with the Indian government in New Delhi in 1964.

Political leader of the second Naga mission through Kachin State to China 1967–69. "Finance minister" of the FGN 1971–76. Vice president of the NNC 1976; president 1976–78. Founding member of the National Socialist Council of Nagaland and its chairman since January 1980, based in northern Sagaing Division. Retreated along with NSCN general secretary, Thuingaleng Muivah, down to Somra Tract opposite Manipur following a split between the Indian and the Burmese Nagas in 1989.

CHIT, Thakin

Burman. Born in 1910 in Thanatpin, Pegu District. School teacher in Mandalay; joined the People's Revolutionary Party in the 1940s and later the Socialist Party. Member of the CPB in September 1946; leader of the All-Burma Trade Union Congress. Went underground in March 1948; member of the central committee and elected to the politburo in 1951. Leader of the cadres in the Pegu Yoma. Became secretary of the central committee after Thakin Than Tun's death in October 1968. Killed in the Pegu Yoma on 15 March 1975.

DAVIES, Michael (a.k.a.) Khun Sa (a.k.a.) Wun Sa

Anglo-Shan. Born in 1941 in Na Hpan, east of the Salween river, of a Welsh father and a Shan mother. Educated at Kambawza College in Taunggyi. Went underground in 1959 in the Tachilek area with the 6th Battalion of *Noom Suk Harn*. Returned to Kengtung but rejoined the Shan underground in the late 1960s. Deputy commander of the 768 Brigade of the Communist Party of Burma's army. Joined the March–April 1989 mutiny but was assassinated on 12 May at Möng Pyen by ex-rebels who favoured an alliance with the Rangoon government.

DEWING, Bo

Shan. Born in 1921 in Möng Ma near Möng Yai, northern Shan State. Gained local fame in the battle of Tang-yan in 1959, the first major clash between the Shan guerrillas and the Burmese army. Freebooter who joined forces with Khun Sa in 1964. Fell out with Khun Sa and fled to Thailand in 1966. Tried unsuccessfully to set up a Shan army in the Tachilek area in the late 1970s. Surrendered during the 1980 amnesty; went underground again and joined the Shan State Army in 1985. Appointed figurehead leader of Khun Sa's Shan State Restoration Council in July 1992, but resigned in December 1993.

DUAN XIWEN (Tuan Shi-wen)

Kuomintang Chinese. Born in 1912 in Yiliang country, Yunnan. Accompanied Gen. Li Mi's forces when they retreated from Yunnan into Shan State in 1950. Took part in the Taiwan-US planned efforts to build up a "secret" KMT army in Burma. Commander of the 5th KMT when the Nationalist Chinese movement on the Thai-Burma border was reorganised in the late 1950s. Established Mae Salong northwest of Chiang Rai, the main KMT settlement in northern Thailand. Actively involved with Thai, Taiwan and US intelligence agencies, and the drug trade, until his death in a Bangkok hospital on 18 June 1980.

GHOSHAL, Hamendranath (a.k.a.) *yebaw* Ba Tin

Burma-born Bengali from Rangoon. Graduated from Rangoon University; joined the Communist Party of Burma in 1939. Fled to India during the Japanese occupation and became member of the Communist Party of India. Returned to Burma after World War II and organised the All-Burma Trade Union Congress. Member of the central committee and the politburo in 1946. Claimed that strikes and demonstrations rather than armed struggle would bring down the government in Rangoon, but nevertheless went underground with the CPB in March 1948. Briefly expelled from the party for advocating a peace settlement with the government. Branded "Burma's Liu Shaoqi" and executed in the Pegu Yoma on 18 June 1967.

HEARN KHAM, Sao Nang

Shan. Born in 1917 in Hsenwi. Daughter of the *saohpa* of Hsenwi. Married Sao Shwe Thaike, the *saohpa* of Yawnghwe, in 1937. Became the first lady of Burma in 1948 when Sao Shwe Thaike was nominated the Union president. A leading Shan politician, MP and involved with the Shan student movement in Rangoon in the 1950s; known as the "Mahadevi of Yawnghwe". Her husband was arrested when the military took over in March 1962; he died in military custody in October. She escaped to Thailand in early 1964 and became chairman of the central military council of the Shan State Army when it was set up on 25 March 1964. Left for Canada in 1969 and handed over most of her duties to her son, Sao Hsö Wai (a.k.a.) Khun Loum Hpa.

HLA PE, U

Pa-O. Born in 1909 in Thanpayapinseik village, Thaton. Served as minister of forestry in Dr Ba Maw's government during the Japanese occupation. Worked closely with Saw Ba U Gyi after the war; vice chairman of the Karen National Union. Went up to southern Shan State to organise the Pa-Os after the death of Saw Ba U Gyi in August 1950. Led the Pa-O rebellion there until he surrendered in 1958. Arrested after the military take-over in 1962, released before the 1963 peace talks but rearrested in the same year. Released in 1970 and went underground again in 1972. Revitalised the Pa-O rebellion. Died of asthma on 25 September 1975.

HSÖ HTEN, Sao (a.k.a.) Sai Sam (a.k.a.) Sai Kyaw Sein

Shan. Born in 1930 in Hsipaw, northern Shan States. Educated at Rangoon University; joined the *Noom Suk Harn* in 1958. One of the founders of the Shan State Independence Army in 1960. Attended the 1963 peace talks in Rangoon and became a major in the Shan State Army when it was set up in 1964. Surrendered along with Bo Lai Oo and became a *Ka Kwe Ye* home guard commander in 1966. Rejoined the SSA in 1968. In October 1973 he led the first SSA delegation to the Panghsang headquarters of the Communist Party of Burma (along with thirty-seven men from the Karen National United Party). Visited China in December. Returned to Panghsang in May 1975. Quit the SSA and joined the CPB. Rejoined the SSA in 1985. Led the bulk of the SSA's fighting force into a peace agreement with Burma's military authorities on 2 September 1989. Now lives in Rangoon.

HSÖ KHAN, Sao (a.k.a.) Khun On Paung (a.k.a.) Sai Myint Aung

Shan. Born in Hsipaw in 1936. Science student at Rangoon University in the 1950s; active in the Shan student movement. Went underground in 1958 with the *Noom Suk Harn* in the Thai border areas. Joined the Shan State Independence Army in 1960 and became its most important field commander. Joined the Shan State Army in 1964. Vice president of its political wing, the Shan State Progress Party, in 1971. Negotiated an alliance with the Communist Party of Burma in 1975; the SSPP-CPB pact was formally announced on 16 January 1977. Killed in action on 5 December 1978.

HSÖ LANE, Sao (a.k.a.) Sai Hla Aung

Shan-Palaung. Born in 1935 in Namhsan, Tawngpeng state (northern Shan States). Geology student at Rangoon University; took part in the Shan national resurgence movement in the mid-1950s. Joined the Shan rebellion (*Noom Suk Harn*) in 1958 and became an officer in the Shan State Independence Army in 1960. Set up the Palaung National Front in 1962 (then part of the Shan State Army). Commander of the SSA in 1979 and president of the Shan State Progress Party from August 1981 to April 1983. Surrendered in June 1983 and settled in Lashio. Formed his own, legal political party, the Shan State Democratic Party, in 1988.

HSÖ NOOM, Sao

Shan-Wa. Born in 1947 in Nam Lao, the Wa Hills. Son of the last *saohpa* of the Wa state of Möng Leün. Joined the Shan State Independence Army in 1963 at the age of sixteen. Became commander of the 2nd Battalion of the Shan State Army in 1964. Surrendered and became a *Ka Kwe Ye* home guard commander in 1967. Rejoined the SSA in 1970 and led the Shan resistance forces in the Wa Hills and northern Shan State. Became allied with the Communist Party of Burma. Commander of the SSA after Sao Hsö Lane's ouster in April 1983. Died from cirrhosis of the liver on 12 November 1983 at Wan Pan near Hsipaw.

HSÖ WAI, Sao (a.k.a.) Khun Loum Hpa (a.k.a.) Chao Tzang (a.k.a.) Eugene Thaike

Shan. Born in 1939 in Yawnghwe, southern Shan State. Son of Sao Shwe Thaike, the *saohpa* of Yawnghwe (and the president of Burma 1948–52) and Sao Nang Hearn Kham. Educated at Rangoon University, where he became a leader of the Shan students. Participated in the 1962 movement at the university against the military take-over. Went underground in 1963 to join the Shan State Independence Army; represented the SSIA at the peace talks in Rangoon in the same year. Helped found the Shan State Army on 25 March 1964. Became commander of the SSA's 1st Brigade in 1967. Promoted to vice chief of staff of the SSA and general secretary of the Shan State Progress Party when it was set up on 16 August 1971. Resigned in 1976 and left for Thailand. Now lives in Canada.

HSÖ WAN, Sao (a.k.a.) Sai Kyaw Tun

Shan. Born in 1939 in Möng Yai. Nephew of the last *saohpa* of Möng Yai. Student leader and outstanding sportsman in Rangoon in the 1950s. Went underground with the *Noom Suk Harn* in 1958 and captured Tang-yan (together with Bo Maung) in 1959. Founded the Shan State Independence Army together with Khun Kya Nu in 1960. The first Shan university student to be killed in action in July 1960.

HTAY, *yebaw*

Burman from Sagaing. Joined the Communist Party of Burma during World War II; became a member of the central committee at the second congress in July 1945. Initiated the "Peace and Coalition Government" line in the 1950s; leader of the CPB's delegation to the August–November 1963 peace talks in Rangoon. Branded "Durma's Deng Xiaoping" by the party's radical faction and executed on 18 June 1967 in the Pegu Yoma.

HTUN AUNG GYAW

Burman. Born in 1954 in Rangoon. Geology graduate who participated in the U Thant "uprising" in December 1974 and the Shwe Dagon Pagoda demonstrations in June 1975. In Insein Jail 1975–80. Founding member of the Freedom Fighters of Burma on 3 April 1988. Escaped to the Thai border after the 18 September 1988 coup and elected chairman of the All-Burma Students Democratic Front on 5 November. Resigned on 13 October 1989. In 1992 left for the US, where he now lives.

HUNTER THAMWE, Saw (a.k.a.) Saw Musso Kawkasa

Karen. Born in 1905 in Bassein. Educated in Bassein and at Judson College in Rangoon. District educational inspector in Henzada after World War II. Joined the Karen National Union in 1947 and the Karen uprising in January 1949. Leader of the Karen forces in the Irrawaddy delta region. Chairman of the KNU and its administrative body, the Karen Revolutionary Council 1956–63. Belonged to the Karen right wing. Surrendered to the government after the peace talks in 1963. Died in Rangoon on 2 January 1980.

JAFAR HUSSAIN (a.k.a.) Jafar Kawwal

Rohingya. Born in 1915 in Ali Chaung village near Buthidaung, Arakan. Attended high school in Akyab (Sittwe). Became a famous practitioner of Qawwali, the devotional music of the Sufis, an ascetic Muslim sect (hence "Kawwal" added to his name). Organised the *Mujahid* Party among the Muslims in Arakan on 20 August 1947 and led them into rebellion the following year. Assassinated on 11 October 1950.

KAN CHIT (a.k.a.) Bo Kan Zeik

Sino-Shan. Born in 1937 in Loi Sanien near Lai Hka. Joined the Karen-inspired Pa-O uprising in southern Shan State in 1952. Later joined Moh Heng's Communist-allied Shan force. Remained in the underground when Moh Heng surrendered in 1958; joined the *Noom Suk Harn* in 1960 and the Shan State Army in 1964. Local resistance leader in the Lai Hka-Möng Küng area (Loi Sanien mountain). A faithful Moh Heng follower, he broke away from the SSA and in 1989 joined the Shan United Revolutionary Army, which became the Tai Revolutionary Council in April 1984. Commander under Khun Sa when he joined the TRC (now the Shan State Restoration Council) in March 1985.

KHAPLANG, Shangwang Shangyung

Naga. Born in 1940 in Waktham village near Pangsau Pass, northern Sagaing Division. Attended the Baptist Mission School in Myitkyina, Kachin State, 1959–60, and a missionary school near Kalemyo, southern Sagaing Division, 1961–62. Went underground in the Pangsau-Namyung area in 1963. One of the first leaders of the Naga Defence Force when it was set up in 1964; vice chairman of the Eastern Naga Revolutionary Council 1965–68 and its chairman 1968–72. Vice chairman of the Eastern Naga National Council 1972–74 and its chairman 1974–78. Alternately fought and cooperated with the Kachin Independence Army. Merged his forces with the federal government of Nagaland (which was dominated by Nagas from the Indian side) and became president of the united Naga movement in 1978. Vice chairman of the National Socialist Council of Nagaland in January 1980. His men drove the Indian Nagas, led by Isaac Chishi Swu and Thuingaleng Muivah, out of northern Sagaing Division in 1989.

KHIN MAUNG GYI

Burman. Born in 1927 in Rangoon. His father was an inspector of land records in the Rangoon Development Trust. Joined the anti-Japanese struggle in 1944 while working for the East-Asiatic Youth League. Became a member of the Communist Party of Burma in late 1945. Passed 2nd MBBS at the Junior Medical College in Rangoon in 1949; executive member of the All-Burma Students' Union. Was nominated to represent the ABSU at the International Union of Students in Prague and tried to go to Czechoslovakia in 1950. Reached Calcutta, but had to return to Burma because of financial difficulties.

Joined the CPB unit in Prome and went to China in 1953. Studied Marxism-Leninism at the Higher Party School in Beijing until 1957. Left for Moscow, where he studied Marxism-Leninism 1957–60; attended Moscow's Academy of Social Sciences, 1961–63; wrote thesis on agrarian problems in Burma and worked for a few months at the Institute of World Economy in Moscow. Returned to Beijing in 1963 and became Thakin Ba Thein Tin's personal secretary as well as member of the "leading group of five" set up in China in November. Visited Hanoi in 1965; attended the fifth congress of the Albanian Party of Labour in Tirana in 1967 along with Thakin Pe Tint.

Vice political commissar of the first CPB unit that entered Burma from China on 1 January 1968. Became member of the central committee and the politburo in 1975. Second vice chairman of the CPB from 1975 to the third congress in 1985 when the post was abolished. In the Central Bureau, 1980–84; returned to Panghsang to attend the third congress. Secretary to the central committee from the third congress to the 1989 mutiny, when he fled to China. The CPB's main theoretician since early 1960s. Now lives in Kunming.

KHUN MAHA, Long

Shan. Born in 1912 in Möng Yai, northern Shan State. "Chief minister" under the Möng Yai *saohpa*. Writer and poet; first chairman of the Shan State Independence Army in 1960. Arrested at Mingaladon Airport in the same year when he went to negotiate with the Union government. Released shortly afterwards and went to Taunggyi to work as an announcer for the Shan language department of the Burma Broadcasting Service. Returned to the Thai-Burma border in 1976 and settled in Khun Sa's Ban Hin Taek headquarters. Token "Shan adviser" to Khun Sa for several years. Died in Chiang Mai, Thailand, on 23 July 1990.

KHUNSUK, Sao

Shan. Born in 1910 in Kengtung. Belonged to the ruling family of Kengtung and educated at the Shan Chiefs' School, Taunggyi. Served with the Burma Frontier Force with the rank of captain before World War II. Retreated with the British to India when the Japanese invaded Burma. Returned to Burma with the Allied forces in 1945. Administered Kengtung state after independence on behalf of his nephew, Sao Sai Long, who was a minor. Imprisoned for two months in 1958 during Ne Win's Caretaker Government. Left for Thailand after his release and took part in the formation of the early Shan resistance movement. Close to Gen. Sarit Thanarat and other high-ranking Thai military officers in the 1960s. Died in Chiang Mai, Thailand, in 1991.

KYA DOE, Saw Henson

Karen. Born in 1907 in Myaungmya, the son of a secondary school headmaster. Enlisted at the age of sixteen as a recruit in the Training Battalion (Burma Rifles) in 1924; selected to enter the Royal Military College at Sandhurst, England, in 1930; passed out as second lieutenant from Sandhurst in 1932. Served with several regiments in India and Burma till the outbreak of World War II. Stayed behind when the Japanese invaded Burma and served with the Burma Defence Army. Joined the anti-Japanese resistance in March 1945 and became vice chief of staff and chief of operations after the war. Released from the army altogether in 1951. Went into business in Rangoon but joined U Nu's resistance along the Thai border in the late 1960s. Surrendered during the 1980 amnesty and returned to Rangoon. Appointed member of the Elections Commission in September 1988.

KYA NU, Khun (a.k.a.) Sao Hseng Suk

Shan. Born in 1935 in Hsipaw, northern Shan States. The son of Khun Kya Pu, chief officer of the Shan State Agricultural Department and an elder Shan statesman (signed the Panglong Agreement). Attended Rangoon University 1956–59. Went underground to join the *Noom Suk Harn* in 1959; founding member of the Shan State Independence Army in 1960. Took part in the 1963 peace talks in Taunggyi as a representative of the Shan National United Front, a body that had been set up to unite the various Shan factions. Commander of the 3rd Brigade when the Shan State Army was founded in 1964. Chief of staff of the SSA and president of its political wing, the Shan State Progress Party, when it was set up on 16 August 1971. Resigned along with the SSPP's general secretary, Sao Hsö Wai, in March 1976. Moved to Thailand, where he now lives. He now heads the Shan State Organisation, which consists of Shan exiles in Thailand, Australia and the United States.

KYAW MYA

Arakanese. Born in 1915 in Paletwa, now Arakan State. Entered Rangoon University in 1934 and obtained a BA in English (honours) in 1940. Worked as clerk at Kyaukpyu, Arakan, until World War II broke out. Participated in the anti-Japanese struggle; joined the Communist Party of Burma in 1946. District party secretary in Sittwe, 1946–51; CPB leader of Arakan, 1951–79. Alternate member of the central committee in 1955; member of the central committee and the politburo in 1975. Left Arakan for Bangladesh in 1979; flew via Dhaka and Karachi to Beijing and continued through China to Panghsang. Settled in China shortly before the 1989 mutiny.

KYAW ZAN RHEE

Arakanese from Myebon, Arakan State. Peasant background; World War II veteran. Joined the Communist uprising in Arakan State in the late 1940s. Broke away from the Communist Party (Red Flag) in 1956 and set up a separate Communist group to fight for an independent, socialist republic in Arakan. The Communist Party of Arakan formally came into existence on 11 March 1962 and was active mainly in Myebon township. Surrendered during the 1980 amnesty. Participated in the 1988 movement for democracy in Arakan. Co-founder (with *Bonbauk* Tha Gyaw and others) of the legal Arakan People's United Organisation in 1988, which, however, failed to win any seats in the 1990 election.

KYAW ZAW (a.k.a.) Thakin Shwe

Burman. Born in 1919 in Saingsu, Thonze township, Tharrawaddy District. Active in the *Dohbama Asiayon*e; one of the Thirty Comrades who went to Japan for military training in 1941. Commander of the No. 4 Military Region of the Burma National Army in 1945. Joined the Communist Party of Burma in 1944 and elected member of the central committee at the second congress in July 1945 but never participated in party activities. Southern commander of the Burma Army from independence until 1952; then northern commander and in charge of the operations against the Kuomintang in Shan State. Accused of leaking news to the CPB and forced to leave the army in 1956. Officially dismissed on 7 June 1957. Lived in retirement in Sanchaung, Rangoon, until July 1976 when he went to Man Hio and joined the CPB. Member of the central committee and the central military commission. Vice chief of general staff of the CPB until the 1989 mutiny when he fled to China. Now lives in exile in Kunming.

KYIN MAUNG (a.k.a.) *yebaw* Tun

Sino-Burmese. Born in 1924 in Sagaing. Joined the Burma Independence Army in 1942 and the Communist Party of Burma in 1943. Went underground in March 1948 and became vice political commissar of the CPB forces in the Kyawkku-Lawng Long-Nawng Wu area of Shan State. Member of the central committee and the politburo in 1975. Chief of propaganda and publicity. Stayed at the Northern Bureau (Möng Ko) until 1987 when he was transferred to Panghsang. Fled to China during the 1989 mutiny.

LAI OO, Bo

Wa. Born around 1925 in Manghseng, southern Wa Hills. Follower of Bo Maung and a local warlord in the Tang-yan area. Closely connected with the opium network of the Kuomintang. Became a *Ka Kwe Ye* home guard commander in 1966 and allied himself with Lo Hsing-han. Retired in 1973 when the KKY programme was abandoned. Assassinated in 1974, most probably by Khun Sa's men.

LAW YONE, Edward

Sino-Burmese. Born in 1911 in Myitkyina. Educated in missionary schools; worked for Burma Railways in the 1930s. Served with the Allied forces during World War II. Founder and editor of the daily *The Nation* in 1948. Arrested in 1963, released in 1968 and was instrumental in setting up U Nu's Thai-border based resistance in the late 1960s. In August 1970 left for the US where he died in June 1980.

LEK, Sai

Shan. Born in 1941 in Mang Pang village near Hsipaw, northern Shan States, of an Indian father and a Shan mother. Joined a local band in the Hsipaw area in 1960. Became commander of the 3rd Brigade of the Shan State Army in 1979 and member of the central committee of the Shan State Progress Party in 1982. Led several Shan delegations to the Communist Party of Burma headquarters at Panghsang. Became general secretary of the SSPP in April 1984. Remained in the underground when the rest of the SSPP/SSA signed a peace agreement with Rangoon in September 1989.

LET YA, Bo

Burman. Born in 1911 in Pyapon. Active in the *Dohbama Asiayone*. Founding member of the CPB on 15 August 1939 but never participated in party activities. One of the Thirty Comrades. Deputy prime minister after the assassination of Aung San in July 1947. Governor's counsellor for defence. Negotiated Defence Agreement with the British at Kandy in 1945. Deputy prime minister and minister for defence immediately before independence (1947–48). Resigned from all posts in 1948 and became a businessman. Joined U Nu's non-communist resistance against the military government in the 1960s; commander of the rebel Patriotic Liberation Army in 1969; chairman of the People's Patriotic Party in March 1973. Killed by Karen rebels near the Thai border on 29 November 1978.

LI MI

Kuomintang Chinese. Born in 1902 in Tengchong, Yunnan. General and World War II hero. Fled Kunming by plane to Hong Kong in the wake of the Communist victory in China in 1949. Men from his 8th KMT Army, and the 26th Army, retreated into northeastern Burma where he rejoined them in early 1950. Set up a string of bases along the Sino-Burmese frontier and built up the "secret" KMT army in Burma. Led several unsuccessful cross-border raids into Yunnan before he left for Taiwan in 1952. The KMT forces left along the Thai-Burma border were later taken over by generals Duan Xiwen and Li Wenhuan. Died in Taiwan in 1973.

LI WENHUAN (Lee Wen-huan)

Kuomintang Chinese. Born in 1917 in Yunnan. Vice governor of Tseung-kan county near the Kokang border in Yunnan during the KMT era. Fled to Burma after the Communist take-over in China and joined the KMT forces there. Became commander of the 3rd KMT, which has been based at Tam Ngob on the Thai-Burma border since the early 1960s. Closely connected with Thai, Taiwanese and US intelligence agencies. One of the most powerful drug warlords of the Golden Triangle.

While based at Tam Ngob as well as in Chiang Mai, Thailand, he worked through proxy armies inside Shan State: Moh Heng's Shan United Revolutionary Army, Mahasang's Wa United Army and various *Ka Kwe Ye* home guard units which carried opium down to refineries under his control in the area around Tam Ngob and Pieng Luang. His fortified residence in Chiang Mai, northern Thailand, was bombed by his rival, Khun Sa, in March 1984. He still lives in Chiang Mai.

LI ZIRU

Chinese. Born in 1946 in Baoshan in China's Yunnan province. Joined the Communist Party of Burma as volunteer in 1968 along with Zhang Zhiming and Lin Mingxian. Attached to the CPB's "special forces" which captured Panghsai/Kyu-hkok in March 1970. Political commissar of the 4045 Battalion (under the 683 Brigade) which in accordance with the "7510 Plan" crossed the Salween river in 1975. Became vice chief of staff of the Central Bureau forces in 1980; later military commander of the Central Bureau. Became an alternate member of the central committee during the third congress in 1985. Joined the mutiny in 1989 and became one of the leaders of the Panghsang-based Burma National United Party, renamed the United Wa State Party on 3 November 1989. Now government-recognised militia commander and prominent drug trafficker.

LIN MINGXIAN (a.k.a.) Sai Leün (a.k.a.) U Sai Lin

Sino-Shan from Panghsai on the Chinese border in northern Shan State. Member of a Red Guard-style organisation in Yunnan during the Cultural Revolution. Joined the Communist Party of Burma in 1968 as a volunteer together with Zhang Zhiming, Li Ziru and other Chinese Red Guards. One of the Communists' ablest field commanders; in charge of the CPB's 815 War Zone (eastern Shan State). Married Pheung Kya-shin's daughter. Joined the 1989 mutiny and now a militia commander close to the government in Rangoon. One of the most important heroin traffickers in eastern Shan State today.

LIN TIN

Karen. Born in 1925 in Thamaing near Rangoon. No higher education. One of the few Karens who served with the Japanese during World War II; interpreter for the Kempetai. Joined the Karen National Defence Organisation in 1948 and the Karen rebellion in 1949. Commander of the Karen's 5th Brigade in the Thaton area in 1956. A well-known combat leader who even raided Mae Sot town in Thailand in 1961. Surrendered together with Saw Hunter Thamwe in 1963. Married Naw Louisa Benson. Killed in Thaton in September 1965 by agents from the Burma Army.

LO HSING-HAN

Kokang Chinese. Born in 1934 in Ta Tsu Chin village, Kokang. Joined the local Kokang Army of the Yang family in the early 1960s. Defected to the Burmese government in 1963 and was appointed commander of the Kokang *Ka Kwe Ye* home guards. One of the KKY commanders who benefited the most from the opium deal with Rangoon; emerged as a prominent drug trafficker in the early 1970s. Went underground when Rangoon decided to disband the KKY in 1973 and teamed up with the Shan State Army. In August 1973 crossed the border to Thailand, where he was arrested and extradited to Rangoon. Sentenced to death for "rebellion against the state" in 1976. Pardoned during the 1980 amnesty. Acted as go-between for Rangoon to negotiate with Communist Party of Burma mutineers in 1989. Now back in the drug business together with Pheung Kya-shin, Pheung Kya-fu and other former CPB commanders who became government militia commanders.

LO HSING-MINH

Kokang Chinese. Lo Hsing-han's younger brother. Commander in his *Ka Kwe Ye* unit in the late 1960s and early 1970s. Stayed on at Mae Aw on the Thai border with a small band of Kokang troops (called the Shan State Revolutionary Army) after the arrest of his brother in August 1973. Surrendered with his men during the 1980 amnesty. Now closely allied with the Rangoon government and back in the drug business.

MA CHING-KO

Kuomintang Chinese. Born in 1915 in Yunnan. Commander of the KMT's 1st Independent Unit in Shan State, which was directly controlled by the Intelligence Mainland Operation Bureau (IMOB) under the Ministry of Defence in Taipei. Established bases from the Lao border up to Loi Sae near Tang-yan in northern Shan State, where he cooperated closely with KMT remnants as well as the Loi Maw *Ka Kwe Ye* of Khun Sa. Now lives in retirement in Chiang Mai.

MAHASANG

Wa. Born in 1946 in Kwan Mau village near Vingngun, the Wa Hills. The second son of Sao Maha, the last *saohpa* of Vingngun. Commander of Vingngun *Ka Kwe Ye* in the late 1960s–early 1970s. Driven out of his area by the Communists in 1972. Went underground with Lo Hsing-han in 1973 and came down with him to the Thai border. First allied with the Shan State Army, which helped him set up the Wa State Army in 1974. Broke with the SSA in 1977 and joined forces with the Kuomintang and Moh Heng's Shan United Revolutionary Army. The political wing of the WNA, the Wa National Organisation, joined the National Democratic Front in 1983. Mahasang went to Panghsang to negotiate with the CPB mutineers in May–June 1989, was arrested by them but managed to escape and reached Thailand a few months later. He now lives in Chiang Mai.

MAUNG, Bo

Wa. Born in 1919 in Sopwa village near Man Hpang-Möng Mau, northern Wa Hills. An officer in the paramilitary Union Military Police. Fought against the Kuomintang in the 1950s. Went underground with the Shan students and led the attack on Tang-yan in 1959 together with Hsö Wan. Overall military commander of the Shan State Independence Army 1960–64. Based in the Wa Hills and cooperated with the Shan State Army in the late 1960s. Wounded in a battle with Khun Sa's forces in 1967 and surrendered. Died in Maymyo in the late 1970s.

MAW REH, Saw

Karenni. Born in 1920 in In-gyaw village, Toungoo District. Took part in the anti-Japanese resistance during World War II and joined the Karen Rifles of the Burma Army after the war. Formed the Karenni National Organisation in 1947 and the United Karenni States' Independence Army in 1948; allied with the Karen National Defence Organisation. Captured by government forces and imprisoned in February 1949. Released in December 1953 and re-joined the Karenni movement. Chairman of the Karenni National Progressive Party 1960–77 and 1978–86. Chairman of the National Democratic Front 1987–91. "President" of the Karenni government since July 1992.

MIN MAUNG

Karen. Born in 1915 in Toungoo. Took part in the first Wingate expedition during World War II; awarded the Military Cross by the British. Lieutenant-colonel and commander of the 1st Karen Rifles after the war. Joined the Karen uprising in January 1949. General and commander in chief of the Kawthoolei Armed Forces until his death in combat on 13 April 1961.

MOE THI ZON (a.k.a.) Myo Than Htut

Burman. Born in 1962 in Rangoon; also known as Myo Than Htut. Prominent student leader in Rangoon during the 1988 uprising. Set up the Democratic Party for a New Society, a legal party, after the 18 September 1988 coup. Fled to the Thai border in April 1989 and became chairman of the All-Burma Students' Democratic Front in November. Chairman of one faction when the front split in August–October 1991.

MOH HENG (a.k.a.) Kwon Zerng

Shan. Born in 1923 in Htanaw village, Hopong township. Went underground with the Communist Party of Burma in 1952. Broke with the CPB in 1956 and set up his own Shan State Communist Party in the Lai Hka-Möng Küng area. Surrendered in early 1958, but went underground again in November 1958, this time with the Shan insurgents (*Noom Suk Harn*). Lost his left arm in a battle with the Burma Army near Punghpakyem in 1960. Broke away from the Shan State Army to set up his own Shan United Revolutionary Army on 20 January 1969 with support from the Kuomintang. Set up base at Pieng Luang on the Thai border northwest of Chiang Dao. Merged his SURA with the SSA's 2nd Brigade on 1 April 1984 and formed the Tai Revolutionary Council. Broke with the KMT and allied his TRC with Khun Sa on 25 March 1985. Chairman of the TRC until his death at Wieng Heng near Pieng Luang on 12 July 1991.

MOHAMMED JAFAR HABIB

Rohingya Muslim. Born in 1935 in Ali Chaung village near Buthidaung in Arakan. Studied at Buthidaung and attended high school in Dhaka (then East Pakistan, now Bangladesh). Studied political science, history and philosophy at Rangoon University where he was active in the Rohingya Students' Union. After graduation worked as a translator at the Egyptian embassy in Rangoon. In March 1963, founded and became chairman of the Rohingya Independence Force which became the Rohingya Patriotic Front in 1974. Chairman of the RFP until the movement split in 1985–86; died in Chittagong, Bangladesh, on 6 November 1987.

MOHAMMED YUNUS

Rohingya Muslim. Born in 1945 in Baguna, Maungdaw township of Arakan State. Studied medicine in Rangoon; medical doctor in Arakan 1970–75. Went underground with the Rohingya Patriotic Front in 1975. Broke away in 1982 together with Nurul Islam and set up the Rohingya Solidarity Organisation. When Nurul Islam in June 1986 merged his faction of the RSO with RPF remnants to form the Arakan Rohingya Islamic Front in August 1987, Mohammed Yunus retained the name RSO for his faction, which subsequently grew stronger than the ARIF. Now based along the Bangladesh-Burma border.

MUIVAH, Thuingaleng

Naga of the Tangkhul tribe (India). Born in 1936 in Somdal village, the Naga-inhabited area of the Indian state of Manipur. Educated at Somdal, Ukhrul, and at Barapani Christian College, Shillong. Obtained a BA in political science from St. Anthony's College, Shillong, in 1961 and an MA from Gauhati University in 1963. Joined the Naga underground in 1964; general secretary of the Naga National Council 1964–78. Political leader of the first Naga mission through Kachin State to China 1966–71. Unofficial Naga representative in Beijing 1967–70. Founder of the National Socialist Council of Nagaland in January 1980. Its general secretary and main theoretician; based in northern Sagaing Division until infighting between the Indian and the Burmese Nagas drove him and Isaac Chishi Swu down to Somra Tract, opposite Manipur, in 1989.

MYA, Bo

Karen. Born in 1927 in Hti Mu Khi village in the Papun hills. Educated up to 4th Standard. Police constable during the Japanese occupation and at the same time gave information to the Allied forces. Later joined Force 136. Went underground with the Karen National Union in 1949. Zone commander with the rank of colonel in 1960. Born an animist, he converted to Christianity in 1961. Broke with the KNU in 1966 on differences regarding the relationship with the CPB. Set up the Karen National United Front on 21 June 1968 together with Mahn Ba Zan. Vice chairman of the re-united KNU in 1975 and its chairman since August 1976. Chairman of the National Democratic Front 1976–87 and chairman of the Democratic Alliance of Burma since November 1988.

MYINT, Khun

Shan. Born in 1930 in Möng Mang in Yunnan, China. Moved to Möng Yang, Burma's Shan State, in 1935. Educated at a Buddhist monastery. Joined the Shan rebellion and became a local commander of the Kengtung-based Shan National Army in 1961. Based at Huei Nam Khun on the Thai border in the mid-1960s. Merged his forces with the Shan State Army and became its eastern commander in 1971. Set up the Shan People's Liberation Army in 1974 and forged an alliance with the Communist Party of Burma. The SPLA became the CPB's 768 Brigade in August 1976. Civil administrator in the CPB's Hsaleü base area east of Möng Yang although he never joined the party. Joined the 1989 mutiny.

MYO MYINT (a.k.a.) *yebaw* Aung

Burman. Born in 1924 in Letpadan, Tharrawaddy District. Active in the student and youth movement in his home town. Joined the Burma Defence Army in 1942; attended the Japanese-run Officers' Training School in Rangoon. Joined the Communist Party of Burma in 1943. Member of the central committee from 1948 onwards. Participated in the uprising in the Pyinmana area together with Thakin Pe Tint, 1948–53, and became political commissar of the CPB's 3rd Division (southern Pegu Yoma, Pegu and Hanthawaddy-Rangoon). Chairman of the CPB's northern region, 1953–67. Returned to the Pegu Yoma, 1967–71; attached to the Pa-O national movement in Shan State, 1971–75; member of the politburo since 1975. Based at the Northern Bureau (Möng Ko), 1975–87, and at Panghsang from 1987 until the 1989 mutiny when he fled to China.

NAG, Dr. (a.k.a.) *yebaw* Tun Maung.

Bengali. One of the founders of the Communist Party of Burma on 15 August 1939. Spent the wartime years in India where he obtained an MBBS and practised medicine. Returned to Burma in 1947 to work at Rangoon General Hospital. Went underground in March 1948 and reached the CPB's headquarters in the Pyinmana area in May. Leading Communist organiser in Burma in the 1950s and chief of the CPB's central medical staff. Educated the Communists' first medics. Political commissar of the northwest military region (Magwe and Sagaing) under Bo Thet Tun. Killed in action when the Burma Army attacked his camp in the Pegu Yoma in 1969.

NAW HPA, Eric

Palaung. Born in 1942 in Namhsan, Tawngpeng state (northern Shan States), where his father was the *saohpa*. Educated at Kambawza Shan Chiefs' School, Taunggyi, and in Rangoon and in Germany. Joined the Palaung National Front in 1968 and Moh Heng's Shan United Revolutionary Army in 1973. Became general secretary of SURA in 1976 and of its successor, the Tai Revolutionary Council, from April 1984 until his death from cancer on 7 October 1988.

NAW SENG

Kachin. Born in 1922 in Man Peng Loi village, Lashio township, Shan State. Joined the Burma Frontier Force, Lashio Battalion. Led resistance against the Japanese in the Kachin Hills during World War II; Jamedar in the British-organised Northern Kachin Levies. Twice awarded the Burma Gallantry Medal by the British for his role in the anti-Japanese resistance. Captain in the 1st Kachin Rifles in 1946; fought against the Communist Party of Burma in the Irrawaddy delta region in 1948.

Defected to the Karen rebels along with his battalion in February 1949. Led the Upper Burma Campaign against the Rangoon government and set up the

Pawngyawng National Defence Force (the first Kachin rebel army in Burma) in November 1949. Retreated into China from Möng Ko in northeastern Shan State in April 1950.

In exile along with a few hundred followers in China's Guizhou province until 1968. Vice military commander (under Than Shwe) of the first CPB unit that entered Burma on 1 January 1968. Military commander of the northeastern command in September 1969. Died under mysterious circumstances in the Wa Hills on 9 March 1972.

NGAR KHAM, Sao (a.k.a.) U Gondara

Shan. Born in 1928 in Kengtung. A Buddhist monk (under the name U Gondara), abbot of Yang Kham monastery and head of Kengtung's Buddhist orphanage. Went underground in 1961 with the Shan State Independence Army. Set up his own Kengtung-based Shan National Army shortly afterwards. Went to Laos in the same year and to Chiang Rai, northern Thailand, where he set up base at Huei Nam Khun near the Burmese border. Assassinated at Ban Huei Krai opium caravan station near Huei Nam Khun in 1964.

NOI, Sao (a.k.a.) Saw Yanda

Shan. Born in 1924 in Yunnan, China. Moved to Burma and participated in the literacy movement for Shan youths in the Bhamo area of Kachin State in the 1950s. Set up the *Noom Suk Harn* at Möng Kyawt village near the Thai border on 21 May 1958. The group faded away in the 1960s, as the Shan students who had initially joined him broke away to set up their own Shan State Independence Army in 1960. Settled in Chiang Dao, northern Thailand. In 1968 he tried a comeback with the help of Gen. Lee Wen-huan of the 3rd Kuomintang and Moh Heng. When the Shan United Revolutionary Army was formed in 1969, Moh Heng became its chairman and Sao Noi its vice chairman. But he was soon pushed out and now lives in retirement in Chiang Dao.

NOL LAR, Nai (a.k.a.) Nai Seik Noh

Mon. Born in 1917 in Hni Pa Daw village, Mudon township. Headman of his home village before he went underground with Nai Aung Tun and Nai Shwe Kyin in August 1948. Founding member of the Mon People's Front in 1952. Surrendered in July 1958. Imprisoned in 1962, released in 1967 and re-joined the Mon underground. Vice chairman of the New Mon State Party; chairman of one faction following a split in April 1981. Vice chairman of the re-united NMSP in December 1987. Died of a heart attack during a ceremony held at Three Pagodas Pass on 8 August 1989 to commemorate the first anniversary of the mass uprising for democracy in Rangoon.

NOOM PAN, Sai (a.k.a.) Lao Kham

Shan. Born in 1940 in Möng Yang, eastern Shan State. One of the very few Christian (Roman Catholic) Shans. Educated in Roman Catholic schools and at Rangoon University, where he participated in the July 1962 demonstrations. Joined the Shan National Army in Kengtung in 1967 and worked briefly for the CIA in Laos. Returned to Shan State after less than a year to became a military commander under Khun Myint. Commander of the Communist Party of Burma's 768 Brigade when it was set up in August 1976, but never joined the party. Joined the March–April 1989 mutiny but disagreed with the decision to make peace with the government in Rangoon. Committed suicide in April 1990.

NU, U

Burman. Born in 1907 in Wakema, Myaungmya district. Educated at Rangoon University. President of the Rangoon University Students' Union 1935–36 and active in the *Dohbama Asiayone* and later the Anti-Fascist People's Freedom League. Prime minister 1948–56; 1957–58 and 1960–62. Formed the *Pyidaungsu* (Union) Party in 1960. Deposed by Gen. Ne Win in March 1962; in prison 1962–66. Left Burma on 11 April 1969 and set up the Parliamentary Democracy Party on 29 August; led resistance against Ne Win from Thailand 1969–73; in exile in the US 1973–74 and in India 1974–80. Returned to Burma during the 1980 amnesty. Retired in Rangoon but re-emerged as a political leader during the 1988 uprising. Placed under house arrest in December 1989. Released in April 1992. Now lives in Rangoon.

NURUL ISLAM

Rohingya Muslim. Born in 1948 in Maungdaw, Arakan State. Studied law at Rangoon University and graduated in 1973. President of the Rohingya Students' Association in Rangoon 1969–70. Practised law in Rangoon and Maungdaw 1973–74. Went underground with the Rohingya Patriotic Front in late 1974. In 1982 set up the Rohingya Solidarity Organisation, which in June 1986 merged with the remnants of the RPF to become the Arakan Rohingya Islamic Front in August 1987. Chairman of the ARIF since 1987.

NYA MAUNG MAE

Karen from Kayah (Karenni) State. Born in 1952 in a village near Mawchi, Kayah State. Worked in the Mawchi mines until he joined the then undivided Karenni rebel movement in 1970. Sided with the pro-Communist faction when the Karenni movement split in 1978. Chairman of the Karenni State Nationalities People's Liberation Front after the death of its founder, Than Nyunt, in April 1982. Resigned in 1992.

OKKER, Hkun

Pa-O. Born in 1946 in Thaton. Attended Rangoon University 1964–69; expelled because of involvement in underground student activities. Studied law and passed Higher Grade Pleadership exams; practised law for a year. Joined U Hla Pe's Pa-O rebels in March 1972; central committee member of the Pa-O National Organisation in 1977. Pa-O representative to the National Democratic Front 1978–88 and to the Democratic Alliance of Burma 1988–91. Visited Kachin State in 1984–85. Remained along the Thai border when the main PNO entered into a peace agreement with Rangoon in March 1991. Formed the Pa-O People's Liberation Organisation on 18 June 1991 and became its president when the new organisation was announced officially on 10 October.

PE TINT, Thakin

Burman. Born in 1916 in Thaton. Grew up in Ye Ni between Pyinmana and Toungoo, where in the 1930s he participated in the nationalist movement. Secretary in one of the ministries in Dr Ba Maw's puppet government during the Japanese occupation; later joined the anti-Japanese struggle and was sent to Bhamo in the Kachin Hills to contact Detachment 101 (the US-organised resistance in northern Burma). Communist Party of Burma secretary in the Pyinmana area after World War II.

Went underground in March 1948 and became member of the central committee in the same year. Peasant organiser in the Pyinmana area in the 1950s and later in the Pegu Yoma. Sent to China in 1965 to cement ties between exiles in Beijing and units at home. Went to Tirana in 1967 together with Khin Maung Gyi to attend the fifth congress of the Albanian Party of Labour. Elected vice chairman after the death of Thakin Zin and Thakin Chit in 1975.

Stayed in China with Thakin Ba Thein Tin until 1978, when the CPB's central office moved to Panghsang headquarters. Led a three-man CPB delegation which held peace talks with the government in Lashio in May 1981. Left for China for medical treatment in 1986 and died in Beijing on 5 July 1990.

PHEUNG KYA-SHIN (Peng Jai-sheng)

Kokang Chinese. Born in 1931 in Hong Seu Htoo Haw village, Kokang. Officer in Jimmy Yang's Kokang Revolutionary Force in the 1960s; contacted by Communist Party of Burma cadres in China in July 1967 and promised arms and ammunition. Went to Beijing along with his younger brother Pheung Kya-fu shortly afterwards. Entered Kokang from China on 5 January 1968 as commander of the Kokang People's Liberation Army, which officially merged with the CPB's army in August of same year. Led civil administration in Kokang although he never joined the party. Entered the heroin trade in the early 1970s. Initiated the mutiny in March 1989 together with Pheung Kya-fu. Became a government-recognised militia commander and one of Burma's most prominent drug traffickers. Lost out to the Yang clan in late 1992, and escaped to the area north of Kengtung which is controlled by his son-in-law, Lin Mingxian. Now lives near Hsipaw in northern Shan State.

PO KUN, Bo

Burmese. Born in 1898. Active in the nationalist movement in the 1930s and prominent in the Burma Independence Army during the Japanese occupation. Leader of the People's Volunteer Organisation after Aung San's death in July 1947. Councillor for education in the pre-independence cabinet, July 1947; minister for public works and rehabilitation from August 1947 to July 1948, when he led the "White" PVO into rebellion against the government. His 2,000-strong force, which had been loosely allied with the Communists, surrendered between July and October 1958. Joined the Burma Socialist Programme Party after the 1962 coup d'etat and was appointed ambassador to Thailand.

PU KYAUNG LONG

Lahu from Loi Kham Long in the Möng Hsat-Möng Ton area of southern Shan State. The *payah* (politico-religious leader) of the Lahus. Commander of a *Ka Kwe Ye* home guard force until he initiated a Lahu rebellion in southern Shan State in January 1973. Based at Doi Lang on the Thai-Burma border west of Fang until his death on 7 July 1980, reputedly at the age of 120.

PYAN, Bo
Padaung (Kayan). Born around 1915 in Pekon, southwestern Shan State. A local Roman Catholic village headman who participated in the anti-Japanese resistance during World War II. Initiated resistance among the Padaung following the demonetisation of the 50 and 100 Kyat banknotes in 1964. Surrendered shortly afterwards. Re-entered politics during the 1988 uprising for democracy and rejoined the Padaung underground. Now lives in a refugee camp in Mae Hong Son, Thailand.

SAM MÖNG, Sao (a.k.a.) Sai Kyaw Khin
Shan. Born in 1941 in Kyaukme, Shan State. One of the many secondary school students who joined the Shan underground in the wake of the Tang-yan battle in 1959. Became the most competent military commander of the Shan rebels and was appointed chief of operations of the Shan State Army. Went to the Panghsang headquarters of the Communist Party of Burma in 1975 with an SSA delegation. Fell out with the CPB and came down to the Thai border in early 1978. Disappeared (together with Lieut-Col. Pan Aung, the other main military commander of the SSA) on his way to Khun Sa's Ban Hin Taek headquarters in August 1978.

SANKEY, Saw
Karen. Born in 1914 in Amherst, Moulmein. Attended Rangoon University 1930–35. Manager for Rangoon Electric Transport 1935–37. Captain with Force 136 during World War II. Member of the Frontier Areas Committee of Enquiry. Became leader of the Karen National Union and commander in the Karen National Defence Organisation in 1947. Went underground in January 1949 and was killed together with Saw Ba U Gyi near Kawkareik on 12 August 1950.

SAW LU (a.k.a.) Saul (a.k.a.) Ta Pluik
Wa. Born in 1942 in Kengtung. Studied at Dr. Gordon Seagrave's missionary school at Namkham and later at the Karen Baptist School in Myaungmya. Became a *Ka Kwe Ye* home guard commander in Saohpa (Pangwei) in the Wa Hills in 1964. Driven out by the Communists in 1969. Later high-ranking official in the ruling Burma Socialist Programme Party. Helped set up the Wa National Development Party and the Lahu National Development Party (his wife Mary is a Lahu) in 1988.
Arrested by the military authorities in Lashio on 21 January 1992 and charged with "cooperating with the CIA and the DEA". Released after pressure from Wa commander Chao Ngi Lai (who had captured Saohpa in 1969) on 16 March 1992. Joined the United Wa State Party in April and now serves as its chief international liaison officer.

SEIN DA, U
Arakanese. Born in 1902 in Yinbwe village, Minbya township in Arakan. Buddhist monk in 1922 and Arakanese nationalist leader; led resistance in Arakan to Japanese, British and AFPFL governments. Active in the legal Arakan National Congress, but broke away in November 1945 to set up his own Arakan People's Liberation Party. Went underground in 1946 to fight against British and for an independent Arakan. Arrested in May 1947. Released later and rejoined the under-

ground. Nicknamed the "King of Arakan". Surrendered on 25 January 1958 along with 400 armed followers. Died as a monk at Shwebontha monastery in Rangoon in 1964.

SETKYA, Bo (a.k.a.) Thakin Aung Than

Burman. Born in 1916 in Rangoon. Student leader in the 1930s. One of the Thirty Comrades. Vice minister for national defence under the Japanese. Secretary to Aung San in London, January 1947. Entered business after independence. President of the Port Workers' Union and treasurer of the Trade Union Congress (Burma). MP in 1951. Went to the Thai border in the late 1960s to join the Burman resistance against the military government in Rangoon. Died of heart failure in 1969 in Bangkok.

SGAW LER TAW

Karen. Born in 1914 in Kyaukpya village, Toungoo district. Studied at Judson College in Rangoon and became headmaster of Tharrawaddy Karen High School in 1940. With Force 136 during World War II; resumed his work as headmaster in Tharrawaddy after the war. Joined the Karen uprising in January 1949. Acting chairman of the Karen National Union 1953–56. Leading official of the Karen National United Party in the Pegu Yoma. Led a Karen delegation to the Communist Party of Burma's eastern base area and to China in 1971–75. Arrived in the KNU's eastern base area along the Thai border in June 1975 and remained there until his death on 7 March 1989 at Manerplaw headquarters.

SHWE, Saw

Karenni. Born in 1919 in Kyebogyi. *Sawphya* [prince] of the Karenni state of Kyebogyi. One of the first leaders of the Karenni rebellion against Rangoon in August 1948; in alliance with the Karen National Defence Organisation from 1949. Leader of the Karenni rebel movement from the arrest of Saw Maw Reh in February 1949 till his death from malaria in 1956.

SHWE AYE (a.k.a.) Naing Hlu Ta

Padaung (Kayan). Born in 1938 in Möng Pai. Student activist in Rangoon in the late 1950s and early 1960s. Went underground with Bo Pyan's Padaung (Kayan) forces after the demonetisation of 1964. Set up the Kayan New Land Council with support from the Karenni rebels the same year. Forged an alliance with the Communist Party of Burma in 1977. Based in the Pinlaung area of southwestern Shan State. Following the collapse of the CPB insurgency in 1989, his KNLC joined the National Democratic Front 20 June 1991.

SHWE KYIN, Nai (a.k.a.) Nai Ba Lwin

Mon. Born in 1913 in Phekata village near Thaton. Arts student at Rangoon University 1933–34. Went underground in August 1948 together with Nai Aung Tun and Nai Ngwe Thein. In jail 26–31 August 1948 and January 1949 to November 1951. Founding member of the Mon People's Front in 1952. The only Mon leader who did not surrender in 1958. Set up the New Mon State Party in July 1958. Participated in the 1963 peace talks in Rangoon. Established his headquarters at Three

Pagodas Pass on the Thai border in 1965. Signed a joint Mon-Karen-Burman agreement with Mahn Ba Zan of the Karen National Union and U Nu of the Parliamentary Democracy Party on 27 May 1970. Leader of one NMSP faction when the party split in April 1981; chairman of the reunited NMSP on 9 December 1987. Vice chairman of the Democratic Alliance of Burma in November 1988. Became chairman of the National Democratic Front in July 1991.

SOE, Thakin

Mon. Born in 1905 in Moulmein. Educated up to 7th Standard in an Anglo-Vernacular school. Employee of the Burmah Oil Company. Joined the *Dohbama Asiayone* and the Communist Party of Burma in the 1930s. Organised anti-Japanese guerrillas in Pyapon district, 1943–45; split with the main CPB in August 1946, set up the Communist Party (Red Flag) and went underground in the Irrawaddy delta region. Captured by the Burma Army in November 1970 at his Than Chaung camp near the Arakan Yoma. Imprisoned but released during the 1980 amnesty. In retirement until he re-entered politics in August 1988. Patron of the Unity and Development Party in September; died in Rangoon on 4 May 1989.

SOE AUNG, U

Arakanese Roman Catholic, married to a Karen. Born 1926 in Akyab (Sittwe). Educated in Rangoon; studied arts at Rangoon University. Joined the Karen National Union in 1946 and the Karen uprising in January 1949. With the 4th Brigade of the Karen forces in the Henzada region and the Arakan Yoma until 1968. In the Pegu Yoma 1968–75; leading official in the Karen National United Party. Went to the Thai border after the fall of the Pegu Yoma in 1975. Member of the central committee of the reunited Karen National Union since 1976. Led a delegation of the National Democratic Front to Kachin State and to the Panghsang headquarters of the Communist Party of Burma in 1985–87. Died of cancer in April 1993 at the KNU's Manerplaw headquarters.

SOE THEIN

Burman. Born in 1925 in Sagaing. Joined the Burma Independence Army in 1942 and the Communist Party of Burma in 1943. Fought against the Japanese in upper Burma together with his cousin Kyin Maung. Both went underground with the CPB in March 1948. CPB brigade commander in the Meiktila-Mandalay-Kyaukse area in 1950. Vice secretary of the Kyaukse district party committee. Went to the Pegu Yoma in April 1950 and to China in 1951. Stayed in Sichuan until 1968, when the northeastern base area was set up. Political commissar of the first CPB until it entered the northeast in 1968. Became vice political commissar of the northeastern command in September 1969, and member of the central committee in 1975. Became political commissar of the northeastern region in 1985. Arrested by the mutineers in the Wa Hills in April 1989. Now in exile in China.

TA KALEI

Karen from Bawgali village, Toungoo District. Worked as a *mahout* (elephant driver) before he joined the Karen National Defence Organisation in 1949. Together with his two brothers, he was sent by the KNDO in the early 1950s to contact the

Pa-Os near Taunggyi in the Shan states. Joined the Pa-O national movement under U Hla Pe. Ta Kalei's elder brother, Bo Special, became one of the ablest commanders of the newly formed Pa-O guerrilla army. During the second Pa-O uprising in 1966, Ta Kalei became its military commander. Fell out with the political leader of the Pa-O movement, U Hla Pe, and joined forces with the Communist Party of Burma in 1973. Headed a CPB-affiliated group called the Shan State Nationalities People's Liberation Organisation until the 1989 CPB mutiny. His SSNPLO was allied with Khun Sa for a short while in 1991; he now operates independently.

TAIK AUNG
   Burman. Born in 1927 in Waw, Pegu District, of a peasant family. Educated in a village monastery. Joined the Communist Party of Burma in the 1940s; went to China in 1953. Stayed in Sichuan, 1953–63. One of the Beijing Returnees. Led the bloody purges in the Pegu Yoma in the 1960s. Went to the northeastern base area in 1969; member of the central committee in 1975. Commander of the Panghsang security force and second in command of the northeastern command; considered a hardliner. Went to the Central Bureau along with Khin Maung Gyi and Mya Min in 1980; returned to Panghsang after suffering a stroke in August 1983. Left for China to get medical treatment in the same year.

TAMLA BAW
   Karen. Born in 1920 in Moulmein. Lance corporal in the 2nd Burma Rifles before World War II; joined Maj. Hugh Seagrim's guerrilla force during the Japanese occupation. Captured by the Japanese in 1944 and imprisoned for four months. Escaped and joined Force 136. Lieutenant in the 1st Karen Rifles after the war. Joined the Karen uprising in January 1949; participated in the Upper Burma Campaign. Active in the Toungoo area in the 1950s; commander of the Karens' 2nd brigade in 1961. Joined Bo Mya's Karen National Liberation Army in 1968. Vice chief of staff of the KNLA and member of the central committee of the Karen National Union since 1969. Lieutenant-general.

THA GYAW, *Bonbauk*
   Arakanese from Akyab. Fought against the Japanese with the Lion Brigade of Force 136 during World War II. Joined U Sein Da's Arakan People's Liberation Party in 1946 but defected to the Red Flag Communists in 1947. Led the Red Flag insurrection in Arakan until he surrendered in 1955 with eighty followers. Re-entered politics during the 1988 uprising for democracy, when he gave speeches and participated in the demonstrations in Akyab (Sittwe). Member of the Internal Peace Committee in Arakan in 1963. Co-founder (with Kyaw Zan Rhee and others) of the legal Arakan People's United Organisation in 1988, which, however, failed to win any seats in the 1990 election.

THAN AUNG, Saw
   Karen. Born in 1928 in Insein. Educated at an Indian school in Rangoon; fluent in Hindustani and Tamil. Ran a transport company in Rangoon and Pegu when he joined the Karen uprising in January 1949. With Saw Hunter Thamwe in the Toungoo-Papun area in the 1950s. In the Pegu Yoma in the 1960s; leading official of the Karen Na-

tional United Party. Came over to the Thai border with Mahn Ba Zan in 1968. General secretary of the reunited Karen National Union 1975–84. Vice president of the KNU from 1984 until his death from cancer in a Chiang Mai hospital on 2 April 1992.

THAN MYAING, Thakin

Burman. Born in 1918 in Kyaukse. Active in the *Dohbama Asiayone*. In charge of radio propaganda for Dr Ba Maw's puppet government during the Japanese occupation. Became a member of the central committee of the Communist Party of Burma at its second congress in 1945 and a member of the politburo in 1953. Went to China in 1953; stayed in Sichuan province. Became a member of the "leading group of five" in China in November 1963; purged for "revisionism" in 1967. Interned in a Chinese prison camp until 1973, when he was released. Settled in Da Shang, Sichuan, where he died on 3 May 1991.

THAN SHWE

Burman. Born in 1922 in Henzada. Joined the Burma Independence Army in 1942 and attended the Officers' Training School in Rangoon during the Japanese occupation. Joined the Communist Party of Burma and became commander of the Tharrawaddy battle front in 1949. Went to China with *yebaw* Aung Gyi in 1950. In Sichuan, China 1950–68. Became member of the 'leading group of five' in China in November 1963. Became military commander of the first CPB unit that entered Burma from China on 1 January 1968. Appointed political commissar of the northeastern command in September 1969. Became a member of the central committee in 1975; demoted to ordinary party member in 1980 for advocating a peaceful settlement with the government. Left the party in 1985 and retired in China.

THAWDA, Khun (a.k.a.) Pi Sai Long (a.k.a.) Pichai Khunseng

Shan. Born in 1925 in Hsipaw. Nephew of Sao Kya Seng, the last *saohpa* of Hsipaw. Studied at Rangoon University and in the United States. Teacher at Kambawza (Shan Chiefs') College in Taunggyi. Went underground with the *Noom Suk Harn* in 1959. Head of the Shan State Independence Army 1960–64. Participated in the 1963 peace talks with the government in Rangoon. Member of the Shan State War Council when the Shan State Army was formed in March 1964. Survived an assassination attempt in Fang in June 1964. Settled in Bangkok in 1968, where he worked for many years for United Press International.

THAN TUN, Thakin

Mon. Born in 1911 in Kanyut Kwin near Pyinmana. School teacher and member of the *Dohbama Asiayone*. Joined the Communist Party of Burma shortly after its foundation on 15 August 1939. Active in the anti-Japanese resistance during World War II. Aung San's brother-in-law. General secretary of the Anti-Fascist People's Freedom League from May 1946 until the CPB was expelled from the front in August. Went to Calcutta in February 1948 to attend the second congress of the Communist Party of India. *De facto* leader of the CPB after the second congress in 1945. Took the CPB underground in March 1948. Elected first party chairman in 1950 (prior to this, the party had been headed by a general secretary) and retained that post until he was assassinated by a government agent in the Pegu Yoma on 24 September 1968.

THEIN PE, Thakin (a.k.a.) Thein Pe Myint
  Burman. Born in 1914 in Budalin, Lower Chindwin District. Attended Mandalay Intermediary College and graduated from Rangoon University in 1934. One of the leaders of the 1936 student strike in Rangoon; active in the *Dohbama Asiayone*. Studied law at Calcutta University; closely associated with revolutionary organisations in Bengal. Became a member of the Communist Party of Burma in 1939, but was not one of its founders. Went to India during World War II to obtain Allied assistance in the struggle against the Japanese.
  Elected general secretary of the CPB in absentia at the second congress in 1945. Returned to Burma shortly afterwards and became editor of the party's theoretical organ, *People's Power* or *Pyithu Ana*. Councillor for agriculture and rural economy in Aung San's pre-independence cabinet, September–October 1946. Left the CPB on 26 March 1948, two days before it resorted to armed struggle.
  One of Burma's leading writers in the 1950s and 1960s. Elected to parliament for Budalin on a National Unity Front ticket in 1956. Editor of the leftist *Vanguard* newspaper. Became adviser to Ne Win's military government after the 1962 coup d'etat and joined the Burma Socialist Programme Party. Died in Rangoon in 1978. Considered Burma's first communist.

THWIN, U
  Burman. Born in 1921 in Pyinmana. A leader of the 1938 student strike and studied at Rangoon University up to 1941. Joined the Burma Independence Army during World War II and at one stage was close to Thakin Soe's Red Flag Communists. Civil servant after independence in 1948 and elected MP in 1951 and 1956. Secretary in U Nu's government and became minister for trade development and supplies in 1960. In jail 1962–68. Joined U Nu's resistance along the Thai border in 1969. The only prominent People's Patriotic Party member who did not surrender during the 1980 amnesty. Edited the *Democracy Journal* from Bangkok in the 1980s and became third vice-chairman of the Democratic Alliance of Burma in November 1988. Died in Bangkok on 18 August 1992.

TIN MAUNG WIN
  Burman. Born in 1938 in Rangoon. The son of U Win, a former Burmese ambassador to the USA. Involved in the 1962 student uprising; in jail 1965–68. Went underground with U Nu along the Thai border in 1969, and joined the rebel Parliamentary Democracy Party in 1970. Leader of its youth wing, the Patriotic Youth Front. Left for the USA in 1976. A founding member of the Committee for Restoration of Democracy in 1985 and its chairman since 1987.

TIN MYA, Thakin
  Burman. Born in Danubyu. Member of the *Dohbama Asiayone* in the 1930s. Became political commissar of the No. 7 Military Region of the Burma National Army in 1945. Became an alternate member of the central committee of the Communist Party of Burma in 1945. Joined Thakin Soe's Red Flag faction in March 1946 but was expelled in 1949 and rejoined the CPB. Arrested in 1957; released in 1960. Briefly re-arrested in 1962. Joined the ruling Burma Socialist Programme Party and became a member of its central committee. Author of a five-volume work on the anti-

Japanese struggle during World War II. Participated briefly in the 1988 uprising for democracy. Lives in retirement in Rangoon.

TIN YEE (a.k.a.) Ne Win

Burman. Born in 1922 in Pegu District. Participated in the "1300 Movement" and the *Dohbama Asiayone* in Pegu. Joined the Communist Party of Burma during the anti-Japanese struggle in 1943. Went to China in 1951 and stayed in Sichuan until 1968. Became a member of the 'leading group of five' in China in November 1963. Political commissar of the 404 War Zone (the Kokang forces), 1968–69; he was then known as "Yang Koang". Became political commissar of the northeastern command in 1971; became a member of the central committee and the politburo in 1975. Chief of general staff of the CPB's army from 1986 until the April 1989 mutiny, when he fled to China.

TING YING

Kachin of the Ngochan tribe from the Yunnan frontier. Broke with the Kachin Independence Army and joined the Communist Party of Burma in early 1968. Established the CPB's 101 War Zone in the Panwa-Kambaiti area of eastern Kachin State together with Zalum, another KIA defector. Joined the 1989 mutiny, and his former CPB unit, now renamed the New Democratic Army, was legalised on 15 December 1989 and became a government-recognised militia force.

TU JAI

Kachin. Born in 1930 in Kutkai, Shan State. Studied at Kutkai middle school up to 8th Standard. Joined the 4th Kachin Rifles in 1950 and became lance corporal in 1956. Joined the Kachin rebel movement in 1961. Brigade commander (the Kachin Independence Army) in the Putao area of Kachin State in 1973. Became chief of staff of the KIA in 1975; handed over his duties to Zau Mai in 1980. Member of the central committee of the Kachin Independence Organisation since 1975.

WEI HSUEH-LONG

Chinese from Yunnan. Fled across the frontier to Burma following the Communist take-over in China. Based for many years at Vingngun in the Wa Hills together with his two brothers, Wei Hsueh-kang and Wei Hsueh-yin. The three Wei brothers were connected with the Kuomintang-CIA spy network along the Yunnan frontier until the Burmese Communists drove them out in the early 1970s. First based at Khun Sa's base at Ban Hin Taek (Wei Hsueh-kang served for several years as Khun Sa's treasurer), they later broke away to establish their own heroin empire along the Thai border. Lacking their own army inside Burma, the Wei brothers made use of their old Wa contacts and bankrolled the build-up of the Wa National Army in the early 1980s. They are now connected with the United Wa State Army of Chao Ngi Lai and Pao Yochang.

YAN AUNG, Bo (a.k.a.) Thakin Hla Myaing.

Burman. Born in 1908 in Syriam. Active in the *Dohbama Asiayone*; organised the oil workers in Syriam. Joined the Communist Party of Burma in 1939. Went with Aung San to Amoy, China, and on to Japan in 1940. One of the Thirty Comrades.

Arrested when the CPB went underground on 28 March 1948, but was freed shortly afterwards to negotiate with the party, which he subsequently rejoined. Remained with the CPB, but was considered almost a "traitor". He was nevertheless elected to the central committee and stayed in the Pegu Yoma until he was executed there on 26 December 1967.

YAN NAING, Bo

Burman. Born in 1918 in Thayetmyo. Educated at Government High School, Prome, and became a student leader in Rangoon in the 1950s. General secretary of the All-Burma Students' Union 1940–41. One of the Thirty Comrades. Major in the Burma Independence Army; fought against British forces in Pa-an, Henzada, Myanaung, Shwedaung and Pauk. Colonel in the Burma Defence Army and served as principal of the Military College, Mingaladon, 1944–45. Leader of the *Maha Bama* party after the war. Married the daughter of Dr Ba Maw, the wartime head of state of Burma. Went into business after independence.

Fled to the Thai border in 1965 together with his brother-in-law Zali Maw and a Karen ex-brigadier-general, Saw Kya Doe, to organise resistance against the military government. Joined U Nu's Parliamentary Democracy Party. Returned to Burma during the 1980 amnesty. Took part in the 1988 pro-democracy movement in Rangoon. Died in Rangoon 28 January 1989.

YANG, Jimmy (a.k.a.) Yang Kyin-sein

Kokang Chinese. Born in 1920 in Kokang. Belonged to the ruling family of Kokang; educated at the Shan Chiefs' School in Taunggyi, Rangoon University and Chungking University in wartime China. Elected MP for Kokang in 1950 and became a banker (founder of the East Burma Bank) later in the 1950s. Founded the Kokang Revolutionary Force in October 1963 and went underground in 1964 with the Shan State Army; commander of its Kokang-dominated 5th Brigade. Retired from the SSA and became manager of the Rincome Hotel in Chiang Mai in 1966. Rejoined the underground in 1969 as commander of the northern forces of U Nu's resistance. Left for Paris in 1973 but returned to Burma during the 1980 amnesty. Died in Rangoon in 1985.

YANG, Olive (a.k.a.) Yang Kyin-hsui

Kokang Chinese. Born in 1927 in Kokang. Jimmy Yang's younger sister. Educated in Kokang and then at the Guardian Angel's Convent, Lashio. Arrested in 1952 for supporting the Kuomintang and held in Mandalay jail for five years. Ruled Kokang 1960–62; she was the first local militia commander to organise lorry convoys that carried opium to the Thai border. Titular head of Kokang in 1960. Arrested again in 1963 and released in 1968. Played some role in negotiating the peace treaty between the Rangoon government and the Kokang unit of the former Communist Party of Burma following the 1989 mutiny.

YANG MO LIAN

Kokang Chinese. Born in 1951 in Kokang. Attended primary school in Tashwehtang and joined the Kokang army in 1966. Military officer in the People's Army of the Communist Party of Burma until the 1989 mutiny. Defeated Pheung

Kya-shin in the 1992 "Opium War" in Kokang. Now commander in chief of the Kokang forces.

YE HTUT, Bo (a.k.a.) Thakin Aung Thein

Burman. Born in 1922 in Rangoon. Member of the *Dohbama Asiayone*; one of the Thirty Comrades. Commanding officer in the Burma Army after independence. One of the mutineers from the 3rd Burifs (Burma Rifles) who went underground in 1949. Vice chief of general staff when the Revolutionary Burma Army joined the Communists' People's Liberation Army of Burma in 1950 to become the People's Army. Surrendered in June 1963. Later joined the ruling Burma Socialist Programme Party and became a member of its central committee. Quit the BSPP and participated in the 1988 pro-democracy uprising in Burma.

YE TUN (a.k.a.) Thakin Tun Nu

Burman. Born in 1912 in Kyauntaphek village, Lewe township, Pyinmana. Educated in a village monastery. Member of the *Dohbama Asiayone*. Joined the Burma Independence Army during the Japanese occupation and became a member of the Communist Party of Burma in 1944. Led peasant struggles in the Pyinmana area in the late 1940s. Left for the northeast in 1968; stayed in the 108 War Zone until 1975. Became a member of the CPB's central committee in 1975 and transferred to Panghsang. Based in Beijing as as an official representative of the CPB from 1975 until the 1989 mutiny. Member of the CPB delegation that held peace talks with the government in Lashio in May 1981. Retired in China after the 1989 mutiny.

ZALI MAW

Burman. Born in 1928 in Rangoon. The son of Dr Ba Maw, the Japanese-installed figurehead of Burma during World War II. Educated in Rangoon and in England. A lawyer by profession. Went to the Thai border in 1965 together with Saw Kya Doe and Bo Yan Naing to organise resistance against the military government. Legal adviser to U Nu's Parliamentary Democracy Party when it was set up on 29 August 1969. Surrendered during the 1980 amnesty, but left almost immediately for Bangkok where he continued to work as a lawyer. Chairman of the Alliance for Democratic Solidarity (Union of Burma) since 19 January 1989.

ZAU DAN

Kachin. Born in 1940 in Hu Bren Pung Shwe village near Kutkai, northeastern Shan State. One of Gen. Zau Seng's younger brothers. Graduate of Mandalay University. Founded the Kachin Independence Army in 1961 together with his brothers Zau Seng and Zau Tu. Commander of the KIA forces in northeastern Shan State and considered one of the ablest officers in the Kachin rebel movement; killed in action with the Communist Party of Burma on 1 March 1975.

ZAU MAI (1)

Kachin. Born in 1936 in Manhkring village near Myitkyina. Studied at the Baptist High School in Myitkyina; obtained a BA degree from Rangoon University in 1959. Government official in Sinlumkaba, Kachin State, in 1959. Joined the Kachin Independence Army in 1962. Participated in the 1963 peace talks with the Rangoon government. Commander of the KIA's 4th Brigade (northeastern Shan State) in 1972. Fought battles with Communist forces in the area until a peace treaty was reached in 1976. Became vice chairman of the Kachin Independence Organisation in 1975 and chief of staff of the KIA in 1980. Led the KIO delegation which held talks with the military authorities in Myitkyina in September 1993.

ZAU MAI (2)
Kachin. Born in 1932 in Kutkai, northeastern Shan State. Joined Naw Seng's forces in 1949. Stayed with him in China, 1950–68. Entered Möng Ko on 1 January 1968 together with Naw Seng's troops and political commissars from the Communist Party of Burma. Became vice military commander of the northeastern command in September 1969. Succeeded Naw Seng as commander after the latter's death in 1972. Became a member of the central committee in 1975. Joined the 1989 mutiny and became one of the leaders of the new Burma National United Party, later renamed the United Wa State Party.

ZAU SENG
Kachin. Born in 1928 in Kapna Bang Shau village near Hsenwi, northeastern Shan State, where his father, Balawng Du, was a Baptist pastor. Studied up to 7th Standard in Hsenwi and served with the US-organised Detachment 101 as a junior intelligence officer during World War II. Joined the 1st Kachin Rifles after the war and went underground with its commander, Naw Seng, in 1949. Remained behind with Karen and Karenni rebels in Burma when Naw Seng retreated to China in 1950.

Closely connected with right-wing circles in Thailand in the 1950s; attended meetings with the World Anti-Communist League in Saigon and Taiwan. Returned to Kachin State in 1958 to organise an uprising there; formed the Kachin Independence Army on 5 February 1961 together with his brothers Zau Tu and Zau Dan.

President of the Kachin Independence Organisation and commander of the KIA. Returned to the Thai border in 1965 to set up base at the Tam Ngob headquarters of the 3rd Kuomintang. Assassinated near Tam Ngob along with Zau Tu and KIO general secretary Pungshwi Zau Seng on 6 August 1975.

ZAU SENG, Gauri
Kachin. Born in 1942 in Myitkyina. Science student at Rangoon University in the early 1960s; active in the Kachin student movement. Went underground in 1964 with the Kachin Independence Army. Succeeded Zau Tu as commander of the KIA's 2nd Brigade (western Kachin State) in 1975. Became member of the central committee of the Kachin Independence Organisation 1977. Led a Kachin delegation to the Thai border in 1983, the first since the assassination of Zau Seng, Zau Tu and Phungshwi Zau Seng in 1975. The main Kachin representative in Thailand since 1983. Became vice chairman of the National Democratic Front in July 1991.

ZAU SENG, Pungshwi
Kachin. Born in Hu Bren Pung Shwe near Kutkai in northeastern Shan State. Studied engineering, art, philosophy and political science at Rangoon University in 1955–59. Civil servant in northeastern Shan State before he joined the Kachin

rebellion in 1961. General secretary of the Kachin Independence Organisation and staunch anti-communist. Accompanied Zau Tu to the Thai border in 1973. Assassinated on 6 August 1975 near Tam Ngob along with Zau Seng and Zau Tu.

ZAU TU

Kachin. Born in 1937 in Kapna Bang Shau village near Hsenwi, northeastern Shan State. Studied at Rangoon University. Gen. Zau Seng's younger brother and one of the founders of the Kachin Independence Army in 1961. Provided the funds for the uprising by robbing the treasury in Lashio of 90,000 Kyats. Led the Kachin rebels in the north after his brother had left for the Thai border in 1965. Fought battles with the Burma Army, the Shan State Army, Naga insurgents and Rawang village militia in northern Kachin State. Left for Tam Ngob on the Thai border 1973. Assassinated on 6 August 1975.

ZAWNG HRA

Kachin of the Maru tribe. Born in 1935 in Sumprabum, Kachin State. Studied at the Kachin Baptist School in Myitkyina before being admitted to Rangoon University in 1955. Acquired a BA degree a few years later and worked for a while as sub-divisional officer of Sumprabum. Joined the Kachin rebels in 1963. General secretary of the Kachin Independence Organisation since 1976; attended peace talks in Rangoon in 1980. Accompanied Brang Seng abroad in 1987; returned to Kachin State in 1988.

ZEYA, Bo (a.k.a.) Thakin Hla Maung

Burman. Born in 1920 in Mandalay. Educated at Rangoon University and president of the Students' Union, 1940–41. One of the Thirty Comrades. Chief of general staff of the Burma Defence Army, 1942–43. Commander of the 3rd Burifs (Burma Rifles) after the war. Joined the army mutiny in 1949 and set up the Revolutionary Burma Army and became second vice chairman of the "Central People's Revolutionary Military Commission" when the RBA and the People's Liberation Army of Burma (of the Communist Party of Burma) merged to become the People's Army on 1 September 1950. Went to China in 1953; one of the Beijing Returnees who participated in the 1963 peace talks. Killed in action near the Pegu Yoma on 16 April 1968.

ZHANG ZHIMING (a.k.a.) Kyi Myint

Chinese. Born in 1950 in Wanting, China's Yunnan province. Joined the Communist Party of Burma in 1968 as a Red Guard volunteer along with Li Ziru and Lin Mingxian. One of the CPB's ablest military officers. Commander of the 2nd Brigade at Möng Paw; led the assault on Hsi-Hsinwan in November 1986. Supported the mutiny in April 1989 and joined Lin Mingxian's forces in the former CPB's 815 Region (Mekong River Division) in eastern Shan State in May. Now government-recognised militia commander and prominent drug trafficker.

ZIN, Thakin

Sino-Burmese. Born in 1912 in Daik-U. Timber merchant. Active in the *Dohbama Asiayone*. Joined the Communist Party of Burma in 1943. Became a member of the central committee at the second congress in 1945. Organiser in the All-Burma Peasants' Organisation. Went underground in March 1948. Political commissar of the CPB's southern Burma command in the 1950s. Party chairman after the death of Thakin Than Tun in October 1968. Killed in the Pegu Yoma on 15 March 1975.

Notes on names in Burma:

U, Ko and *Maung* are used to mean "mister", depending on the rank and age of the man addressed, and his relationship to the speaker. Thus, Nu would be called *Maung* Nu by his mother, *Ko* Nu by his friends and *U* Nu when addressed formally or by subordinates. *Daw* and *Ma* are used similarly for women. *Daw* Aung San Suu Kyi is the formal designation while *Ma* Aung San Suu Kyi would have been used when she was younger or by her friends.

Bo and *Bohmu* are military titles for officers which are often carried into civilian life, like *Bogyoke*, which means supremo or chief and is more respectful than general, a military designation only. *Thakin* is a title used by the young nationalists in the 1930s (*Thakin* Nu, for instance); it means master and was originally reserved for the British. Some of the Communist leaders, who once were members of the early nationalist movement, thus are referred to as *thakins* as well.

Yebaw means comrade and is used by the Communists and, until 1988, was also used within the ruling Burma Socialist Programme Party. Shans are titled *Sai* (literally "brother"; *Nang* means sister).*Sao* and *Khun* are Shan titles originally reserved for the ruling families but later used by military officers in the insurgency. *Sara* (in Burmese: *Saya*) means "teacher".

Karens are titled *Saw* (men) and *Naw* (women). *Mahn* is the Pwo Karen equivalent of *Saw*. *P'doh* is used for addressing officials in the Karen rebel administration. Mon males are titled *Nai* ("mister"). The Burmans, Shans, Arakanese, Mons, Karens, Karennis, Was, Padaungs (Kayans), Palaungs and most smaller tribes do not have any family names. The Chins, Kachins and Nagas, on the other hand, have surnames as well as clan names.

Appendix 3:
Rebel Armies and Other
Anti-Government Groups in Burma

Communist and pro-Communist:

Communist Party of Burma (CPB): Set up on 15 August 1939 in Rangoon. Played an important role in the anti-Japanese struggle during World War II. Went underground on 28 March 1948 and was formally outlawed in October 1953. Strongholds in the Pegu Yoma, the Arakan Yoma, the Irrawaddy delta and in upper Burma until these were recaptured by government forces in the mid 1970s. A new, 20,000 square-kilometre base area was established in northeastern Shan State during the period 1968–73. The party ceased to exist as an armed insurgent force inside Burma after a mutiny in March–April 1989. Strength: 15–18,000 (1950); 4–5,000 (1960); 23,000 (1978); 10,000 (1989). Leaders: Thakin Than Tun 1945–68; Thakin Zin 1968–75; Thakin Ba Thein Tin 1975–89. In the wake of the 1988 uprising for democracy, some students fled to areas in Shan and Kayah states controlled by CPB allies; 250 of them were organised by the CPB into the short-lived **Democratic Patriotic Army (DPA)**, which disintegrated after the 1989 mutiny. Following the 1989 mutiny, the former CPB's "People's Army" broke up into four local armies based along ethnic lines:

New Democratic Army (NDA) in the former 101 War Zone in Kachin State. Led by Ting Ying and based at Pangwa, Hpimaw and Kambaiti pass on the Chinese border northeast of Myitkyina. Strength: 300–400. Involved in timber and drug trade with China.

Myanmar National Democratic Alliance Party/Army (MNDAP/MNDAA) in the Kokang area, led by Pheung Kya-shin and his younger brother, Pheung Kya-fu until December 1992 when they were driven out by the rival Yang clan led by Yang Mo Lian. Strength: 1,500–2,000. The main drug trafficking organisation inside Burma today.

United Wa State Party/Army (UWSP/UWSA) in the Wa Hills, led by Chao Ngi Lai and Pao Yu-chang, two Wa ex-CPB leaders. Strength: 10,000–15,000 plus about the same number of local militia forces.

National Democratic Alliance Army, Military and Local Administration Committee, Eastern Shan State (the former 815 War Zone north of Kengtung in eastern Shan State), led by Lin Mingxian (Sai Leün or Sai Lin) and Zhang Zhiming (Kyi Myint). Strength: 3,500–4,000. Not the biggest, but the best-organised drug trafficking organisation inside Burma today. Closely connected with mainland Chinese intelligence.

Communist Party (Red Flag): A radical CPB faction, led by Thakin Soe, which broke away from the main party in February 1946 and went underground. It established strongholds in the Arakan Yoma, Upper Burma, and especially around Dedaye north of Thegon in the Irrawaddy delta region, where Thakin Soe had fought against the Japanese during World War II. Strength in the early 1950s: 1,500–2,000. Thakin Soe was captured in November 1970, after which the party virtually collapsed. He was released during the 1980 amnesty and became the patron of the legal Unity and Development Party in September 1988. Thakin Soe died in Rangoon on 4 May 1989. The last remnants of the CP(RF), based along the Bangladesh border and led by *yeni* Thaw Da, joined the People's Liberation Front (PLF) on 7 November 1990.

People's Volunteer Organisation (PVO)/People's Comrade Party (PCP): The PVO was set up on 1 December 1945 as an association for wartime veterans but, in effect, it became a militia force loyal to Aung San until his assassination on 19 July 1947. It then split into two factions: a "Yellow Band" PVO led by Bohmu Aung, one of the Thirty Comrades who was close to the Socialist Party, and the much more left-leaning "White Band" PVO led by another of the Thirty Comrades, Bo La Yaung, and Bo Po Kun, also a veteran of World War II (but not one of the Thirty Comrades). The White Band PVO went underground on 28 July 1948 (4,000 men, or approximately 60% of the PVO's total main force), allying itself loosely with the Communists as a member of the People's Democratic Front (PDF), and was active all over central Burma. Bo La Yaung surrendered in the early 1950s; Bo Po Kun continued the struggle under the new banner, PCP, until August 1958, when he also surrendered. Several PCP leaders later entered legal politics and some became members of the Burma Socialist Programme Party (BSPP) after the 1962 military take-over. The name PVO reappeared during the 1988 uprising for democracy; some veterans even had it registered as a political party, but it failed to win any significant support.

Shan State Communist Party (SSCP): Set up in 1956 by Moh Heng, a local CPB commander in the Lawksawk area, when the main party rejected the demand for a separate Shan party committee. Moh Heng and 400 SSCP followers surrendered to the government on 10 May 1958. Moh Heng joined the non-communist Shan resistance (*Noom Suk Harn*) in November 1958 (see Shan groups).

Chin National Vanguard Party (CNVP): A small pro-Communist group set up in March 1956 by lowland Chins in the Thayetmyo area of Magwe Division. Participated in the 1963 peace talks but was absorbed by the Communist Party of Burma later the same year.

Communist Party of Arakan (CPA): Formally set up on 11 March 1962 by Kyaw Zan Rhee and others who had in effect already broken away from Thakin Soe's Red Flag Communists in 1956 to fight for an independent socialist republic of Arakan. It was active mainly in Myebon township (Kyaukpyu) and almost disintegrated after Kyaw Zan Rhee's surrender during the 1980 amnesty. Its last known activity inside Arakan was an attack in May 1986 on a police station in Minbya town. The remnants of the CPA, now in exile in Bangladesh, joined the National United Front of Arakan (NUFA) when it was set up on 8 September 1988.

Non-Communist Burman:

Parliamentary Democracy Party (PDP): The formation of the PDP was announced in London on 29 August 1969 by U Nu, who became its president. Other leading personalities include Bo Let Ya of the Thirty Comrades (vice president); the former editor of *The Nation*, Law Yone (general secretary); former commerce minister U Thwin (joint secretary); a former chief of the air force, Air Commodore Tommy Clift (foreign and financial affairs); Dr Ba Maw's son, Zali Maw, in charge of legal affairs; and Bohmu Aung, another of the Thirty Comrades. Its armed wing, the **Patriotic Liberation Army (PLA)**, was commanded by Bo Let Ya with former Brig.-Gen. Kya Doe as chief of staff and Bo Yan Naing (also of the Thirty Comrades) as vice chief of staff. The PLA established bases in Mon and Karen territory along the Thai border and had more than 3,000 men in arms in the early 1970s. A pact was signed with Mon and Karen rebels on 25 May 1970, leading to the formation of the **National United Front (NUF)**, nominally chaired by Karen leader Mahn Ba Zan. The movement began to dwindle when U Nu left for India in 1973.

People's Patriotic Party (PPP): The new name for U Nu's PDP in late 1974, now led by Bo Let Ya. It disintegrated after the death of Bo Let Ya on 29 November 1978. Many of its most prominent members went into exile in Europe, Australia and the US. The remnants in Thailand surrendered during the 1980 amnesty and returned to Rangoon. Only U Thwin remained in Thailand, where he continued to edit the PPP's magazine, the *Democracy Journal*, until the 1988 uprising for democracy. U Thwin's PPP joined the Democratic Alliance of Burma on 18 November 1988.

People's Unity and Peace Front: A smaller group which was active in the mid-1970s, led by David Zaw Tun, a Rangoon University graduate. Active in the hills east of Pyinmana and based mainly in the Karenni rebel area opposite Mae Hong Son. The group disintegrated in 1975.

Burma Liberation Army (BLA): A small group based near Chumphon near the Thai border and led by Bo Htwe, a former PPP/PLA commander.

People's Liberation Front (PLF): A small left-leaning group set up on 6 July 1973 by Aye Saung, formerly of the CP(RF), and a group of students at Mandalay University. Aye Saung joined the Shan State Army (SSA) in 1978 but left for Thailand in 1982 to rebuild the PLF. Existed in name only until the 1988 uprising for democracy when it was joined by some dissident air force personnel who escaped to the Thai border. Became a member of the Democratic Alliance of Burma on 18 November 1988. Based north of Mae Sot on the Thai-Burma border. The last remnants of the CP(RF) on the Bangladesh border joined the PLF on 7 November 1990.

Committee for Restoration of Democracy in Burma (CRDB): Set up in the US in 1985 but officially announced on 4th January 1987. Umbrella organisation of overseas Burmese dissidents in the US, the UK, Germany, Australia, Thailand and Bangladesh. Joined the Democratic Alliance of Burma on 18 November 1988. Chairmen: Kyaw Win 1987–88; Tin Maung Win 1988-. General secretary 1987–92: Ye Kyaw Thu.

All-Burma Students' Democratic Front (ABSDF): Set up on 5 November 1988 at Wangkha on the Thai border; an umbrella organisation of students who fled to the Thai, Chinese and Bangladesh border areas after the military take-over in September 1988. Claims to have 4,800 members in Karen, Mon, Kachin, Shan, Kayah and Arakan States, and Tenasserim Division. Possibly 500–600 are armed. Became a member of the Democratic Alliance of Burma on 18 November 1988. First chairman: Htun Aung Gyaw 1988–89. Moe Thi Zun was elected chairman in 1989 but refused to step down during the ABSDF's second congress, which lasted from 14 August to 24 October 1991. The ABSDF subsequently split into two factions, one led by Moe Thi Zun and the other by Dr. Naing Aung.

Alliance for Democratic Solidarity (Union of Burma) (ADS [B]): Set up on 19 January 1989 by U Nu's son, U Aung, and some former PDP/PPP cadres in Thailand. Based in Bangkok and in Mon rebel territory near Three Pagodas Pass on the Thai-Burma border. Chairman: Zali Maw. General secretary: U Aung. Other prominent members include Bo Khin Maung, a former AFPFL MP who escaped to the Thai border in late 1988, and Zaw Oo, a student activist who took part in the 1988 uprising for democracy.

People's Defence Force (PDF): Set up by Sein Mya, a former colonel of the Burma Army who escaped to Three Pagodas Pass with Bo Khin Maung in late 1988. Sein Mya first joined the ADS(B) but broke away in 1989 to form the PDF. It consisted of army defectors who fled to the Thai border after the 1988 uprising for democracy, plus a few students. Sein Mya died of malaria in December 1993.

Akha:

The Akha tribe of the Kengtung area of eastern Shan State never formed any properly organised rebel army. However, an Akha rebellion broke out in Pa Lu-Pa-Le near the Burma-Laos-China triborder junction in 1967 against Kuomintang rule in the area. These forces, led by Lao Er Ji Pyao, began receiving support from the Communist Party of Burma in 1970 and became part of the Communist 815 Region when it was set up on 5 October 1971. Following the March–April 1989 mutiny, these forces became part of Lin Mingxian's and Zhang Zhiming's drug trafficking group, the National Democratic Alliance Army, Military and Local Administration Committee, Eastern Shan State.

Arakanese:

Arakan People's Liberation Party (APLP): More commonly known as just the PLP. Set up in 1945 by U Sein Da, an Arakanese monk and nationalist leader. Resorted to armed struggle against the British in 1946; continued the fight for a separate Arakan state after Burma's independence in 1948. U Sein Da and 400 of his last followers surrendered in 1958.

Arakan National Liberation Party (ANLP): Set up in June 1960 when some former APLP activists decided to go underground again. Led by Maung Sein Nyunt, they established a few bases in the Arakan Yoma but soon retreated to the Bangladesh border. Joined the NUFA in September 1988.

Arakan Independence Organisation (AIO): Set up on 20 May 1970 by a group of Arakanese students at Rangoon University and trained by the Kachin Independence Organisation (KIO). They were ambushed on their way back to Arakan from Kachin State in 1977, and only a handful survived. The first chairman, Tun Shwe Maung, surrendered in 1980 and was succeeded by Kyaw Hlaing. The AIO maintained a camp on the Bangladesh border until the late 1980s. The last remnants joined the NUFA in September 1988.

Arakan Liberation Party/Army (ALP/ALA): Set up in July 1972 by Khaing Moe Lin and trained by the Karens at Kawmoorah (Wangkha) on the Thai-Burma border. They were sent back to Arakan in 1977 but were intercepted by the Burma Army in Chin State and wiped out. The remnants along the Thai border received backing from the Karen National Union and new units were established in Karen rebel camps on the Thai-Burma border, where they still remain. Strength: 50–60 men. The first chairman, Khaing Moe Lin, was cornered in Chin State in 1978 and committed suicide. Khaing Ye Khaing became new chairman (he now lives in Mizoram, India). Joined the NUFA in September 1988.

National United Front of Arakan (NUFA): Set up on 8 September 1988, uniting five small groups based on the Bangladesh-Burma border: the AIO, the ALP, the ANLP, the Communist Party of Arakan (CPA) and a faction of the Tribal Nationality Party of Arakan (a tribal organisation in the Arakan Yoma led by former Communist Party of Burma cadres in Arakan; another TNPA faction remains with the CPB in Arakan). The combined army is called **the New Arakan Construction Army (NACA)**, but its presence in Arakan is negligible. The forces of the former ALA are still fighting with the Karens along the Thai-Burma border. Became a member of the Democratic Alliance of Burma on 18 November 1988. A break-away group, led by Khaing Ra Za, formed in 1991 the **Arakan Army (AA)** which collects taxes on trading boats in the Mergui archipelago off the coast of southern Tenasserim Division.

Chin:

Chin Independence Army (CIA): Set up by Lieut.-Col. Son Ka Pao in the Falam area of northern Chin State in 1961. He was arrested in 1963 and released in 1970. Lian Mang took over the CIA in 1963 and sent several delegations to Thailand to get outside support, which failed. In 1967, CIA became **the Zomi National Armed Force (ZNAF, or the Zomi National Force, the ZNF)**, which on 7 July 1977 became **the Committee for Restoration and Protection of the Sovereignty and Independence of Occupied Zoram (CRPSIOZ)**, led by Lian Mang. It soon dwindled away and never managed to establish any foothold inside Chin State ("Zoram").

Chin National Front/Army (CNF/CNA): The CNF was formed in 1985 and its armed wing, the CNA, was set up on 14 November 1988. The Kachin Independence Army (KIA) trained about 100 Chin rebels in 1989; they were sent back to Chin State later that year, and some fighting erupted. The CNF became a member of the National Democratic Front (NDF) and the Democratic Alliance of Burma on 2 March 1989. Initially led by John Khaw Kim Thang, the group has now broken up into several different factions.

Chinese:

Kuomintang (KMT): Nationalist Chinese troops from southern China entered northeastern Shan State from Yunnan following their defeat in the Chinese civil war in 1949–50. They established bases along the Sino-Burmese border in Shan State and on the Thai border in the south, where they worked closely together with Taiwan intelligence, Thai military authorities and the CIA. The KMT also built up the Shan State opium trade. Their first leader, Gen. Li Mi, returned to Taiwan in 1952 and was succeeded by Lieut.-Gen. Liu Yuanlin, a graduate of the fourth year of the Central Army Officers' Training School. Liu, a Fukkienese, came from Chiang Kai-shek's personal security force and was therefore trusted by the high command in Taipei to unofficially succeed the high-profile Li Mi.

Most KMT forces in Burma were driven out by a joint mainland China-Burma military operation in 1961 and re-established themselves in northern Thailand: the 3rd KMT at Tam Ngob, west of Fang and the 5th KMT at Doi Mae Salong, northwest of Chiang Rai. Inside Shan State the KMT has been acting through proxies since the 1960s and 1970s: Moh Heng's Shan United Revolutionary Army (SURA); *Ka Kwe Ye* units dominated by ethnic Chinese, Mahasang's Wa National Army (WNA); and even elements of the Communist Party of Burma (CPB).

Rival KMT groups maintain close links with Khun Sa, whose most powerful military commanders are also Chinese with KMT connections: for instance Chang Shu-chuan (a Manchurian who is also known by his Shan name Sao Hpalang) and Leng Chong-ying (*aka* Leng Seün; an ex-KMT from the Beijing area).

Kokang Revolutionary Force (KRF): A local insurgent group based in the Chinese-dominated Kokang district of northeastern Shan State, and founded in December 1963 by Jimmy Yang of Kokang's ruling family. It became the 5th Brigade of the Shan State Army (SSA) in 1964, but soon split into different factions. Jimmy Yang became the northern commander of U Nu's National United Front (NUF) in 1970; Pheung Kya-shin and his brother Pheung Kya-fu had joined the Communist Party of Burma in 1967. Another commander, Lo Hsing-han, had already defected to the government in 1963 and set up a *Ka Kwe Ye* home guard unit in Kokang.

Jimmy Yang returned to Rangoon during the 1980 amnesty. Lo Hsing-han broke with the government when the *Ka Kwe Ye* programme was abandoned in February 1973 and linked up with the SSA in May. He was arrested in July in Thailand, extradited to Burma and sentenced to death in 1976. He was released during the 1980 amnesty and now is the "godfather" of the drug trade from Kokang.

Kokang People's Liberation Army (KPLA): Set up by Pheung Kya-shin and Pheung Kya-fu in late 1967 in China with backing from the CPB. Entered Kokang from China on 5 January 1968, and officially merged with the CPB's army in August.

Shan State Revolutionary Army (SSRA): Set up on 2 August 1976 by Lo Hsing-han's younger brother, Lo Hsing-minh, and other remnants of the Kokang *Ka Kwe Ye*, who had been stranded at Mae Aw on the Thai border near Mae Hong Son following Lo Hsing-han's arrest in 1973, plus Jimmy Yang's nephew Donald Yang and his followers. Closely allied with Taiwan intelligence and active in the opium trade. Lo Hsing-han was released during the

1980 amnesty and Lo Hsing-minh returned to Lashio from the Thai border with 200 of his men.

Chang Chifu (Khun Sa): A half-Chinese, half-Shan warlord from the Loi Maw area north of Tang-yan. He has led a number of private armies which have been involved in opium smuggling and heroin trafficking. In 1963, he set up a *Ka Kwe Ye* home guard unit in Loi Maw under the aegis of the Burma Army. He was arrested in October 1969, and his men went underground and forged an alliance with the Shan State Army (SSA).

In 1972, they set up the **Shan United Army (SUA)**, commanded by Chang Shu-chuan, an ex-KMT Chinese from Manchuria. Chang was released in 1974 and rejoined his men in 1976, assuming the Shan name "Khun Sa". The SUA was based at Ban Hin Taek inside Thailand, northwest of Chiang Rai, until January 1982, when Thai forces launched an attack and drove them across the border to Burma.

On 25 March 1985, the SUA joined the **Tai Revolutionary Council (TRC)**, an alliance between the former SURA of Mo Heng and the SSA's 2nd Brigade (see Shan groups). The renewed TRC's army was also called the **Shan State Army (SSA)** on 21 July 1985, but it became the **Möng Tai Army (MTA)** in 1987.

Mo Heng was the official chairman of the TRC until his death in July 1991. Khun Sa succeeded Moh Heng in September, but "resigned" in July 1992 in favour of Bo Dewing. The TRC was renamed the **Shan State Restoration Council (SSRC)** in 1991 and Khun Sa was re-elected chairman on 12 December 1993. Strength: approximately 18,000–20,000 men, but not all are armed. Most soldiers are Shans but there are also many Was, Palaungs and even Kachins in the MTA.

Kachin:

Pawngyawng National Defence Force (PNDF): Set up by Naw Seng in northeastern Shan State on 15 November 1949 to fight for Kachin independence. The group was cornered in northeastern Shan State, and Naw Seng with 300 followers retreated across the border into China in April 1950. Naw Seng returned to Burma in January 1968 as military head of the Communist Party of Burma's units in the northeast. Many former PNDF cadres served as officials in the CPB's civil administration in the Sino-Burmese border areas until the 1989 mutiny. Some remain in the Wa area while others have retired in China.

Kachin Independence Organisation/Army (KIO/KIA): Set up in the Hsenwi area of northeastern Shan State on 5 February 1961 by three brothers: Zau Seng, Zau Tu and Zau Dan. The movement soon spread to Kachin State proper, most of which was taken over by the rebels in the 1960s and 1970s. Strength by the early 1990s: 6,000–7,000 plus local militias. Chairmen: Gen. Zau Seng 1961–75; Brang Seng 1975-. Commanders of the KIA: Gen. Zau Seng 1961–75; Brig. Tu Jai 1975–80; Maj.-Gen. Zau Mai 1980-.

The 4th Brigade of the KIA in northeastern Shan State signed a peace treaty with the Rangoon government on 11 January 1991 and became the **Kachin Democratic Army (KDA)**, led by Mahtu Naw, a former brigade major of the 4th Brigade. The main KIA entered into a similar agreement with Rangoon on 8 April 1993. The cease-fire was finalised on 29 September when Maj.-Gen. Zau Mai met Burma's powerful intelligence chief, Lieut.-Gen. Khin Nyunt, in Myitkyina.

Karen:

Karen National Defence Organisation (KNDO): Set up on 16 July 1947 by Mahn Ba Zan as the private militia of the KNU. Occupied Thaton on 30 August 1948 and Moulmein on the 31st. The KNDO withdrew from those cities a few days later, but went underground in Insein in January 1949. The KNDO made up the core of the Karen rebel forces although the overall name changed several times. Today, the name KNDO is used for the KNU's village militia forces.

Karen National Union (KNU): Set up on 5 February 1947 by Saw Ba U Gyi to safeguard Karen interests in view of Burma's imminent independence. Went underground in January 1949 and took over large parts of central Burma. The movement was reorganised in November 1953 to comprise a front organisation, the KNU, a vanguard political party, the **Karen National United Party (KNUP)**, and the army, the **Kawthoolei Armed Forces (KAF)**. The KAF, in turn, was organised into regular brigades supported by local guerrilla forces and village defence units (KNDO). Strength in the early 1950s: 10,000–12,000. Its administrative organisation was called the **Kawthoolei Governing Body (KGB)** 1950–54 and the **Karen Revolutionary Council (KRC)** 1954–62.

The KAF were officially re-named the **Karen People's Liberation Army (KPLA)** in 1956, although the old name was also used. The KRC chairman, Saw Hunter Thamwe, made peace with Rangoon in 1963 along with a few hundred followers, while the main force of more than 5,000 guerrillas remained underground. The military commander throughout the 1950s, Gen. Min Maung, was killed in action in 1961.

The eastern units, led by Gen. Bo Mya, broke away on 21 June 1968 to set up the **Karen National United Front (KNUF)** with Mahn Ba Zan as chairman and Bo Mya as vice chairman. The army was named the **Karen National Liberation Army (KNLA)**, which also became the name of the combined army when the two factions of the Karen rebel movement were reunited as the KNU in 1975 (following the dissolution of the left-leaning KNUP). Mahn Ba Zan was chairman of the reunited KNU 1975–76; Bo Mya since 1976. Strength today: 4,000–4,500.

Karenni (Kayah):

United Karenni Independent States (UKIS): Proclaimed on 11 September 1946 by Bee Tu Re as a local "government", or rather movement, to preserve the 'independent' status of the Karenni states of Bawlake, Kyebogyi and Kantarawaddy in view of Burma's imminent independence. In November 1947, Saw Maw Reh, another Karenni leader, formed the **Karenni National Organisation (KNO)** to back up the UKIS politically. In late 1948, an armed wing, the **United Karenni States Independence Army (UKSIA)**, was formed by Saw Maw Reh, who subsequently began gathering arms and recruits.

Saw Maw Reh was captured alive by government troops on 9 February 1949, and the Karenni rebels, now led by Saw Shwe, the *sawphya* [prince] of Kyebogyi, then joined forces with the Karen National Defence Organisation. Saw Maw Reh was released in 1953 and rejoined the movement, which was, in effect, a branch of the Kawthoolei Armed Forces and commanded by one of their officers, Bala Sein. Saw Shwe died from malaria in 1956 and was succeeded by his wife, Catherine, who surrendered after three months in office. Her successor, Taw Plo, formed the KNPP (see below), an organisation more independent of the Karen movement.

Karenni National Progressive Party (KNPP): Set up on 29 July 1957 by Taw Plo, who was assassinated in September of the same year. His successor, Mee Ei, was assassinated in March 1958. The next leader, Saw Maw Raw, surrendered in mid-1958. Po Kyaw was elected the new leader in early 1959, but was captured by government forces the following year. Veteran Karenni rebel leader Saw Maw Reh was KNPP chairman 1960–77 and again 1978–86 (the movement split in 1977 and had to be reorganised). Chairman since 1986: Plya Reh.

Its armed wing, the UKSIA, became the **Karenni Army (KA)** in 1974. Commanders: Aung Than Lay 1974–78; Abel Tweed 1978–83; and Bee Htoo 1983-. Present strength: 1,000. The Karenni movement also maintains a "government" whose president since July 1992 is Saw Maw Reh.

Karenni State Nationalities People's Liberation Force (KNPLF): Set up in 1978 by Than Nyunt and others who had broken with the KNPP and allied themselves with the Communist Party of Burma. Than Nyunt was killed in a clash with KNPP forces in April 1982 and Nya Maung Mae became the new chairman. He resigned in 1992 and was replaced by San Tha. Present strength: 400–500. Strongholds near Loikaw in Kayah State. Now cooperates with the Karen National Union (KNU).

Kuki:

Kuki National Organisation/Army (KNO/KNA): Set up in 1987 and trained by the Kachin Independence Army (KIA). Led by Hanglen, a Kuki from the Indo-Burmese border area. Strength: possibly 100 men. Active in the Kuki-inhabited territory of western Sagaing Division as well as in Chandel district of Manipur across the border in India. Fought bitter battles with Muivah's faction of the Nationalist Socialist Council of Nagaland in 1992–93.

Lahu:

Lahu National United Party/Lahu State Army (LNUP/LSA): Set up in February 1973 with assistance from the Shan State Army (SSA). Led by *payah* Pu Kyaung Long until his death in 1980 and then by his son and new *payah* of the Lahus, Char Ui. Based at Doi Lang on the Thai-Burma border northwest of Fang where a number of heroin refineries were established in the 1970s. Became a member of the National Democratic Front (NDF) in 1976. Driven out of Doi Lang by Khun Sa's forces in August 1982, the group surrendered to the Rangoon government in January 1984.

Lahu National Organisation/Army (LNO/LNA): A new Lahu rebel organisation set up by Char Ui when he rejoined the underground in August 1985. Member of the NDF since 1987. Based in Muang Na on the Thai-Burma border west of Chiang Dao; no presence inside Burma apart from a token contingent attached to the Karenni rebels opposite Mae Hong Son.

Mon:

Mon National Defence Organisation (MNDO): The first Mon rebel army, set up in March 1948 and modelled after the Karen National Defence Organisation. Supported the KNDO occupation of Moulmein in August 1948. Went underground with the Karens in early 1949. Three political organisations also represented the Mon nationalists at this time: the Mon United Front (MUF) led by Nai Hla Maung, the Mon Freedom League (MFL) led by Nai Shwe Kyin and the United Mon Association (UMA) led by Mon U Pho Cho.

Mon People's Front (MPF): Set up in November 1952 to replace the MUF, the MFL and the UMA. Chairman 1952–58: Nai Aung Tun. Almost the entire organisation surrendered to the government on 19 July 1958.

New Mon State Party/Mon National Liberation Army (NMSP/MNLA): Set up by Nai Shwe Kyin on 20 July 1958, the day after the MPF surrendered to the government. Nai Shwe Kyin continued the struggle almost alone, but more people, mainly students, went underground after the abortive peace talks in 1963. The NMSP split in April 1981: one faction was led by Nai Shwe Kyin and the other by Nai Nol Lar. Nai Nol Lar's faction joined the National Democratic Front (NDF) in June 1982. The two factions reunited on 9 December 1987 with Nai Shwe Kyin as the chairman. The reunited NMSP is also a member of the NDF.

Muslim (general):

Ommat Liberation Front (OLF): Set up in the mid-1970s by Mohammed Ali Tanggoon, a Kachin Muslim, at the Tam Ngob headquarters of Gen. Li Wenhuan's 3rd Kuomintang. The first attempt to form an all-Burma insurgent army (as opposed to previously existing Rohingya groups in Arakan). Now defunct.

Kawthoolei Muslim Liberation Front (KMLF): Set up on 31 October 1983 under the aegis of the Karen National Union (KNU) in its area at Wangkha, Mae Tha Waw and Three Pagodas Pass along the Thai border. Renamed the **All Burma Muslim Union (ABMU)** after the pro-democracy uprising in 1988; Became a member of the Democratic Alliance of Burma on 18 November 1988. Chairman: Tin Maung Thet (a.k.a. Abdul Razak).

Muslim Liberation Organisation of Burma (MLO): Set up on 5 February 1988 by Kyaw Hla in Karenni rebel territory opposite Mae Hong Son. The group was known previously as the **Arakan Liberation Organisation (ALO)** and is comprised of Muslims from Arakan who do not consider themselves Rohingyas. The group maintains some contact with Islamic circles in Pakistan. Became a member of the Democratic Alliance of Burma on 18 November 1988.

Naga:

Naga National Council (NNC): Set up in the Naga Hills of India in 1946 by Angami Zapu Phizo to safeguard Naga interests in view of India's imminent independence. Proclaimed an independent Nagaland on 14 August 1947, a day before India's independence. Resorted to armed struggle shortly afterwards. A **Federal Government of Nagaland (FNG)** was proclaimed on 22 March 1956. Phizo left for Britain in 1958, but his men in the Naga Hills continued the armed struggle against India.

Naga rebels from India established base areas across the border in the Naga Hills of Burma's Sagaing Division in the early 1960s, first in Somra opposite Manipur and later in the border mountains west and northwest of Singkaling Hkamti. Maintained links with the Kachin rebels until the late 1980s. The NNC split in 1980 and again in 1990, following Phizo's death in London. Its **Federal Naga Army** still maintains a small base on the Burmese side of the border opposite Noklak village in Nagaland's Tuensang district.

Eastern Naga Revolutionary Council (ENRC): The first Burmese Nagas to go underground were S.S. Khaplang and Tungbo, who organised the **Naga Defence Force (NDF)** in the Pangsau Pass area in 1963–64. It became the ENRC in 1965, the **Eastern Naga National Council (ENNC)** in 1972, and merged with the NNC from the Indian side in 1978. Most eastern Nagas joined the NSCN when it was founded in January 1980.

National Socialist Council of Nagaland (NSCN): Set up on 31 January 1980 by Thuingaleng Muivah and Isaac Chishi Swu, who had broken away from the NNC, and ENNC leader S.S. Khaplang. Maintained base areas northwest of Singkaling Khamti, Sagaing Division, and in Somra Tract further to the south, but most fighting consisted of cross-border raids into Manipur and Nagaland in India. The Burmese Nagas broke with their Indian cousins in 1989: Khaplang and his men took over the northern base area (and maintained the name NSCN for their organisation) while Muivah and Isaac fled to Somra, where they now head a much smaller group, also called the NSCN.

Pa-O:

United Pa-O National Organisation/Pa-O National Liberation Army (UPNO/ PNLA): Set up in October 1958 by U Hla Pe. He had gone underground in 1948 to set up the first Pa-O rebel army (called *Pa-O Lam Bhu*, which in English would be the "Pa-O Union") but surrendered in 1958 to form the UPNO, at first a legal organisation. U Hla Pe went underground again in 1972 and joined the armed struggle that had begun again in 1966 under the banner of the **Pa-O National Liberation Organisation (PNLO;** which became the **Shan State Nationalities Liberation Organisation, SSNLO,** in 1968). In 1973 SSNLO was taken over by pro-Communist elements and U Hla Pe formed the **Shanland Nationalities Liberation Front (SNLF).** Another Pa-O rebel army led by Hkun Ye Naung merged with U Hla Pe's group in 1975 to become the PNO/PNA (see below).

Shan State Nationalities People's Liberation Organisation (SSNPLO): Set up in 1968 (see above) but the word "People's" was inserted when Tha Kalei broke away from U Hla Pe's Pa-O rebel arm and joined forces with the Communist Party of Burma in 1974. Strongholds in the hills near Hsi-Hseng in southern Shan State. Strength: 600–700 men.

Pa-O National Organisation/Army (PNO/PNA): The new name of the combined Pa-O movement (UPNO plus Hkun Ye Naung) since 1976. Joined the National Democratic Front (NDF) in the same year. Chairman after U Hla Pe's death in 1975 and until December 1977: Kyaw Sein. Chairman since December 1977: Aung Kham Ti. Strength: 500–600 men, based in the Kyauktalong area south of the Shan State capital of Taunggyi and at Mae Kong-Loi Kae near Lai Hka-Namsang. Decided on a peace treaty with the Rangoon government on 27 March 1991. It was subsequently legalised and withdrew from the NDF as well as the Democratic Alliance of Burma.

A handful of Pa-O rebels, led by Col. Hkun Okker, who refused to honour the pact with Rangoon, reorganised themselves as the **Pa-O People's Liberation Organisation (PPLO)** on 18 June 1991 (announced officially on 10 October 1991). Their camp is near Na Awn on the Thai border opposite Mae Hong Son.

Padaung (Kayan):

Kayan Newland Party (KNLP): The first Padaung (Kayan) rebel units were organised by Bo Pyan after the demonetisation of the 50 and 100 Kyats banknotes in 1964. He was joined by some Padaung university students, among them the present chairman, Shwe Aye (Naing Hlu Ta). The KNLP was formally formed on 8 August 1964 with backing from the Karenni rebels. It resigned from the National Democratic Front to join forces with the Communist Party of Burma in 1977. Following the 1989 mutiny, it rejoined the NDF on 20 June 1991. Strength: approximately 100–200 men, based in the Pekon-Möng Pai area of southwestern Shan State.

Palaung:

Palaung National Front (PNF): Set up by a Shan-Palaung, Sao Hsö Lane, on 12 January 1963 as a group subordinate to the Shan State Independence Army. Became the 5th and 6th Battalions of the 1st Brigade of the Shan State Army (SSA) when it was formed in March 1964. Led by Kwan Tong, who later broke with the SSA and allied himself with the Kachin rebels.

Palaung State Liberation Organisation/Army (PSLO/PSLA): Set up on 12 February 1976 based on the old PNF and led by Kwan Tong. Closely allied with the Kachin Independence Army (KIA). It became the **Palaung State Liberation Party/Army (PSLP/PSLA)** on 31 October 1986. Based in the Palaung-inhabited mountains south of the Shweli river in northern Shan State. Strength: 700–800 men. Chairmen: Kwan Tong 1976–79; Than Lwin 1979–82; Aung Khaing 1983; Kyaw Hla (a.k.a. Khrus Sangai) 1983–86; Ai Möng 1986-.

The PSLP/PSLA signed a peace treaty with the government in Rangoon on 21 April 1991 and was subsequently legalised. A few Palaungs who disagreed with the truce organised the **Palaung State Liberation Front (PSLF)**, but its armed strength is negligible.

Rohingya (Arakanese Muslim):

Mujahid Party: The first Muslim resistance army in the Arakan area, set up on 20 August 1947 in Buthidaung by Jafar Hussain (a.k.a.) Jafar Kawwal, a popular singer. The Muslim rebellion in Arakan soon spread all over the areas bordering East Pakistan (now Bangladesh). Kawwal was assassinated on 11 October 1950 and replaced by Cassim. Strength in 1950: 2,000. This first Muslim rebellion in Arakan petered out in the 1950s.

Rohingya Independence Force (RIF): Set up on 26 March 1963 by Mohammad Jafar Habib on the border with East Pakistan (now Bangladesh) as a direct result of the 1962 military take-over in Rangoon and the subsequent banning of the until then legal Rohingya groups: the Rohingya Students' Union and the Rohingya Youth League.

Rohingya Patriotic Front (RPF): The new name of the RIF since 1974. Chairman until the group split in 1985 into several different factions: Mohammad Jafar Habib. Based along the Burma-Bangladesh border.

Rohingya Solidarity Organisation (RSO): Set up in 1982 when Nurul Islam, Mohammed Yunus and others broke away from the RPF. Nurul Islam's faction joined forces with the remnants of the RPF in June 1986 to set up the ARIF (see below), while Mohammed Yunus' faction has retained the name RSO. The present-day RSO, led by Mohammed Yunus, maintains a string of bases along the Burma-Bangladesh border and has close connections with Jamaat-i-Islami in Bangladesh. Armed strength: about 100 men with many more activists in the border areas.

Arakan Rohingya Islamic Front (ARIF): Nurul Islam (formerly of the RSO) and Shabbir Hussain (formerly of the RPF) signed a joint agreement on 30 June 1986 leading to the formation of the ARIF on 22 August 1987. Based along the Burma-Bangladesh border. Armed strength: less than 50 men, but like the RSO it has many more activists in the Burma-Bangladesh border areas. Chairman: Nurul Islam.

Shan:

Noom Suk Harn **("The Young Brave Warriors"):** Set up on 21 May 1958 by Sao Noi (Saw Yanda) and Pu Ling Gung Na at Möng Kyawt village, across the Thai-Burma border from Chiang Dao. They were joined by some university students from Rangoon and camps were established along the border. The students soon fell out with Sao Noi and broke away to form the SSIA in March 1960. Some of Sao Noi's followers joined Moh Heng's SURA when it was set up in 1969.

Shan State Independence Army (SSIA): Set up on 24 April 1960 near Pangtawng on the Thai border by Shan students who had broken away from Sao Noi's *Noom Suk Harn*. Active mainly in central and northern Shan State. Leaders: Long Khun Maha 1960; Sao Khun Thawda (Pichai Khunseng) 1960–64. Merged with the SSA in 1964.

Shan National United Front (SNUF): Set up on 16 July 1961 in the Lai-Hka area north of Taunggyi, not as a separate group but as a forum to unite the various Shan armies at the time. Led by Moh Heng (*Noom Suk Harn*) and Khun Kya Nu (SSIA). Absorbed by the SSA in March 1964.

Shan National Army (SNA): Local Shan rebel group in the Kengtung area of eastern Shan State. Set up in 1961 by Sao Ngar Kham (U Gondara), who was assassinated in 1964 at Ban Huei Krai opium caravan station, northern Thailand. The remnants either stayed at Huei Nam Khun village north of Chiang Rai in northern Thailand (near Ban Huei Krai) as the **Shan State Army (Eastern)**, or they joined Khun Myint's SPLA (see below).

Shan State Army/Shan State Progress Party (SSA/SSPP): The SSA was set up on 25 March 1964, combining the SSIA, the SNUF and Jimmy Yang's Kokang Revolutionary Force (KRF). Strongholds in central and northern Shan State. A political wing, the SSPP, was set up on 16 August 1971. Armed strength during its heyday in the 1970s: 5,000–6,000 men. Commanders of the SSA: Sao Nang Hearn Kham 1964–69; Lieut.-Col. Sam Möng early 1970s–1978; Sao Hsö Lane 1979–83; Sao Hsö Noom 1983; Sao Gaw Lin Da 1983–88. Leaders of the SSPP: Sao Hseng Suk 1971–76; Sao Boon Tai 1976–79, Sao Hsö Lane 1979–83; Sao Hsö Noom 1983; Sao Sai Lek 1983-. Member of the National Democratic Front (NDF) since its inception in 1976 until 1991, when it was expelled from the front.

The vast majority of the SSPP/SSA (led by Sao Hsö Hten) made peace with the Rangoon government on 2 September 1989; only a handful, led by Sai Lek, remain in the underground, mainly along the Chinese border in the north. Other SSA remnants joined the Möng Tai Army of Khun Sa.

Shan National Independence Army (SNIA): Set up in 1966 when Sao Noi (Saw Yanda) was ousted from the *Noom Suk Harn* by some better educated, younger followers. Active in southern Shan State and led by Hseng Saw, a Shan from Yunnan in China who had joined the *Noom Suk Harn* in 1959. In 1968, with the help of Gen. Li Wenhuan of the 3rd Kuomintang, Sao Noi captured the SNIA's main base at Pieng Luang on the Thai border west of Chiang Dao. They were disarmed by Moh Heng, the then SSA chief of staff. Moh Heng pushed Sao Noi out in late 1968, broke away from the SSA and set up the SURA at Pieng Luang.

Shan United Revolutionary Army (SURA): Set up on 20 January 1969 by Moh Heng to act as a proxy inside Shan State for the 3rd KMT of Gen. Li Wenhuan. About 1,000–1,200 strong, and headquartered at Pieng Luang; area of operation extended up to the Salween river, and to Loi Sanien and at Wan Yung-Pang Mau east of Lawksawk in central Shan State.

The SURA merged with the 2nd Brigade of the SSA on 1 April 1984 to become the **Tai-land Revolutionary Council/Army (TRC/TRA)** with about 1,500–2,000 men. The Shan United Army (SUA) of Chang Chi-fu alias Khun Sa joined the TRC on 25 March 1985. Chairman of the SURA 1969–83 and chairman of the TRC 1983–91: Moh Heng.

Chairman of the TRC (now renamed the **Shan State Restoration Council, SSRC**, and the **Möng Tai Army, MTA**), 1991–92: Khun Sa; 1992–93: Bo Dewing; 1993-: Khun Sa. Thousands of new recruits have been drafted to the MTA since 1985, bringing the total troop strength to nearly 19,000 men, but not all are armed.

Shan People's Liberation Army (SPLA): Set up by Khun Myint in 1974 in the Möng Yang area north of Kengtung. Allied with the CPB; became the 768th Brigade of its People's Army in August 1976. Military commander: Sai Noom Pan. Following the 1989 CPB mutiny, the old 768 Brigade briefly assumed the old name *Noom Suk Harn* but was soon absorbed by Lin Mingxian's more powerful forces of the former 815 Military Region. Sai Noom Pan committed suicide in April 1990. His deputy, Michael Davies a.k.a. Sao Won Sa, was killed in May 1989 most probably because of his opposition to the alliance with the Rangoon government.

Tai Independence Army (TIA): Set up in 1978 by Priwat Kasemsri, a Thai *Mom Ratchawong*, who also used the name Sao Yawt Pha. Active in the Tachilek area and used by the Shan rebels as a bridgehead for cooperation with Thai authorities. Now defunct.

Shan State Revolutionary Army (SSRA): see Chinese groups.

Shan United Army (SUA): see Chinese groups.

Wa:

Wa National Organisation/Army (WNO/WNA): Grew out of the Vingngun *Ka Kwe Ye*, which was recognised as a government militia force in February 1969 in Tang-yan and led by Mahasang, the son of the last *sawbwa* of Vingngun. Mahasang went underground with Lo Hsing-han in 1973 and came down to the Thai border, where the WNA was organised on 29 July 1974 with assistance from the Shan State Army (SSA). Broke with the SSA in 1977 to team up with the 3rd Kuomintang of Gen. Li Wenhuan. The WNA's political wing, the WNO, joined the National Democratic Front (NDF) in 1983. Based along the Thai border, but not in the Wa Hills, which were controlled by the Communist Party of Burma (CPB) until the 1989 mutiny.

Wa National Council (WNC): Officially the administrative arm of the WNO, but in effect a separate organisation based along the Thai-Burma border near Fang. Led by Ai Kyaw Hsö, they joined forces with the Wa units of the former CPB following the March–April 1989 mutiny and became the UWSP/UWSA in November.

United Wa State Party/Army (UWSP/UWSA): Set up on 3 November 1989, combining Ai Kyaw Hsö's WNC forces along the Thai border and the Wa units of the former CPB. Chairman of the party: Chao Ngi Lai. Commander of the army: Pao Yu-chang. Recognised as a government militia force and first legalised under the name the Myanmar National Solidarity Party on 9 May 1989.

Fronts:

People's Democratic Front (PDF): A pro-Communist alliance set up on 24 March 1949 in Prome, comprising the Communist Party of Burma (CPB), the Communist Party (Red Flag), the People's Comrade Party (PCP), the Arakan People's Liberation Party (APLP) and the Revolutionary Burma Army (RBA; which merged with the CPB in 1950). Ceased to exist following the surrender of the APLP and the PCP in 1958.

Democratic Nationalities United Front (DNUF): A loosely organised non-communist front set up in 1956 and comprising the Karen National Union (KNU), the Karenni National Progressive Party (KNPP), the Mon People's Front (MPF) and U Hla Pe's Pa-O rebels. Ceased to exist when the Mons and the Pa-Os surrendered in 1958.

National Democratic United Front (NDUF): A Communist-inspired front organisation set up in 1959 (to replace the old PDF) by the Communist Party of Burma (CPB), the Chin National Vanguard Party (CNVP), the Karen National United Party (KNUP), the Karenni National Progressive Party (KNPP), the New Mon State Party (NMSP), and Pa-O rebels. The front was dissolved in 1975 and several groups joined the RNA, the FNDF and in 1976 the NDF. The Pa-O rebels split in the 1970s: one faction joined the CPB and the other the NDF.

Nationalities Liberation Alliance (NLA): A loose front in the early 1960s of the Kachin Independence Organisation (KIO), the Shan *Noom Suk Harn*, the Kawthoolei Revolutionary Council (KRC) and the Karenni National Progressive Party (KNPP). Ceased to exist when KRC chairman Saw Hunter Thamwe surrendered in 1963.

United Nationalities Front (UNF): Set up in 1965 and dissolved a year later. Members: Karen National Union (KNU), the Karenni National Progressive Party (KNPP), the Kayan New Land Party (KNLP), the Zomi National Front (ZNF) and the Shan State War Council of the Shan State Army (SSA).

Nationalities United Front (NUF): A front of ethnic groups which was set up in 1967 and dissolved in 1975 when the RNA was established. Its members were the Karen National United Party (KNUP), the Karenni National Progressive Party (KNPP), the Kayan New Land Party (KNLP), the New Mon State Party (NMSP; left in 1969), the Shan State Nationalities People's Liberation Organisation (SSNPLO) and the Zomi National Front (ZNF).

Revolutionary Nationalities Alliance (RNA): Forerunner to the NDF (see below); set up at Kawmoorah (Wangkha) on the Thai-Burma border in May 1973 by the Karen National Union (KNU), the Karenni National Progressive Party (KNPP), the Kayan New Land Party (KNLP) and the Shan State Progress Party (SSPP). Succeeded by the Federal National Democratic Front (FNDF) in May 1975.

Federal National Democratic Front (FNDF): Set up in Karen-held territory on the Thai border in May 1975 by the Karen National Union (KNU), the Karenni National Progressive Party (KNPP), the New Mon State Party (NMSP), the Arakan Liberation Party (ALP) and the Shan State Progress Party (SSPP). Became the NDF in 1976.

National Democratic Front (NDF): Set up on 10 May 1976 at the Manerplaw headquarters of the Karen rebels by the Arakan Liberation Party (ALP), the Karen National Union (KNU), the Karenni National Progressive Party (KNPP), the Lahu National United Party (LNUP), the Palaung State Liberation Organisation (PSLO), the United Pa-O National Organisation (UPNO) and the Shan State Progress Party (SSPP).

The UPNO resigned in 1977; its successor, the Pa-O National Organisation (PNO) became a member in October 1980. The New Mon State Party (NMSP) joined the NDF in June 1982, the Kachin Independence Organisation (KIO) in 1983; the Wa National Organisation (WNO) in 1983; the Lahu National Organisation (LNO) in 1987 (replacing the LNUP which had resigned from the front in 1984) and the Chin

National Front (CNF) in 1989. The KNLP resigned in 1977 but rejoined the NDF in June 1991.

The PNO, the PSLP and the SSPP were expelled from the NDF in 1991 because of their peace treaties with the government. Members in 1993: the National United Front of Arakan (NUFA; succeeded the ALP in September 1988), the NMSP, the KNU, the KNPP, the WNO, the LNO, the KNLP, the KIO and the CNF.

Chairmen: Bo Mya (KNU) 1976–87; Saw Maw Reh (KNPP) 1987–91; Nai Shwe Kyin (NMSP) 1991-.

Democratic Alliance of Burma (DAB): Set up on 18 November 1988 at Klerday, comprising all members of the NDF (except the Karenni National Progressive Party) plus the All-Burma Students' Democratic Front (ABSDF), the Committee for Restoration of Democracy in Burma (CRDB) and about a dozen smaller Burman and Muslim opposition groups. Chairman: Bo Mya (the Karen National Union); vice chairman: Brang Seng (the Kachin Independence Organisation).

All Nationalities Peoples' Democratic Front (PDF): A front of pro-Communist groups in Shan and Kayah states. Set up in 1989 by the Shan State Nationalities People's Liberation Organisation (SSNPLO), the Karenni State Nationalities People's Liberation Force (KNPLF), the Kayan New Land Party (KNLP), the Democratic Patriotic Army (DPA; set up by the Communist Party of Burma after the 1988 uprising for democracy), and remnants of the CPB in southern-central Shan State who did not join the 1989 CPB mutiny. The KNLP joined the NDF in 1991; the SSNPLO signed an agreement with Khun Sa in 1992 but later began to operate independently; the KNPLF joined forces with the Karen National Union (KNU) in 1992.

Democratic Front of Burma (DFB): Set up at Manerplaw on 18 December 1990 by the DAB plus members of the National League for Democracy (NLD) who had fled to the Thai border after the 1990 election. At the same time a parallel government was formed, made up of MPs who had been elected in May 1990 but later prevented from assuming power in Rangoon: the **National Coalition Government of the Union of Burma (NCGUB)**, headed by Aung San Suu Kyi's cousin, Sein Win. The DFB was renamed **the Anti-Military Dictatorship National Solidarity Committee (ANSC)** on 22 February 1991. Chairman: Bo Mya (KNU); general secretary: Win Khet (NLD); joint general secretary: Moe Thi Zon (ABSDF).

Appendix 4:
Burma's "Thirty Comrades"

Thakin Aung San (alias Bo Teza). Went to Amoy in 1940; was taken to Tokyo by the Japanese, and returned to Burma to pick up more recruits in 1941. Colonial Burma's prime minister until his assassination on 19 July 1947.

Thakin Hla Myaing (Bo Yan Aung). Went with Aung San to Amoy; remained behind in Bangkok and Tokyo when Aung San returned to Burma in 1941. Joined the CPB and went underground in 1948. Accused of being a "revisionist" and executed by the party in the Pegu Yoma on 26 December 1967.

Thakin Hla Pe (Bo Let Ya). In the first batch that left on 9 March 1941 aboard the Shunten Maru. Originally a member of the CPB, he became deputy prime minister after independence. Joined U Nu's resistance in 1969 and became military chief of the Patriotic Liberation Army, which was based on the Thai border. Killed in battle with Karen rebels on 29 November 1978.

Thakin Aye Maung (Bo Moe). In the first batch that left on 9 March 1941 aboard the Shunten Maru. Killed in action in Burma in 1942.

Thakin Ba Gyan (Bo La Yaung). In the first batch that left on 9 March 1941 aboard the Shunten Maru. Leader of the PVO and led them underground on 28 July 1948. Surrendered in the early 1950s and joined the legal National Unity Front. Participated in the peace movement of 1963 and later worked for the Trade Department under the Revolutionary Council. Died on 9 July 1969.

Thakin Tun Shein (Bo Yan Naing). In the first batch that left on 9 March 1941 aboard the Shunten Maru. Married Dr. Ba Maw's daughter after the war. Joined U Nu's resistance on the Thai border in the late 1960s. Surrendered during the 1980 amnesty. Died in Rangoon on 28 January 1989.

Thakin Saw Lwin (Bo Min Gaung). In the second batch that left on 13 April 1941 aboard the Kairu Maru. Entered politics after the war; joined U Nu's "Clean AFPFL" in 1958. Minister in several cabinets. Died in Rangoon in 1983.

Thakin Than Tin (Bo Mya Din). In the second batch that left on 13 April 1941 aboard the Kairu Maru. Died from fever in Chiang Mai, Thailand, on the way back from Formosa (Taiwan).

Thakin Shwe (Bo Kyaw Zaw). In the second batch that left on 13 April 1941 aboard the Kairu Maru. Prominent Burma Army commander in the 1950s. Dismissed from the army in 1957. Joined the CPB in 1976 and now lives in exile in Kunming, China.

Thakin Soe (Bo Myint Aung). In the second batch that left on 13 April 1941 aboard the Kairu Maru. Committed suicide when the British returned in 1945.

Thakin Tun Shwe (Bo Lin Yon). In the second batch that left on 13 April 1941 aboard the Kairu Maru. Settled in Rangoon after the war, where he died on 8 April 1974.

Ko Aung Thein (Bo Ye Htut). In the second batch that left on 13 April 1941 aboard the Kairu Maru. Joined the CPB in 1948. Surrendered in 1963. Participated in the 1988 pro-democracy uprising. Now lives in Rangoon.

Ko Tin Aye (Bo Phone Myint). In the second batch that left on 13 April 1941 aboard the Kairu Maru. Entered politics after the war, but retired following the AFPFL split in 1958 to become a timber trader. Appointed president of the Socialist Economy Construction Council under the Revolutionary Council after the 1962 coup d'etat. Now lives in Rangoon.

Thakin Aung Than (Bo Setkya). Arrived between the second and third batch. MP for Thayetmyo in the 1950s. Later retired from politics to set up the Thiri Setkya Company. Joined U Nu's resistance along the Thai border; died in Bangkok in 1969.

Thakin Than Tin. Arrived between the second and third batch. Member of the Ba Sein-Tun Oke faction. Died from malaria in Formosa (Taiwan).

Thakin Hla Maung (Bo Zeya). In the third batch that left in June 1941 aboard the Kosai Maru. Joined the CPB after the war. Burma Army commander after independence. Went underground with the CPB in 1949. In China in the 1950s; returned in 1963. Killed in action on 16 April 1968.

Thakin San Mya (Bo Tauk Htein). In the third batch that left in June 1941 aboard the Kosai Maru. MP from Pyinmana in the 1950s. Joined the 1988 pro-democracy uprising and became a member of the Democracy Party, which was close to U Nu. Now lives in Pyinmana.

Thakin Khin Maung Oo (Bo Taya). In the third batch that left in June 1941 aboard the Kosai Maru. Went underground after independence and surrendered in the 1950s. Elected MP in 1960. Now a writer, he lives in Rangoon.

Ko Saung (Bo Htein Win). A Burmese drama student in Tokyo who also joined the group— but he did not go to Hainan for military training.

Thakin Shu Maung (Bo Ne Win). In the fourth and last batch that arrived on 7 July 1941 aboard the Koreyu Maru. Member of the Ba Sein-Tun Oke faction. Commander in chief of the Burma Army after 1949. Burma's undisputed strongman since the 1962 coup d'etat.

Thakin Tun Khin (Bo Myint Swe). In the fourth and last batch that arrived on 7 July 1941 aboard the Koreyu Maru. Member of the Ba Sein-Tun Oke faction. Settled in Rangoon after the war. Elected MP in 1960. Died on 23 January 1973.

Thakin Ngwe (Bo Saw Aung). In the fourth and last batch that arrived on 7 July 1941 aboard the Koreyu Maru. Member of the Ba Sein-Tun Oke faction. Fell in battle at Shwegyin in 1945.

Thakin Thit (Bo Saw Naung). In the fourth and last batch that arrived on 7 July 1941 aboard the Koreyu Maru. Member of the Ba Sein-Tun Oke faction. Retired from the army after the war. Served in the Trade Department under Ne Win's Revolutionary Council after the 1962 coup d'etat. Now dead.

Thakin Kyaw Sein (Bo Moe Nyo). In the fourth and last batch that arrived on 7 July 1941 aboard the Koreyu Maru. Member of the Ba Sein-Tun Oke faction. Worked at a home for the disabled after independence. Died in Rangoon in 1960.

Thakin San Hlaing (Bohmu Aung). In the fourth and last batch that arrived on 7 July 1941 aboard the Koreyu Maru. Defence minister in the 1950s. Joined U Nu's resistance on the Thai border in the late 1960s. Surrendered during the 1980 amnesty. Participated in the 1988 uprising for democracy. Now lives in Rangoon.

Thakin Tun Lwin (Bo Bala). In the fourth and last batch that arrived on 7 July 1941 aboard the Koreyu Maru. Retired from the army in 1958 with the rank of major. Elected MP in 1960. Now lives in Rangoon.

Thakin Maung Maung (Bo Nyana). In the fourth and last batch that arrived on 7 July 1941 aboard the Koreyu Maru. Fell in battle between the Burma Independence Army and Karen guerrillas in 1942.

Thakin Tun Oke. In the fourth and last batch that arrived on 7 July 1941 aboard the Koreyu Maru. Did not undergo military training in Hainan (hence he did not have any *nom de guerre*). Leader of the Ba Sein-Tun Oke faction. Connected with SEATO and the CIA in the 1950s and 1960s. Died in 1971 in Rangoon.

Ko Hla (Bo Min Yaung). In the fourth and last batch that arrived on 7 July 1941 aboard the Koreyu Maru. Retired from the army after the war. Served with the State Timber Board under Ne Win's Revolutionary Council following the 1962 coup d'etat. Died on 6 January 1988.

Ko Than Nyunt (Bo Zin Yaw). In the fourth and last batch that arrived on 7 July 1941 aboard the Koreyu Maru. MP and businessmen after the war. Manager of Bo Setkya's Thiri Setkya Company. Deputy manager of the State Timber Board under Ne Win's Revolutionary Council following the 1962 coup d'etat. Now lives in Rangoon.

On 6 September 1988, nine out of the eleven survivors of the Thirty Comrades called on the army to join the pro-democracy uprising: Bo Yan Naing, Bo Ye Htut, Bo Phone Myint, Bo Tauk Htein, Bo Saw Naung, Bo Taya, Bohmu Aung, Bo Bala and Bo Zin Yaw. They also denounced Ne Win and his regime. Only Kyaw Zaw, who was then at the CPB's Panghsang headquarters, was unable to join the appeal against their erstwhile comrade-in-arms.

Bibliography

Books and independent studies:

Aye Saung. *Burman in the Back Row: Autobiography of a Burmese rebel.* Hong Kong: Asia 2000; Bangkok: White Lotus, 1989. 296 pp. The autobiography of a Burmese rebel who spent several years in the 1970s and early 1980s with Communist-affiliated organisations as well as the Shan State Army.

Becka, Jan. *The National Liberation Movement in Burma during the Japanese Occupation Period (1941–1945).* Prague: The Oriental Institute in Academia, 1983. 387 pp. A comprehensive account of the early years of the Burmese resistance movement, including useful notes on the Communists.

Bless, Roland. *Divide et Impera? Britische Minderheitenpolitik in Burma 1917–1948.* Stuttgart: Franz Steiner Verlag, 1990. 376 pp. An academic thesis on Burma's minority problems and British policy prior to independence.

Bo Yang. *Golden Triangle: Frontier and Wilderness.* Hong Kong: Joint Publishing Company, 1987. 204 pp. An account of a journey in early 1982 up to the Kuomintang's bases along the Thai-Burmese border as seen from a Taiwan perspective.

Boucaud, André & Louis. *Burma's Golden Triangle: On the Trail of the Opium Warlords.* Hong Kong: Asia 2000, 1988. 187 pp. A personal account of several treks together with Karenni, Karen, Pa-O and Shan rebels.

Cady, John F. *A History of Modern Burma.* Ithaca and London: Cornell University Press, 1958. 682 pp. One of the most complete books on Burmese history.

Candlin, A.H. Stanton. *Psycho-Chemical Warfare: The Chinese Communist Drug Offensive against the West.* New Rochelle, New York: Arlington House, 1973. An attempt to blame the Golden Triangle drug trade on the Chinese Communists.

Chakravarty, N.R. *The Indian Minority in Burma: the Rise and Decline of an Immigrant Community.* London: Oxford University Press, 1971. 214 pp. A solid account of the role of the Indian community in Burma during the 1900–41 period.

Clements, Alan. *Burma: The Next Killing Fields?* Berkeley, California: Odonian Press, 1992. 96 pp. A very personal account of Burma's recent turmoil written by an American who was a Buddhist monk in Burma for seven years.

Cochrane, W.W. *The Shans.* Rangoon: Superintendent, Government Printing, 1915. Reprint, New York: AMS Press, 1981. 227 pp. Useful notes on the customs and history of the Shans.

Coloquhoun, Archibald Ross. *Amongst the Shans.* New York: Paragon Book Reprint Corp, 1970; first published in 1885. 392 pp. An account of a journey from northern Thailand to China in the late nineteenth century.

Fellowes-Gordon, Ian. *Amiable Assassins: The Story of the Kachin Guerrillas of North Burma.* London: Robert Hale, 1957. 159 pp. A British officer's account of service with the Kachin Levies in Burma during World War II. Includes a description of how opium was used by British and American forces to pay their locally recruited troops as well as civilians in the war zone.

————. *The Battle for Naw Seng's Kingdom.* London: Leo Cooper, 1971. 176 pp. A slightly revised, second edition of *Amiable Assassins.*

Fischer, Edward. *Mission in Burma: The Columban Fathers' Forty-three Years in Kachin Country.* New York: Seabury Press, 1980. 164 pp. About Irish Roman Catholic fathers in Kachin State.

Fistié, Pierre. *La Birmanie ou la Quete de l'unité,* Paris: École Française d'Extreme-Orient, 1985. 462 pp. An academic study of Burma's ethnic minority problem from a pro-military point of view.

Fleischmann, Klaus. *Arakan: Konfliktregion zwischen Birma und Bangladesh.* Mitteilungen des Instituts für Asienkunde, Hamburg No. 121, 1981. 222 pp. About the conflict in Arakan and border problems with Bangladesh.

————. *Die Kommunistische Partei Birmas: Von den Anfängen bis zur Gegenwart.* Mitteilungen des Instituts für Asienkunde No. 171, Hamburg, 1989. 427 pp. A not too successful attempt to write the history of Burma's Communist movement.

Fleischmann, Klaus, ed. *Documents on Communism in Burma 1945–1977.* Mitteilungen des Instituts für Asienkunde No. 172, Hamburg, 1989. 278 pp. An incomplete and haphazard collection of original Communist publications which, however, contains some important early documents.

Grabner, Sigrid. *Hoffnung am Irrawaddy.* East Berlin: Verlag Neues Leben, 1980. 260 pp. A short history of the upheavals immediately before Burma's independence as seen from an East European point of view.

Hanson, Rev. Ola. *The Kachins: Their Customs and Traditions.* Rangoon: American Baptist Mission Press, 1913. Reprint. New York: AMS Press, 1982. 225 pp. An account of the Kachin people written by one of the first missionaries in northernmost Burma.

Izumiya, Tatsuro. *The Minami Organ.* Rangoon: Higher Education Department, 1981. 214 pp. An account of World War II in Burma seen from a Japanese perspective.

Katoh, Hiroshi. *Kawthoolei.* Tokyo: Dojidai-Sha Co Ltd, 1982. 155 pp. A photobook about the Karen rebel movement.

Khin Maung Gyi. *Agrarnye Otnosenija i Borba Trudjascichsja Mass Krestjanstva za Korennoe Resenie Ograrnogo Voprosa v Birme* ("The Agricultural Situation in Burma and the Peasants' Mass Struggle for a Solution to Burma's Agricultural Problems"). Moscow: the Academy of Social Sciences, 1963. Unpublished thesis, 307 pp.

Kin Oung. *Who Killed Aung San?* Bangkok and Cheney: White Lotus, 1993. 101 pp. Examines the mystery of Aung San's assassination and Burma's subsequent legacy of violence.

Kuhn, Delia & Ferdinand. *Borderlands.* New York: Alfred A. Knopf, 1962. 335 pp. Contains an interesting chapter on nationalist sentiments among the Shan and the Kachins in the early 1960s.

Lamour, Catherine & Lamberti, Michel R. *The Second Opium War.* London: Allen Lane, 1974. 278 pp. About the Golden Triangle opium trade but not up to the standard of McCoy's book (in French: *Les Grandes Manoeuvres de l'Opium.* Paris: Éditions du Seuil, 1973).

Lamour, Catherine. *Enquete sur une Armée Secrete.* Paris: Éditions du Seuil, 1975. 288 pp. A detailed and very personal account of the KMT in Burma.

Leach, Edward R. *Political Systems of Highland Burma.* London: The London School of Economics and Political Science, 1954; revised edition 1964. 324 pp. A study of Kachin social structure.

Leary, William M. *Perilous Missions: Civil Air Transport and CIA Covert Operations in Asia.* Montgomery: University of Alabama Press, 1984. 281 pp. Contains useful information about the American involvement with the Kuomintang in Burma in the early 1950s.

Lehman, Frederick K. *Military rule in Burma since 1962.* Singapore: Maruzen Asia, 1981. 83 pp. Six essays on modern Burma, including one about Burma's minority problems by Josef Silverstein.

Lintner, Bertil. *Land of Jade: A Journey through Insurgent Burma.* Edinburgh: Kiscadale Publications; Bangkok: White Lotus, 1990. 315 pp. An account of an eighteen-month trek, from October 1985 to April 1987, through rebel-held areas in Sagaing Division, Kachin State and Shan State.

————. *Outrage: Burma's Struggle for Democracy.* London: White Lotus UK, 1990. 208 pp. An account of the 1988 pro-democracy uprising in Burma. It also contains notes on the civil war and the minorities.

————. *The Rise and Fall of the Communist Party of Burma.* Ithaca, New York: Cornell University Southeast Asia Programme, 1990. 124 pp. A history of Burma's Communist movement, including maps, pictures and biographies of major Communist leaders.

McCoy, Alfred W. *The Politics of Heroin in Southeast Asia.* New York: Harper & Row, 1972. 472 pp. A detailed and authoritative account of the narcotics trade in Southeast Asia in the 1970s.

————. *The Politics of Heroin: CIA Complicity in the Global Drug Trade.* New York: Lawrence Hill Books, 1991. 634 pp. A revised and updated version of McCoy's first book.

Marshall, Rev. Harry Ignatius. *The Karen People of Burma: A Study in Anthropology and Ethnology.* Ohio: University of Columbus, 1918. Reprint. New York: AMS Press, 1980. 329 pp. An outdated but interesting account of the Karens written by a Baptist missionary.

Maung Maung, Dr. *Grim War Against the Kuomintang.* Rangoon: Nu Yin Press, 1953. 86 pp. The anti-KMT struggle seen from the Burma Army's point of view.

————. *Burma and General Ne Win.* Bombay: Asia Publishing House, 1969. 332 pp. The official biography of Gen. Ne Win written by one of his closest associates.

————. *To a Soldier Son.* Rangoon: Sarpay Beikman Press, 1974. 158 pp. Contains useful information about the history of the Burma Army.

Maung Maung (ex-Brig.-Gen.). *From Sangha to Laity: Nationalist Movements of Burma 1920–1940.* New Delhi: (for the Australian National University), 1980. 311 pp. This study traces the origin of the Burmese nationalist movement, showing how it moved away from the influence of the *sangha* (order of monks) and took a different ideological influence.

————. *Burmese Nationalist Movements 1940–1948.* Edinburgh: Kiscadale Publications, 1990. 395 pp. A detailed account of Burma's struggle for independence, and the various parties and political personalities in the 1940s, including the Karen rebels.

Milne, Leslie. *The Shans at Home.* 1910. New York: Paragon Book Reprint Corp., 1970. 289 pp. Anthropological notes on Shan customs and traditions.

Minn Latt. Burma in Battle. (Unpublished manuscript). Prague, early 1950s. 192 pp. A history of the early CPB written by a Burmese Communist exiled in Czechoslovakia.

Mirante, Edith T. *Burmese Looking Glass: A Human Rights Adventure and a Jungle Revolution.* New York: Grove Press, 1993. 333 pp. A lively and very personal account of several trips to rebel bases along the Thai-Burma border.

Morrison, Ian. *Grandfather Longlegs: The Life and Gallant Death of Major H.P. Seagrim.* London: Faber & Faber, 1947. 239 pp. The moving account of a British officer who stayed behind with Karen guerrillas in the Papun hills during Japan's occupation of Burma.

Morse, Eugene. *Exodus to a Hidden Valley.* London: Collins, 1975; Terre Haute, Indiana: North Burma Christian Mission, 1985. 224 pp. The story of the Morse missionary family who spent several years with the Kachins in northernmost Burma.

Moscotti, Albert D. *Burma's Constitution and Elections of 1974.* Singapore: Institute of Southeast Asian Studies, 1977. 184 pp. Includes the complete text of the 1974 constitution.

Nibedon, Nirmal. *Nagaland: The Night of the Guerrillas.* Second edition. New Delhi: Lancers Publishers, 1983. 404 pp. A fascinating and lively—but not always accurate—account of the Naga guerrillas of India's northeast and their relations with other tribes across the border in Burma.

————. *Mizoram: The Dagger Brigade.* New Delhi: Lancers Publishers, 1983. 269 pp. A similar book about the Mizos and their relationship with rebel groups in Burma's Arakan State.

Owen, Frank. *The Campaign in Burma.* Dehra Dun: Natraj Publishers, 1974. 165 pp. A lively account of the Allied campaign to recapture Burma from the Japanese.

Peers, William R. & Brelis, Dean. *Behind the Burma Road: The Story of America's Most Successful Guerrilla Force.* Boston: Little Brown, 1963. 246 pp. About Detachment 101 and the US-trained Kachin guerrillas during World War II. Includes information on the use of opium by the US army.

Phillips, C.E. Lucas. *The Raiders of Arakan.* London: Heinemann, 1971. An excellent account of events in Arakan during World War II. Essential for the understanding of the conflict between Muslims and Buddhists in the area.

Saimong Mangrai, Sao. *The Shan States and the British Annexation.* Ithaca, New York: Cornell University Southeast Asia Programme, Data Paper no. 57, 1965. 415 pp. A history of the Shan States written from a Shan point of view.

San C. Po, Dr. *Burma and the Karens.* London: Elliot Stock, 1928. 94 pp. Written by a prominent, pro-British Karen who argues that the Karens want to have a country of their own.

Sarkisyanz, E. *Buddhist Background of the Burmese Revolution.* The Hague: Martinus Nijhoff, 1965. 250 pp. A study of Burmese political thought and intellectual history.

Shwe Lu Maung. *Burma: Nationalism and Ideology.* Dhaka: University Press Ltd, 1989. 117 pp. An analysis of Burma's society, culture and politics written by an Arakanese national.

Silverstein, Josef. *Burma: Military Rule and the Politics of Stagnation.* Ithaca and London: Cornell University Press, 1977. 224 pp. A comprehensive introduction to modern Burmese politics.

————. *Burmese Politics: The Dilemma of National Unity.* New Brunswick: Rutgers University Press, 1980. 263 pp. An analysis of Burma's struggle for political unity up to the military take-over in 1962.

Sitte, Fritz. *Rebellenstaat in Burma-Dschungel.* Graz: Verlag Styria, 1979. 240 pp. A rather superficial account of a visit to the Karen rebels.

Smeaton, Donald MacKenzie. *The Loyal Karens of Burma.* London: Kegan Paul, Trench & Co., 1887. 264 pp. One of the first British accounts of the Karens. Contains some interesting social and anthropological data.

Smith, Charles B. *The Burmese Communist Party in the 1980s.* Singapore: Institute of Southeast Asian Studies, 1984. 126 pp. Although it contains English translations of some important CPB documents, it is an incomplete and largely inaccurate account of Burma's Communist movement.

Smith, Martin. *Burma: Insurgency and the Politics of Ethnicity.* London: Zed Press, 1991. 492 pp. An outstanding study of Burma's civil war and its ethnic problems.

Smith-Dun, Gen. *Memoirs of the Four-Foot Colonel.* Ithaca, New York: Cornell University Southeast Asia Programme, Data Paper no. 113, 1980. 126 pp. A comprehensive history of the Karens by the first chief of the Burma Army.

Steinberg, David I. *Burma: A Socialist Nation of Southeast Asia.* Boulder, Colorado: Westview Press, 1982. 150 pp. A useful introduction to various aspects of Burmese history and politics.

Stevenson, H.N.C. *The Hill Peoples of Burma.* London: Longmans, Green & Co. Burma Pamphlets no. 6, 1945. 51 pp. A brief introduction to Burma's various hill peoples.

Taylor, Robert H. *Marxism and Resistance in Burma 1942–1945.* Ohio University Press, 1984. 326 pp. Contains an English translation of Thakin Thein Pe's *Wartime Traveller.*

————. *The State in Burma.* London: C. Hurst & Company, 1987. 395 pp. An account of Burmese political systems from the pre-colonial era to 1987.

Tegenfeldt, Herman G. *A Century of Growth: The Kachin Baptist Church of Burma.* South Pasadena, California: William Carey Library, 1974. 512 pp. The best available history of the Kachins, their customs and religions.

Tinker, Hugh. *Burma: The Struggle for Independence 1944–1948.* London: Her Majesty's Stationery Office, 1984. Two volumes: 1,078 pp. and 921 pp. An almost complete collection of documents on Burma's relations with Britain during the years immediately before independence.

————. *The Union of Burma.* London: Oxford University Press, 1957. 424 pp. A comprehensive history of Burma in the late 1940s and the 1950s.

Trager, Frank. *Burma: From Kingdom to Republic.* London: Pall Mall Press, 1966. 455 pp. A historical and political analysis of modern Burma.

Tuchman, Barbara W. *Stilwell and the American Experience in China 1911–45.* New York: Bantam Books, 1972. 794 pp. A detailed account of America's China policy and involvement with the Kuomintang.

Vumson. *Zo History.* Aizawl, Mizoram (by the author), India. N.d. 347 pp. A personal history of the Chins written by a Burma-born Chin.

Winnington, Alan. *The Slaves of the Cool Mountains.* East Berlin: Seven Seas Books, 1959. 262 pp. Although the author visited only the minority areas of southern

Yunnan, China, this is one of the few books which contains material about the customs and the traditions of the Was.

Woodman, Dorothy. *The Making of Burma.* London: Cresset Press, 1962. 594 pp. An authoritative account of Burma's political history, including useful notes on the frontier areas.

Yawnghwe, Chao Tzang. *The Shan of Burma. Memoirs of a Shan Exile.* Singapore: Institute of Southeast Asian Studies, 1987. 276 pp. A comprehensive study of the Shans, their history and rebellion against Rangoon.

Yegar, Moshe. *The Muslims of Burma.* Wiesbaden: Otto Harrassowitz, 1972. 151 pp. A detailed history of Burma's various Muslim communities.

U. S. Congress. House. Committee on International Relations. Sub-committee on Future Foreign Policy Research and Development Hearings, April 22 and 23. 94th Cong., 1st sess., 1975. Contains letters and documents on the Shan rebellion and the Golden Triangle opium problem, including detailed material submitted by the Shan State Army.

————. House. Select Committee on Narcotics Abuse and Control. Hearings, July 12 and 13. 95th Cong., 1st sess., 1977. As above, but with more information on Khun Sa.

————. House. Committee on Foreign Affairs. Hearings, June 30 and July 15. 100th Cong., 1st sess., 1987. Contains Bo Gritz's account of his journey to Khun Sa's headquarters, documents from Khun Sa's group and other information about the Golden Triangle drug trade.

Papers and selected articles:

Aung-Thwin, Maureen. Burmese Days. *Foreign Affairs,* Spring 1989. A brief account of the 1988 pro-democracy uprising and its aftermath.

Cowell, Adrian. Report on a Five Month Journey in the Shan State of Kengtung with the Shan National Army. Typescript, 1965.

Forbes, Andrew. The "Cin-Ho" (Yunnanese Chinese) Caravan Trade with North Thailand. Typescript, 1985.

Lintner, Bertil. The Shans and the Shan State of Burma. *Contemporary Southeast Asia* 5, no. 4. Mar. 1984. A 48-page history of the Shan nationalist movement.

————. *Cross-border Drug Trade in the Golden Triangle.* Durham, England: Boundaries Research Press, for International Boundaries Research Unit, Department of Geography, University of Durham, 1991. 65 pp.

————. The Internationalization of Burma's Ethnic Conflict. In *Internationalization of Ethnic Conflict.* London: Pinter Publishers for International Centre for Ethnic Studies, Sri Lanka (edited by K.M. de Silva and R.J. May), 1991.

————. Heroin and Highland Insurgency in the Golden Triangle. In *War on Drugs: Studies in the Failure of US Narcotics Policy* (edited by Alfred W. McCoy and Alan A. Block). Boulder, San Francisco and Oxford: Westview Press, 1992.

'A Special Correspondent' (Lintner, Bertil). The Return of Lo Hsing-han. *Focus,* Bangkok, Aug. 1981. Rangoon releases a former opium warlord.

'P. Vichit-Thong' (Lintner, Bertil). Shifts in the Shan States. *Focus,* Bangkok, Oct. 1981. The Shan State Army breaks with the Communists.

Lintner, Bertil. Leadership tussle at Three Pagodas. *Focus,* Jan. 1982. The Mon rebel movement splits.

'P. Vichit-Thong' (Lintner, Bertil). The Persistent Karenni/Crackdown at Ban Hin Taek. *Focus,* Bangkok, Feb. 1982. About the Karenni rebel movement and the campaign against Khun Sa.

'A Special Correspondent' (Lintner, Bertil). The Kachin dilemma. *Focus,* Bangkok, Apr. 1982. About the Kachin rebel movement.

Lintner, Bertil. New Years—New Fears. *Business in Thailand,* Feb. 1983. About Khun Sa and the narcotics trade.

'A Correspondent' (Lintner, Bertil). The Karenni Connection. *Far Eastern Economic Review,* 18 June 1982. Deals with a link-up between Burmese and Thai Communists, the return of Lo Hsing-han, and includes an interview with Shan State Army commander Sai Hla Aung (Sao Hsö Lane).

Lintner, Bertil. Alliances of convenience, *Far Eastern Economic Review,* 14 Apr.1983. An overview of Communist as well as ethnic insurgent groups.

———. The amiable assassins, *Far Eastern Economic Review,* 18 Aug. 1983. About the Kachin rebel movement.

Lintner, Bertil & Tasker, Rodney. Calm before the storm? *Far Eastern Economic Review,* 5 Apr. 1984. About a major Burma Army offensive against Karen rebels.

Lintner, Bertil. In the dragon's wake. *Far Eastern Economic Review,* 26 Apr. 1984. Arakan State and the Bangladesh border.

'A Correspondent' (Lintner, Bertil). The borderline case. *Far Eastern Economic Review,* 10 May 1984. Khun Sa and official complicity in the drug trade.

Lintner, Bertil. Backs to the wall/Goodbye to all that. *Far Eastern Economic Review,* 6 Sep. 1984. Burma Army offensive against Karen rebels, and Bangkok decides to clamp down on the Kuomintang.

———. Old comrades never die. *Far Eastern Economic Review,* 13 Sept. 1984. The CPB celebrates its 45th anniversary.

———. Bangkok, Taipei, Peking: The unsettling eternal triangle. *Far Eastern Economic Review,* 24 Jan. 1985. The Kuomintang in the Golden Triangle.

———. Headhunting and tales of Burma's wild people. *Far Eastern Economic Review,* 7 Feb. 1985. About the Was and the Sino-Burmese border.

———. The turbulent tribes. *Far Eastern Economic Review,* 21 Aug. 1985. About the Nagas and the Indo-Burmese border.

———. War in the North, *Far Eastern Economic Review,* 28 May 1987. Cover story about the Kachins, the Shans and other ethnic insurgents. Interview with Kachin rebel leader, Brang Seng.

———. The rise and fall of the communists. *Far Eastern Economic Review,* 4 June 1987. About the CPB, including an interview with its chairman, Thakin Ba Thein Tin.

———. Praise the Lord and pass the ammunition. *Far Eastern Economic Review,* 21 Jan. 1988. About Christian missionary influence among the Nagas, Kachins and Karens.

———. Rebels with a cause. *Far Eastern Economic Review,* 30 Mar. 1989. The first report about the CPB mutiny.

———. Left in disarray. *Far Eastern Economic Review,* 1 June 1989. About the collapse of the Communist insurgency.

————. Asian narcotics: Protected industry. *Far Eastern Economic Review*, 28 June 1990. Cover story on official complicity in the Golden Triangle drug trade.

————. Season of fear. *Far Eastern Economic Review*, 27 Dec. 1990. An offensive is expected against dissident students and ethnic rebels along the Thai border.

————. Burma road to ruin. *Far Eastern Economic Review*, 28 Mar. 1991. Cover story on the drug trade from Burma to China.

————. Forgotten frontiers. *Far Eastern Economic Review*, 16 May 1991. About road construction and casinos in the Golden Triangle.

————. Spiking the guns. *Far Eastern Economic Review*, 23 May 1991. Cease-fire agreements are reached between the government and some rebel groups.

————. Diversionary tactics. *Far Eastern Economic Review*, 29 Aug. 1991. Rohingya Muslims begin to flee to Bangladesh.

————. Tension mounts in Arakan State. *Jane's Defence Weekly*, 19 Oct. 1991. Rebels and refugees along the Burma-Bangladesh border.

————. Return to the Delta. *Far Eastern Economic Review*, 14 Nov. 1991. Karen rebels launch attacks in the Irrawaddy delta.

————. Poisons and politics. *Far Eastern Economic Review*, 14 Nov. 1991. Reviews of books on the Golden Triangle drug trade.

————. Burma's rebels in advance. *Jane's Defence Weekly*, 7 Dec. 1991. Karen rebels and government forces clash in the Irrawaddy delta.

————. Burma's new front. *Far Eastern Economic Review*, 9 Jan. 1992. Arakan Muslims resort to armed raids.

————. Fields of dreams. *Far Eastern Economic Review*, 20 Feb. 1992. The heroin trade flourishes along the China-Burma border.

————. Military guns silent. *Far Eastern Economic Review*, 28 May 1992. The government calls off an offensive against Karen rebels.

————. Loss of innocence. *Far Eastern Economic Review*, 16 July 1992. Power struggle among dissident students in Kachin State leads to murder.

————. Smack in the face. *Far Eastern Economic Review*, 5 Nov. 1992. New, ex-CPB narcotics chieftains usurp traditional drug barons.

————. Tracing new tracks. *Far Eastern Economic Review*, 18 Mar. 1993. Ex-CPB warlords smuggle drugs to Laos and Cambodia.

————. Neighbours' interests. *Far Eastern Economic Review*, 1 Apr. 1993. China and Thailand to mediate in Burma's civil war.

————. New calls for democray. *Far Eastern Economic Review*, 20 May 1993. Lahu and Wa representatives shun the SLORC's constitution.

————. A fatal overdose/Chinese takeaway. *Far Eastern Economic Review*, 3 June 1993. New drug routes from the Golden Triangle.

Overholt, William H. Burma: The Wrong Enemy. *Foreign Policy*, no. 77, Winter 1989–90. An interesting criticism of official US policy towards Burma's national minorities.

Selth, Andrew. Race and resistance in Burma, 1942–1945. *Modern Asian Studies* 20, no. 3, Cambridge, 1986. A brief background to Burma's ethnic minority problem during the years immediately before independence.

Silverstein, Josef. Politics in the Shan State: The Question of Secession from the Union of Burma. *Journal of Asian Studies* 18, no. 1, Nov. 1958.

————. Burmese Student Politics in a Changing Society. *Dædalus* 97, no. 1, Winter 1968.

———. Burmese and Malaysian Student Politics: A Preliminary Comparative Inquiry. *Journal of Southeast Asian Studies* 1, no. 1, Mar. 1970.

———. Burma's Six Domestic Challenges in the 1990s. Paper submitted to a seminar organised by the Institute of Strategic and International Studies, Kuala Lumpur, 11–13 July 1990. Deals with the question of federalism.

Silverstein, Josef and Wohl, Julian. University Students and Politics in Burma. *Pacific Affairs* 37, no. 1, Spring 1964.

———. The Burmese University Student: An Approach to Personality and Subculture. *The Public Opinion Quarterly* 30, Summer 1966.

Smith, Martin. Sold down the river: Burma's Muslim borderland. *Inside Asia*, July–Aug. 1986. About Arakan State and the Bangladesh border.

———. Peace in Burma: A possibility? The position of the armed opposition groups. Unpublished paper submitted to a Burma seminar organised by *Stiftung Wissenschaft und Politik* in Bonn, 22–24 July 1988.

Taylor, Robert H. *Foreign and Domestic Consequences of the Kuomintang Intervention in Burma.* Ithaca, New York: Cornell University Southeast Asia Programme, Data Paper no. 93, 1973. 77 pp.

Thant Myint-U. *US Policy Towards Burma since 1945* (unpublished paper, undated but probably written in 1990), 20 pp.

———. *Marxism, Nationalism and the Political Economy of British Burma.* BA thesis, Harvard College, Cambridge, Mar. 1988. 147 pp.

Thaung, U. *Army's Accumulation of Economic Power in Burma (1950–1990).* Paper presented at a Burma seminar on 20 Oct. 1990 in Washington, D.C.

Thayer, Nate. Diverted Traffic. *Far Eastern Economic Review*, 18 Mar. 1993. Indochina supplants Thailand as conduit for Burma's drugs.

Yawnghwe, Chao Tzang. Politics of Burma and Shan State: Effects on North Thailand and Thailand. *Political Science Review*, Chiang Mai University, Thailand, Sep. 1982.

———. *Ne Win's Tatmadaw Dictatorship.* MA thesis. University of British Columbia, Vancouver, Apr. 1990), 223 pp.

———. *Politics and the Informal Economy of the Opium-Heroin Trade: Impact and Implications for Shan State of Burma.* Paper presented to the Fifth Annual Conference of the Northwest Consortium for Southeast Asian Studies, Vancouver, 16–18 Oct. 1992. 34 pp.

Burmese government publications:

In English/before 1962

The Shan States and Karenni. List of Chiefs and Leading Families (Corrected up to 1939). Simla: The Manager, Government of India Press, 1943. 78 pp.

Frontier Areas Committee of Enquiry. Rangoon: Superintendent, Government Printing and Stationery, 1947. Report presented to the British government. Part II: Appendices include hearings with minority representatives.

The Constitution of the Union of Burma. Rangoon: Superintendent, Government Printing and Stationery, 1947. 78 pp. Independent Burma's first, democratic constitution.

Burma and the Insurrections. Rangoon: Government of the Union of Burma publications, Sep. 1949. 63 pp. An official survey of the various insurgent political and ethnic movements.

KNDO Insurrection. Rangoon: Government Printing and Stationery, 1949.

Karen Race Special Enquiry Commission Report of 1950. Rangoon: Superintendent, Government Printing and Stationery, 1951.

The Pyidawtha Conference: August 4–17, 1952. Rangoon: Ministry of Information, 1952. The first national conference called to discuss programmes and plans for the creation of a "new Burma". Includes speeches and resolutions of the participants.

The Kuomintang Aggression Against Burma. Rangoon: Ministry of Information, 1953. 222 pp. Burma's case before the United Nations on the KMT presence in the Shan states.

The First Interim Report of the Administration Re-organisation Committee. Rangoon: Superintendent, Government Printing and Stationery, 1954. An official study of the inherited colonial administrative system and recommendations of ways to improve it.

The Final Report on the Administration Re-organisation Committee. Rangoon: Superintendent, Government Printing and Stationery, 1955. Final recommendations of necessary changes to make the administration of Burma more democratic.

Enquiry Commission for Regional Autonomy, Report, 1952. Rangoon: Superintendent, Government Printing and Stationery, 1955.

The National Ideology and the Role of the Defence Services. An important document outlining the "ideology" of the Burma Army. Rangoon, 1960. Originally distributed at the Defence Services conference held at Meiktila, 21 October 1958.

Is Trust Vindicated? The Chronicle of trust, striving and triumph. Rangoon: Director of Information, 1960. 567 pp. An official account of Ne Win's 1958–60 Caretaker Government, including claimed gains against the insurgents.

Report of the Public Services Enquiry Commission. Rangoon: Superintendent, Government Printing and Stationery, 1961. A re-examination of the administration with a view to recommending ways to improve it.

In English/after 1962

Ba Than. *The Roots of the Revolution.* Rangoon: Government Printing Press, 1962. 86 pp. A brief and partisan history of the Burma Army and the first year of military rule.

The System of Correlation of Man and and His Environment. Rangoon: Burma Socialist Programme Party, 1964. 77 pp. A document that provides the basis for the ideology of the military and its BSPP. The book also includes *The Burmese Way to Socialism*, a policy declaration of the 1962 Revolutionary Council.

International Peace Parley (Historical Documents no. 1), Rangoon, 1963. Mimeo. Documents from the 1963 peace talks.

The Constitution of the Socialist Republic of the Union of Burma. Rangoon: Printing and Publishing Corp., 1974. Burma's one-party constitution that was abolished in September, 1988.

Burma Communist Party's Conspiracy to take over State Power. Rangoon: Ministry of Information, 1989. 174 pp. Speech by intelligence chief Khin Nyunt on 5 August, 1989. An attempt to prove that the Communists were behind the 1988 movement for democracy in Burma. Contains some interesting biographies of Communist leaders.

The Conspiracy of Treasonous Minions within the Myanmar naing-ngan and Traitorous Cohorts Abroad. Rangoon: Ministry of Information, 1989. 332 pp. Speech by Khin Nyunt on 9 September, 1989. An attempt to show that the 1988 pro-democracy uprising was a rightist plot. Contains some useful biographies of various opposition leaders and ethnic insurgents.

In Burmese

သခင်သန်းထွန်း၏ နောက်ဆုံးနေ့.များ; (The Last Days of Thakin Than Tun). 2 vols., Rangoon: Mya Ya Pin Sarpay, 1969. 1,436 and 654 pp. Ostensibly written by some CPB defectors but the actual author is a former intelligence chief, Brig.-Gen. Tin Oo. A detailed and comparatively accurate account of the purges in the Pegu Yoma in the 1960s.

ဇင်+ချစ် နောက်ဆုံး (၂) (Zin and Chit—the Last Two) Rangoon: Mahananda, 1976. 348 pp. A sequel to Tin Oo's first two books on the CPB.

Selected rebel publications:

Some Facts about Ne Win's Military Government. 8 pp. Published by the CPB in Beijing, 1962.

A Short Outline of the History of the Communist Party of Burma. 6 pp. A brief history of the CPB, published by the CPB in Beijing, June 1964.

တပါတီလုံးသွေးစည်းညီညွတ်ပြီး အောင်ပွဲအရယူရေးအတွက် ချီတက်ကြပါစို့. (The Entire Party! Unite and March to Achieve Victory!) Political report of the politburo of the CPB, submitted by Chairman Thakin Ba Thein Tin on 1 Nov. 1978. The CPB's printing press, Panghsang, 13 Sep. 1979. 139 pp. Contains statistics and data on the various areas controlled by the CPB.

ကိုယ့်ဦးကိုယ်ချုန် အဆင်းရဲအပင်ပန်းခံ လုံးပမ်းတိုက်ခိုက်တဲ့ ၄၈၄၉ စိတ်ဓါတ်တွေကိုမွေးမြူ့ကြ(The Spirit of 1948–49 Was One of Self-reliance and Enduring Hardships). The CPB's printing press, Panghsang, Aug. 1979. Outlines the CPB's difficulties in the wake of the Chinese reduction of aid to the party in the late 1970s.

Historical Facts about the Shan State. Published by the Tai Revolutionary Council in 1986. 121 pp. Contains some reliable data on geographical features as well as copies of original documents of the Panglong conferences but the historical material is partisan to Khun Sa.

Independence of Determination of the Karenni States. Published by the Karenni National Revolutionary Council in 1974. 55 pp. Mimeo. A partisan history of the Karenni movement.

Karenni Manifesto and Karenni History. Published by the Karenni Provisional Government in 1990. A revised and updated version of the first Karenni rebel history.

The Mon National Liberation Movement. Published by the New Mon State Party, n.d. 22 pp. Mimeo. A partisan history of the Mons and their rebel movement.

Lonsdale, Michael: *The Karen Revolution.* Sam Art, Singapore. 30 pp. An overview of the Karen movement, including a chronology.

Rolly, Mika. *The Pa-O People.* Printed in Chiang Mai, Thailand, 1986 or 1987. 92 pp. A partisan and quite fanciful Pa-O history which contains some useful information on the Pa-O rebel movement.

Notes

Chapter 1: "The Rangoon Government"

1. Related to the author (New Delhi, 21 Feb. 1992) by one of H.N. Ghoshal's relatives in India, Baladas Ghoshal, a prominent Indian academic who teaches at Jadavpur University, Calcutta.

2. Interview with Khin Maung Gyi, Kunming, China, 10 Jan. 1992. Khin Maung Gyi became a politburo member in 1975 and was the CPB's main theoretician in the 1970s and 1980s. The description of the CPB headquarters in 1948, and the factionalism that existed within the CPB at the time, is also based on several lengthy interviews with Thakin Ba Thein Tin, Panghsang, Dec. 1986–Feb. 1987 (ref. also subsequent quotes from the former CPB chairman).

3. Correspondence with Aung Htet, Thakin Ba Thein Tin's personal assistant, 4 May 1992. See also U Nu, *Saturday's Son: Memoirs of the Former Prime Minister of Burma* (Bombay: Bharatiya Vidya Bhavan, 1976), pp. 143–146.

4. Thein Pe Myint, တော်လှန်ရေးကာလနိုင်ငံရေးအတွေ့အကြုံများ; ("Political Experiences of the Revolutionary Era"), p. 446.

5. For a full text of the ultimatum, see Klaus Fleischmann, *Documents on Communism in Burma 1945–1977* (Hamburg: Mitteilungen des Instituts für Asienkunde, no. 172, 1989), pp. 41–42.

6. Interview with Thakin Ba Thein Tin, Panghsang, 24 Dec. 1986. See also Thein Pe Myint, op. cit. p. 562: "Thakin Than Tun's Communists raise the slogan 'For a Protracted Civil War'."

7. This and subsequent quotes from Ye Tun: interviews with him, Panghsang, 21 Jan. 1987. Ye Tun served as the CPB's representative in Beijing for several years in the 1970s and 1980s. He now lives in exile in Sichuan, China.

8. British sources, however, usually describe "Operation Flush" as a successful campaign; see for instance Hugh Tinker (ed.), *Burma: The Struggle for Independence 1944–1948*, Vol. II (London: Her Majesty's Stationery Office, 1984), pp. 314–315. But the document nevertheless adds that Operation Flush was "a ruthless effort".

9. Interview with Thaung Htut, a native of Pyinmana, New York, 21 March 1992.

10. *Burma and the Insurrections* (Rangoon: Government of the Union of Burma, 1949), p. 23. See also Martin Smith, *Burma: Insurgency and the Politics of Insurgency* (London and New Jersey: Zed Press, 1991), pp. 107–108. However, the latter source states erroneously that Bo Po Kun was one of the Thirty Comrades; he was a BIA veteran. The same mistake occurs in Hugh Tinker, *The Union of Burma: A Study of The First Years of Independence* (London: Oxford University Press, 1957), p. 396.

11. U Nu, op. cit. pp. 161–162.

12. Maung Maung, *Burmese Nationalist Movements 1940–1948* (Edinburgh: Kiscadale, 1989), p. 157.

13. U Nu, op.cit. p. 155.

14. Ibid. p. 159.

15. Interview with Kyaw Sein (a 3rd General Transport Company mutineer who later joined the CPB; now in exile in China), Möng Ko, 20 Nov. 1987. For the government's version: see. *Burma and the Insurrections,* p. 23.

16. For a moving account of Maj. Seagrim's exploits, see: Ian Morrison, *Grandfather Longlegs: The Life and Gallant Death of Major H.P. Seagrim* (London: Faber & Faber, 1947). For BIA atrocities at this time, see also Tinker, op. cit. pp. 9–10.

17. Smith, op. cit. pp. 80–87. Maung Maung, op. cit. p. 346.

18. Maung Maung, op. cit. p. 215.

19. Interview with Nai Shwe Kyin, Manerplaw, 7 May 1992. Subsequent quotes from him are also from the same interview, plus another interview in Bangkok, 8 June 1992. Nai Shwe Kyin later became president of the New Mon State Party and from 1991 also chairman of the National Democratic Front. Other sources include *Burma and the Insurrections,* and Tinker, op. cit. pp. 37–47.

20. Tinker, *The Union of Burma,* p. 39.

21. U Nu, op. cit. p. 171.

22. Ibid. p. 173.

23. Interview with Kaser Doh, Manerplaw, 8 May 1992.

24. Interview with Saw Ba Thin, Manerplaw, 9 May 1992. Saw Ba Thin is now the general secretary of the KNU and prime minister of the rebel Kawthoolei government.

25. Interview with Lydia, Mae Sot, 6 Nov. 1992. Lydia is now a leader of the KNU's women's organisation along the Thai border.

26. Interview with N'Chyaw Tang, ex-1st Kachin Rifleman, Pa Jau, 23 April 1986. N'Chyaw Tang is now an officer of the Kachin Independence Army. See also Tinker, *The Union of Burma,* p. 41.

27. Interview with Tamla Baw, Manerplaw 9 May 1991. Tamla Baw is now deputy commander in chief of the Karen National Liberation Army with the rank of lieutenant-general.

28. Smith, op. cit. pp. 139–140.

29. Interview with Sgaw Ler Taw, Manerplaw, 1 Aug. 1984.

30. U Nu, op. cit. p. 176.

31. Ibid. p. 187.

32. Minn Latt, *Burma in Battle* (unpublished manuscript written in Prague in the early 1950s; a copy was passed on to me by Czech Burma scholar Jan Becka in Jan. 1992), p 74.

33. Ibid. pp. 87–88.

34. *Burma and the Insurrections,* p. 36.

35. *The Nation,* 23 Sept. 1956.

36. Minn Latt, op. cit. p. 187, quoting "The Order of the Day to Members of the People's Army, issued by Thakin Than Tun." The only date given is "1950".

37. *Burma and the Insurrections,* p. 37.

Chapter 2: The Burmese Jigsaw

1. Charles B. McLane, *Soviet Strategies in Southeast Asia* (Princeton, New Jersey: Princeton University Press, 1966), p. 352.

2 .The square has since been renamed Raja Subodh Mullick Square; Raja Subodh Mullick, a *zamindar* landowner and an ardent nationalist, also donated the land on which the Jadavpur University in Calcutta was built.

3 .Ruth McVey, *The Calcutta Conference and the Southeast Asian Uprisings* (Ithaca, New York: Cornell Modern Indonesia Project, Interim Report Series, 1958), p. 8.

4. Brimmel, J.H., *Communism in Southeast Asia* (London: Oxford University Press, 1959), p. 257.

5. တက်ဘုန်းကြီး ["The Modern Monk"], (Rangoon: New Light of Burma Press, 1937).

6. Robert H. Taylor, *Marxism and Resistance in Burma 1942–1945* (Athens, Ohio: Ohio University Press, 1984), p. 6.

7. Gene D. Overstreet and Marshall Windmiller, *Communism in India* (Berkeley: University of California Press, 1959), p. 267.

8. Letter to the author from Khin Maung Gyi, dated Kunming, 15 April 1992.

9. Thakin Thein Pe (Thein Pe Myint), "Letter to Comrade Dange", Rangoon Oct. 1950 (in တော်လှန်ရေးကာလနိုင်ငံရေးအတွေ့အကြုံများ, [Political Experiences during the Revolutionary Era], pp. 441–448). Thein Pe claims that this line was adopted by the politburo on Ghoshal's return to Burma; Thakin Ba Thein Tin and Khin Maung Gyi say he was reprimanded for the article: interviews with Thakin Ba Thein Tin, Panghsang, 24 Dec. 1986, and Khin Maung Gyi, Kunming, 17 Jan. 1992.

10. Letter from Khin Maung Gyi, dated Kunming, 15 April 1992. Many authors have assumed that Ghoshal attended the meetings in Calcutta in February 1948 (see for instance Klaus Fleischmann, *Documents on Communism in Burma 1945–1977*. Hamburg, Institut für Asienkunde, 1989, p. 123), which the CPB denies. Documents from these meetings do not mention Ghoshal: he was in Rangoon at the time organising strikes and demonstrations. It is equally wrong that Ghoshal and Than Tun attended a CPI central committee meeting in December 1947, as claimed by Fleischmann, op. cit., p. 123. Ghoshal visited Bombay in December 1947–January 1948 and Than Tun went to Calcutta in February, after Ghoshal had returned to Burma.

11. Brimmell, op. cit., pp. 262–263.

12. Bo Aung Min served as general secretary of the People's Volunteer Organisation (PVO) in the 1940s; later leader of the CPB's *tat-ni* ("Red Guards"). He became chief of general staff of the CPB's "People's Army" in 1951, and surrendered to the government in 1955.

13. Interview with Thakin Ba Thein Tin, Panghsang, 23 Dec. 1986. Letter from Khin Maung Gyi, dated 20 April 1993.

14. See, for instance, Victor Purcell, *Malaya: Communist or Free?* (Stanford, California: Stanford University Press, 1954), pp. 60–61: "A strong delegation from Russia is said to have attended [the Calcutta Youth Conference], and a resolution was passed, advocating 'the capture of power by the peasants and workers by any means". He goes on to describe the "plan" that was laid down in Calcutta to achieve this aim. However, no "strong Russian delegation"

attended the meeting, and no such resolution was adopted. In the absence of any proof of a "Soviet conspiracy", Gene D. Overstreet and Marshall Windmiller suggest in their *Communism in India* (Berkeley: University of California Press, 1959), an otherwise excellent account of the CPI, that "it is at least possible that Yugoslav directives triggered Communist guerrilla-style revolution throughout Southeast Asia". (p.274).

15. Aleksandr Kaznacheev, *Inside a Soviet Embassy: Experiences of a Russian Diplomat in Burma* (London: Robert Hale, 1962), p. 160.

16. Ruth McVey, op. cit., p. 7 and 9.

17. Interview with Baladas Ghoshal, Bangkok, 7 March 1993.

18. Sumanta Banerjee, *In the Wake of Naxalbari* (Calcutta: Subarnarekha, 1980), p. 82.

19. For a full text of Thakin Than Tun's speech, see the *People's Age*, 29 Feb. 1948. U Nu in his *Saturday's Son: Memoirs of the Former Prime Minister of Burma* (Bombay: Bharatiya Vidya Bhavan, 1976) distorts Thakin Than Tun's speech, exaggerating the language which the Communist leader used: "He [Thakin Than Tun] went on to accuse the U Nu government in Burma of being 'the running dogs of Anglo-American imperialism', and to say that thousands of Communist guerrilla fighters were 'ready to strike'." (p. 141).

20. Overstreet and Windmiller, op. cit., pp. 271–272.

21. Interview with Thakin Ba Thein Tin, Panghsang, 23 Dec. 1986. See also Bertil Lintner: "A Product of Moneylending", *Far Eastern Economic Review*, 4 June 1987 (the only published interview with Thakin Ba Thein Tin). Olga Chechetkina, a Soviet journalist specialising in Indonesia, was present in Calcutta at this time, according to McVey, op. cit., p. 2.

22. See for instance John F. Cady, *A History of Modern Burma* (Ithaca and London, Cornell University Press, 1978), p. 582. Many other writers (e.g. Fleischmann, op. cit.,, pp. 123) have also stated incorrectly that Ghoshal participated in the CPI's second congress.

23. Interview with Thakin Ba Thein Tin, Panghsang, 23 Dec. 1986.

24. McLane, op. cit., p. 381.

25. McVey, op. cit., p. 10.

26. Ibid., p. 24.

27. Cady, op. cit., p. 134.

28. Kin Oung, *Who Killed Aung San?* (Bangkok and Cheney: White Lotus, 1993), pp. 16–24. The following account of Burma's freedom struggle is partly based on Kin Oung's book, which this writer helped edit.

29. Josef Silverstein, *Burma: Military Rule and the Politics of Stagnation* (Ithaca and London: Cornell University Press, 1977), p. 9.

30. Ibid., p. 10.

31. Ibid., p. 10.

32. Shwe Yoe, *The Burman: His Life and Notions* (Arran, Scotland: Kiscadale Publications, 1989), p. 286.

33. David I. Steinberg, "Literacy Tradition," *Far Eastern Economic Review*, 27 Nov. 1987.

34. Maung Maung, *Burma's Constitution* (The Hague: Martinus Nijhoff, 1961), pp. 15–16.

35. U Le Pe Win, *History of the 1920 University Boycott* (Rangoon: Student Press, 1970), p. 43.

36. For background to the Saya San rebellion, see Cady, op. cit., pp. 312–321. For an analysis as seen from a Burmese perspective, see Aung San Suu Kyi, *Freedom From Fear* (London: Penguin Books, 1991), pp. 143–144.

37. Lucien W. Pye, *Politics, Personality and Nation Building: Burma's Search for Identity*. (New Haven, Connecticut: Yale University Press, 1962). p. 259.

38. Kin Oung, op. cit., p. 20.

39. Ibid., p. 20.

40. Aung San Suu Kyi, op. cit., p. 144.

41. Kin Oung, op. cit., p. 21.

42. *A Short Outline of the History of the Communist Party of Burma*: Official party document dated June 1964, and printed in Beijing.

43. Express Letter from the Chief Secretary to the Govt. of Burma, Police Department, No 173-C-34, dated 17 March 1934. Reproduced in *Communism in India: Unpublished Documents 1925–1934*, National Book Agency, Calcutta 1980, p. 170.

44. According to Bo Let Ya, apart from himself, Thakins Thein Pe, Ba Hein, and Aung San, an unnamed "friend from Calcutta" participated in this meeting (Bo Let Ya, "Snapshots of Aung San" in *Aung San of Burma*, ed. Dr. Maung Maung [The Hague: Martinus Nijhoff, 1962]). According to Ba Thein Tin, interview, Panghsang, 23 Dec. 1986), Thakin Aung San, Thakin Hla Pe (Bo Let Ya), Thakin Ba Hein, Thakin Bo, H.N. Ghoshal, and Dr. Nag alias Tun Maung, another Bengali revolutionary who had lived in Burma for a long time, were present at the "first congress". Ba Thein Tin also says that Thakins Soe and Than Tun did not participate in this meeting but joined the party shortly afterwards. According to Thakin Thein Pe (Thein Pe Myint) ("Critique of the Communist Movement in Burma," dated 1973, in Fleischmann, op. cit., p. 224, Burma's first Communist cell included Thakin Aung San, Thakin Soe, Thakin Ba Hein, Thakin Hla Pe (Bo Let Ya), and H.N. Ghoshal. Thakin Thein Pe also states that he himself initiated this meeting but "was left out from the first party cell for his individualism and sectarianism on the part of some comrades," and that Thakin Than Tun was "not Communist enough to be in the first cell".

45. *Communism in India: Unpublished Documents 1925–1934*, pp. 177–178. The document does not give the Chinese name for the newspaper. It ceased publication in November 1929.

46. Izumiya Tatsuro, *The Minami Organ* (Rangoon: Translation and Publications Department, Higher Education Department, 1985), p. 14.

47. Kin Oung, op. cit., p. 27.

48. Interview with Bo Kyaw Zaw, one of the Thirty Comrades, Panghsang, 1 Jan. 1987.

49. Interview with Bo Kyaw Zaw, Panghsang, 1 Jan. 1987.

50. *Japan's Scheme for the Liberation of Burma: The Role of the Minami Kikan and the Thirty Comrades* by Won. Z. Yoon, unpublished paper from Ohio University Center for International Studies, 1973, p. 7–9.

51. Izumiya, op. cit., pp. 20–22; and U Ba Than, *The Roots of Revolution* (Rangoon: The Guardian Press, 1962), p. 10.

52. Bo Let Ya in Maung Maung (ed.), *Aung San of Burma*, p. 47.

53. Kin Oung, op. cit., p. 30.

54. Original edition: Aung San Suu Kyi, *Burma and India: Some Aspects of Intellectual Life Under Colonialism* (Shimla and New Delhi: Indian Institute of Advanced Study in association with Allied Publishers, 1990). Reprinted in Aung San Suu Kyi, *Freedom from Fear*, pp. 82–139.

55. Aung San Suu Kyi, *Freedom from Fear*, p. 133.

56. Shelford Bidwell, *The Chindit War: Stilwell, Wingate and the Campaign in Burma in 1944* (New York: Macmillan Publishing, 1979), p. 18.

57. Richard Rhodes James, *Chindit: The explosive truth about the last Wingate expedition* (London: Sphere Books, 1981), p. 53.

58. Bidwell, op. cit., p. 24

59. Ibid., p. 17.

60. Ibid., p. 19.

61. Robert Taylor, *The State of Burma* (London: C. Hurst & Company, 1987),p. 100.

62. တို့ဗမာအစည်းအရုံးသမိုင်း (အကျဉ်းချုပ်) [A Brief History of the Dohbama Asiayone] (Rangoon: Sarpay Beikman, 1976), p. 215. See also *The Guardian* monthly (in Burmese), Rangoon, Feb. 1971: "The word *myanma* signifies only the Burmese, whereas *bama* embraces all indigenous nationalities."

63. *Working People's Daily*, 27 May 1989.

64. Josef Silverstein, *Burmese politics: The Dilemma of National Unity* (New Brunswick, New Jersey: Rutgers University Press, 1980), p. 9. It should be noted, however, that the 1931 census followed the Indian method of asking people what language they "habitually" spoke at home; thus, the census was based on language rather than ethnicity. The Mons were classified as Burmans under this system, as were the Arakanese. Many Karens in the delta would also speak Burmese "habitually" at home.

65. Ibid., p. 14.

66. Ibid., p. 14.

67. Harry Marshall, *The Karens of Burma* (New York: AMS Press, reprint 1980; original published by the University of Columbus, Ohio, 1922), pp. 5–6.

68. Gen. Smith-Dun, *Memoirs of the Four-Foot Colonel* (Ithaca, New York: Cornell University Southeast Asia Programme, Data Paper no. 113, 1980), pp. 1–2.

69. Silverstein, *Burmese politics*, p. 16.

70. San C. Po, *Burma and the Karens* (London: Elliot Stock, 1928), p. 1.

71. Bertil Lintner, "Praise the Lord and pass the ammunition", *Far Eastern Economic Review*, 21 Jan. 1988.

72. Quoted in Smith-Dun, op. cit., pp. 6–7.

73. Quoted in San C. Po, op. cit., p. 23.

74. J. Russel Andrus, *Burmese Economic Life* (Stanford, California: Stanford University Press, 1948), p. 27.

75. George A. Theodorson, "Minority Peoples in the Union of Burma" (paper presented at the First International Conference of Southeast Asian historians, Singapore, Jan. 1961).

76. San C. Po, op. cit., pp. 77 and 81.

77. Rong Syamananda, *A History of Thailand* (Bangkok: Chulalongkorn University, 1977), p. 7.

78. Ibid., p. 8.

79. Eric Seidenfaden, *The Thai Peoples* (Bangkok: Siam Society, 1967), p. 7.

80. For a complete list of the Shan states, see *Shan and Karenni: List of Chiefs and Leading Families* (Simla: Government of India Press, 1943).

81. Silverstein, *Burmese Politics*, p. 18.

82. Bertil Lintner: The Shans and the Shan State of Burma, *Contemporary Southeast Asia* 5, no 4. Singapore, Mar. 1984. See also Chao Tzang Yawnghwe: *The Shan of Burma: Memoirs of a Shan Exile.* Institute of Southeast Asian Studies, Singapore, 1987.

83. Quoted in "A Cockpit of Anarchy", *Asiaweek*, 29 May 1981.

84. Frank N. Trager: *Burma: From Kingdom to Independence* (London: Pall Mall Press, 1960), p.41.

85. *Shan and Karenni: List of Chiefs and Leading Families*, pp. 75–78.

86. For a succinct history of Shan-Burman relations during the British era, see Chao Tzang Yawnghwe, op. cit., pp. 45–82.

87. Ibid., See also Bertil Lintner, "The Shans and the Shan State of Burma", *Contemporary Southeast Asia* 5, no. 4, Mar. 1984.

88. G.E. Harvey, "The Wa People of the Burma-China Border", *St. Antony's Papers No. II, Far Eastern Affairs, No. One.* London: Chatto & Windus, 1957, p. 129.

89. *A Collection of Treaties, Engagements and Sanads Relating to India and Neighbouring Countries*, compiled by C.U. Aichison, Vol. XII, (Calcutta: Government of India Central Publication Branch, 1931), p. XII. Note that only the Western Karenni states—Kyebogyi and Bawlake—were recognised as "independent"; the eastern state of Kantarawaddy had a separate agreement with the British Crown. See Sao Saimong Mangrai, *The Shan States and the British Annexation* (Ithaca, New York: Cornell University Southeast Asia Programme, Data Paper no. 57, 1965), pp. xliii–xlv.

90. Ronald D. Renard, *Socio-Economic and Political Impact of Production, Trade and Use of Narcotic Drugs in Burma* (UN Research Institute for Social Development, June 1992), pp. 35–36.

91. Seidenfaden, op. cit., p. 124.

92. Alfred McCoy, *The Politics of Heroin: CIA Complicity in the Global Drug Trade* (New York: Lawrence Hill Books, 1991), pp. 83–86. See also Maurice Collis, *Foreign Mud* (London: Faber and Faber, 1946), pp. 66–66; and *The Opium War* (Beijing: Foreign Languages Press, 1976), pp. 4–6.

93. Collis, op. cit., p. 303: "In 1850 the Government of India was deriving five and a half millions [pounds] of revenue from opium out of a total revenue of twenty-seven and a half millions. Without these five and a half million, it was innocently asked, how could the Government continue its beneficent plans for education and hospitals and put the Indians on the road to civilization?"

94. Sterling Seagrave, *The Soong Dynasty* (London: Sidgwick & Jackson, 1985), p. 4.

95. J.M. Scott, *The White Poppy: A History of Opium* (New York: Funk & Wagnalls, 1969), pp. 84–85.

96. McCoy, op. cit., p. 82; Catherine Lamour and Michel R. Lamberti, *The Second Opium War* (London: Allen Lane, 1974), p. 41.

97. *The Opium War* (Beijing), pp. 37–38.

98. Richard Hughes, *Borrowed Place, Borrowed Time: Hong Kong and its many faces* (London: Andre Deutsch, 1968), p. 119.

99. Scott, op. cit., p. 100.

100. Hughes, op. cit., p. 105.

101. Ibid., pp. 105–106. See also Scott, op. cit., pp. 22–30.

102. Leonard P. Adams, "China: The Historical Setting of Asia's Profitable Plague" in Alfred McCoy, *The Politics of Heroin in Southeast Asia* (New York: Harper and Row, 1972), p. 361.

103. McCoy, *The Politics of Heroin: CIA Complicity in the Global Drug Trade*, p. 80.

104. Chiran Prasertkul, *Yunnan Trade in the Nineteenth Century: Southwest China's Cross-boundaries Functional System* (Bangkok: Institute of Asian Studies, Chulalongkorn University, 1989), p. 62.

105. Jackie Yang Rettie, "Kokang", *Thai-Yunnan Newsletter*, March 1991, p. 11. Ronald D. Renard, op. cit., p. 35.

106. Hugh Tinker, *The Union of Burma: A Study of The First Ten Years of Independence* (London: Oxford University Press, 1957), p. 371. Jackie Yang Rettie, op. cit., p. 11.

107. Bertil Lintner, "Letter from Kokang", *Far Eastern Economic Review*, 6 Aug. 1987. For a brief history of Kokang, see Jackie Yang Rettie, "Kokang", *Thai-Yunnan Newsletter*, March 1991.

108. G.E. Harvey, op. cit., p. 129.

109. Chiranan Prasertkul, op. cit., p. 63.

110. McCoy, *The Politics of Heroin: CIA Complicity in the Global Drug Trade*, p. 93: "In 1905–1906, for example, opium sales provided 16 percent of taxes in French Indochina, 16 percent for Netherlands Indies, 20 percent for Siam, and 53 percent for British Malaya."

111. For a full text of these laws, see *The Opium Manual. Containing the Opium Act and the Rules and Directions thereunder in force in Burma* (Rangoon: Superintendent, Central Press, 1964).

112. *The Burma Gazetteer: The Bhamo District* (Rangoon: Superintendent, Government Printing and Stationery, reprint 1960), p. 82.

113. Leslie Milne, *The Shans at Home* (New York: Paragon Book Reprint, 1970), p. 180.

114. Gross revenue in North Hsenwi State totalled 690,889 Rupees annually before World War II, compared to 427,879 Rupees for the much larger state of Kengtung, or 126,513 Rupees for the relatively prosperous, agricultural (non-poppy growing) central state of Yawnghwe (*Shan States and Karenni: List of Chiefs and Leading Families*, pp. 5, 12 and 65).

115. H.N.C. Stevenson, *The Hill Peoples of Burma* (Calcutta: Longmans & Green, 1945), p. 9.

116. Ibid., p. 9.

117. For a comprehensive study of the Kachins, see Edward R. Leach, *Political Systems of Highland Burma: A Study of Kachin Social Structure* (London: G.Bell, 1954).

118. For a detailed history of the Kachin Baptist church, see Herman G. Tegenfeldt, *A Century of Growth: The Kachin Baptist Church of Burma* (South Pasadena, California: William Carey Library, 1974.

119. George A. Theodorson, op. cit., pp. 14–15.

120. Vumsom, *Zo History* (Aizawl, India: Published by the author, undated), pp. 184–185.

121. Stevenson, op. cit., p. 15.

122. For a description of the Burmese Nagas, see Bertil Lintner, *Land of Jade: A*

Journey through Insurgent Burma (Edinburgh and Bangkok: Kiscadale and White Lotus, 1991), pp. 87–88.

123. When I trekked through the Naga Hills in 1985, villagers often asked me if I was "Indian or Burmese", the only two countries they had heard of. Hardly anyone spoke Burmese, and they clearly considered Burma an alien country.

124. Theodorson, op. cit., p. 12.

125. For a comprehensive account of the Rohingyas and other Muslim communities in Burma, see Moshe Yegar, *The Muslims of Burma: A Study of a Minority Group* (Wiesbaden: Otto Harrassowitz, 1972).

126. Ibid., p. 19.

127. For a comprehensive history of the Indian community in Burma, see Nalini Ranjan Charkravarti, *The Indian Minority in Burma: The Rise and Decline of an Immigrant Community* (London: Oxford University Press, 1971).

128. Theodorson, op. cit., p. 9.

129. Stevenson, op. cit., p. 3.

130. Charles Cruickshank, *SOE in the Far East* (Oxford: Oxford University Press, 1983), p. 5.

131. Andrew Selth, "Race and Resistance in Burma 1942–1945", in *Modern Asian Studies*, Cambridge, 20, 3 (1986), p. 502.

132. His son Chatichai Choonhavan later became a prominent politician and served as prime minister of Thailand 1988–91.

133. Frank Owen, *The Campaign in Burma* (Dehra Dun: Natraj Publishers, 1974), p. 76.

134. Charles M. Simpson, *Inside the Green Berets* (New York: Berkeley Books, 1983), p. 14.

135. Ian Fellowes-Gordon, *Amiable Assassins* (London: Robert Hale Ltd, 1957), p. 87–88.

136. Interview with Lasang Ala, Pa Jau, 23 June 1986.

137. William R. Peers and Dean Brelis, *Behind the Burma Road: The Story of America's Most Successful Guerrilla Force* (Boston and Toronto: An Atlantic Monthly Press Book, Little, Brown & Co, 1963), p. 69.

138. Ibid., p. 69.

139. Interview with Tamla Baw, Manerplaw, 9 May 1992.

140. "DSO Colonel Faces Fraud Charges", *Daily Mail*, 9 Aug. 1952.

141. Kin Oung, op. cit., p. 30.

142. Jan Becka, *The National Liberation Movement in Burma during the Japanese Occupation Period*. The Oriental Institute in Academia, Publishing House of the Czechoslovak Academy of Sciences, Prague 1983, p. 53.

143. Ibid., p. 223.

144. *A Short Outline of the History of the Communist Party of Burma*, pp. 2–3

145. Becka, op. cit., p. 145.

146. Interview with Thakin Ba Thein Tin, Panghsang, 23 Dec. 1986.

147. Becka, op. cit., p. 170.

148. Interview with Thakin Ba Thein Tin, Panghsang, 23 Dec. 1986.

149. McLane: op. cit., pp. 326–327.

150. *Burma and the Insurrections* , (Rangoon: Government of Burma publications, Sept. 1949), p.3.

151. Becka, op. cit., p. 258.

152. Ian Fellowes-Gordon, *The Battle for Naw Seng's Kingdom* (London: Leo Cooper, 1971), p. ix.

153. Governor of Burma to Secretary of State for Burma, Telegram IOR:M/4/2422, dated 6 Feb. 1946 (in Hugh Tinker, *Burma: The Struggle for Independence 1944–1948*, London: Her Majesty's Stationery Office, 1983, Vol. I, p. 642)

154. Ibid., p. 642.

155. Michael Lonsdale, *The Karen Revolution in Burma* (Singapore: Sam Art, undated), p. 29.

156. Josef Silverstein, *Burmese Politics: The Dilemma of National Unity* (New Brunswick: Rutgers University Press, 1980), p. 84.

157. Interview with Inge Sargent, last Mahadevi of Hsipaw, Boulder, Colorado, 13 March 1992.

158. Quoted in Silverstein, op. cit., p. 85.

159. P.G.E. Nash to Sir Gilbert Laithwaite, IOR: M/4/3023, dated Rangoon 12 Aug. 1946. (in Hugh Tinker, *Burma: The Struggle for Independence*, Vol. I, p. 949–950).

160. Ibid., p. 950.

161. Interview with Saw Thra Din, Sangkhlaburi, 11 Jan. 1981.

162. "Observation by H.N.C. Stevenson on Karen Resolution, adopted on 25 April 1946" (in Hugh Tinker, *Burma: The Struggle for Independence*, Vol. I, p. 850).

163. For a comprehensive history of these turbulent years, see Silverstein, *Burmese Politics*, pp. 93–101. For the schism within the CPB, see Bertil Lintner, *The Rise and Fall of the Communist Party of Burma* (Ithaca, New York: Cornell University Southeast Asia Programme, 1990), pp. 10–11.

164. The Karen National Union to the Prime Minister (via Governor of Burma), IOR: M/4/3023 (in *Hugh Tinker, Burma: The Struggle for Independence*, Vol. II, pp. 418–419).

165. For the full text of the Panglong Agreement, see Silverstein, *Burmese Politics*, . p. 107–108.

166. *The Constitution of the Union of Burma* (Rangoon: Supt., Govt. Printing and Stationery, 1947), pp. 56–57 (Chapter X: Right of Secession).

167. Silverstein, *Burmese Politics*, p. 109.

168. Ibid., pp. 104–105, 108. Bottomley has since then frequently expressed his admiration for Ne Win, whom he considers "my personal friend".

169. *Frontier Areas Committee of Enquiry, Part II: Appendices* (Rangoon: Supt. Govt. Printing and Stationery, 1947), p. 2.

170. Ibid., pp. 5–6 and 85.

171. Ibid., pp. 128–129.

172. Ibid., pp. 37–39.

173. Silverstein, *Burmese Politics*, p. 116.

174. "Press Release: the Karen National Union for Reuters, 25 June 1947", in *Hugh Tinker, Burma: The Struggle for Independence*, Vol. II, pp. 610–611: "We, the Karens of Burma, strongly resent the gross misrepresentation of our cause by Lt Col David Rees-Williams, Chairman of the Burma Frontier Areas Committee of Enquiry as expressed in his recent article, reported to be published in London about the 22nd June 1947 as reported by Reuter in the Monday issue of the *Rangoon Monitor* of 23rd June 1947." Rees-Williams's article had stated, among other things: "The Chins are

so divided geographically that it is difficult for them to effect any cohesion among themselves. The Karens are equally at variance politically; the Animist Karens have no interest in the Constitutional issue, the Buddhist Karens are inclined to side with the Burmans, while the Christian Karens, who are about 25 per cent of the whole, and the educated ones at that, are divided among themselves into two groups, one of which supports Aung San and the other is against him."

175. For a complete text of the speech, see Maung Maung Pye, *Burma in the Crucible* (Rangoon: Khittaya Publishers, 1952), pp. 204–207.

176. Interview with Saw Maw Reh, Mae Hong Son, 10 Nov. 1992.

177. Bertil Lintner, "In the dragon's wake", *Far Eastern Economic Review*, 26 April 1984. See also Moshe Yegar, op. cit., p. 96.

178. *A Short Outline of the Communist Party of Burma*, p. 3. Interview with Thakin Ba Thein Tin, Panghsang, 23 Dec. 1986.

179. *Burma and the Insurrections* , pp. 4–5. For a full text of the so-called "Ghoshal Thesis", see Fleischmann, op. cit., pp. 83–128.

180. Moreover, Thakin Ba Thein Tin, one of the three members of the politburo, was still on his way back from Calcutta by sea when the Pyinmana meeting took place (Than Tun had returned earlier by air)—so it is impossible that a politburo meeting took place in Pyinmana at the same time as the peasant rally: such an important decision would have to be taken by a meeting attended by all members of the politburo. For a text of the resolutions passed at the Pyinmana meeting, see *Burma and the Insurrections*, p. 41. The resolution called for the formation of peasant unions, and support for the "BOC strike and other strikes which are prevailing in Rangoon". No one mentioned guerrilla warfare in rural areas, which followed after 28 March 1948.

181. Even McLane admits this in his *Soviet Strategies*: "It appears to this writer to be an authentic document, although some uncertainty naturally attaches the question inasmuch as the Burmese Communists have never published the paper." (p. 371). It is also possible that the importance of the thesis has been grossly overstated simply because it was the only CPB document to which most Western scholars until recently had access: it was distributed in Rangoon by Thakin Thein Pe, who had resigned from the party shortly before the outbreak of the civil war.

182. Letter to the author from Aung Htet, personal assistant to the CPB's last chairman, Thakin Ba Thein Tin, 10 July 1992. Khin Maung Gyi, the CPB's last secretary, wrote to the author in a letter dated Kunming, 15 April 1992, upon receiving a copy of the Ghoshal thesis: "Many thanks for this document. As for us, it is the first time that we have got the opportunity to read the so-called 'Ghoshal Thesis', which was non-existing inside our party and is merely a fabrication with the aim of accusing the CPB of instigating the civil war in Burma as directed by an external Communist Party."

Chapter 3: "Peace Within One Year"

1. U Ba Than, *Roots of the Revolution* (Rangoon: Director of Information, 1962), p. 67. For a list of units that mutinied, see also *The Nation*, 23 Sept. 1956. In addition to the regular units listed here, *The Nation* also lists the 9th and 1st UMP, the whole

Sitwundan Corps in Thayetmyo and Magwe, plus elements of the Monywa *Sitwundan*.

2. Maung Maung, *To A Soldier Son* (Rangoon: Sarpay Beikman, 1974), p. 143.

3. U Nu, *Saturday's Son: Memoirs of the Former Prime Minister of Burma* (Bombay: Bharatiya Vidya Bhavan, 1976), p. 192. See also B.R. Nanda (ed.), *Indian Foreign Policy: the Nehru Years* (New Delhi: Radiant Publishers and the Nehru Memorial Museum and Library, 1976): "In Burma, within three months of independence, communists attemped to overthrow the government through armed rebellion. The Indian government supplied the U Nu government with arms, ammunition and monetary assistance. And later, in March 1950, India's mediation resulted in the decision of five Commonwealth countries to lend Burma six million pounds as assistance to meet the communist threat to that country. India contributed one-sixth of that sum." (p. 83).

4. *Chin National Journal*, No. 1, March 1992. See also Vumson, *Zo History* (Aizawl, Mizoram: Published by the author, undated), pp. 207–211.

5. Hugh Tinker, *The Union of Burma: A Study of The First Years of Independence* (London: Oxford University Press, 1957), pp. 325–326.

6. Dr. Maung Maung, *Grim War Against the Kuomintang* (Rangoon: Nu Yin Press, 1953), p. 4. But even some of the *Sitwundans* defected: "The whole *Sitwundan* Corps in Thayet district under Bo Aung Thein defected . . . the whole of *Sitwundan* Corps in Magwe under Bo Pe Aung was overpowered. Bo Pe Aung was executed by the Communists. *Sitwundan* Corps in Monywa under Bo Kyaw Kyaw was overpowered. Bo Kyaw Kyaw was executed by the Communists." (*The Nation*, 23 Sept. 1956). Nevertheless, the *Sitwundans* proved to be quite effective as counter-insurgency forces.

7. Dr. Maung Maung, op. cit., p. 34.

8. "A Brief History of Tatmadaw Leadership", *Working People's Daily*, 14 Jan. 1991.

9. For an account of the early expansion of the Burma Army, see Tinker, op.cit. p.323–330. The training of Burmese army officers in Malaya has never been officially acknowledged, but Brig.-Gen. Kyaw Zaw stated in an interview with the author (Panghsang, 1 Jan. 1987) that at least one high-ranking officer, Lieut.-Col. Tin Maung, was attached to a Malayan battalion. Kyaw Zaw (then southern command commander of the Burma Army) himself went to Malaya to inspect the small Burmese contingent there in 1952. It was later transferred to Singapore, where training of Burmese intelligence personnel continued even well after Ne Win's coup in 1962. There is only one official document that mentions the training in Malaya— but then in an indirect quote from Taiwan's UN representative, Dr. Tingfu F. Tsiang, in a debate in the General Assembly on 17 April 1953: "I have before me a newspaper despatch published in an English newspaper in Hong Kong. Its dateline is Singapore, March 27, that is, a little over two weeks ago. I quote from the despatch: . . . Captain Tin Koko, who is attached to the Burma Army Officers Training School in Rangoon, spent three weeks with British and Gurkha troops in the Malayan jungles observing British techniques against the Malayan Communists. He and his colleague, Major Tin Sha, left here by Comet for Rangoon this morning." *The Kuomintang Aggression Against Burma* (Rangoon: Ministry of Information, 1953), p.45.

10. Robert Taylor, *The State of Burma* (London: Hurst & Company, 1987), p. 262.

11. Robert Taylor, *Domestic and Foreign Consequences of the Kuomintang Intervention in Burma* (Ithaca, New York: Cornell University Southeast Asia Programme, Data Paper No. 93), pp. 6–7. See also Dept. of State Letter 3/d 2876, 5 May 1950 and *National Intelligence Estimate: Prospects for Survival of a Non-Communist Regime in Burma* (the Central Intelligence Agency: NIE-36, 1 Aug. 1951).

12. Quoted in Andrew Selth, *Assisting the Defence of Australia: Australian Defence Contacts with Burma 1945–1987* (Canberra: The Australian National University, Working Paper No 218, 1990), pp. 1–2.

13. Ibid., p. 2. However, Burma did not become a full member of the Colombo Plan until 1952.

14. Dept of State Letter, 5 May 1950.

15. Tinker, op. cit., p. 48.

16. Frank Trager, *Burma: From Kingdom to Republic* (London: Pall Mall Press, 1966), p. 216.

17. Ibid., pp.154–156.

18. Interview with Mika Rolley, Mae Hong Son, 9 Nov. 1992.

19. Letter to the author from Anthony Stonor, 22 Nov. 1992.

20. Interview with Mika Rolley, Mae Hong Son, 9. Nov. 1992. Also letter to the author from Anthony Stonor, 22 Nov. 1922. Sterling Seagrave writes in a letter to the author dated 27 May 1992: "According to Bo Set Kya, one of the most astute of the Thirty Comrades . . . who spent many evenings talking with me in my living room over several months, one 'cell' in the British secret service including former members of the SOE and Wingate's Chindits who had lost many close friends to the Japanese and their Burmese allies, were committed to getting their revenge. . . . Set Kya said this 'cell' was bitterly opposed to granting Burma independence but had to work in secret to avoid collision with the postwar Labour government's Burma policy." Undoubtedly, differences existed beween Labour and Conservatives in regards to Burma, but it is still uncertain to what extent the "anti-Burman" lobby was willing to support, for instance the Karens. Whether Tulloch belonged to this group is also unclear: his arrest and subsequent conviction on fraud charges seem to indicate that he was a lone free-booter.

21. Letter to the author from Anthony Stonor, 22 Nov. 1992.

22. Interview with Mika Rolley, Mae Hong Son, 9 Nov. 1992.

23. Interview with Sgaw Ler Taw, Manerplaw, 26 May 1987.

24. Interview with Sgaw Ler Taw, Manerplaw, 26 May 1987.

25. Interview with Mika Rolley, Mae Hong Son, 9 Nov. 1992. Stonor writes that in Nov. 1949 he received a letter from Tulloch, urging him to fly to Bangkok, which he did. In Bangkok, he met Col. L.M. Coffey, a British engineer, with whom Baldwin had been staying before crossing the border into Karen-held areas of eastern Burma shortly before Stonor's arrival in Thailand.

26. Interview with Mika Rolley, Mae Hong Son, 9 Nov. 1992; interview with Paw Moo Thoo, a Karen veteran of World War II and the early Karen insurrection, Three Pagodas Pass, 15 Jan, 1981. See also Martin Smith, *Burma: Insurgency and the Politics of Ethnicity* (London and New Jersey: Zed Books, 1991), pp. 143–144. Sein Lwin, the Burma Army officer who led the raid, later became a prominent state and party leader under Ne Win; he also served as president of Burma for 18 days during the turmoil of July–August 1988.

27. *Reuters*, Rangoon, 15 Aug. 1950.

28. See for instance "The KNU Insurgents: Conditions soon after independence",*Working People's Daily*, 4 & 5 Nov. 1988. In fact, David Vivian stayed with the Karens until the mid-1950s after which he returned to Britain via Thailand. Vivian died in Swansea, Wales, in the late 1980s.

29. *Daily Telegraph*, Aug. 1952.

30. See, for instance, *yebaw* Thit Maung, "The KNU Insurgents: From the First to the Second Programme", the *Working People's Daily*, 6 Nov. 1988: "The KNU insurgents had their embryo formed in the womb of the divide-and-rule policy of imperialists and they were born and nurtured by the imperialists." The same article mentions the activities of Campbell and Tulloch.

31. Chaine Dun is now a well-to-do engineer living in New Jersey. Oliver Ba Than, the KNU's secret envoy to London in 1948, was killed in action near Daik-U in February 1949.

32. Smith, op. cit., p. 114.

33. Interview with Zau Mai, Panghsang, 3 Jan. 1987. Zau Mai retreated with Naw Seng to China in 1950, and returned with him to Burma in January 1968 as a military commander in the CPB's army. He should not be confused with Maj.-Gen. Zau Mai, the chief of staff of the non-communist Kachin Independence Army (KIA); see Appendix III.

34. Letter from Sterling Seagrave (Gordon Seagrave's son) to the author, 4 Dec. 1992.

35. U Nu, op. cit., p. 192.

36. Letter from Sterling Seagrave to the author, 4 Dec. 1992.

37. For an account of Seagrave's exploits during World War II, see his book *Burma Surgeon* (New York: W.W. Norton & Co, 1943). I met and interviewed several of his old nurses when I trekked through CPB territory in 1986–87; they had followed Naw Seng into exile in China in May 1950, and returned with him to Burma in 1968 to join the CPB.

38. Letter from Sterling Seagrave to the author, 4 Dec. 1992.

39. Interview with Zau Mai, Panghsang, 3 Jan. 1987. Out of the 400 who crossed to China, about 100 filtered back into Burma after a while. But 300 were resettled in Guizhuo province and returned to Burma on 1 Jan. 1968: see Chapter Six.

Smith suggests in op. cit. (p. 141) that Naw Seng's retreat into China was negotiated "secretly" by Kachins who had remained loyal to the government, including *Duwa* Sinwa Nawng. This seems highly unlikely; Sinwa Nawng, or any other Burmese citizen for that matter, was hardly in a position to negotiate the exile in China of ethnic rebels from Burma. Zau Mai also refutes the claim and insists that the only contacts that existed at the time were between the rebels themselves and local authorities across the frontier in Yunnan. Higher authorities in Beijing learned about the mini-exodus only later, Zau Mai says.

40. Minn Latt (Min Lat), *Burma in Battle* (unpublished manuscript, Prague: see bibliography).

41. Interview with Thakin Be Thein Tin, Panghsang, 24 Dec. 1986.

42. Catherine Lamour, *Enquete sur une Armée Secrete* (Paris: Éditions du Seuil, 1975), pp. 17–18. Lu Han's predecessor, Gen. Long Yun, had ruled Yunnan as a semi-independent territory from 1927 until 1945. Abandoning the KMT, he went to Beijing in 1950, spending his remaining life there.

43. Interview with Francis Yap, KMT veteran, Bangkok, 18 Apr. 1993.

44. Lamour, op. cit., p. 18.

45. Lamour calls the place Möng Pang in op. cit., p. 18. Francis Yap says the right name is Möng Pong. Description of the location of the camp also from interview with Francis Yap, Bangkok, 18 Apr. 1993.

46. Lamour, op. cit., p. 22.

47. McCoy, *The Politics of Heroin in Southeast Asia* (New York: Harper and Row, 1972), p. 128. Most of these KMT troops were interned on Phu Quoc island off the coast of Cambodia until they were eventually repatriated to Taiwan in June 1953. However, other reports indicate that a fairly large number of KMT stragglers settled in northern Laos, especially in Phong Saly province, which borders both Vietnam and China (interview with Bill Young, Chiang Mai, 13 Oct. 1992).

48. Lamour, op. cit., p. 25.

49. For the Burmese government's version of the KMT intervention, see *The Kuomintang Aggression Against Burma*. Other sources include Robert Taylor, *Foreign and Domestic Consequences of the Kuomintang Intervention in Burma*, and Dr. Maung Maung, op.cit.

50. Lamour, op. cit., pp. 18–22.

51. It has been generally assumed that Gen. Li Mi fled to Burma along with his men from the 93rd Division of the 26th Army. His former men, however, tell a different story. According to them, he flew from Kunming to Hong Kong when the Communists entered Yunnan and travelled later via Bangkok to Möng Hsat; interview with ex-KMT officer Francis Yap, Bangkok 30 Oct. 1992. See also Bo Yang, *Golden Triangle: Frontier and Wilderness* (Hong Kong: Joint Publishing Co., 1987), p. 109: "Lu Guoquan ... appointed Peng Cheng [Li Mi], who had remained in Hongkong, as divisional commander." There is also some confusion regarding the KMT units that entered Burma in 1950. Usually all of them are referred to as 'the 93rd Division'. The original 93rd Division was included in the Chinese expeditionary forces which entered Burma to fight the Japanese, and this may be the reason why it has left such a mark in the region. The forces which fled to Burma at this time came mainly from various forces of the 26th Army (including elements of the 93rd Division) and the 193rd Division of the 8th Army, but other local units were also included. The 26th Army's 278th Regiment was later redesignated as the "new" 93rd Division with Gen. Li Mi as its commander. However, many troops from this "new" 93rd Division came from the legendary, "old" 93rd; see Bo Yang, op. cit. pp. 108–111 (Chapter 24: "The Strange 93rd Division"). Burmese records from the early 1950s, for instance *The Kuomintang Aggression*, are inaccurate on this account and their mistakes have been repeated by many writers since then.

52. *Kuomintang Aggression*, p. 195.

53. Bo Yang, op. cit., p. 109. Interview with Francis Yap, Bangkok, 28 Oct. 1992.

54. It has now been revealed that US and Soviet air forces clashed directly in Korea. The Russians admit to having lost 354, while claiming they shot down 1,300 American planes. Jon Halliday, "A Secret War", *Far Eastern Economic Review*, 22 April 1993.

55. Trager, op. cit., p. 114.

56. Quoted in Dr. Maung Maung, op. cit., p. 9.

57. Taylor, *The Kuomintang Intervention*, p. 42.

58. Dr. Maung Maung, op.cit., p. 14.

59. Quoted in Taylor, *The Kuomintang Intervention*, p. 42.

60. McCoy, op. cit., p. 167–168.

61. U.S. Congress, House. Committee on Un-Anerican Activities. *International Communism (Communist Encroachment in the Far East)*: "Consultations with Maj.-Gen. Claire Lee Chennault, United States Army". 85th Cong., 2nd sess., 23 Apr. 1958, pp. 9–10.

Chapter 4: The Secret War

1. *Kuomintang Aggression Against Burma* (Rangoon: The Ministry of Information, 1953), p. 10 and 15: "During their first assault on Yunnan in May and June 1951, it was also observed that unidentified four-engined aircraft kept dropping supplies to KMT troops in the forward areas of Kokang and Wa States inside Union territory."

2. Letter to the author from Sterling Seagrave, 22 Aug. 1992.

3. Quoted in *Kuomintang Aggression*, pp. 37–38.

4. Ibid., p. 38.

5. Some confusion exists in this regard. Several sources refer to Gen. Li Mi as the "ex-Governor of Yunnan", which he never was. The last KMT governor of Yunnan was Lu Han who defected to the Communists (see Chapter Three). Taipei later appointed Li Mi "Governor of Yunnan", but he was then based at Möng Hsat in the southern Shan states.

6. *Kuomintang Aggression*, pp. 37–38 and 13.

7. Catherine Lamour, *Enquete sur une Armée Secrete* (Paris 1975: Éditions du Seuil), p. 80. She quotes Gen. Li Mi as saying that original troops from the 8th and 26th Armies numbered 8,000 men; locally recruited Sino-Burmese who were mostly muleteers: 2,500; plus local hill-tribe recruits as well as refugees from China, who were still in the early 1950s coming across the border in large numbers.

8. Ibid., p. 186.

9. Ibid., p. 198.

10. For a picture of Chiang Ching Kuo in Möng Hsat, see Lamour, op. cit., picture 10 after p. 160.

11. Lamour, op. cit., p. 42.

12. William M. Leary: *Perilous Missions: Civil Air Transport and CIA Covert Operations in Asia* (Montgomery: Alabama University Press, 1984), p. 129. The clandestine air-lift was code-named "Operation PAPER". "Dutch" Brongersma later flew Air America planes during the secret war in Laos in the 1960s; see Christopher Robbins, *Air America* (London: Corgi Books, 1988), p. 116.

13. Leary, op. cit., pp. 129–130.

14. Jonathan Marshall: *Drug Wars: Corruption, Counterinsurgency and Covert Operations in the Third World* (San Francisco: Cohen and Cohen, 1991), pp. 54 and 60. Helliwell later returned to Florida to take part in covert operations against Fidel Castro's Cuba. See Alfred W. McCoy, *The Politics of Heroin: CIA Complicity in the Global Drug Trade* (New York: Lawrence Hill Books, 1991), p. 470. Another prominent American intelligence operative connected with SEA Supplies was Sherman B. Joost, a Princeton graduate.

15. Barbara W. Tuchman, *Stilwell and the American Experience in China 1911–45* (New York: Bantam Books, 1972) p. 334.

16. Ibid. p. 334. This was in March 1942, before the retreat to India. The Soong family produced many prominent leaders and businessmen in Nationalist China: T.V. Soong later became prime minister and his younger brothers T.L. Soong and T.A. Soong became prominent financiers in Taiwan. T.V. Soong's three elder sisters all married prominent people: Ai-ling Soong became the wife of Taiwan's finance minister, H.H. Kung; Ching-ling Soong married KMT founder Sun Yat-sen and remained a revolutionary even after the Communist victory in China; and May-ling Soong married Chiang Kai-shek.

17. Ibid., p. 483.

18. Ibid., p. 483.

19. Ibid., p. 475.

20. McCoy, op. cit., p. 167

21. Ibid., p. 167. The official buyer of CAT was the OPC (a CIA subsidiary), Leary, op. cit., pp. 103–104.

22. Tuchman, op. cit., p. 238.

23. McCoy states in op. cit, pp. 166–167, that "in November 1950, President Truman authorised an expansion of covert action capabilities and approved a plan put forward by the Office of Policy Coordination (OPC) and the CIA for the invasion of southern China using the KMT remnants in Burma." While this may be correct, Truman was nevertheless more pragmatic than, for instance, the hawks of the China Lobby. The OPC was an intentionally vague designation that masked the US government's covert action arm. It was eventually absorbed by the CIA (Leary, op. cit., pp. 70 and 131–132).

24. For the full text of Key's statement, see Leary, op. cit., p. 131. Assistant Secretary of State Dean Rusk supported the CIA's cover story. According to Leary, op. cit., p. 131: "After an 'exhaustive investigation,' he [Rusk] replied to Key on August 22, the State Department was able to authorize the ambassador 'categorically to deny to GOB [the Government of Burma] that there is or could be in future any official or unofficial US Govt connection with this force.' The departmet, he promised, would take action to prevent 'gunrunning' by private American citizens."

25. *New York Herald Tribune*, 22 March 1953.

26. Letter to the author from Sterling Seagrave, dated 27 May 1992. Seagrave, a well-known author and the son of "the Burma Surgeon", Gordon Seagrave, married Law-Yone's daughter in 1965.

27. Robert Taylor, *Foreign and Domestic Consequences of the KMT Intervention in Burma* (Ithaca, New York: Cornell University Southeast Asia Programme, Data Paper no. 93, 1973), p. 39.

28. Interview with Mika Rolley, Mae Hong Son, 9 Nov. 1992.

29. Interview with Mika Rolley, Mae Hong Son, 10 Nov. 1992.

30. Interview with Francis Yap, Bangkok, 30 Oct. 1992.

31. See for instance Taylor, op. cit, p. v. Mika Rolley says that the only weapons the Karens got from the KMT were a few small firearms which were given to Ohn Pe and his bodyguards when they returned to the Karen Hills in 1954. However, they strayed into Thailand, where they were disarmed by the Thai police before being sent back to KNU-held territory inside Burma. Most of the aid seems to have been given to the Mons and, later, the Kachins under Zau Seng.

32. Interview with Mika Rolley, Mae Hong Son, 9 Nov. 1992. See also Smith, *Burma: Insurgency and the Politics of Ethnicity* (London and New Jersey: Zed Books, 1991), pp. 153. The Burmese government, on the other hand, has always maintained that the Karens benefitted from KMT support (see, for instance, the *Working People's Daily*, 6 Nov. 1988: "When [the Karen rebels] began to lose military operations and their old master [the British] did not help them, the KNU hopefully turned to their new master, the KMT aggressor, for help." Taylor supports this view in op. cit., p. 18.

33. Interview with Brig.-Gen. Kyaw Zaw, Panghsang, 2 Jan. 1987.

34. Interview with Francis Yap, Bangkok, 30 Oct. 1992.

35. Interview with Sgaw Ler Taw, Manerplaw, 1 Aug. 1984.

36. Interview with Thakin Ba Thein Tin, Panghsang, 24 Dec. 1986.

37. Interview with Thakin Ba Thein Tin, Panghsang, 24 Dec. 1986. The decision to distribute land to the tillers had been taken during a meeting with peasants and village elders at Myetkyagon village in Pyinmana district shortly after the outbreak of the civil war in March 1948.

38. Interview with Aye Ngwe, Panghsang, 4 Jan. 1987.

39. *Kuomintang Aggression Against Burma*, p. 1.

40. Taylor, op. cit., p. 26.

41. Ibid., p. 38. See also Maung Maung, *Grim War Against KMT* (Rangoon: Nu Yin Press, 1953), p. 67. For a reproduction of the picture of the three dead Caucasians, see c. Lamour and M.R. Lamberti, *Les grandes manœuvres de l'opium* (Paris: Éditions du Seuil, 1972), p. 107.

42. *Kuomintang Aggression Against Burma*, p. 41.

43. Ibid., pp. 44–45.

44. Ibid., p. 95.

45. "The UN Through Burmese Eyes", pp. 8–9, quoted in Taylor, op. cit., p. 28.

46. McCoy, *The Politics of Heroin in Southeast Asia* (New York: Harper & Row, 1972), p. 136. Lamour, op. cit., p. 42.

47. G. William Skinner, *Leadership and Power in the Chinese Community of Thailand* (Ithaca, New York: Cornell University Press, 1958), pp. 99–100.

48. *In Memory of Chin Sophonpanich* (special supplement to the *Bangkok Post*, 9 April 1988), p. 7 and 12.

49. Ibid., p. 12. See also Lamour, op. cit., p. 109: "Le président de le Bangkok Bank lui est aussi totalement dévoué. C'est lui qui avance a Phao les fond nécessaires pour financer le commerce de l'opium." In 1955, Chin Sophonpanich also founded the Chinese language newspaper *Universal Daily News*, which is still being published in Bangkok. In more recent years, the *Universal Daily News* has arranged trips for foreign journalists to meet Khun Sa in the Golden Triangle.

50. Quoted in Maung Maung, op. cit., pp. 70–71.

51. *Kuomintang Aggression Against Burma*, p. 11, 37.

52. Ibid., p. 37.

53. Leary, op. cit., p. 131.

54. For a discussion of the early years of the opium trade in Burma, see *War On Drugs: Studies in the Failure of US Narcotics Policy* (Boulder, San Francisco & Oxford: Westview Press, 1992), pp. 237–317; Alfred McCoy: "Heroin as a Global Commodity: A History of Southeast Asia's Opium Trade", and Bertil Lintner: "Heroin and Highland Insurgency in the Golden Triangle".

55. Ibid., p. 288.
56. McCoy, *The Politics of Heroin: CIA complicity in the Global Drug Trade*, p. 101.
57. Ibid., p. 101.
58. Ibid., pp. 101–102. See also J.N. Scott, *The White Poppy: A History of Opium* (New York: Funk & Wagnalls, 1969), p. 136: "A fifth of Thailand's total revenue of about £7,000,000 in 1922–3 came from opium".
59. McCoy, *The Politics of Heroin in Southeast Asia*, p. 67.
60. McCoy, *The Politics of Heroin: CIA complicity in the Global Drug Trade*, p. 103. See also Elaine T. Lewis, "The Hill Peoples of Kengtung State", *Practical Anthropology* 4, No. 5 (Nov.–Dec. 1957): "At the time the Chinese Communists occupied Yunnan Province to the border of Kengtung State in 1950, a great flood of hill people came down to Kengtung State." The KMT invasion of Kengtung State caused many of them to flee again, Lewis writes: "For many years there have been large numbers of Chinese Nationalist troops in the area demanding food and money from the people. The areas in which these troops operate are getting poorer and poorer and some villagers are finding it necessary to flee. . . . Many hill people from the area have found their way into the hills of Thailand, so that now one may find substantial numbers of Lahus, Akhas, Meau [Hmong], Was, and other hill tribes originally from Kengtung in the hills in northern Thailand."
61. McCoy, *The Politics of Heroin in Southeast Asia*, p. 138.
62. *New York Times*, 16 Oct. 1953.
63. Interview with Nai Shwe Kyin, Bangkok 8 June 1992. Siddhi Savetsila later served with the National Security Council and was foreign minister of Thailand from 1980 to 1988.
64. Bertil Lintner, "Oiling the Buffers", *Far Eastern Economic Review*, 3 Dec. 1992.
65. McCoy, *The Politics of Heroin: CIA complicity in the Global Drug Trade*, pp. 168–169
66. Interview with Francis Yap, Bangkok, 28 Oct. 1992.
67. Hugh Tinker, *The Union of Burma: A Study of The First Years of Independence* (London: Oxford University Press, 1957), p. 368.
68. Taylor, op. cit., p. 46.
69. *New York Times*, 8 July 1953.
70. Taylor, op. cit., p. 47.
71. Interview with Kyaw Zaw, Panghsang, 2 Jan. 1987.
72. Dr Maung Maung, op. cit., p. 43.
73. Interview with Kyaw Zaw, Panghsang, 2 Jan. 1987.
74. Tin Oo served as chief of staff and defence minister 1974–76, he was imprisoned 1976–80, and became chairman of the National League for Democracy (NLD) in September 1988.
75. Taylor, op. cit., p. 49.
76. Interview with an American resident in Chiang Mai, who witnessed the evacuation in 1953, Chiang Mai, 22 Apr. 1993.
77. Leary, op. cit., p. 196.
78. Ibid., p. 196.
79. McCoy, *The Politics of Heroin: CIA complicity in the Global Drug Trade*, p. 175.
80. Interview with Kyaw Zaw, Panghsang, 2 Jan. 1987.
81. Interview with Kyaw Zaw, Panghsang, 2 Jan. 1987.

82. Taylor, op. cit., p. 50.

83. Taylor, op. cit., p. 50.

84. Li Mi returned to Taiwan in late 1952, but continued to be involved in the covert operation in Burma's Shan State for at least two more years from his office in Taipei.

85. Interview with Francis Yap, Bangkok, 30 Oct. 1992.

86. Bo Yang, op. cit. p. 109; of these units only the 3rd and the 5th remain today. The 3rd is based at Tam Ngob southeast of Fang and the 5th has its headquarters at the tourist destination Doi Mae Salong. Officially, these units have been renamed several times since the 1950s, first as "Chinese Irregular Forces" (CIF) and more recently as the quaintly named "*Sakura* [cherry blossom] Force".

87. Interview with Kyaw Zaw, Panghsang, 2 Jan. 1987.

88. Interview with Kyaw Zaw, Panghsang, 2 Jan. 1987.

89. The operation against the CPB, code-named *Aung Marga* (Victory Path) was launched in 1956. It led to the dismissal of Kyaw Zaw from the army; see Chapter Five.

90. Interview with Kyaw Zaw, Panghsang, 2 Jan. 1987.

91. Interview with Kyaw Zaw, Panghsang, 2 Jan. 1987.

92. Interview with Kyaw Zaw, Panghsang, 2 Jan. 1987.

93. For a break-down of Burmese budgets 1949–54, see Tinker, op. cit., p. 100.

94. Andrew Selth, *"Assisting the Defence of Australia": Australian Defence Contacts with Burma, 1945–1987* (Canberra: The Research School of Pacific Studies, Australian National University, Working Paper no. 218, 1990), p. 2.

95. Ibid., p. 2.

96. Ibid., p. 5.

97. Interview with Kyaw Zaw, Panghsang, 1 Jan. 1987.

98. Tinker, op. cit., p. 333.

99. For an overview of Japan-Burma relations since the war, see "The Odd Couple" by Bertil Lintner in *Japan in Asia: the Economic Impact on the Region* (Hong Kong: Review Publishing, 1991), pp. 162–171.

100. Ibid., p. 333.

101. Interview with Khin Maung Gyi, Panghsang, 28 Dec. 1986.

102. Interview with Kyaw Zaw, Panghsang, 1 Jan. 1987.

103. Peter Janssen, "Singular Story of a Foreign Success", *Asian Business*, Hong Kong, June 1985.

104. U Thaung, *Army's Accumulation of Economic Power in Burma* (1950–1990). Paper presented at a Burma seminar in Washington on 20 Oct. 1990.

105. Ibid.

106. Central Intelligence Agency: *National Intelligence Estimate: Prospects for Survival of a Non-Communist Regime in Burma*. NIE-36, 1 Aug. 1951.

Chapter 5: Retreat to the Jungle

1. For a brief history of these years, see D.G.E. Hall, *A History of Southeast Asia* (London: MacMillan Press, 1981), pp. 909–912.

2. Ibid., p. 911.

3. Ibid., pp. 910–911.

4. Ibid., p. 911.

5. U Nu, *Saturday's Son: Memoirs of the Former Prime Minister of Burma* (Bombay: Bharatiya Vidya Bhavan, 1976), p. 247.

6. Quoted in James Barrington, "The Concept of Neutralism," an *Atlantic Monthly* supplement, 1958, p. 29.

7. Ibid., p. 30.

8. *The Times*, 2 Nov. 1955.

9. Hugh Tinker, *The Union of Burma: A Study of The First Years of Independence* (London: Oxford University Press, 1957), pp. 376–378.

10. စင်+ချစ် နောက်ဆုံး (၂) ("Zin and Chit: the Last Two"; Rangoon: Mahananda Publishers, 1976), pp. 52–53.

11. Interview with Thakin Ba Thein Tin, Panghsang, 24 Dec. 1986.

12. Martin Smith, *Burma: Insurgency and the Politics of Ethnicity* (London and New Jersey: Zed Books, 1991), p. 454–455.

13. The letter, dated 20 Jan. 1956, was quoted in *The Nation*, 23 Sept. 1956.

14. *The Nation*, 23 Sept. 1956.

15. For an analysis of the shift in Moscow's Asia policy in the 1950s, see A. Doak Barnett (ed.), *Communist Strategies in Asia: A Comparative Analysis of Governments and Parties* (New York: Frederick A. Praeger Publishers, 1964).

16. Chan Aye took part in the pro-democracy movement of 1988 and became a prominent member of the National League for Democracy (NLD). Ex-Brig.-Gen. Aung Gyi capitalised on Chan Aye's past membership in the CPB when he decided to quit the NLD in Dec. 1988 to set up his own political party. Chan Aye was imprisoned by the military government in 1989.

17. Smith, op. cit., p. 167.

18. For complete election results, see Josef Silverstein, *Burma: Military Rule and the Politics of Stagnation* (Ithaca and London: Cornell University Press, 1977), pp. 70–71.

19. Interview with Thakin Chit Maung, Rangoon, 20 Apr. 1989.

20. Tinker, op. cit., p. 91

21. Alkesandr Kaznacheev, *Inside a Soviet Embassy* (London: Robert Hale, 1962) p. 63.

22. Ibid., p. 153.

23. Ibid., p. 155. Ba Tin still lives in Rangoon and continues to be an ardent admirer of Lenin and Stalin, even after the collapse of the Soviet Union in 1991–92. Interview with Igor Zouev, TASS Rangoon correspondent, Bangkok, March 1992.

24. A copy of this unpublished manuscript was sent by Czech Burma scholar Jan Becka in 1992 to the author.

25. *Outline of Word Construction in Modern Burmese* (Prague: the Oriental Institute, 1963). Min Lat rejoined his CPB comrades in Beijing in 1968, leaving behind his Czech wife and their son in Prague. Min Lat was executed by the CPB for "revisionism" in 1972 in the northern Wa Hills. Two other Burmese students in Prague, CPB members Tun Shein and Khin Win, had left for China in Dec. 1956. Interview with Khin Win, Panghsang, 9 Jan. 1987. Also interview with Jan Becka, one of Min Lat's Burmese language students, Prague, 1 Sept. 1992.

26. Interview with Thakin Ba Thein Tin, Panghsang, 24 Dec. 1986.

27. Letter to the author from Aung Win, Moscow, 7 July 1992.

28. Interview with Khin Maung Gyi, Panghsang, 28 Dec. 1986.

29. Interview with San Thu, Panghsang, 5 Jan. 1987.

30. John H. Badgley, "Burma's Radical Left: a Study in Failure", *Problems of Communism* X, 2 (Mar.–Apr. 1961), pp. 53–54.

31. Interview with KNU veteran Soe Aung, Manerplaw, 2 Aug. 1984.

32. Interview with KNU veteran Soe Aung, Manerplaw, 2 Aug. 1984.

33. Interview with Saw Ba Thin, Manerplaw, 11 May, 1992. See also Smith, op. cit., pp. 171–172.

34. Interview with KNU veteran Soe Aung, Manerplaw, 2 Aug. 1984.

35. Interview with Bo Mya, Manerplaw, 10 May 1992.

36. Bertil Lintner, "In the Dragon's Wake," *Far Eastern Economic Review*, 26 Apr. 1984. The article is based on numerous interviews with refugees, rebel leaders and local people during a trip to the Burma-Bangladesh border in February 1984.

37. Silverstein, op. cit., pp. 79, 153. See also the official publication *Is Trust Vindicated?* (Rangoon: Director of Information, 1960), pp. 223–228

38. For a comprehensive overview of the Indonesian army and its ideology, see David Jenkins, *Suharto and His Generals: Indonesian Military Politics 1975–1983* (Ithaca: Cornell Modern Indonesia Project, 1987).

39. Samuel P. Huntington, *Political Order in Changing Societies* (New Haven: Yale University Press, 1968), pp. 100–102. For an insight into the thoughts of Lucien W. Pye, see his *Asian Power and Politics: The Cultural Dimensions of Authority* (Cambridge, Massachusetts: The Belknap Press of Harvard University, 1985).

40. Intriguingly, the state-run *Working People's Daily* reprinted as late as 1993 an article by Robert G. Neumann, which expressed these anachronistic views: "Many of these [developing] countries view a military dictatorship, not as an act of retrogression, but rather as a progressive step. . . . The army and the military dictator may constitute the only feasible unifying principle (sic) capable of moderating influence." (Robert G. Neumann: "Is Democracy Possible and Desirable in Newly Emerging Nations?", *Working People's Daily*, 25 March 1993).

41. *Archiv Orientalni* (Academia Praha), vol. 49/1981.

42. Andrew Selth, *"Assisting in the Defence of Australia": Australian Defence Contacts with Burma, 1945–1987* (Canberra: The Research School of Pacific Studies, Australian National University, Working Paper no. 218, 1990), p. 6.

43. Interview with Kyaw Zaw, Panghsang, 2 Jan. 1987. See also Mya Win, "A Brief History of Tatmadaw Leadership-3", *Working People's Daily*, 15 Jan. 1991.

44. *Burma: the Eight Anniversary 1956* (Rangoon: the Government of the Union of Burma Central Publishing Office, 1956), p. 102.

45. Bertil Lintner, *Outrage: Burma's Struggle for Democracy* (London: White Lotus UK, 1990), p. 34.

46. Silverstein, op. cit., pp. 69–72.

47. Frank N. Trager, *Burma: From Kingdom to Republic* (London: Pall Mall Press, 1966), pp. 178–179.

48. Quoted in the foreword of *Is Trust Vindicated?*

49. *The National Ideology and the Role of the Defence Services* (Third edition. Rangoon, 30 Jan. 1960).

50. For a full text of the speech, see *Is Trust Vindicated?*, pp. 545–549.

51. Silverstein, op. cit., p. 32.

52. *The National Ideology and the Role of the Defence Services*, pp. 19–20

53. Sein Win, *The Split Story* (Rangoon: The Guardian Ltd., 1959), p. 48.

54. Ibid., p. 67.

55. U Nu, op. cit., p. 327.

56. *Is Trust Vindicated?*, p. 19 and 31. The break-down was as follows: CPB 3,050; CP(RF) 750; Karens 3,700; Mons 30; *Mujahids* 120; and KMT 1,350. These figures were probably well below the actual numbers—and the listings of surrenders and casualties were grossly inflated.

57. Ibid., pp. 21–22 and 27.

58. Ibid., p. 3.

59. The 1988 movement against the military and for democracy was especially strong in these areas, and some of the worst killings by the army took place there as well.

60. U Law Yone, "Burma's Socialist Democracy", *Atlantic Monthly Supplement*, 1958, p. 62.

61. Josef Silverstein, op. cit., pp. 70–71.

62. Ibid., p. 72.

63. Interview with Chao Tzang Yawnghwe, Bangkok, 7 March 1993. Chao Tzang now lives in exile in Vancouver, Canada and is attached to the University of British Columbia.

64. Maung Maung, *Grim War Against KMT* (Rangoon: Nu Yin Press, 1953), p. 65.

65. Sai Pan, "Shan State Today and Tomorrow", *Tai Youth Magazine*, 1957. Young dames who "would sob in hiding leaving the pursuing *yebaws* [Burma Army troops] furious with demands" is a euphemism for soldiers demanding sexual favours from village girls. A year later, Sai Pan went underground to join the Shan rebels along the Thai border where he assumed the *nom de guerre* of Sao Boon Tai and became a prominent rebel leader. He was assassinated in Chiang Mai, northern Thailand, in August 1983.

66. *Historical Facts about Shan State* (Tai Revolutionary Council, 1986), pp. 71–73.

67. Quoted in Josef Silverstein, "Politics in the Shan State: The Question of Secession from the Union of Burma", *Journal of Asian Studies* 18, no. 1, 1958.

68. Delia and Ferdinand Kuhn, *Borderlands* (New York: Alfred A. Knopf, 1962), p. 136.

69. According to Chiang Mai sources who have requested anonymity, Bo Ling Gung Na's official connections in Thailand were mainly with a police lieutenant called Nai Motpadung.

70. Interview with Sao Khun Thawda, Bangkok, 15 April 1993. Many other Shan war veterans also remember "Harry" who returned to Britain in late 1960, following the death of Sai Kyaw Tun. His whereabouts today are unknown. "Harry's" involvement with the early Shan rebels was never picked up by the War Office in Rangoon, in which case some kind of "foreign conspiracy" would most probably had been concocted.

71. Delia and Ferdinand Kuhn, op. cit., pp. 137–138.

72. Surachart Bamrungsuk, *United States Foreign Policy and Thai Military Rule 1947–1977* (Bangkok: Editions Duang Kamol, 1988), p. 62.

73. Ibid., pp. 62–63.

74. Ibid., pp. 63.

75. David Morell and Chai-anan Samudavanija, *Political Conflict in Thailand: Reform, Reaction, Revolution* (Cambridge, Massachusetts: Oegeschlager, Gunn & Hain Publishers, 1981), pp. 50–51.

76. Ibid., p. 52.

77. Surachart Bamrungsuk, op. cit., p. 77.

78. Hall, op. cit., p. 948.

79. Ibid., p. 949.

80. Charles F. Keyes, *Thailand: Buddhist Kingdom as Modern Nation-State* (Bangkok: Editions Duang Kamol, 1991), p. 113: "The size of direct US military aid and military investment in Thailand was enormous, totalling over US$2 billion for the period between 1951 and 1971."

81. Interview with Khun Kya Nu, Chiang Mai, 15 Jan. 1993.

82. Interviews with Shan veterans, Pieng Luang, 24 Apr. 1993. The meeting was held in Bangkok in March 1959, and it was obvious that the Thai representatives viewed the Shans' political demands as unrealistic. M.R. Kukrit Pramoj later became a prominent political leader and prime minister of Thailand.

83. Interview with Khun Kya Nu, Chiang Mai, 14 Jan. 1993.

84. Interview with Sao Hsö Lane, Möng Mai, 12 Mar. 1983. Hsö Lane took part in the campaign and later became commander of the Shan State Army. He surrendered in April 1983.

85. Interview with Sao Hsö Lane, 12 Mar. 1983.

86. Interview with Khun Kya Nu, Chiang Mai, 23 Apr. 1993. Long Khun Maha later joined Khun Sa's Shan United Army.

87. There are many stories, and myths, about the death of Sai Kyaw Tun. According to one version, he was hiding in a barn in a paddy field when it was surrounded by government forces. Rather than give himself up, he had heroically pulled a hand-grenade and blown himself to pieces. Other sources discount this story, asserting that the Shan rebels at this time did not have any hand-grenades. According to another story, he died while trying to defend Harry, his English friend. However, Harry, who had gone with Sai Kyaw Tun up to Möng Hpayak shortly after the formation of the SSIA, had returned to the Thai border in June 1960, a month before the death of Sai Kyaw Tun. Whatever the case, the gallantry medal of the Shan rebels has since then been named after 'Sao Hsö Wan" a.k.a. Sai Kyaw Tun (Chao Tzang, op. cit. 197)

88. Interview with Chao Tzang Yawnghwe, Bangkok, 18 Mar. 1993.

89. Interview with Brang Seng, Kachin rebel leader, Pa Jau, 7 May 1986.

90. Interview with Malizup Zau Mai, Na Hpaw, 17 Oct. 1986. Also interview with N'Chyaw Tang, one of Naw Seng's men, Pa Jau, 25 Apr. 1986. Zau Mai joined the Kachin insurrection in 1961 and became commander in chief of the Kachin Independence Army (KIA) in 1980.

91. The villages were Hpimaw, Kangfang and Gawlum, a 153 sq.km. area on the Chinese frontier northeast of Myitkyina. At the same time, the Panhung-Panglao area (189 sq.km.) in the Wa Hills was also handed over to China. For details about the border agreement, see Bertil Lintner, *Cross-Border Drug Trade in the Golden Triangle (S.E. Asia), Territory Briefing Number 1* (University of Durham: International Boundaries Research Unit, 1991).

92. For more details, see Bertil Lintner, *Land of Jade: a Journey through Insurgent Burma* (Edinburgh and Bangkok: Kiscadale and White Lotus, 1990), pp. 167–168.

93. Interview with N'Chyaw Tang, Pa Jau, 25 Apr. 1986.

94. Silverstein, *Burma: Military Rule and the Politics of Stagnation*, p. 175. During my trek through the hills north of Kengtung in March–April 1987, I interviewed numerous villagers who vividly described the PLA intervention in 1961. Acting on reliable intelligence, the PLA targeted all major KMT camps in the hills around Möng Yang and Möng Wa. The villagers said casualties were heavy on the PLA's side, but the determination of the Chinese Communists to press on was unmistakable. The KMT was beaten despite the PLA's heavy losses. See also *National Intelligence Estimate, no. 50–61, 28 March 1961: Outlook in Mainland Southeast Asia* (US intelligence document, declassified on 6 Mar. 1990): "Acting under a secret agreement providing for joint action to protect the teams engaged in demarcating the Sino-Burmese border, the Chinese Communists launched an attack into Burma against the Nationalist [KMT] units in December 1960. The Burmese Army later joined in. By February 1961, the forces of the two countries had succeeded in capturing the major Nationalist bases and driving most of the irregulars across the Mekong into Laos and Thailand, although this was apparently done at the cost of severe casualties to the Burmese Army. Substantial quantities of Nationalist arms and equipment, much of it US made, were captured by the Burmese. . . . The fact that Chinese Communist troops helped the Burmese Army in the attack on the irregulars has been kept from the Burmese public and U Nu has publicly and emphatically denied the presence of any Chinese Communist troops on Burmese soil."

95. Central Intelligence Agency, Office of Current Intelligence: *Chinese Irregulars in Southeast Asia* (NLK-77-320: 29 July 1961).

96. Ibid.

97. For a discussion of these events from a Shan point of view, see Chao Tzang Yawnghwe, *The Shan of Burma: Memoirs of a Shan Exile* (Singapore: Institute of Southeast Asian Studies, 1987), pp. 114–118.

98. Interview with Chao Tzang Yawnghwe, Bangkok, 9 March 1993.

99. U Nu, op. cit., p. 340.

100. This and subsequent quotes from an interview with Inge Sargent, Denver, Colorado, 13 March, 1992. She was born in Austria as Inge Eberhard, and met Sao Kya Seng in the US in the early 1950s. They were married in 1953. Sao Kya Seng was one of two Shan leaders to "disappear" after the military take-over in 1962. His widow now lives in Denver, Colorado, and has remarried to Tad Sargent, an American. For an account of the disappearance of her husband and her efforts to shed light on the mystery, see Bertil Lintner, "Burma keeps mum on the fate of the prince of Hsipaw", *Bangkok Post*, 18 Aug. 1988.

Chapter 6: The Military Takes Over

1. Sao Shwe Thaike "expired" in police custody in October 1962. The authorities never explained why and how he died. His family suspect that he was extrajudicially executed. See testimony by his daughter, Sao Nang Ying Sita, in *Hearings Before the Subcommittee on Future Foreign Policy Research and Development of the Committee on International Relations*. (U.S. Congress. House. 94th Cong., 1st sess., 22 and 23 April 1975.) pp. 137–149.

2. Letter from Sai Tzang to author, also quoted in Bertil Lintner, *Outrage: Burma's Struggle for Democracy* (London: White Lotus UK, 1990), pp. 13–14.

3. Dr. Maung Maung, *Burma and General Ne Win* (Bombay: Asia Publishing House, 1969), p. 292.

4. David I. Steinberg, "Burma Under the Military: Towards a Chronology", *Contemporary Southeast Asia* . 3, no. 3, Dec. 1981, p. 249.

5. Bertil Lintner, "Burma Keeps Mum on Fate of the Prince of Hsipaw", *Bangkok Post*, 18 Aug. 1988.

6. For a detailed description of the Revolutionary Council, see Josef Silverstein, *Burma: Military Rule and the Politics of Stagnation* (Ithaca and London: Cornell University Press, 1977), pp. 88–90.

7. *The System of Correlation of Man and His Environment* (Rangoon: the Burma Socialist Programme Party, 1963).

8. This and following quotations from Sai Tzang come from Lintner, op. cit., p. 38–39 and are based on a long letter to the author from Sai Tzang.

9. Steinberg, op. cit., pp. 250–251.

10. Sein Lwin was also the officer who had managed to kill the Karen rebel leader Saw Ba U Gyi on 12 Aug. 1950. Sein Lwin rose to prominence after this feat, and soon became one of Ne Win's closest associates.

11. David Steinberg, *Burma: A Socialist Nation in Southeast Asia* (Boulder: Westview Press, 1982), p. 76.

12. Josef Silverstein and Julian Wohl, "University Students and Politics in Burma", *Pacific Affairs* 1/1964.

13. *Some Facts about Ne Win's Military Government*, Central Committee, Communist Party of Burma (1962) (For Information Abroad), pp. 6 and 8.

14. *The Nation* (Rangoon), 8 Aug. 1963.

15. *The Guardian*, 31 Aug. 1963.

16. Interview with Thakin Ba Thein Tin, Panghsang, 24 Dec. 1986.

17. Martin Smith, *Burma: Insurgency and the Politics of Ethnicity* (London and New Jersey: Zed Press, 1991), pp. 208–209.

18. *A Short Outline of the History of the Communist Party of Burma*: official party document dated June 1964, and printed in Beijing.

19. Interview with San Thu, Panghsang, 26 Feb. 1987.

20. Interview with Zau Mai, Panghsang, 3 Jan. 1987.

21. For an excellent biography of Kang Sheng and his role in China and Southeast Asia, see John Byron & Robert Pack, *The Claws of the Dragon* (New York: Simon & Schuster, 1992). Kang Sheng's role in building up the CPB was mentioned frequently by party veterans when I visited Panghsang in Dec.1986–Mar. 1987.

22. Interview with Ma San Yi (an ethnic Chinese from Bassein in the Irrawaddy delta region), Panghsang, 26 Feb. 1987. Ma San Yi spent several years in the Shweli river guerrilla zone before being transferred to Panghsang, where she met and married San Thu, the Moscow returnee who had surveyed the border in late 1963.

23. Interview with Omar Farouk, Bangkok, 12 Dec. 1988.

24. Aye Saung, *Far Eastern Economic Review*, 25 Aug 1988.

25. For a brief history of Burma's press, see Bertil Lintner, "Proud Past, Sad Present", *Far Eastern Economic Review*, 28 March 1985.

26. Chao Tzang Yawnghwe, "Politics of Burma and Shan State: Effects on North Thailand and Thailand", *Political Science Review* (Chiang Mai University), Sep. 1982.

27. Interview with Bo Mya, Manerplaw, 8 May 1992.

28. Naw Louisa Benson later married Glenn Craig, an American, and settled in the US. She is now active in the pro-democracy movement abroad.

29. Adrian Cowell, *Report on a Five Month Journey in the State of Kengtung with the Shan National Army*, typescript, 1965.

30. Alfred McCoy, *The Politics of Heroin in Southeast Asia* (New York: Harper & Row, 1972), pp. 308–311.

31. For instance "Dutch" Brongersma; see Chapter Four.

32. This was still the case when I first visited Huei Krai in Jan. 1980.

33. Interview with the Mahadevi's son, Chao Tzang Yawnghwe (Sai Tzang), Bangkok, 14 March 1993.

34. Interview with Sai Tzang, Bangkok, 14 March 1993.

35. Interview with Sai Tzang, Bangkok, 14 March 1993.

36. Interview with Sai Tzang, Bangkok, 14 March 1993.

37. Thak Chaloemtiarana, *Thailand: The Politics of Despotic Paternalism* (Bangkok: the Social Science Association of Thailand, 1979), pp. 336–337; Rong Syamananda, *A History of Thailand* (Bangkok: Thai Watana Panich, 1977), p. 182.

38. According to numerous testimonies by local and foreign residents in northern Thailand who I have interviewed over the last ten years. See also Alfred McCoy, op. cit. 143 and 158.

39. Ibid. p. 158.

40. Thak, op. cit., pp. 339–340.

41. David Morell & Chai-anan Samudavanija, *Political Conflict in Thailand: Reform, Reaction, Revolution* (Cambridge, Mass.: Oelgeschlager, Gunn & Hain, 1981), pp. 53–54.

42. Ibid., p. 54.

43. *In Memory of Chin Sophonpanich* (special supplement to the *Bangkok Post*, 9 April 1988), p. 22.

44. "An Outline of the Political History of the Shan State From World War II to the Present", in *Hearings*, April 1975, pp. 253–266.

45. Interview with Aung Gyi, Rangoon, 24 April 1989. The story about Olive Yang and Wa Wa Win Shwe's relationship is not a secret; it is commonly known, and frequently discussed, among most of her generation in Rangoon.

46. Anthony Paul, "The Sinister Warlord Behind Asia's Drug Traffic", *Reader's Digest*, May 1973, pp. 30–34.

47. Lo Hsing-ko was later assassinated and his widow, Chao Chih-yuan, moved to Bangkok, where she married Yang Ming-pang, the honorary chairman of the Yunnanese Association of Thailand and a prominent drug trafficker. Yang Ming-pang became a heroin addict himself and died in Bangkok in early 1993.

48. Interview with Yang Jenn-swe, a.k.a. Peter Yang, a native of Kokang, Chiang Mai, 10 July 1981.

49. McCoy, op. cit., pp. 336–337; and also *Focus* (Bangkok, August 1981): " . . . Only about 600 of the 1,374 men of the KKY in the Kokang region were paid by the government at the rate of 50 Kyats (about US$7) a month. The remainder earned their living by trafficking in opium or smuggling other goods."

50. Paul, op. cit., p. 32.

51. Interview with Khun Sa, Möng Mai, 14 Dec. 1993.

52. A Special Correspondent (Bertil Lintner), "The Return of Lo Hsing-han", *Focus* (Bangkok, August 1981).

53. *Political Science Review*, (Chiang Mai University, Thailand), Sep. 1982.

54. Interview with N'Chyaw Tang, Pa Jau, 26 Apr. 1986.

55. "The Kachin Dilemma", *Focus* (Bangkok, Apr. 1982).

56. For a history of the jade trade, see Bertil Lintner, "Burma's Jade Trail", *Gemological Digest* (Bangkok, no. 4, 1989).

57. Scott Anderson & Jon Lee Anderson, *Inside the League* (New York: Dodd, Mead & Co., 1986), p. 47. This succinct and revealing study of the APACL and the WACL is highly recommended for background on Taiwan's and South Korea's designs for Asia during the Cold War.

58. Catherine Lamour, *Enquete sur une Armée Secrete* (Paris: Éditions du Seuil, 1975), p. 204.

59. Interview with Bill Young, former CIA officer in Laos, Chiang Mai, 3 June 1992. Interview with Chang Shu-chuan (a.k.a. Sao Hpalang), a veteran of BS 111, Möng Mai 14 Dec. 1993. See also Lamour, op. cit., p. 210.

60. Ibid., pp. 217–218.

61. The Wei Brothers, operating through Wa mercenaries, later became leaders of one of the most powerful drug trafficking networks in Southeast Asia.

62. Lamour, op. cit., p. 218.

63. *Weekend Telegraph* (London), 10 Mar. 1967.

64. Estimates by Sao Hsö Lane, commander of the Shan State Army (SSA), in an interview at Möng Mai, 18 Apr. 1982.

65. Interview with Sao Hsö Lane, 18 Apr. 1982.

66. Interview with Sao Hsö Lane, 18 Apr. 1982

67. Catherine Lamour and Michel R. Lamberti, *The Second Opium War* (London: Allen Lane, 1974), pp. 96–97.

68. "Taiwan links in Lo trial", *Bangkok Post*, 25 Jan. 1974.

69. Patya Saihoo, "The hill tribes of northern Thailand and the opium problem", *Bulletin of Narcotics* (Dec. 1967), p. 41: "Of the opium-producing tribes, the Lisu and the Black Lahu consume the least of their own produce (about 5%), the Red Lahu the most (30–40%) and the Meo [Hmong] and the Yao in between." The highest figure would correspond to a 70–80% addiction rate in a middle-sized Red Lahu village.

70. Roger Faligot & Rémi Kauffer, *The Chinese Secret Service* (London: Headline Publishing, 1989), p. 462.

71. Interview with Thakin Ba Thein Tin, Panghsang, 24 Dec. 1986.

72. Andrew Selth, *Assisting in the Defence of Australia: Australian Defence Contacts with Burma, 1945–1987* (Canberra: The Research School of Pacific Studies, the Australian National University, Working Paper no. 218, 1990), p. 7.

73. Interview with Thakin Ba Thein Tin, Panghsang, 24 Dec. 1986.

74. Interview with Khin Maung Gyi, Panghsang, 28 Dec. 1986.

75. *A Short Outline*, p. 5.

76. သခင်သန်:ထွန်:၏ နောက်ဆုံ:နေ့များ: (The Last Days of Thakin Than Tun; Rangoon: Mya Ya Pin Sarpay, 1969), pp. 520–526. Also, interview with Than Maung, one of

the *tat ni lunge* who participated in the killings in the Pegu Yoma at the time, Panghsang, 25 Dec. 1986.

77. Several authors have assumed that Thakin Than Myaing was executed during the Cultural Revolution (for instance, Klaus Fleischmann, *Die Kommunistische Partei Birmas: Von den Anfängen bis zur Gegenwart* [Hamburg: Mitteilungen des Instituts für Asienkunde, 1989], p. 421). However, he languished in his labour camp until he was released and rehabilitated in 1973. He died from natural causes in Da Shang, Sichuan, on 3 May 1991.

78. Silverstein, *Burma: Military Rule and the Politics of Stagnation*, p. 161–162.

79. Ibid., p. 179. See also David Steinberg, "Burma Under the Military: Towards a Chronology", *Contemporary Southeast Asia* 3, no. 3, Dec. 1981, p. 262.

80. Interview with Mowu Gwizan, ex-commander of the Naga Army, Kohima, Nagaland, 18 Oct. 1985. Mowu was the person who the Chinese contacted in Karachi in 1962.

81. Interview with Thuingaleng Muivah, Kesan Chanlam in the Naga Hills of Burma, 5 Nov. 1985.

82. Interview with Brang Seng, Pa Jau, 14 June 1986.

83. Interview with Brang Seng, Pa Jau, 14 June 1986.

84. The news about the imminent CPB thrust into northeastern Burma was brought from China to the Pegu Yoma by a messenger, Aung Sein, in 1967. See Chapter Seven.

85. *The Last Days of Thakin Than Tun*, pp. 653–654

Chapter 7: The Communist Juggernaut

1. This account of the attack on Möng Ko is based on interviews with Yang Ta-ban, Lee Kya-shan and Yang Shwe-ji, three local villagers who remember the event (Möng Ko, 20 Nov. 1986). They insisted that they saw Naw Seng and Khin Maung Gyi directing the thrust into Möng Ko on 1 January 1968, and that they heard Naw Seng speak to the villagers in the morning. Khin Maung Gyi, however, said in an interview with the author in Kunming on 17 January 1992 that "Naw Seng and I did not participate in the first assault on Möng Ko. We arrived on the scene a few months later." This revision of history may have been prompted by the fact that some serious mistakes were made immediately after the attack on Möng Ko, for instance, a bloody campaign against guerrillas of the Kachin Independence Army (KIA) in the area, who were supposed to be the CPB's allies according to an agreement reached in Beijing in November 1967 between the two rebel armies.

2. For a history of the CPB's northeastern base area, see Bertil Lintner, *The Rise and Fall of the Communist Party of Burma* (Ithaca, New York: Cornell University Southeast Asia Programme, 1990), pp. 25–37.

3. Interview with Ohn Kyi, Panghsai, 4 Nov. 1986.

4. Interview with Dashi Gam (one of Naw Seng's men who took part in the ambush), Panghsang, 6 Jan. 1987.

5. Interview with KIA officer Malizup Zau Mai (who fought against the CPB in the Kutkai area in the early 1970s), Na Hpaw, 17 Oct. 1986. Zau Mai is the present chief of staff of the KIA, and no relation to Zau Mai of the CPB, who is a follower of Naw Seng.

6. Non-communist opposition sources made even more astonishing claims at the time, possibly in the hope of obtaining Western sympathy. See, for instance, an interview with a Karen rebel in *Daily Telegraph's* 15 April 1970 issue, in which he claimed that the CPB's bases in the northeast had "electronic equipment, dish antennae, and air-strips for planes which are secured in hangars built in caves." The source also claimed that some 20,000 Chinese irregulars were operating in Burma's Shan and Kachin states. While there was a large number of Chinese in the late 1960s and early 1970s, the actual number was probably more in the order of 5,000–10,000. The rest of the story is pure fiction.

7. David I. Steinberg, "Burma Under the Military: Towards a Chronology", *Contemporary Southeast Asia* 3, no. 3, Dec. 1981, p. 263.

8. For an account of the death of Thakin Than Tun, see သခင်သန်းထွန်း၏ နောက် ဆုံးနေ့များ (The Last Days of Thakin Than Tun; Rangoon: Mya Ya Pin Sarpay, 1969), pp. 1415–1417. This comprehensive history of the CPB was ostensibly written by three communist defectors—Tin Shein, Maung Mya and Bo Khet—but in reality by Burma's former intelligence chief, Brig.-Gen. Tin Oo. It is a largely factual and correct account of the history of the CPB, but, needless to say, it heavily reflects the government's interpretation of these events. Maung Mya, an ethnic Chin whose real name was Nga Mya, was the government agent who killed Thakin Than Tun. In the late 1970s, he showed up in the Karen area along the Thai border, possibly with similar instructions from Rangoon. This was at a time when the Karens had an alliance with U Nu's and Bo Let Ya's ethnic Burman resistance. Nga Mya was arrested and executed by the Karen rebels.

9. Interview with Aung Sein, Panghsang, 25 Dec. 1986.

10. Interview with Than Maung, Panghsang, 25 Dec. 1986.

11. Interview with Aung Sein, Panghsang, 25 Dec. 1986.

12. Steinberg, op. cit., p. 263.

13. San Yu served as chief of staff and defence minister 1972–74, and president of Burma 1981–88.

14. For an account of Lo Hsing-han's activities and his relationship with the Burma Army, see Anthony M. Paul, "The Sinister Warlord Behind Asia's Drug Traffic", *Reader's Digest*, May 1973; Jon Swain, "At the Court of the Opium King", *Bangkok Post*, 25 Jan. 1974; and A Special Correspondent (Bertil Lintner), "The Return of Lo Hsing-han", *Focus* (Bangkok), Aug. 1981.

15. Interview with Wa officers, Mae Hong Son, 9 Nov. 1992.

16. Interview with Col. Sai Pao, Wa officer, Chiang Mai, 19 Apr. 1990.

17. Interview with Sao Hsö Lane, Shan rebel leader, Möng Mai, 14 Apr. 1981. Interview with Ai Pao, Wa leader, Chiang Mai, 12 June 1992.

18. Interview with Peter Yang a.k.a. Yang Jenn-swe, a native of Kokang, Chiang Mai, 20 July 1981. See also "Taiwan links in Lo trial," *Bangkok Post* 25 Jan. 1974: "Part of the KKY ran up against a government force on May 11 [1973] in Lashio . . . and lost 10 dead and several wounded. . . . The group fled toward the Lwese [Loi Sae] hills to the southeast where it joined agents of Taiwan's Ministry of National Defence at a village called Man Palawang." This article was written during Lo Hsing-han's trial in 1974.

19. John Byron & Robert Pack, *The Claws of the Dragon* (New York: Simon & Schuster, 1992), pp. 355–356.

20. Interview with Khin Maung Gyi, Kunming, 18 Jan, 1992. An internal document from China's Public Security Bureau ("Brief on Reactionary Organisations by the First Department of the Public Security Bureau", Beijing, 1985; in Chinese), lists all the initial CPB bases in the northeast as strongholds of a quasi-political religious sect, the Yi Guan Dao. The document states that the overall leader of this network, which was also allegedly involved in espionage and drug trafficking, was Liu Binghong, former KMT mayor of Zhen An in Longling County between Mangshi and Baoshan in Yunnan.

21. Ibid.

22. For a discussion about this "think-tank", see Josef Silverstein, *Burma: Military Rule and the Politics of Stagnation* (Ithaca and London: Cornell University Press, 1977), pp. 117–118.

23. Ibid., p. 118. See also Martin Smith, *Burma: Insurgency and the Politics of Ethnicity* (London and New Jersey: Zed Books, 1991), p. 275.

24. Letter to the author from Law Yone's son-in-law, Sterling Seagrave, dated 27 May 1992.

25. Ibid.

26. Silverstein, op. cit. p. 118; Bertil Lintner, *Outrage: Burma's Struggle for Democracy* (London: White Lotus UK, 1990), p. 50. Seagrave and other sources have questioned the sum which I mentioned in *Outrage*—US$10 million—which came from several Mon and Karen rebel sources I interviewed along the Thai border in 1981–83. Whatever the case, the amount of money and the degree of outside support which Law Yone received was much less than most observers appear to have assumed.

27. This is based on interviews with Edward Law Yone's daughter, Wendy Law Yone-O'Connor, Washington, 15 March 1992; and an interview with Sterling Seagrave, Paris, 11 Dec. 1992. Both sources reject claims by Smith in op. cit., pp. 273–278, that the CIA was "behind" Law Yone's and U Nu's attempt to build up a non-communist resistance in the late 1960s and early 1970s. Liaison with the groups was, however, maintained through one "Mr. Kamal", a Turkish-American who was suspected of being a CIA operative. More precisely, Kamal belonged to an entangled network of past or present intelligence operatives, arms merchants and covert operation types, whose activities were not always approved by Washington, or the CIA's headquarters in Langley, Virginia. During the Indochina War, they included John Singlaub (later of World Anti-Communist League fame), Theodor Shackley (CIA station chief in Laos in the 1960s), William Colby (CIA chief in the 1980s), adventurer Ray Cline of the China Lobby, and Richard Secord, who ran covert operations in Laos, Cambodia and Vietnam (and who was later convicted in the Iran-Contra affair). Lacking official support and approval from Washington (and sometimes even Langley) for their cloak-and-dagger operations, they had turned to powerful interests in the Middle East to raise funds for their activities—which later became a national scandal in the US when the Iran-Contra affair was revealed by the *Washington Post*. However, contacts with wealthy Middle East business circles had been maintained since oil was discovered in that part of Asia in the 1960s. Among them were arms merchant Manuchar Gorbanifar and his middleman Adnan Khashoggyi (later connected with the discredited Bank of Credit and Commerce International, the BCCI, which collapsed in 1991). Kamal was one of Khashoggyi's cronies who set up shop in Southeast Asia to maintain liaison between the two

groups. He transferred black money between the Middle East and Southeast Asia. He also went to places where the CIA for obvious reasons did not want to be seen. Since Law Yone was trying to sell Burma's oil fortunes, it was perhaps natural that people like him would take an interest. But sources close to Law Yone's operation in the late 1960s assert that they received no significant monetary, or military, assistance from Kamal.

28. Interview with Sao Hseng Harn (a.k.a. Sai Nyan Win, the Shan medical student who had accompanied the Yawnghwe Mahadevi to Thailand in 1964), one of the SSA officers who went to Tang-yan to contact Khun Sa in 1969, Chiang Mai, 29 Jan. 1982; interview with Sao Hsö Lane, 28 Feb. 1982. See also Chao Tzang Yawnghwe, *The Shan of Burma: Memoirs of a Shan Exile* (Singapore: Institute of Southeast Asian Studies, 1987), p. 189.

29. Details about Than Shwe come from an interview with his old comrade-in-arms, Khin Maung Gyi, Panghsang, 28 Dec. 1986. Than Shwe later disagreed with the CPB's policy of armed struggle and retired in Chengdu, Sichuan, in 1985.

30. This account of the Kyinshan battle is based on an interview with ex-Col. Khin Maung Soe, Bangkok, 1 May 1992, and with CPB commanders on the other side of the frontline whom I interviewed in Kokang, Kyinshan and Möng Mau in Nov.–Dec. 1986.

31. In 1988, Tun Yi became a leading member of the army-backed National Unity Party (NUP), the new name of the BSPP after the turmoil of August–September of that year. He failed to win a seat in the May 1990 election.

32. Interview with Mya Thaung, CPB Political Commissar of the Northern Wa Hills, Möng Mau, 4 Dec. 1986.

33. Interview with ex-Col. Khin Maung Soe, Bangkok, 1 May 1992. It is uncertain where the napalm came from, but many sources, from the Burma Army as well as the rebels, assert that napalm was used extensively during the war in northern Shan State in the 1970s.

34. His son "Dickie" became a BSPP official and ran for elections in Hopang in May 1990 on a NUP ticket. He became one of only ten NUP candidates who were elected, securing 3,336 votes in this small constituency. The only other candidate in Hopang was Saw Philip of the pro-democracy Wa National Development Party, who got 2,324 votes (see the *Working People's Daily*, 6 June 1990).

35. Interview with ex-Col. Khin Maung Soe, Bangkok, 1 May 1992.

36. Interview with ex-Col. Khin Maung Soe, Bangkok, 1 May 1992. See also Chao Tzang Yawnghwe, "Politics of Burma and Shan State: Effects on North Thailand and Thailand", *Political Science Review* (Chiang Mai University), Sep. 1982.

37. Interview with ex-Col. Khin Maung Soe, Bangkok, 1 May 1992.

38. This account of the CPB's expansion in the northeast is based on several interviews with officers and soldiers who took part in the campaign. The most detailed account came from the files of Khin Maung Gyi, secretary to the CPB's central committee.

39. Interview with Mya Thaung, Möng Mau, northern Wa Hills, 4 Dec. 1986.

40. Interview with Mya Thaung, Möng Mau, northern Wa Hills, 4 Dec. 1986.

41. Interview with Lao Er Ji Pyao, Man Hpai, 4 April 1987.

42. For instance the introduction of Kyats 45 (4+5=9) and 90 (9+0=9) banknotes in 1987.

43. The other bridge is at Ta-Kaw on the Taunggyi-Kengtung road.

44. Interview with ex-officer Aung Myint (not his real name), Bangkok, 10 Oct. 1992.

45. See Adrian Cowell and Chris Menges' excellent film "The Opium Warlords", which contains an interview with Khun Hseng, Khun Sa's uncle. While listening to radio messages, he gets the information: "At present the Burmese troops are also moving in to help the Kokang Ka Kwe Ye to carry down the opium" [sic]. That the Burma Army in the early 1970s directly participated in defending the opium convoys from the north to the Thai border has also been confirmed by several former Burma Army officers I have interviewed in Bangkok.

46. Bertil Lintner, *Land of Jade: A Journey Through Insurgent Burma* (Kiscadale and White Lotus: Edinburgh and Bangkok, 1990), pp. 168–169. This theory was suggested by many Kachins I met during my trek through northern Burma in 1985–87. Even if it is not true, it has certainly affected Kachin perceptions of the CPB ever since. The news about Naw Seng's death, based on a CPB radio broadcast, was prominently displayed in the official *Working People's Daily* of 27 Apr. 1972.

47. Interview with Aung Htet, Panghsang, 19 Jan. 1987. Aung Htet is the son of Ludu U Hla and Daw Ama, two prominent leftist writers and newspaper publishers in Mandalay. Aung Htet later joined the CPB and became Thakin Ba Thein Tin's personal assistant. He now lives in exile in China. The director of the Coco Islands Prison Department, Col. Tun Tin Law (a Pa-O national), later became a prominent BSPP leader and head of the Shan State People's Council. This description of the penal colony on the Coco Islands is also based on an interview with Tin Zaw a.k.a. Hla Pe (another political prisoner who was there from Feb. 1969 to Dec. 1971), Manerplaw, 11 May 1991.

48. Interview with Mahn Nyein Maung (one of the two Karens who escaped from the Coco Islands in Sep. 1970), Manerplaw, 11 May 1991.

49. Smith, op. cit., pp. 264–265.

50. Ibid., p. 297.

51. Klaus Fleischmann, ed., *Documents on Communism in Burma* (Hamburg: Mitteilungen Des Instituts für Asienkunde, 1989), p. 177.

52. Interview with Sgaw Ler Taw, who led the KNUP mission to the northeast, Manerplaw 2 Aug. 1984.

53. My wife Hseng Noung lived and went to school in Möng Ton at the time of the Lahu raid. This account is based on what she remembers of the attack.

54. Interview with some of Jimmy Yang's old associates who have requested anonymity, Chiang Mai, 14 June 1992. See also McCoy, *The Politics of Heroin in Southeast Asia* (New York: Harper & Row, 1972), p. 340.

55. Interview with Sao Hsö Lane, Möng Mai, 28 Feb. 1982. Former SSA-leader Hsö Lane knew Pu Kyaung Long well, both as an ally and as an enemy.

56. Interview with Saw Shwe, one of Pu Kyaung Long's lieutenants, Manerplaw, 16 June 1982. See also Bertil Lintner, "Laying down arms", *Far Eastern Economic Review*, 2 Feb. 1984.

57. A Special Correspondent (Bertil Lintner), "The Return of Lo Hsing-han", *Focus*, Aug. 1981.

58. *Domestic Council Drug Abuse Task Force 1975: White Paper on Drug Abuse. A Report to the President.* Washington: 1975. Copy of the passage passed on to

author by Doris Buddenberg, EC drugs consultant in Islamabad, Pakistan. UNFDAC is now called the United Nations International Drug Control Programme (UNDCP).

59. Interview with Peter Yang, Chiang Mai, 20 June 1981. See also "The Return of Lo Hsing-han", *Focus*, Aug. 1981.

60. The offer, and the development leading up to it, have been described in detail in Adrian Cowell and Chris Menges' award-winning documentary "The Opium Warlords" (filmed in Shan State in 1972–73).

61. For the full text of the proposal, see *Hearings Before the Subcommittee on Future Foreign Policy Research and Development of the Committee on International Relations*, (U.S. Congress. House. 94th Cong., 22–23 Apr. 1975, pp. 16–17).

62. Interview with Sai Tu, Pa Jau, 29 Apr. 1986. Sai Tu was later released and rejoined the Shan rebellion. I met him at the KIO headquarters at Pa Jau when he was there as Shan liaison officer with the Kachins.

63. Interview with Sai Tu, Pa Jau, 29 Apr. 1986. More specifically, Lo was charged under Section 122/1 ("Anti-national activities and waging war against the State") and 15/1 ("Damaging Burma's socialist economy") of the Burmese Penal Code. Opium was never mentioned during his trial.

64. *Focus* (Thailand), Feb. 1982.

65. The original "Khun Sa" is supposed to have been a Shan brigand leader in the Möng Yai area who cooperated with the Japanese during the occupation. He was executed when the war was over.

66. Yawnghwe, op. cit., p. 136.

67. Interview with Sgaw Ler Taw, Manerplaw, 2 Aug. 1984. Interviews with Shan officers who took part in the mission, Möng Mai, 3 Jan. 1983.

68. ဇင်+ချစ်နောက်ဆုံး: (၂) (Zin+Chit: the Last Two), Rangoon: Mahananda Publishers, 1976, pp. 342–347. Following the death of Thakins Zin and Chit, the people from all the fourteen villages in the Pegu Yoma (mostly ethnic Karens) were resettled in the lowlands south of the mountain range. Until recently, surviving village elders from the Pegu Yoma were always especially invited to attend Union Day celebrations in Rangoon. The mountain range remains unpopulated to this day.

69. David I. Steinberg, "Burma: Ne Win After Two Decades", *Current History*, Dec. 1980, p. 181.

70. For an excellent account of the U Thant movement, see Andrew Selth, *Death of a Hero: The U Thant Disturbances in Burma, December 1974* (Brisbane: Griffith University, Australia-Asia Papers no. 49, 1989).

71. Interview with Zaw Win, Möng Ko, 19 Nov. 1986.

72. Interview with Li Ziru, Panghsang, 8 Jan. 1987.

73. This account is based on the original radio messages, which I read at Pa Jau in May 1986, plus additional interviews with Maj. N'Chyaw Tang.

74. Fleischmann, ed., op. cit., pp. 185–186.

75. John Byron & Robert Pack, *The Claws of the Dragon* (New York: Simon & Schuster, 1992), p. 324.

76. The Thais returned to Thailand in the early 1980s while the Indonesians left for China at about the same time. The *Suara Revolusi Malaya* fell silent in the mid-1980s.

77. Ye Tun, a veteran peasant organiser from Pyinmana (see Chapter One), was the CPB's official representative in Beijing until the 1989 mutiny.

78. For a detailed account of the power struggle that was raging in China at this time, see Byron & Pack, op. cit., pp. 410–426.

79. *Beijing Review*, 30 July 1976.

80. *Beijing Review*, 30 Sep. 1976.

81. *Beijing Review*, 26 Nov. 1976.

82. ကိုယ့်ဥ္းကိုယ်ချွန် အဆင်းရဲအပင်ပန်းခံ လုံးပမ်းတိုက်ခိုက်တဲ့ ၄၈၄၉ စိတ်ဓါတ်တွေကိုမွေးမြူကြ (The Spirit of 1948–49 was one of self-reliance and enduring hardships), the CPB's printing press, Panghsang, August 1979.

Chapter 8: Guns, Drugs, and Ethnic Resistance

1. David Morell & Chai-anan Samudavanija, *Political Conflict in Thailand: Reform, Reaction, Revolution* (Cambridge, Mass.: Oelgeschlager, Gunn & Hain, 1981), p. 66. See also James Mills, *The Underground Empire* (New York: Dell Books, 1987), p. 787: "... the Border Patrol Police, which is in fact an organization created, paid for, and controlled by the CIA".

2. Paisal Sricharatchanya, "An Unusual Career Indeed" (interview with Sudsai Hasdin), *Week* (Bangkok), 16 June 1980.

3. Quoted in Eric Wakin, *Anthropology Goes to War: Professional Ethics & Counterinsurgency in Thailand* (Madison: University of Wisconsin, Centre for Southeast Asian Studies, Monograph no. 9, 1992), p. 192. This excellent study details the controversial role which many anthropologists have played in counter-insurgency programmes.

4. These thirteen groups were the Arakan Liberation Party, the Arakan National Liberation Party (ANLP), the Karenni National Progressive Party, the Karen National Union, the Kachin Independence Organisation, the Kayan Newland Party, the Lahu National United Party, the New Mon State Party, the Palaung State Liberation Organisation, the Shan State Progress Party, the Shan United Army (SUA), the Shan United Revolutionary Army (SURA), and the United Pa-O National Organisation. The ANLP did not join, nor did Khun Sa's SUA or Moh Heng's SURA.

5. Interview with Sgaw Ler Taw, Manerplaw, 1 Aug. 1984.

6. Paisal, op. cit. Sudsai willingly admits his role in the 6 Oct. 1976 massacre. He told me during an interview in Bangkok on 31 Oct. 1992: "It was better to kill a few dozen Communist students in Bangkok than to let them seize power and kill thousands."

7. Charles F. Keyes, *Thailand: Buddhist Kingdom as Modern Nation-State* (Bangkok: Editions DK, 1991), p. 99.

8. Quoted in Paisal, op. cit.

9. Interview with Sao Hpalang, Möng Mai, 14 Dec. 1993. Sao Hpalang, a fluent Japanese speaker, was trained in Japan and sent to Korea as an intelligence officer during the Korean War. He served in Laos from 1955 to 1961.

10. Alfred McCoy, *The Politics of Heroin in Southeast Asia* (New York: Harper & Row, 1972), p. 323. This account of the opium war of 1967 comes from McCoy's book and several interviews in Chiang Mai in 1981–82 with Peter Yang a.k.a. Yang

Jenn-swe, a Kokang Chinese who had served as an officer in Khun Sa's army—and took part in the 1967 opium war.

11. This remarkable set-up was not mentioned in the Thai press until after the Thai army had stormed Ban Hin Taek in early 1982. See, for instance, the *Bangkok Post*, 28 Jan. 1982: "Illegal jade, drugs found in Khun Sa's home". *The Nation* of 29 Jan. 1982 mentioned that Khun Sa also maintained a house off Sukhumvit Road in Bangkok.

12. Statement of Sao Nang Ying Sita in *Hearings Before the Subcommittee of Future Foreign Policy Research and Development on International relations*, (U.S. Congress. House. 94th Cong., 1st sess., 22 and 23 April 1975), p. 145.

13. A recently published book in Thai, *Doi Mae Salong nai atit San Santikiri* (Chiang Mai: Watanachai Puwakun, 1992) by Kanchana Pragaswutisarn, a retired police officer, has a wonderful collection of pictures of KMT troops saluting Gen. Kriangsak in Mae Salong, of his villa and other scenes.

14. Quoted in Richard Nations, "Politics and the Poppy", *Far Eastern Economic Review*, 15 Apr. 1977.

15. Testimony by Lester Wolff, ibid., pp. 47–49.

16. Chao Tzang Yawnghwe, "Politics and the Informal Economy of the Opium-Heroin Trade: Impact and Implications for Shan State of Burma". Paper presented at the 5th Annual Conference of the Northwest Regional Consortium for Southeast Asian Studies, Vancouver, 16–18 Oct. 1992, p. 32.

17. These and other details about Khun Sa's networks come from "Statement of Hon. Lester L. Wolff, a Former Representative in Congress from the State of New York" in *Hearings Before the Committee on Foreign Affairs* (U.S. Congress. House. 100th Cong., June 30 and July 15, 1987). pp. 55–63.

18. Ibid., p. 61. See also James Mills, *The Underground Empire* (New York: Dell Publishing, 1987), p. 33.

19. *Hearings Before the Select Committee on Narcotics Abuse and Control* (U.S. Congress. House. 95th Cong., 12 and 13 July 1977.), pp. 215–216.

20. Bo Yang, *Golden Triangle and Wilderness* (Hong Kong: Joint Publishing, 1987), p. 147.

21. Martin Booth, *The Triads: The Chinese Criminal Fraternity* (London: Grafton Books, 1990), pp. 8–9. For a more scholarly account of the Triads and their history, see W.P. Morgan, *Triad Societies in Hongkong* (Hong Kong: Government Press, 1960; reprinted 1982 and 1989).

22. Booth, op. cit., p. 72.

23. Jules Nadeau, *Twenty Million Chinese Made in Taiwan* (Montreal: Montreal Press, 1990), p. 271–272. In 1949, when the Communists marched into Shanghai, Tu Yueh-sheng (or Du Yuesheng) fled to Hong Kong, where he died in 1951. Two years later, the remains of "the most influential resident of the French concession in Shanghai", (to quote an official Taiwan yearbook), were flown to Taiwan and the monument honouring "the Chinese Al Capone" was erected in Xizhi.

24. Morgan, op cit., p. 80.

25. Lynn Pan, *Sons of the Yellow Emperor*, (Boston: Little, Brown & Co., 1990), p. 338.

26. Gerald L. Posner, *Warlords of Crime* (London: Penguin Books, 1988), pp. 156–157.

27. Ibid., p. 160.

28. The most recent such attack occurred when in October 1984 American-Chinese writer Henry Liu was murdered in his Daly City (California) home just as he was about to publish documents which would prove embarrassing to the Taiwan government. It was only after heavy pressure from the US government that the hitmen (who belonged to the Bamboo Union) were prosecuted in Taiwan, but all their contacts with higher authorities were conveniently covered up. David E. Kaplan describes the Henry Liu case in his latest book, *Fires of the Dragon: Politics, Murder, and the Kuomintang* (New York: Atheneum, 1993).

29. *Hearings*, 1987, p. 61.

30. Melinda Liu, "The Triangle's Pecking Order", *Far Eastern Economic Review*, 14 Sept. 1979.

31. A Thai lawyer and legal expert, who prefers to remain anonymous, once told me that "the reason why Asian crime gangs such as the Triads and the Japanese Yakuza have never managed to entirely control drugs, prostitution and similar activities in Thailand was because they were up against an even better organised gang here: the Thai police". This does not exclude the fact that Thailand has had honest and dedicated policemen as well, but their survival (professionally as well as physically) has often depended on the protection and support they have received from foreign colleagues. For an account of the Chiu Chao underworld, see Sterling Seagrave, *The Soong Dynasty* (London: Sidgwick & Jackson, 1985), pp. 19–20. He adds: "When Westerners imagined wicked Chinese pirates smuggling gold, drugs, and frightened maidens, and lurking in the dark recesses of the Spice Islands, they were picturing the chiu chao. To this day chiu chao kingpins heading major banks in the region control the international narcotics trade from the Golden Triangle . . . through Bangkok to Amsterdam and other drug centres. Western drug-enforcement agencies look the other way."

32. The King of Thailand initiated the first crop substitution programme in 1967. This was followed in 1972 by projects sponsored by UNFDAC, USAID, and the West German government. By 1981, substitute crops had been introduced in 450 hill-tribe villages in the north (*Focus* magazine, Bangkok, June 1981). By 1983, Thailand's production was a mere 35 tons, down from 57 tons before the projects began (*Bangkok Post*, 1 Dec. 1983). By comparison, the 1982–83 opium harvest yielded 500–600 tons in Burma, up from 300 tons in 1980.

33. The interview was filmed by British film-makers Adrian Cowell and Chris Menges, and was shown as a TV documentary called "Opium: the Politicians" (a sequel to "Opium: the Warlords", which had been shot in 1972–73.

34. *Focus* magazine (Bangkok), Feb. 1982.

35. *Hearings*, 1977, p. 54.

36. Ibid., p. 13.

37. *Hearings*, 1975, p. 59

38. Interviews with former employees of the Directorate of Procurement, Ministry of Defence in Rangoon. After the upheaval of 1988 and the subsequent cut-off of all American assistance to Rangoon, US Department of Defence personnel have also admitted that such support was forthcoming in the 1970s.

39. *Hearings*, 1975, p. 59.

40. One US-supplied Bell helicopter was shot down by the Karens in xxx and serial numbers and other details were sent to the US embassy in Bangkok. There was no response or comment from US authorities.

41. *Hearings*, 1977, p. 188.

42. John McBeth, "Drugs: the new connections", *Far Eastern Economic Review*, 14 Sep. 1979.

43. UNFDAC: *Review of the UNFDAC/Burma Programme for Drug Abuse Control*, Oct./Nov. 1983, p. 4.

44. *Far Eastern Economic Review*, 26 Apr. 1984.

45. *Forward* magazine (Rangoon), Aug. 1978

46. *Far Eastern Economic Review*, 14 July 1978.

47. *Far Eastern Economic Review*, 9 June 1978.

48. *Asiaweek*, 9 June 1978.

49. According to the author of one of these articles. He has requested anonymity, and says that he later realised that he had been manipulated.

50. Letter to the author, dated 1 July 1985.

51. Mills, op. cit., p. 779. Also interview with Peter Yang, Chiang Mai, 10 Aug. 1981.

52. See Bo Yang, op. cit., pp. 151–159, for a detailed description of the KMT's participation in the battle for Khao Ya. This account of the battle is based on Bo Yang's book, and several interviews with Chai Min, Te Shin Liu and other KMT war veterans in Ban Mai Nong Bua southwest of Fang on 27 Sep. 1984.

53. Bo Yang, op. cit., pp. 157–158.

54. "B 50,000 price on Khun Sa approved", *The Nation* (Bangkok), 11 July 1981.

55. "New campaign to capture drug kingpin", *Bangkok Post*, 6 Aug. 1981.

56. "Drug reward limit puzzles agents", *Bangkok Post*, 16 Sep. 1981.

57. John Hail, "Long and hazardous hunt for the opium warlord", *Bangkok Post*, 11 Jan. 1982.

58. I lived in Chiang Mai at this time, and most local people had heard the story.

59. See "Revival of the SUA as a fighting force", *Bangkok Post*, 19 June 1983. "A Special Correspondent" is me. I visited the SUA's new camps in the Mae Hong Son area in March 1983.

60. Paul Jasvinder, "Moonshine, gambling and heroin", *Bangkok Post*, 8 Nov. 1981.

61. "Drug kingpin Lao Su killed", *The Nation* (Bangkok), 13 Feb. 1983.

62. He later also fell out with Khun Sa and opened a road-side store in the vicinity of Doi Lang. In the late 1980s, he was assassinated on the road to Mae Salong.

63. I was staying at Möng Mai in February 1983 when Leng's SUA unit marched in.

64. André and Louis Boucaud, *Burma's Golden Triangle: On the Trail of the Opium Warlords* (Hong Kong: Asia 2000, 1988), pp. 169–170. It is uncertain, however, whether Khun Sa himself participated in the Möng Ton meeting. Spokesmen for his group deny this. In any event, a meeting did take place at Möng Ton and an agreement was no doubt reached.

65. "Burmese troops seize Khun Sa's HQ", *Bangkok Post*, 20 May 1984.

66. Interviews with several Bangkok-based narcotics officials, 20–25 May 1984.

67. *Brief on Reactionary Organisations: Internal Document of the Public Security Bureau* (in Chinese; Beijing: the First Department of the Public Security Bureau, 1985).

68. Interview with Chao Tzang Yawnghwe, Bangkok, 14 Mar. 1993.

69. For a discussion of the beginning of the fall of the CPT, see "Thailand: The Challenge of the 1980s," special issue of the *Southeast Asia Chronicle*, Oct. 1981.

70. *Peace is Our Gift to the People*, pamphlet published by the Royal Thai Army, 1982.

71. Interview with Brang Seng, Pa Jau, 12 Aug. 1986.

72. Interview with Brang Seng, Pa Jau, 12 Aug. 1986.

73. Interview with Ye Tun, a CPB delegate to the talks in Lashio, Panghsang, 31 Jan. 1987.

74. Bertil Lintner, "A gathering of rebels", *Far Eastern Economic Review*, 22 May 1986. I arrived at Pa Jau shortly after the NDF delegation had left, but caught up with some of them at Panghsang in December 1986.

75. Interview with Brang Seng, Pa Jau, 12 Aug. 1986.

76. I was present at Zhang Zhiming's command post the morning Hsi-Hsinwan was attacked on 16 Nov. 1986, and had many long conversations with him before and after the battle.

77. I stayed in Panghsai for several days in November 1986.

Chapter 9: Burma in Upheaval

1. Radio Rangoon home service, as monitored by the BBC, 5 Sep. 1987. FE/9666/B/1.

2. Quoted in David Steinberg, "Neither Silver Nor Gold: the 40th Anniversary of the Burmese Economy", in Josef Silverstein, ed., *Independent Burma at Forty Years: Six Assessments* (Ithaca, New York: Cornell University Southeast Asia Programme, 1989), p.35.

3. This description of the teashop incident is based on interviews with Min Sein and Tun Oo, two RIT students who fled to the Thai border after the September 1988 military take-over; Three Pagodas Pass, 28 Nov. 1988. For a fuller account of the events of March 1988, see Bertil Lintner, *Outrage: Burma's Struggle for Democracy* (London: White Lotus UK, 1990), pp. 1–12.

4. These views were expressed by many students I interviewed in the Thai border areas in September and December 1988. Tun Naing, for instance, said: "My own uncle is an army officer and he knows what the people think about the government; I never thought he would obey orders to shoot at us." Three Pagodas Pass, 28 Nov. 1988

5. In an official video tape called "Loss of State Fund and Property in Burma" (sic), which was distributed to foreign visitors by the SLORC after the September 1988 massacre, foreign minister Ohn Gyaw claimed that the army had first told the demonstrators to disperse before firing warning shots over the heads of the demonstrators, then rubber bullets and, at last when nothing else helped, live ammunition. No eyewitnesses back up this official version: they all say the troops fired their automatic rifles and machine-guns right into the crowd without any warning or provocation.

6. Interview with Peter Conard, Bangkok, 15 Sept. 1988. Also quoted in Lintner, op. cit., p. 94.

7. Interview with Ko Lin, Bangkok, 5 Jan. 1989. This account of the events in Rangoon in August 1988 is based on numerous interviews with Burmese who

participated in the demonstrations, and with foreign diplomats in Rangoon who observed them.

8. Richard Gourley, "Troops fire on crowds in Rangoon", *Financial Times*, 10 Aug. 1988.

9. The State Department's Human Rights Statement, Feb. 1989.

10. This and the following are quotes from a mimeographed English translation of her speech, which was distributed in Rangoon at the same time. Copy in my possession.

11. Interview with Ko Lin, Bangkok, 5 Jan. 1989.

12. "Ne Win dumped by independence heros", *Bangkok Post*, 7 Sep. 1988.

13. See, for instance, Jon Wiant, "Tradition in the Service of Revolution: the Political Symbolism of *Taw-hlan-ye-khit*", in F.K. Lehman, ed., *Military Rule in Burma since 1962* (Singapore: Maruzen Asia, 1981).

14. It is a matter for conjecture why Kyaw Zaw joined the CPB in 1976. Younger CPB sources, whom I interviewed in Panghsang in early 1987, claimed that he had been forced to leave Rangoon in the wake of an abortive coup attempt in 1976. Kyaw Zaw had not been involved in it, but the plotters, when asked who they would like to see as leaders of the country as opposed to Ne Win, had replied: "Brig. Kyaw Zaw and Gen. Tin Oo." Tin Oo had then just been ousted from the army for refusing to use troops against student demonstrators in the mid-1970s. Having fought the KMT, Kyaw Zaw most probably thought he would be welcome in China, from where he intended to continue on to the Thai border to join his old comrade-in-arms, Bo Let Ya. However, the Chinese appear to have ordered him to go to Panghsang and join the CPB. This was at a time when the Chinese were withdrawing their military instructors and "volunteers" from Burma so the CPB badly needed an experienced, indigenous military leader. Kyaw Zaw fled to China after the April 1989 mutiny and now lives in retirement in Kunming.

15. Wiant, op. cit., p. 68.

16. See Robert Taylor, *The State of Burma* (London: C. Hurst & Co., 1987). The last chapter is even called "Reasserting the State, 1962–1987".

17. Michael Aung-Thwin, "The British 'Pacification' of Burma: Order Without Meaning", *Journal of Southeast Asian Studies*, Sep. 1985, p. 258: "Ne Win of course takes his role as military administrator/leader from Aung San, the modern embodiment of great Burmese unifiers. Aung San is seen as the fourth great unifier after Aniruddha of 11th century Pagan, Bayinnaung of 16th century Taungoo (sic), and Alaunghpaya of 18th century Shwebo. Ne Win is regarded as the fifth. . . . Incidentally, the Buddha of the future, Metteya, is the fifth and last Buddha of this *kappa*."

18. A Western diplomat I interviewed in September 1988 told me that before he went to Burma, a Burmese diplomat in his home country had told him that "you can earn some extra money by selling antiques abroad. Not a lot, but a little bit is OK."

19. Note Verbale, Embassy of the Federal Republic of Germany, Rangoon/Burma, Wi 445 BIR 57/VN No. 318/88, 28 Oct. 1988. The note continues: "The Embassy regrets to have to lodge a firm protest with the Government of Burma. It reserves all rights to later claim full compensation, on behalf of the Government of the Federal Republic of Germany, for the damage done to the Plant Protection and Rodent

Control Project and for losses of public property and damage incurred by the project." The Burmese foreign ministry replied feebly on 10 February 1989 that it regretted "that the Embassy had to jump to the conclusion and lodged a firm protest." The German embassy repeated its claim in an even more strongly worded Note Verbale dated 8 March 1989.

20. Copies of these leaflets are in the author's possession. English translations of the crude leaflets were compiled by the British embassy in Rangoon at the time and circulated among the diplomatic community.

21. Capt. Si Thu was later promoted to major. In early 1993, he served as "guide and interpreter" for a visiting TV crew from Singapore.

22. Interview with Gen. Saw Maung, *Asiaweek*, 27 Jan. 1989.

23. Melinda Liu, "Inside Burma: An On-Scene Report on the Crisis", *Newsweek*, 3 Oct. 1988.

24. *Bangkok Post*, 22 Sep. 1988.

25. *Drug Control: Enforcement Efforts in Burma Are Not Effective* (Washington: US General Accounting Office, Sep. 1989), pp. 15 and 27."

26. For a collection of personal experiences from the pro-democracy movement of 1988 and the flight to the border areas, see *Voices From the Jungle: Burmese Youth in Transition* (Tokyo: Centre for Christian Response to Asian Issues, 1981). My account of the movement and the exodus is based mostly on more interviews with dozens of student refugees along the Thai, Chinese and Bangladesh borders during several trips to these areas in 1988–1990.

27. This line had been reaffirmed at the CPB's third congress at Panghsang in September/October 1985. See Bertil Lintner, *The Rise and Fall of the Communist Party of Burma* (Ithaca, New York: Cornell University, Southeast Asia Programme, 1990), p. 36. The account is based on original CPB congress documents, which are in my possession.

28. *Working People's Daily*, 20 Nov. 1989. A transcript of the entire discussion was published in the *Working People's Daily* of 18, 19, 20 and 21 Nov. 1989. Surprisingly, the government-run newspaper published this in order to show that the CPB was behind Burma's pro-democracy movement.

29. "Khun Sa: An Interview With Burma's Number One Drug Czar", *Dateline Bangkok* 15, Jan.–Mar., 1989.

30. Interviews with people from Möng Yang, Jinghong (Sipsongpanna), 15 May 1989.

31. Letter from Sai Noom Pan, dated 20 Oct. 1988.

32. *News Release: The People's Voice of Burma, The Organ of the Communist Party of Burma*, no. 5/88, 22 Dec. 1988. The rebel claims concurred with estimates by Rangoon-based diplomats.

33. The Möng Yang and Maw Tha Waw battles were reported extensively in the *Working People's Daily* in October and December 1988. For obvious reasons, however, the Kongsa battle went unreported in the official media.

34. "Clash between Tatmadaw and Laotian insurgent group in Mong Hpayak Township," *Working People's Daily*, 5 Oct. 1988. The same news was broadcast over Radio Rangoon, but never appeared in Foreign Broadcast Information Service (FBIS) transcripts. It was the first time FBIS thought it necessary to censor an important news item.

35. See, for instance, the *Working People's Daily*, 4 Nov. 1988 (two couriers captured together with 1.535 kg of heroin in Lashio) and 14 Dec. 1988 (3.5 kg of heroin seized in Lashio). For an unusually favourable DEA document, see *Foreign Situation Report: Burma 1990* (Rangoon: Drug Enforcement Administration). Written by the country attaché at that time, Angelo Saladino, it states: "Non assistance to the present Government of Burma in anti-narcotic matters serves no practical purpose in terms of the US Government's interest in narcotics suppression and is contrary to the US Government's stated international narcotics strategy." It then goes on to list "achievements" in drug suppression in Burma, mainly seizures, arrests of couriers and public drug burning shows.

36. It was only in early 1991 that the State Department dismissed John Htin Aung following a polygraph examination which proved deception regarding his affiliation with the secret police, the DDSI (see Chapter Ten).

37. Hamish MacDonald, "Blood and Timber: How Burma bought friends", *Far Eastern Economic Review*, 22 Feb. 1990.

38. *Bangkok Post*, 21 Dec. 1988.

39. Interviews with foreign refugee officials, Bangkok, 2 Apr. 1989.

40. Interview with Soe Thein, political commissar of the Northeastern base area, Panghsang, 5 Jan. 1987.

41. တပါတီလုံး သွေးစည်းညီညွတ်ပြီး အောင်ပွဲအရယူရေးအတွက် ချီတက်ကြပါစို့ (The Entire Party! Unite and March to Achieve Victory!) Political report of the politburo of the CPB, submitted by Chairman Thakin Ba Thein Tin on 1 Nov., 1978. The CPB's printing press, Panghsang, 13 Sep. 1979, pp. 104–105.

42. Interview with Khin Maung Gyi, Kunming, 18 Jan. 1992.

43. Interview with Mya Thaung, political commissar of the Northern Wa District, Möng Mau, 4 Dec. 1986.

44. Interview with Soe Thein, political commissar of the CPB's northeastern base area, Panghsang, 5 Jan. 1987.

45. A theme often repeated by CPB soldiers I talked to during my trek through the area in 1986–87: "The Chinese come and pick up our leaders in limousines on the border. We don't dare to oppose them."

46. Hand-written minutes from this meeting were passed on to the author during a visit to Jinghong, Yunnan, China, in May 1989.

47. SWB, FE/0439B/1, 20 April 1989.

48. FBIS-EAS-89-081, 28 April 1989.

49. Martin Smith, *Burma: Insurgency and the Politics of Ethnicity* (London and New Jersey: Zed Press, 1991), p. 379.

50. *Focus* (Bangkok), Aug. 1981, *Far Eastern Economic Review*, 18 June 1982.

51. Interview with Aung Gyi, Rangoon, 24 Apr. 1989.

52. Bertil Lintner, "Left in disarray," *Far Eastern Economic Review*, 1 June 1989. See also *Working People's Daily* (Rangoon), 23 Apr. 1989.

53. For instance, see *Working People's Daily* (Rangoon), 28 Aug. 1989.

54. Interview with Ai Pao, Wa leader, Chiang Mai, 19 Apr. 1990.

55. Soe Tun Ni, "All that Glitters is not Gold - 2", *Working People's Daily* (10 May 1989): "The [CPB] insurgents are doing opium business. . . . They have get understanding with the KMT White Chinese and the Wa insurgents with whom they quarrelled and now are trafficking in opium with their help" [sic]. In what

could have been an oversight by the editor of the state-run newspaper, its 5 December 1989 issue published a vitriolic attack on a [former] CPB commander, Zhang Zhiming (Kyi Myint), who was described as a "bull on heat when it comes to female matters". The commander in question participated in unofficial peace talks in Rangoon with the military authorities on the day the article appeared in the *Working People's Daily*.

56. I met Zhang Zhiming in Jinghong (Sipsongpanna), when he came down from the north in mid-May 1989.

57. Bertil Lintner, "A fix in the making", *Far Eastern Economic Review* (28 June 1990); interviews with former CPB cadres at Mangshi, Yunnan, Jan. 1991.

58. International Narcotics Strategy Report, Mid-Year Update (Sep. 1990), US Department of State, Bureau of International Narcotics Matters, p.56.

59. *Far Eastern Economic Review*, 28 June 1990.

Chapter 10: The Strife Continues

1. I was in Burma in Apr. 1989 when this movement was gathering momentum.

2. "Death awaits Burmese demonstrators," *Bangkok Post*, 19 July 1989.

3. The Conspiracy of Treasonous Minions within the Myanmar naing-ngan and Traitorous Cohorts Abroad: *State Law and Order Restoration Council Secretary (1) Brig.-Gen. Khin Nyunt's statement* (Rangoon: Ministry of Information, 1989). Among the dead "traitorous cohorts" were Sao Khun Hkio, the Shan leader who served as foreign minister in the 1950s.

4. *Burma Communist Party's Conspiracy to take over State Power: State Law and Order Restoration Council Secretary (1) Brig.-Gen. Khin Nyunt's statement* (Rangoon: Ministry of Information, 1989), p 79. The official document says: "In 1987–88 . . . she made contact with the political leaders and handed in the letters sent from the BCP [i.e. the CPB] and contributed cash towards the BCP UG [underground] fund. And these caused her detention [sic] on 21 July 1989." There is, however, no evidence to back up this allegation, and CPB leaders I interviewed in Kunming in January 1991 and January 1992 said they were unaware of any connection with Daw Kyi Kyi. Most probably, she and her family were arrested simply because she was the widow of Thakin Zin, a name with which most Burmese—and many foreigners—were familiar.

5. See, for instance, "US Embassy Reports Torture in Burmese Jails", *New York Times*, 26 Aug. 1989.

6. For an overview of the differences between the DEA and the State Department, see Susumu Awanohara, "Getting their hands dirty", *Far Eastern Economic Review*, 28 June 1990.

7. *The Sunday Star-Ledger*, 27 Aug. 1989.

8. News Release, 16 Mar. 1990 (Bangkok: United States Information Service).

9. *Bangkok Post*, 6 Mar. 1987.

10. *Bangkok Post*, 28 Feb. 1987.

11. *Bangkok Post*, 12 Mar. 1987.

12. Interview with "Bo" Gritz, Chittagong (Bangladesh), 21 Jan. 1990. See also James "Bo' Gritz, *A Nation Betrayed* (Boulder City, Nevada: Lazarus Publishing, 1989), p. 84.

13. Ibid., pp. 85–86.

14. Ibid., p. 86.

15. *Hearing before the Committee on Foreign Affairs* (U.S. Congress. House. 100th Cong., 1st sess., June 30 and July 15, 1987.), p. 109. Wrobleski belonged to the "old school" of State Department officials whose views differed little from the DEA's uncritical approach. It is highly unlikely that a currently serving State Department official would have made such an innocent statement.

16. *Bangkok Post*, 3 Feb. 1991.

17. Angelo Saladino was later recalled to New York for his alleged involvement in drafting a memorandum for Burma's secret police chief, Maj.-Gen. Khin Nyunt, outlining ways of "silencing the regime's most biased critics". Saladino's memorandum also contains suggestions about how best to manipulate the US government and various US agencies.

18. See, for instance, Alan Dawson, "American Hero in Burma", *Bangkok Post*, 1 Oct. 1988.

19. The CBS was represented by its Tokyo correspondent Bill Whitaker, producer Mary Walsh, Bangkok-based cameraman Derek Williams and soundman Brian Robbins. The *Time* photographer was Peter Charlesworth.

20. The ambassador, Burton Levin, had in December 1988 (a few months after the massacre in Rangoon) had the former country attache, Greg Korniloff, dismissed for not obeying orders from the embassy. Korniloff left the country within four days.

21. *The Nation* (Bangkok), 25 May 1990.

22. I met and talked to the CBS team before and after their visit to Rangoon. They also showed me their tapes from the visit. Also note that Charles Rangel visited Rangoon in January 1988—a few months before the upheaval—and then praised the government's "anti-drug efforts". He said that the Burma Army's "war on drugs" was a war not only for the Burmese people but also for the entire international community.

23. *Working People's Daily* (Rangoon), 6 June 1990.

24. Summary of World Broadcast (SWB), Rangoon Home Service, 27 July 1990 (FE/0829 B/1, 30 July 1990).

25. SWB, 22 Sept. 1988 (FE/0265 B/1, 24 Sep. 1988).

26. A copy of the Gandhi Hall Declaration is in my possession.

27. A complete list of the wounded, beaten and arrested monks is in my possession. The list was compiled by monks in Mandalay immediately after the incident.

28. SWB 8 Aug. 1990 (FE/0839 B/1, 10 Aug. 1990).

29. *Report of the Committee on the Human Rights of Parliamentarians*, 86th Inter-Parliamentary Conference, Santiago, Chile, 7–12 Oct. 1991.

30. *Bangkok Post*, 21 Oct. 1990.

31. *Bangkok Post*, 23 Oct. 1990.

32. Letter to me from Hla Myint, director of Associated Business Consultancy Services (a company run by Aye Zaw Win, Gen. Ne Win's son-in-law), 15 Jan. 1990.

33. *International Narcotics Strategy Report* (Washington: US Department of State, Bureau of International Narcotics Matters, Mar. 1991), pp. 230–231.

34. Bertil Lintner, "The busy border", *Far Eastern Economic Review* , 8 June 1989.

35. *Working People's Daily* (Rangoon), 1 Oct. 1989.

36. Bertil Lintner, "Block and load", *Far Eastern Economic Review*, 13 Sep. 1990.

37. *Far Eastern Economic Review*, 13 Sep. 1990, 6 Dec. 1990, and 6 June 1991; *Jane's Defence Weekly*, 18 Sep. 1990, and 15 June 1991.

38. *Working People's Daily* (Rangoon), 24 Nov. 1990.

39. A typescript of his speech is in my possession.

40. *Working People's Daily* (Rangoon), 24 Nov. 1990.

41. According to former CPB cadres from Kokang who were interviewed in Mangshih and Ruili, Yunnan, China, in Jan. 1991.

42. *Working People's Daily* (Rangoon), 2 Feb. 1991.

43. *Working People's Daily* (Rangoon), 2 Feb. 1991.

44. Interviews in Mangshi and Ruili with local residents of Möng Ko, Jan. 1991. According to correspondence this writer received from Kokang in February 1991, the military authorities paid 100,000 Kyats a kilogram for the drugs which were burnt at the first ceremony in November 1990. The sources also alleged that military officers from Rangoon did not burn all the heroin they bought; they took substantial quantities with them when they left the area by helicopter.

45. Passenger lists for the helicopters that went up to Möng Ko in January 1991 are in my possession. John Htin Aung is listed as a DEA representative.

46. *Bangkok Post*, 3 Feb. 1991.

47. Statement from Sen. Daniel P. Moynihan's office, Washington, 22 Mar. 1990.

48. *Bangkok Post*, 14 July 1989.

49. Figures from the US State Department's Bureau for International Narcotics Matters.

50. Bertil Lintner, *Outrage*, pp. 67–68.

51. *The Los Angeles Times*, 24 June 1990.

52. *Working People's Daily* (Rangoon), 24 Nov. 1990. *Bangkok Post* of Feb. 3 1991 published pictures of intelligence chief Khin Nyunt and Burma's Bangkok ambassador, Nyunt Swe, destroying poppies "in a field near Chinsweho". The poppies, however, looked conspicuously small and few had flowers or real pods; the field appeared to have been grown not for commercial purposes but for the benefit of the foreign visitors (DEA and UNFDAC personnel).

53. According to the *Working People's Daily*, 19 Mar. 1991: "The UN experts visited Mongla [Möng La] by helicopter on 13 March morning. They were briefed on the measures being taken for the development of border areas and national races in Mongla by leaders of local nationals U Sai Lin and U Kyi Myint."

54. *Working People's Daily* (Rangoon), 12 July 1991.

55. Excerpts of this document are in my possession.

56. In a letter to the "Honest Ballot Association", dated, appropriately, 1 April 1993, Horn lists a number of the SLORC's "achievements" and goes on to laud the Burmese government's anti-drug efforts.

57. According to a statement issued by the KIA in early February 1991, six companies from its 4th Brigade (based in northeastern Shan State) agreed to a cease-fire with the SLORC. The main KIA, or 8,000–9,000 troops in Kachin State proper, were not affected by the defection, the statement said.

58. *Bangkok Post*, 19 Dec. 1991.

59. *Bangkok Post*, 21 Dec. 1991. BBC 19 Dec. 1991.

60. Bertil Lintner and Rodney Tasker, "General Malaise", *Far Eastern Economic Review*, 13 Feb. 1992.

61. *Working People's Daily* (Rangoon), 22 Jan. 1992.

62. I visited Teknaf in late July 1991 to interview Rohingya refugees. See Bertil Lintner, "Diversionary tactics", *Far Eastern Economic Review*, 8 Aug., 1991.

63. *Asia Yearbook 1992* (Hong Kong: Review Publishing, 1992), p. 92.

64. *Far Eastern Economic Review*, 7 May 1992.

65. Bertil Lintner, "Triangular ties", *Far Eastern Economic Review*, 28 Mar. 1991. This article is based on numerous interviews conducted in the Sino-Burmese border areas in January 1991.

66. "Burma-India: A Fourth Side to the Golden Triangle", *The Geopolitical Drugwatch* (Paris), Dec. 1992.

67. *The New York Times*, 9 Aug. 1990; Uttam Sengupta, "Spreading Scourge", *India Today*, 15 Dec. 1990; Harbinder Baweja and Arun Katiyar, "The Indian face of AIDS", *India Today*, 30 Nov. 1992.

68. "Cambodia: Mekong Pipeline", *The Geopolitical Drugwatch* (Paris), Feb. 1993.

69.

70. "Cambodia: Mekong Pipeline", *The Geopolitical Drugwatch* (Paris), Feb. 1993; Nate Thayer, "Diverted traffic", *Far Eastern Economic Review*, 18 Mar. 1993.

71. Bertil Lintner, "A Fatal Overdose", *Far Eastern Economic Review*, 3 June 1993. This article is based on several interviews conducted along the Thai-Burma border in May 1993.

72. Ammar Siamwalla and Chaiyuth Punyasavatsut, "The 'Drug Money'—How Much and to Whom?" *TDRI Quarterly Review*, June 1991.

73. Interview with Saw Lu, Chiang Mai, 25 May 1993.

74. A copy of Saw Lu's proposal is in my possession.

Epilogue

1. Michael Levine, *Deep Cover* (New York: Delacorte Press, 1990), pp. 19 and 16; and "The Betrayal of Michael Levine", *Esquire*, Mar. 1991.

2. Peter Dale Scott and Jonathan Marshall, *Cocaine Politics: Drugs, Armies and the CIA in Central America* (Berkeley: University of California Press, 1991), p. 172.

3. Stanton Candlin, *Psycho-chemical Warfare: The Chinese Drug Offensive against the West* (New Rochelle: Arlington House, the Conservative Book Club, 1973), p. 245.

4. Ibid., p. 459.

5. See Alfred McCoy, *The Politics of Heroin in Southeast Asia* (New York: Harper & Row, 1972), pp.147–148.

6. Melinda Liu, "The Curse of China White", *Newsweek*, 14 Oct. 1991.

7. *Bangkok Post*, 26 July 1992.

8. Interview with Australian narcotics officials in Thailand, 23 Apr. 1993.

9. *US Department of Justice: Registration Statement 3690*, dated 9 Feb. 1993.

10. John Barron, *KGB Today: The Hidden Hand* (London: Hodder and Stoughton, 1983), p. 254.

11. *Report to the Honest Ballot Association Regarding Narcotics & Human Rights in Myanmar*, dated 6 May 1993, and signed by Donald A. MacDonald, and former congressmen Seymour Halpern and Robert Leggett.

12. Wolff's first propaganda trip to Burma in November 1992 included US Congressman Charles Rangel, who even had an official meeting with heroin trafficker Pheung Kya-shin (FBIS, 13 Nov. 1992). Less than a month later, Pheung was ousted from his position of power in Kokang by a rival heroin gang led by Yang Mu Lian.

13. *Hearings Before the Subcommittee on East Asian and Pacific Affairs jointly with the Subcommittee on Terrorism, Narcotics and International Operations, 9 March 1990* (Washington: Anderson Reporting Company, 1990), p. 17.

14. *Bangkok Post*, 23 Mar. 1990.

15. *Statement of Sherman M. Funk, Inspector General, US Department of State Before the Subcommittee on East Asian and Pacific Affairs and the Subcommittee on Terrorism, Narcotics and International Operations of the Senate Committee on Foreign Relations, 9 March 1990*, pp. 11–12.

16. *Programme of the National League for Democracy* mimeo, 1989, pp. 2–3.

Index

About the Book and Author

The product of thirteen years of research, interviews, and experience, this is the most authoritative book ever written on the interrelationship of drugs, insurgency, counterinsurgency, and politics in Burma. Widely respected as one of the world's leading experts on Burma, Bertil Lintner has drawn on his extensive travels and personal meetings with rebel commanders, ethnic leaders, and other key figures to present a compelling and comprehensive picture of politics and society in a poor and bitterly divided country.

Fighting between the central government and myriad political and ethnic insurgencies entered its forty-seventh year in 1994, with no solution in sight. While other countries in the region are developing into freer, more open societies, once-democratic Burma has been ruled by a medieval military dictatorship since 1962. The complex nexus between the drug problem, military rule, and Burma's civil war has rarely been considered when international narcotics agencies have evaluated the drug problem in the Golden Triangle. Consequently, millions of dollars have been wasted in a misguided effort to treat the problem as a localized vice, rather than addressing the underlying historical, social, and economic factors behind the drug explosion. Meanwhile, opium production is increasing steadily, year by year.

This book aims to explore the inextricable links among Burma's booming drug production, insurgency, and counterinsurgency and to explain why the country has been unable to shake off over thirty years of military rule to build a modern democratic society. Burma's ethnic strife, the author argues, is not a peripheral problem confined to the country's border areas. Without a lasting solution to ethnic divisions and the civil war they have fueled, Burma will remain a source of political despair—and the opium it grows will continue to flood the markets of the world.

Bertil Lintner is a freelance writer based in Thailand who contributes regularly to the *Far Eastern Economic Review* and has written three previous books on Burma.